Contents

THE COMPANION TO DEVELOPMENT STUDIES

Second Edition

EDITED BY

VANDANA DESAI
ROBERT B. POTTER

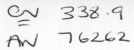

HODDER
EDUCATION
RE UK

First published in Great Britain in 2008 by
Hodder Education, part of Hachette Livre UK,
338 Euston Road, London NW1 3BH

www.hoddereducation.com

British Library Cataloguing in Publication Data
A catalogue record for this book is available from the British Library

Library of Congress Cataloging-in-Publication Data
A catalog record for this book is available from the Library of Congress

ISBN 978 0340 88914 5

1 2 3 4 5 6 7 8 9 10

Typeset in 10 on 12 pt Minion by Phoenix Photosetting, Chatham, Kent
Printed and bound in Malta

What do you think about this book? Or any other Hodder Education title?
Please send your comments to the feedback section on www.hoddereducation.com

Contributors

Dr Isabella Aboderin, Oxford Institute of Ageing, University of Oxford, UK

Martin Adams, Mokoro Ltd, Oxford, UK

Dr Katharine Adeney, Department of Politics, University of Sheffield, UK

Giles Atkinson

Donald W. Attwood, Professor of Anthropology, McGill University, Canada

Professor Hazel Barrett, Professor of Development Geography, Department of Geography, Environment and Disaster Management, Faculty of Business, Environment and Society, Coventry University, UK

Geraldine de Bastion, Deutsche Gesellschaft für Technische Zusammenarbeit (GTZ) GmbH, Germany

B.S. Baviskar, Senior Fellow, Institute of Social Sciences, New Delhi, India, formerly Professor of Sociology, University of Delhi, India

Professor Anthony Bebbington, School of Environment and Development, University of Manchester, UK

Harriot Beazley, School of Social Work and Applied Human Sciences, University of Queensland, Australia

Professor J.A. (Tony) Binns, Professor of Geography, University of Otago, New Zealand

Dr Richard Black, Co-director, Sussex Centre for Migration Research, University of Sussex, UK

Dr Morten Bøås, Fafo Institute for Applied International Studies, Oslo, Norway

Professor John Briggs, Department of Geographical and Earth Sciences, University of Glasgow, UK

Dr Lynne Brydon, Senior Lecturer, Centre of West African Studies, University of Birmingham, UK

Peter Burnell, Professor of Politics, University of Warwick, UK

Terry Cannon, Reader in Development Studies, and Research Fellow of the Natural Resources Institute, University of Greenwich, London, UK

Dr Raff Carmen, Senior Lecturer, Vocational. Professional and Lifelong Learning Group, University of Manchester, UK

Dr Erlet Cater, Department of Geography, University of Reading, UK

Professor Michael M. Cernea, Senior Social Development Advisor, Middle East and North Africa Region, World Bank, Washington DC, USA

Sylvia Chant, Professor of Development Geography, London School of Economics, UK

John D. Clark, Social Development, The World Bank, Washington DC, USA

Stephen J. Connor, International Research Institute for Climate and Society (IRI), The Earth Institute at Columbia University, New York, USA

Professor Dennis Conway, Professor of Geography, Indiana University, USA

Stuart Corbridge, Professor of Development Studies, London School of Economics, UK

Sonia Corrêa is a research associate at ABIA – Brazilian Interdisciplinary Association for HIV/AIDS, and the co-ordinator of Sexuality Policy Watch. She is also a coordinator of the Sexual Reproductive Health and Rights program, of DAWN – Development Alternative with Women for a New Era

Dr Marina Della Giusta, Department of Economics, University of Reading Business School, UK

Dr Vandana Desai, Lecturer in Development Geography, Royal Holloway, University of London, UK

Dr Stephen Devereux, Institute of Development Studies, University of Sussex, UK

Klaus Dodds, Professor of Geopolitics, Royal Holloway, University of London, UK

Dr Caroline Dyer, Senior Research Fellow, POLIS, University of Leeds, UK

Dr Jennifer A. Elliott, Principal Lecturer in Geography, University of Brighton, UK

Gerrit Faber, University of Utrecht, The Netherlands

Dr Tim Forsyth, Lecturer in Geography, London School of Economics, UK

Margaret Foster

Dr Alan F. Fowler, Hon. Professor, Centre for Civil Society, University of KwaZulu Natal, South Africa

V. Gayathri

Professor Alan Gilbert, Professor of Geography, University College London, UK

Dr Alan Grainger, Senior lecturer in Geography, University of Leeds, UK

Professor David Greenaway, Professor of Economics, University of Nottingham, UK

Dr Robert N. Gwynne, Reader in Latin American Development, University of Birmingham, UK

Dr Jane Haggis, Associate Professor in Sociology, Flinders University, Adelaide, Australia

Professor Björn Hettne, Department of Peace and Development Research, Gothenburg University, Sweden

Nikolas Heynen

Dr Susie Jacobs, Senior Lecturer in Sociology, Department of Sociology, Manchester Metropolitan University, UK

Professor Rob Jenkins, Professor of Political Science, Birkbeck College, University of London, UK

Dr Gareth A. Jones, Senior Lecturer in Development Geography, London School of Economics, UK

Peris Jones, Lecturer in Human Rights, Institute of Commonwealth Studies, University of London, UK (writing while at the University of Oslo, Norwegian Centre for Human Rights)

Ray Kiely, Professor of International Politics, Queen Mary, University of London, UK

Professor Tony Killick, Senior Research Associate, Overseas Development Institute, UK

Thomas Klak, Professor of Geography, Miami University, Ohio, USA

Dr Phoebe Koundouri, Senior Lecturer, DIEES, Athens University of Economics and Business, Greece

Yiannis Kountouris

Tiziana Leone, Lecturer in Population Studies, London School of Economics, UK

Dr Philipp Lepenies, Development Economics Policy Department, KFW Entwicklungsbank, Frankfurt, Germany

Dr Sally Lloyd-Evans, Lecturer in Geography, University of Reading, UK

Alex Loftus, RCUK Academic Fellow, Department of Geography, Royal Holloway, University of London, UK

Dr Kenneth Lynch, Senior Lecturer in Geography, University of Gloucestershire, Cheltenham, UK

Dr Don D. Marshall, Senior Research Fellow, Sir Arthur Lewis Institute of Social and Economic Studies, University of the the West Indies, West Indies

Duncan Matthews, Intellectual Property Institute, Centre for Commercial Law Studies, Queen Mary, University of London, UK

Dr Cheryl McEwan, Lecturer in Geography, University of Durham, UK

Dr Duncan McGregor, Senior Lecturer in Geography, Royal Holloway, University of London, UK

Dr Cathy McIlwaine, Reader in Human Geography, Queen Mary, University of London, UK

Dr Candace Miller, Department of International Health, Boston University, Boston MA, USA

Professor Chris Milner, Professor of International Economics, University of Nottingham, UK

Dr Giles Mohan, Senior Lecturer in Development Studies, The Open University, Milton Keynes, UK

Dr Stephen Morse, Reader in Development Studies, University of Reading, UK

Dr Joe Mullen, Senior Lecturer in Rural Development/Poverty, Institute for Development Policy and Management, University of Manchester, UK

Viviana Munoz Tellez, Innovation and Access to Knowledge Programme, South Centre, Geneva, Switzerland

Barry Munslow, Emeritus Professor of Politics, Liverpool School of Tropical Medicine, UK

Dr Paul J. Nelson, Associate Professor, Graduate School of Public and International Affairs, University of Pittsburgh, USA

Tim O'Dempsey, Liverpool School of Tropical Medicine, UK

Phil O'Keefe, Professor of Economic Development and Environmental Management, Northumbria University, UK

Dr Michael J.G. Parnwell, Reader in East Asian Studies, University of Leeds, UK

Professor Jane L. Parpart, Professor of History, International Development Studies and Women's Studies, Dalhousie University, Halifax, Canada, and visiting Professor in Political Science at Stellenbosch University, South Africa

Professor Tulsi Patel, Professor of Sociology, Delhi School of Economics, University of Delhi, India

Dr Mark Pelling, Reader in Human Geography, King's College, London, UK

Robert B. Potter, Professor of Human Geography, University of Reading, UK

Dr Marcus Power, Lecturer in Human Geography, University of Durham, UK

Jules Pretty, Professor in Environment and Society, University of Essex, UK

Dr Shirin M. Rai, Reader in Politics, University of Warwick, UK

Professor Carole Rakodi, International Development, University of Birmingham, UK

Michael Redclift, Professor of International Environmental Policy, King's College, London, UK

Dr Jonathan Rigg, Reader in Geography, Durham University, UK

Paul Rogers, Professor of Peace Studies, University of Bradford, UK

Joanne Rose, ECT UK Ltd, North Shields, UK

Susan Rose-Ackerman, Law School and Department of Political Science, Yale University, New Haven CT, USA

Dr Barbara Rugendyke, Senior Lecturer in Geography and Planning, University of New England, Armidale, Australia

Dr Lora Sabin, Department of International Health, Boston University, Boston MA, USA

Professor David Sapsford, Department of Economics, Management School, University of Liverpool, UK

Dr David Satterthwaite, Human Settlements Programme, International Institute for Environment and Development (IIED), London, UK

Dr Susanne Schech, Associate Professor in Geography, Flinders University, Adelaide, Australia

Dr Frans J. Schuurman, Senior Lecturer in Development Studies, University of Nijmegen, The Netherlands

Andrew Scott, International Programmes and Policy Director, Intermediate Technology Development Group, Schumacher Centre for Technology Development, UK

David Seddon, Professor of Development Studies, University of East Anglia, UK

Professor Timothy M. Shaw, Institute of International Relations, University of the West Indies, Trinidad & Tobago, and Royal Roads University, Victoria BC, Canada

Kay Sharp

Prakash Shetty, Professor of Nutrition, Public Health, University of Southampton, UK

Dr Deborah Sick

James D. Sidaway, Professor of Human Geography, University of Plymouth, UK

David Simon, Professor of Development Geography, Royal Holloway, University of London, UK

Rachel Slater, Overseas Development Institute, London, UK

David M. Smith, Emeritus Professor of Geography, Queen Mary, University of London, UK

T.T. Sreekumar

Dr Kathleen Staudt, Professor of Political Science, University of Texas at El Paso, USA

Professor B. Sudhakara Reddy, Dean, Indira Gandhi Institute of Development Research, Mumbai, India

Professor Tim Swanson, Department of Economics, University College London, UK

Dr Dirk Willem te Velde, Overseas Development Institute, London, UK

Professor Anthony P. Thirlwall, Professor of Applied Economics, University of Kent, UK

Dr Emma Tomalin, Lecturer in Religious Studies, University of Leeds, UK

Dr D. Alissa Trotz, Associate Professor, Sociology and Equity Studies, Ontario Institute for Studies in Education and Women and Gender Studies, Director of Carribean Studies at the University of Toronto, Canada

Dr Maya Unnithan-Kumar, Reader in Social Anthropology, University of Sussex, UK

Professor Tim Unwin, Professor of Geography, Royal Holloway, University of London, UK

Dr Pitou van Dijck, CEDLA, Amsterdam, The Netherlands

Dr Alison Van Rooy, article based on work as Senior Researcher, The North-South Institute, Ottawa, Canada

Dr Ann Varley, Reader in Geography, UCL (University College London), UK

Eduardo A. Vasconcellos, advisor for ANTP, the Brazilian Association of Public Transport, São Paulo, Brazil

Dr Sudhir Wanmali, Consultant, Rural Development and Planning, Rockville, USA

Dr Howard White, Fellow, Institute of Development Studies, University of Sussex, UK

Jim Whitman, Department of Peace Studies, Bradford University, UK

Steve Wiggins

Dr Katie D. Willis, Reader in Development Geography, Royal Holloway, University of London, UK

Andrew Wyatt, Department of Politics, University of Bristol, UK

Dr Kate Young, Vice-chair, National Alliance of Women's Organisations, UK

Professor Annelies Zoomers, Utrecht University (Human Development, International Development Studies), and Radboud University Nijmegen (Regional Development Policy and International Migration), The Netherlands

Preface

The first edition of *The Companion to Development Studies* has been very well received, both critically and in the marketplace. Indeed, the major criticism we encountered suggested that we had made it all too easy for students of development studies – a limitation that we could more than happily live with! Further, the original volume has given rise to at least one other companion to development studies, and we take this as a form of flattery.

Hence, our intention in the second edition has primarily been to bring the volume up to date. The structure has, therefore, largely been retained, and the chapters are divided into ten major parts. However, some of the titles of the parts have been modified. For example, Part 4 now deals with 'Globalization, employment and development' rather than 'Industrialization and employment', and Part 10 with 'Governance and development' rather than 'Agents of development'. In addition, the parts of the book dealing with the environment and the political economy of violence have both seen considerable expansion.

The first edition of *The Companion* consisted of 107 chapters, and this has increased to 115 in this volume. Around 40 new chapters were commissioned especially for this edition, although in a few cases this represented an existing author being asked to prepare what amounted to an essentially new chapter under a modified title. The new chapters deal with pressing contemporary topics such as: the New Institutional Economics; the Millennium Development Goals; culture and development; ICT and development; the Labour Party and development; indigenous knowledge; social exclusion; free trade and fair trade; pro-poor globalization; migration and transnationality; illegal workers; urban bias; urban-rural interaction; urban transport; international regulation and the environment; biodiversity; water management; energy; forest management; tourism and environment; livelihood strategies; agricultural sustainability; GM crops; famines; gender and globalization; ageing; health inequalities; gender and age-based violence; conflict development and aid; humanitarian aid; ethnicity, identity and nationalism; faith; the global war on terrorism; corruption; non-government public action networks; public–private partnerships; multilateral institutions; challenges to the World Trade Organization; intellectual property rights and multilateral institutions; and universal human rights.

Our goal as editors of *The Companion* has remained to bring together leading scholars from around the world in an effort to provide a truly international and interdisciplinary overview of the major issues that have a bearing on development theory and practice in the twenty-first century. From the outset it was envisaged that the book would offer a one-stop reference guide for anyone with a practical, professional or academic interest in development studies. We hope that this revised edition will remain of relevance to those in the fields of development studies, sociology, government, politics and international relations, and economics, along with practitioners in NGOs, and those in donor agencies.

Just as we recorded in the first edition, *The Companion* recognizes the existence of numerous good general texts on development studies, including readers. However, the volume aims to perform a unique function in bringing together in an accessible format, a wide range of concisely written overviews of the most important issues in the field. We hope that the book remains an invaluable course text, while with the exercise of critical judgement, it can be treated as a source of readings and discussion pieces in connection with higher-level options and training courses, for example, at master's level. It remains our hope that students following certain programmes may well be able to make use of the volume over the duration of their studies and not just for a single option or module. Each chapter is followed by suggestions for further reading, lists of references cited in the text, along with details of useful websites.

One of the principal strengths of the volume is that it has been written by well-known and respected authors from both the 'Global South' and the 'Global North'. For both editions, we specifically targeted authors from around the world. As with the first edition, we were delighted – and just a little amazed – that our invitations to take part in the project were so overwhelmingly greeted with a positive response. For the first edition we felt sure that the excellent response from our invited contributors reflected the fact that there was a real gap in the development studies literature. We sincerely hope that the enthusiasm we encountered this second time round means that our invitees believe that *The Companion to Development Studies* has gone a long way to filling this gap.

Over and above the contributors, three people have been vital in the production of the second edition. Susan Millership adopted the project from her predecessor and was enthusiastic from the outset. Liz Wilson covered a wide array of editorial tasks and made major logistical contributions from the very beginning of the project. Towards the end, Alison Thomas copy-edited the text with care and professionalism. All three demonstrated patience – and at times resilience – beyond that which should rightfully have been expected of them, for which we express our sincere gratitude.

Vandana Desai and Rob Potter
July 2007

Vandana Desai

For Ian, Nayantara & Dhruva

Rob Potter

For Virginia & Katherine

The nature of development and development studies

Editorial introduction

The chapters in this first section of the book explore and comment on two closely linked themes: first, the nature and progress of development studies as a distinct avenue of enquiry; and second, how development itself can be defined and conceptualized. In respect of the first of these two topics, it is important to stress the origins of the First, Second and Third Worlds in the politics of the cold war, and the later transition to a North–South dichotomy following the Brandt Commission. With the collapse of the Berlin Wall and the near total demise of the socialist Third World, it is now best to talk in terms of 'developing countries', and even more so perhaps, 'poor nations'.

Early views of development within the field of development studies undoubtedly stressed catching up with, and generally imitating, the 'West'. The failure of development in so-called Third World countries, together with the postmodern critique and trends of globalization, are customarily regarded as having given rise to a major impasse in development studies in the 1980s. Recent approaches have been somewhat more liberating in terms of the world views promulgated, and there are trends to link development studies with cultural studies, for example, in respect of the condition of postmodernity and the vital nature of issues of peace and security. Further, the trend of globalization, the reduction in the importance of the state, and the associated alienation of the state from civil society, all mean that development studies face a battery of issues, not least whether these trends are real and inescapable phenomena, or constructs designed to legitimize the logic of the neoliberal market.

Stemming from these various trends, since the early 1990s, it has become increasingly fashionable to criticize 'Western' development imperatives, and this has given rise to a variety of what can be referred to as 'postist-stances', including post-development, antidevelopment and beyond development. In truth, these positions should not be seen as new, but rather as joining earlier Marxist and feminist critiques of the status quo nature of development. Further, some would argue that, whatever its sins, the 'development project' has brought financial aid and technological assistance, which have sought to raise standards of living in the South, even if they have only been successful locally. Some argue that new technologies will afford poor countries the chance to catch up in ways different from those of the past.

If development is defined in terms of poor countries, an enduring problem remains the need to measure and understand poverty. This is especially so today, with poverty 'alleviation' and 'elimination' programmes, and the difficulties of heavily indebted poor countries (HIPCs) being stressed by the international development agencies. Poverty means that in spite of overall global trends, it still matters where you live, especially if you fall into the poorest third or so of people, living in tropical Africa and Asia. Addressing poverty requires political will, and many would maintain that this remains the real obstacle to development. The Millennium Development Goals are major indicators that are being employed to assess the progress with specific development targets in the twenty-first century.

The issues on which a growing consensus appears to be emerging include the fact that economic growth is a necessary, but not sufficient, condition for development. Without redistribution of income and wealth, inequalities are not going to be reduced, and there is much evidence that it is inequalities that hurt. Thus, development must be regarded as synonymous with enhancing human rights and welfare, so that self-esteem, self-respect and improving entitlements become central concerns. In such a guise, participatory planning is a vital prerequisite, in particular, in coming to appreciate the value of indigenous knowledge.

1.1 The Third World, developing countries, the South, poor countries

Klaus Dodds

The power of words

In October 2001, British Prime Minister Blair, while addressing the Labour Party Conference, described Africa as 'the scar on the conscience of the world'. He pledged to make 'Africa' a foreign and development policy priority for his second term of administration. Over the next five years, the Blair Government promoted an increase in overseas aid spending, debt reduction and trade reform in an attempt to promote the Millennium Development Goals, which include reducing extreme poverty, halting the spread of HIV/AIDS and providing universal primary education, all by the target date of 2015. With his own unique brand of personalized diplomacy, Prime Minister Blair used the G8 summit in July 2005 to push for further progress towards debt forgiveness and overseas aid increases. Unfortunately, the London bombings on 7 July rather overshadowed the substance of the summit, and critics contended that the febrile announcements on debt cancellation rather over-egged the scale of the gesture – the deal only includes *some* of the debts of *some* poor countries. It will release about $1 billion a year to combat poverty, compared to the minimum of $10 billion debt cancellation per year needed to help developing countries achieve the Millennium Development Goals. However, a new Prime Minister, Gordon Brown, has pledged to keep this issue high on the international agenda.

There is a long way to go before we witness either widespread debt cancellation or overseas aid spending at approximately 0.7 per cent of GDP. Britain and the United States have yet to reach that target with regard to overseas aid and indeed there are many commentators who believe that increasing aid spending is not necessarily a worthwhile objective. Euro-American trade markets and the role that agricultural subsidies play therein deserve more critical attention. At the December 2005 meeting of the World Trade Organization in Hong Kong, developing countries gained little from the small concessions made by richer nations such as the United States and members of the European Union. Billed as the 'development round', critics of the Hong Kong meeting complained that the concessions to the poor countries, including most of Africa, were modest and usually followed by demands by the wealthier nations and groupings expecting further openings in the markets of the Global South.

While it is now commonplace to comment on Millennium Development Goals, the World Trade Organization and the 'Doha Round' of trade talks, 60 years earlier such terms and institutions did not exist. Instead, the term 'Third World' had been coined to signify a new geopolitical imagination based on a geography of global politics divided into three camps – the United States and its allies, the Soviet Union and the Communist world and a 'Third World' of post-colonial states in Africa, Asia and Latin America.

This chapter seeks to remind readers of this period, characterized by cold war and superpower competition, and consider how the fate of the Third World has changed since the mid-twentieth century. With the ending of the cold war, it was widely hoped that questions pertaining to development, poverty reduction and debt cancellation would enjoy a greater political profile. This has been achieved, but has not led to the profound changes hoped for by many activists, campaigners and governments in the Third World and beyond. Arguably, the recent preoccupation in the United States with a 'global war on terror', is not likely to assist those seeking more fundamental changes to the terms and conditions attached to global trade and development. For one thing,

American geopolitical priorities are focused on particular parts of the world, such as the Middle East and Central Asia, and comparatively modest amounts of funding and investment have been channelled into Africa compared to the military budget enjoyed by the Pentagon.

The invention of the Third World

In the aftermath of the Korean conflict (1950–53, and arguably ongoing), a new geopolitical imagination began to emerge as the conflict between the Soviet Union and the United States spread around the globe. Key geographical designations, such as 'First World' and 'Third World', were deployed by Western social scientists in an attempt to highlight the profound differences between the United States and the Soviet Union. Newly decolonized countries in South Asia, Africa and Asia were seen as providing opportunities for both sides to project influence, extend trading opportunities and recruit for the purpose of defending particular parts of the earth's surface from the influence of the ideologies of either Communism (in the case of the Soviets) or liberal democracy and capitalism (in the case of the United States). Billions of dollars and roubles were spent over the next 50 years in pursuit of that geopolitical objective. Both sides used the existence of this cold war to plan and implement development programmes, aid assistance, volunteer groups, trade stimulation, academic exchanges and/or arms sales.

During the cold war, the experiences of the Third World were never uniform, with some countries and regions receiving greater attention than others (Westad 2005). In the case of Latin America, for instance, US administrations were adamant (particularly following the 1959 Cuban Revolution) that they would not tolerate any further socialist governments in the hemisphere. President Johnson ordered 20,000 US Marines to overthrow the government of the Dominican Republic in 1965, and President Nixon approved the overthrow of the socialist President of Chile, Salvador Allende, on 11 September 1973. During the 1960s, countless efforts were made either to assassinate or overthrow Cuba's Fidel Castro, especially in the aftermath of the Bay of Pigs fiasco, which witnessed US-backed anti-Castro forces being routed by the armed forces loyal to the socialist leader. When the United States was not attempting to promote revolution and/or turmoil, it was content to support violent anticommunist military regimes in Argentina, Brazil, Chile and Uruguay. In other parts of the world, regional allies such as Israel, Pakistan, South Korea and Taiwan received substantial financial and military forms of assistance because they were judged to be significant in the wider struggle to prevent the Soviet Union from extending its global influence.

While certainly not unique to the United States, the Soviets were also engaged in a programme of aid, development and intervention in an attempt to project a global communist revolution. Some Third World states welcomed Soviet largesse – India was one such beneficiary and many of its citizens were subsequently trained in Soviet universities and institutions. Soviet allies such as Cuba also assisted in this global mission – Cubans were based in Angola and played a vital role in buttressing the national security capability of the country in the 1970s, when it faced South African forces who used South West Africa (Namibia) to launch covert raids against the country, which was consumed by civil war for much of its post-colonial existence. Elsewhere, the Soviet Union provided support for revolutionary movements in Central America, South East Asia and sub-Saharan Africa for much of the cold war period.

Not surprisingly, many members of the expanding Third World did not welcome the intensification of the cold war. In 1961, the Non-Aligned Movement (NAM) was created after an earlier Afro-Asian conference in Indonesia. NAM was important in so far as it signalled a resistance to the bipolar strictures of the cold war. Recently decolonized states resented and resisted pressures from the superpowers to align with one side or the other. The purpose of NAM was to find a 'third way', and one which respected their independence from extraterritorial influence. It also sought to promote a different vision of development, based on fairness, information and technological exchange, and a reformed international political system. By the early 1970s, NAM was joined by the so-called 'Group of 77' in the United Nations and advocates of a New International Economic Order (NIEO). Unfortunately for those campaigners, the early 1970s were turbulent years, as rich countries such as the United States were rattled by oil shortages, the Vietnam debacle and the Watergate crisis. There was no mood, in the United States in particular, to address the demands explicit in the calls for an NIEO.

It was also evident by the latter stages of the cold war that the 'Third World' was a highly diverse group of countries that had enjoyed very different development trajectories. The political-economic condition of oil-producing states such as Nigeria, Saudi Arabia and Venezuela differed markedly from South East Asian states such as Singapore and Taiwan. Sub-Saharan Africa and Central America probably contained some of the poorest states in the world, which were also immersed in damaging civil wars and/or damaged by corrupt and violent dictatorships and military regimes. The cold war provided an opportunity for these schisms and uncertainties to be exploited by the rich countries as they sought to extend ideological and economic influence. Tragically, millions perished as basic needs such as access to clean drinking water proved less politically attractive than expenditure on the latest tank, ship or missile.

The South

Amidst a general feeling of despair and pessimism among many development advocates and Third World academics, the United Nations-sponsored Brandt Commission reported on the state of the world in 1980 and 1983. Significantly, the Commission depicted a world divided between North and South, and not a First, Second and Third World. In other words, whatever the ideological differences between the Soviet Union and the United States and their respective allies, the world was really divided between the rich North and poor South. The Commission called for the North, in particular, to recognize that the world was more interdependent than ever (globalization had not been coined as a term by that stage) and to promote a more equitable form of global political economy. The message of the two reports, although hard-hitting and significant, was a victim of geopolitical timing.

With the Soviet invasion of Afghanistan in 1979, the cold war appeared to have entered a new and more dangerous phase. A new US president, Ronald Reagan, was committed to confronting what he described as the 'evil empire'. American and Soviet military spending increased and American financial assistance was used to fund anti Soviet forces in Afghanistan and anticommunist movements in places such as Nicaragua. The decision to fund anti-Soviet forces in Central Asia was particularly significant and arguably contributed to the emergence of the Al-Qaeda terror network in the 1980s and 1990s (Johnson 2000). What all this meant for the South was fairly straightforward – American and Soviet energies were directed towards this global struggle and any thought of reconstructing the world economy or pursuing global development strategies was an irrelevance.

By the late 1980s, the Soviet Union was bankrupt and regimes in Eastern and Central Europe were crumbling. In 1989, Germans on both sides of the divide tore down the Berlin Wall, the most practical and symbolic illustration of a divided Europe. The so-called Velvet Revolution led to the undoing of all those former communist governments, including the more brutal ones in Romania and East Germany. Elsewhere, military regimes in Latin America were crumbling and democratic governments emerged. The ending of the cold war was apparently completed when the Soviet Union folded in 1991. Some analysts, such as Francis Fukuyama, were swift to declare 'the end of history', in so far as it signalled the triumph of liberal democracy and market-based capitalism over state socialism and global communism (Fukuyama 1989). Whether or not that claim was justifiable, the ending of the cold war did begin to bring to an end a confrontation that had claimed millions of lives through proxy wars, government intervention and/or bombings. Democratic change in the 1990s was widespread and owed as much to the ending of the cold war as it did to a host of circumstances specific to particular places and regions.

Poor countries

Notwithstanding expressions of optimism regarding a global democratic revolution, the 1990s brought to the fore a stark realization – the world remained highly divided, despite all the attempts of governments and policy advocates to promote development. Even if the cold war did not help at one level, it did nonetheless provide both superpowers with an added incentive to channel aid and assistance to their favoured allies. More broadly, endeavours to promote the reduction of poverty and inequalities were modest in scope and extent. Since the mid-1980s, far more attention has been devoted towards inequalities and mal-development, but the results have been mixed. On the one hand, international organizations such as the International Monetary Fund (IMF) have promoted structural adjustment and good governance in return for economic assistance and aid spending. The 1996 initiative designed to promote debt relief for a select number of highly indebted poor countries (HIPC) was criticized for demanding a range of measures, such as privatization, in return for modest debt cancellation. This has led to accusations that these agencies are exercising a neocolonial influence on countries in the Global South. On the other hand, there have unquestionably been improvements in the basic conditions of many people, including access to drinking water, improved life expectancy and poverty reduction. It would be foolish to pretend otherwise, even if profound inequalities remain stubbornly in place.

While access to Northern markets is not the panacea for poverty reduction, it clearly does not help poor countries if access to consumer markets is hindered by trade barriers and subsidies given to Northern producers, especially farmers (Gowan 1999). The World Trade Organization (WTO) continues to attract considerable criticism from antiglobalization protestors, especially in the aftermath of the Seattle meeting in November/December 1999. However, a credible WTO, with the willingness to tackle trade inequities and Northern dominance, would help to create conditions more favourable to the Global South. Notwithstanding unfair subsidies and trade barriers, Global South members of the WTO also face a further profound disadvantage: it is expensive and time-consuming to attend WTO summits and meetings, and small states with modest resources simply do not have the same access to knowledge networks and negotiating teams that countries such as the United States and groupings such as the European Union take for granted. This is profoundly important in terms of who participates and what gets discussed at each summit. There can also be over 1000 WTO meetings ever year, and these include discussions on dispute settlement, international standardization and trade liberalization. David Harvey has argued that these institutions encourage 'accumulation by dispossession', by forcing open markets while simultaneously refusing to 'open up' domestic markets (Harvey 2003).

While we often talk of international bodies such as the WTO and the IMF having a profound impact on the poor in the Global South, it is also worth noting that those same communities have also been aided and abetted by their respective diasporas. In London, for example, it is estimated that there are over 500,000 West Africans, many of whom are sending monies and other objects back to their families across the region. Globally, it is estimated that over 1 million Ethiopians are also contributing remittances to their home country and families therein. There has been a great deal of research on the role of overseas remittance and the contribution it makes to families around the world, including the Caribbean and South Pacific (Conway and Connell 2000). Ultimately, it may well be these modest flows of money and support that make a more meaningful difference to many citizens in those poor countries.

Conclusions

There is a great deal more to be said on this topic and this chapter has only touched on the cold war origins of development and the subsequent connections between North and South (Power 2003). The ending of the cold war did not bring the profound changes that many campaigners hoped for in respect of substantial reforms in the terms and conditions of international trade and generous debt reduction. Antiglobalization campaigners, alongside others such as Make Poverty History and the Jubilee Campaign, have helped to capture global media attention and pressurize Northern governments into making concessions on debt, trade and aid spending. However, these concessions are usually modest and are often nullified by the terms and conditions attached to aid and debt cancellation.

The war on terror now preoccupies the United States, and many countries are on the receiving end of aid and investment, especially when they are judged strategically significant with regard to preventing further terror attacks on the United States (Gregory 2004). The cold war may be over, but a similar process of labelling some parts of the Global South more useful than others continues, albeit against a backdrop informed by a fear of Islamic militancy rather than godless Communism. While America is preoccupied with terror networks, it is at the same time seeking to promote a selective form of international order, which takes seriously intellectual property rights, resource rights to oil and natural gas, and trade tariffs, but is less inclined to worry when human rights are abused, by either the US or its allies in the Global South. This selective approach carries with it inherent dangers and does nothing to enhance America's reputation in the wider world. More importantly, for poor countries in the Global South, a rules-based international order is absolutely critical in ensuring that poverty reduction and development (however modest) can gain some sort of momentum. Very few political leaders (such as Hugo Chávez of oil-rich Venezuela) have the luxury of calling the President of the United States a 'devil', or the time to read Noam Chomsky (Chomsky 2001).

GUIDE TO FURTHER READING

For an insightful guide to development geographies and the contested geopolitics of neoliberalism, see Power, M. (2003) *Rethinking Development Geographies*, London: Routledge.

An excellent account of the impact of the cold war on the Third World can be found in Westad, O. (2005) *The Global Cold War*, Cambridge: Cambridge University Press.

On the impact of the war on terror and its connections to older patterns of colonial violence, see Gregory, D. (2004) *The Colonial Present*, Oxford: Blackwell.

USEFUL WEBSITES

G8: www.g8.gov.uk
Make Poverty History: www.makepovertyhistory.org
World Trade Organization: www.wto.org

REFERENCES

Chomsky, N. (2001) *9–11*, New York: Seven Stories Press.
Conway, D. and Connell, J. (2000) 'Migration and remittances in island microstates: A comparative perspective on the South Pacific and the Caribbean', *International Journal of Urban and Regional Research*, 24(1): 52–78.
Fukuyama, F. (1989) 'The end of history', *The National Interest*, Summer, available at: www.wesjones.com/eoh.htm
Gowan, P. (1999) *The Global Gamble: Washington's Bid for Global Dominance*, London: Verso.
Gregory, D. (2004) *The Colonial Present*, Oxford: Blackwell.
Harvey, D. (2003) *The New Imperialism*, Oxford: Oxford University Press.
Johnson, C. (2000) *Blowback: The Costs and Consequences of American Empire*, New York: Henry Holt.
Power, M. (2003) *Rethinking Development Geographies*, London: Routledge.
Westad, O. (2005) *The Global Cold War*, Cambridge: Cambridge University Press.

1.2 Current trends and future options in development studies

Björn Hettne

Development studies in retrospect

At the beginning of the twenty-first century we are in an era which, rather depressingly for development theorists, has been described as 'post-development' (Escobar 1995). There is a need to reconsider purpose, content, agency and context in a reconstituted field of development studies. The classical discourse, which had its roots in the late 1940s and was institutionalized in the 1950s and 1960s, assumed the possibility of an autonomous, (inter)disciplinary field, containing a set of theoretical cores with development economics as a respected member of the family. The relevant theoretical schools, competing, yet in dialogue, were: *modernization*, *structuralism*, *dependency* and '*another development*', all normatively concerned with the specific problem of national development in the so-called 'Third World'.

The reconstruction of war-torn Europe provided the model for state-directed modernization of the 'new nations'. In this model, development was largely sociological and political in nature, and underdevelopment was defined in terms of differences between rich and poor nations. Development implied the bridging of the gap by means of an imitative process, in which the less developed countries gradually assumed the qualities of the developed. Marxist theory essentially shared this perspective. For structuralism, which dominated the early phase of development economics (still influenced by Keynesianism), a certain amount of intervention was considered necessary, due to institutional conditions which made growth in the poor areas less automatic than it was assumed to be in the so-called developed countries. From the late 1960s, modernization theory and structuralism were challenged by the Latin American *dependencia school*, which, together with the more global *world system theory*, articulated the weak structural position of Third World countries in the world system. The 'dependentistas', or 'neo-Marxists', asked for a radical political transformation within these countries, as well as a 'de-linking' of their economies from the world market (Blomström and Hettne 1984; Kay 1989). With its focus on state-driven industrialization, dependency theory did not differ much from the modernization and structuralist schools with respect to the content of development. In contrast, 'another development', a counterpoint to this modernist view, was defined as need-oriented, endogenous, self-reliant, ecologically sound and based on structural transformation (Nerfin 1977). However, the main concern for this and subsequent 'alternative' approaches was the many problems created in the course of mainstream development, and what to do with people who were excluded from development. Here the imperative of intervention reached a high degree of utopianism, but still it can be argued that the normative basis, against inequality and for emancipation, remains significant for development studies (Schuurman 2000).

Development and globalization

The interventionist approach was challenged by the rise of neoliberalism in the 1980s, a theoretical shift associated with a deepening of internationalization (globalization) and referred to as the 'counter-revolution' in development economics (Toye 1987). This was a purified neoclassical discourse, according to which development was an inherently universal and increasingly global economic process. Development economics was thus deprived of its autonomous status and removed from the interdisciplinary family. The development problem was seen as primarily domestic, created by 'rent-seeking' bureaucrats and corrupt politicians, with no blame at all put on the 'world system'. Another problem with the old interventionist approach was that in a 'globalized' world, the nation state no longer constituted the dominant framework for analysis and action. Development theory found itself at an impasse, and the subsequent debate was about escaping it (Booth 1985).

Much of what is new is summarized in the rather elusive concept of *globalization*. This is clearly a long-term historical process, but at the same time a qualitatively new one, in the sense that it is tooled by new information and communication technologies and a new organizational logic: networking (Castells 1996). The global and the local are enmeshed in a shrinking world. A related dimension of importance is the rise of supraterritoriality (Scholte 2000).

Globalization, as influenced by neoliberal economic policies, has become the new word for mainstream development. *Globalism* as development ideology implies the growth of a world market, increasingly penetrating and dominating 'national' economies. In contrast with the interventionist bias of the classical discourse, (ideological) globalists consider 'too much government' as a systemic fault. Good governance is thus defined as less government. In accepting this ideology, the state becomes the disciplining spokesperson of global economic forces, rather than the protector against these forces. It is not much of an exaggeration to say that, whereas a five-year plan was previously a must for a developing country expecting international assistance, after the 'counter-revolution' it would have disqualified that country from receiving aid.

From this perspective, classical development studies stands out as a non-starter, and as the new discourse reached a hegemonic position, the classical one ebbed away. Postmodern critics even claimed that what they referred to as 'the modern project' had collapsed. Others wanted to save it, arguing for a return of the political in some transnational form. According to this approach, development must be analysed within a larger space than the nation and merged with the international political economy (IPE). This could amount to a 'counter counter-revolution' (Krugman 1992) and a revival of the modern project. Many doubts remain, however.

Development and security

The classical discourse on development and security viewed global poverty and 'underdevelopment' as a threat to the liberal world order in the context of the emerging cold war (Hettne 2001). This was a hierarchical world order of centres and peripheries, which, together with bipolarity, shaped the general pattern of conflict, a struggle for power and at the same time a competition between different socio-economic systems. None of the theories constituting this discourse, summarized above, proved to be of much instrumental value for development in the poor countries. They were ultimately replaced by the policy of *structural adjustment*, a purified modernization paradigm of disciplined economic development, completely divorced from security concerns. These concerns reappeared soon enough in the form of food riots (the 'IMF riots'), but also in more traumatic forms of societal stress and violence. This disturbing reality has been referred to as 'postmodern conflict', 'neo-mediaevalism' or 'durable disorder' (Cerny 1998; Duffield 1998), a multitude of concepts which could indicate a paradigm shift in the making, reflecting an emerging globalized, chaotic world. The new 'political economy of warlordism' can be found in most parts of the world.

What could be the meaning of development in a world where the nation state is abdicating, people act in a vacuum, where global inequalities are increasing, where 'new wars' multiply and the poverty problem in development aid has been reduced to a civil form of intervention in 'complex humanitarian emergencies'? According to the conventional view, disintegration of the state leads to chaos and, consequently, non-development. The typical reaction among donors is that development aid also has to include conflict management and efforts to 'normalize' the situation. But non-state-centric analyses of 'real' substantive economies suggest a more complex picture of emerging local (or rather 'glocalized') economies, delinked from state control, run by new entrepreneurs, supported by private military protection and drawing on international connections. This is only the most obvious example of increasing global chaos, contradicting everything that the concept of development represented.

Development and culture

One theoretical way of accommodating the new uncertainties is postmodernism. Development thinking is undoubtedly a child of the Enlightenment, or the 'modern project', that is, the increasing capacity to design societies in accordance with rationalist principles. The credit for having deconstructed this magnificent myth, or grand narrative, is shared between feminism, postmodernism and cultural studies, emerging trends with a great deal of overlap.

The introduction of cultural studies to the study of development marked a significant change, going far beyond the 'cultural factor' in development (Tucker 1996). The cultural approach also implied a deconstruction of 'development' and the 'Third World'. Postmodern theory, which dominates cultural studies, is relativizing the whole business of development theorizing, thus making the project of 'development' rather senseless. Other theorists reject the relativism of postmodern thinking and look for a combination of political economy and cultural studies in order to get rid of the bathwater but keep the baby. The significance of culture and identity in development has to do not so much with the cultural factor in the process of development, as with abandoning Eurocentric development thinking (i.e. development as catching up and imitation), and instead conceiving and conceptualizing development as an inclusive, liberating process, in which different world views are accommodated and constitute a dialogical process (Munck and O'Hearn 1999). The new emphasis on culture has far-reaching implications, and may constitute the greatest challenge to the rethinking of development. The early development theorists were not self-critical enough on this issue, inter alia neglecting the fact that development is necessarily culture- and context-specific and that the specificity concerns the observer as well. Today, however, few social scientists would dispute that social theorizing will be significantly marked by the particular intellectual and practical context from which it emerges.

Development and world orders

Globalization implies the 'unbundling' of traditional state functions, a changed relationship between the state and civil society, and, in particular, a tendency for the state to become increasingly alienated from civil society. In this process of change, legitimacy, loyalty, identity and even sovereignty are transferred up or down in the system, to political entities other than the state (i.e. to macro-polities or micro-polities), at present with the latter predominating. Taking these diverging trends as a point of departure, one can think of three major routes towards a new world order. They do not determine content, but provide different global contexts, enabling some and excluding other solutions. Each of them thus contains variations on the main theme.

The first route is some sort of regression into pre-Westphalianism (which in most of the Third World corresponds to 'pre-colonial') – a world order with a drastically reduced role for the nation state as we know it, and little to compensate for this defect at the global level. Thus it does not permit effective global regulation. This route can be divided into two contrasting forms: one malevolent, implying a diffuse and turbulent system of changing authority structures in sometimes violent competition; and one benevolent, implying a better functioning multilevel order with a strong local base. The mode of development possible in the first context may be some sort of 'primitive accumulation', at best promising development in a distant future. In contrast, the benevolent decentralized model would give more room for 'alternative' forms of development, including protection of local resources, indigenous groups and other subnational regional interests, risking exclusion in mainstream development.

The second is a neo-Westphalian order, reformed and stabilized either by a reconstituted UN system or by a more loosely organized concert of dominant powers, assuming the privilege of intervention by reference to a shared value system focused on order. Here most of us would consider the former as the more benevolent form, since the latter lacks legitimacy. Furthermore, an assertive multilateralism would facilitate participation of the marginalized regions of the world.

The third is a post-Westphalian alternative, where the locus of power lies more firmly at the transnational level. The state can either be substituted by a regionalized order of political blocs, or by a strengthened global civil society, in both cases representing a step towards supranational governance either on a regional or a global level (Hettne et al. 1999; Nederveen Pieterse 2000). The regional approach contains both negative and positive communitarian forms; the cosmopolitan, certainly an attractive model, so far lacks both supportive institutions and emotional underpinnings. Could the two meet and merge?

A new start?

One problem in understanding qualitative/structural change in the globalized condition is a lack of appropriate social science terminology. The nation-state system and the establishment of capitalism gave rise to a conceptual framework devoted to the analysis of national space and – rather as an addition – international (interstate) relations, creating the great debate between 'statist' and 'transnational' approaches to the international system. The recent popularity of the word 'globalization' illustrates the disturbing lacuna with regard to appropriate concepts relevant for understanding contemporary structural change and providing a scientific basis for grasping a future order beyond the current turbulence. This conceptual poverty also implies a lack of political solutions to problems in the real world 'out there', since the novelty of the situation is not even grasped.

This is a challenge for all social sciences, but for development studies in particular. This field has changed in everything except its normative concern with emancipation from inequality and poverty. The emerging approach can be described as transcendence: development studies as a precursor of a comprehensive and universally valid historical social science, devoted to the contextual study of different types of societies in different phases of development, struggling to improve their structural position within the constraints of one world economy and one, albeit multilayered, world order. Furthermore, development theory needs to be reconstructed in terms of content as well. Some of the building blocks for a reconstitution, ultimately contributing to a unified historical and comprehensive social science, or 'global social theory', as discussed above, are: certain strands of international political economy (IPE) theory; a theory of the new development-related conflicts (and the links between peace and development); a new emphasis on cultural studies; and (reflecting the relevance of alternative thinking) a continuing concern for the excluded (including the difficult question of what the excluded shall then be included in). The question of development must, finally, be related to the issue of world order, since the framework within which development is analysed and acted on will no longer be the nation state only. The nature of this larger framework is still open, but undoubtedly of great importance for the future of development. Global development can be defined as improvement in the quality of international relations, which would require a strengthening of the welfare dimensions of world order – the provision of global public goods. This goal was expressed in the 2000 Millennium Declaration, the relevance of which was underlined dramatically by the threat of terrorism after September 11 the following year.

GUIDE TO FURTHER READING AND REFERENCES

The following text references provide the basis for further reading.

Blomström, M. and Hettne, B. (1984) *Development Theory in Transition. The Dependency Debate and Beyond: Third World Responses*, London: Zed Books.

Booth, D. (1985) 'Marxism and development sociology: Interpreting the impasse', *World Development*, 13(7): 761–87.

Castells, M. (1996) *The Rise of the Network Society*, Vol. 1: *The Information Age*, Oxford: Blackwell.

Cerny, P.G. (1998) 'Neomedievalism, civil war and the new security dilemma: Globalization as durable disorder', *Civil Wars* 1(1): 36–64.

Duffield, M. (1998) 'Post-modern conflict: Warlords, post-adjustment states and Private Protection', *Civil Wars* 1(1): 65–102.

Escobar, A. (1995) *Encountering Development: The Making and Unmaking of the Third World*, Princeton, NJ: Princeton University Press.

Hettne, B. (2001) 'Discourses on peace and development', *Progress in Development Studies* 1(1): 21–36.

Hettne, B., Inotai, A. and Sunkel, O. (eds) (1999) *Globalism and the New Regionalism*, London: Macmillan.

Kay, C. (1989) *Latin American Theories of Development and Underdevelopment*, London: Routledge.

Krugman, P. (1992) *Toward a Counter Counter-revolution in Development Theory*, Washington, DC: World Bank.

Munck, R. and O'Hearn, D. (eds) (1999) *Critical Development Theory: Contributions to a New Paradigm*, London: Zed Books.

Nederveen Pieterse, J. (2000) *Global Futures: Shaping Globalization*, London: Zed Books.

Nerfin, M. (ed.) (1977) *Another Development: Approaches and Strategies*, Uppsala: Dag Hammarsköld Foundation.

Scholte, J.A. (2005) *Globalization: A Critical Introduction*, second edition, London: Macmillan.

Schuurman, F.J. (2000) 'Paradigms lost, paradigms regained? Development studies in the twenty-first century', *Third World Quarterly*, 21(1): 7–20.

Toye, J. (1987) *Dilemmas of Development: Reflections on the Counterrevolution in Development Theory and Policy*, Oxford: Basil Blackwell.

Tucker, V. (1996) 'Introduction: A cultural perspective on development', *European Journal of Development Research*, 8(2): 1–21.

1.3 The impasse in development studies

Frans J. Schuurman

Introduction

Development studies is a relatively new branch of the social sciences. Coming into being in the late 1960s and early 1970s, it inherited many features of post-Second World War developments within the social sciences. Modernization theory contributed to its developmental orientation and its comparative methodology. From dependency theory it inherited its normative and progressive political character and its interdisciplinary conceptual frameworks.

In the 1970s, with dependency theory denouncing modernization theory as crypto-imperialist, and modernization theorists hitting back by accusing dependency authors of being populist pseudo-scientists, development studies found fertile ground and grew into an increasingly accepted new discipline of the social sciences. Universities – often under pressure from leftist professors and students – created Third World Centres. Debates about the nature and impact of development assistance became popular, and the existence of many dictatorial regimes in the South led to numerous solidarity committees in the North. In the 1980s, things started to change for development studies. A number of occurrences in that decade, which will be dealt with in the following paragraphs, led to an increasingly uneasy feeling within the discipline that old certainties were fading away. It was felt that development theories in the sense of a related set of propositions of the 'if...then' kind, could ever less adequately explain experiences of development and underdevelopment. Whether it concerned modernization theories or neo-Marxist dependency theories, both sets of development theories were losing out in terms of their explanatory power. From the mid-1980s onwards, the so-called 'impasse in development studies' was talked about. The contours of this impasse were sketched for the first time in a seminal article by David Booth in 1985. In the years which followed, other authors continued the discussion, which took on new dimensions with the end of the cold war and the debate on globalization.

Reasons for the impasse

Three reasons can be held responsible for having changed the panorama for development studies to such an extent that it created this theoretical impasse. Chronologically they were: (i) the failure of development in the South and the growing diversity of (under)development experiences; (ii) the postmodernist critique on the social sciences in general and on the normative characteristics of development studies in particular, and, finally, (iii) the rise of globalization in its discursive as well as its ontological appearance. Each of these issues is considered in the account that follows.

The failure of development in the South

Although until the 1980s developing countries realized average improvements in life expectancy, child mortality and literacy rates, more recent statistics have shown that these improvements were less valid for the poorest of these countries and, more specifically, for the lowest income groups. In fact, in the 1980s there was a reversal in some of the development indicators. It was realized that given the growth rates of that time, it would take another 150 years for Third World countries to achieve even half the per capita income of Western countries. Modernization theories failed to account for these figures and trends. Instead of a self-sustained growth (a much favoured concept of modernization), many developing countries were up to their ears in debt, which served to paralyse development initiatives.

Problems such as unemployment, poor housing, human rights offences, poverty and landlessness were increasing at alarming rates. UNICEF estimated a fall of 10–15 per cent in the income of the poor in the Third World between 1983 and 1987. In 1978, the Third World received 5.5 per cent of the world's income; in 1984 this had fallen to 4.5 per cent. The 'trickle-down' process (another favoured concept of modernization) had failed miserably. In 1960, the income ratio between the world's rich and poor countries was 20:1; in 1980 it increased to 46:1; and in 1989, the ratio was as high as 60:1.

Although dependency theory could certainly not be accused of an over-optimistic view concerning the developmental potentials of developing countries, it could not really account for the growing difference between Third World countries, nor were the developmental experiences of so-called socialist countries particularly enviable. In addition, Marxist and neo-Marxist development theories were dealt a heavy blow when the fall of the Berlin Wall meant the delegitimization of socialism as a political project of solving the problem of underdevelopment.

The postmodernist critique of the social sciences

The 1980s witnessed the advancement of postmodernism within the social sciences, bringing with it a tendency to undermine the 'great narratives' of capitalism, socialism, communism, and so forth. The basic argument was that there is no common reality outside the individual. As such, political alternatives, which always exist by the grace of a minimum of common perception, were manoeuvred out of sight. Development theories based on meta-discourses or on the role of a collective emancipatory agency lacked, according to the postmodern logic, a sound basis. The Enlightenment ideal of the emancipation of humanity (shared by modernization and dependency theory alike) had not been achieved, nor could it be achieved. In addition, in its quest for hidden metaphors, the postmodern method of deconstruction revealed that the notion of development contained a number of hidden and unwarranted evolutionist, universalist and reductionist dimensions, which would definitely lead anyone working with this notion down the wrong path. As such, development studies became a direct target for a wide range of views furthering the notion of 'alternative development'. Under postmodernist, or perhaps better put, antimodernist pressures, the central object of development studies – unequal access to power, to resources, to a humane existence – became increasingly substituted by something like socio-economic diversity. Apparently, the notion of diversity was considered to avoid the hidden universalist (read: Western or imperialist) and reductionist dimensions which inequality brought with it. At the same time, others considered this switch to a voluntarist and pluralist approach to the development problem not only anathema, but also inferior to a universalistic emancipation discourse.

Globalization

In the 1990s, the forces which had led to the impasse in development theories were joined by the discourse on globalization. Although the most recent factor, it probably represents the most important positive challenge to development studies. Whether globalization is a real phenomenon (cf. Hirst and Thompson 1996), or nothing more than a discourse to legitimize neoliberal market logic, it is undeniable that it has had a major influence on development studies in the 1990s. To understand why this is so, it is important to realize the significance of the (nation) state for social science theories in general, and for development studies in particular.

It is the declining, or at least changing, position and status of the (nation) state which has been, and still is, at the core of the literature on globalization. As an interdisciplinary branch of the social sciences, theories within development studies try to connect economic, political and cultural aspects of inequality and development trajectories. The connection between these aspects is realized by using the (nation) state as a linchpin. As such, theories of economic development became focused on the workings of the national market and on economic relations between countries. In theories of political development, the role of the state and the process of nation-building were central objects of study. In more culturalistic development theories, the notion of a national identity was crucial in understanding the differences between development trajectories. This importance of the (nation) state became visible in modernization theories, in neo-Marxist and Marxist development theories alike. Globalization changed all that. Many authors writing about globalization agree on the decreasing, or at least the changing, economic, political and cultural importance of (nation) states. The central role of the state, it is said, is being hollowed out from above as well as from below. In a political sense, there is the increasing importance of international political organizations which interfere politically and also militarily in particular states. In this way, they relegate to the past the Westphalian principles about the sovereignty of (nation) states and their monopoly on the use of institutionalized violence within their borders. The national state is hollowed out from below by the growing phenomenon of decentralization and local government.

Economically, the state is seen as disappearing as an economic actor through privatization supported by deregulation. Also, there is the growing importance of the global financial market, where about $1500 billion is shifted daily around the globe. Culturally, the idea of national identity as the central element in identity construction for individuals or groups is quickly eroding, in favour of cosmopolitanism on the one hand and/or the fortification of ethnic, regional and religious identities on the other.

It is not only that the globalization debate gives reason to suppose that the role of the (nation) state has been, and still is, declining, but also that, as a consequence, the former conjunctive dynamic (i.e. following the same spatial and time paths) of economy, polity and culture – on which the interdisciplinary character of many a development theory was based – has been replaced by a disjunctive dynamic (cf. Appadurai 1990). Development studies has yet to redefine its object and its subject – as have the other social sciences – vis-à-vis globalization, but this quest presents much more of a challenge than the former impasse ever did.

Conclusion

The impasse in development studies can in fact be traced back to a crisis of paradigms. The three reasons which were mentioned as being responsible for the impasse and its deepening – the lack of development and increasing diversity in the South, the postmodernist critique on 'grand narratives', and globalization – challenged, respectively, three post-Second World War developmental paradigms. These were:

1   the essentialization of the Third World and its inhabitants as homogeneous entities;
2   the unconditional belief in the enlightenment concepts of progress and the 'makeability' of society;
3   the importance of the (nation) state as an analytical frame of reference and a political and scientific confidence in the state to realize progress.

Each of these paradigms came in for criticism, one after the other. Development theories related to these paradigms (such as modernization and dependency theories) became automatically tainted as well, initiating the so-called impasse in development studies.

However, in spite of this impasse, an important number of authors in the field of development studies have continued their work, some using more grounded theories, others trying to elaborate on new concepts like civil society, global governance and global social movements. Many feel that the growing inequality between, as well as within, North and South is enough of a reason to continue with development studies. To fit this effort in with the new reality shaped by globalization presents a new and exciting challenge, and one which relegates the impasse to the past.

GUIDE TO FURTHER READING

Corbridge, S. (1989) 'Marxism, post-Marxism and the geography of development', in R. Peet and N. Thrift (eds) *New Models in Geography*, Vol. 1, London: Unwin Hyman, pp. 224–54. Identifies and elaborates on three dimensions in Booth's critique of neo-Marxist development theories, i.e. essentialism, economism and epistemology.

Edwards, M. (1989) 'The irrelevance of development studies', *Third World Quarterly*, 11(1): 116–36. Approaches development theories from the point of view of the practitioner.

Munck, R. and O'Hearn, D. (eds) (1999) *Critical Development Theory: Contributions to a New Paradigm*, London: Zed Books.

Schuurman, F.J. (ed.) (1993) *Beyond the Impasse: New Directions in Development Theory*, London: Zed Books. Provides a general overview of the dimensions of the impasse and the attempts to develop new theories, as well as the problems and possibilities of these attempts.

Simon, D. and Närman, A. (eds) (1999) *Development as Theory and Practice. Current Perspectives on Development and Development Co-operation*, Harlow: Longman.

Vandergeest, P. and Buttel, F. (1998): 'Marx, Weber, and development sociology: Beyond the impasse', *World Development*, 16(6): 683–95. Focuses on Booth's critique on the underlying meta-theoretical assumptions of Marxism, pointing out the necessity of looking within the heterogeneity of developing countries for common denominators.

Willis, K. (2005) *Theories and Practices of Development*, London: Routledge.

REFERENCES

Appadurai, A. (1990) 'Disjuncture and difference in the global cultural economy', in M. Featherstone (ed.) *Global Culture, Nationalism, Globalization and Modernity*, London: Sage, pp. 295–311.

Booth, D. (1985) 'Marxism and development sociology: Interpreting the impasse', *World Development*, 13: 761–87.

Hirst, P. and Thompson, G. (1996) *Globalization in Question*, Cambridge: Polity Press.

1.4 Post-development

James D. Sidaway

Instead of the kingdom of abundance promised by theorists and politicians in the 1950s, the discourse and strategy of development produced its opposite: massive underdevelopment and impoverishment, untold exploitation and repression. The debt crisis, the Sahelian famine, increasing poverty, malnutrition, and violence are only the most pathetic signs of the failure of forty years of development (Escobar 1995: 4).

Development occupies the centre of an incredibly powerful semantic constellation... at the same time, very few words are as feeble, as fragile and as incapable of giving substance and meaning to thought and behavior (Esteva 1992: 8).

Along with 'anti-development' and 'beyond development', post-development is a radical reaction to the dilemmas of development. Perplexity and extreme dissatisfaction with business-as-usual and standard development rhetoric and practice, and disillusionment with alternative development are keynotes of this perspective. Development is rejected because it is the 'new religion of the West'...it is the imposition of science as power...it does not work... it means cultural Westernisation and homogenisation...and it brings environmental destruction. It is rejected not merely on account of its results but because of its intentions, its worldview and mindset. The economic mindset implies a reductionist view of existence. Thus, according to Sachs, 'it is not the failure of development which has to be feared, but its success' (1992: 3) (Nederveen Pieterse 2000: 175).

Jan Nederveen Pieterse goes on to explain how, from these critical perspectives, 'development' often requires the *loss* of 'indigenous' culture, or of environmentally and psychologically rich and rewarding modes of life. Development is also seen as a particular vision, and one that is neither benign nor innocent. It reworks, but is never entirely beyond prior colonial discourses (see Kothari 2005). Development comprises a set of knowledges, interventions and world views (in short, a 'discourse') which are also powers – to intervene, to transform and to rule. It embodies a geopolitics, in that its origins are bound up with Western power and strategy for the Third World, enacted and implemented through local elites (see Slater 1993). Western agencies, charities and consultants often dominate the agendas (see Jackson 2005).

Development came to the fore in the Third World after 1945, as a powerful combination of policy, action and understanding. These configurations are changing fast with globalization, posing analytical and practical challenges (Sidaway 2007). Related to concepts of antidevelopment and post-colonial criticisms, post-development is, above all, a critique of the standard assumptions about progress, who possesses the keys to it and how it may be implemented. This critical understanding has also proven suggestive for thinking about the politics of local and regional development in (relatively peripheral parts of) Western Europe (see Donaldson 2006).

Of course, as a number of people have pointed out, many of these critiques represent reformulations of scepticisms and alternatives that have long been evident. According to Marshall Berman (1983), an example is the myth of Faust, which crops up repeatedly in European cultures. Faust is a man who would develop the world and himself, but must also destroy all that lies in his path to this goal, and all who would resist him. The myth of Faust, who sells his soul for the earthly power to develop, bears witness to a very long history of critics of progress and modernity. Throughout the twentieth century, populist ideas of self-reliance and fulfilling 'basic needs' have also been sceptical of many of the claims of development, particularly when the latter takes the forms of industrialization and urbanization (see Kitching 1989). Subsequently, the history of ideas of dependency has been, in part, a rejection of Western claims of development as a universal panacea to be implemented in a grateful Third World. From Latin American roots (see Kay 1989), dependency ideas were disseminated very widely, and sometimes took the form of a rejection of Western modernization/development as corrupting and destructive (see Blomstrom and Hettne 1984; Leys 1996; Rist 1997), or as a continuation of colonial forms of domination (Rodney 1972). In particular, writers from predominantly Islamic countries (most notably Iran) saw the obsession with development as part of a misplaced 'intoxification' with the West (see Dabashi 1993). Likewise, more conventional Marxist accounts have long pointed to the 'combined and uneven' character of development and its highly contradictory consequences (see Lowy 1980). Feminist writings have also criticized the ways in which the so-called 'Third World woman' is represented as needing 'development' and Western-style 'liberation' (Mohanty 1988), and have opened up alternative ways of conceptualizing the economic and social change of 'development'.

Some critics have therefore complained that 'post-development' is not really beyond, outside or subsequent to development discourse. In this view, post-development is merely the latest version of a set of criticisms that have long been evident *within* writing and thinking about development (Kiely 1999; Curry 2003). Development has always been about choices, with losers, winners, dilemmas and destruction, as well as creative possibility. Gavin Kitching (1989: 195), who is concerned to put post-Second World War debates about development into a longer historical perspective (stressing how they also reproduce even older narratives from the nineteenth century), argues:

> It is my view that the hardest and clearest thinking about development always reveals that there are no easy answers, no panaceas whether these be 'de-linking', 'industrialization', 'rural development', 'appropriate technology', 'popular participation', 'basic needs', 'socialism' or whatever. As I have had occasion to say repeatedly in speaking on and about this book, development is an awful process. It varies only, and importantly, in its awfulness. And that is perhaps why my most indulgent judgements are reserved for those, whether they be Marxist-Leninists, Korean generals, or IMF officials, who, whatever else they may do, recognize this and are prepared to accept its moral implications. My most critical reflections are reserved for those, whether they be western liberal-radicals or African bureaucratic elites, who do not, and therefore avoid or evade such implications and with them their own responsibilities.

In this sense, perhaps, post-development is chiefly novel not for its scepticism towards grand narratives about development, but for the theoretical frames (the analysis of discourse) which it brings to bear in problematizing these. For post-development writers, not only are there 'no easy answers', but the whole question of 'development' should be problematized and/or rejected.

There are a number of more fundamental objections to post-development. The first is that it overstates the case. Such arguments usually accept that development is contradictory (that it has winners and losers), but refuse to reject all that goes under its name. To reject all development is also seen as a rejection of the possibility for progressive material advancement and transformation; or to ignore the tangible transformations, in life chances, health, wealth and material well-being that have been evident in parts of the Third World, notably South East Asia (Rigg 2003). Moreover, development itself is so varied, and carries so many meanings (see Williams 1976), that analysts need to be specific about what they mean when they claim to be anti- or post-development.

In this context, Escobar's (1995) work, in particular, is often criticized. One objection is that he understates the potential for change within development discourse (see Brown 1996). Escobar's work reflects his experiences as an anthropologist in Colombia. As a rendition of Colombia, a society of ongoing violent civil war and foreign intervention, whose main export (by value) is cocaine, Escobar's critique of development would seem suggestive. But perhaps there is a risk that it obscures the diversity of experiences of development, not all of which are as problematic and contradictory as the Colombian experience.

The second objection involves rejecting post-development as yet another intellectual fad, of limited (or no) relevance to the poor in the Third World. Sometimes this objection draws attention to the fact that many of those who write about or disseminate post-development ideas live precisely the cosmopolitan, middle-class, relatively affluent lives that development promises to deliver. Such questions parallel the critique of *post-colonialism* as an intellectual fashion most useful to the careers of Western-based intellectuals.

However a few counter-arguments are in order here. First, a whole set of writings and ideas are grouped together under the rubric of post-development. Michael Watts (2000: 170) explains:

> There is of course a polyphony of voices within this post-development community – Vandana Shiva, Wolfgang Sachs, Arturo Escobar, Gustavo Esteva and Ashish Nandy, for example, occupy quite different intellectual and political locations. But it is striking how intellectuals, activists, practitioners and academics within this diverse community participated in a global debate.

Moreover, it is important to point out that for Escobar (1995) and others exploring the (geo)politics of development, to criticize development is not necessarily to reject change and possibility. Rather, it is to make us aware of the consequences of framing this as 'development'. Alternative visions, considering, for example, democracy, popular culture, resourcefulness and environmental impacts, would transform the imagined map of more or less developed countries. Recognition that development is but one way of seeing the world (and one which carries certain consequences and assumptions) can open up other perspectives. What happens, for example, to the perception of Africa when it is seen as *rich* in cultures and lives whose diversity, wealth and worth are not adequately captured by being imagined as more or less *developed*? Alternatively, why are poverty and deprivation (or, for that matter, excessive consumption among the affluent) in countries like the USA or the UK not issues of 'development' (see Jones 2000)? What is taken for granted when the term 'development' is used? It often seems that, in Escobar's (1995: 39) words, development has 'created a space in which only certain things could be said or even imagined'. Post-development literatures teach us not take this 'space' and its contours for granted.

GUIDE TO FURTHER READING

Crush, J. (ed.) (1995) *Power of Development*, London and New York: Routledge. An introduction and collection of 14 essays that examine the 'power' of development discourses. The essays show how development's claims to be a solution to problems of national and global poverty, disorder and environmental degradation, are often illusions.

Escobar, A. (1995) *Encountering Development: The Making and Unmaking of the Third World*, Princeton, NJ: Princeton University Press. Written by a Colombian anthropologist, and drawing on the trajectory of that country (while making more general claims), this critique uses the ideas of Michel Foucault to understand 'development' as a discourse and therefore as a particular (Western) regime of truth, power and knowledge.

Ferguson, J. (1990) *The Anti-Politics Machine: 'Development', Depoliticization and Bureaucratic Power in Lesotho*, Cambridge: Cambridge University Press. Like Escobar, this is another book-length critique of the discourse of development written by an anthropologist. It is less sweeping in its claims than Escobar, but no less persuasive in its arguments. Subsequent texts by this author, *Global Shadows: Africa in the Neoliberal World Order* (2006) and *Expectations of Modernity: Myths and Meanings of Urban Life on the Zambian Copperbelt* (1999), are also rewarding.

Rahnema, M. and Bawtree, V. (eds) (1997) *The Post-Development Reader*, London: Zed Books. An introduction plus 440 pages, comprising 37 short extracts (and an afterword) from thinkers, politicians and activists who problematize development. Each reading has a short introduction that helps to contextualize it (written by the editors). This is probably the best place to start a course of further reading and/or to get a flavour of 'post-development'.

Saunders, K. (ed.) (2002) *Feminist Post-Development Thought: Rethinking Modernity, Post-colonialism and Representation*, London: Zed Books. Seventeen essays examining intersections between feminism, post-development and post-colonialism.

REFERENCES

Berman, M. (1983) *All That Is Solid Melts Into Air: The Experience of Modernity*, London: Verso.

Blomstrom, H. and Hettne, B. (1984) *Development Theory in Transition: The Dependency Debate and Beyond: Third World Responses*, London: Zed Books.

Brown, E. (1996) 'Deconstructing development: Alternative perspectives on the history of an idea', *Journal of Historical Geography*, 22(3): 333–9.

Curry, G.N. (2003) 'Moving beyond postdevelopment: Facilitating indigenous alternatives for "development"', *Economic Geography*, 79(4): 405–23.

Dabashi, H. (1993) *Theology of Discontent: The Ideological Foundation of the Islamic Revolution in Iran*, New York and London: New York University Press.

Donaldson, A. (2006) 'Performing regions: Territorial development and cultural politics in a Europe of the regions', *Environment and Planning A*, 38(11): 2075–92.

Escobar, A. (1995) *Encountering Development: The Making and Unmaking of the Third World*, Princeton, NJ: Princeton University Press.

Esteva, G. (1992) 'Development', in W. Sachs (ed.) *The Development Dictionary: A Guide to Knowledge as Power*, London: Zed Books, pp. 6–25.

Jackson, J.T. (2005) *The Globalizers: Development Workers in Action*, Baltimore, MD: Johns Hopkins University Press.

Jones, P.S. (2000) 'Why is it alright to do development "over there" but not "here"? Changing vocabularies and common strategies of inclusion across the "First" and "Third" Worlds', *Area*, 32(2): 237–41.

Kay, C. (1989) *Latin American Theories of Development and Underdevelopment*, London and New York: Routledge.

Kiely, R. (1999) 'The last refuge of the noble savage? A critical account of post-development', *European Journal of Development Research*, 11(1): 30–55.

Kitching, G. (1989) *Development and Underdevelopment in Historical Perspective: Populism, Nationalism and Industrialization*, revised edition, London and New York: Routledge.

Kothari, U. (2005) 'From colonial administration to development studies: A post-colonial critique of the history of development studies', in U. Kothari (ed.) *A Radical History of Development Studies: Individuals, Institutions and Ideologies*, London: Zed, pp. 47–66.

Leys, C. (1996) *The Rise and Fall of Development Theory*, London: James Currey.

Lowy, M. (1980) *The Politics of Combined and Uneven Development: The Theory of Permanent Revolution*, London: New Left Books.

Mohanty, C.P. (1988) 'Under western eyes: Feminist scholarship and colonial discourses', *Feminist Review*, 30: 61–88.

Nederveen Pieterse, J. (2000) 'After post-development', *Third World Quarterly*, 21(2): 175–91.

Rigg, J. (2003) *Southeast Asia: The Human Landscape of Modernization and Development*, second edition, London and New York: Routledge.

Rist, G. (1997) *The History of Development: From Western Origins to Global Faith*, London: Zed Books.

Rodney, W. (1972) *How Europe Underdeveloped Africa*, London: Bogle L'Ouverture.

Sidaway, J.D. (2007) 'Spaces of postdevelopment', *Progress in Human Geography*, 31(3): 1–17.

Slater, D. (1993) 'The geopolitical imagination and the enframing of development theory', *Transactions of the Institute of British Geographers*, New Series, 18: 419–37.

Watts, M. (2000) 'Development', in R.J. Johnson, D. Gregory, G. Pratt and M. Watts (eds) *The Dictionary of Human Geography*, Oxford: Blackwell, 167–71.

Williams, R. (1976) *Keywords*, London: Fontana.

1.5 New institutional economics and development

Philipp Lepenies

New institutional economics (NIE) strongly influences current development theory and policy. It is an expansion of traditional neoclassical economic theory and its merits stem from the fact that it has identified efficient institutions to be a prerequisite for development.

What is NIE?

NIE attempts to incorporate a theory of institutions into economics. It is a deliberate attempt to make neoclassical economic theory more 'realistic'. Neoclassical economic theory assumed that information flows freely between the actors in competitive markets and that, as a result, institutions do not matter. In contrast, NIE postulates that information is distributed asymmetrically (asymmetrical information) and that market transactions come at a cost (i.e. the cost of gathering information, or transaction costs). Consequently, institutions have to be formed to reduce these costs.

NIE retains the neoclassical assumptions that individuals seek to maximize their utility from scarce resources subject to budget constraints and that collective outcomes rest on the choices made by rational individuals (i.e. methodological individualism). However, it discards the concept of instrumental rationality, which implies that the choices made by each individual are completely foreseeable. With all information readily available to everyone (perfect information), there is no uncertainty in human actions. Institutions become unnecessary and efficient markets characterize economies.

The necessity for a modification of neoclassical theory arose from the fact that so-called social dilemmas could not be explained by it. Social dilemmas are situations in which the choices made by rational individuals yield outcomes that are socially irrational. This is obvious in the case of market failures that can be caused by negative externalities (i.e. a cost arising from an activity which does not accrue to the person or organization carrying on the activity, e.g. pollution) and public goods (i.e. goods that are open to all, free of charge and thus not usually supplied by the market), but also applies to cases of asymmetrical or imperfect information (i.e. information is not fully available to everyone). Imperfect information might cause moral hazards (i.e. the danger that one of two parties of a contract knowingly alters her behaviour in order to maximize her utility at the other party's expense); adverse selection (e.g. imperfect health insurance contracts attract those who have high health risks); and/or principal-agent dilemmas (i.e. the problem of how a 'principal' can motivate an 'agent' to act for the principal's benefit rather than following his or her self-interest).

NIE's core argument is that institutions provide the mechanisms whereby rational individuals can transcend social dilemmas and economize on transaction costs (Bates 1995: 29). Institutions are thus 'the rules of the game of society...the humanly devised constraints that structure human interaction. They are composed of formal rules (statute law, common law, regulations), informal constraints (conventions, norms of behaviour and self-imposed rules of conduct), and the enforcement characteristics of both' (North 1995: 23).

The term 'new institutional economics' was coined in the 1970s by Oliver Williamson to distinguish it from an earlier attempt to incorporate institutions into economic theory at the beginning of the twentieth century, the so-called '(old) institutional economics', whose main authors were Thorstein Veblen and John R. Commons.

The concept of NIE came into being in 1937, when Ronald Coase explained the existence of firms. Ironically, neoclassical theory could not explain why firms existed and why market transactions were not carried out solely by individuals, as methodological individualism suggests. Coase departed from the Walrasian notion of market transactions being made costless on the spot by an invisible and omniscient auctioneer (i.e. the idea of perfect information). Instead he assumed that 'the main reason why it is profitable to establish a firm would seem to be that there is a cost of using the price mechanism' (Coase 1937: 390). Transactions thus involve the cost of discovering what the relevant prices are.

With time, the idea of transaction costs, probably the single-most important concept of NIE, was developed further. Some authors distinguish different transaction costs in accordance with the three big areas of analysis within NIE – the market, the firm and the state. Thus there are:

* market transaction costs, which are those described by Coase;
* management transaction costs within a firm that come as a result of administrative procedures, strategic planning and supervision of the workforce;
* political transaction costs, which are the costs of establishing, enforcing and utilizing a political system.

Others identify transaction costs according to the process of transacting (i.e. information and search costs, costs of negotiating contracts and the costs of enforcing them). Yet all transaction costs 'have in common that they represent resources lost due to lack of information' (Dahlman 1979: 148).

It is important to point out that NIE is not a homogeneous school of thought. Rather, it consists of a variety of theoretical writings by a large number of different authors. NIE includes research on transaction costs, political economy, contract theory, property rights, hierarchy and organizations, public choice and development.

NIE and development

Since the 1990s, NIE has had a tremendous impact on development policy and theory. This can be demonstrated by tracing out the obvious influence that NIE has had on the World Bank, by presenting Douglass C. North's NIE-inspired theory of development and by describing the relevance of NIE for development practitioners.

NIE and the World Bank

Since free markets alone could not be relied on to ensure development, NIE emphasizes the necessity for development policy to design favourable growth-inducing institutional settings. This was reflected in the new role ascribed to the state in the World Bank's *World Development Report*

(WDR) *The State in a Changing World* (1997). Therein, the state, having been viewed as an obstacle to the functioning of competitive markets in the years before, was suddenly identified as an important facilitator of favourable institutional arrangements.

The appointment of Joseph Stiglitz, a major theorist of NIE, as chief economist of the World Bank, also reflected the influence of NIE on the Bank's policy. In 1986, Stiglitz stated that the assumptions of neoclassical economics were 'clearly irrelevant' for the analysis of developing countries. Instead he showed that asymmetrical information prevailed in most markets (1986: 257). During his spell as chief economist of the World Bank, the bank began to define itself as a 'knowledge bank', whose responsibility was to gather and disseminate information transparently on a global scale. NIE dominated the WDR 1998/1999, *Knowledge for Development*, which highlighted the general importance of overcoming asymmetrical information in development. The influence of NIE was also obvious in the WDR 1999/2000, *Entering the 21st Century*, which summarized the lessons learned from the previous 50 years of global development policy. One lesson plainly read: 'Institutions matter' (World Bank 1999: 1).

Explaining institutional change and underdevelopment

A major branch of NIE is concerned with the analysis of institutional change and underdevelopment. Its most prominent author is Douglass C. North, who added a historical perspective to neoclassical economics. Historically, societies had to learn how to solve the problem of scarcity.

> The key…is the kind of learning that organisations acquired to survive. If the institutional framework made the highest pay-off for organisation's piracy, then organisational success and survival dictated that learning would take the form of being better pirates. If on the other hand productivity-raising activities had the highest pay-off, then the economy would grow (North, 1995: 21).

Thus, developmental outcomes in the world differ according to how people learn to cope with scarce resources.

For North, the Western capitalist system has been flexible enough to adapt itself to the institutional necessities induced by the higher division of labour, minute specialization, impersonal exchange and worldwide interdependence. However, in a country with inefficient institutions, only a process of internal re-contracting can change the institutional setting. As long as those holding the bargaining power have an incentive to defend the status quo, and inefficiencies are perceived to be rewarding, the situation will not improve (path dependence). This is a major deviation from the neoclassical notion of long-term equilibrium – and a more pessimistic one where underdevelopment becomes plausible.

The practical relevance of NIE for development

The practical relevance of NIE is twofold. First, concepts such as asymmetrical information, transaction costs, adverse selection, moral hazard and principal-agent dilemmas are currently widely used tools for socio-economic analysis. Second, they serve as the basis for individual project design. Institution-building itself has become the *raison d'être* of many development projects since the late 1990s.

Parting from the definition of 'institutions', any attempt to establish 'rules of the game' and their enforcement characteristics (be it new laws, regulations or governance structures) can consequently be seen as an application of NIE.

A prominent case where concepts of NIE are used is that of the analysis of financial services for the poor. The banking sector usually does not offer financial services to the informal sector because information is asymmetrically distributed between the potential borrower and lender. The lender does not have sufficient information on the borrower, whom he does not know personally, who usually does not keep written accounts or business plans and who cannot offer physical collateral. Thus, the lender cannot calculate the risk of default. As a result, credit to the informal sector is rationed since lenders are reluctant to give out credit. If financial services to the poor are to be provided, these problems have to be addressed with adequate institutional design.

In the absence of physical collateral, for instance, group-based lending could be an institutional design option to overcome the problems of asymmetrical information. By introducing peer-monitoring as a control mechanism of the borrowers, and by linking future payments to group members to the repayment performance of the entire group during monitored weekly meetings, the risks posed by the lack of information described above are minimized.

However, just as NIE is a heterogeneous theory, there is also no such thing as a clear-cut NIE approach to development. Few development practitioners or theorists who make use of NIE concepts would define themselves as being 'of the NIE'. Yet the fact that elements of NIE are used so widely, and that the importance of institution-building has been generally acknowledged, is arguably the strongest sign of how much NIE has already become commonplace in development.

Critique and conclusion

NIE has 'challenged the dominant role ascribed to the market…[by highlighting that] neither state nor market is invariably the best way in which to organise the provision of goods and services', and that efficient institutions are the key to successful development (Harris, Hunter and Lewis 1995: 1). It is, without a doubt, the strongest merit of NIE to have put the issue of institutions on the development agenda.

However, NIE is not without limitations. As noted before, NIE is an attempt to change neoclassical economics from within. This alone is praiseworthy. Yet, as it maintains the basic assumption that individuals rationally pursue the maximization of their utility at all times, little or no room is given to any behaviour which might not be guided by the individual's rationally calculated quest for utility maximization. Hence, NIE is still not realistic enough as it maintains a simplistic and incomplete model of human behaviour.

The major flaw of NIE, be it in development or elsewhere, is that many concepts of NIE are hard to measure, sometimes even hard to define, as 'a clear cut definition of transaction costs does not exist' (Eggertsson 1990: 14). From this derives the difficulty in measuring exactly what transaction costs are. The same applies to the notion of asymmetrical information, or the simple question, what 'information' means – especially when one takes into account that 'information' might mean different things to different people. Research which utilizes concepts of NIE might thus bring forth insights for a special case. Nevertheless, it is often not comparable with other findings.

Laudably, NIE's historical analysis of development and institutional change rejects the simple idea of market-driven institutional progress. All the same, the attempt to explain persistent underdevelopment by analysing if and how institutions have used resources efficiently in the past is not as straightforward as it seems. A major problem arises out of the way in which history is interpreted. Different interpretations of the past might give rise to various interpretations of the present, especially concerning the reasons for underdevelopment. Therefore, a historical interpretation might not be shared by everyone. Any historical analysis is just one possible point of view – among many others.

In North's (1995) approach, the reasons for persistent underdevelopment are by assumption endogenous. As long as the bargaining power rests with those forces of society that have an interest in perpetuating inefficient institutions, no efficient institutions can emerge. Yet the role that external factors (e.g. international political or economic power structures) can play in the explication of underdevelopment is not particularly highlighted – a severe omission given the global economic and political interdependencies. More problematic still is his notion of path-dependence. With this idea, it seems that countries are trapped in their inefficiencies. This view is overly pessimistic and eclipses the possibility of active development or development cooperation.

Notwithstanding, NIE undoubtedly provides useful explanatory tools for research. It has also rightly identified institution-building as a necessary developmental activity. Nevertheless, identifying a problem through NIE-inspired analysis does not automatically lead to infallibly designed institutions. Therefore, when attempts are made at institution-building, caution is advised when the newly created 'rules of the game' presuppose economically rational and utility-focused behaviour of the target group. Humans do not necessarily behave as assumed in neoclassical economics. The more practitioners take note of the complexities of human nature when designing institutions, and the more they part from the assumptions about human behaviour underlying NIE, the more probable it will be that their institutions function as desired. However, were it not for NIE, practitioners might still not bother about institutions at all.

GUIDE TO FURTHER READING

Furobotn, E.G. and Richter R. (1998) *Institutions and Economic Theory. The Contribution of the New Institutional Economics*, Ann Arbor: Michigan University Press. A very thorough and detailed analysis of practically all aspects of NIE.

REFERENCES

Bates, R.H. (1995) 'Social dilemmas and rational individuals: An assessment of the new institutionalism', in J. Harris, J. Hunter and C.M. Lewis (eds) *The New Institutional Economics and Third World Development*, London: Routledge, pp. 27–48.

Coase, R. (1937) 'The nature of the firm', *Economica*, 4: 386–405.

Dahlman, C. (1979) 'The problem of externality', *Journal of Law and Economics*, 22: 141–62.

Eggertsson, T. (1990) *Economic Behavior and Institutions*, Cambridge: Cambridge University Press.

Harris, J., Hunter, J. and Lewis, C.M. (1995) 'Introduction: Development and significance of NIE', in J. Harris, J. Hunter and C.M. Lewis (eds) *The New Institutional Economics and Third World Development*, London: Routledge, pp. 1–13.

North, D.C. (1995) 'The new institutional economics and Third World development', in J. Harris, J. Hunter and C.M. Lewis (eds) *The New Institutional Economics and Third World Development*, London: Routledge, pp. 17–26.

Stiglitz, J.E. (1986) 'The new development economics', *World Development*, 14: 257–65.

World Bank (1997) *World Development Report 1997: The State in a Changing World*, Oxford: Oxford University Press.

World Bank (1998) *World Development Report 1998/1999: Knowledge for Development*, Oxford: Oxford University Press.

World Bank (1999) *World Development Report 1999/2000: Entering the 21st Century*, Oxford: Oxford University Press.

Note: The views expressed in this contribution are the author's own. Contact: philipp.lepenies@kfw.de

1.6 The measurement of poverty

Howard White

Introduction

The importance of the task of poverty reduction means that we must be clear as to what we mean by poverty, who the poor are and the best way to help them escape poverty. This chapter is concerned with the first of these points – the meaning and measurement of poverty. The first section outlines key concepts which underpin the various poverty measurements discussed in the subsequent section. Finally, some data on poverty trends are presented.

Poverty concepts

In everyday usage, the term 'poverty' is synonymous with a shortage of income. But the development literature stresses the multidimensionality of poverty. In addition to material consumption, health, education, social life, environmental quality, spiritual and political freedom all matter. Deprivation with respect to any one of these can be called poverty.

Some dispute the use of multidimensionality, arguing that income poverty (i.e. lack of material well-being) is what really matters. Arguments supporting this view include the high correlation between income and other measures of well-being, such as health and education status, and the view that governments can do something about income (i.e. support growth), but are less able to enhance spiritual well-being.

But there are good arguments in defence of multidimensionality. First, the correlation with income is not that strong for some indicators. Second, poor people themselves often rank other dimensions as being more important than income. Most famously, Jodha (1988) showed with Indian data that the welfare of the poor had risen by measures they considered important – such as wearing shoes and separate accommodation for people and livestock – whereas surveys showed their income to have fallen. Participatory approaches to poverty measurement seek to identify the things that matter to poor people. Different perceptions matter since the poverty concept adopted will influence policy. When poverty is defined solely in terms of income, then it is unsurprising that economic growth is found to be the most effective way to reduce poverty. But if basic needs such as health and education are valued, then the development strategy is likely to put more emphasis on social policy.

Two further conceptual issues are: absolute versus relative poverty; and temporary versus permanent poverty. Absolute poverty is measured against some benchmark – such as the cost of getting enough food to eat, or being able to write your own name for literacy. Relative poverty is measured against societal standards; in developing countries the basket of 'essentials' comprises food and a few items of clothing, whereas in developed countries it includes Christmas presents and going out once a month.

The distinction between the temporarily and the permanently poor is linked to the notion of vulnerability. The vulnerable are those at risk of falling into poverty. If there are poverty traps – such that once someone falls into poverty they cannot get out again – then there is a good case for antipoverty interventions to prevent this happening.

Poverty measures

National-level measures

The most commonly reported development statistic is a country's GNP per capita. While a case may be made for using GNP as an overall development measure, it is not a good measure of poverty for two reasons. First, as an average, the statistic takes no account of distribution. Hence two countries can have the same level of GNP per capita, but in one of the two, a far greater proportion of the population fall below the poverty line if income is less equally distributed. Second, GNP is an income measure which ignores other dimensions of poverty.

The most common income-poverty measure is the headcount, that is, the percentage of the population falling below the poverty line. However, this measure takes no account of how far people are below the poverty line – so that a rise in the income of the poor which leaves them in poverty appears to have no effect. Hence another measure, the poverty gap, is often used, which can be variously interpreted as the product of the headcount and the average distance of the poor below the poverty line (expressed as a percentage of the poverty line) and the benefit of perfect targeting. The poverty severity index is a similar measure which puts greater weight on those furthest below the poverty line. These three measures – the headcount, the poverty gap and the poverty severity index – are known collectively as the Foster-Greer-Thorbecke poverty measures, and labelled P_0, P_1 and P_2 respectively.

Over the years, a number of composite measures of development have been proposed (a composite being an average of a number of different measures). A previous measure, the physical quality of life index (PQLI), has been superseded in recent years by the United Nations Development Programme's (UNDP) human development index (HDI). The HDI is a composite of GDP per capita, life expectancy and a measure of educational attainment (which is an average of literacy and average enrolment rate for primary, secondary and tertiary education). However, just as income per capita takes no account of distribution, neither does the HDI: schooling can show an increase by the already well educated extending their university education, rather than access expanding among those with little or no education. However, UNDP has also proposed a human poverty index (HPI), which focuses on deprivation. Specifically, the HPI is calculated as the average of the percentage of the population not expected to live to 40, the percentage who are illiterate and what is called the 'deprivation in living standard' (the average of those without access to water and health care, and the percentage of under-fives who are underweight).

Although the HDI is widely used there have been criticisms of its construction (which are summarized in a technical appendix to the 1996 *Human Development Report*), one of which concerns problems in using a composite. There are three main problems: which variables to put in the index; the necessarily arbitrary choice of weights in constructing the average; and that information is lost by combining three or four pieces of data into a single number. Thus it may be preferable to report a small range of social indicators, such as life expectancy, infant and child mortality, and literacy, rather than attempt to combine these in an overall poverty index.

The measurement of income poverty

The income-poverty headcount is the percentage of the population whose income is below the poverty line. This calculation is fraught with difficulties.

First, poverty lines must be defined (it is common practice to use two lines), which is done either absolutely, with reference to the cost of a basket of goods, or relatively, to mean income or a certain share of the population. In the former case, the basket can be calculated either as the cost of acquiring a certain number of calories or of a basket of goods and services. In the first example, the resulting poverty line (food poverty line) is often used as the line for the extreme poor. It is then divided by the share of food in the budget of the poor (or the population as a whole, though strictly defined it should be that of a person on the poverty line) to get the upper poverty line.

In applying the poverty line, consumption (expenditure) is commonly used rather than income. First, this is because survey respondents will have a far clearer idea of their expenditure than their income. Second, when income is uneven households will smooth consumption (i.e. even it out over time), so that at any point in time current consumption is likely to be a more accurate measure of well-being than current income.

In practice, data are collected at the level of the household rather than the individual. Doing so ignores problems of intra-household allocation. There are no data on the number of women or children living in poverty (despite the tendency of some international organizations to report such figures), only data on the percentage of women and children living in households whose income is below the poverty line. The use of household-level data introduces problems of household composition and size. Household composition matters since the consumption requirements of different individuals vary – specifically, children consume less than adults and, more controversially, women may need to consume less than men. This problem is catered for by the use of an adult equivalents scale, which expresses the consumption needs of women and children as a fraction of those of an adult male. Household size matters as there are economies of scale in household consumption – that is, two can live together more cheaply than they could apart as there are shared expenses (living space, utilities and many household items). Failure to take account of these economies will overstate poverty in large households.

Finally, prices vary across time and space. Allowance must be made for these price differences in order for the poverty line to be comparable. There are even greater difficulties in comparing between countries, partly since market exchange rates do not reflect differences in purchasing power. Rather, purchasing power parity (PPP) exchange rates should be used, which are not uniformly available.

Comparisons across time and space also require that consumption is measured in a comparable way. If survey designs differ greatly, then 'aggregate consumption' may mean quite different things. It is commonly recognized that own-production should be measured as this is an important part of total consumption. But 'wild foods' (collected in nature) and festivals can also form an important source of food and are commonly overlooked. Similarly, sources of income from common property, or the provision of free social services, vary between countries and so introduce another source of incomparability.

It may seem from this discussion that measurement of income poverty is so difficult that it may be better to stick to some other measure. Certainly a small survey should stick to a proxy for income, such as housing quality and ownership of a few household items. But other indicators are not without problems; indeed data quality is far worse for many social indicators than it is for income/expenditure.

Some data

Estimates of 'dollar a day' poverty are calculated only for the developing world. The proportion of absolutely poor in developed countries by this measure is nil or negligible. In the figure showing the evolution of 'dollar a day' poverty since the early 1980s, the most striking trend is the dramatic fall in poverty in East Asia, powered largely by reductions in the number of poor in the world's most populous country, China, but assisted by more recent declines in neighbouring Vietnam. There has been a slower, but still marked, decline in the poverty headcount in south Asia, including in the world's second largest country, India. By the mid-1990s, the rate of decline was sufficient for the absolute number of poor people in south Asia to start falling. Asia thus makes up the vast bulk of poverty reduction in the closing decades of the last century. During the 1990s, global poverty fell from 27.9 per cent in 1990 to 21.1 per cent in 2001, but excluding China these figures

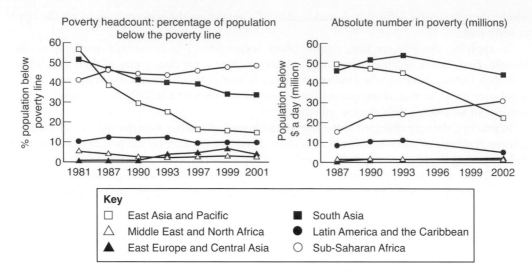

'Dollar a day' poverty by region, 1983–2002
Source: World Bank data

were 26.1 and 22.2 per cent respectively. That is, almost half the fall in poverty came from China alone. Indeed, sub-Saharan Africa, which has suffered economic hardship since the 1970s, saw a rise in income poverty, with close to half the people on the subcontinent now living on less than a dollar a day. Africa's poor performance lays behind the low overall fall in the number of poor from 1.2 billion in 1987 to 1.03 billion in 2002. Africa's share in this total rose from 12 to 30 per cent over this period (whereas Asia's fell from 80 to 64 per cent). The final trend of note is the resurgence of poverty in the formerly centrally planned economies, following the collapse of communist governments, though there has been some remission since the turn of the century.

The Africanization of poverty is also evident when considering other poverty measures. Health is commonly measured by infant mortality (the number of children who die before their first birthday per 1000 live births) and child mortality (deaths between first and fifth birthdays per 1000 children); these two indicators are combined to make under-five mortality. The United Nations Population Division reports population data, including mortality, from 1950, with projections to 2050. The positive news is that, in line with the long-run improvement in social indicators across the developing world, mortality rates have been falling (see figure showing 'child mortality rate'), though some African countries experienced a reversal in the 1990s as a result of HIV/AIDS and worsening health systems after three decades of economic decline. In Africa as a whole, the decline in mortality rates has been insufficient to keep up with population growth, so that the number of deaths has continued to rise. A turnaround is expected around the time of writing (2006), but the situation in Africa will improve less than elsewhere, so the continent will account for close to two-thirds of the world's under-five deaths in the coming decades.

GUIDE TO FURTHER READING AND REFERENCES

Most of the literature on poverty measurement concerns income poverty, the most comprehensive, though technical, treatment being Ravallion (1992). A critique of income measures is given by Jodha (1988) and a discussion of alternatives is in Chambers (1995). More general analysis of both concepts and measurement is available in Baulch (1996) and White (1999). For a broader coverage of poverty issues, consult the series of poverty briefings produced by the Overseas Development Institute, including 'The meaning and

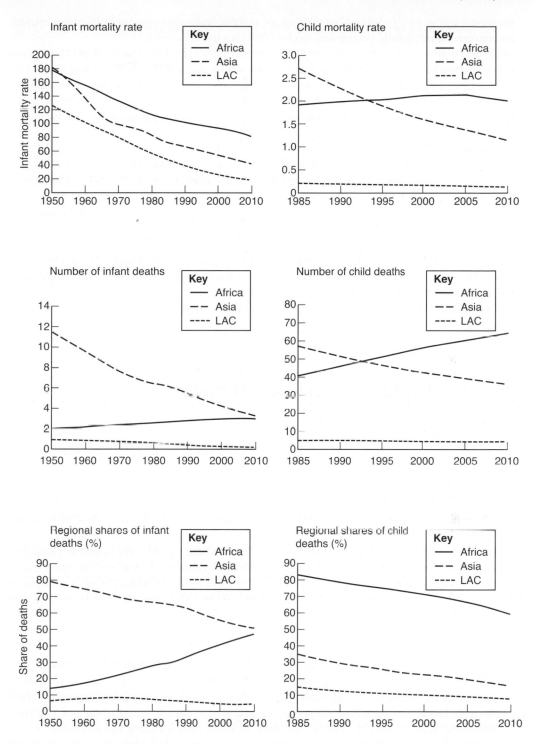

Trends in infant and child mortality rate (per 1000)

measurement of poverty' by Simon Maxwell (these are available from www.odi.org.uk/publications/briefing/poverty/index.html). Finally, Gordon and Spicker (1999) is a useful resource.

The main data sources are the UNDP's *Human Development Report* and the World Bank's *World Development Indicators*, both of which are published annually (with the latter available on CD-ROM). Past issues of the *Human Development Report* contain discussions of the various indices presented, including the HDI and HPI, while *World Development Indicators* contains useful information on data sources. The World Bank's poverty data are available from www.worldbank.org/poverty, which includes many useful links to poverty-related material.

The following text references provide the basis for further reading.

Baulch, B. (1996) 'The new poverty agenda: A disputed consensus', *IDS Bulletin*, 27: 1–10.

Black, R. and White, H. (2004) *Targeting Development: Critical Perspectives on the Millennium Development Goals*, London: Routledge.

Chambers, R. (1995) *Poverty and Livelihoods: Whose Reality Counts?* Brighton: Institute of Development Studies, Discussion paper 347.

Gordon, D. and Spicker, P. (eds) (1999) *International Glossary on Poverty*, London: Zed Books.

Jodha, N.S. (1988) 'Poverty debate in India: A minority view', *Economic and Political Weekly*, 22(45–47): 2421–8.

Ravallion, M. (1992) *Poverty Comparisons: A Guide to Concepts and Methods*, Washington, DC: World Bank, Living Standards Measurement Study, Working Paper 88.

White, H. (1999) 'Global poverty reduction: Are we heading in the right direction?', *Journal of International Development*, 11: 503–19.

1.7 The Millennium Development Goals

Jonathan Rigg

Deriving the goals

The Millennium Development Goals (MDGs) were adopted by the General Assembly of the United Nations on 18 September 2000, at the UN Millennium Summit. Nearly 190 countries have since signed up to the resolution. The eight goals, to be achieved by 2015, are linked to 18 targets, and these, in turn, to 48 indicators (Table 1). While the individual goals may not be new, the collective agreement by almost 190 countries to strive to meet these goals was – and is – unprecedented. The MDGs arose from a wish, clearly expressed at the Millennium Summit, that at the turn of the millennium good intentions had to be matched by concrete actions. Under 'values and principles', the UN General Assembly agreed that:

> We believe that the central challenge we face today is to ensure that globalization becomes a positive force for all the world's people. For while globalization offers great opportunities, at present its benefits are very unevenly shared, while its costs are unevenly distributed…only through broad and sustained efforts to create a shared future, based upon our common humanity in all its diversity, can globalization be made fully inclusive and equitable.
>
> We will spare no effort to free our fellow men, women and children from the abject and dehumanizing conditions of extreme poverty, to which more than a billion of them are currently subjected. We are committed to making the right to development a reality for everyone and to freeing the entire human race from want (http://www.un.org/millennium/declaration/ares552e.pdf).

Table 1 The MDGs: 8 goals, 18 targets, 48 indicators

Goals (8)	Targets (18)	Indicators (48)
1. Eradicate extreme hunger and poverty	1. Reduce by half the proportion of people living on less than a dollar a day	1. Proportion of population below $1 (PPP) per day 2. Poverty gap ratio, $1 per day 3. Share of poorest quintile in national income or consumption
	2. Reduce by half the proportion of people who suffer from hunger	4. Prevalence of underweight children under five years of age 5. Proportion of the population below minimum level of dietary energy consumption
2. Achieve universal primary education	3. Ensure that all boys and girls complete a full course of primary schooling	6. Net enrolment ratio in primary education 7. Proportion of pupils starting grade 1 who reach grade 5 8. Literacy rate of 15- to 24-year-olds
3. Promote gender equality and empower women	4. Eliminate gender disparity in primary and secondary education, preferably by 2005, and at all levels by 2015	9. Ratio of girls to boys in primary, secondary and tertiary education 10. Ratio of literate women to men 15–24 years old 11. Share of women in wage employment in the non-agricultural sector 12. Proportion of seats held by women in national parliaments
4. Reduce child mortality	5. Reduce by two-thirds the mortality rate among children under five	13. Under-five mortality rate 14. Infant mortality rate 15. Proportion of 1-year-old children immunized against measles
5. Improve maternal health	6. Reduce by three-quarters the maternal mortality ratio	16. Maternal mortality ratio 17. Proportion of births attended by skilled health personnel
6. Combat HIV/AIDS, malaria and other diseases	7. Halt and begin to reverse the spread of HIV/AIDS	18. HIV prevalence among 15- to 24-year-old pregnant women 19. Condom use rate of the contraceptive prevalence rate and population aged 15–24 years with comprehensive correct knowledge of HIV/AIDS 20. Ratio of school attendance of orphans to school attendance of non-orphans aged 10–14 years
	8. Halt and begin to reverse the incidence of malaria and other major diseases	21. Prevalence and death rates associated with malaria 22. Proportion of population in malaria risk areas using effective malaria prevention and treatment measures 23. Prevalence and death rates associated with tuberculosis 24. Proportion of tuberculosis cases detected and cured under directly observed treatment short courses
7. Ensure environmental sustainability	9. Integrate the principles of sustainable development into country policies and programmes; reverse loss of environmental resources	25. Forested land as percentage of land area 26. Ratio of area protected to maintain biological diversity to surface area 27. Energy supply (apparent consumption; kg oil equivalent) per $1000 (PPP) GDP

76262

Table 1 – *continued*

		28. Carbon dioxide emissions (per capita) and consumption of ozone-depleting CFCs
	10. Reduce by half the proportion of people without sustainable access to safe drinking water	29. Proportion of the population with sustainable access to and improved water source
		30. Proportion of the population with access to improved sanitation
	11. Achieve significant improvement in lives of at least 100 million slum dwellers, by 2020	31. Slum population as percentage of urban population (secure tenure index)
8. Develop a global partnership for development	12. Develop further an open trading and financial system that is rule-based, predictable and non-discriminatory, includes a commitment to good governance, development and poverty reduction – nationally and internationally	*Official development assistance* (ODA)
		32. Net ODA as percentage of OECD/DAC donors' gross national product (targets of 0.7% in total and 0.15% for LDCs)
	13. Address the least developed countries' special needs. This includes tariff- and quota-free access for their exports; enhanced debt relief for heavily indebted poor countries; cancellation of official bilateral debt; and more generous official development assistance for countries committed to poverty reduction	33. Proportion of ODA to basic social services (basic education, primary health care, nutrition, safe water and sanitation)
		34. Proportion of ODA that is untied
		35. Proportion of ODA for environment in small island developing states
		36. Proportion of ODA for transport sector in landlocked countries
		Market access
	14. Address the special needs of landlocked and small island developing states	37. Proportion of exports (by value and excluding arms) admitted free of duties and quotas
	15. Deal comprehensively with developing countries' debt problems through national and international measures to make debt sustainable in the long term	38. Average tariffs and quotas on agricultural products and textiles and clothing
		39. Domestic and export agricultural subsidies in OECD countries
		40. Proportion of ODA provided to help build trade capacity
	16. In cooperation with the developing countries, develop decent and productive work for youth	*Debt sustainability*
		41. Proportion of official bilateral HIPC debt cancelled
	17. In cooperation with pharmaceutical companies, provide access to affordable, essential drugs in developing countries	42. Total number of countries that have reached their HIPC decision points and number that have reached their completion points (cumulative) (HIPC)
	18. In cooperation with the private sector, make available the benefits of new technologies – especially information and communications technologies	43. Debt service as a percentage of exports of goods and services
		44. Debt relief committed under HIPC initiative
		45. Unemployment of 15- to 24-year-olds, each sex and total
		46. Proportion of population with access to affordable, essential drugs on a sustainable basis
		47. Telephone lines and cellular subscribers per 100 population
		48. Personal computers in use and Internet users per 100 population

Source: Extracted and adapted from http://www.un.org/millenniumgoals/index.html
Notes: DAC = Development Cooperation Directorate; HIPC = heavily indebted poor countries; OECD = Organization for Economic Cooperation and Development

At the time of the Summit, United Nations Secretary General Kofi Annan stated: 'We will have time to reach the Millennium Development Goals – worldwide and in most, or even all, individual countries – but only if we break with business as usual.'

Progress towards the MDGs

At the time of writing (2006), more than five years have passed since the MDGs were adopted by the UN General Assembly, a sufficient period of time to assess whether they are likely to be achieved – and where. To put it another way, is there evidence that the world community has broken with 'business as usual', as Kofi Annan exhorted?

The baseline year for measuring progress towards most of the targets is 1990 and the latest data come from 2004. On this basis, the simple answer is that while there has been significant progress with respect to some of the goals, and in some parts of the world, it is also necessary to admit that overall progress has been slow, halting and patchy. Table 2 summarizes progress in 2005 towards goals 1–7 in ten regions of the world. In only 55 instances are targets likely to be met by 2015 at current rates of progress; in 81 cases, the target is not expected to be met given prevailing trends, and, of these, in 33 cases there has actually been a deterioration in progress. Table 3 shows that there is a clear – at least in terms of this level of aggregation – regional pattern to achievement and failure. In sub-Saharan Africa, South Asia, West Asia, Oceania and CIS Asia the balance of success is negative: more targets will not be met by 2015 than will be met, at least given prevailing trends.

It is goal 8, relating to the derivation of a global partnership for development and its associated indicators and targets, which directs attention to the responsibility of the wider international community and, particularly, richer countries. Again, progress has been made, but, many commentators feel, not sufficiently far or fast enough to meet the MDGs. Aid has increased significantly but not by enough; trade barriers remain largely in place, particularly for products deemed strategically important to rich countries (such as farm products); and while the debt burden of heavily indebted countries in Africa has fallen, it remains too high and an impediment to progress.

Criticizing the self-evidently desirable

Few would contest that the desires and objectives contained within the MDGs are laudable – they are self-evident 'goods'. Perhaps because of this, scholars have tended to shy away from criticizing them. However, from the start, there have been critics who have questioned whether, first, the MDGs are fit for purpose; second, whether we have the available data to measure the achievement of the targets identified; third, whether the targets set adequately assess the goals to be achieved; and fourth, whether there is a mechanism in place – beyond exhortation and moral persuasion – to support and propel the achievement of the MDGs, especially in relation to goal 8.

Jeffrey James (2006) directs his criticism at what he perceives to be a failure to distinguish between means and ends, or between *actual* achievements (ends) and *potential* achievements. Some of the MDG targets are ends manifested and measurable at the level of the individual. This applies, for example, to the targets associated with goals 4, 5 and 6 (all health related) and also target 2 under goal 1 (referring to hunger) (see Table 1). But many of the other goals are, in James's view, means rather than ends. So, for example, he draws a distinction between completing primary school (target 3 under goal 2) and the acquisition of basic literacy and numeracy. The former (primary school education) may lead to the latter (literacy and numeracy), but if schooling is inadequate, as it so often is in the poorest countries, then this may not be achieved. In other words, the mere meeting of a target – universal primary-level education – may not deliver the desired end of an adequate education for the modern world. The same argument can be applied to the goals of gender equality and empowerment, and of environmental sustainability (goals 3 and 7).

Table 2 MDG progress chart (2005)

Goals and targets	Number of regions in each category (out of ten world regions)			
	Target met or close to being met	Target expected to be met if prevailing trends persist	Target not expected to be met if prevailing trends persist	No progress, or deterioration or reversal in trends
Goal 1: Reduce by half the proportion of people living on less than a dollar a day	2	2	3	2
Goal 1: Reduce by half the proportion of people who suffer from hunger	0	5	3	2
Goal 2: Ensure that all boys and girls complete a full course of primary schooling	0	4	5	1
Goal 3: Eliminate gender disparity in primary education	5	2	3	0
Goal 4: Reduce by two-thirds the mortality rate among children under five	0	3	6	1
Goal 4: Measles immunization	4	2	2	2
Goal 5: Reduce by three-quarters the maternal mortality ratio	0	3	5	2
Goal 6: Halt and begin to reverse the spread of HIV/AIDS	0	0	2	6
Goal 6: Halt and begin to reverse the incidence of malaria	0	5	4	1
Goal 6: Halt and begin to reverse the incidence of tuberculosis	0	3	4	3
Goal 7: Reverse loss of forests	3	0	3	4
Goal 7: Reduce by half the proportion of people without sustainable access to safe drinking water	0	7	1	2
Goal 7: Reduce by half the proportion of people without sanitation	0	3	2	5
Goal 7: Achieve significant improvement in lives of slum dwellers	0	2	5	2
Total	**14**	**41**	**48**	**33**

Source: Millennium Development Goals: Progress Chart (2005) http://www.un.org/millenniumgoals/mdg_chart_sept.pdf
Notes: Some regions' progress is not assessed under some of these targets because of insufficient data. These targets do not conform exactly to those agreed at the UN Millennium Summit and listed in Table 1.

In defence of this means-based approach, it has been suggested that cross-country data are simply not always available to target ends and that such means-based measures are a broad and generally applicable indicator of success. But even here there are reasons to be cautious. For example, doubts have been expressed about whether we have sufficiently robust data to assess the achievement of the targets set. And, of course, the absence of robust data is particularly severe in

Table 3 Progress chart by region (2005)

Goals and targets	Number of regions in each category (out of ten world regions)			
	Target met or close to being met	Target expected to be met if prevailing trends persist	Target not expected to be met if prevailing trends persist	No progress, or deterioration or reversal in trends
North Africa	1	10	2	0
Sub-Saharan Africa	0	0	4	10
East Asia	3	5	5	1
South East Asia	2	6	5	1
South Asia	0	2	10	2
West Asia	0	4	5	4
Oceania	0	2	4	6
Latin America and Caribbean	2	5	6	1
CIS – Europe	3	4	4	3
CIS – Asia	3	3	3	5
Total	**14**	**41**	**48**	**33**

Source: Millennium Development Goals: Progress Chart (2005) http://www.un.org/millenniumgoals/mdg_chart_sept.pdf

the poorest countries where the need to meet the MDGs is most acute. Satterthwaite (2003: 184–5), for example, writes of 'nonsense' statistics, such as the levels of urban poverty and urban service provision in Africa (linked to goal 7, targets 10 and 11), which are then used to measure progress towards the MDGs: 'if monitoring is based on inappropriate indicators or indicators based on inappropriate assumptions, it will not serve to monitor poverty reduction with regard to adequate income levels or service provision levels' (p. 189).

A related criticism is whether the rather mechanical, target-based approach places a characteristically instrumentalist gloss on the achievement (or otherwise) of the goals. The achievement of the poverty target, for example (goal 1, target 1), is income-based and related to official data and basic needs as ascertained by 'experts'. Other forms of deprivation (linked to social exclusion, political marginality and cultural rights) are ignored, and the inequalities in power which are often the root cause of poverty, overlooked (ibid.: 182). It also means that governments and agencies are likely to focus their energies on interventions that will improve the chances of meeting the MDGs, rather than on more deep-seated, political and problematic manifestations of deprivation. Moreover, it is not just *what* is done – reducing poverty, eradicating hunger, reducing maternal mortality – but *how* it is done. The general criticism that development has become a technocratic project informed by experts, driven by governments and multilateral agencies, and based on measures of success that pay little heed to local desires is equally apposite to the MDG initiative (see the papers in Hasan, Patel and Satterthwaite 2005).

It is important to appreciate that the MDGs are not discrete, stand-alone goals, but are interlinked so that the failure to meet one is likely to have knock-on effects for some of the other goals. Thus, the failure to meet the goal of universal primary school education will compromise the achievement of targets related to infant mortality, child malnutrition, gender equality, HIV/AIDS, and so forth (Delamonica, Mehrotra and Vandemoortele 2004). Furthermore, high maternal mortality in sub-Saharan Africa reflects not just a shortage of the necessary medical infrastructure, but also the low status of women in those societies and women's lack of control over their reproductive decisions (Simwaka et al. 2005). The goals, therefore, not only link with each other, but are implicated in some deeper and arguably even more profound aspects of inequality.

To achieve the MDGs there needs to be a commitment from both donors, in terms of increased assistance, and, of course, from developing country governments. Regarding the former, the UN Millennium Project calculated that aid needed to rise from US$69 billion in 2003, to US$135 billion in 2006, to US$195 billion in 2015 if the MDGs were to be met. Furthermore, this increase in aid needs to be targeted at the right places – the neediest countries and those that are likely to use it most effectively and efficiently. The evidence is that on both counts donor nations are failing. Total aid to developing countries in 2005 was US$106 billion. Baulch (2006) also argues that the United States and the European Commission, particularly, disperse the bulk of their aid budgets to middle-income countries that either have met, or are on track to meeting the MDGs.

Summary

The MDGs represent the first collective and integrated attempt to improve the lives and life chances of the world's poor. That must be counted, in itself, a success. It already seems, however, that many of the poorest countries will not meet the majority of the goals by the target date of 2015. Furthermore, since 2000 there have emerged a number of critiques of the goals themselves, the way that the targets have been framed, the reliability of the data on which progress is assessed, and the failure of the wider international community to sign up to the MDGs in terms of material commitment.

GUIDE TO FURTHER READING

A great deal of valuable material on the MDGs can be gleaned from the UN, World Bank and other websites. For more hard-hitting assessments, however, it is best to look at academic papers.

Hasan, A., Patel, S. and Satterthwaite, D. (eds) (2005) 'Meeting the Millennium Development Goals in urban areas', *Environment and Urbanization*, 17(1), special issue. A valuable set of papers which takes a critical look at the MDGs from an urban perspective and questions the assumptions on which some of the goals and targets are based.

James, J. (2006) 'Misguided investments in meeting Millennium Development Goals: a reconsideration using ends-based targets', *Third World Quarterly*, 27(3): 443–58. An interesting alternative take on the MDGs and whether the targets set really represent the ends the world community wishes to achieve.

UN (2006) *Millennium Development Goals Report*, New York: United Nations, http://unstats.un.org/unsd/mdg/Resources/Static/Products/Progress2006/MDGReport2006.pdf. A summary of progress towards the goals based on a 'master' data set compiled by an 'Inter-Agency and Expert Group on MDG Indicators'.

USEFUL WEBSITES

The main UN MDG website, with background information on the initiative, the UN resolution and the Secretary General's interventions, can be found at http://www.un.org/millenniumgoals/index.html

A useful 2005 progress chart on the Millennium Development Goals can be downloaded from http://www.un.org/millenniumgoals/mdg_chart_sept.pdf

The latest (and past) UN reports on progress towards the MDGs can be downloaded from http://www.un.org/millenniumgoals/documents.html http://unstats.un.org/unsd/mdg/Resources/Static/Products/Progress2006/MDGReport2006.pdf

A fact sheet on the role of the UN in implementing the Millennium Development Goals can be found at http://www.un.org/millenniumgoals/MDGs-FACTSHEET1.pdf

The World Bank also has a full section on the MDGs, with links to relevant studies, accessible from http://ddp-ext.worldbank.org/ext/GMIS/home.do?siteId=2

REFERENCES

Baulch, B. (2006) 'Aid distribution and the MDGs', *World Development*, 34(6): 933–50.

Delamonica, E., Mehrotra, S. and Vandemoortele, J. (2004) 'Education for all: How much will it cost?', *Development and Change*, 35(1): 3–30.

Hasan, A., Patel, S. and Satterthwaite, D. (eds) (2005) 'Meeting the Millennium Development Goals in urban areas', *Environment and Urbanization*, 17(1), special issue.

James, J. (2006) 'Misguided investments in meeting Millennium Development Goals: A reconsideration using ends-based targets', *Third World Quarterly*, 27(3): 443–58.

Satterthwaite, D. (2003) 'The Millennium Development Goals and urban poverty reduction: Great expectations and nonsense statistics', *Environment and Urbanization*, 15(2): 181–90.

Simwaka, B.N., Theobald, S., Amekudzi, Y.P. and Tolhurst, R. (2005) 'Tackling gender inequalities is key to reducing maternal mortality in sub-Saharan Africa', *British Medical Journal*, 331: 708–9.

1.8 Development and economic growth

A.P. Thirlwall

The economic and social development of the world's poorest countries is perhaps the greatest challenge facing society at the present time. Over one billion of the world's six billion population live in absolute poverty; the same number suffer various degrees of malnutrition, and millions have no access to safe water, health care or education. This poverty is concentrated largely in countries described as 'developing', and coexists with the affluence enjoyed by the vast majority of people in countries described as 'developed'.

The standard of living of people is commonly measured by the total amount of goods and services produced per head of the population, or what is called gross domestic product (GDP) per capita (or gross national product (GNP) per capita, if net income from abroad is added). This, in turn, is determined by the number of people who work, and their productivity. The basic proximate cause of the poverty of nations is the low productivity of labour associated with low levels of physical and human capital (education) accumulation, and low levels of technology.

Income per head in a country is naturally measured in units of its own currency, but if international comparisons of living standards are to be made, each country's per capita income has to be converted into a common unit of account at some rate of exchange. The convention is to take the US dollar as the unit of account and convert each country's per capita income into dollars at the official exchange rate. A country's official exchange rate, however, is not necessarily a good measure of the relative purchasing power of currencies, because it only reflects the relative prices of goods that enter into international trade. But many goods that people buy are not traded, and the relative price of these non-traded goods tends to be lower the poorer the country, reflecting much lower relative labour costs. An exchange rate is required which reflects the purchasing power parity (PPP) of countries' currencies, and this is now provided by various international organizations, such as the World Bank, which uses US$1 per day measured at PPP, to define the level of absolute poverty.

The economic growth of countries refers to the increase in output of goods and services that a country produces over an accounting period, normally one year. If a country is said to be growing at 5 per cent per annum, it means that the total volume of its domestic output (GDP) is increasing at this rate. If population is growing at 2 per cent per annum, this means that output per head (or the average standard of living) is growing at 3 per cent per annum.

Economic growth, however, is not the same as economic development. The process of economic (and social) development must imply a growth in living standards, but it is a much wider concept than the growth of per capita income alone. Growth, it might be said, is a necessary condition for the economic and social development of nations, but it is not a sufficient condition because an aggregate measure of growth or per capita income pays no attention to how that output is distributed among the population; it says nothing about the composition of output (whether the goods are consumption goods, investment goods or public goods such as education and health provision), and it gives no indication of the physical, social and economic environment in which the output is produced. In short, the growth rates of nations cannot be taken as measures of the increase in the welfare of societies because the well-being of people is a much more inclusive concept than the level of income alone.

If the process of economic and social development is defined in terms of an increase in society's welfare, a concept of development is required which embraces not only economic variables and objectives, but also social objectives and values for which societies strive. Many economists and other social scientists have attempted to address this issue, and here we mention the ideas of two prominent thinkers in the field: Denis Goulet and Amartya Sen (who in 1998 won the Nobel Prize in economics for his work on the interface between welfare and development economics).

Goulet (1971) distinguishes three basic components or core values that he argues must be included in any true meaning of development, which he calls life sustenance, self-esteem and freedom. Life sustenance is concerned with the provision of basic needs. No country can be regarded as fully developed if it cannot provide all its people with such basic needs as housing, clothing, food and minimal education. A country may have a relatively high average standard of living and an impressive growth performance over several years, but still have a poor provision of basic needs, leaving large sections of the population in an underdeveloped state. This issue is closely related to the distribution of income in societies measured by the share of total income going to the richest and poorest sections of society. The distribution of income is much more unequal in poorer developing countries than in richer developed countries, and it is perfectly possible for a poor country to be growing fast, yet its distribution of income to be worsening because the fruits of growth accrue to the rich. Such a country would have grown, but it would not have developed if the provision of basic needs for the poorest groups in the community had not improved.

Self-esteem is concerned with feelings of self-respect and independence. A country cannot be regarded as fully developed if it is exploited by others or cannot conduct economic relations on equal terms. In this sense, the colonization of large parts of Africa, Asia and South America kept the countries in these regions of the world in an underdeveloped state. Colonialism has now virtually ended, but some would argue that there are modern equivalents of colonialism, equally insidious and antidevelopmental. For example, the International Monetary Fund (IMF) and the World Bank dominate economic policymaking in many developing countries, and many of the policies that the countries are forced to pursue are detrimental to development. Also, multinational corporations that operate in many developing countries often introduce consumption patterns and techniques of production which are inappropriate to the stage of development of the countries concerned, and to that extent impair welfare. In international trade, poor and rich countries do not operate on a level playing field, and the strong may gain at the expense of the weak. The distribution of the gains from trade is not equitable, not least because the terms of trade of primary producing developing countries (i.e. the price of their exports relative to the price of imports) tends to deteriorate through time (at an average rate of about 0.5 per cent per annum for at least the last century).

Freedom refers to the ability of people to determine their own destiny. No person is free if they are imprisoned on the margin of subsistence with no education and no skills. The great benefit of material development is that it expands the range of choice open to individuals and to societies at large. For the economic and social development of a country, however, all must participate in and benefit from the process of growth, not just the richest few. If the majority are left untouched, their choices remain limited; and no person is free if they cannot choose.

Sen (1983, 1999) argues in a similar vein to Goulet that economic growth should not be viewed as an end in itself, but as the means to the achievement of a much wider set of objectives by which economic and social development should be measured. Development should focus on, and be judged by, the expansion of people's 'entitlements' and the 'capabilities' that these entitlements generate, and income is not always a good measure of entitlements. Sen defines entitlements as 'the set of alternative commodity bundles that a person can command in a society using the totality of rights and opportunities that he or she faces'. For most people, the crucial determinants of their entitlements depend on their ability to sell their labour and on the price of commodities. Employment opportunity, and the level of unemployment, must therefore be included in any meaningful definition of development. Entitlements also depend on such factors as what individuals can extract from the state (in the form of welfare provision); the spatial distribution of resources and opportunities, and power relations in society. Sen (1984) has analysed major world famines, using the concept of entitlements, and finds that several famines have not been associated with a shortage of food, but rather with a lack of entitlements because the food supply has been withdrawn from certain parts of the country or sections of society, or food prices have risen.

The thinking of Goulet, Sen and others has led to the construction of alternative measures of economic and social development to supplement statistics on growth rates and levels of countries' per-capita income. The most notable of these measures are the human development index (HDI) and the human poverty index (HPI), compiled by the United Nations Development Programme (UNDP) and published in its annual *Human Development Report*. These alternative indices of the economic well-being of nations do not always correlate well with per-capita income. The same growth rate and per-capita income of countries can be associated with very different levels of achievement in other spheres, such as life expectancy, death rates, literacy and education. As the UNDP says in its 1997 report: 'although GNP growth is absolutely necessary to meet all essential human objectives, countries differ in the way that they translate growth into human development'.

The UNDP's human development index is based on three variables: life expectancy at birth; educational attainment, measured by a combination of adult literacy and combined primary, secondary and tertiary school enrolment rates; and the standard of living measured by real per-capita income measured at PPP. These variables are combined in a composite index that ranges from 0 to 1 (see Thirlwall 2006 for details). Comparing the ranking of developing countries by their HDI and per-capita income shows some interesting divergences. Many oil-producing countries, for example, have much lower HDI rankings than their per-capita income rank, while some poor countries rank relatively high by their HDI because they have deliberately devoted scarce resources to human development. Countries such as Cuba, Venezuela, Jamaica and some former states of the Soviet Union fall into this category.

The UNDP's human poverty index is also based on three main indices: the percentage of the population not expected to survive beyond the age of 40; the adult illiteracy rate; and a deprivation index based on an average of three variables – the percentage of the population without access to safe water, the percentage of the population without access to health services, and the percentage of children under the age of five years who are underweight through malnourishment. The ranking of countries by their HPI also shows some striking contrasts with their ranking by per-capita income. The UNDP has calculated that the cost of eradicating poverty across the world is relatively small compared to global income – not more than 0.3 per cent of world GDP – and concluded that political commitment, not financial resources, is the real obstacle to poverty eradication.

To summarize, economic growth is not the same as economic development. The annual growth rate of a country is a very precise measure of the growth of the total volume of goods and services produced in a country during a year, but it says nothing about its composition or distribution. Growth is a necessary condition for real income per head to rise, but it is not a sufficient condition for economic development to take place, because development is a multidimensional concept which embraces multifarious economic and social objectives, concerned with the distribution of income, the provision of basic needs, and the real and psychological well-being of people. Many poor countries in the last quarter of the twentieth century experienced quite a respectable rate of growth in living standards – averaging 2–3 per cent per annum – but the absolute number in poverty has continued to rise, and the distribution of income has become more unequal. At the global level, there is little evidence of the convergence of per-capita incomes across nations. The poor countries have been growing, but the rich countries have been growing as fast, if not faster in per-capita terms. While the eradication of poverty – and the narrowing of the rich–poor country divide – remains one of the great challenges of the new millennium, economic growth in poor countries is not enough by itself for development to take place when viewed in a broader framework.

GUIDE TO FURTHER READING AND REFERENCES

The topics covered here can be taken further by recourse to the following texts.

Goulet, D. (1971) *The Cruel Choice: A New Concept on the Theory of Development*, New York: Atheneum.

Sen, A. (1983) 'Development: which way now?', *Economic Journal*, December.

Sen, A. (1984) *Poverty and Famines: An Essay in Entitlement and Deprivation*, Oxford: Clarendon Press.

Sen, A. (1999) *Development as Freedom: Human Capability and Global Need*, New York: Knopf.

Thirlwall, A.P. (2006) *Growth and Development: With Special Reference to Developing Economies*, eighth edition, London: Macmillan.

United Nations Development Programme (1997, 1999) *Human Development Report*, New York: Oxford University Press.

1.9 Development and social welfare/human rights

Jennifer A. Elliott

Critical development studies

In the early years of the twenty-first century, human well-being (including individual civil and political liberties), as well as meeting the physical and material needs of human society, are accepted concerns for development, both as outcomes and conditions for sustained progress (World Bank 1998; UNDP 2000). Issues of egalitarian development, democracy, participation, ethics and human rights suffuse development theory, the pronouncements of major development institutions such as the United Nations and the World Bank, and the activities of new social movements alike. In short, the practice and discourses of development have become more morally informed, particularly since the late 1980s.

In part, the 'insertion of a critical sensibility' (Radcliffe 1999: 84) into development studies is a product of the recognition that many of the world's citizens continue to lack even the most fundamental goods and opportunities. Integral to this understanding has been the expansion in tools and measures for monitoring deprivation and progress worldwide, such as those developed and reported annually by the United Nations Development Programme (UNDP).

Theoretical developments have also been important in prompting an emphasis on human welfare and human rights concerns. The legitimacy and universal acceptance of the 'big ideas' of progress and development, for example, that characterized the modernist tradition in development theory for so long, were to a degree overturned by the postmodern movement, particularly through the 1990s (Simon 1999). 'Rights-based development', as a concept and as a policy directive, has also gained strength through the rethinking and critique of neoliberalism and its agents (Manzo 2003).

In short, while a concern for human dignity and well-being in development studies is not entirely new, it is only recently that 'many new problems *as well as* old ones' (Sen 1999: xi, emphasis added) are being so widely conceptualized in terms of human rights and freedoms.

Rights and development as separate concerns

Although human rights and well-being were undoubtedly concerns in the 1940s and 1950s within international institutions, among governments of newly independent countries and in the emergent discipline of development studies, it has been argued that the predominant ideas and practices of development at that time were often devoid of ethical considerations and separate from those 'marked out for development' (Corbridge 1999: 69). For example, ideas of progress during that period were generally synonymous with economic growth and the modernization of traditional societies. In so far as welfare and rights issues were considered, it was assumed that these would follow as outcomes of the linear process of economic development. In turn, development and underdevelopment were quantified (and as reported by the World Bank and United Nation's reports) in terms of the level of gross national product (GNP) per capita.

During this period, the traditional view of human rights centred on civil and political (CP) rights (the right to life, liberty and security, for example; the right to vote, to a free press and freedom of speech) and on legal rights such as due process of law and the presumption of innocence until proven guilty. In short, the debates were led by the West, they emphasized material well-being and took place alongside, rather than being integrated with, the agendas of international development. Although two key international covenants were adopted by the United Nations in 1966 (on CP rights and on economic, social and cultural (ESC) rights), work focused on the ratification and inscription of CP rights into constitutional and legal frameworks. ESC rights, such as the right to an adequate standard of living, the right to education, to work and equal pay, and the right of minorities to enjoy their own culture, religion and language, were less prominent and tended to be considered separately to CP rights (Maxwell 1999).

The basic needs approach

By the end of the 1960s, however, there was growing disillusionment with the practice of development and with indicators of development that took no account of the distribution of national wealth. It became widely agreed that the economic growth that actually took place in most developing countries seemed to go together with increases in absolute and relative poverty. In response to this dilemma, it was argued that a *direct* approach was required to the delivery of welfare outcomes. In due course, what became known as the basic needs approach (BNA) drew together theorists and practitioners from a range of traditions, academic centres and institutions of development, searching for more human-centred and locally relevant processes and patterns of development (see for example, Stohr's (1981) 'development from below'). In short, under the basic needs approach, development was redefined as a broad-based, people-oriented or endogenous process, as a critique of modernization and as a break with past development theory.

As a result of the influence of the BNA, the 1970s saw a 'vast array' (Escobar 1995) of programmes focused on households and covering aspects of health, education, farming and reproduction practices, designed to create a minimum level of welfare for the weakest groups in society. Development practice became characterized by district and regional planning (supported by major international donor institutions), by proliferating field bureaucracies and by development solutions through targeting (of social groups – particularly women and children, of sectors and of regions) to overcome the recognized inadequacies of the 'planning fantasies of the 1960s' (Chambers 1993: 108). Concurrently, a series of social indicators for development appeared, most notably within annual reports of the World Bank and the UNDP, as concepts of absolute and relative poverty were redefined to include the distribution of access to education and clean water, for example, in addition to income.

Buying and selling welfare

The BNA did much to put poverty, human needs and rights back on official development agendas in the 1970s. However, many assert that the decade of the 1980s was one of development 'reversals' rather than achievements, with evidence, particularly in Africa, of falling school enrolments and literacy levels, for example (Simon 1999). Similarly, development theory was proposed to have reached an 'impasse' (Schuurman 1993) through the predominance and power of neoliberal development ideas.

Progressively throughout the decade, basic human rights such as access to safe water and sanitation, which had been identified in the early 1980s as essential to bringing marginal groups into dominant cultures, became 'commodities subject to the rigours of the market' (Bell 1992: 85). Donors, for example, came under increasing pressure to find new methods of financing and providing welfare both at home and abroad. Governments of developing nations were also required to cut state expenditures under conditions for access to multilateral development finance. While these pressures opened up spaces for new project types, processes and programmes in development, it has been suggested that the more radical aspects of the original BNA philosophies were often devalued in practice, 'reducing them from agendas for change and empowerment into little more than shopping lists that are hawked to donors for implementation, commonly more in line with donors' than recipients' priorities' (Simon 1999: 27).

Converging agendas through the 1990s

If the 1980s were an impasse in development thinking, it could be suggested that the 1990s made up for it with a whole set of theoretical 'turns' that generated much debate and (often divergent) ideas on how development could be achieved, and even on the meaning of development itself. Smith (2000: 2), however, was cautious regarding the prospects for change in practice: 'while the affluent endure post-modern ambiguity and uncertainty in comfort, for those at the coal-face of human misery what constitutes progress is still likely to be self-evident'.

In 1986, the United Nations adopted the UN Declaration on the Right to Development, within which development itself was identified as an inalienable human right. The articles that supported the Declaration drew on wider debates about development at that time, in particular through engaging with the emerging critique of conventional development and of neoliberalism, with understandings of the uneven impacts and limits of globalization and in the support it gave to notions of 'people centred' development and human empowerment (Manzo 2003). However, out of respect for international human rights law and the Charter of the UN, the Declaration also emphasized the primary role of the state for creating the national and international conditions favourable to realizing the rights to development. Subsequently, the fiftieth anniversary of the 1948 Universal Declaration of Human Rights provided an opportunity for key players within the UN to reaffirm society's obligations to respond to the inalienable rights of individuals and the commitment of the UN to efforts to mainstream rights-based development across the institution (Manzo 2003).

Throughout the 1990s, agencies of the UN (such as the UNDP) made important contributions to changing ideas on the meaning and goals of development and in raising understanding of the non-income indicators of human well-being, through changes in its annual reporting of development progress, for example. In 1990, it introduced the human development index (HDI), a composite index designed to reflect achievements in the most basic human capabilities, defined as leading a long life, being knowledgeable and enjoying a decent standard of living. In 1995, the gender-related human development index (GDI) and gender empowerment measure (GEM) were introduced, encompassing the recognition that gender equality is a measure of and means for human and national development. In 1997, the human poverty index (HPI) was introduced to measure deprivation, in terms of the percentage of population not expected to live until the age of 40, illiteracy rates, the percentage of people lacking access to health services and safe water, and the percentage of children under five years who are moderately or severely underweight. These developments are evidence of how, increasingly, 'development' became conceived in terms of human rights and freedoms and of the recognition of the interconnectedness and multidimensional nature of these component issues.

Poverty is now understood as a human rights violation, and working to ensure freedom from poverty (and its impacts on human opportunity and environmental resources) worldwide in the future is encapsulated in the Millennium Development Goals around which multilateral and bilateral aid are increasingly focused. Poverty Reduction Strategy Papers are now the framework through which eligibility for debt relief and further funding from the World Bank and the International Monetary Fund is coordinated, for example; these require recipient countries to establish coherent plans focused on poverty reduction and to identify the financing needs required.

Table 1 displays a number of quotations that further illustrate the converging agendas of welfare and human rights issues in international development into the twenty-first century.

Conclusion

In this short chapter, it has not been possible to do justice to the decades of work done in the fields of poverty, participation, gender and democracy, for example, which have all been extremely important in bringing about a much more holistic and moral agenda for development. However,

Table 1 The multidimensional and interdependent nature of human rights and human development

- Political freedoms (in the form of free speech and elections) help to promote economic security. Social opportunities (in the form of education and health facilities) facilitate economic participation. Economic facilities (in the form of opportunities for participation in trade and production) can help to generate personal abundance as well as public resources for social facilities. Freedoms of different kinds can strengthen one another. (Sen 1999: 11)
- Civil and social education will help people better understand their rights and increase their choices and income-earning capacity. At the same time, developing and implementing equal opportunity laws will empower people to gain more equitable access to productive resources. (UNDP 1998: 10)
- Sustainable human development and human rights will be undone in a repressive environment where threat of disease prevails, and both are better able to promote human choices in a peaceful and pluralistic society. (UNDP 1998: 6)
- The levels of ill-health experienced by most of the world's people threatens their country's economic and political viability and this in turn affects economic and political interests of all other countries. (Brundtland 2000: 3)
- A fundamental human freedom is freedom from want. Poverty is a human rights violation, and freedom from poverty is an integral and inalienable right. (UN Declaration on the Right to Development, 1986)
- Every step taken towards reducing poverty and achieving broad-based economic growth is a step towards conflict prevention. (Annan 2000: 45)

this brief analysis has highlighted how such an agenda has shifted the focus away from determining any *particular* means or 'specially chosen list of instruments' (Sen 1999: 3) for development, towards more concern for the overarching ends of development. Critically, these ends are plural and fluid in the sense that different societies at any particular time may assign varied importance within conceptions of human rights, for example, to the obligations of individuals to self and other, or to material well-being over personal liberty. But rather than debating the primacy of one right, good, opportunity or resource over another, the debates are now more regularly focused on questions of appropriate entry points or sequencing in development interventions in recognition of the reinforcing and interdependent nature of these issues. As Sen has highlighted, the (inter-related) sources of people's 'unfreedoms' may be extremely varied. Development involves expanding these freedoms, as liberties to be valued in their own right and as the principal means (free agency, capability and choice) through which the overarching goals of development, for individuals to 'lead the kinds of lives they have reason to value' (ibid.: 10), will be achieved.

GUIDE TO FURTHER READING

Bell, M. (1992) 'The water decade valedictory, New Delhi 1990: Where pre- and post-modern met', *Area*, 24(1): 82–9. This paper gives a nice review of the thinking behind, and outputs from, the International Drinking Water Supply and Sanitation Decade.

Hausermann, J. (1998) *A Human Rights Approach to Development*, London: Rights and Humanity. Prepared for the Department for International Development as part of the consultation process behind the first White Paper, this text provides a very clear and comprehensive source of information and ideas on human rights, evolving approaches to development and the opportunities for greater integration of these areas.

Manzo, K. (2003) Africa in the rise of rights-based development, *Geoforum*, 34: 437–56. A paper that explores the rise of rights-based development, the debate surrounding the concept and the varied way in which it is being endorsed by prominent international organisations like DFID, the World Bank and the United Nations. It explores in detail its origins within the critique of neoliberalism, but points also to how many of the elements of that agenda are actually being perpetuated in the name of rights-based development.

The Office of the United Nations High Commissioner for Human Rights (OHCHR) is a department of the UN Secretariat that is mandated to promote and protect all rights established in the Charter of the United Nations and in international human rights laws and treaties. The Declaration on the Right to Development as well as work under the Vienna Declaration and Programme of Action can be found via www.ohchr.org

Simon, D. (1999) 'Development revisited', in D. Simon and A. Narman (eds) *Development as Theory and Practice*, Harlow: Longman, pp. 17–54. A nice starting point to put the explicit issues of welfare and human rights into a wider context. The overview chapter gives a challenging account of changes in development thinking and practice.

Smith, D.M. (2000) 'Moral progress in human geography: Transcending the place of good fortune', *Progress in Human Geography*, 24(1): 1–18. A recent paper, from an author well known for his contributions over time in this area, which raises many questions for individual researchers, disciplines and institutions of development if 'gaps are to be narrowed'.

Wolfe, M. (1996) *Elusive Development*, London: Zed Books. A readable book that reflects in some detail on the successes and failures of the Basic Needs Approach to development.

REFERENCES

Annan, K. (2000) '*We the Peoples*': The role of the United Nations in the twenty-first century, Washington, DC: United Nations.

Bell, M. (1992) 'The water decade valedictory, New Delhi 1990: Where pre- and post-modern met', *Area*, 24(1): 82–9.

Brundtland, G.H. (2000) *Health and Population*, Reith Lecture, http://news.bbc.co.uk/hi/english/static/events/reith_2000

Chambers, R. (1993) *Challenging the Professions: Frontiers for Rural Development*, London: Intermediate Technology Publications.

Corbridge, S. (1999) 'Development, post-development and the global political-economy', in P. Cloke, P. Crang and M. Goodwin (eds) *Introducing Human Geographies*, London: Edward Arnold, pp. 67–75.

Escobar, A. (1995) 'Development planning', in S. Corbridge (ed.) *Development Studies: A Reader*, London: Edward Arnold, pp. 64–78.

Hausermann, J. (1998) *A Human Rights Approach to Development*, London: Rights and Humanity.

Manzo, K. (2003) Africa in the rise of rights-based development, *Geoforum*, 34: 437–56.

Maxwell, S. (1999) *What Can We Do with a Rights-based Approach to Development?* Briefing Paper 1993(3), September, London: Overseas Development Institute.

Radcliffe, S.A. (1999) 'Re-thinking development', in P. Cloke, P. Crang and M. Goodwin (eds) *Introducing Human Geographies*, London: Edward Arnold, pp. 84–92.

Schuurman, F. (ed.) (1993) *Beyond the Impasse: New Directions in Development Theory*, London: Zed Books.

Sen, A. (1999) *Development as Freedom*, Oxford: Oxford University Press.

Simon, D. (1999) 'Development revisited', in D. Simon and A. Narman (eds) *Development as Theory and Practice*, Harlow: Longman, pp. 17–54.

Smith, D.M. (2000) 'Moral progress in human geography: Transcending the place of good fortune', *Progress in Human Geography*, 24(1): 1–18.

Stohr, W.B. (1981) 'Development from below: The bottom-up and periphery-inward development paradigm', in W.B. Stohr and D.R.F. Taylor (eds) *Development from Above or Below?*, Chichester: John Wiley, pp. 39–72.

UNDP (United Nations Development Programme) (1998) *Integrating Human Rights with Sustainable Human Development*, New York: UNDP.

UNDP (United Nations Development Programme) (2000) *Human Development Report: Human Rights and Human Development*, New York: UNDP.

World Bank (1998) *Development and Human Rights: The role of the World Bank*, Washington, DC: The World Bank.

1.10 Participatory development

Giles Mohan

At the dawn of the 21st century, calls for more active engagement of poor people in development have come of age. Participation in development has gained a new respectability and legitimacy, and with the status of development orthodoxy (Cornwall 2002a: 15).

Introduction

Since the mid-1970s, a wide range of organizations have started involving local people in their own development, so much so, as Cornwall's quote above shows, that it is new 'orthodoxy'. This chapter begins by looking at different definitions of participatory development and examines through what sorts of organization it is achieved. As there are many possible approaches, I have included case studies which demonstrate different facets of participation. This brings us on to a critique and an overview of where things seem to be heading.

Participatory development in theory

The emergence of participatory development (PD) is tied into critiques of both theory and practice.

The emergence of participation

According to the strongest advocates of PD, 'normal' development is characterized by biases – Eurocentrism, positivism and top-downism – which are disempowering (Chambers 1997). The tendency is to equate development with the modernity achieved by 'Western' societies and to copy them through planning by experts. The flip side is that 'non-expert', local people were sidelined and their only role was as the objects of grandiose schemes.

As it became apparent that programmes had yielded limited benefits, the volume of criticism grew. In the 1970s, radicals such as Paulo Freire (1970) advocated participatory action research, which created new learning environments for people to express their needs and achieve development. Even mainstream organizations like the World Bank argued for basic needs approaches which targeted marginalized groups. Added to this were academics, most notably Robert Chambers, who argued that 'putting the last first' was necessary for rural development. Since then, the acceptance of participation has widened (Hickey and Mohan 2005).

Contested definitions

Participation is a plastic concept, which is generally deemed 'a good thing', but it has multiple meanings. Understanding how participation is used, therefore, is more than an academic exercise, but central to its possible impacts. In terms of development, a key question is: if people participate, what are they aiming to gain by participating? One view is about *efficiency and effectiveness* of 'formal' development programmes (Cornwall 2002a). The goals of development are valid, although the institutions are felt to be malfunctioning, but can be improved by involving the beneficiaries. For example, the German agency, GTZ, defined participation as 'co-determination and power sharing throughout the programme cycle' (1991: 5, cited in Nelson and Wright 1995: 4). Here, participation involves external and local agencies working together on a project basis, the implication being that the project was reasonably circumscribed. Another view concerns *mutual learning*, in which participation is an epistemological and practical issue of understanding where others are coming from and, ideally, learning from one another to achieve a better outcome (Chambers 1997; Cornwall 2002a). Others take this further in seeing participation as more *transformative* (Hickey and Mohan 2005). That is, 'development' is flawed and only by valorizing other voices can meaningful social change occur.

Despite these differences, there has been a growing acceptance regarding the importance of local involvement. Underlying this 'consensus' is the belief in not relying on the state. So, it might not be coincidental that PD gained popularity around the same time as the neoliberal counter-revolution of the 1980s, with its discourse of self-help and individualism.

Powerful processes

It needs emphasizing that whichever approach to participation we adopt, PD is fundamentally about power (Nelson and Wright 1995). Participation involves struggle whereby the powerful fight to retain their privileges. Even many supposedly participatory development agencies show a marked reluctance to release control. Cornwall (2002b) usefully distinguishes between 'invited' and 'claimed' spaces of participation. Invited spaces are the more formal events where development agents create forums for stakeholders to contribute and, ideally, reach a consensus in an orderly fashion. By contrast, claimed spaces are more organic and involve the poor taking control of political processes, without necessarily being invited in. Here, participation is conflictual, although in practice, political struggle usually has elements of both.

Participatory development in practice

In this section I discuss the institutional arrangements involved in PD and the processes through which it attempts to change power relations.

Grass-roots civil society

In rejecting the statism and top-downism of 'normal' development, the focus for PD has become the grass-roots level which permits a plurality of developmental goals to be realized, as well as giving communities the self-determination they need. Hence, PD has become associated with civil society. If state structures are inflexible, bureaucratic, urban-biased and unaccountable, then civil society organizations are believed to be smaller, more accountable and hands-on. Although civil society has multiple meanings, it has largely been interpreted as the realm of non-governmental organizations (NGOs), with many Southern-based ones relying on funding and institutional support from Northern partners.

New knowledges

The first step in reversing the biases marginalizing the poor concerns rethinking knowledge generation. The expert systems of modernity relied on scientific approaches, where planners worked from normative social models so that the recipients of development were treated as passive or, more often, conservative and obstructive. PD reverses this. The research methods for accessing local knowledges were inspired by Paulo Freire and have grown into a veritable industry (Chambers 1997), but all centre on trying to see the world from the point of view of those directly affected by the developmental intervention.

The most widely used methodology is participatory rural appraisal (PRA). As Chambers (1997: 103) explains:

> The essence of PRA is change and reversals – of role, behaviour, relationship and learning. Outsiders do not dominate and lecture; they facilitate, sit down, listen and learn. Outsiders do not transfer technology; they share methods which local people can use for their own appraisal, analysis, planning, action, monitoring and evaluation. Outsiders do not impose their reality; they encourage and enable local people to express their own.

PRA relies on many visual and oral techniques for generating knowledge because it is felt that the medium of written language is prejudicial to free expression. Methods such as mapping, ranking of preferences and oral histories are all part of PRA. So, PD seeks out diversity rather than treating everybody as uniform objects of development.

Participation in action

So far I have outlined the theory of PD, but what happens when it is practised in the 'real' world? These brief case studies demonstrate different facets of PD. The Aga Khan Rural Support Programme (India) has used participation to enhance the effectiveness of predetermined projects. The approach relates to 'consensus building', whereby the role of participatory approaches was 'to find a meeting ground to negotiate terms of collaboration' (Shah 1997: 75). In a dam scheme the farmers were not given an option regarding water payments, but the participatory exercise helped them to reach mutually agreeable solutions. As Shah (1997: 77) concludes, 'What has this exercise achieved? Certainly not true empowerment where villagers decide and prioritise development proposals with minimal external support and facilitation.' Shah suggests that while transformatory participation might be desirable, it is rarely viable where external agents are time-bound and accountable to funders. But that is not to say that they are dictatorial and that the lack of true empowerment detracts from real benefits.

A similar issue is raised where participatory approaches have been 'scaled up'. In the mid-1990s, the major lenders initiated poverty reduction strategies (PRSs), which responded to the criticism of their predecessors – structural adjustment programmes – of being imposed on countries. Instead, formulation of PRSs is to be 'owned' by the countries concerned, which means scaling up the invited spaces in which citizens and their representative organizations have a voice (Hickey and Mohan 2005). However, these mass participation exercises are often piecemeal, late in the policy process, and involve only 'safe' civil society organizations who will not question the neoliberal logic of PRSs.

By contrast, Village Aid, a small, UK-based NGO working in West Africa, has been trying to promote deeper participation, which leaves the development trajectories more open-ended. It became aware 'that a particular project undertaken in the past had not been a high priority for the village, but was undertaken at the suggestion of an NGO' (Village Aid 1996: 7). These were very much invited spaces. Instead, it sought to develop a situation where 'village communities set the agenda and outside agencies become responsive' (ibid.: 8). This process encourages the claiming of spaces and moves beyond a rigid PRA framework which is based on the values and communication capacities of outsiders.

The problems of participatory development

Having looked at these case studies, it will be worth drawing together some of the major problems that have emerged with PD.

The first is tokenism. As PD has become popular, some agencies use the rhetoric of participation with limited empowerment. Although PRA started as a challenge to expertise, it has become so routinized that many agencies treat it as a rubber stamp to prove their participatory credentials. As the Village Aid study showed, some NGOs have grown sceptical about the abuse of PRA, as it still relies on methods (e.g. voting) which are non-local (Cooke and Kothari 2001). And in the PRS process, which champions participation and ownership, most representatives of the poor are either hand-picked to ensure agreement or are brought in too late to change anything (Hickey and Mohan 2005).

Second, much PD has treated communities as socially homogeneous. While community empowerment might be an improvement on unresponsive bureaucracies, there have been cases where support for 'the community' has meant that resources have passed to elites. More sensitive PRA picks up on heterogeneity, particularly gender differences at the household and community level (Mosse 1994).

Third, the emphasis on civil society can create competition between local organizations. With aid being channelled through such organizations, it is the better organized or more acceptable which capture resources. The result is that weaker organizations are further undermined. Allied to this is that many 'partnerships' between Northern and Southern NGOs are heavily loaded in favour of the former. Not only does the Northern NGO usually control the finances, but it often retains de facto veto power over its counterpart. Financially, intellectually and politically, many partnerships are anything but participatory, with the Southern NGO acting as a delivery mechanism for a predetermined agenda.

Fourth is whether participation is an end in itself or also a means to an end. From a democratic perspective, simply being able to participate is a major achievement, but for the poor their lack of resources means that any participatory process must yield tangible benefits. In turn, this forces us to consider people not as idealized political subjects, but as embodied agents, shaped and constrained by material and cultural structures. Furthermore, as Brett (2003) warns, simply participating is meaningless unless there is some institutionalized accountability. He argues that we should focus on 'the nature of the institutional constraints that determine how much leverage users can exercise over agencies, whether these operate in the state, market or voluntary sector' (Brett 2003: 18).

The final problem is broader and relates to the causes of underdevelopment. PD seeks to give local people control, but many processes affecting their (or our) lives are often not readily tackled at the local level. For example, it is very hard for a small cooperative in Africa to change the rules governing international trade when the World Trade Organization is dominated by the developed economies. The emphasis on grass-roots society can leave important structures untouched and do nothing to strengthen states and make them more accountable to their citizens.

Citizenship and the future of participatory development

It becomes clear that while PD has brought benefits to some communities, it has been abused and does little to address extra-local processes. This recognition that development will involve broader questions of citizenship and sovereignty has seen agencies building the capacity of the state rather than bypassing it in their eagerness to empower civil society. This involves state–society 'synergy' to produce more lasting development by bolstering citizenship.

Reframing participation as citizenship is about combining the advantages of invited and claimed participatory spaces. It situates PD in a broader range of socio-political practices, or expressions of agency (Gaventa 2002), through which people extend their status and rights as members of particular political communities, thereby increasing their control over socioeconomic resources. This unites a 'liberal' theory of citizenship, stressing formal rights and political channels, with 'civic republican' approaches that emphasize the collective engagement of citizens in the determination of their community affairs. The focus here is on substantive rather than procedural forms of citizenship, a participatory notion that offers the prospect that citizenship can be claimed 'from below', through the efforts of the marginalized in organized struggles, rather than waiting for it to be conferred 'from above'.

A further development on the limitations of localized participatory approaches has been the move by NGOs into advocacy and lobbying. Given that 'local' problems have global causes, the most useful thing that a relatively powerful, non-local organization can do is use its political weight to raise awareness and campaign for reform of global institutions. This sees ever more complex networking between NGOs, which generates new forms of participation which are not rooted in place, but stretched across transnational space where 'community' may exist only in a 'virtual' sense. In all these cases, the challenges for participatory development multiply.

GUIDE TO FURTHER READING AND REFERENCES

The following text references provide the basis for further reading.

Brett, E.A. (2003) 'Participation and accountability in development management', *Journal of Development Studies*, 40(2): 1–29.

Chambers, R. (1997) *Whose Reality Counts? Putting the First Last*, London: Intermediate Technology Publications.

Cooke, W. and Kothari, U. (2001) *Participation: The New Tyranny?* London: Zed Books.

Cornwall, A. (2002a) *Beneficiary, Consumer, Citizen: Perspectives on Participation for Poverty Reduction*, SIDA Studies no. 2, Stockholm: Swedish International Development Cooperation Agency.

Cornwall, A. (2002b) 'Making spaces, changing places: situating participation in development', *IDS Working Paper 170*, Brighton: Institute of Development Studies.

Freire, P. (1970) *The Pedagogy of the Oppressed*, New York: The Seabury Press.

Gaventa, J. (2002) 'Exploring citizenship, participation and accountability', *IDS Bulletin*, 33(2): 1–11.

GTZ (1991) *Where There is no Participation*, Eschborn: Deutsche Gessellschaft für Technische Zusammenarbeit.

Hickey, S. and Mohan, G. (2005) 'Relocating participation within a radical politics of development', *Development and Change*, 36(2): 237–62.

Mosse, D. (1994) 'Authority, gender and knowledge: Theoretical reflections on the practice of participatory rural appraisal', *Development and Change*, 25: 497–526.

Nelson, N. and Wright, S. (1995) 'Participation and power', in N. Nelson and S. Wright (eds) *Power and Participatory Development: Theory and Practice*, London: Intermediate Technology Publications, pp. 1–18.

Shah, A. (1997) 'Developing participation', *PLA Notes*, 30: 75–8.

Village Aid (1996) *Beyond PRA: A New Approach to Village-led Development*, unpublished business plan, Village Aid.

1.11 Culture and development

Susanne Schech and Jane Haggis

The role of culture in development has become an important subject in the development literature since the mid-1990s. Scholars increasingly recognize culture's interconnectedness with the many and varied economic, political and social changes which developing societies are experiencing in their quest to modernize, and the impossibility of understanding such changes without taking 'the cultural factor' into account. As Tim Allen (1992: 337) points out in an early contribution to the literature on culture and development, 'religion and kinship are just as significant as economic transactions and the political life of nation states, and in fact these things are not really separable or comparable'.

Even though many development scholars accept that culture matters in development, there is still much debate over *how* it matters. Some argue that cultural values, attitudes, orientations and opinions are a key variable in determining economic progress, and can explain why some countries succeed in their quest for development and others fail (Harrison and Huntington 2000). But Amartya Sen (2004: 43) warns against such cultural determinism, and points out that 'the temptation toward using cultural determinism often takes the hopeless form of trying to fix the cultural anchor on a rapidly moving boat'. His concept of culture takes into account that cultures are constantly changing and are not internally homogeneous, and that culture alone does not determine our lives and identities – class, gender and politics also shape us, as do institutions and incentives. However, in the eyes of other scholars, Sen's concept of culture is too limited. Rather than seeing gender as separate from culture, feminist critiques of the male bias of mainstream economic development acknowledge gender as an important cultural variable in the development process. If gender can be seen as cultural, then so can institutions. Arturo Escobar (1995) argues that the 'Third World' is produced 'by the discourses and practices of development' embedded in institutions such as the World Bank. Techniques of definition and categorization, such as the international poverty line, operate to stereotype millions of people by criteria not of their own making. In this way, the 'Third World' becomes a cultural artefact of

the West, revealing more about the cultural blinkers of the West than the objective circumstances of the 'Rest'. These examples demonstrate the need to understand where scholars are
coming from when they consider culture and development.

Looking back on culture and development

A focus on culture is not a new move in development studies. In the 1950s and 1960s, the role of
culture in development received considerable attention within a development studies dominated
by modernization theory. Here, the main challenge was perceived to be to explain why some societies were developed and others were not, and how underdeveloped societies can become modern
and developed. Culture played an important role in distinguishing 'traditional' from 'modern' societies. Daniel Lerner's anthropological study of the Turkish village of Balgat, caught in the 1950s on
the brink of its incorporation into the modernizing capital city of Ankara, exemplifies this
approach. His study typecasts the village head as a 'traditional man', defined by Islamic religiosity,
patriarchal authority, austerity, obedience and patriotic loyalty, whose cosmos is the village of
Balgat. In contrast, the 'modern man' is a shopkeeper, who dreams of material wealth, moving to
the USA and knowing the world. This binary contrasting traditional and modern is based on a
notion of culture as a bounded, discrete entity, 'consisting of particular sets of structures of social
relations, practices and symbolic systems which forge a cohesive unity for the group, whether as
society, nation, community, or class' (Schech and Haggis 2000: 35, 22).

Modernization studies took for granted that development was accompanied by the acquisition
of Western cultural traits and values, which would result in developing societies eventually resem-
bling Western Europe and the United States. One way of explaining this was by seeing modern patterns of social relations as a 'universal social solvent' which erases the traditional cultural traits of
Third World societies through contact. Thus the traditional/modern was not a binary of equals,
but hierarchical: traditional societies or 'cultures' placed at the bottom of the hierarchy were
labelled evolutionary dead ends, which would either be left to die out or be 'bred out' of a people
through more or less well-meaning policy interventions (Schech and Haggis 2000: 18–19). A more
positive depiction of non-Western cultures was as romanticized Other, whose unchanging reposi-
tories of 'tribal', 'peasant' or 'traditional' ways of living and belief systems were presumed to exist
outside modernity, where they could be imagined as part of pure nature. Both these conceptualizations of 'traditional' society are based on the same notion of culture as a discrete, bounded
entity.

In the 1970s and 1980s, the battle between Marxist-inspired studies of underdevelopment and
dependent development on the one hand, and neoliberalism on the other, drove culture off the
mainstream development agenda dominated by economist and political-economy analyses. With
this debate at an impasse, some scholars turned to the new fields of cultural studies, post-colonial
studies and globalization for new analytical tools to explore development. This provided for a
much more dynamic and broad definition of culture as 'a network of representations – texts,
images, talk, codes of behaviour, and the narrative structures organising these – which shapes every
aspect of social life' (Frow and Morris 1993: viii). Culture, from this perspective, is productive, in
the sense of being an active component in the production and reproduction of social life, and the
sense people make of it.

The significance attached to representation and power in this definition of culture reflects the
impact of post-colonial studies, which critiques Western cultural domination and cultural representations of developing societies, and thus places power relations at the centre of analysis (Said
1978; Hall 1992). Stuart Hall reveals how European colonization not only involved economic and
political domination of the New World, but that 'Europe brought its own cultural categories, languages, images, and ideas into the New World in order to describe and represent it' (Hall 1992:
293–4). How the colonial territories and peoples were seen, thought about and represented in art,

literature and scientific studies reflected the interests Europe had in them. Edward Said's study of Orientalism, which he describes as a way of knowing the Orient and simultaneously 'a Western style of dominating, restructuring, and having authority over the Orient' (Said 1978: 3), exposes and challenges a politics of representation which continues to use colonizing strategies in describing developing countries and problems of development.

The rise of globalization studies, and the processes of globalization themselves, have also influenced the ways scholars look at the connection between culture and development. The deregulation of financial capital and trade, and the reconfiguration of social relationships in terms of space, time and speed, has challenged the binary models of modernity and tradition, core and periphery, which underpinned modernization and Marxist development theories. The connection with the global makes the parameters of people's lived experience more permeable than ever before, expanding the awareness of other circumstances, experiences, images and ways of living. Thus, Arjun Appadurai, Stuart Hall and others have argued that the global flows of ideas, people and goods further undermine the utility of a concept of culture as a distinct, discrete and nationally bounded entity, fostering instead a fluid and complex notion of culture as constantly being transformed by multi-directional, cultural interactions, which weave the local and the global together in a multitude of different, and often rather unstable, configurations. Alan Pred (1992: 109) captures this notion of culture in his inimical style:

> Culture does not stand   isolated
>   on its own, immutable and uncontested.
> It is neither fixed, nor confined to the traditional,
>   neither completely stable, nor a unified monolith of coherence.
> It is not an autonomous entity,
>   existing in a territory of its own,
> beyond the realms of materiality and social reality.
> Culture is embodied and lived,
>   actively produced and expressed,
> through all social practices,
> through all that is concrete and everyday,
> through all that is enmeshed in power relations
>   and their associated discourses,
>   their associated representations and rhetorics. (...)

Looking through a culture and development lens

As Pred and others have pointed out, the 'cultural' in development studies is connected to the uneven articulations of capitalist economic processes, which are never just physical – labour, capital, goods, technologies, and so on – but also take on cultural forms. As late capitalist economies switch their focus from production to consumption, 'culture gains a heightened salience in differentiating consumers and driving the ever-changing goods through which modernity and identity are appraised' (Radcliffe 2006: 229). At the same time, discontent, contestation and resistance to the inequalities and injustices produced by the forces of capitalism and modernity are increasingly expressed and channelled through culture. Friedman's (1990) study of *Les Sapeurs*, a men's group in Brazzaville in the People's Republic of the Congo, illustrates this dialectic relationship. As Les Sapeurs acquire European designer clothes at great expense, sacrificing the majority of their income as migrant workers in Paris, only to display the brand names in ritualized practices of 'lumpen-proletarian dandyism' on their return to Brazzaville, they lock themselves into the global cultural economy as consumers and workers. But they also indigenize Western consumerism in ways that challenge the established norms of elite status in Congolese society (Schech and Haggis 2000: 61).

Culture is not only a product or a vehicle of accommodation and contestation, but is increasingly used as a development tool by a variety of development actors (international agencies, governments, non-governmental organizations and grass-roots activists) (Radcliffe 2006). As Sarah Radcliffe argues, since the 1990s, development planners and scholars have increasingly treated culture as a kind of glue that holds societies together and gives them a coherent structure which can be used for development interventions. For example, the World Bank moved towards a more social notion of development in the 1990s that considered the influence of gender, ethnicity and other forms of diversity on economic development and poverty. The Bank commissioned a study of the *Voices of the Poor* (Narayan et al. 2000), which identifies the common threads and themes in the world views of the poor, as well as acknowledging that representation is a critical issue in development policymaking and practice. The study reveals that poor people are often ambivalent about the cultural norms relating to gender, class, ethnicity, caste, and so on, of the societies they live in – sceptical and ironical on the one hand, but compliant on the other. Drawing on this study, the *World Development Report 2000* argues that the fight against poverty must build on the social capital that bonds poor communities together – the ties connecting family members, neighbours, close friends and business associates – onto which vertical ties can be grafted between the poor and people in positions of influence in formal organizations who make decisions relating to their welfare.

While the World Bank has incorporated elements of the perspective of poor people into its model of development, as Appadurai (2004: 66) points out: 'The poor are recognized, but in ways that ensure minimum change in the terms of redistribution.' He uses the example of a pro-poor alliance of housing activists based in Mumbai, India, and linked to a global network, the Slum/Shackdwellers International, to show how the poor become development actors by using culture to expand the spaces of agency and representation. One of the strategies the Alliance employs to increase the voice of Mumbai slum residents and expand their capacity to aspire is the housing exhibition, which provides a public space for poor people to discuss their housing needs and interests with politicians, donor agencies, local planners, architects and professional builders. Hijacking what is essentially an upper-class form and placing slum residents at its centre enhances their visibility and recognition, as well as cleverly subverting the dominant class cultures in India.

GUIDE TO FURTHER READING

Appadurai, A. (1996) *Modernity at Large: Cultural Dimensions of Globalization*, Minnesota: University of Minnesota Press.

Ferguson, J. (1990) *The Anti-Politics Machine: 'Development', Depoliticization, and Bureaucratic Power in Lesotho*, Cambridge: Cambridge University Press.

Goudge, P. (2003) *The Whiteness of Power: Racism in Third World Development and Aid*, London: Lawrence & Wishart.

Lerner, D. (1958) *The Passing of Traditional Society: Modernizing the Middle East*, New York: Free Press.

Liechty, M. (2003) *Suitably Modern: Making Middle Class Culture in a New Consumer Society*, Princeton, NJ: Princeton University Press.

REFERENCES

Allen, T. (1992) 'Taking culture seriously', in T. Allen and A. Thomas (eds) *Poverty and Development in the 1990s*, Oxford: Oxford University Press, pp. 331–46.

Appadurai, A. (2004) 'The capacity to aspire: Culture and the terms of recognition', in V. Rao and M. Walton (eds) *Culture and Public Action*, Stanford, CA: Stanford University Press, pp. 59–84.

Escobar, A. (1995) *Encountering Development: The Making and Unmaking of the Third World*, Princeton, NJ: Princeton University Press.

Friedman, J. (1990) 'Being in the world: Globalization and localization', *Theory, Culture and Society*, 7: 311–28.

Frow, J. and Morris, M. (1993) *Australian Cultural Studies: A Reader*, St Leonards, Australia: Allen & Unwin.

Hall, S. (1992) 'The West and the rest: Discourse and power', in S. Hall and B. Gieben (eds) *Formations of Modernity*, Cambridge: Polity Press, pp. 275–311.

Harrison, L.E. and Huntington, S.P. (eds) (2000) *Culture Matters: How Values Shape Human Progress,* New York: Basic Books.

Narayan, D. et al. (2000) *Voices of the Poor, Vols. 1–3*, New York: Oxford University Press.

Pred, A. (1992) 'Capitalisms, crises, and cultures II: Notes on local transformation and everyday cultural struggles', in A. Pred and M.J. Watts (eds) *Reworking Modernity: Capitalisms and Symbolic Discontent*, New Brunswick, NJ: Rutgers University Press.

Radcliffe, S.A. (2006) 'Conclusions: The future of culture and development', in S.A. Radcliffe (ed.) *Culture and Development in a Globalizing World: Geographies, Actors, and Paradigms*, London: Routledge, pp. 228–37.

Said, E.W. (1978) *Orientalism: Western Conceptions of the Orient*, New York: Pantheon Books.

Schech, S. and Haggis, J. (2000) *Culture and Development: A Critical Introduction*, Oxford: Blackwell.

Schech, S. and Haggis, J. (eds) (2002) *Development: A Cultural Studies Reader*, Oxford: Blackwell.

Sen, A. (2004) 'How does culture matter?', in V. Rao and M. Walton (eds) *Culture and Public Action*, Stanford, CA: Stanford University Press, pp. 37–58.

1.12 Information and communication technologies for development

Tim Unwin and Geraldine de Bastion

In his acceptance speech for the 2006 Nobel Peace Prize, Mohammed Yunus, the founder of the Grameen Bank in Bangladesh, commented:

> Information and communication technology (ICT) is quickly changing the world, creating a distanceless, borderless world of instantaneous communications. Increasingly, it is becoming less and less costly. I saw an opportunity for the poor people to change their lives if this technology could be brought to them to meet their needs.
>
> As a first step to bring ICT to the poor we created a mobile phone company, Grameen Phone. We gave loans from Grameen Bank to the poor women to buy mobile phones to sell phone services in the villages. We saw the synergy between microcredit and ICT.
>
> The phone business was a success and became a coveted enterprise for Grameen borrowers. Telephone ladies quickly learned and innovated the ropes of the telephone business, and it has become the quickest way to get out of poverty and to earn social respectability. Today there are nearly 300,000 telephone ladies providing telephone service in all the villages of Bangladesh (http://nobelprize.org/nobel_prizes/peace/laureates/2006/yunus-lecture-en.html).

This is a prominent example of the ways in which information and communication technologies (ICTs) have recently come to the fore as a vehicle for improving the lives of poor people, and thereby contributing to 'development'. However, ICT for development (ICT4D) has not been without its critics, many of whom argue that the use of such technologies merely reinforces existing patterns of social and economic inequality.

There has been much discussion of the notion that ICTs have played a central part in the processes associated with globalization. The use of the Internet has transformed the ways in which people interact, with flows of information and communication taking place across the world at ever increasing speeds. However, it is also possible to argue that, rather than being an exogenous force of change, the emergence of such technologies has been a direct response to the needs of those in power, notably businesses and the world's dominant states, to increase their control of the world economy. Castells (2000) has argued that these processes have ushered in a profoundly new Information Age. He suggests that

> Towards the end of the second millennium of the Christian era several events of historical significance transformed the social landscape of human life. A technological revolution, centred around information technologies, began to reshape, at accelerated pace, the material basis of society. Economies throughout the world have become globally interdependent, introducing a new form of relationship between economy, state, and society, in a system of variable geometry (Castells 2000: 1).

More recently, Friedman (2006) has commented that around the year 2000, certain forces had come together to act in a mutually reinforcing way to lead to a flattening of the world, moving it from being a primarily vertical system to one instead dominated by horizontal processes associated with connecting and collaborating. For Friedman (2006: 205), these ten key forces were 'the fall of the Berlin Wall, the rise of the PC, Netscape, work flow, outsourcing, offshoring, uploading, insourcing, supply-chaining, in-forming, and the steroids' of computing, instant messaging and file sharing, Voice over Internet Protocol (VoIP), videoconferencing, new computer graphics and wireless technologies. It is not easy to determine who will be the winners and the losers in these new social, economic, political and cultural contexts. Friedman (2006) certainly makes the case that the USA can retain its dominance of the global economy, but he also argues that developing countries can benefit from the potential of the 'Flat World' if they are able to get the infrastructure, education and governance conditions right for their people to benefit.

Two contrasting sets of ideas can help us to understand these options. On the one hand are 'normalization' arguments that suggest that the social profile of digital and online communities will gradually broaden over time, so that the use of these technologies will come to reflect society as a whole, be that locally or globally. Thus, in more developed societies, the Internet could eventually become as ubiquitous as television is today, as a result of falling costs for hardware, software and services. For enthusiasts like Jean Michel Billaut, the introduction of fibre-optic cables across Europe would thus transform the ways in which we communicate and work (http://billaut.typepad.com). Drawing in part on his experiences in the southern French community of Pau – where an optical and wireless network offering 100 megabits per second for US$30 per month for everybody has provided dramatically enhanced functionality, including VoIP, DVD quality streaming, web conferencing, music, e-health, e-administration and interactive 3D for commerce – Billaut envisages a future where everyone can benefit from the potential of high bandwidth connectivity. In contrast, social diffusion models, drawing particularly on the work of Rogers (2003, but first published in 1962), have suggested that the adoption of new technologies often reinforces existing economic advantages. Thus, characteristics such as education, levels of literacy and social status all constrain access to the essential financial and information resources that are necessary to enable people successfully to benefit from new technologies. In highly stratified societies it is therefore common for innovations to reinforce existing socio-economic differences. However, one of the key conclusions of this body of literature is that active initiatives to level the playing field and enable disadvantaged communities to benefit from innovations may have a positive impact in equalizing these benefits.

Von Braun and Torero (2006: 1) have emphasized that ICTs have become an increasingly important component of contemporary development practice for four main reasons: their inherent public-good characteristics; their economies of scale effects; their ability to promote 'interactive communication unhindered by distance, volume, medium, or time'; and their role in facilitating better decision making.

> ICT has the potential to accelerate growth, create jobs, reduce migration pressure from rural to urban areas, increase agricultural and industrial productivity, increase services and access to them, facilitate the diffusion of innovations, increase public administration efficiency and the effectiveness of economic reforms, strengthen competition in developing countries, and encourage greater public participation and democracy (von Braun and Torero 2006: 1).

Given this potential, it is not surprising that numerous global initiatives over the last decade have sought to channel the potential of ICTs in the development arena. One of the earliest specific references to the role of ICTs can be found in the Millennium Development Goals agreed by the UN Development Summit in 2000. These explicitly include the aspiration that the international development community should, 'In cooperation with the private sector, make available the benefits of new technologies – especially information and communications technologies', as part of Goal 8 to develop a global partnership for development (http://www.un.org/millenniumgoals). It is crucial here to emphasize that ICTs are mentioned explicitly in the context of private-sector involvement in development partnerships. This has given rise not only to very many initiatives that have sought to implement such partnerships (see Schware 2005; Weigel and Waldburger 2004; http://topics.developmentgateway.org/ict), but also to a considerable raft of criticism that the emphasis on ICTs has been driven primarily by the interests of the private sector in expanding their markets and reducing labour costs (see Cline-Cole and Powell 2004). In 2000, the G8 established its Digital Opportunity Task Force (DOT Force) to take forward these agendas, and in 2001 the UN took up the mantle with the creation of its ICT Task Force (http://www.unicttaskforce.org/welcome/), whose main mission was to determine how the global community could 'harness this extraordinary force, spread it throughout the world, and make its benefits accessible and meaningful for all humanity, in particular the poor'. This, in turn, gave rise to the World Summit on the Information Society (WSIS) held in Geneva in 2003 and Tunis in 2005 (http://www.itu.int/wsis/), which provided a declaration of principles, a plan of action and an agenda focusing particularly on financial mechanisms for meeting the challenges of ICT4D, as well as recommendations on Internet governance, including the creation of an Internet Governance Forum. As one of its main follow-ups to WSIS, the UN launched the Global Alliance for ICT and Development (GAID) in 2006, to provide a truly global forum to address cross-cutting issues relating to ICT in development. 'It will do so by providing an inclusive, multi-stakeholder global forum and platform for cross-sectoral policy dialogue and advocacy and by catalyzing multi-stakeholder action oriented partnerships encouraged under the GAID umbrella' (http://www.un-gaid.org/).

There are two main ways through which ICTs can contribute to development agendas. First, if development is defined primarily in terms of economic growth, ICTs can play a very significant role in contributing to development both through its ability to enhance productivity, and also as a means to generate employment in developing countries. Business Process Outsourcing (BPO) has thus played a very significant role in the economic growth of parts of southern India such as Bangalore, as well as in other areas of Asia. This is typified by the emerging role of countries such as the Philippines, with companies like People Support moving most of their activities from the USA – in 2006, People Support employed more than 7000 people in its centres in Manila and Cebu. In explaining this move, they emphasize the way in which the Philippines has modelled many of its systems on those in the USA, the country's large pool of skilled college graduates who speak English with minimal accents, the strong work ethic, a consultative and customer mindset, government support and incentive, and a robust technical infrastructure. Such initiatives undoubtedly play a significant role in helping to develop local economic activity, and the multiplier effect provides substantial benefits. However, many analysts still point to the generally low impact that investment in ICTs appears to be having on economic growth in the poorest countries. In their comprehensive study, Torero, Chowdhury and Bedi (2006: 47–8) thus comment that 'Marginal improvements in telecommunications infrastructure are unlikely to yield discernible growth effects. Moreover, given the even lower penetration level of other forms of ICT, growth effects will remain elusive without widespread increases in access to these technologies in low-income countries.' There is therefore still a long way to go before the poorest countries can be expected to reap the benefits that ICTs might offer them. Indeed, it remains very uncertain whether they will ever be able to achieve this, given the emphasis that some of the most economically powerful are continuing to place on remaining competitive knowledge economies. The European Commission has recognized that 'The fast development of the Information and Communication Technology (ICT) has brought about deep **changes in our way of working and living**, as the widespread diffusion of ICT is accompanied by organisational, commercial, social and legal innovations', and the Lisbon European Council in March 2000 set a strategic goal for Europe 'to become the most competitive and dynamic knowledge-based economy in the world, capable of sustaining economic growth with more and better jobs and greater social cohesion' by 2010 (http://ec.europa.eu/employment_social/knowledge_society/index_en.htm). This is scarcely an agenda that emphasizes the value of sharing knowledge and information in order that poor and marginalized communities may gain equal benefit from it (see also Mansell and Wehn 1998).

Second, there are many ICT4D initiatives across the globe that have sought to focus explicitly on alternative mechanisms that can be used directly to support poor and marginalized communities, thereby empowering them to benefit from the new technologies through which they can communicate and share information (see, for example, Greenberg 2005; ITU 2005; Milward-Oliver 2005; Torero and von Braun 2006). Despite being well intentioned, many of these initiatives have so far proved not to be sustainable without continuing donor support or civil society intervention. In part, this is because far too many of them have been externally driven and supply-led, without paying sufficient attention to the real needs of user communities. There have undoubtedly been some initiatives that have become highly successful, such as the Grameen Phone example used to open this chapter, but too many have wasted valuable resources because they have focused more on the technologies than on user needs (Souter et al. 2005). Another problem has tended to be the duplication of effort resulting from many different donors and organizations wishing to provide ICT-based resources, but doing so independently. Achieving an integrated approach to the provision of appropriate ICT infrastructures that can be used for health, education, governance and rural development programmes has so far eluded most governments in the poorest countries of the world. In this context, it is also crucial that local demands should drive the initiatives, rather than some externally imposed conceptualization of what those demands are. There have been remarkably few studies that have actually sought to identify what the information needs of poor people are (for an exception, see Schilderman 2002). Until ICT4D initiatives really focus on developing innovation technological solutions to deliver these needs in a cost-effective and sustainable way, it is likely that many more such initiatives will continue to flounder. As experiences in the richer countries of the world have shown, for example, ICTs can dramatically transform the lives of people with disabilities, but, as yet, negligible attention has been paid to rolling out these life-transforming innovations for people with disabilities in the poor countries of the world.

In conclusion, this chapter has sought to argue that ICTs have considerable potential to change the lives of poor people and communities across the world. Experience suggests that to date such technologies have been used primarily to sustain existing economic advantages, but the dramatic expansion in the use of mobile devices, computers and the Internet since the mid-1990s has provided immense opportunities to develop new means of empowering poor and marginalized communities. The full potential of these innovations has yet to be realized in ways that will enable everyone to benefit from them, but if we concentrate our attention on the information and communication needs of the least privileged, we can at least begin to redress the balance in emphasis that has led to the failure of all too many ICT4D initiatives.

GUIDE TO FURTHER READING

Greenberg, A. (2005) *ICTs for Poverty Alleviation: Basic Tool and Enabling Sector*, Stockholm: Sida.

Torero, M. and von Braun, J. (eds) (2006) *Information and Communication Technologies for Development and Poverty Reduction*, Baltimore, MD: Johns Hopkins University Press for IFPRI.

Weigel, G. and Waldburger, D. (2004) *ICT4D – Connecting People for a Better World*, Geneva: Swiss Agency for Development and Cooperation and Global Knowledge Partnership. (See also the ICT4D Collective website at http://www.ict4d.org.uk)

REFERENCES

Castells, M. (2000) *The Rise of the Network Society. The Information Age: Economy, Society and Culture Volume I*, second edition, Oxford: Blackwell.

Chowdhury, S.K. and Bedi, A.S. (2006) 'Telecommunications infrastructure and economic growth: A cross-country analysis', in M. Torero and J. von Braun (eds) *Information and Communication Technologies for Development and Poverty Reduction*, Baltimore, MD: Johns Hopkins University Press for IFPRI, pp. 21–63.

Cline-Cole, R. and Powell, M. (eds) (2004) 'ICTs, "Virtual Colonisation" and Political Economy', special issue of *Review of African Political Economy*, 99.

Development Gateway Topic – ICT for Development, http://topics.developmentgateway.org/ict

Friedman, T.L. (2006) *The World is Flat: The Globalized World in the Twenty-first Century*, London: Penguin.

Greenberg, A. (2005) *ICTs for Poverty Alleviation: Basic Tool and Enabling Sector*, Stockholm: Sida.

ITU (ed.) (2005) *Digital Reach*, Leicester: Tudor Rose for ITU.

Mansell, R. and Wehn, U. (1998) *Knowledge Societies: Information Technology for Sustainable Development*, Oxford: Oxford University Press.

Milward-Oliver, G. (ed.) (2005) *Maitland+20 – Fixing the Missing Link*, Bradford on Avon: Anima.

Rogers, E. (2003) *Diffusion of Innovations*, fifth edition, New York: Free Press.

Schilderman, T. (2002) *Strengthening the Knowledge and Information Systems of the Urban Poor*, London: DFID and ITDG.

Schware, R. (ed.) (2005) *e-Development: From Excitement to Effectiveness*, Washington, DC: IBRD, World Bank Group.

Souter, D. with Scott, N., Garforth, C., Jain, R., Mascarenhas, O. and McKerney, K. (2005) *The Economic Impact of Telecommunications on Rural Livelihoods and Poverty Reduction: A Study of Rural Communities in India (Gujarat), Mozambique and Tanzania*, London: CTO and DFID.

Torero, M., Chowdhury, S.K. and Bedi, A.S. (2006) 'Telecommunications infrastructure and economic growth: A cross-country analysis', in M. Torero and J. von Braun (eds) *Information and Communication Technologies for Development and Poverty Reduction*, Baltimore, MD: Johns Hopkins University Press for IFPRI, pp. 21–63.

von Braun, J. and Torero, M. (2006) 'Introduction and overview', in M. Torero and J. von Braun (eds) *Information and Communication Technologies for Development and Poverty Reduction*, Baltimore, MD: Johns Hopkins University Press for IFPRI, pp. 1–20.

Weigel, G. and Waldburger, D. (2004) *ICT4D – Connecting People for a Better World*, Geneva: Swiss Agency for Development and Cooperation and Global Knowledge Partnership.

World Summit on the Information Society, http://www.itu.int/wsis/

Note: all Internet sites were accessed on 22 January 2007.

1.13 The Labour Party and development

David Seddon

The early years

The early labour movement combined radical and reformist strands – from the Independent Labour Party (ILP) to the Fabians. Influenced by nonconformism, it rejected militarism, seeking an end to poverty and oppression, at home and abroad. Some criticized aggressive foreign policy and the quest for capitalist profit overseas; but many also saw imperialism as a force for good, bringing progress to backward peoples and territories. Established in 1906, the Labour Party was overshadowed by the Liberals. A member of the Second International, its socialist credentials were always questionable.

In 1914, initially opposed to an alliance with Tsarist Russia against relatively progressive Germany, the membership's overwhelming pro-war sentiments forced the resignation of Labour's leader, Ramsay MacDonald. His replacement, Arthur Henderson, joined the 'war cabinet'. Labour opposed conscription initially, but in 1916 accepted it. After the war, Labour supported the formation of the League of Nations, to help regulate conflicts between states. Government responsibility for colonial development was recognized with the Colonial Development Act of 1929. That year, Labour won the general election and Sidney Webb, a Fabian intellectual, became Colonial Secretary. His period in office was unremarkable. Worldwide depression affected Britain, and the government was inevitably blamed. Labour split over economic policy, and in May 1931 a 'National Government' was formed. Labour did badly in the next two elections, and remained in the political wilderness until 1945.

Growing interest in colonial development

During the interwar years, African and Asian nationalists were welcomed in left-wing Labour circles, which expressed increasing interest in 'overseas' issues and support for colonial independence. The Labour Party Advisory Committee on Colonial Affairs was established, but only two of its members were active in parliament. One was Arthur Creech Jones, MP for Shipley. Colonial or imperial themes enjoyed little prominence in the party's manifestos or policy literature: support for 'an extension of the mandate system to colonial territories' was the only reference to 'overseas development' in Labour's 1935 election manifesto.

Clement Atlee became party leader and few, apart from Winston Churchill, saw a growing threat from fascism. Labour argued for disarmament. By 1939, Britain was at war. Over the next five years, the resources of the Empire proved a major strength to Britain. The Colonial Office increased in size and importance. In 1940, the Fabians established a Colonial Research Bureau, and Arthur Creech Jones addressed himself, as no Labour politician had done before, to development issues. He became a major influence. Creech Jones was the main architect of the Colonial Charter, considered (but not adopted) at the party conference in 1942. The Bureau 'provided the Party with exciting new blueprints for a positive colonial policy, based on long-term economic, technological and educational development' (Morgan 1985: 190).

The Labour Government of 1945–1951

Labour came to power in 1945. With Creech Jones in the Colonial Office, initiatives were taken to dismantle the Empire and create a new Commonwealth of independent states. India gained independence in 1947, but partition left Kashmir a disputed territory. Burma and Ceylon achieved independence more easily. In 1948, Britain terminated its Mandate over Palestine ingloriously, abandoning it to war, the forced exodus of thousands of Palestinians and the declaration of the state of Israel. The continuing troubles of Kashmir and Israel/Palestine are, partly, a Labour legacy.

Nevertheless, colonial independence was initiated. In 1945, 457 million people lived under British rule; at the end of 1951, the number was 70 million. Morgan suggests (1985: 231) that

> it may be that it is in the more arcane or specialist areas of policy in promoting colonial freedom and economic development between 1945 and 1951 that the most significant of Labour's legacies for the future of the world can be discerned. No aspect of its achievement glows more brightly in the later twentieth century.

Creech Jones – assisted by Andrew Cohen, head of the Africa Division – was largely responsible. There was a dynamism about the Colonial Office now, with development economists, journalists, intellectuals and others, including African and Asian leaders, enjoying easy access to government ministers. In many ways, the Colonial Office was the Fabian Colonial Research Bureau, writ large.

A key element in Labour's development strategy was the creation of powerful, centrally funded corporations – the Overseas Food Corporation (OFC) and the Colonial Development Corporation (CDC). In Africa, ambitious schemes were promoted. Some proved dramatic failures, doing Creech Jones and his corporate approach to 'development' considerable harm. But they provided a stimulus to economic growth, in Africa in particular. In Asia, development plans were established for India, Pakistan, Ceylon, Malaya, Singapore and British North Borneo at the Colombo Conference (1950). These schemes and plans, like Labour's development strategy as a whole, were largely 'top-down', poorly grounded in local realities and marked by a strong element of British self-interest. The approach was an extension of a distinctive party tradition: 'enlightened' policymakers combining self-interest with 'doing good', or – as *Tribune* (4 July 1947) put it – 'Fabianising the Empire'.

The push for colonial freedom accelerated, based on earlier initiatives taken by the Colonial Office. Constitutional reform was promoted where possible, more tentative changes proposed where white settlers constituted an impediment. By 1950, change was under way in Sierra Leone, Uganda, Northern Rhodesia, Nyasaland and Zanzibar. In Nigeria, independence was within sight. Newfoundland and Malta were already independent. When Creech Jones lost his seat in the 1950 general election, Bevin said that he had been 'too undemonstrative' and had hidden his light 'under a bushel'. He was not reselected.

A radical opposition: 1951–1964

The Conservatives made slow progress towards independence for the remaining colonial territories, and relatively little effort towards promoting 'overseas development'. It was easy for Labour, in opposition, to be critical. Harold Wilson, a rising star in the party, urged that money should be spent on poor countries, not on arms, and that there should be no pandering to the Americans; and he asked whether 'the underfed coolie' could be blamed for snatching at Communism (Pimlott 1992: 171). Wilson served briefly as Chairman of the Bevinite Group and sparred with development economists Thomas Balogh and Dudley Seers. In 1952, the left-wing Association for World Peace published his pamphlet, *War on Want*. This called for an International Development Agency, and for 10 per cent of the arms budget and 2 per cent of national income to be allocated for the relief of world poverty. It argued that world problems required 'something other than the free price mechanism'. The pamphlet was widely discussed, and gave rise to the 'development' pressure group, War on Want. In August 1953, a book based on the pamphlet was published as *The War on World Poverty*.

At a May Day rally in 1954, Wilson denounced French imperialism in Indochina and warned against proposals for a US-led anticommunist alliance in Asia (Pimlott 1992: 187). Wilson was not the only Labour leftist espousing anticolonialism and anti-imperialism. Barbara Castle argues that 'one of the consuming interests of the Labour left in the 1950s was colonial freedom' (Castle 1991: 258). She records how she became aware of 'the new currents of thought on colonial development, which were swirling around, particularly in the Fabian Society, and of the number of outstanding people who were challenging the old paternalistic approach' (pp. 258–9).

Eden's efforts, in 1956, to 'protect' the Suez Canal against nationalization by President Nasser, revealed the extent to which some remained wedded to the old imperialism. But 'Suez' marked the end of an era. Ghana gained independence in 1957, and even the Conservatives recognized the 'winds of change' blowing through Africa. In 1961, they established a Department of Technical Cooperation (DTC) to coordinate their aid programme and all 'development' activities previously undertaken by the Commonwealth Relations Office (CRO) and the Colonial Office (CO).

The Wilson years: 1964–1970

Elected party leader in 1963 and Prime Minister in October 1964, Harold Wilson was now able to translate his commitment to Third World issues into action. Once in office, 'Wilson gave [development] a budget, a place round the Cabinet table and one of the most energetic and persuasive members of his ministerial team, Barbara Castle' (Hennessey 1990: 409). Castle saw the Ministry as 'a guarantee that overseas aid was no longer to be regarded as a charitable donation from rich to poor but an essential motor to world development' (ibid.: 407). Castle was assisted by Sir Andrew Cohen. The intention was clear: to regain the commitment and vision of the Creech Jones era. The ministry was built on a model developed by the Fabian Society in the early 1960s. When Castle arrived on her first day, a despatch rider was sent to the Society's headquarters to collect six copies of the relevant pamphlet.

Within nine months, however, 'development' was to prove a casualty of economic crisis, resulting from the overvaluation of the pound. In July 1965, Castle confronted a hostile Public Expenditure Committee, which threatened her aid budget. With Wilson's support, she fought back, and the eventual allocation was in her favour. But in December 1965, she was moved to transport, and replaced by Anthony Greenwood. Soon, Castle herself would be arguing for cuts in foreign expenditure, 'even though it would include overseas development...' (Crossman 1979: 219). In August 1966, Greenwood was also moved. The ministry was no longer to spearhead a new regime of international cooperation, providing 'an essential motor to world development'. The power moved elsewhere. In 1968, the CRO and FO merged, to become the Foreign and Commonwealth Office (FCO). In October 1969, Crossman noted laconically: 'Judith [Hart] is out of Cabinet and into the Overseas Department' (ibid.: 652).

Labour's continuing commitment

The Conservatives under Edward Heath won the 1970 election. One of Heath's few successes in office was to pass a bill enabling Britain to join the EEC. A minority of Labour MPs supported him. Labour was divided on other issues as well. But in 1972, in the first issue of *Third World*, a new Fabian Society journal, Wilson reasserted his commitment to development and 'the war on world poverty'. Under Heath, aid was administered by the Overseas Development Administration (ODA), under FCO auspices. Wilson argued that, 'as a subservient department, the ODA has inevitably been denied the powerful cutting edge it needs. We shall therefore re-establish a separate ministry in its own right, but it will also be essential to re-establish a Select Committee on Aid and Development in one form or another.' He remarked that a specialist subcommittee under Judith Hart was already preparing the 'development' section of Labour's Green Paper on foreign policy.

When Labour returned to office in October 1974, Wilson made good his promises regarding 'overseas development'. Hart was brought back as minister, with a place in Cabinet. Economic crisis again intervened, however, following substantial oil price increases; and, after a bitter struggle to maintain its commitment to the 'social contract' and public expenditure, the government approached the IMF for a loan, subjecting itself to conditions that were to become part of the new monetarist 'consensus'. In March 1975, Wilson resigned, and was replaced by James Callaghan. Hart resigned in June. She returned in February 1977, remaining minister until May 1979, when Labour lost the election to the Conservatives under Margaret Thatcher.

In its 1979 manifesto, Labour still proposed 'to create the conditions necessary to free the world from hunger, poverty, inequality and war' (Labour Party 1979: 35). Its stance was essentially moral: 'it cannot be right that 15 million children in poorer countries die before they are five – yet the world spends so much on the means of destruction. There is a compelling moral need to raise the standard of life of all the world's citizens – no matter where they live' (ibid.: 4). Aid was to be focused on 'the poorest countries and the poorest people, with the emphasis on rural development'. Labour would 'seek to implement the UN target of 0.7 per cent of the GNP for official aid, as soon as economic circumstances permit'. It promised to consider human rights when giving aid, and to help the victims of repressive regimes. It approached the 'North-South dialogue' in 'a spirit of cooperation' and planned to 'actively participate in UNCTAD 5 and other negotiations seeking to establish a more just world trading system which recognises the needs of poorer countries' (ibid.: 36).

But Labour was replaced by a party whose leader's very different vision of the world and Britain's role in it was to dominate the next decade, and profoundly influence those who came afterwards. Under Thatcher, overseas aid and development were, once again, subordinate to the FCO. Cuts in aid rapidly took spending to below £10 billion for the first time since 1974. By the early 1990s, annual flows to developing countries were between £2 and 3 billion only. Public expenditure on aid as a proportion of GNP slumped to 0.31 per cent (from 0.52 in 1979). The net flow of funds to developing countries reached its lowest level ever in 1992 – putting the UK in joint 12th place with Italy and Portugal. Thatcher's priority in foreign policy was building relationships with the strong, not developing an inclusive approach to international relations and contributing to the economic and social development of the Third World. 'Poverty alleviation' was acceptable; but strength, self-reliance and enterprise were to be rewarded abroad as they were at home.

New Labour: 1997–2006

When New Labour eventually came to office in 1997, it emphasized its commitment to 'aid and development' and 'poverty alleviation', while keeping tight controls on public spending. Clare Short, an MP with left-wing credentials, became minister at the Department for International Development (DFID), with a seat in Cabinet. A White Paper was published, *Eliminating World Poverty: A Challenge for the 21st Century* (DFID 1997). The title evoked both Wilson's own publications and the series of reports initiated by the Brandt Report, *North-South: A Programme for Survival* (1980). Commitments to 'the South' were to be based on morality and the mutual self-interest of North and South, rather than the radical transformation of capitalism.

Various initiatives by the UN in the 1990s failed to undermine the 'Washington consensus' on the fundamental role of markets in promoting greater equity and alleviating poverty, despite evidence to the contrary. Unlike Wilson's vision, aid was now to complement a global strategy, in which private enterprise, not state intervention, would provide 'the motor for development'. In 2000, the DFID produced a second White Paper, *Eliminating World Poverty: Making Globalisation Work for the Poor,* which made clear its belief that poverty elimination could be achieved by embracing globalization and 'making it work for the poor' – or, more cynically, making the poor work for globalization.

In February 2001, Labour introduced the International Development Bill, promoting the combination of private sector, civil society (or NGO) and state initiatives for the relief of global poverty. Internationally, New Labour supported the 'new Washington consensus' around framework agreements and standardized recipes for poverty alleviation in developing countries (the Poverty Reduction Strategy Papers, or PRSPs), particularly after the widespread adoption of the UN Millennium Development Goals. Prime Minister Blair's Commission on Africa expressed concern for the continent that had 'performed' least well, and initiatives for debt relief were strongly supported, with the UK's finance minister, the then Chancellor of the Exchequer, Gordon Brown, in the forefront. But attempts to achieve significant concessions by the developed countries on trade and access to their own markets generally failed. The focus of 'the international development community' turned away from promoting development through reform of the international order, towards ensuring national 'good governance' through stricter conditionality.

The foreword (by Tony Blair) to the 2006 White Paper – *Eliminating World Poverty: Making Governance Work for the Poor* – states that 'eliminating world poverty is in Britain's interests – and is one of the greatest moral challenges we face'. But the growing sense of global 'insecurity' associated with the rise of international terrorism and 'failing states' has shifted the emphasis towards more overtly political and security-related concerns. The first substantive chapter of the White Paper ('building states that work for poor people') provides a top-down vision of political engineering that differs markedly from more traditional notions of democracy. It declares that the UK will support the UN in its peacekeeping as well as its developmental role, but fails to mention the realities of UN impotence or of successive military interventions of dubious legality by 'Western' states (including Israel), and the consistent undermining of the UN by those prepared to take military action in the name of 'security'.

The old commitment of Labour to resist militarism and to uphold basic democratic rights has weakened. The Fabian vision of top down 'solutions', managed and directed by bureaucratic elites in the name of the people, remains strong. What is different today is the key role attributed to private enterprise and the priority accorded to 'security', in whose name both democracy and development risk being severely compromised.

GUIDE TO FURTHER READING AND REFERENCES

Brandt, W. et al. (1980) *North-South: A Programme for Survival*, London and Sydney: Pan Books.

Castle, B. (1991) *Fighting All the Way*, London: Macmillan.

Crossman, R.H.S. (1979) *The Crossman Diaries: Selections from the Diaries of a Cabinet Minister 1964–1970*, London: Methuen.

DFID (Department for International Development) (1997) *Eliminating World Poverty: A Challenge for the 21st Century*, London: DFID.

DFID (2000) *Eliminating World Poverty: Making Globalisation Work for the Poor*, London: DFID.

DFID (2006) *Eliminating World Poverty: Making Governance Work for the Poor*, London: DFID.

Hennessey, P. (1990) *Whitehall*, London: Fontana Press.

Labour Party (1979) *Manifesto*, London: Labour Party.

Morgan, K.O. (1985) *Labour in Power, 1945–1951*, Oxford: Oxford University Press.

Pimlott, B. (1992) *Harold Wilson*, London: HarperCollins.

Seddon, D. (2005) 'Japanese and British overseas aid compared', in D. Arase (ed.) *Japan's Foreign Aid: Old Continuities and New Directions*, London: Routledge.

Wilson, H. (1953) *The War on World Poverty*, London: Victor Gollancz.

Theories and strategies of development

Editorial introduction

It is generally appreciated that ideas about how development can be put into practice have long been both controversial and highly contested. Development involves a range of actors, from international agencies, through the state, down to the individual, all of whom have a vested interest in how change and development are to proceed. Thus, all facets of development depend not only on political ideology, but on moral and ethical prescriptions too. Thus, ideas about development over time have tended to accumulate and accrue, and not fade away. These sorts of ideas are considered at the outset in this part of the book, before turning to some of the major theories and strategies of development that have been followed and popularized.

Right-wing stances on development can be regarded as having their origins in the Enlightenment and the era of modernity that followed. The eighteenth-century Enlightenment saw an increasing emphasis placed on science, rationality and detailed empiricism. It also witnessed the establishment of the 'West' and 'Europe' as the ideal. It was during this period that the classical economists, Adam Smith and David Ricardo, writing in the 1700s, developed ideas surrounding the concept of comparative advantage, which stressed the economic efficacy of global free trade and, in many senses, gave rise to the earliest capitalist strategies of economic development. These were followed by a plethora of dualistic and linear conceptualizations of the development process, including modernization theory, unbalanced and unequal growth, and top-down and hierarchical formulations. Together, such approaches are generally referred to as neoclassical. Whatever one's critical view on modernization, the approach usefully pinpointed the salience of change as a necessary factor in the development equation. Such approaches are, of course, still alive and kicking, in the form of the 'new right' orthodoxy, involving the 'magic of the market' and the neoliberal policies of structural adjustment, and very recently, poverty reduction strategies. All these approaches can be traced directly to the works of Smith and Ricardo.

The antithesis to classical and neoclassical views was provided by radical dependency approaches in the 1960s. It is a reflection of the Eurocentricity of development theory that Andre Gunder Frank has become the name most closely associated with dependency. This is despite the fact that the approach essentially stemmed from the writings of structuralists in Latin America and the Caribbean. In respect of process, dependency theory was couched in terms of inverted cascading global chains of surplus extraction, and, again, it was all too easy to reduce this to simple dichotomous terms, involving polar opposites such as 'core–periphery', 'rich–poor' and 'developed–underdeveloped'. It was left to world systems theory to stress that contemporary development has involved the emergence of a substantial semi-periphery, consisting of the newly industrializing countries (NICs) of east Asia and Latin America.

The era of postmodernity may not be regarded as fitting the realities of the developing world or poor countries in all respects, but the existence of these notions cannot be ignored in the analysis of the conditions faced by such nations. Early standpoints taking a less generic, less monumental and less linear view of the development process included what are referred to under the headings 'bottom-up' and 'agropolitan' approaches, which have come to include ideas of 'another' development. All these approaches stressed the importance of local indigenous knowledge. More recently, the 'postist' stance afforded by post-colonialism has been added to the critique. This argues that the production of Western knowledge has been inseparable from the exercise of Western power. And development is closely interconnected with reducing the forms of social exclusion that exist within societies. Ethical and moral considerations surface once more, this time in terms of the responsibilities we carry for so-called 'distant others'. Most of us have been trained to favour people close to home, our 'nearest and dearest', as opposed to those strangers who may be deemed more needy, but who live far away. Many of the practical problems that are to be faced in the field of humanitarian assistance stem from this basic but enduring conundrum of development. Finally, it is notable that evolving conceptualizations of the roles of the state, civil society and social capital underpin continuing debates concerning development theory.

2.1 Theories, strategies and ideologies of development

Robert B. Potter

A major characteristic of the multi- and interdisciplinary field of development studies since its establishment in the 1940s has been a series of sea-level changes in thinking about the process of development itself. This search for new theoretical conceptualizations of development has been mirrored by changes in the practice of development in the field. Thus, there has been much debate and controversy about development, with many changing views as to its definition, and the strategies by means of which, however development is defined, it may be pursued. In short, the period since the 1950s has seen the promotion and application of many varied views of development. And the literature on development theory and practice has burgeoned, particularly since the mid-1980s (see, for example, Apter 1987; Preston 1987, 1996; Lesson and Minogue 1988; Schuurman 1993; Crush 1995; Escobar 1995; Hettne 1995; Streeten 1995; Brohman 1996; Cowen and Shenton 1996; Leys 1996; Rapley 1996; Potter et al. 2004). A major theme is that ideas about development have long been controversial and highly contested.

It is also necessary to stress that development covers both theory and practice, that is, both ideas about how development should or might occur, and real-world efforts to put various aspects of development into practice. This is conveniently mapped into the nomenclature suggested by Hettne in his overview of *Development Theory and the Three Worlds* (1995). In reviewing the history of development thinking, he suggested that 'development' involves three things: *development theories*, *development strategies* and *development ideologies*. Before going any further, these three basic terms can usefully be defined and clarified.

Following the general definition of a theory as a set of logical propositions about how the real world is structured, or the way in which it operates, *development theories* may be regarded as sets of ostensibly logical propositions, which aim to explain how development has occurred in the past, and/or how it should occur in the future. Development theories can either be *normative*, that is, they can generalize about what should happen or be the case in an ideal world, or *positive*, in the sense of dealing with what has generally been the case in the past. This important distinction is broadly exemplified in the figure that accompanies this account. Hettne (1995) remarks that 'development studies is explicitly normative', and that teachers, researchers and practitioners in the field 'want to change the world, not only analyse it' (Hettne 1995: 12). The arena of development theory is primarily, although by no means exclusively, to be encountered in the academic literature, that is, in writing about development. It is, therefore, inherently controversial and contested.

On the other hand, *development strategies* can be defined as the practical paths to development which may be pursued by international agencies, states in both the so-called developing and developed worlds, non-government organizations and community-based organizations, or indeed individuals, in an effort to stimulate change within particular nations, regions and continents. Thus, Hettne (1995) provides a definition of development strategies as efforts to change existing economic and social structures and institutions in order to find enduring solutions to the problems facing decision makers. As such, Hettne argues that the term 'development strategy' implies an actor, normally the state. In order to sound less top-down, it is necessary to think in terms of a wider set of development-oriented actors, including all those listed above.

Different development agendas will reflect different goals and objectives. These goals will reflect social, economic, political, cultural, ethical, moral and even religious influences. Thus, what may be referred to as different *development ideologies* may be recognized. For example, both in theory and in practice, early perspectives on development were almost exclusively concerned with promoting economic growth. Subsequently, however, the predominant ideology within the academic literature changed to emphasize political, social, ethnic, cultural, ecological and other dimensions of the wider process of development and change. Theories in development are distinctive by virtue of the fact that they involve the intention to change society in some defined manner. One of the classic examples is the age-old battle between economic policies which increase growth but widen income disparities, and those wider policy imperatives which seek primarily to reduce inequalities within society.

Perhaps the only sensible approach is to follow Hettne (1995) and to employ the overarching concept of *development thinking* in our general deliberations. The expression 'development thinking' may be used as a catch-all phrase indicating the sum total of ideas about development, that is, including pertinent aspects of development theory, strategy and ideology. Such an all-encompassing definition is necessary due to the nature of thinking about development itself. As noted at the outset, development thinking has shown many sharp twists and turns during the twentieth century. The various theories that have been produced have not commanded attention in a strictly sequential-temporal manner. In other words, as a new set of ideas about development has come into favour, earlier theories and strategies have not been totally discarded and replaced. Rather, theories and strategies have tended to stack up, one upon another, coexisting, sometimes, in what can only be described as very convoluted and contradictory manners. Thus, in discussing development theory, Hettne (1995: 64) has drawn attention to the 'tendency of social science paradigms to accumulate rather than fade away'.

This characteristic of development studies as a distinct field of enquiry can be considered in a more sophisticated manner by referring to Thomas Kuhn's ideas on the *structure of scientific revolutions*. Kuhn (1962) argued that academic disciplines are dominated at particular points in time by communities of researchers and their associated methods, and they thereby define the subjects and the issues deemed to be of importance within them. He referred to these as 'invisible colleges', and he noted that these serve to define and perpetuate research which confirms the validity of the existing paradigm, or 'supra-model', as he referred to it. Kuhn called this 'normal science'. Kuhn noted that only when the number of observations and questions confronting the status quo of normal science becomes too large to be dealt with by means of small changes to it, will there be a fundamental shift. However, if the proposed changes are major and a new paradigm is adopted, a scientific revolution can be said to have occurred, linked to a period of what Kuhn referred to as 'extraordinary research'.

In this model, therefore, scientific disciplines basically advance by means of revolutions in which the prevailing normal science is replaced by extraordinary science and, ultimately, a new form of normal science develops. In dealing with social scientific discourses, it is inevitable that the field of development theory is characterized by evolutionary, rather than revolutionary change. Evidence of the persistence of ideas in some quarters, years after they have been discarded elsewhere, will be encountered throughout the development literature. Given that development thinking is not just about the theoretical interpretation of facts, but rather about values, aspirations, social goals and, ultimately, that which is moral, ethical and just, it is understandable that change in development studies leads to the parallel *evolution* of ideas, rather than *revolution*. Hence, conflict, debate, contention, positionality and even moral outrage are all inherent in the discussion of development strategies, and associated plural and diverse theories of development.

There are many ways to categorize development thinking through time. Broadly speaking, it is suggested here that four major approaches to the examination of development thinking can be recognized, and these are shown in the figure. This framework follows that suggested by Potter and Lloyd-Evans (1998) (see also Potter et al. 2004). The framework first maps in the distinction previously made between *normative development theories* (those focusing on what should be the case) and *positive theories* (which ponder what has actually been so). Another axis of difference between theories is seen as relating to whether they are *holistic* or *partial*, and most partial theories emphasize the economic dimension. This is also intimated in the figure.

These two axes can be superimposed on one another to yield a simple matrix or framework for the consideration of development theories, as shown. Following Potter et al. (2004: Chapter 3), as noted, four distinct groupings of development theory can be recognized by virtue of their characteristics with regard to the dimensions of holistic–economic and normative–positive. The approaches are referred to as: (i) the classical–traditional approach; (ii) the historical–empirical approach; (iii) the radical political economy–dependency approach; and finally, (iv) bottom-up and alternative approaches. Following the argument presented in the last section, each of these approaches may be regarded as expressing a particular ideological standpoint, and can also be identified by virtue of having occupied the centre stage of the development debate at particular points in time. Classical–traditional theory, embracing dualism, modernization theory, top-down conceptualizations, the new right and neoliberal imperatives, is seen as stressing the economic and, collectively, existing midway between the normative and positive poles. In direct contrast, according to this framework, radical–dependency approaches, embracing neo-Marxism, and the articulation of the modes of production, are seen as being more holistic. At the positive end of the

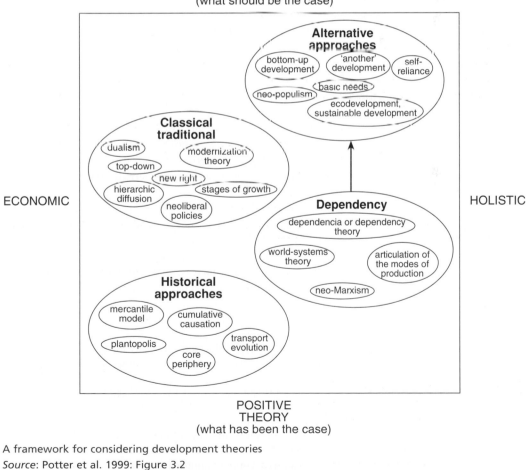

A framework for considering development theories
Source: Potter et al. 1999: Figure 3.2

spectrum exist those theories which are basically historical in their formulation, and which purport to build on what has happened in the past. These include core–periphery frameworks, cumulative causation and models of transport evolution, especially the mercantile model. In contrast, once again, are theories which stress the ideal, or what should be the case. These are referred to as 'alternative approaches', and basic needs, neo-populism, 'another development', ecodevelopment and sustainable development may be included in this category.

However, each approach still retains currency in particular quarters. Hence, in development theory and academic writing, left-of-centre socialist views may well be more popular than classical and neoclassical formulations, but in the area of practical development strategies, the 1980s and 1990s have seen the implementation of neoliberal interpretations of classical theory, stressing the liberalization of trade, along with public-sector cutbacks, as a part of structural adjustment programmes (SAPs), aimed at reducing the involvement of the state in the economy (Pugh and Potter 2000). Such plurality and contestation are an everyday part of the field of development studies. In the words of Hettne (1995: 15), 'theorizing about development is therefore a never-ending task'.

GUIDE TO FURTHER READING

Hettne, B. (1995) *Development Theory and the Three Worlds: Towards an International Political Economy of Development*, second edition, Harlow: Longman. Briefly introduces the concepts of development theories, strategies and ideologies (see pp. 15–16), before presenting an overview of Eurocentric development thinking, the voice of the 'other', globalization and development theory, and 'another development'.

Potter, R.B., Binns, T., Elliott, J. and Smith, D. (2004) *Geographies of Development,* second edition, Harlow: Prentice Hall. An introductory textbook on development, designed mainly for undergraduates. In terms of overall remit, the book seeks to stress the plural and contested nature of development theory and practice. As part of this approach, Chapter 3 overviews theories and strategies of development, stressing their diversity and value-laden character. The structure of the account is based on the figure employed in the present account.

Preston, P.W. (1996) *Development Theory: An Introduction*, Oxford: Blackwell. Sets out to provide an overview of the intellectual resources available to developmentalists working with reference to the classical European tradition of social theorizing. Accordingly, the first part of the book treats social theory in general terms. Thereafter, contemporary theories of development are summarized, followed by what are referred to as new analyses of complex change.

REFERENCES

Apter, D. (1987) *Rethinking Development: Modernization, Dependency and Postmodern Politics*, Newbury Park, CA: Sage.

Brohman, J. (1996) *Popular Development: Rethinking the Theory and Practice of Development*, Oxford: Blackwell.

Cowen, M.P. and Shenton, R. (1996) *Doctrines of Development*, London: Routledge.

Crush, J. (1995) *Power of Development*, London: Routledge.

Escobar, A. (1995) *Encountering Development*, Princeton, NJ: Princeton University Press.

Hettne, B. (1995) *Development Theory and the Three Worlds: Towards an International Political Economy of Development*, second edition, Harlow: Longman.

Kuhn, T. (1962) *The Structure of Scientific Revolutions*, Chicago: University of Chicago Press.

Lesson, P.E. and Minogue, M.M. (eds) (1988) *Perspectives on Development: Cross-Disciplinary Themes in Development*, Manchester: Manchester University Press.

Leys, D. (1996) *The Rise and Fall of Development Theory*, Oxford: James Currey.

Preston, P.W. (1987) *Making Sense of Development: An Introduction to Classical and Contemporary Theories of Development and their Application to Southeast Asia*, London: Routledge.

Preston, P.W. (1996) *Development Theory: An Introduction*, Oxford: Blackwell.

Potter, R.B. and Lloyd-Evans, S. (1998) *The City in the Developing World*, Harlow: Prentice Hall.

Potter, R.B., Binns, T., Elliott, J. and Smith, D. (2004) *Geographies of Development*, second edition, Harlow: Prentice Hall.

Pugh, J. and Potter, R.B. (2000) 'Rolling back the state and physical development planning: The case of Barbados', *Singapore Journal of Tropical Geography*, 21: 183–99.

Rapley, J. (1996) *Understanding Development: Theory and Practice in the Third World*, London: UCL Press.

Schuurman, F. (1993) *Beyond the Impasse: New Directions in Development Theory*, London: Zed Books.

Streeten, P. (1995) *Thinking About Development*, Cambridge: Cambridge University Press.

2.2 Enlightenment and the era of modernity

Marcus Power

Introduction: The 'rough and tumble' of early industrialism

Just as light cuts through darkness, the philosophy of the Enlightenment was seen as something that would open the eyes of the world's poor and free them from unjust rule. During the 'century of Enlightenment', educated Europeans awoke to a new sense of life and many wrote of 'enlightening' the world and the need to disseminate knowledge among 'enlightened peoples'. According to Gay (1973: 3), at this time educated Europeans experienced 'an expansive sense of power over nature and themselves: the pitiless cycles of epidemics, famines, risky life and early death, devastating war and uneasy peace – the treadmill of human existence – seemed to be yielding at last to the application of critical intelligence'. Fear of change began to give way to fear of stagnation. It was a century of commitment to enquiry and criticism, of a decline in mysticism, of growing hope and trust in effort and innovation (Hampson 1968). One of the primary interests was social reform, and the progression and development of societies built around an increasing secularism and a growing willingness to take risks (Gay 1973). There is no monolithic 'spirit of the age' that can be discerned, however. Enlightenment ideas and writings comprise a fairly heterogeneous group, but did form a set of interconnected ideas, values, principles and assumptions. In its simplest sense, the Enlightenment was the creation of a new framework of ideas and secure 'truths' about the relationships between humanity, society and nature, which sought to challenge traditional world views dominated by Christianity.

New cultural innovations in writing, painting, printing, music, sculpture and architecture, and new technological innovations in warfare, agriculture and manufacture, had a major impact on the *philosophes*, the free-thinking 'men of letters' who had brokered this enlightened awakening. Reaching its climax in the mid-eighteenth century in Paris and Scotland, but with foundations in many European countries, 'the Enlightenment' was thus a sort of intellectual fashion, or 'a tendency towards critical inquiry and the application of reason' (Black 1990: 208), rather than a coherent intellectual movement or institutional project. The modern idea and narration of 'development' can thus be traced back to these tendencies and critical enquiries, and back to where it was invented 'amidst the throes of early industrial capitalism in Europe' (Cowen and Shenton 1996: 5). The metaphor of the 'light of reason' shining brightly into all the dark recesses of ignorance and superstition in 'traditional' societies was a powerful and influential one at this time. In Europe, the light that 'development' brought was intended to 'construct order out of the social disorders of rapid urban migration, poverty and unemployment' (ibid.: 5).

The *philosophes* sought to redefine what was considered as socially important knowledge, to bring it outside the sphere of religion and to provide it with a new meaning and relevance. They believed that through this 'enlightenment', Europe had broken through the 'sacred circle' (Gay 1973) where dogma had previously circumscribed European thought. In this sense, as Hall and Gieben (1992: 36) point out, there are four main areas which distinguish the thought of the *philosophes* from earlier intellectual approaches:

- anticlericalism;
- a belief in the pre-eminence of empirical, materialist knowledge;
- an enthusiasm for technological and medical progress;
- a desire for legal and constitutional reform.

There is clearly a risk of applying the term 'the Enlightenment' too loosely or too widely, as if it had touched every intellectual society and every intellectual elite of this period equally. The Enlightenment is thus best considered as an amorphous, dynamic and variegated entity (Porter 1990). There were, however, many common threads to this patchwork of enlightenment thinking: the primacy of reason/rationalism, a belief in empiricism, the concept of universal science and reason, the idea of progress, the championing of new freedoms, the ethic of secularism and the notion of all human beings as essentially the same (Hall and Gieben 1992: 21–2). Thinkers such as Kant, Voltaire, Montesquieu, Diderot, Hume, Smith, Ferguson, Rousseau and Condorcet found a receptive audience in many European cities for their 'new style of life' (Hampson 1968). They produced a large collection of novels, plays, books, pamphlets and essays for the consumption of nobles, professionals (especially lawyers), academics and the clergy. It is important to remember, however, that this new style of life was in the main reserved for the fortunate and the articulate – the rural and urban masses had little share. It was not until the eve of the French Revolution in the 1780s that a new social group emerged, concerned with popularizing enlightenment ideas. Similarly, though many women played a major part in the development and diffusion of enlightenment ideas, applying such ideas to their social conditions meant negotiating a number of contradictory positions within patriarchal societies.

The emancipatory potential of this knowledge thus turned out to be limited in that it was conceived of as abstract and utilitarian, as a mastery over nature which thus becomes characterized by power. As Doherty (1993: 6) has argued:

> Knowledge is reduced to technology, a technology which enables the *illusion* of power and of domination over nature. It is important to stress that this is an illusion. This kind of knowledge does not give actual power over nature... What it does give in the way of power is, of course, a power over the consciousness of others who may be less fluent in the language of reason... Knowledge thus becomes caught up in a dialectic of mastery and slavery. (emphasis in original)

Many enlightenment thinkers viewed the remedy for the disorder brought on by industrialization as related to the 'capacity' to use land, labour and capital in the interests of society as a whole. Only certain kinds of individuals could be 'entrusted' with such a role (Cowen and Shenton 1996). Property, for example, needed to be placed in the hands of 'trustees', who would decide where and how society's resources could be utilized most effectively. In eighteenth-century France, the prevailing social orders were represented as three 'estates' – clergy, nobility and the 'third estate', which comprised everyone else, from wealthiest bourgeois to poorest peasant (Hall 1992). This 'dialectic of mastery and slavery', and this gap between the *philosophes* (who were often members of the second estate) and the peasantries of European eighteenth-century societies, are both important parts of the historical context of enlightenment thinking. Although they appeared to represent a threat to the established order, these ideas and writings sought evolutionary rather than revolutionary change, arguing that progress and development could come about within the existing social order through the dissemination of ideas among 'men of influence' (Hall and Gieben 1992).

'Modernity' and the rise of the social sciences

The influential economist John Maynard Keynes (1936: 570), once wrote that '[p]ractical men, who believe themselves to be quite exempt from any intellectual influences, are usually the slaves of some defunct economist'. So it is with much development thinking today. A variety of twenti-eth-century movements, including neoclassicism (of which Keynes was an important part) and liberalism, can trace their origins back to the Enlightenment. The foundations of many modern disciplines (including development studies) were intimately bound up with the Enlightenment's concept of progress, and the idea that development could be created through the application of reasoned and empirically based knowledge. The Enlightenment had forged the intellectual condi-tions in which the application of reason to practical issues could flourish through such 'modern' institutions as the academy, the learned journal and the conference. In turn, a 'modern' audience was constituted for the dissemination of social and political ideas alongside a class of intellectuals that could live from writing about them (Hall 1992). Through the Enlightenment, state bureaucra-cies began to use social statistics to provide the evidence necessary for 'rational' choices in the allo-cation of resources. These 'official' labels were – and still are – generally portrayed and accepted as objective facts, though many are rooted in intensely political processes. For example, many con-ventional racial and group classifications were created in the imperial and colonial periods, when authorities counted, categorized, taxed and deployed slave, servile and forced labour, often over vast geographical areas (IDS 2006).

The emergence of an idea of 'the West' was also important to the Enlightenment in that it was a very European affair, which put Europe and European intellectuals at the pinnacle of human achievement. This view sees 'the West' as the result of forces largely internal to Europe's history and formation (Hall 1992) rather than as a 'global story' involving other cultural worlds. In the mak-ing of nineteenth-century European 'modernity', Europeans had a sense of difference from other worlds (e.g. 'Africa'), which shaped the ways in which they were viewed as distant, uncivilized and immature stages in the progress of humanity. The establishment of modern modes of scientific enquiry, of modern institutions and the modern 'development' of societies in nineteenth century Europe thus partly incorporated a contrast with the 'savage' and 'uncivilized' spaces of the non-Western world.

Modernist reason was not as inherently good as the 'enlightened' thinkers believed and has been used for a wide variety of purposes. Reason can be imperialist and racist (as in the making of the idea of 'the West'), taking a specific form of consciousness for a universal, a standard that all must aspire to reach. Reason was also a potent weapon in the production of social normativity during 'the Enlightenment', driving people towards conformity with a dominant and centred 'norm' of behaviour (Doherty 1993). Modernist reason was therefore dependent on the 'othering' of non-conformists, of cultures and societies that were not informed by this reason and social norms, and were thus banished to the lower echelons of humanity, defined as 'backward', 'undeveloped' or 'uncivilized'. The emergence of new ideas about social, political and economic development was therefore bound up with these pressures to conform to particular notions of knowledge, reason and progress, and with the making of a 'third estate' or 'Third World' of nonconformity as the alter ego of a developed 'West'.

Conclusions: Completing the Enlightenment beyond Europe

Much contemporary development thinking has its roots in the Enlightenment as the 'age of reason', which shaped concepts of progress, growth and social change. Modernist thought also envisaged a process of enlightenment, of becoming more modern and less traditional, and saw a group of enlightened Western scientists 'guiding' the paths to progress of distant others. Arturo Escobar (1995: 2–4) has even argued that the post-1945 development project is 'the last and failed attempt to complete the Enlightenment in Asia, Africa and Latin America'. 'Development' represents more than a singular post-war historical experience, however, and has complex roots in the emergence of 'the Enlightenment' at the dawn of European industrial capitalism, and in the rise and formation(s) of European modernity. It is also important to remember that European and Western identities have been formed by contrasting modernity with the tradition and backwardness of the 'Third World' as 'other'.

Even today, the work of enlightenment thinkers like Adam Smith (with his free-market economics) remains very relevant to 'international development' for some observers. Examples of this can be found in some of the key global development institutions, such as the World Bank, which see their (neoclassical) knowledges as potentially enlightening. Consider the following quotation from a speech given by the World Bank President James Wolfensohn in 1996: 'Knowledge is like light. Weightless and intangible, it can easily travel the world, enlightening the lives of people everywhere. Yet billions of people still live in the darkness of poverty – unnecessarily' (quoted in Patel 2001: 2). Thus the knowledge and expertise of contemporary development practitioners is seen as something almost universal that easily traverses borders, extinguishing the darkness of poverty wherever it shines. For some theorists and practitioners of development today, people and places can become 'developed' simply though acquiring scientific and technical knowledges about the 'normal' or correct series of developmental stages. If only it were that simple.

GUIDE TO FURTHER READING

For an excellent introduction and overview to early development discourses and ideas, see Rist, T. (1997) *History of Development*, London: Routledge.

Cowen, M.P. and Shenton, R.W. (1996) *Doctrines of Development*, London: Routledge. Provides an accessible discussion of enlightenment ideas, exploring their bearing on the construction of particular development approaches and doctrines.

Doherty, T. (ed.) (1993) *Modernism/Postmodernism*, Hemel Hempstead: Harvester Wheatsheaf. Offers clear and accessible definitions of modernism in the Introduction.

Hall, S. and Gieben, B. (1992) *Formations of Modernity*, Cambridge: Open University/Polity. Focuses on the making of modernity in the non-Western world.

Kors, A.C. (2003) *Encyclopedia of the Enlightenment*, New York: Oxford University Press. A four-volume edited encyclopedia of the Enlightenment.

REFERENCES

Black, J. (1990) *Eighteenth-century Europe 1700–1789*, London: Macmillan.
Cowen, M.P. and Shenton, R.W. (1996) *Doctrines of Development*, London: Routledge.
Doherty, T. (1993) 'Postmodernism: An introduction', in T. Doherty (ed.) *Modernism/Postmodernism*, Hemel Hempstead: Harvester Wheatsheaf, pp. 1–31.
Escobar, A. (1995) *Encountering Development: The Making and Unmaking of the Third World*, Princeton, NJ: Princeton University Press.
Fieldhouse, D.K. (1999) *The West and the Third World: Trade, Colonialism, Dependence and Development*, London: Blackwell.
Gay, P. (1973) *The Enlightenment: A Comprehensive Anthology*. New York: Simon & Schuster.
Hall, S. (1992) 'The West and the rest: Discourse and power', in S. Hall and B. Gieben (eds) *Formations of Modernity*, Cambridge: Open University/Polity, pp. 275–331, Chapter 6.
Hall, S. and Gieben, B. (1992) *Formations of Modernity*, Cambridge: Open University/Polity.

Hampson, N. (1968) *The Enlightenment*, London: Penguin.

IDS (Institute of Development Studies) (2006) 'The power of labelling in development practice', IDS Policy Briefing, Issue 28 (April).

Keynes, J.M. (1936) *The General Theory of Employment, Interest and Money*, London: Macmillan.

Patel, R. (2001) 'Knowledge, power, banking', *Z Magazine*, (20 July 2001) (available at http://www.zmag.org/ZSustainers/ZDaily/2001–07/20patel.htm).

Porter, R. (1990) *The Enlightenment*, London: Macmillan.

Rist, T. (1997) *History of Development*, London: Routledge.

2.3 Smith, Ricardo and the world marketplace, 1776–2007: Back to the future?

David Sapsford

Introduction

Why do countries trade with one another? What determines the terms on which trade between countries is conducted in the world marketplace? These two questions are perhaps the most fundamental to be considered in any analysis of international trade, be it trade *between* developed and developing countries or trade *among* countries in either the developing or the developed world. These questions are of special importance in the context of economic development, since if there are 'gains from trade' to be had, the distribution of such gains between trading partners carries important implications for living standards and economic welfare within the participating countries.

The classical economists, most notably Adam Smith (1723–90) and David Ricardo (1772–1823) considered these two questions, and their analyses are outlined in the following section. Subsequent sections consider the available evidence regarding the changes that have occurred over the long run in the terms on which trade between developed and developing nations has been conducted, exploring the implications of this for economic development in the developing world.

Absolute and comparative advantage

The foundations of the economic theory of international trade were laid by Adam Smith in *The Wealth of Nations* (1776). Smith's analysis of the division of labour is well known, and to a large extent he saw the phenomenon of international trade as a logical extension of this process, with particular regions or countries (rather than particular individuals) specializing in the production of particular commodities. Smith's view is clearly demonstrated by the following quotation:

> It is the maxim of every prudent master of a family, never to attempt to make at home what it will cost him more to make than buy... What is prudence in the conduct of every private family, can scarce be folly in that of a great kingdom. If a foreign country can supply us with a commodity cheaper than we ourselves can make it, better buy of them with some part of the produce of our own industry, employed in a way in which we have some advantage (Smith 1776: 424).

Thus, according to Smith, countries engage in trade with one another in order to acquire goods more cheaply than they could produce them domestically, paying for them with some proportion of the output that they produce domestically by specializing according to their own 'advantage'. Central to this view is the notion that relative prices determine trade patterns, with countries buying abroad when foreign prices are below domestic ones. In addition, Smith argued that by expanding the size of the market, international trade permits greater specialization and division of labour than would otherwise have been possible. This is perhaps one of the earliest arguments in favour of globalization as a process by which the size of the world marketplace is increased.

Economics textbooks abound with simple two-country/two-good examples that illustrate Smith's argument. Suppose that the world consists of only two countries (say, the UK and the USA) and only two goods (say, food and clothing). Within this (over)simplified framework, let us assume that the USA is more efficient than the UK at producing food (in the sense that fewer resources are needed to produce a unit of food in the USA than in the UK) and (in the same least resource-cost sense) that the UK is more efficient than the USA at producing clothing. In economists' terminology, this example represents the case where the UK possesses *absolute advantage* in the production of clothing, while the USA possesses absolute advantage in the production of food. To further simplify, let us assume that labour is the only factor of production and that within each country it is mobile between the two industries. Assume also that wages are the same in both countries and that transport costs are zero. On the basis of this battery of assumptions, the USA will be the cheaper source of food and the UK of clothing. It is a matter of simple arithmetic to show that if both countries are initially producing some of each good, it is always possible to increase output of both goods if each country specializes in the production of that good for which it possesses absolute advantage. It also follows that by trading, each country can consume the bundle of clothing and food that it consumed in the absence of trade (that is, under *autarky*), while still leaving some of each product over! Each country thus has the potential to increase its consumption of both goods and, assuming that more of each good is preferable to less, in principle, trade can allow both trading partners to increase their *economic welfare*. As already noted, the distribution of this surplus (that is, the distribution of the *gains from trade*) between the two countries is an important matter, especially in the context of economic development. We return to this issue in the following section.

The case analysed by Adam Smith considered, quite naturally at the time he was writing, the situation where one country possesses absolute advantage in the production of one good, while the other country possesses it in the production of the other good. Writing four decades later, David Ricardo considered the rather more tricky analytical case in which one of the two countries (say, the UK) is more efficient at producing *both* goods. According to Adam Smith's absolute advantage argument, both goods should be produced by the UK. However, this situation can clearly not represent a feasible state of affairs in the long run since although the USA will seek to purchase both goods from the UK, the UK will not wish to buy anything from the USA in return. Ricardo (1817) was the first economist to provide a formal analysis of this case, and by so doing he derived his famous *Law of Comparative Advantage*.

According to Ricardo's Law of Comparative Advantage, which encompasses Adam Smith's analysis of absolute advantage as a special case, world output, and therefore (on the basis of the assumption discussed above) world economic welfare, will be increased if each country specializes in the production of that good for which it possesses *comparative* advantage. The concept of comparative advantage is basically concerned with comparative efficiency, and Ricardo's law follows from recognizing the fact that differences in the relative prices of the two goods as between the two countries opens up the possibility of mutually beneficial trade. To take a concrete example, suppose that the labour required to produce 1 unit of each good in each country is as set out in Table 1. Notice that the UK requires less labour than the USA in both industries.

On the basis of these figures (and assuming that labour productivity in each industry does not alter with the level of output) we can see that in the absence of trade, each unit of food within the UK trades for 2.5 units of clothing, since each is equivalent to the output of five people. Likewise, in the USA, 1 unit of food trades for 0.5 unit of clothing, each being the output of six people. It is the difference between these two relative prices (or internal terms of trade) that opens up the possibility for mutually beneficial trade. For example, if US prices prevail in the world outside the UK, a UK citizen in possession of 1 unit of food can exchange this within the UK for 2.5 units of clothing, which could then be sold in the USA for 5 units of food; thereby providing a gain equal to 4 units of food. Likewise, if UK relative prices prevail, a US producer employing 12 people to make 1 unit of clothing could switch to the food industry and thereby produce 2 units of food, which could then be sold in the UK for 5 units of clothing, thus realizing a gain of 4 units of clothing. At intermediate relative prices (or terms of trade), both countries can gain from trade, although not to the extent shown in the respective examples given above.

In a nutshell, according to Ricardo's analysis, each country shifts its production mix towards the good for which it possesses comparative advantage. In our example, the UK has comparative advantage in the production of clothing, whereas the USA's comparative advantage is in food, where it is *less inefficient*. Reading across the rows in Table 1, we see that this follows because the UK requires five-sixths of US unit inputs in food, but only one-sixth in clothing.

Table 1 Labour requirements matrix

| | Labour per unit of output | |
	UK	USA
Food	5	6
Clothing	2	12

Who gains from trade?

While the elegance of Ricardo's analysis and its correctness within the confines of its own assumptions cannot be faulted, it does beg a question that is vitally important in the context of trade that takes place between countries of the developed/industrialized world and countries of the developing world. While the analysis demonstrates quite clearly the *potential* benefits to trading partners from engaging in international trade in the world marketplace, it has nothing whatsoever to say about the division of these potential gains between them. As we saw in the preceding example, if relative prices in the world marketplace were equal to US relative prices, the UK would effectively appropriate all the gains from trade for herself, whereas, at the opposite end of the spectrum, the USA would scoop all the gains if UK relative prices prevailed.

In order to focus our ideas, let us consider trade between the countries of the developed/industrialized world and those of the developing world, and, for simplicity, assume that the former produce manufactured goods while the latter produce primary commodities. The fact that Ricardo's analysis did not shed any light on the issue of how the potential gains from trade are shared out in practice did not seem to constitute a problem in the minds of classical economists, since in a related context, Ricardo, like Smith before him, had argued that as an inevitable consequence of the twin forces of diminishing returns in the production of primary commodities from a fixed stock of land (including mineral resources) as population increased, and the downward pressures on production costs in manufacturing generated by the moderating influences of surplus population and urbanization on wages, the price of primary products would rise over the long run in relation to the price of manufactured goods, thereby giving rise to an upward drift in the net barter terms of trade between primary commodities and manufactured goods.[1] On the above assumptions, this movement will translate into an improvement in the terms of trade of developing countries vis-à-vis the developed countries. On the basis of this argument, there was little, if any, reason to be concerned about the plight of developing countries in the context of their trading relations with the industrialized world, since it predicted that over the long run, the terms of trade would shift steadily in their favour, with the result that they would enjoy an increasing proportion of the potential gains from trade.

However, in the early 1950s, the classical prediction of a secular improvement was challenged by both Prebisch (1950) and Singer (1950). Both argued forcefully that in direct contravention of the then still prevailing classical prediction, the terms of trade had actually, as a matter of statistical fact, been historically subject to (and could be expected to continue to be subject to) a declining trend. Both analyses therefore implied that, contrary to the classical view, developing countries were actually obtaining a falling proportion of the potential gains from their trade with the countries of the developed world.

A number of theoretical explanations have been put forward in the literature to account for the observed downward trend in the terms of trade of developing countries, relative to developed countries, and these can be conveniently summarized under the following four headings:

1 *differing elasticities of demand for primary commodities and manufactured goods* (with the inelastic nature of the former resulting in a tendency for increases in the conditions of commodity supply to be felt more strongly in price decreases than in quantity increases);
2 *differing rates of growth in the demands for primary commodities and manufactured goods* (with the demand for primaries expanding less rapidly than the demand for manufactures due to their lower income elasticity of demand – especially so in the case of agricultural commodities due to the operation of Engel's Law – plus the development of synthetic substitutes and the occurrence in manufacturing of technical progress of the raw materials-saving sort);
3 *technological superiority* (the argument being that the prices of manufactured goods rise relative to those of primaries because they embody both a so-called Schumpeterian rent element for innovation, plus an element of monopolistic profit arising from the monopoly power of multinational producers);
4 *asymmetries in market structure* (the argument here is that differences in market structure – with primary commodities typically being produced and sold under competitive conditions, while manufacturing in industrialized countries is often characterized by a high degree of monopoly by organized labour and monopoly producers – mean that while technical progress in the production of primary commodities results in lower prices, technical progress in manufacturing leads to increased factor incomes as opposed to lower prices).

Policy implications

Although space constraints do not allow the discussion in any detail of the policy implications of the observed worsening trend in the terms on which trade is conducted in the world marketplace between primary commodity-producing countries and manufacturing countries, it is important to note that the Prebisch–Singer hypothesis is sometimes advanced as one argument in favour of development policies of the import-substituting industrialization as opposed to export promotion variety (Sapsford and Balasubramanyam 1994). However, the policy issues here are not clear-cut, and the fact that all four of the above explanations relate as much, if not

1 For brevity, I refer hereafter to the net barter terms of trade between primary commodities and manufactured goods (i.e. the ratio of the price of primary commodities to the price of manufactured goods) as simply their terms of trade.

more, to the characteristics of different types of countries as to the characteristics of different types of traded goods, highlights the need to devise and implement policies that address differences and imbalances of the former as opposed to the latter sort.

It is now the case that at least some of the international agencies involved in the world trading system have come to accept that primary commodity producers in developing countries do face real and significant uncertainties and risks regarding the prices that they will actually receive for their products when they come to the world market. At the time of writing, a task force set up under the auspices of the World Bank is investigating a range of possible 'market-based' approaches for dealing with the price risks faced by primary commodity producers in developing countries. As pointed out by Morgan (2001), these approaches appear to represent an attempt to confront price risk by modifying the financial environment within which primary producers in less developed countries operate. However, it remains to be seen whether such approaches will prove any more, or less, successful than the various policies which have preceded them.

1776–2007: Back to the future?

Some 231 years have elapsed since Adam Smith laid the initial foundations of trade theory as we know it today. It is testament to the logical correctness of his analysis, especially as extended by Ricardo, that this theoretical framework is still pivotal to twenty-first-century thinking in both trade theory and policy formulation. As we have seen, the central prediction of this approach is that provided the world terms of trade lie within the limits imposed by domestic opportunity cost ratios, international specialization and exchange via trade provides an opportunity for both trading partners to benefit from increased output (and therefore economic welfare) with given resource/factor endowments. However, we have also seen that that there is a school of thought surrounding the Prebisch-Singer hypothesis suggesting that, in practice, the actual terms of trade have drifted, within the range delineated by the Ricardian analysis, in favour of the industrialized (manufacturing) nations to such an extent that these nations have appropriated for themselves the lion's share of the gains from trade, leaving only small pickings for the (primary-commodity-dependent) poorer countries of the developing world.

What does current experience tell us in relation to the fundamental question of who has gained what from participating in international trade? The basic structure of international institutions that currently oversee/govern the day-to-day conduct of international trade and commerce were laid down in 1944 at the famous Bretton-Woods Conference. Prominent among these institutions is what is now known as the World Trade Organization[2] (WTO) whose mission, in a nutshell, is to provide an arena and set of processes and rules designed to achieve multilateral reductions in trade barriers. The underlying philosophy here, squarely in the spirits of both Smith and Ricardo, is to maximize the potential global gains from trade by minimizing (if not completely eliminating) impediments to free trade, such as import tariffs, quotas, and so on.

We have now accumulated more than 60 years of experience of the operation of this process of tariff reduction via multilateral trade negotiations under the auspices of the WTO and its predecessors. Although advocates of free trade see the WTO as having achieved considerable success in its mission to reduce average tariff levels, experience since the mid-1990s might be interpreted as suggesting an altogether less rosy picture when one comes to ask the important question as to who has actually harvested the global gains generated by this move closer to free trade in the sense understood by Smith and Ricardo. Although a detailed discussion of the operation of the WTO is

2 Previously known as the General Agreement on Tariffs and Trade (GATT), although originally named (by Keynes as the principal architect of the Bretton-Woods system) the International Trade Organization (ITO). See Chen and Sapsford (2005).

beyond the scope of the current chapter, it should be noted that it seeks to achieve multilateral reductions in tariff (and other non-tariff) barriers via a series of negotiating rounds. In 1994, the trade deal that came out of the so called Uruguay Round of negotiations was signed, although the negotiations had appeared to be on the verge of collapse as late as 1990. One major factor that surfaced during the Uruguay Round was the view of poor, primary-commodity-dependent countries that the proposed package would bestow substantial benefits on the industrialized countries, while offering them very little. In 1999, pressure to offer a better deal to poor counties led to a summit meeting in Seattle, which ended in failure (accompanied by public disorder). In 2001, in an attempt to reinvigorate the process of multilateral tariff reductions, WTO members agreed to launch fresh talks, known as the Doha Development Round. Despite this initiative, however, the 2003 ministerial summit in Cancun, Mexico, collapsed in acrimony over the developed countries' intransigency over the issue of removal of subsidies paid to their farmers. In response to this, the 2004 deadline for agreement was pushed back in an attempt to inject new life into the Doha Round. In 2005, the latest ministerial summit in Hong Kong just about managed to keep the process alive. However, in June 2006, the WTO director general, Pascal Lamy, publicly declared the whole process of multilateral negotiations in crisis, while at the subsequent G8 summit, representatives of these major industrial nations called on countries to return to the negotiating table. In July 2006, representatives of six key member countries met at the WTO's offices in Geneva for what was envisaged as the first of a series of meetings designed to get the process back on the road. However, talks finally broke down after 14 hours, with no (obvious) common ground having been established.

What is to be made of this tale? At the time of writing (December 2006) the picture is clearly one where the very continued existence of the process of tariff reductions via multilateral negotiations is hanging by little more than a thread. The current stumbling block from the perspective of the poor countries is the refusal of the major developed countries (including the EU and USA) to remove the trade barrier imposed by the still substantial subsidies paid to their farmers. However, there is a wider view, according to which this particular issue is but a symptom of a more fundamental problem: namely, that after participating in the process of multilateral tariff reduction for at least half a century, the poor countries of the world have continually seen the gains from the trade being appropriated by their richer trading partners. Indeed, some commentators are predicting that such is their degree of dissatisfaction with a process which has delivered so little to them relative to their richer trading partners, that group(s) of poor countries are on the verge of withdrawing altogether from the process, in favour of going it alone.

Whether the thread eventually breaks remains to be seen. I wonder what Adam Smith and David Ricardo would make of this twenty-first-century situation!

GUIDE TO FURTHER READING

Detailed discussion of both the theoretical arguments and statistical evidence underlying the declining trend in terms of trade hypothesis can be found in the following texts.

Sapsford, D., Sarkar, P. and Singer, H. (1992) 'The Prebisch–Singer terms of trade controversy revisited', *Journal of International Development* 4(3): 315–32.

Sapsford, D. (2007) 'Terms of trade and economic development', in A. Dutt and J. Ros (eds) *International Handbook of Development Economics*, Cheltenham: Edward Elgar.

Singer, H. (1987) 'Terms of trade and economic development', in J. Eatwell, M. Milgate and P. Newman (eds) *The New Palgrave: A Dictionary of Economics*, London: Macmillan, pp. 626–8.

Spraos, J. (1983) *Inequalizing Trade?* Oxford: Oxford University Press.

Comprehensive discussion of a wide range of issues relating to the relationship between economic development and international trade may be found in the following text.

Greenaway, D. (ed.) (1988) *Economic Development and International Trade*, London: Macmillan.

Highly accesible discussion of the main issues involved in the globalization debate, seen from either side of the fence, can be found in the following two references.

Bhagwati, J. (2004) *In Defense of Globalization*, New York: Oxford University Press.

Stiglitz, J. (2003) *Globalization and its Discontents*, London: Penguin Books.

REFERENCES

Chen, J. and Sapsford D. (eds) (2005) *Global Development and Poverty Reduction: The Challenge For International Institutions*, Cheltenham: Edward Elgar.

Morgan, W. (2001) 'Commodity futures markets in LDCs: A review and prospects', *Progress in Development Studies*, 1(2): 139–50.

Prebisch, R. (1950) 'The economic development of Latin America and its principal problem', United Nations Economic Commission for Latin America; also published in *Economic Bulletin for Latin America*, 7(1), 1962: 1–22.

Ricardo, D. (1817) *On the Principles of Political Economy and Taxation*, reprinted 1971, London: Penguin.

Sapsford, D. and Balasubramanyam, V.N. (1994) 'The long-run behavior of the relative price of primary commodities: Statistical evidence and policy implications', *World Development*, 22(11): 1737–45.

Singer, H. (1950) 'The distribution of gains between investing and borrowing countries', *American Economic Review, Papers and Proceedings*, 40: 473–85.

Smith, A. (1776) *The Wealth of Nations*, reprinted 1961, London: Penguin.

2.4 Dualistic and unilinear concepts of development

Tony Binns

The development imperative

After the Second World War, Europe embarked on a massive programme of reconstruction, instrumental to which was the Marshall Plan, launched by the US Government on 5 June 1947. While the Marshall Plan was heralded as US financial help to the devastated economies and infrastructures of Western Europe, this 'goodwill gesture' was also designed to stimulate markets for America's burgeoning manufacturing sector. The Marshall Plan, which injected US$17 billion mainly into the UK, France, West Germany and Italy between 1948 and 1952, generated much confidence in the role of overseas economic aid (Hunt 1989; Rapley 1996). Another landmark in the recognition of the need for richer countries to play an active role in the development of poorer countries came less than two years later, on 20 January 1949, when US President Truman, in 'Point Four' of his Inaugural Address, proclaimed:

> we must embark on a bold new program for making the benefits of our scientific advances and industrial progress available for the improvement and growth of underdeveloped areas. More than half the people of the world are living in conditions approaching misery. Their food is inadequate. They are victims of disease. Their economic life is primitive and stagnant. Their poverty is a handicap and a threat both to them and to more prosperous areas. For the first time in history, humanity possesses the knowledge and skill to relieve the suffering of these people... I believe that we should make available to peace-loving peoples the benefits of our store of technical knowledge in order to help them realize their aspirations for a better life (Public Papers of the Presidents of the United States 1964: 114–15).

'Point Four' probably inaugurated the 'development age', and 'represents a minor masterpiece...in that it puts forward a new way of conceiving international relations' (Rist 1997: 71–2).

The neoclassical paradigm

The so-called neoclassical paradigm dominated much thinking about development in the two or three decades after the Second World War. Adam Smith, the founding father of the classical school, writing in his *Wealth of Nations* (1776) in the early years of the Industrial Revolution, saw manufacturing as capable of achieving greater increases in productivity than agriculture. He emphasized the expansion of markets as an inducement for greater productivity, which he believed would lead to greater labour specialization and productivity. More than a century later, in 1890, Alfred Marshall, in his influential book, *Principles of Economics*, spelt out the neoclassical perspective, emphasizing the desirability of maximizing aggregate economic welfare, while recognizing that this was dependent on maximizing the value of production and raising labour productivity. Technological change was recognized as being vital to raising productivity and meeting the demands for food and raw materials from a growing population. There was also a strong belief that free trade and the unimpeded operation of the market were necessary for maximizing efficiency and economic welfare (Hunt 1989).

Dualism

Another theme that emerged in the post-war period was that underdeveloped economies were characterized by a 'dichotomous' or 'dualistic' nature, where advanced and modern sectors of the economy coexisted alongside traditional and backward sectors. A strong proponent of the dualistic structure of underdeveloped economies was the West Indian economist Arthur Lewis, whose seminal paper 'Economic development with unlimited supplies of labour' was published in 1954. Like others who followed him, Lewis did not differentiate between economic growth and development. The paper, which, significantly, opens with the statement, 'This essay is written in the classical tradition', envisages a division of the economic system into two distinct sectors – capitalist and subsistence. The subsistence sector, according to Lewis, consists predominantly of small-scale family agriculture, and has a much lower per-capita output than the capitalist sector, where manufacturing industry and estate agriculture, either private or state-owned, are important elements. The process of development, Lewis suggested, involves an increase in the capitalists' share of the national income due to growth of the capitalist sector at the expense of the subsistence sector, with the ultimate goal of absorption of the latter by the former. Since most labour for the capitalist sector would come from underemployed labour in subsistence agriculture, changes within the latter sector were seen as essential for the process of overall economic development.

The Lewis model had a significant influence on development thinking in the 1950s and 1960s, but it has been criticized for failing to appreciate the positive role of small-scale agriculture in the development process. With such agronomic successes as the Green Revolution, it was realized that raising the productivity of the rural subsistence sector could actually be an important objective rather than a constraint in development policy.

The concept of dualism is also apparent in some early spatial development models, focusing on the different qualities and potential of contrasting regions, rather than economic sectors as in the Lewis model. While some would argue that the development of certain areas at the expense of others is likely to inhibit the growth of the economy as a whole, others regarded initial regional inequality as a prerequisite for eventual overall development. Both Gunnar Myrdal and Albert Hirschman, for example, advocated strategies of 'unbalanced growth'. Myrdal's (1957) 'cumulative causation' principle suggested that once particular regions have, by virtue of some initial advantage, moved ahead of others, new increments of activity and growth will tend to be concentrated in already expanding regions because of their derived advantages, rather than in other areas of the country. Thus, labour, capital and commodities move to growing regions, setting up so-called 'backwash effects' in the remaining regions, which may lose their skilled and enterprising workers and much of their locally generated capital. However, Myrdal recognized that such less dynamic areas may benefit from centrifugal 'spread effects', in that by stimulating demand in other, particularly neighbouring regions, expansion in the growing areas may initiate economic growth elsewhere.

Hirschman (1958), working independently of Myrdal, followed similar thinking, proposing a strategy of 'unbalanced growth', and suggesting that the development of one or more regional centres of economic strength is essential for an economy to lift itself to higher income levels. He envisaged spatial interaction between growing 'Northern' and lagging 'Southern' regions in the shape of 'trickle-down' and 'polarization' effects, similar to Myrdal's spread and backwash effects. Keeble (1967) argued that Hirschman's model,

> far from assuming a cumulative causation mechanism, implies that if an imbalance between regions resulting from the dominance of polarization effects develops during earlier stages of growth, counter-balancing forces will in time come into operation to restore the situation to an equilibrium position. Such forces, chief of which is government economic policy, are not to be thought of as intensified trickling-down effects, but as a new element in the model, arising only at a late stage in development. Their inclusion, together with the exclusion of any cumulative mechanism, represents the model's chief structural differences from that of Myrdal (Keeble 1967: 260).

A significant policy implication of Hirschman's unbalanced growth model is that governments should not necessarily intervene to reduce inequalities, since the inevitable search for greater profits will lead to 'a spontaneous spin-off of growth-inducing industries to backward regions' (Potter et al. 2004: 84).

The spatial models of Myrdal and Hirschman have strong parallels with the work of François Perroux and other French economists in the 1940s and 1950s, who pointed out that growth did not appear everywhere simultaneously, but instead is frequently located in a 'growth centre or pole' (*pôle de croissance*). In essence, the growth centre model depicts the transmission of economic prosperity from a centre, most commonly an urban-industrial area, as a result of the interplay of spread and backwash effects. The model singles out crucial variables in the development of spatial variation in economic prosperity within a region and specifies how they operate. A particular 'growth industry', such as motor manufacturing, is likely to attract other linked industries, such as those which supply it with inputs and/or derive their inputs from it. Other agglomeration economies may encourage further growth, while technological change is encouraged through close proximity and interaction between the various industrial enterprises.

Unilinear models

Much post-war development thinking was strongly 'Eurocentric' in that, often inappropriately, 'theories and models [were] rooted in Western economic history and consequently structured by that unique, although historically important, experience' (Hettne 1995: 21). Walt Rostow's (1960) 'unilinear' model (see figure) is probably the best-known attempt to show how a country's economy and society progress through a series of stages, and is firmly based on the Euro-American experience. It was undoubtedly the most influential modernization theory to emerge in the early 1960s. It is interesting to note that Rostow entitled his book *The Stages of Economic Growth: A Non-communist Manifesto*, and, '[his] perception of the purpose of the United States' promotion of economic development in the Third World was governed by a strongly anti-communist stance' (Hunt 1989: 96). Indeed, early in his book, Rostow asserts that he is aiming to provide 'an alternative to

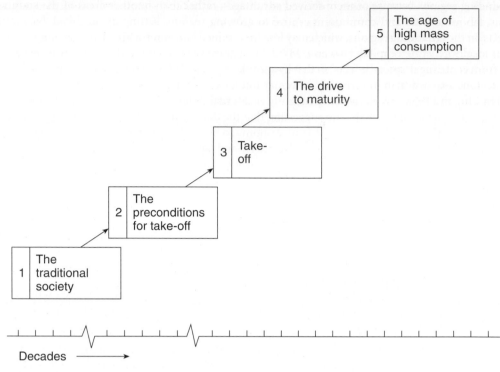

Rostow's unilinear model

Karl Marx's theory of modern history' (Rostow 1960: 2). The key element in Rostow's thinking was the process of capital formation, represented by five stages through which all countries pass in the process of economic growth.

- *Stage 1 – Traditional society*: Characterized by primitive technology, hierarchical social structures, production and trade based on custom and barter, as in pre-seventeenth-century Britain.
- *Stage 2 – Preconditions for take-off*: With improved technology and transport, and increased trade and investment, economically based elites and more centralized national states gradually emerged. Economic progress was assisted by education, entrepreneurship and institutions capable of mobilizing capital. Often traditional society persisted side by side with modern economic activities, as in seventeenth- and eighteenth-century Britain, when the so-called 'agricultural revolution' and world exploration (leading to increased trade) were gaining momentum. While the preconditions for take-off were actually endogenous in Britain, elsewhere they were probably the result of 'external intrusion by more advanced societies' (Rostow 1960: 6).
- *Stage 3 – Take-off*: The most important stage, covering a few decades, when the last obstacles to economic growth are removed. 'Take-off' is characterized by rapid economic growth, more sophisticated technology and considerable investment, particularly in manufacturing industry. The share of net investment and saving in national income rise from 5 per cent to 10 per cent or more, resulting in a process of industrialization, as in early nineteenth-century Britain. Agriculture becomes increasingly commercialized and more productive with increasing demand from growing urban centres.
- *Stage 4 – Drive to maturity*: A period of self-sustaining growth, with increasing investment of between 10 and 20 per cent of national income. Technology becomes more sophisticated,

there is greater diversification in the industrial and agricultural sectors and falling imports, as in late nineteenth- and early twentieth-century Britain.

- *Stage 5 – Age of high mass consumption*: The final stage, characterized by the increasing importance of consumer goods and services, and the rise of the welfare state. In Britain and Western Europe, this stage was not reached until after the Second World War (post-1945), but in the USA, mass production and consumption of consumer goods, such as cars, fridges and washing machines, came earlier, during the 1920s and 1930s.

Despite its considerable influence on development planning at the time, Rostow's model has been strongly criticized for a number of reasons. First, it is a 'unilinear' model, implying that 'things get better' over time, which is by no means always true, as, for example, the experience of many sub-Saharan countries indicates. Increases in per-capita income have scarcely kept pace with world trends and the AIDS pandemic has had a devastating effect on mortality and life expectancy rates. Most sub-Saharan countries are relatively worse off in the early twenty-first century than in the 1960s, when many gained their independence. Second, it is a 'Eurocentric' model, suggesting that all countries will imitate the experience of Europe and America. It is quite inappropriate to apply such a model to countries which have been subjected to colonial rule and whose economies (and societies) have been manipulated to serve the demand for agricultural and mineral resources from the growing manufacturing sectors in the metropolitan countries. Third, the model suggests that all countries progress through these stages in the same sequence as happened in Europe and North America. But in some developing countries the sequence of events has not been so straightforward, with rapid change in the agricultural, industrial and service sectors, for example, happening at the same time, rather than sequentially. While modern consumer goods, schools and hospitals may be present in towns and cities, in remote rural areas these facilities are frequently absent, and poor farmers still use simple technology to produce food for their families. Finally, it is often wrongly seen as a 'development' model, whereas it is actually an 'economic growth' model. Rostow was concerned more with economic progress and increasing industrial investment, rather than human welfare and other non-economic indicators of development. Some countries have experienced periods of rapid economic growth, yet much of the population has felt little benefit from this – what might be called 'growth without development' (Binns 1994). The real significance of the Rostow model was that it seemed to offer every country an equal chance to develop.

From dualism to basic needs

The lack of distinction and explanation drawn by Rostow and others between the processes of 'growth' and 'development' led some writers to try to clarify the situation. There was also growing concern that economic growth, which had been the main preoccupation of Lewis, Hirschman, Myrdal and Rostow, did not necessarily eliminate poverty, and that the so-called 'trickle-down' effects of growth generally failed to benefit the poor in both spatial and social terms. Dudley Seers provided much-needed clarification on the meaning of development, suggesting that poverty, unemployment and inequality should be key foci in the development debate, and that there should be greater concern for the fulfilment of basic needs (notably food, health and education) through the development process (Seers 1969, 1972). The basic needs approach gained momentum in the mid-1970s. The International Labour Organization's 1976 conference on World Employment adopted the Declaration of Principles and Programme of Action for a Basic Needs Strategy of Development, highlighting poverty alleviation as a key objective for all countries in the period up to the year 2000. Possibly the main weakness of the basic needs strategy was its top-down approach, 'which made it vulnerable to changing fashions in the international aid bureaucracy' (Hettne 1995: 180). In spite of such limitations, the debates surrounding the meaning and process of development and the question of basic needs did much to move development thinking and policy away from the dualistic, unilinear and essentially Eurocentric approaches of the 1950s and 1960s.

GUIDE TO FURTHER READING

For detailed consideration of development theory, see Hettne (1995) and Hunt (1989). Keeble's (1967) chapter in Chorley and Haggett's *Socio-economic Models in Geography*, though written nearly half a century ago, is still helpful. A more recently written overview is provided in Chapter 3 of Potter et al.'s *Geographies of Development* (2004). Hirschman (1958), Lewis (1954), Rostow (1960) and Smith (1776) are justifiably regarded as 'classic' texts, while Alfred Marshall's (1890) *Principles of Economics* was a key undergraduate textbook for more than 50 years.

REFERENCES

Binns, T. (1994) *Tropical Africa*, London: Routledge.
Hettne, B. (1995) *Development Theory and the Three Worlds: Towards an International Political Economy of Development*, London: Longman.
Hirschman, A.O. (1958) *The Strategy of Economic Development*, New Haven, CT: Yale University Press.
Hunt, D. (1989) *Economic Theories of Development*, London: Harvester Wheatsheaf.
Keeble, D.E. (1967) 'Models of economic development', in R.J. Chorley and P. Haggett (eds) *Socio-economic Models in Geography*, London: Methuen, pp. 243–305.
Lewis, W.A. (1954) 'Economic development with unlimited supplies of labour', *The Manchester School of Economic and Social Studies*, 22(2), May; reprinted in A. Agarwala and S. Singh (eds) (1958) *The Economics of Underdevelopment*, Oxford: Oxford University Press, pp. 400–49.
Marshall, A. (1890) *Principles of Economics*, eighth edition, reprinted 1920, London: Macmillan.
Myrdal, G. (1957) *Economic Theory and Underdeveloped Regions*, London: Duckworth.
Potter, R.B., Binns, T., Elliott, J.A. and Smith, D. (2004) *Geographies of Development*, London: Pearson.
Public Papers of the Presidents of the United States (1964) *Harry S. Truman, Year 1949*, 5, Washington, DC: United States Government Printing Office.
Rapley, J. (1996) *Understanding Development: Theory and Practice in the Third World*, London: UCL Press.
Rist, G. (1997) *The History of Development*, London: Zed Books.
Rostow, W. (1960) *The Stages of Economic Growth: A Non-communist Manifesto*, Cambridge: Cambridge University Press.
Seers, D. (1969) 'The meaning of development', *International Development Review*, 11(4): 2–6.
Seers, D. (1972) 'What are we trying to measure?', *Journal of Development Studies*, 8(3): 21–36.
Smith, A. (1776) *The Wealth of Nations*, 2 vols, reprinted 1961, London: Methuen.

2.5 Neoliberalism, structural adjustment and poverty reduction strategies

David Simon

The rise of neoliberalism

The dramatic oil price increases of 1973 and 1979 triggered a slowdown and then a severe recession in the North and the world economy as a whole, and precipitated the so-called 'debt crisis' in the South in 1981–82.

Profound disillusionment in the North with the record of state involvement in economic and social life led to a simplistic and rather naive belief in 'the magic of the market' as the most efficient economic regulator. Keynesian-style state involvement in the economy was held to be inefficient, bureaucratic and an unnecessary drain on public coffers. Hence, by selling off loss-making and inefficient public enterprises and parastatal corporations, and restricting the role of the state to regulation and economic facilitation, taxes could be cut substantially.

This is the essence of neoliberalism, an economic creed that seeks to deregulate markets as much as possible to promote 'free' trade. It harks back to the ideas of Adam Smith and David Ricardo, in other words, to the very historical roots of neoclassical economics – hence neo(new)liberalism. This ideology rapidly became the economic orthodoxy in the North and was exported to the global South via aid policies and the measures formulated to address the debt crisis.

Structural adjustment and economic recovery programmes

Initial responses to the debt crisis

In late 1981, Brazil and Mexico – soon followed by Poland – announced that they could no longer service their official debts, triggering panic among Northern creditor governments and the transnational banks that had advanced enormous commercial loans to the debtor countries. They feared that if rapid countermeasures were not taken and strict penalties imposed, there could be a domino effect among debt-ridden countries that would drive individual banks into bankruptcy and undermine the entire international financial system.

The International Monetary Fund (IMF) assumed the lead role in addressing the debt crisis. Its analysis – which was echoed by the multilateral banks and leading creditor governments – hinged on Northern self-interest and a determination to protect the international financial system. The problem of default was diagnosed as entirely the fault of the debtor countries, on account of their governments being corrupt, interventionist, bloated by bureaucracy and weighed down by inefficient, often loss-making state enterprises; they had also pursued inappropriate policies. The dramatic interest rate increase was noted, but was not regarded as sufficient explanation; nor was the fact that the loans in question had been willingly contracted by both parties. The banks, which had actively sought to lend out their surplus petrodollars, were not in any sense held liable for their own misfortune or lack of foresight. They were even able to write off their losses of up to £1 billion annually against tax.

Moreover, the IMF's policy response was geared to maximizing the prospects for, and amounts of repayment by, debtor countries. For many years there was, accordingly, an almost total unwillingness to consider writing off the debts of even the most impoverished and debt-ridden countries for fear of evoking a chorus of 'can't pay, won't pay'.

The anatomy of structural adjustment programmes

These new policies, known as structural adjustment programmes (SAPs), were designed to cut government expenditure, reduce the extent of state intervention in the economy, and promote liberalization and international trade. SAPs were explicit about the necessity of export promotion based on the Ricardian notion of comparative advantage. Accordingly, each country should specialize in and export those commodities that it can produce more cheaply in real terms than its competitors. However, international trade is often unbalanced and inequitable in its impacts; this depends on many factors, not least market share and power, and the terms of trade.

SAPs comprised four main elements:

1 the mobilization of domestic resources;
2 policy reforms to increase economic efficiency;
3 the generation of foreign exchange revenue from non-traditional sources through diversification, as well as through increased exports of traditional commodities;
4 reducing the active economic role of the state and ensuring that this is non-inflationary.

The instruments designed to achieve these objectives were generally divided into two categories (Simon 1995: 5), as follows.

Stabilization measures: these were immediate, short-term steps designed to arrest the deterioration in conditions and to provide a foundation on which longer-term measures could act:

- a public-sector wage freeze – to reduce wage inflation and the government's salary bill;
- reduced subsidies on basic foods and other commodities, and on health and education – to reduce government expenditure;
- currency devaluation – to make exports cheaper and hence more competitive, and to deter imports.

Adjustment measures: these were generally to be implemented as a subsequent, second phase, designed to promote economic structural adjustment (restructuring) and economic competitiveness:

- export promotion – through incentives (including easier access to foreign exchange and retention of some of the hard currency obtained from export revenues) and diversification;
- downsizing the civil service – through retrenchments following a consolidation and rationalization of the public sector, in order to reduce 'overstaffing', duplication, inefficiency and cronyism in job allocation;
- economic liberalization – relaxing and eventually removing many regulations and restrictions on economic activity, both domestic and international, in the name of efficiency; examples include import quotas and tariffs, import licences, state monopolies, price fixing, implicit or hidden subsidies, restrictions on the repatriation of profits by foreign-owned firms;
- privatization – selling off state enterprises and parastatal corporations, especially loss-making ones, in order to reduce direct economic activity and resource use by the state, and to reduce the size of the civil service;
- tax reductions – to create incentives for individuals and businesses (both local and foreign) to save and invest.

Adoption and implementation of an IMF-approved SAP became a prerequisite for obtaining financial support. The World Bank (WB), regional development banks and most major Northern bilateral donors followed suit. This *economic conditionality* was complemented in 1990 by *political conditionality*, the prerequisite imposed by the British and other donor governments for so-called 'good governance' as well as approved economic policies.

Refining SAPs and economic recovery programmes

SAPs were refined in the late 1980s and 1990s, taking better account of local circumstances and social development needs, seeking to soften the negative impacts of specific measures and supporting continuity of policies and funding. To this end, a distinction emerged between SAPs, which became the initial programme implemented by a country over three to four years, and follow-up economic recovery programmes (ERPs) of similar duration, which were designed to promote broader economic restructuring. The principal funding mechanism became the Enhanced Structural Adjustment Facility (ESAF) (Wood 1997).

Some countries have sought, often with only short-lived success, to avoid the pain of formal SAPs and to retain more sovereignty over economic policy by implementing home-grown equivalents. South Africa remains exceptional in not having any structural adjustment loans.

Particularly with respect to South East Asia, the analyses offered by the international financial institutions (IFIs) have changed contradictorily: during the economic boom, the rapidly industrializing countries were held up as models of market-led development; as soon as the crisis of 1997 struck, the problems were blamed on interventionist states, cronyism and inappropriate policies (Dixon 1999; Mohan et al. 1999).

The take-up of SAPs and ERPs

Despite their unpopularity with debtor countries, the rapid take-up rate of SAPs reflected the dire straits in which an increasing number of countries found themselves, as well as the perceived (and often real) lack of alternatives. By 1987 the World Bank had approved 52 structural adjustment loans and 70 sectoral adjustment loans. During the period 1980–89, 171 SAPs were introduced in sub-Saharan Africa; a further 57 had been initiated by the end of 1996.

Evaluating SAPs and ERPs

The impacts of SAPs were frequently harsh. Many ordinary people, rather than the elites or the state, bore the brunt of the adjustment burden, although some did benefit. Even the IMF has acknowledged that the early SAPs were excessively economistic and neglected or retarded social development. Initially, packages of palliative measures were hastily created (for example, the Ghanaian Programme of Actions to Mitigate the Social Costs of Adjustment (PAMSCAD) in the mid-1980s), and later SAPs were redesigned to contain a social development component.

The initial presumption, which provided a powerful lever for the IFIs, was that successful adjustment would lead to rapidly increasing foreign direct investment; this has not occurred in most countries (Simon 1995; Wood 1997).

Many of the adjustment measures took far longer to have a tangible impact, whereas the pain of stabilization measures, often implemented too hastily and in one fell swoop rather than in stages, was immediate. One indirect – and arguably desirable – effect was to adjust the rural–urban terms of trade substantially, by eliminating much of the urban bias implicit in traditional policies of infrastructural provision and price subsidization.

Among the worst-affected groups were the urban poor and – predominantly – urban-based civil servants, who have lost jobs, suffered severe salary erosion and faced steep commodity price increases as commodity subsidies have been slashed, and transport fares and utility prices have been commercialized. Conversely, the principal beneficiaries have been large traders and import–export merchants (as a result of liberalization and improved foreign exchange availability), and rural agricultural producers, including peasants who have a saleable surplus, on account of higher producer prices for their crops.

Economists evaluated SAPs and ERPs almost exclusively on a sector-by-sector basis at the national scale. However, this is inadequate and precludes assessment of the impacts on different social groups and subnational spaces (urban, rural, regional) in a situation where there is no reason to believe the effects to be socially and geographically neutral (Simon 1995; Bracking 1999; Mohan et al. 1999).

However, in some countries, food security was undermined by IMF insistence that food crop production be switched to cash crops for export if comparative advantage existed. For example, Zimbabwe was pressurized into selling its maize surplus from the bumper 1991–92 harvest rather than retaining it as a buffer stock. When the rains failed over the following two years, massive maize imports became necessary at a price far higher than that obtained for exporting the previous surplus. Zimbabweans, not the IMF, bore the cost.

The environment suffered in different ways, as a result of marginal land being brought into cultivation or fallow periods being squeezed in order to grow more food to compensate for lost subsidies or to yield a surplus for export. Tropical forests were logged at a faster rate to generate export earnings (Reed 1992).

Finally, economic and political conditionalities attached to SAPs and ERPs represented an unprecedented invasion of the hitherto sacrosanct right of sovereign states to determine their own economic and political policies (Bracking 1999; Mohan et al. 1999). This argument was exploited by many government leaders seeking to deflect the hostility of protesters against food price increases and other measures.

Poverty reduction strategies: Substantive change or business as usual?

During 1999, image management and changing fashion led to the introduction of a new vocabulary and objective. SAPs and ERPs were summarily superseded by an apparently more positive and cooperative approach known as poverty reduction strategies (PRSs). This fits well with the major donors' reinvention of development assistance (previously aid) as 'partnerships' since the late 1990s (Kifle et al. 1997; Närman 1999), and also the adoption of poverty reduction or elimination as the *leitmotiv* of development policies by several donors, most notably the British 'New' Labour Party Government that took office in 1997 (Burnell 1998).

Inevitably under such circumstances, poverty reduction means different things in different contexts. However, the IMF and WB adopted PRSs as the successor to SAPs, and the ESAF was renamed the Poverty Reduction and Growth Facility. Continuity of underlying donor policy, however, is strong. For instance, lending remains conditional on adoption and approval of a Poverty Reduction Strategy Paper (PRSP).

However, in contrast to SAPs and ERPs, PRSPs must prioritize antipoverty expenditures and are supposed to be prepared through a wide-ranging and deep process of consultation with civil society. The extent to which this has occurred varies considerably, and there are numerous examples of superficial or minimalist 'consultation' designed to enable the government to claim compliance and legitimacy.

Many parts of civil society remain cynical, not least because the underlying approach and agenda (including conditionality) have changed too little, and on account of perceived fickleness by the IFIs. For instance, during preparation of the PRSP's predecessor in Kenya, the National Poverty Eradication Plan for 1999–2000, civil society NGOs lobbied hard for an approach in which poverty reduction would get priority, in turn promoting economic development. The WB failed to support it.

The rather tenuous assumption underlying PRSs is that neoliberal macroeconomic reform will promote a reduction in poverty as a result of leaner, fitter and more efficient economic management and political governance. However, improvements have been made to the process since the early 2000s (Booth 2005; Driscoll with Evans 2005), and some assessments are more positive (e.g. Craig and Porter 2003), but others (e.g. Fraser 2005; Larmer 2005) see them as a form of social control by IFIs and the participatory process as a Trojan Horse.

Conclusion

The resurgence of the conservative doctrine of neoliberalism at the end of the 1970s was rapidly translated into development and aid policies by the Northern donors and IFIs at the onset of the debt crisis. This required debtor countries to bear the full costs of adjustment and recovery. These market-oriented and trade-integrationist policies were embodied in SAPs and then ERPs, comprising a mixture of short-term stabilization and longer-term adjustment measures. Much hardship was caused, often to some of the most vulnerable people, although many rural producers have benefited from agricultural and marketing reforms. The environmental costs were sometimes substantial too. Urban bias was reduced, however, and, for a short period in the mid- to late 1980s, apparently even reversed in some African countries. The initially crude and economistic policies were gradually refined and more carefully targeted. Since 1999/2000, the language and presentation of macroeconomic reform programmes have been transformed under the guise of PRSs, but despite some positive changes, including having antipoverty measures at the heart of public expenditure plans, the underlying doctrines and conditionalities remain in place, while the degree of civil society consultation and 'buy-in' varies substantially (Paloni and Zanardi 2006).

GUIDE TO FURTHER READING

The following texts represent a selection of useful surveys of particular issues or perspectives.

Booth, D. (2005) *Missing Links in the Politics of Development: Learning from the PRSP Experiment*, Working Paper 256, London: Overseas Development Institute (available at http://www.odi.org.uk/publications/working_papers/wp256.pdf).

Driscoll, R. with Evans, A. (2005) 'Second-generation poverty reduction strategies: New opportunities and emerging issues', *Development Policy Review*, 23(1): 5–25.

Husain, I. and Faruqee, R. (eds) (1996) *Adjustment in Africa: Lessons from Country Case Studies*, Aldershot: Avebury for the World Bank. One of the most useful World Bank outputs, covering Burundi, Côte d'Ivoire, Ghana, Kenya, Nigeria, Senegal and Tanzania.

Mohan, G., Brown, E., Millward, B. and Zack-Williams, A. (eds) (1999) *Structural Adjustment: Theory, Practice and Impacts*, London: Routledge. A recent collection addressing the origins, evolution and especially the negative impacts of SAPs; provides examples, careful critiques and suggested alternatives.

Paloni, A. and Zanardi, M. (eds) (2006) *The IMF, the World Bank and Policy Reform*. London and New York: Routledge. A useful collection of assessments of the Bretton Woods Institutions' role.

Reed, D. (ed.) (1992) *Structural Adjustment and the Environment*, London: Earthscan. This is probably still the only book-length treatment of the environmental consequences of SAPs.

Simon, D., Van Spengen, W., Dixon, C. and Närman, A. (eds) (1995) *Structurally Adjusted Africa: Poverty, Debt and Basic Needs*, London and Boulder, CO: Pluto Press. Studies the implications of SAPs on different parts of Africa at different scales, from the supranational to the regional and local.

REFERENCES

Booth, D. (2005) *Missing Links in the Politics of Development: Learning from the PRSP Experiment*, Working Paper 256, London: Overseas Development Institute (available at http://www.odi.org.uk/publications/working_papers/wp256.pdf).

Bracking, S. (1999) 'Structural adjustment: Why it wasn't necessary and why it didn't work', *Review of African Political Economy*, 26(80): 207–26.

Burnell, P. (1998) 'Britain's new government, new White Paper, new aid? Eliminating world poverty: A challenge for the 21st century', *Third World Quarterly*, 19(4): 787–802.

Craig, D. and Porter, D. (2003) 'Poverty reduction strategy papers: A new convergence', *World Development*, 31(1): 53–69.

Dixon, C. (1999) 'The Pacific Asian challenge to neoliberalism', in D. Simon and A. Närman (eds) *Development as Theory and Practice: Current Perspectives on Development and Development Co-operation*, Harlow: Longman.

Driscoll, R. with Evans, A. (2005) 'Second-generation poverty reduction strategies: New opportunities and emerging issues', *Development Policy Review*, 23(1): 5–25.

Fraser, A. (2005) 'Poverty Reduction Strategy Papers: Now who calls the shots?', *Review of African Political Economy*, 32(104–5): 317–40.

Kifle, H., Olukoshi, A.O. and Wohlgemuth, L. (eds) (1997) *A New Partnership for African Development: Issues and Parameters*, Uppsala: Nordiska Afrikainstitutet.

Larmer, M. (2005) 'Reaction and resistance to neo-liberalism in Zambia', *Review of African Political Economy*, 32(103): 29–45.

Mohan, G., Brown, E., Millward, B. and Zack-Williams, A. (eds) (1999) *Structural Adjustment: Theory, Practice and Impacts*, London: Routledge.

Närman, A. (1999) 'Getting towards the beginning of the end for traditional development aid: Major trends in development thinking and its practical application over the last fifty years', in D. Simon and A. Närman (eds) *Development as Theory and Practice: Current Perspectives on Development and Development Co-operation*, Harlow: Longman.

Paloni, A. and Zanardi, M. (eds) (2006) *The IMF, the World Bank and Policy Reform*, London and New York: Routledge.

Reed, D. (ed.) (1992) *Structural Adjustment and the Environment*, London: Earthscan.

Simon, D. (1995) 'Debt, democracy and development in Africa in the 1990s', in D. Simon, W. Van Spengen, C. Dixon and A. Närman (eds) *Structurally Adjusted Africa: Poverty, Debt and Basic Needs*, London and Boulder, CO: Pluto Press.

Wood, A. (1997) *The International Monetary Fund's Enhanced Structural Adjustment Facility: What Role for Development?*, Briefing Paper, Bretton Woods Project (available on the Project's website at http://www.brettonwoodsproject.org/brief/esaf.html).

2.6 Dependency theories: From ECLA to André Gunder Frank and beyond

Dennis Conway and Nikolas Heynen

Dependency theory, more than a theoretical construct, is a way of understanding historically embedded, political-economic relations of peripheral capitalist countries, especially Latin American countries, within the broader context of the global economy. It is, essentially, a critique of the development paths, policies and strategies followed in Latin America, and elsewhere in the periphery (Amin 1976, 1992 argues the African case). Dependency theory emerged as a critical lens through which the history of Latin American development, marginalized as it was by Western hegemony, could be better understood; the 'development of underdevelopment', no less. The initial theorization was a *structuralist* perspective by economists who were associated with the United Nations Economic Commission for Latin America (ECLA). This was soon transformed, and informed, by more critical *dependency* notions and the spread of Marxist and neo-Marxist critiques of imperialism (Palma 1978).

Perhaps one of dependency theory's most important characteristics is that it was a product of Latin American scholarship (much of it written in Spanish) rather than Western scholars. These authorities theorized on the Latin American condition as 'insiders', as erstwhile, often passionate, native sons. This gave rise to a more informed, and more involved, appreciation of the reasons for Latin American underdevelopment, as *dependistas* dealt with the context of various countries' specific national circumstances, and theorized about Latin America's structures of social organization and localized behaviours. For Caribbean (and English-speaking) readers, Norman Girvan edited a special edition of *Social and Economic Studies* in 1973, with contributions translated from the Spanish. More widely, it was the publication of the writings of André Gunder Frank (and the collection and translation of other Latin American original contributions by North American Latin Americanists) which brought the dependency school's ideas to the notice of North American and European development studies (Chilcote 1984).

Prior to the Second World War, Latin American countries' economic strategies primarily followed a development path based on the export of natural resources and primary commodities to core countries. Many, including Argentinian Raúl Prebisch, Brazilians Paul Singer and Celso Furtado, and Chilean Osvaldo Sunkel, felt that Latin America's historical marginalization and resultant underdevelopment was perpetuated by such unequal commercial arrangements. While free market notions of 'comparative advantage' suggested that Latin America should benefit from their export strategies, ECLA economists argued otherwise. Their structuralist assessments had core countries, particularly Britain and the United States, benefiting at Latin America's expense.

Consequently, Prebisch and other ECLA structuralists insisted that major structural changes in development policy would be necessary to improve Latin America's economic situation. They proposed structural changes which favoured switching to more domestic production under tariff protection as a means of replacing industrial imports. In line with this strategy, capital goods, intermediate products and energy would be purchased with national income revenues from primary exports, and technology transfer would be negotiated with transnational corporations. This development strategy – often referred to as import substitution industrialization (ISI) – became widely practised throughout Latin America and the Third World/global South in general.

Although ECLA structuralist analyses recognized some of the problems underlying Latin American underdevelopment, the proposed ISI remedies brought other, more problematic, forms of dependency. Multinational corporate power and authority over technology transfer and capital investment emerged as a new form of dependency. Fernando Henrique Cardoso (1973) pointed this out in his assessments of power and authority in Brazil, and characterized the situation in such peripheral economies as 'associated dependent development'. Indeed, Cardoso felt that the dependent capitalist process of 'import substitution industrialization' occurred mostly under authoritarian regimes, and further, that state policies would favour multinational capital at the expense of labour.

Prebisch's (1950) identification of core–periphery relations as the global historical heritage behind unequal development meant that Latin America faced a formidable structural reality. Imperialism, colonialism and neocolonialism needed to be challenged more rigorously, because peripheral capitalism was not the answer for Latin American development. Accordingly, alternative critical commentary more deeply rooted within Marxist and neo-Marxist ideologies emerged, to better explain Latin America's subordinate place within the global economy, and to better understand the processes that led to such exploitive and dependent relations. ECLA structuralism was recast in *dependencia* terms.

Baran's influential (1957) *Political Economy of Growth* described the reasons for Latin America's underdevelopment within a Marxist framework as being a consequence of advanced nations' forming special partnerships with powerful elite classes in less developed countries, which benefited the minority class of Latin American elites rather than economic development more generally. Baran felt that such 'partnerships' perpetuated core countries' maintenance of traditional systems of surplus extraction, thereby making domestic resources continuously available to them, while rendering the economic development of Latin American countries unlikely, because any surplus generated was appropriated by the power-elites. Accordingly, Latin American countries remained subordinate and the core's monopoly power grew from the unequal commodity exchanges.

André Gunder Frank (1967, 1979) further developed Baran's ideas, by focusing on the dependent character of peripheral Latin American economies. In Frank's prognosis, '*the development of underdevelopment*' was the concept which best characterized the capitalist dynamics that both developed the core countries and caused greater levels of underdevelopment and dependency within Latin American countries. Frank used this conceptual framework to explain the dualistic capitalist relations which had occurred, and which would continue to occur between Latin American and core countries, as a result of the latter's continued political-economic domination.

Although there was a popular perception that Third World countries regained some sense of self-determination following decolonization, Frank argued that this was a fallacy. Rather, exploitation of many Third World countries by colonial and neocolonial core countries intensified following their achievement of political 'independence', further contributing to greater unequal relations. Thus, given the class-based stratification of Latin American society, which Baran blamed for the development of ties between Latin American elites and capitalist and political leaders from core countries, revolutionary action to remove such elites from power would be needed to forge a reformulation of international capitalist relations.

Besides arguing that the dependent core–periphery relationship was best articulated at the national scale, Frank also posited that a similar metropolis–satellite relationship occurred at smaller (regional) scales. In particular, he described similar dependent circumstances occurring between cities in Latin American countries and their peripheral hinterlands. Within this more localized scenario, the city and its periphery becomes increasingly polarized as a result of the capitalist relations between them, namely the metropolis exploiting its satellites. Dense networks of metropolis-satellite combinations formed what Frank referred to as 'constellations across national space' (Frank 1967).

Frank's notions of *dependencia*, which are perpetuated through global capitalism, ran counter to dualist notions that sought to explain Latin America's peripheral position in terms of modern versus traditional structures. Frank contended that by conceptualizing Latin America's underdevelopment as a function of feudal, or traditional, structures, the dualist perspective failed to truly comprehend the historical significance and transformative impact of capitalism's penetration of the continent's economic, political and social structures. This dependent relationship that Frank posited drew sharp criticism from many, however. Laclau's (1971) analysis is perhaps the most notable.

Laclau asserted that Frank's analytical method has significant shortcomings because it is based on an erroneous characterization of Marx's notion of modes of production. Instead of basing the construction of a mode of production on social or class relations, as Marx did, Laclau claims that Frank's reliance on market relations as the defining quality of the processes under which production occurs is inherently flawed. As a consequence, Laclau concludes that Frank's analysis offers little more than an account of a history that is well reported; in effect, he contributes nothing to theoretical explanation in terms of determining conditions.

The resultant tensions within Frank's analytical framework as a result of arguably incorrect, or less than accurate, usage of Marxist ideology, led the way to other neo-Marxist investigations of the linkages and possible reconciliation between dependency theory and Marxism. One was Ruy Mauro Marini's fundamental thesis in *Dialéctica de la Dependencia* (1973), which concerned the 'super-exploitation' of labour in dependent countries as a necessary strategy for capitalists to partially compensate for the falling rates of profit arising out of unequal exchange. Seeking to 'end the debate', Chilcote (1984) effectively situated the various capitalist and socialist approaches to the 'development of underdevelopment' – structuralism, dependencia, internal colonialism, neo-Marxism, even Trotskyism – as a full set of alternative theories and perspectives on development and underdevelopment. He also finds a place for Wallerstein's more worldly focus in the collection of alternatives. Wallerstein (1974, 1980) adapted dependency notions not only to comment on the commercial relations between the core countries and Latin America, but also to examine world historiography in terms of the dominant and subordinate relations that successive emerging cores, their peripheries and semi-peripheries have experienced, from the long sixteenth century, through eras of capitalism to the present globalizing era (the post-1980s).

Following Chilcote's (1984) insightful synthesis, Ghosh (2001) has further updated the record and provided us with a contemporary critical appraisal and overview of contemporary thoughts on the full set of alternative dependency theories and their 'development of underdevelopment' underpinnings. Agreeing with Ghosh, we feel that the dependency paradigm is still relevant as a partial explanation of the paths to development and underdevelopment that the core and peripheral Latin American nations followed. Furthermore, there are significant 'inter-temporal paradigm shifts' in the theory's wider application in our rapidly globalizing world. As Ghosh reminds us: 'There are indeed many issues and areas of development where dependency plays a major role. Some of these are: aid dependency, technological dependency, dependency for foreign capital investment, trade dependency, dependency for better human capital formation and so forth' (Ghosh 2001: 133).

Ghosh then points out the all-too-obvious connections between the divergent trajectories of capitalism's expansion in the global North as opposed to the global South, with the equally obvious assessment that 'unequal competition' remains an extremely powerful dependency relationship in globalization's transformative, disciplinary and destructive influences (Conway and Heynen 2006). Just as the imperialism of old imposed colonial regimes that fostered dependency and underdevelopment, modern globalization of the post-1980s has several salient features that are de facto successors to these imperial mechanisms:

- a programme of binding individuals, institutions and nations into a common set of market relationships;
- a calculated economic strategy of the capitalist economies, corporations and international financial institutional systems to encourage and stimulate capitalist growth for 'winners' – core and emerging markets – not the 'losers', with no comparative advantages, weak or failed states or the corruption-weakened;
- a means of extracting surplus through the exploitation of the cheap labour, high-quality manpower and resources of the global South (Ghosh 2001: 158).

Both Ghosh (2001) and Taylor (1996) argue convincingly that the evolving world system of core–periphery relationships has entered its postmodern phase of new dependency relationships, ecological uncertainty, rapid technological change, and a multiplicity of cross-cutting flows of information, cultural messages and knowledge exchange, at multiple scales and scopes of influential power and authority – ranging from the global to the local, from the exceptional to the ordinary, and from the elites to the bourgeoisie and working classes. Taylor (1996) draws parallels from the experiences and characteristics of earlier Dutch, British and American hegemonic cycles to chronicle the transition of the world's modern core–periphery system to a new postmodern (and globalized) 'world impasse', where 'all we can be sure of is that there will be many surprises for humanity' (Taylor 1996: 224).

Dependency thinking has come a long way since its initial Latin American interpretations, but even in today's globalizing world, the geopolitical and geo-economic struggles under way in Latin America are anything but predictable, and can no longer be framed so easily in the structural terms of core US hegemony and Latin American dependency. Furthermore, and as a concluding recommendation on how dependency theory might best be reread and refashioned, dependency thinking today requires us to confront the power hierarchies of the recent past (and present), using much more informed critical perspectives on the gendered roles of women, as well as men, in the development process. The primacy of capitalism's system of production and class struggle, which for so long anchored dependency theory's macro-level explanations of inequality and underdevelopment in the global South, needs to be further rethought and scaled down to incorporate micro- and meso-level assessments and examinations of class-based and gendered agency at the household, community and regional levels (Scott 1995). This way, the 'real-life economics' of more than half the globe's six billion people who are dependent and underdeveloped can be more effectively understood and evaluated in terms of their sustainability, democratic participation and accountability, their social power and authority (Ekins and Max-Neef 1992).

GUIDE TO FURTHER READING

Chilcote, R. (1984) *Theories of Development and Underdevelopment*, Boulder, CO, and London: Westview Press.

Ghosh, B. (2001) *Dependency Theory, Revisited*, Aldershot and Burlington, VT: Ashgate.

Kay, C. (1989) *Latin American Theories of Development and Underdevelopment*, London and New York: Routledge.

REFERENCES

Amin, S. (1976) *Unequal Development: An Essay on the Social Formation of Peripheral Capitalism*, New York: Monthly Review Press.

Amin, S. (1992) *Empire of Chaos*, New York: Monthly Review Press.

Baran, P. (1957) *The Political Economy of Growth*, New York: Monthly Review Press.

Cardoso, F.H. (1973) 'Associated-dependent development: Theoretical and practical implications', in A. Stepan (ed.) *Authoritarian Brazil: Origins, Policies, and Future*, New Haven, CT: Yale University Press, pp. 142–76.

Chilcote, R.H. (1984) *Theories of Development and Underdevelopment*, Boulder, CO, and London: Westview Press.

Conway, D. and Heynen, N. (2006) *Globalization's Contradictions: Geographies of Discipline, Destruction and Transformation*, Abingdon and New York: Routledge.

Ekins, P. and Max-Neef, M. (1992) *Real-Life Economics: Understanding Wealth Creation*, London and New York: Routledge.

Frank, A.G. (1967) *Capitalism and Underdevelopment in Latin America: Historical Studies of Chile and Brazil*, New York and London: Monthly Review Press.

Frank, A.G. (1979) *Dependent Accumulation and Underdevelopment*, New York: Monthly Review Press.

Ghosh, B.N. (2001) *Dependency Theory Revisited*, Aldershot and Burlington, VT: Ashgate.

Girvan, N. (1973) 'Dependence and underdevelopment in the New World and the Old', Special Number, *Social and Economic Studies*, 22(1): March.

Kay, C. (1989) *Latin American Theories of Development and Underdevelopment*, London and New York: Routledge.

Laclau, E. (1971) 'Feudalism and capitalism in Latin America', *New Left Review*, May–June: 19–38.

Marini, R.M. (1973) *Dialéctica de la Dependencia*, Mexico: Ediciones Era.

Palma, G. (1978) 'Dependency: A formal theory of underdevelopment or a methodology for the analysis of concrete situations of underdevelopment?', *World Development*, 14(3): 881–924.

Prebisch, R. (1950) *Economic Development in Latin America and its Principal Problems*, Lake Success, NY: UN Department of Economic Affairs.

Scott, C.V. (1995) *Gender and Development: Rethinking Modernization and Dependency Theory*, Boulder, CO: Lynne Rienner.

Taylor, P.J. (1996) *The Way the Modern World Works: World Hegemony to World Impasse*, Chichester: Wiley.

Wallerstein, I. (1974) *The Modern World System, Volume 1. Capitalist Agriculture and the Origins of the European World-Economy in the Sixteenth Century*, New York: Academic Press.

Wallerstein, I. (1980) *The Modern World System, Volume 2. Mercantilism and Consolidation of the European World-Economy, 1600–1750*, New York: Academic Press.

2.7 The New World Group of dependency scholars: reflections on a Caribbean avant-garde movement

Don D. Marshall

This chapter does not aspire to a chronology or a historical sequencing of events. Instead it examines retrospectively the rise and demise of an intellectual movement in the anglophone Caribbean under the animating force of decolonization. Allowance is made for a foray into the reasons behind the thwarted impulses of that age and the present decline of radical critique in the modern neoliberal period.

Introduction: Post-New World intellectual currents

Since the emergence of the New World movement in the early 1960s, it might be reasonable to expect that gathering forces in the international system – shaped by the imperatives of globalization – would present the spectre of the emergence once more of vital new political forces. Then, as now, the region was thrown back into contemplation on the relevance of its development strategy. With the benefit of the backward glance, 'New World' was first founded in Georgetown towards the end of 1962, against the backdrop of a long general strike and growing racial conflict between African-Guyanese and Indian-Guyanese. The early founders aspired to invent an indigenous view of the region, convinced that the modernization ideologies very much in vogue embraced neither a strategy for real, independent development, nor an understanding of the political-economic legacy of the Caribbean, of which more later.

In the first decade of the twenty-first century, Caribbean intellectuals in the main, particularly social scientists, take on the colour of their historical environs: if neoliberal capitalism cannot be challenged successfully, then to all intents and purposes it does not exist; all that remains is the challenge of massaging a link between market liberalization and populist statism. To be sure, this concern among Caribbean scholars and commentators does not preclude expression of despair in some quarters over the sustainability of the island-national project of the Caribbean. This forecast is based on an understanding of the export impetus girding contemporary capitalism, and the difficulties associated with making the transition in political economies dominated by merchant capital.

Decolonization and the rise of New World

The New World movement in the anglophone Caribbean was marked by an optimism of will and intellect. Newly independent governments were seen to be in pursuit of development guideposts to chart a self-reliant future. At the popular level, claims for social equality through redistribution became intensely salient as an expression of justice. And knowledge producers within both the academic and the literary community, no longer under the heel of colonial power, focused their energies on either transformative or ameliorative development agendas. Social dialogue and action seemed governed by an impulse towards West Indian self-definition, manifested in discussions on race, class, culture and the question of ownership and control of the region's resources. The general decolonization horizon within which such mood and thought moved was also marked by raging debates occurring in the academic world between modernization theorists and neo-Marxist scholars. The New World group – largely comprising historians and social scientists – would come to draw from, and intervene in, these debates, combining serious enquiry into the development possibilities under capitalism, with integrative, normative and programmatic thinking on nation building.

Considered by their pragmatic counterparts in government, media and academy as 'radicals', this cluster of writers and commentators across the Caribbean came to be known as the New World Group (NWG). Their thoughts and ideas on socialism, national self-determination and the delimiting horizons of capitalism reached a West Indian mass audience through public lecture series, various national fora, and newspapers and newsletters of their creation. *New World*, a Jamaica-based magazine, first appeared in 1963 and was published fortnightly under the editorship of Lloyd Best, with assistance from a host of University of the West Indies (UWI, Mona Campus) scholars – George Beckford, Owen Jefferson, Roy Augier, Derek Gordon, Don Robotham and Trevor Munroe, to list a few. From 1965, *New World* was published as a quarterly. Bearing the imprint of the UWI, the 'New World' would serve as a loose association attaching its name to anti-imperialist, consciousness-raising activity across the region. Indeed, NWGs were said to be formed in St Vincent, St Lucia, Washington, DC, Montreal, St Kitts, Trinidad, Barbados, Anguilla, Jamaica and Guyana. Other publications that appeared either as complements to or refinements of *New World*'s mission included *Moko* and *Tapia*, Trinidad-based, weekly newspapers appearing in 1969, *Abeng*, a Jamaican newsletter launched in the same year, and the 1970 St Lucia-based *Forum*.

The first issue of *New World* focused on Guyana's development dilemma. The analysis moved beyond conventional state-centric explanations about the country's savings gap, low technologies, unskilled, undifferentiated labour markets and inadequate infrastructure. Guyana's, and indeed the Caribbean's, limited development, it was argued, was a function of the region's structural dependent linkages with Europe in terms of its value system and its economic relations. This point of view resonated with the dependency perspective first advanced by Paul Baran and subsequently extended by others who specialised in Latin American area studies. It was certainly a more assimilable 'angle' for Norman Girvan and Owen Jefferson to deploy in their doctoral theses explaining Jamaican underdevelopment (circa 1972), than the market-deficiency arguments of neoclassical proponents. As Girvan and Jefferson saw it, the move towards self-government and independence could not arrest the process of underdevelopment so long as the domestic economies remained dependent on foreign capital and terms of trade set under colonial rule.

Principally, the path of resistance for New World associates was forged out of opposition to Arthur Lewis's (1955) import substitution industrialization (ISI) model, favoured by Caribbean governments in the 1960s and 1970s. Briefly, the ISI programme required state provision of incentives to transnational enterprises in order to attract offshore industrial operations. The various budgetary and fiscal preparatory statements placed emphasis on the prospects for increased employment, technology transfer and stimulated markets for local inputs.

Beckford (1972) and Best and Levitt (1968) levelled a critique of Lewis's model that was representative of the dominant positions New World associates adopted on the question of Caribbean capitalist development. With epistemic insights drawn from orthodox Marxists and Latin American structuralists, their research fitted the growing canon of work seeking to establish dependency as the source of persistent underdevelopment. Beckford and others in the NWG would enrich this stock argument by anchoring the dependency concept within the plantation experience of Caribbean societies.

Dependency theory and plantation economy

Beckford's (1972) *Persistent Poverty* defined the historic plantation slave economy as a quintessentially dependent economy, the units of which included Caribbean land, African unfree labour and European capital. This is Best and Levitt's (1968) 'pure plantation economy', as no other economic activity occurred outside the sugar plantation. Beckford's work was as much a repudiation of Caribbean development strategies as it was a paradigmatic challenge to the liberal fallacy of 'progress'. For him, the mode of accumulation in the region remained a modified plantation economy variant, as dependent investment and aid ties with London and other metropolitan cities persisted. After lamenting the disarticulation between branch-plant production and the rest of the host economy, and the general mono-product character of local economies, Beckford (and, later, Best and Levitt) outlined other structural features of the plantation economy which generated underdevelopment:

- land requirements of plantation production tended to restrict domestic food production;
- terms of trade often deteriorated as rising food and other imports presented balance of payments difficulties;
- stagnant educational levels tended to foreclose on product diversification options and improvements.

Havelock Brewster (1973), seized by the plantation economy argument, argued that foreign capital could not possibly champion industrialization in accordance with common needs and the utilization of the internal market. This was so, he surmised, because the gridlocked nature of a plantation economy, with its lack of an internal dynamic, its reliance on outdated technologies and hierarchical management practices, guaranteed for the region a subordinate role in its relationships with core firms and countries.

From all this we may gather that, unlike their dependency counterparts in Latin America, most New World associates relied less on external-determinist explanations to explain Caribbean underdevelopment, than on the *internal* workings of Caribbean economies to account for the region's structural dependency, even as they were careful to note that the characteristics of these economies extended back to colonial relations between Britain and the West Indies. *Dependistas* and structuralists, on the other hand, placed the centre–periphery relations they depict within the context of macro-historical forces, intent on locking peripheral societies into an unyielding spiral of exploitation and poverty.

Interestingly enough, Walter Rodney, a Guyanese historian, and Jamaican political scientist, Trevor Munroe, could be said to have framed Caribbean development in such deterministic terms, except that they singled out the social legacy of the plantation experience as especially debilitating for non-white races. Both were inspired by Marx's historical materialist method, but Rodney was inclined to argue that nation building in the region had to be about renewing spirits, constructing grounds for black liberation and pursuing self-reliance. Trevor Munroe's perspective was expressed in more classical but nuanced terms, as he was mindful of the plantation slavery experience. As he would frame it, underdevelopment in the region was the predictable outcome of undeveloped class formation – itself partly perpetuated by that mix of domestic policies which threw the territories back on traditional activity and on traditional metropolitan dependence. The extent of the lag in technological, market, infrastructural and resource development will pose a challenge to aspirant Caribbean societies committed to constructing a capitalist economy.

Of the NWG, however, Best's dependency perspective evinced a deep-seated ambivalence towards Western discourses on development. Perhaps he was self-conscious of the post-colonial scholar's place in such literary transactions, of the dangers of succumbing to the neoclassical association between open economies and automatic economic growth. In the context of plantation economies, such assumptions muddled an already complex situation, Best argued. His dependency perspective was consistently embedded in extended and detailed analyses of ruling circles. Apart from addressing the aforementioned features of neocolonial dependency in the region, he singled out the shared outlook of Caribbean elites and Western development planners as a major brake on effecting meaningful socio-economic transformation. Not surprisingly, his appeal was for a shift in the register of social consciousness on the part of the ruling elite. The colonial hangover apart, Best failed to draw sufficient attention to the degree of class conflict inherent in decolonization as new class forces move to reorient the social system and the values which define that system.

The demise of New World

As the 1970s dawned, the New World movement shuffled to a halt as division arose over strategies, tactics and modes of resistance to neocolonialism. By this time, Best was especially critical of the group, decrying what he saw as New World's fatal attraction for governments, and a tendency to substitute policy-oriented research for contemplative scholarship. Increasingly, such knowledge products, he argued, amounted to exercises in self-justification, and as such were quite explicit disclosures of governmental discourse in action. He was also resistant to the idea that the NWG could move towards the formation of a political party or organization contending for power. In a polemic entitled 'Whither New World', Best (1968: 2) spoke of the tensions of the group, offering the following observation: 'There is among us, much unwitting intolerance, little cool formulation, hardly any attentive listening and even less effective communication.' Munroe would come to lament their facetious pursuit of class unity and vowed to distance himself from what he termed the 'bourgeois idealism' of New World.

The disintegration of the NWG was in part a result of the attention given by many to the immediate realms of the policy process. Mona-based economists, in particular, played key advisory roles in the Michael Manley administration of the 1970s, while others across the region responded to appeals from governments for technical and project management assistance. But there are some scholars who instead place emphasis on the internal arguments between Best and others on the question of New World's relevance and its activist orientation. Their analysis, in my view, falls short precisely because they do not recognize sufficiently that New World, like any avant-garde movement, became compromised not so much by bourgeois acceptance as by *absorption into the intelligentsia*. Attendance to career, administration and public service would spawn a culture marked by keynote address, cocktail attendance and doctoral authority. Consequently, the new radicals were to be found on the outskirts of black power movements, drawn less to its ideology than to the struggle for worker freedom and justice.

On a wider intellectual plane, New World could be said to suffer the slump it did largely because the dependency concept itself lacked lasting explanatory power. Overall, there was a circularity in the dependency argument: dependent countries are those which lack the capacity for autonomous growth, and they lack this because their structures are dependent ones. Other scholars have also made the point about development in the world economy being, in fact, *dependent* development, pointing to foreign investment relationships between core states and firms. By the late 1970s, the emphasis among neo-Marxists shifted away from an independent weight placed on 'dependency' as undesirable, towards either a normative condemnation of state capitalism or an appeal to Third World states to *negotiate* the scope of their dependency.

Summary: Back to the future

If we posit that openings for dissent are as necessary to democracy as securing consent, then Caribbean civil and uncivil society can continue to offer sites for objection and challenge. But there has been no New World equivalent emerging out of the tensions of the present neoliberal period. True the rise and influence of non-governmental organizations (NGOs), particularly women's organizations, trades unions and the galvanizing work of the Caribbean Policy Development Centre, along with that of critical scholars, have served to exert pressure on increasing public transparency and inclusion. To be sure it is not at all clear that NGOs constitute an intrinsically virtuous force for the collective good. These can run a similar course to that of the New World. Beyond a certain point, NGOs may lose the critical element that caused them to come into existence, as they render services to governance agencies, take funds from them or 'cross over' to work for government institutions and organizations which they previously challenged. Market mentalities predominate in government bureaucracies, business firms and academy in the early twenty-first century. Academicians from the UWI, particularly social scientists, are exhorted by media, business and government commentators to give advice and attention to the technicality of social control or constitutional and other reforms. In most issue spaces, ruling discourses of technocratic expertise seem to suppress alternative perspectives arbitrarily. The UWI's role in this is not entirely surprising, as the University's struggle for relevance and its sensitivity to budget efficiency do make for a climate where conformity to the prevailing common sense seems the best course for research programming. Hegemony-affirming research thus continues to triumph. Political and intellectual challenges are foreclosed in the prevailing environment, where priority of survival continues to be asserted both as an operating principle and as a rationale for the absence of radical critique. This is the 'bourgeois villainy' Best would speak of when the case was hardly self-evident among intellectuals of New World. The associates then at least managed a discussion of Caribbean dependency that was enriched by site characteristics of plantation production relations. This added colour to parallel debates in Latin America. For New World associates, the dependency concept had operative power; it encouraged an interesting entry point for challenging the colonial mode of accumulation. It also fashioned an intellectual cachet of dissent in the region, illuminating history and social fact as economic paradigms came under challenge.

GUIDE TO FURTHER READING AND REFERENCES

Beckford, G. (1972) *Persistent Poverty: Underdevelopment in Plantation Economies of the Third World*, Morant Bay, Jamaica, and London: Maroon Publishing House and Zed Press.

Best, L. (1968) 'Forum: Whither New World', *New World*, IV(1): 1–6.

Best, L. and Levitt, K. (1968) 'Outlines of a model of pure plantation economy', *Social and Economic Studies*, 17(3): 283–326.

Blomstrom, M. and Hettne, B. (1984) *Development Theory in Transition*, London: Zed Books.

Brewster, H. (1973) 'Economic dependence: A quantitative interpretation', *Social and Economic Studies*, 22(1): 90–95.

Dookeran, W. (ed.) (1996) *Choices and Change: Reflections on the Caribbean*, Washington, DC: Inter-American Bank.

Hendriks, C.M. (2006) 'Integrated deliberation: Reconciling civil society's dual role in deliberative democracy', *Political Studies*, 54: 486–508.

Lewis, R.C. (1998) *Walter Rodney's Intellectual and Political Thought*, Kingston, Jamaica, and Detroit, MI: University of the West Indies Press and Wayne State University Press.

Lewis, W.A. (1955) *The Theory of Economic Growth*, London: Allen and Unwin.

Marshall, D.D. (2000) 'Academic travails and a crisis-of-mission of UWI social sciences: From history and critique to anti-politics', in G. Howe (ed.) *Higher Education in the Anglophone Caribbean: Past, Present, and Future Directions*, Mona, Jamaica: University of the West Indies Press, pp. 59–84.

Munroe, T. (1990) *Jamaican Politics: A Marxist Perspective in Transition*, Kingston, Jamaica, and Boulder, CO: Heinemann Publishers (Caribbean Limited) and Lynne Rienner Publishers.

Rodney, W. (1972) *How Europe Underdeveloped Africa*, London: Penguin.

2.8 World-systems theory: Cores, peripheries and semi-peripheries

Thomas Klak

Definition

World-systems theory (WST) argues that any country's development conditions and prospects are shaped primarily by economic processes, commodities chains, divisions of labour and geopolitical relationships operating at the global scale. World-systems theorists posit the existence of a single global economic system since at least the start of European industrialization around 1780–90. According to WST doyen Immanuel Wallerstein, and others, the global system dates back even further, to at least 1450, when international trade began to grow, and when Europe embarked on the 'age of discovery' and colonization (Frank and Gills 1993). Contrary to much social science thinking, WST stresses the futility of a 'statist orientation' – that is, the attempt to analyse or generate development by focusing at the level of individual countries, each of which is profoundly shaped by world-system opportunities and constraints (Bair 2005).

WST has identified a number of regularly occurring historical cycles associated with the level and quality of business activity. These cycles account for economic booms and busts of various durations. The main economic periods for WST are *Kondratieff cycles*, named after the Russian economist who discovered them in the 1920s. Each cycle, or *long wave*, lasts about 50 to 60 years and represents a qualitatively different phase of global capitalism, not just a modification of the previous cycle. Kondratieff cycles are themselves divided into a period of expansion and stagnation. There is first an A-phase of upswing, economic expansion and quasi-monopolistic profitability, fuelled by technological innovations and organized by new assymetrical institutional rules. Price inflation increases during the A-phase. This then leads into a B-phase of increased competition, profit decline, economic slowdown and price deflation. The profit squeeze towards the end of the B-phase motivates capitalists and policymakers to create new and innovative ways to accumulate capital. They work to shift investment out of established economic sectors, regulated environments and production locations, and thereby create the conditions for a new Kondratieff cycle (Knox et al. 2003).

The previous Kondratieff cycle began in the 1940s, expanded until 1967–73 (A-phase), and then contracted through the 1980s (B-phase). Each cycle's organizing institutions and rules are both economic and political. For this cold war cycle, key economic rules and structures included the US dollar as the global currency, and supranational bodies such as the World Bank, the IMF and the G7. Political structures included the UN and the geopolitical divisions brokered at the Yalta conference. This divided Europe into US- and Russian-dominated zones, pitted global capitalism against Russian-led state socialism (communism), and presented the developing world as ideologically contested turf. The dawn of the twenty-first century finds the world in a new cycle. New institutions and rules, such as the World Trade Organization (WTO), neoliberal free trade and global financial liberalization, aim to stabilize and ensure quasi-monopolistic profitability and global power for core countries. As in the cold war cycle, the United States remains the preeminent core (and thus global) power, but its hegemony is now contested by other strenghtening core countries and semi-peripheral countries, notably China.

Scholars and disciplines influencing, and influenced by, WST

WST is almost synonymous with its principal architect, Immanuel Wallerstein. Indeed, few influential theoretical perspectives are so closely linked to one contemporary scholar. WST's conceptual roots are largely in Marxism. Wallerstein (1979) says that WST follows 'the spirit of Marx if not the letter'. Evidence of Marx's spirit includes WST's emphasis on class, the state, imperialism and control over the means of production and labour power. WST's objections to classical Marxism include concern over a theoretical component known as *developmentalism*. This is the idea that societies move sequentially through feudalism, capitalism and socialism to communism, and that they can be analysed and transformed individually and separately from the world system. WST's alternative view – that there has been for centuries but one world economy, driven by capital accumulation – employs a concept of mode of production closer to that of Karl Polanyi than that of Marx.

WST has much interdisciplinary relevance, and has therefore attracted both supporters and detractors from across the social sciences. WST complements political-economic analysis rooted in the traditions of *dependency theory* (Cardoso and Faletto 1979), *uneven development* (Smith 1984) and *dependent development* (Evans 1979). A conceptually overlapping, but perhaps less economistic, and highly influential alternative to WST is the *regulation school*. Usually applied at a more local level than WST (i.e. to national or subnational systems), regulation theory seeks to identify phases of capitalism of variable length, based on relations between a particular prevailing method of accumulating capital and an associated 'mode of regulation', that is, a set of state regulations and behavioural norms (O'Hara 2003).

The geography of WST: Three groups of nation states

WST's temporal cycles of systemic integration, order, turbulence, transition and reconstitution of the global economy play out variably across geographical space. The world system is very unequal. Despite (or, world-system theorists argue, *because of*) several centuries of worldwide economic integration and trade, and more than a half-century of World Bank-led international development, global inequalities continue to rise. The difference in per-capita income separating the richest and poorest countries was 3:1 in 1820, 35:1 in 1950, 72:1 in 1992, and 108:1 in 2004 (UNDP 1999, 2006). Within this highly unequal world order are place-specific dynamics. At times, regions can rise and fall in terms of power, development and economic potential. WST describes this globally differentiated space with reference to nation states and regional groupings thereof. These fall into three categories (see figure).

Compared to long waves, the geographical components of the world system are less conceptually refined and empirically specified. With this caveat in mind, general geographical features can be described. Countries of the *core*, or *centre*, are the sites of global economic (and especially industrial) power and wealth, and the associated political and military strength and influence. Core countries feature higher-skill, capital-intensive production. Politically, they collectively establish and enforce the rules of the global order and, through these advantages, appropriate surplus from non-core countries. The *semi-periphery* is positioned between the core's strengths and the periphery's weaknesses. It mixes characteristics of the core (e.g. industry, export power, prosperity) and the periphery (e.g. poverty, primary product reliance, vulnerability to core decision making). The semi-periphery is the most turbulent category, in that its members most frequently rise or fall in the global hierarchy. In semi-peripheral countries, there is much hope for development and joining the core countries, and narrow windows of opportunity to do so. But there are also intense interactions, with core countries bent on fostering their own capital accumulation by maintaining the hierarchical status quo. The *periphery* is the backwater of the world system. It provides low-skill production and raw materials for industries elsewhere. It has poor living conditions and bleak development prospects. The semi-periphery versus periphery distinction for non-core regions is important. It avoids grouping such a heterogeneous set of countries with respect to development, industrialization, trade, resource control and geopolitics. Still, putting the world's 200 countries into just three groups inevitably glosses over much intra-group heterogeneity. Note the regional clustering of countries in the three categories in the figure. At present the core is mainly North America, Western Europe, Australasia and Japan. The semi-periphery is essentially East Asia, Latin America's larger countries and most of the former Soviet realm. The periphery is everything else, particularly Africa.

A nation state's position in the world system is historically *path-dependent*, but not deterministically so. Nation states can move between categories over time, depending on their accumulation regimes, development strategies and international aid and alliances. Indeed, WST is quite useful for analysing the upward and downward movement of countries over time. There is not agreement over each country's categorization, depending on the defining characteristics and their interpretation. In addition, relative positions *within* each of the three categories can also shift over time.

East Asia illustrates the semi-periphery's potential and turbulence (Gwynne et al. 2003). Following massive US aid and industrial export growth in recent decades, South Korea has recently been knocking on the core's gate, although it was set back considerably by the 1997 Asian financial crisis. Indonesia has traditionally been peripheral, but in recent decades it has arguably joined the semi-periphery. Its increased clout derives from economic growth based on industrial exports for Nike and others, large resource endowments, including oil exports, and its status as the world's

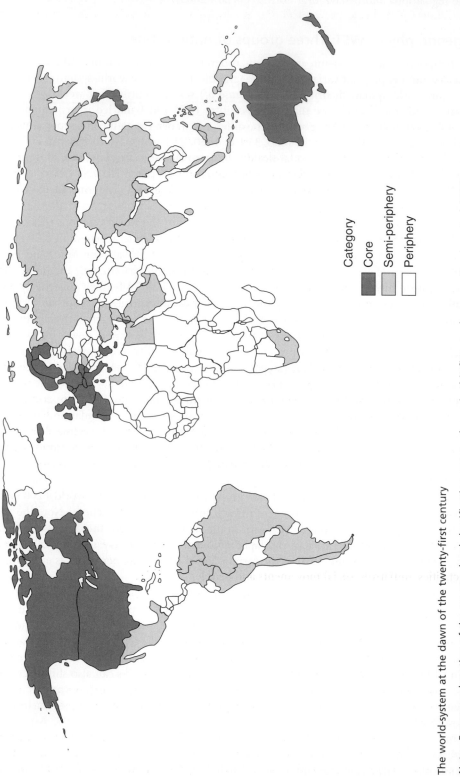

The world-system at the dawn of the twenty-first century

Notes: For an explanation of the country-level classification system shown in this figure, please see Gwynne et al. 2003.

Category

Core

Semi-periphery

Periphery

fourth most populous country (see figure). China's industrial export boom and associated capital accumulation since the 1980s drove it into the semi-periphery. Now many Japanese and US leaders fear China's global resource hunger and ambitions as a soon-to-be core country (Zweig and Jianhai 2005).

Criticisms of WST

One capitalist world economy, divided by Kondratieff cycles, since at least 1450?

Need we subscribe to WST's totalizing global history to employ it effectively to understand recent development? Compared to Wallerstein, few writers employing a WST framework are as deeply historical, and few treat economic activities during previous centuries in such a globally holistic way. Much work, for example, has been done to identify the evolving features of capitalism associated with five Kondratieff cycles extending back only to 1789. Many other WST-influenced scholars focus on the dynamics of contemporary capitalism. WST purists may reject these approaches as insufficiently historical.

While Kondratieff cycles have considerable historical and empirical support (Mandel 1980), they remain controversial. Others have assembled evidence to cast doubt on the existence and significance of long waves, and to suggest instead that capitalism moves through phases of differing lengths, problems and features (e.g. Maddison 1991). As mentioned earlier, the regulation school is one alternative conceptualization of contemporary capitalist dynamics.

Metatheory?

Beyond the considerable empirical analysis of Kondratieff cycles and their associated production and technological features, many WST claims remain untested and are perhaps untestable. Most WST-influenced scholarship focuses on the contemporary global political economy, and the lack of time series data limits testing. Further, how could the simple three-category spatial division of the world system be tested? WST-inspired writing tends to read like an open-ended analysis of unfolding world events. Critics can claim that this method allows one to find and fit the data anecdotally to the theory. Better to think of a world-system *approach*, *analysis* or *perspective* than a world-system *theory*.

Neglect of the local?

Operating at the global level and concerned with economic cycles over decades, if not centuries, WST is too holistic to account for local dynamics. Indeed, WST underplays the generative role of local activities, initiatives, social movements and people.

Conclusion

World-systems theory, with its keen sense of historical, cyclical, technological and geographical patterns, has undoubtedly deepened our understanding of the global political economy. It is a satisfying antidote to the reductionism, ahistoricism and superficiality in most popular interpretations of economic change. WST's historical and holistic perspective and level-headedness serves to counter the recent hyperbole about the uniqueness of globalization and the inevitability of neoliberalism.

In practice, many scholars employing a WST perspective downplay the details and measurement of the cycles of upswing and downswing in the global economy. They focus instead primarily on contemporary trends, and adopt a qualitative approach to understanding business cycles, global systemic change, and the associated realignments of geopolitical and economic power, constraints and potential. Many economists, and some WST purists, would judge a more qualitative version of WST to be insufficiently rigorous and therefore theoretically deficient. WST defenders would counter that a more qualitative approach is suitable, given their aim to see the 'big picture', and to decipher and rectify contemporary economic and political institutions and options.

GUIDE TO FURTHER READING

Gwynne, R., Klak, T. and Shaw, D. (2003) *Alternative Capitalisms: Geographies of 'Emerging Regions'*, London: Hodder Arnold, and New York: Oxford University Press. Employs WST to examine the recent reconfiguration of countries in the semi-periphery of the global economy.

Knox, P., Agnew, J. and McCarthy, L. (2003) *The Geography of the World Economy*, fourth edition, London: Hodder Arnold. Couples WST with economic geography to explore the workings of the contemporary global economy.

Shannon, T.R. (1996) *An Introduction to the World-System Perspective*, second edition, Boulder, CO: Westview Press. Useful overview of WST, endorsed by Wallerstein.

Wallerstein, I. (2004) *World-System Analysis: An Introduction*, Durham, NC: Duke University Press. Wallerstein's own introduction to the field.

Wallerstein, I. (ed.) (2004) *The Modern World System in the Longue Durée*, Boulder, CO: Paradigm Publishers. Wide-ranging set of chapters by leading world-system scholars, providing a useful overview of WST.

USEFUL WEBSITES

Fernand Braudel Center for the Study of Economies, Historical Systems, and Civilizations, Binghamton University, State University of New York, http://fbc.binghamton.edu/index.htm. The Center focuses on 'the analysis of large-scale social change over long periods of historical time'.

Journal of World-Systems Research, Institute for Research on World-Systems, University of California, Riverside, http://jwsr.ucr.edu/index.php. Free online journal devoted to WST.

United Nations Development Programme, *Human Development Reports*, http://hdr.undp.org/. Global and comparative country data for a range of development indicators.

REFERENCES

Bair, J. (2005) 'Global capitalism and commodity chains: Looking back, going forward', *Competition and Change*, 9: 153–80.

Cardoso, F. and Faletto, E. (1979) *Dependency and Development in Latin America*, Berkeley, CA: University of California Press.

Evans, P. (1979) *Dependent Development: The Alliance of Multinational, State, and Local Capital in Brazil*, Princeton, NJ: Princeton University Press.

Frank, A.G. and Gills, B. (eds) (1993) *The World System: Five Hundred Years or Five Thousand?* London: Routledge.

Gwynne, R., Klak, T. and Shaw, D. (2003) *Alternative Capitalisms: Geographies of 'Emerging Regions'*, London: Hodder Arnold, and New York: Oxford University Press.

Knox, P., Agnew, J. and McCarthy, L. (2003) *The Geography of the World Economy*, fourth edition, London: Hodder Arnold.

Maddison, A. (1991) *Dynamic Forces in Capitalist Development*, Oxford: Oxford University Press.

Mandel, E. (1980) *Long Waves of Capitalist Development*, Cambridge: Cambridge University Press.

O'Hara, P. (2003) 'Deep recession and financial instability or a new long wave of economic growth for US capitalism? A regulation school approach', *Review of Radical Political Economics*, 35: 18–43.

Smith, N. (1984) *Uneven Development: Nature, Capital, and the Production of Space*, New York: Blackwell.

UNDP (1999, 2006) *Human Development Report*, New York: Oxford University Press.

Wallerstein, I. (1979) *The Capitalist World-Economy*, Cambridge: Cambridge University Press.

Zweig, D. and Jianhai, B. (2005) 'China's global hunt for energy', *Foreign Affairs*, September/October.

2.9 Indigenous knowledge and development

John Briggs

Interest in indigenous knowledge systems developed particularly during the 1980s, primarily in response to dissatisfaction with modernization as a means of improving living standards for the majority of the population of the Global South. Modernization, through the diffusion of formal scientific and technical knowledges from the North to the Global South, has been seen to be an effective way of eradicating poverty. Consequently, development has frequently been conceptualized as a fundamentally technical issue, driven by the dominant science discourses of Europe and North America. By the 1980s, however, it had become clear that this transfer had not been wholly successful in transforming the lives of many, especially in Africa.

Alternatives were sought, and in promoting local-level, even antidevelopment, approaches, Escobar (1995: 98) perhaps captures the spirit best when he writes: 'the remaking of development must start by examining local constructions, to the extent that they are the life and history of the people, that is, the conditions of and for change'. This highlights the importance of local-level histories, geographies and sociocultural constructs in understanding community-level development, as well as the need for a more explicit acknowledgement of indigenous knowledge as a valid body of knowledge. Despite this, much current development thinking still reflects the dominance of formal science; development remains a technical challenge and the voices of the poor and dispossessed are still little heard. However, the challenge for a new vision remains, and there is increasing sympathy for the view that 'there is now an explicit understanding among many promoters and practitioners that farmer participatory research has clear advantages for the development of appropriate, environmentally friendly and sustainable production systems' (Okali, Sumberg and Farrington 1994: 6).

Although it is only in the last quarter of the twentieth century that the interest in indigenous knowledge has explicitly emerged in the literature, there were elements of an embryonic indigenous knowledge before then. Although William Allan's (1965) classic, *The African Husbandman*, is basically a standard development narrative of its time, focusing on issues of population and land pressure, there is nonetheless an acknowledgement that indigenous agricultural systems demonstrate a considerable knowledge of, and sympathy with, the environment. The first major discussions of indigenous knowledge in development, however, can be traced to a collection of papers in the *IDS Bulletin* in 1979 (see, for example, Howes 1979). This was followed by an important landmark work edited by Brokensha, Warren and Werner (1980). Richards (1985) took the debate forward with a study which showed how African farmers used their own knowledge systems as the basis for successful agricultural production. Interestingly, Richards' study raises the issue as to whether these local knowledge systems are complementary to formal science, or whether they are rather more radical alternatives, which better reflect the needs, aspirations and priorities of local people. Based on much of this pioneering work, indigenous knowledge has become increasingly important in discussions on sustainable development because of the ways in which such knowledge has apparently allowed people to live in harmony with nature while still being able to make a living. If indigenous knowledge has indeed become an accepted part of development, then this can be seen as 'a shift from the preoccupation with the centralised, technically oriented solutions of the past decades that failed to alter life prospects for a majority of the peasants and small farmers of the world' (Agrawal 1995: 414). Whether this shift has taken place, however, is a debatable point.

Unsurprisingly, a number of development agencies have been keen to try to deploy indigenous knowledge in their development strategies. The World Bank (1998: i), for example, argues that there is a need 'not only to help bring global knowledge to the developing countries, but also to learn about indigenous knowledge (IK) from these countries, paying particular attention to the knowledge base of the poor'. Although the broad thrust is very welcome to many, indigenous knowledge is still seen as little more than a list of easily identifiable, mostly technical and discrete knowledges. There is little sense of dealing with embedded knowledges as part of a wider economy and society. Indigenous knowledge in the World Bank's conceptualization is not allowed to offer a fundamental challenge to development, but simply to offer the opportunity for some technical, place-specific solutions where indigenous knowledge can hopefully be integrated into World Bank-supported programmes. This can only come about once the validity of indigenous knowledge has been confirmed, and, of course, this is achieved by scrutinizing that knowledge through the lens of formal science. Only then can indigenous knowledge be judged to be worthy of serious investigation and dissemination (Briggs and Sharp 2004).

Herein, therefore, lies a fundamental problem in deploying indigenous knowledge in development, that of the tensions between formal Western science and indigenous knowledge, a people's science – a tension which may be referred to as the binary divide. Western science is rational, controlled, rigorous and universal; indigenous knowledge is irrational, imbued with folklore and too place-specific to offer any meaningful solution to underdevelopment. Maddox, Giblin and Kimambo (1996) conceptualized this difference as a 'Merrie Africa' and a 'Primitive Africa'. The former, pre-colonial period is dominated by an indigenous knowledge which is in harmony with nature. The latter, conversely, suggests a period of hostile, threatening environments, which, of course, can only be treated successfully by the use of science and technology. Both views, however, seriously underestimate the capacity for constructive transformation from within rural communities themselves; both, ironically, to a greater or lesser extent, are dismissive of the utility of indigenous knowledge. The danger with this position is that if modern Western science is located at one end of the development spectrum, indigenous knowledge is located at the other. It is increasingly apparent, however, that such polar extremes are in reality untenable, and there is greater sympathy for the view that indigenous knowledge represents a complementary, not competing, set of knowledge, and that it somehow represents a sense of additionality (Reij, Scoones and Toulmin 1996).

A problem, however, is that if an overdependence on modernization approaches has failed to deliver significantly improved living standards for the bulk of the world's population since the mid-twentieth century, then an overdependence on indigenous knowledge as an alternative, at the other extreme, may also fail to deliver meaningful development results. The tensions between the two knowledge systems have been exacerbated by the resistance of modernization theorists and practitioners to using indigenous knowledge systems in development. For them, the problem of poverty is to be treated by technology transfer, by capital investment and by the release of productive forces (typically within the framework of International Monetary Fund (IMF) structural adjustment programmes). The development agenda is defined in the corridors of power in the 'North', and, in this, the voice of the 'South' is largely unheard. For example, for many in the North, dryland areas in particular have to be managed in a rational, technocratic manner, as befits fragile and vulnerable environments, using knowledges rooted firmly in formal Western science and technology. No worthwhile contribution can be made by the inhabitants of such areas themselves, as they have little meaningful to offer; indeed, left to their own ways, their management, if that is what it can be called, will result only in further degradation. The voice of the South is to be ignored as it has no worthwhile contribution to make. Proponents of indigenous knowledge argue that the indigenous knowledge of those people resident in particular places can be of equal, or even greater, value than more formal Western scientific knowledge. If this argument is followed through, Western science loses its universal hegemonic position, a position of power, and becomes one of a range of competing and contested knowledge systems. Pretty (1994: 38) has observed that 'the trouble with normal science is that it gives credibility to opinion only when it is defined in scientific language, which may be inadequate for describing the complex and changing experiences of farmers and other actors in rural development'. Consequently, knowledge which is not rooted in Western science is still seen by many in the development community as flawed, other than in instances where straightforward and uncontroversial indigenous technical solutions can be incorporated into development practice.

An additional problem with indigenous knowledge in the context of development is the empirical emphasis of much of the work and the extent to which it is place-specific, and hence not easily transferable over geographic space. Methods of indigenous soil and water management, in particular, have attracted considerable interest, as has research on medicinal plant use. There is now a better understanding of how local people make sense of soil properties and characteristics, using attributes such as colour and feel, rather than chemical factors that Western pedologists might employ. Ostberg (1995), in a fascinating study in Tanzania, for example, discusses how farmers talk about 'cool' land, which is good for cultivation, and land which becomes 'tired', and then 'hot', and which can no longer be cultivated, or at least, should no longer be cultivated. Interesting as these micro-narratives are, there is still a sense of frustration among development practitioners as to how useful they might be in the bigger scheme of things.

In a similar vein, the fact that indigenous knowledge is differentiated within communities makes it difficult to use in development. Although it would be attractive to generate the concept of a community knowledge, shared by all its members, in reality this rarely, if ever, exists, because such knowledge is fragmentary and is cut across by factors such as wealth, production priorities, household circumstances, and so on. All these factors impact on an individual's access to knowledge and that individual's ability to deploy such knowledge. Various studies have also shown that there can be clear gender differences in indigenous knowledge acquisition and how such knowledge is deployed (Briggs et al. 2003). With this kind of fragmentation and differentiation, it becomes difficult to see how indigenous knowledge can be successfully and effectively deployed across a range of rural settings.

The power relations associated with indigenous knowledge are no less problematic, particularly at the local scale. Bluntly put, whose knowledge counts? There is a tendency among some to take the view that indigenous knowledge is somehow an inherently 'good thing', but, of course, this need not be the case at all. An example of local meetings in Tanzania showed that it tended to be a small group of the same male voices that were constantly being heard (Cleaver 1999). Under these circumstances, indigenous knowledge can become the product (and property) of only a small group of powerful individuals.

There has sometimes been a tendency to romanticize indigenous knowledge as a static, unchanging, pristine and untainted knowledge system. Hence, the trick becomes one of how to tease out these knowledges, which will then provide the key to sustainable development in the rural areas of the Global South. The danger with this approach is that it privileges indigenous knowledge in the same way that modernization proponents privilege Western science. It is clear, however, that rural people in the Global South are very open to a whole range of ideas, regardless of their origins, as long as they make economic sense and are culturally acceptable. The notion that indigenous knowledge is static, unchanging, pristine and untainted is very difficult to sustain; instead, it is fluid, dynamic and provisional. People will adopt and experiment with new ideas if they will improve their livelihoods, and so it may be that instead of the term indigenous knowledge, a better term might be local mediated knowledges, deliberately in the plural (Briggs 2005).

Finally, there is the issue of the contextualization of indigenous knowledge. It does not exist separate from the society in which it is found. It is very much embedded in everyday practice and reflects the economic, social, cultural and political characteristics of that village, society, and so on. This is particularly awkward for development because it makes the deployment of indigenous knowledge difficult over different geographic spaces. This highlights one of the key differences between indigenous knowledge and Western science. Whereas the former is deeply embedded within its context, the latter is separated, almost disembodied from its context, and is, therefore, presumably much more universally applicable. This line of reasoning leads inexorably to the conclusion that indigenous knowledge cannot be developed successfully into a development tool, because it has little relevance or applicability outside its immediate area. There is much still to be done and understood before indigenous knowledge becomes an important element of the development armoury.

GUIDE TO FURTHER READING

Briggs, J. (2005) 'The use of indigenous knowledge in development: Problems and challenges', *Progress in Development Studies*, 5: 99–114.

Ellen, R., Parkes, P. and Bicker, A. (eds) (2000) *Indigenous Environmental Knowledge and its Transformations: Critical Anthropological Perspectives*, Amsterdam: Harwood Academic Publishers.

Leach, M. and Mearns, R. (eds) (1996) *The Lie of the Land: Challenging Received Wisdom on the African Environment*, London: International African Institute.

Okali, C., Sumberg, J. and Farrington, J. (1994) *Farmer Participatory Research: Rhetoric and Reality*, London: Intermediate Technology Publications/Overseas Development Institute.

Pottier, J., Bicker, A. and Sillitoe, P. (eds) (2003) *Negotiating Local Knowledge: Power and Identity in Development*, London: Pluto Press.

Reij, C., Scoones, I. and Toulmin, C. (eds) (1996) *Sustaining the Soil: Indigenous Soil and Water Conservation in Africa*, London: Earthscan.

REFERENCES

Agrawal, A. (1995) 'Dismantling the divide between indigenous and scientific knowledge', *Development and Change*, 26: 413–39.

Allan, W. (1965) *The African Husbandman*, London: Oliver and Boyd.

Briggs, J. (2005) 'The use of indigenous knowledge in development: Problems and challenges', *Progress in Development Studies*, 5: 99–114.

Briggs, J. and Sharp, J. (2004) 'Indigenous knowledges and development: A postcolonial caution', *Third World Quarterly*, 25: 661–76.

Briggs, J., Sharp, J., Hamed, N. and Yacoub, H. (2003) 'Changing women's roles, changing environmental knowledges: Evidence from Upper Egypt', *Geographical Journal*, 169: 313–25.

Brokensha, D., Warren, D. and Werner, O. (eds) (1980) *Indigenous Knowledge Systems and Development*, New York: University Press of America.

Cleaver, F. (1999) 'Paradoxes of participation: Questioning participatory approaches to development', *Journal of International Development*, 11: 597–612.

Escobar, A. (1995) *Encountering Development: The Making and Unmaking of the Third World*, Princeton, NJ: Princeton University Press.

Howes, M. (1979) 'The use of indigenous technical knowledge in development', *IDS Bulletin*, 10: 12–23.

Maddox, G., Giblin, J. and Kimambo, I. (eds) (1996) *Custodians of the Land: Ecology and Culture in the History of Tanzania*, London: James Currey.

Okali, C., Sumberg, J. and Farrington, J. (1994) *Farmer Participatory Research: Rhetoric and Reality*, London: Intermediate Technology Publications/Overseas Development Institute.

Ostberg, W. (1995) *Land is Coming Up: The Burunge of Central Tanzania and their Environments*, Stockholm: Stockholm Studies in Anthropology.

Pretty, J.N. (1994) 'Alternative systems of enquiry for a sustainable agriculture', *IDS Bulletin*, 25: 37–48.

Reij, C., Scoones, I. and Toulmin, C. (eds) (1996) *Sustaining the Soil: Indigenous Soil and Water Conservation in Africa*, London: Earthscan.

Richards, P. (1985) *Indigenous Agricultural Revolution: Ecology and Food Production in West Africa*, London: Hutchinson.

World Bank (1998) *Indigenous Knowledge for Development: A Framework for Development*, Knowledge and Learning Center, Africa Region, World Bank (available at http://www.worldbank.org/afr/ik/ikrept.pdf).

2.10 Agropolitan and bottom-up development

Michael J.G. Parnwell

One of the greatest development challenges since the mid-twentieth century has been to find effective means of confronting *uneven development*. Although a perfectly even development may be found only in utopian visions of the world, it is generally the case that most serious development problems tend to be associated with the downside of uneven development (e.g. peripherality, marginality, exclusion and powerlessness). Accordingly, ever since Dudley Seers' (1969) influential reinterpretation of the meaning of 'development', in which inequality (as well as poverty and unemployment) should decline for development to occur, scholars and practitioners have paid increasing attention to distributional criteria (spatial, economic, social) in the theory and praxis of development.

There is a strong body of thought which points to alternative forms of development being necessary if inequality is to be confronted seriously. Uneven development is claimed, in part, to be a by-product of an orthodox capitalist development process which places emphasis on rapid and efficient economic growth, privileges the industrial sector and urban areas, and tends to support the first foremost. Left behind in this process are a host of areas, sectors and social groups which possess neither the means nor the power to keep up with the pace of progress and change. A series of binary descriptors of the *phenomenon* of uneven development has entered common usage, such as core and periphery, rich and poor, mainstream and marginal, dynamic and backward, powerful and powerless. Analysts point also to the *process* of uneven development, with the nature of relationships across these (albeit artificially created) binaries tending disproportionately to serve the interests of the advanced, and work against the neglected or excluded. Given such a situation, the prospects for a reduction in inequality within orthodox capitalist development would appear to be quite weak.

Alternative models of development have tended to opt for the antithesis of the orthodox approach. Thus an urban and industrial bias is replaced with an emphasis on the rural and the agricultural; the top-down directionality and centralized character of development policy is challenged by decentralized, devolved and bottom-up initiatives; capitalism is superseded by socialist ideals; small-scale and particularistic development is seen as preferable to large-scale and universalistic approaches, and so on. In essence, we are presented with another binary, between the orthodox and the alternative. One danger of this, as we shall see below, is that the very real gains from orthodox development are seriously downplayed in favour of sometimes idealistic and neo-populist alternative visions of the future.

Initial efforts to confront the spatial manifestations of uneven development centred on 'growth centre' strategies, and drew heavily on the relatively successful Western European experiment with 'growth poles'. The aim was to facilitate economic development in peripheral regions of the developing world (and at the same time ease some of the pressures of over-rapid metropolitan growth) by encouraging firms to locate in or relocate to designated growth centres. The strategy manifestly failed to achieve a significant reversal in the process of uneven development – indeed, some analysts claim that it may have worsened the situation by intensifying the 'trickle-up' process wherein the resources and resourcefulness of the periphery became sequestered by the core. This 'alternative' strategy was, in reality, no such thing: it was simply a scaled-down version of the orthodox model, with capitalism, cities, industries, growth and economic efficiency at its heart. Little wonder, then, that its outcome was little different from that of its orthodox precursors. Something more radical was clearly needed (Stöhr and Fraser Taylor 1981).

Agropolitan development formed part of the radical critique of development, and centred on the premise (elaborated above) that the functional integration of peripheral and marginal areas into national and supranational systems in a weak and dependent manner contributes fundamentally to their relative economic backwardness. To overcome this, the local must be privileged over the national. By selectively closing localities to external domination and competition, it was argued that a self-reliant form of development may ensue which could deliver basic needs, social equality and a solid foundation for future growth and progress. The strategy centred around seemingly contradictory concepts such as 'rural urbanization' and 'rural industrialization', with absolute priority being given to agriculture and small-scale artisanal activities, rural settlement, labour-intensive activities and appropriate technology, local democracy and popular participation in the decision-making process. It was strongly based on socialist principles of access to the means of production (e.g. collective ownership of land) and to the locus of power, and drew on what the principal architect of the concept, John Friedmann, called 'collective consciousness' (Friedmann and Douglass 1978).

The essential building block of the agropolitan approach was the 'agropolitan district' – a territorial unit with a population of 40,000–60,000 people, which was small enough to be self-contained, self-reliant and conducive to face-to-face contact in the process of development, but large enough to bestow certain economies in the provision of essential services, infrastructure, and both agricultural and industrial production. In line with basic democratic principles, the community itself would determine the allocation of productive resources and the utilization of any generated surplus. Human needs were to be placed first and foremost, and, where necessary, ahead of economic growth per se. The aim was not to create isolated 'mini republics', but instead to afford localities the opportunity to 'get the basics right' and be protected from external competition during their embryonic stage before (if at all) venturing back into the wider competitive world. Large-scale heavy industry was to be set aside in 'enclaves' with which the agropolitan districts would be functionally integrated but fundamentally protected. The *ujamaa* villagization programme in Tanzania, introduced in the late 1960s, provides the closest (not altogether successful) working example of agropolitan development in practice (Lea and Chaudhri 1983).

This ideal world model was not without its shortcomings. Resource endowments and development potential are not evenly distributed to start with, and it was accepted that some agropolitan districts would inevitably be more successful than others, the latter perhaps struggling to satisfy even a minimum acceptable level of human needs. Strong state intervention was thus required in order to influence the allocation of resources and support according to need rather than potential, and to restrict migration between agropolitan districts. However, the required controlling hand of the state ran contrary to one of the fundamental principles of agropolitan development: namely the devolution of political power and control to the communities themselves. State-initiated bottom-up development remains an oxymoron.

Other criticisms levelled at this radical model of alternative development include its highly idealistic, neo-populist, Eurocentric, even utopian nature. The romantic visions of egalitarian and corporate rural communities of the past, which were to be recreated through agropolitan development – a form of 'back to the future' – often had little foundation in reality. The notion that local power holders would readily and altruistically cede power and influence in the interests of the wider community was also somewhat naive. The sacrificing of orthodox development (narrowly defined as modernization and economic growth) in the interests of 'distributive justice', as determined by external visionaries, also sometimes ran counter to the aspirations of the communities themselves, and may well have led to everyone becoming equally poor. Analysts have also criticized the overemphasis on the spatial dimension in the agropolitan model, and the consequent downplaying of class, gender, ethnicity, ecology and history, and the important role of human agency. John Friedmann has countered the criticism of agropolitan development as a utopian concept by suggesting that the world will never change unless there is a vision to provide guidance for future action.

The notion of *bottom-up development* goes a stage further than the agropolitan model by fundamentally challenging the directionality of development decision making. It is argued that large-scale, universal, government-driven national programmes of (especially rural) development frequently fail to meet the particular needs and wants of local communities, and are only rarely tailored to local conditions and contexts. Centralized development decision making, often involving city-based 'experts', is generally too detached from local contextual realities. It is frequently encumbered by a 'planning arrogance', where technocrats think they know best what is in the interests of people at the grass-roots level. State-driven development initiatives may also reflect the prevailing orthodox development paradigm, and may be strongly influenced by misconceptions and stereotypes of life in the countryside. Their paternalistic nature engenders a culture of dependence in local communities, stifling initiative, innovation and self-reliance. Finally, the top-down channelling of commands and support fails to provide a mechanism for evaluating the effectiveness of development initiatives, and for ascertaining to what extent they match local people's needs, expectations and aspirations. Local people are thus seen as passive recipients of development, who are powerless to control their own destinies.

What is required is another antithetical development which is localized and contextually rooted, small in scale, flexible, culturally sensitive, democratic and participatory, and which centres on the empowerment of the poor. Bottom-up development is thus centred on, and emerges from, the communities themselves. Conscientization enables the poor to understand the root causes of their problems, and to design appropriate solutions. The decision-making role of the community yields a greater sense of ownership and identity with the process of development, and people are more likely to contribute the enthusiasm, commitment and endeavour that it requires to succeed. Examples of bottom-up/grass-roots development activities include the Grameen Bank, which was established in 1976 to provide much-needed credit facilities to the rural poor in Bangladesh; the Appropriate Technology Association in Thailand, which sought to promote agro-ecology in rural areas; various rural industrialization schemes, which have attempted to strengthen the non-farm sector and thus provide alternatives to outmigration; small-scale irrigation schemes; AIDS/HIV support; housing associations; ethnic and human rights organizations; environmental movements, and so on (see Holloway 1989; ODI, Non-Governmental Organizations Series 1993).

Bottom-up development has gained in momentum and prominence since the 1970s, to the extent that it now challenges orthodox approaches as the mainstream paradigm in many parts of the developing world. Central to the role and function of bottom-up development has been the explosive growth of *non-governmental organizations* (NGOs). NGOs initially took the shape of charitable, often religious bodies, from the countries of the North, targeted at particular development problems, such as destitution, persecution, hunger, homelessness and disaster. Some were diametrically opposed to governments and state institutions, most particularly in authoritarian and dictatorial regimes, and were often mirrored by, or linked to, locally based political movements. Through the 1980s, political space started to open up for Southern NGOs to form and flourish. Initially these relied on alliances with, and support from, the organizations of the North, including the international development agencies, but the NGOs of the South have come to predominate, and in some instances are so numerous, diverse and effective that they are challenging the state's historical prominence and legitimacy. Meanwhile, many governments have started to relax their initial suspicion of, and antagonism towards, the non-governmental movement, and increasingly partnerships are being forged between the state and certain grass-roots organizations.

NGOs have many theoretical advantages over the cumbersome and amorphous institutions of the state in terms of delivering development at the grass-roots level. They are seen to be more flexible, adaptable and nimble, have shallower decision-making hierarchies and shorter lines of communication, are largely autonomous, and are typically less costly to run because of a high contribution of voluntary inputs into their activities. Their philosophy centres around altruism, democracy, popular participation (learning together rather than the simple transfer of knowledge), empowerment, conscientization, contextual groundedness, responsiveness rather than prescriptiveness, and the promotion of self-reliance.

There are also several weaknesses which again serve to undermine the ideal of bottom-up development when set in real-world situations. Whatever the theoretical advantages of grass-roots organizations, as embodied in their philosophical approach, critics have claimed that they simply represent a new form of top-down, paternalistic development occurring further down the development hierarchy. Participation emerges more prominently in words than in tokenistic deeds, and is often coerced rather than natural. There is often a considerable level of rivalry within the non-governmental sector, as organizations vie for funds, prestige and space, and this may draw energy and commitment away from the underlying mission. Pre-existing structures, such as in the distribution of political power, economic and asset wealth or in gender relations, are very difficult to wish away by the best intentions of grass-roots activists, and indeed may become reinforced by their activities. Meanwhile, recognizing the dynamism and potential power of the bottom-up movement, governments have attempted to restyle themselves as grass-roots aware, liberally incorporating the rhetoric of participation and self-reliance in their revamped policy statements. However, we return again to the fundamental contradiction of state-driven bottom-up development, not least when developing countries, and the world economy into which they are increasingly being incorporated, are still driven by a narrow development orthodoxy. There is little doubt that the bottom-up philosophy is beginning to have a profound effect on development praxis, but it is unrealistic to suggest that 'alternative development' is set to become the mainstream paradigm. A pragmatic articulation of orthodox and alternative development, with strengthening linkages between the governmental and non-governmental sectors, would appear to be the most realistic way forward.

GUIDE TO FURTHER READING AND REFERENCES

The following few items should prove of interest to readers wanting to go further.

Friedmann, J. and Douglass, M. (1978) 'Agropolitan development: Towards a new strategy for regional planning in Asia', in F.C. Lo and K. Salih (eds) *Growth Pole Strategy and Regional Development Policy*, Oxford: Pergamon Press, pp. 163–92.

Holloway, R. (ed.) (1989) *Doing Development: Governments, NGOs and the Rural Poor in Asia*, London: Earthscan.

Lea, D.A.M. and Chaudhri, D.P. (1983) *Rural Development and the State*, London: Methuen.

ODI, Non-Governmental Organizations Series (1993) J. Farringdon and D.J. Lewis (eds) *Non-Governmental Organizations and the State in Asia: Rethinking Roles in Sustainable Agricultural Development*; A. Bebbington and G. Thiele (eds) *Non-Governmental Organizations and the State in Latin America: Rethinking Roles in Sustainable Agricultural Development*; K. Wellard and J.G. Copestake (eds) *Non-Governmental Organizations and the State in Africa: Rethinking Roles in Sustainable Agricultural Development*, London: Routledge.

Seers, D. (1969) 'The meaning of development', *International Development Review*, 11(4): 2–6.

Stöhr, W.B. and Fraser Taylor, D.R. (eds) (1981) *Development from Above or Below? The Dialectics of Regional Planning in Developing Countries*, Chichester: John Wiley.

2.11 Community participation in development

Vandana Desai

Introduction

Community participation (CP) is an indispensable part of many development programmes and projects encouraged by national governments, the World Bank, UN agencies and non-governmental organizations (NGOs). Despite the differing perspectives of these various agencies, all agree that CP should be encouraged. Actions by the poor to influence decision making through direct and informal means have emerged as an alternative way by which they can gain access to decision-making processes and to resources, and thereby improve their well-being.

This chapter aims to analyse the nature and role of the participants in CP. The most critical issue is whether or not CP can achieve real improvements in well-being and social conditions. A major gulf exists between reality and the way in which community participation is supposed to operate, particularly in light of the resource cutbacks experienced by most developing countries as they cope with debt and structural adjustment policies.

There are various reasons why CP is deemed desirable from the point of view of development agencies and governments. These include the following.

- CP has become an important ingredient in poverty reduction strategies espoused by governments, in the context of decentralization policies adopted in the post-structural adjustment programmes of the 1990s, and through the good governance policies encouraged by multilateral aid agencies such as the World Bank.
- People have a right to participate in decision making which directly affects their living conditions.
- Social development can be promoted by increasing local self-reliance. Since people themselves know best what they need, what they want, what is most suitable for their needs and what they can afford, only close cooperation between project implementers and the community can lead to project effectiveness and sustainability. This gives communities a sense of ownership over their projects and maintains mobilization.
- It also demonstrates that people can form partnerships with governments, development agencies, private-sector organizations and NGOs to bring about development and poverty reduction in developing countries.
- It enhances accountability and transparency in developmental projects at the grass roots (Brett 2003).

Definition of community participation

Participation is defined in a United Nations report (1979: 225) as 'sharing by people in the benefits of development, active contribution by people to development and involvement of people in decision making at all levels of society'. Clearly, much more information is needed if we are to ascertain who participates, what participation entails and how it is to be promoted.

The arguments on participation seem to converge on the relationship between three key concepts in CP, namely taking part, influence and power. Moreover, any participation process seems to have two components, irrespective of the context, situation or objective: a decision-making process and an action process to realize the objective decided on. When participants are unequal in their endowments, participation means the less endowed taking part and influencing the decision-making process in their favour. Stiefel (1981: 1–2) defines participation in terms of 'organised efforts to increase control over resources and regulative institutions in given social situations on the part of the groups and movements hitherto excluded from such decision making processes'.

People with different perspectives assume very different virtues of CP. Consequently, opinions on who should participate, in what and how, vary widely between and among development agencies and residents (Parfitt 2004). Literature from non-governmental sources tends to emphasize the need for 'true' participation (i.e. a bottom-up approach, grass-roots development). CP can also be broken down into state-initiated and grass-roots-initiated.

The shift in participation, however, is towards the empowerment of the less powerful and poverty reduction (Cornwall and Brock 2005; Mohan and Hickey 2000). In developing countries, resources for development have always been very scarce, but pressures for their allocation from various interested groups have increased progressively. The poor, since they have neither socio-economic nor political power, do not generally gain access to the decision-making processes and hence are unable to influence them. Therefore, the poor have not benefited from economic growth, but in fact have become worse off. Oakley and Marsden (1984: 88) state in this regard: 'meaningful participation is concerned with achieving power: that is the power to influence the decisions that affect one's livelihood'.

Community organizations and community leaders

The purpose of community organizations (COs) is to increase unity and solidarity. Mobilization is a key input in the process of empowerment. The collective nature of the community could increase poor people's bargaining power, including their input into the local decision-making process. The question that arises is, to what extent do COs succeed in their demand making, and to what degree are COs linked to the wider partisan-political system? Are COs sustainable organizations?

Considerable attention is given to the role of COs in articulating demands and mobilizing resources. Mobilization is intended for social capital formation and to relieve scarce government resources. Many COs are issue based. There is usually an interplay of many forces – local, linguistic, regional and even religious – in the functioning of COs. In all these set-ups, political forces may creep in. Generally, COs defend rights and win some concessions, and they politicize some individuals, especially community leaders. The existence of an organization does not guarantee that it represents the entire community, however. Men, for example, tend to be over-represented in such organizations, but there can also be exclusively women's groups within communities (Parpart 2000).

Those high up in social and economic stratification hierarchies possess greater resources and motivation, and therefore are more likely to participate in and take greater advantage of the opportunities than those lower in the hierarchy of socio-economic stratification. The only people who can afford to be active in COs are perhaps the richer among the poor: businessmen, shopkeepers and landlords. Consequently, community leaders are often not representative of the population, but rather represent particular interest groups (Desai 1995).

Community leadership is an important ingredient in the level and form of CP, and in successful demand making. Some key issues in the nature of leadership need to be analysed. The first relates to the sources of leaders' power within each community. Do leaders maintain power through force, through charisma and popularity in the community, or because they have influential friends outside the community or are linked to a political party apparatus? Do patterns of leadership vary with the circumstances of the settlement? Do strong authoritarian leaders emerge at times of crisis and for the achievement of major services? Over what time period do they lead the community?

Role of the state in community participation

Few systematic attempts have been made to examine the relationship between the state and community initiatives. This is partly because CP theorists are implacably opposed to the idea that the state can contribute effectively to the promotion of CP. State responses to CP in development have often been haphazard and poorly formulated, and there are substantial variations in the extent to which these ideals have been applied in different countries. They have also enjoyed greater or lesser popularity, depending on the preferences of senior administrators, politicians and planners.

A number of observers have argued that CP in urban development invariably results in a concerted effort by the state to subvert and manipulate local people. Gilbert and Ward (1984: 239) argue on the basis of the study of three Latin American cities (Bogotá, Mexico City and Valencia) that the state effectively uses the mechanisms of CP as a means of social control. They found that, in each of the three cities, the state had been successful in deflecting opposition by making concessions, by providing services, by co-opting leaders or, in the last resort, through repression. Such tactics can also make the state stronger (Williams 2004).

For the role of the state/government to become one of facilitator, supporter, interpreter and constructive critic within CP, it needs to recognize that it will have to implement substantial structural changes in its administration, bureaucracy and operational style. This is reflected in the lack of suitable personnel (e.g. social workers and community organizers) and the working approaches of professional staff who have been trained in conventional techniques which involve little, if any, CP, and who have a limited understanding of how to incorporate CP in their planning and their role in the day-to-day functioning of participatory projects. Usually the poor are expected to participate actively in project implementation and maintenance, but are often left out of the design stage – obviously the most critical phase from the point of view of ensuring that programmes meet 'real' needs. Thus the state/government must restructure itself (and its field branches) to create a more responsive, public service-oriented administration, which involves beneficiaries more directly, and it must be held accountable.

The fact that COs are the common level of social organization, above that of the household, means that inevitably they act as a magnet for supralocal political parties, which seek to gain an advantage by working through them. However, the issue is whether communities are likely to enhance their chances of securing more resources from outside through engaging in the use of party political linkages or NGOs.

There are two important mechanisms used by governments to gain support from these COs and leaders. These are co-optation and clientelism. Co-optation plays a key role in maintaining a small elite in power, and its manifestations vary widely. Clientelism takes different forms, but it has a long tradition in many societies, with clients expected to offer consistent political loyalty for their part.

Co-optation may occur when community leaders believe, often mistakenly, that formal affiliation will further the interests of those whom they represent, by providing better access to the agencies distributing resources. Political parties and government departments may be eager to co-opt leaders as a means of extending their influence over local constituencies. The community may lose its autonomy and become subject to the orthodoxy of the co-opting body. In some cases, co-optation to the governing party may well reduce the chances of successful demand making. It may also provide an important foothold for successful negotiation where political support is exchanged for services to the community.

The other form of support is based on clientelism. A patron–client relationship is an enduring dyadic bond, based on informally arranged personal exchanges of resources between actors of unequal status. In the case of the poor communities, the leader, or 'broker', maintains a personal relationship with the politicians or administrators, who control limited resources required by the community or members of the community. This is the principal form of linkage between aspirant politicians and high-ranking government officials, and the poor. The leader or patron benefits in so far as he is able to demand the loyalty of those dependent on him and to mobilize that loyalty on behalf of his superiors. Clients benefit as long as they gain access to influential people who may intercede on their behalf and increase the chances of a successful outcome to their demand making. It must be said that *all* political systems depend on a degree of co-optation and clientelism. The crucial irony is that 'participation by representation' is a contradiction in terms, because the represented perceive of their representatives as unique and distinct from themselves.

The role of NGOs in community participation

Through NGOs, existing community organizations can be guided to exert pressure on the government in order to encompass joint decision making. It is argued that NGOs provide effective opportunities for the implementation of CP ideals, and that these organizations are more likely to promote authentic forms of participation than the state. While it is true that NGOs have played a major role in the promotion of CP, it cannot be claimed that their involvement has been faultless.

Many NGOs, especially the larger ones, function bureaucratically and use formal procedural rules to carry out their tasks. Non-government organizations are prone to ossification, particularly if they are dominated and controlled by charismatic leaders who are unresponsive to new ideas and view innovation as a threat to their authority. Middle-class individuals whose views are liberal and paternalistic, rather than radically egalitarian, run many NGOs. The assumption that they are usually politically progressive and enhance participation needs to be questioned.

Conclusion

Although the idea of CP is exceedingly popular in development today, it raises difficult issues. Most governments appear to have a limited view of participation; there is a lack of political will to distribute power and resources. Popular initiatives towards participation are often co-opted by, and in the end serve, the interests of the high-income groups, rather than those of the poor.

The basic problem is that many of the ideologists of participation want politics without politics. *All* organizations larger than a handful of people necessarily and inevitably involve:

- a degree of delegated power to leaders (even if leaders are replaceable democratically) – the representation of interests is always indirect;
- the organization itself having interests different from the perceived interests of some/all of its members.

Participation is often treated as if it could be implemented in a vacuum, with all actors agreeing on its precise meaning and goals. Any discussion of participation is a discussion of politics and the exercise of power. CP has been treated as a technical issue, or as a social project component. Too often it is forgotten that CP as 'citizens' control' or 'people's power' is little short of very significant social and political change.

While the arguments covered here may be depressing, it would be wrong to conclude that nothing can be achieved through CP. Participatory programmes, whether sponsored by the state or the NGO sector, have brought tangible benefits to people in many parts of the world, but have also experienced a great many difficulties that belie the idealism of their advocates. These conclusions suggest that the limits of participation need to be recognized and accommodated. As governments move away from the role of provider to that of facilitator, new management skills need to be developed and more flexible planning tools devised to encourage community participation.

GUIDE TO FURTHER READING AND REFERENCES

Brett, T. (2003) 'Participation and accountability in development management', *Journal of Development Studies*, 40(2): 1–29.

Cooke, B. and Kothari, U. (eds) (2001) *Participation: The Tyranny?* London and New York: Zed Books.

Cornwall, A. and Brock, K. (2005) 'What do buzzwords do for development policy? A critical look at "participation", "empowerment" and "poverty reduction"', *Third World Quarterly*, 26(7): 1043–60.

Desai, V. (1995) *Community Participation and Slum Housing: A Study of Bombay*, New Delhi, London and Thousand Oaks, CA: Sage Publications.

Gilbert, A. and Ward, P. (1984) 'Community action by the urban poor: Democratic involvement, community self-help or a means of social control?', *World Development*, 12: 8–20.

Hickey, S. and Mohan, G. (eds) (2004) *Participation: From Tyranny to Transformation? Exploring New Approaches to Participation in Development*, London: Zed Books.

Mohan, G. and Hickey, S. (2000) 'Participatory development and empowerment: The danger of localism', *Third World Quarterly*, 21(2): 247–68.

Oakley, P. and Marsden, D. (1984) *Approaches to Participation in Rural Development*, Geneva: International Labour Office.

Parfitt, T. (2004) 'The ambiguity of participation: A qualified defence of participatory development', *Third World Quarterly*, 25(3): 537–56.

Parpart, J. (2000) 'Rethinking participation, empowerment, and development from a gender perspective', in J. Freeman (ed.) *Transforming Development: Foreign Aid for a Changing World*, Toronto: University of Toronto Press, pp. 222–34.

Stiefel, M. (1981) 'Editorial', in *Dialogue About Participation*, 1, Geneva: United Nations Research Institute for Social Development.

United Nations (1979) *1978 Report on the World Social Situation*, New York: United Nations.

White, S. (2000) 'Depoliticising development: The uses and abuses of participation', in D. Eade (ed.) *Development, NGOs, and Civil Society*, Oxford: Oxfam. Also in *Development in Practice* (1996), 6(1).

Williams, G. (2004) 'Evaluating participatory development: Tyranny, power and (re)politicisation', *Third World Quarterly*, 25(3): 557–78.

2.12 Postmodernism and development

David Simon

Postmodernism: Panacea, placebo or perversity?

Postmodernism became a major social scientific theoretical paradigm during the 1990s, although its prominence has now waned somewhat. In development studies it gained prominence as one of the routes for transcending the so-called theoretical 'impasse' that emerged in the mid- to late 1980s. However, the concept assumed diverse meanings, a factor contributing substantially to the often heated but unenlightening debates over its usefulness in the context of development.

The alliterative heading to this section aptly synthesizes the divergent positions on the relevance of postmodernism to development studies. Few theoretical propositions have elicited such strongly polarized views: some have embraced it enthusiastically, while others argue strongly that it is irrelevant and/or pernicious. Yet, many academics and practitioners profess no interest in, or understanding of, the issues, while the raft of new development textbooks appearing since the late 1990s have devoted surprisingly little attention to postmodernism (Simon 1999: 38–43). Some make no mention of postmodernist and other 'post-' or 'antidevelopmentalist' approaches at all, while others include only a few pages or a single chapter, almost as an afterthought. Very few give fuller coverage, with the result that most current students continue to have little exposure to these debates.

Postmodernism first emerged in art, architecture and literature in the mid-1970s, where it found expression as a rejection of the then dominant modernist paradigm. The concepts of ideals, absolutes, order and harmonization, which had given rise to increasing alienation of the individual, were challenged by architects such as Charles Jencks and Vincent Scully. The objective became a celebration of diverse forms and sharp contrasts, in order to rupture conventional expectations. This is generally achieved through the juxtaposition of radically different styles in street facades, something that was, and remains, anathema to most urban planners and local authority planning codes; or the literal turning inside out of a building, in terms of which its previously hidden infrastructure is boldly displayed as an art form. Perhaps the best-known examples of this style are the Pompidou Exhibition Centre in Paris and the Lloyd's Building in the City of London, although the positioning of glass-walled lifts in the atria of office blocks and shopping malls for dramatic panoramic effect has now become a common worldwide architectural feature.

In literature, Latin American writers like Gabriel García Márquez and Carlos Fuentes pioneered a literary style that broke with the established tradition of a single, chronological flow to novels, and replaced it with multiple, cross-cutting strands, flashbacks, forward leaps and previews in structurally much more complex forms.

In the social sciences, postmodernism gained a foothold as part of the ferment in discourse that included post-structuralist rejection of modernist meta-theories and grand narratives of a single mode of explanation or 'truth'. Other elements of this discursive revolution were critical social theory; concern with the deconstruction of ideology and official discourses; a growing cynicism about established orders and vested power; concern at increasing alienation within Northern societies and, partly as a result, the so-called 'cultural turn', in terms of which renewed attention has been paid to the explanatory value of cultural factors, rather than the political and economic. The work of Michel Foucault, Henri Lefebvre, Jacques Derrida and Jean Baudrillard looms large in the foundations of postmodernism. Among the most widely reputed social scientific accounts of postmodernism are those of Frederic Jameson (1984), Jean-François Lyotard (1984), David Harvey (1989) and Ed Soja (1991). Most situate it explicitly within the (cultural) logic of late capitalism, as part of the search for profit accumulation in a context of globalized production and consumption. As such, they are critical and see it as having limited social explanatory value, serving mainly to justify conspicuous self-expression, rather than representing a profound new paradigm.

Significantly, several leading advocates of postmodernism and postcolonialism in cultural studies, sociology and allied disciplines, including Homi Bhabha, Trin Minha, Gyatri Spivak and the late Edward Said, hail from the global South, even though generally now working in Northern universities. Among geographers, sociologists and development specialists, and especially those working in Latin America, some of the most trenchant critics of conventional development espoused postmodernism as the way forward during the 1990s – in particular, Santiago Colás, Arturo Escobar, Gustavo Esteva and David Slater. However, the book that established Escobar's (1995) anti-development reputation is principally a critique of 'the development project', offering little insight into a revisioned future beyond an invocation of new social movements. By contrast, Colás (1994) interprets postmodern developments in different spheres of Argentinian society, while

Esteva and Prakash (1998) provide one of the very few detailed expositions of regional and local-level postmodernism in practice as social action. Slater (1992, 1997) has taken forward geopolitical and development debates across the North–South divide. Other authors have been cautious about the relevance of postmodernism relative to postcolonialism. Escobar's more recent work has moved substantially beyond antidevelopment, forming part of the increasing consensus around the need for alternative approaches, or post-development.

Nevertheless, most social scientists working in, or concerned with, poor regions of the world have tended to ignore postmodernism or to dismiss it as an irrelevance. The latter sentiment is based on one or both of two main considerations.

1 Postmodernism literally means 'after the modern'; however, in the Global South, the majority of people are still poor and struggling to meet basic needs and enjoy the fruits of modernization so powerfully held up to them as the outcome of development. In such situations, modernity has yet to be widely achieved, so that which follows on from the modern can have little relevance (e.g. King 1995).
2 Postmodernism is yet another fashionable Northern paradigm, which finds expression mainly in aesthetic/architectural terms, and as playful, leisured heterodoxes and new forms of consumption centred on individualism which can best be described as self-indulgence by the well-off. Such preoccupations are seen as irrelevant to the Global South, if not actually harmful in terms of distracting attention from survival and 'development' agendas and the macro-processes which impact on them. Moreover, as with many other academic fashions, it will soon pass.

These positions are understandable, but do reveal misunderstandings or confusion about the diverse meanings and applications of postmodernism which, in turn, reflect the diversity of usage

A conceptual schema

The following typology distinguishes the different connotations of postmodernism/postmodernity in order to facilitate understanding. Postmodernity describes the 'condition' or manifestation, while postmodernism is the ideology or intellectual practice. At least three broad interpretations of the postmodern can be distinguished in the vast and multidisciplinary literatures.

The chronological approach

This is the most literal interpretation, in terms of which the postmodern necessarily follows the modern. This is usually taken to apply to time periods, but could also refer to artistic and architectural styles. In practice, however, no clean break between eras can be distinguished: there was no dramatic event to act as signifier, and there has been no agreement on the basis of transition. At best, one might be able to conceptualize a transitional phase of some years' duration, the precise timing and length of which reflects the sphere of interest or discipline(s) involved.

In terms of globalization and mass consumption, for instance, the traditional mass-market air package holiday would be modern, whereas the more differentiated and personalized small-group luxury tour, complete with ecotourist credentials and/or sanitized versions of conflictual local histories in distant countries for the benefit of international tourists, might be conceived of as postmodern.

The aesthetic approach

The second basic understanding of postmodernism is as a form of expression in the creative and aesthetic disciplines like art, architecture and literature. This perspective reflects the considerations

– and is exemplified by the authors and buildings – cited in the introduction to this chapter. Inevitably, perhaps, most such attention has been centred on elite and middle-class consumption, especially in terms of leisure activities, but also, increasingly, in the working environment and public spaces. Terms most frequently associated with this movement include pastiche, melange, playfulness, commodity-signs, imaginaries and spectacles. Theme parks, pleasure domes and other purpose-built leisure complexes which offer decontextualized time–space representations of various places and experiences (Featherstone 1995; Watson and Gibson 1995), often in sanitized form, are characteristic of this approach, in much the same way as great exhibitions of global exploration, scientific discoveries and industrial achievements were hallmarks of Victorian modernity.

Postmodernism as intellectual practice

The approach of postmodernism as *problematique* or intellectual practice is the most relevant from the perspective of development studies. Here, the postmodern supposedly represents fundamentally different ways of seeing, knowing and representing the world. The modern approach, rooted in Enlightenment thinking about rationality, is concerned with a search for universal truths, linked to positivist scientific methodology and neoclassical economics. Proponents of different theories held them to be superior to all their competitors, to have global relevance even if based on limited empirical evidence from specific contexts, and ultimately to represent *the* truth. Such universalizing, globalizing approaches are often referred to as meta-narratives.

In theory, at least, postmodern practice rejects such singular explanations in favour of multiple, divergent and overlapping interpretations and views. Simplicity should give way to complexity and pluralism, in terms of which these different accounts are all accorded legitimacy. The privileging of official and formal discourses should be replaced by approaches lending credence to both the official and unofficial, formal and informal, dominant and subordinate, central and marginal groups, and to their discourses and agendas. Top-down development, so closely associated with official national and international agendas of modernization, has been discredited over a long period; instead, bottom-up approaches, or some hybrid of the two, should be encouraged.

As such, postmodernism can become a fruitful approach for addressing the conflictual and divergent agendas of social groups, be it in relation to access to productive resources and/or the bases for accumulating social power, mediating the impacts of large development schemes, evolving complementary medical services that harness the most appropriate elements from both Western and indigenous systems, or addressing long-standing conflicts between statutory and customary legal systems (Esteva and Prakash 1998; Simon 1998, 1999). Empowerment of the poor and powerless should be the objective.

Such discourses have much in common with earlier, liberal pluralism, basic needs and grassroots development paradigms, although the emphasis on coexistence and multiple modes of explanation is different. Equally, there are considerable areas of overlap with some strands of post-colonialism), which is centrally concerned with the cultural politics and identities of previously subordinated groups.

Extreme postmodernism can become almost indistinguishable from anarchism, in that all forms of social or collective action become impossible, due to the inability to agree – or conceive of agreeing – on any shared rationality or even basic rules of what is, and is not, acceptable behaviour. Extreme relativism means that everyone's views are equally valid; without some decision-making rules, any social action not gaining unanimity or consensus becomes impossible.

For this reason, and because of the emphasis by some authors on playful, leisured self-fulfilment, postmodernism is sometimes regarded, with justification, as a conservative ideology embedded within late capitalism – another reason for its rejection by many critics. Ley (2003) even wrote its perhaps premature epitaph because of its perceived fad status, and because of problems operationalizing it in meaningful distinction from the modern, a term widely used to denote recent or present-day. Postmodernism may indeed have lost much of its social scientific prominence since the early 2000s, in favour of the closely related umbrella of post-colonialism, but that does not deny that it retains much of value, especially in terms of understanding contemporary social dynamics and complexities. Gabardi's (2001: xxi) articulation of 'critical postmodernism', 'not only as a product of the modern-postmodern debate, but also as a theoretical and ideological response to our current late modern/postmodern transition and a practical tool for negotiating this transition', is the most detailed and spirited recent articulation of that perspective.

Conclusion

Postmodern discourses arose within changing intellectual and geopolitical circumstances. An important problem has been the multiple uses and meanings of postmodernism, with resultant confusion and misinterpretation. Although of Northern intellectual origin, it has found favour among some leading artistic and intellectual voices, who have contributed greatly to its refinement and prominence. However, it is also true that many Northern writers linking postmodernism to globalization and other politico-economic changes have, either implicitly or explicitly, assumed their Northern research and arguments to have global relevance.

'Moderate' forms of postmodern intellectual practice do indeed have global relevance in the cause of problem analysis, development promotion and empowerment. This may be a radically different agenda from that of official agencies, as it lends legitimacy to different social groups and their voices rather than merely seeking a compatible mouthpiece to support external interventions in the name of 'development'. However, therein lie the prospects to transcend the shortcomings of discredited official 'rapid modernization as development' and to facilitate local communities to develop according to their own conceptions, governed by acceptable rules of conduct. Of course, such processes are not free from conflict, nor can there be room for any nostalgia for long dead traditions and heritages. What is required is an adaptation to dynamic realities.

Extreme postmodernism is unduly relativistic and permissive; it may preclude any social contract or action and should rightly be rejected.

GUIDE TO FURTHER READING

The following sources provide a useful range of perspectives, with particular reference to development studies.

Esteva, G. and Prakash, M.S. (1998) *Grassroots Postmodernism: Remaking the Soil of Cultures*, London: Zed Books. One of the few book-length treatments of postmodern practice, linking new social movements, grass-roots organizations and regionally based rebellions against inequitable and oppressive national governments in Latin America and Asia.

Harvey, D. (1989) *The Condition of Postmodernity*, Oxford: Blackwell. This remains an important reference guide to postmodernity as a function of late capitalism. Although focused on the North, it does have an implied global salience.

Pieterse, J.N. (2001) *Development Theory: Deconstructions/Reconstructions*, London: Sage. Brings together a series of the author's articles, several of which address the limitations and oversimplifications of critiques of 'the development project' as in anti-/post-development.

Simon, D. (1998) 'Rethinking (post)modernism, postcolonialism and posttraditionalism: South–North perspectives', *Environment and Planning D: Society and Space*, 16(2): 219–45. A detailed exposition of much of the ground covered in this chapter.

Slater, D. (1997) 'Spatialities of power and postmodern ethics – rethinking geopolitical encounters', *Environment and Planning D: Society and Space*, 15(1): 55–72. Develops themes of post-cold war geopolitical change and its implications across the North–South divide, including postmodern concerns for distant strangers.

Watson, S. and Gibson, K. (eds) (1995) *Postmodern Cities and Spaces*, Oxford: Blackwell. An innovative and important collection of essays, both conceptual and applied, addressing different approaches to postmodernism in a range of diverse urban contexts, both North and South.

REFERENCES

Colás, S. (1994) *Postmodernity in Latin America: The Argentine Paradigm*, Durham, NC: Duke University Press.
Escobar, A. (1995) *Encountering Development: The Making and Unmaking of the Third World*, Princeton, NJ: Princeton University Press.
Esteva, G. and Prakash, M.S. (1998) *Grassroots Postmodernism: Remaking the Soil of Cultures*, London: Zed Books.
Featherstone, M. (1995) *Undoing Culture: Globalization, Postmodernism and Identity*, London: Sage.
Gabardi, W. (2001) *Negotiating Postmodernism*, Minneapolis: Minnesota University Press.
Harvey, D. (1989) *The Condition of Postmodernity*, Oxford: Blackwell.
Jameson, F. (1984) 'Postmodernism, or the cultural logic of late capitalism', *New Left Review*, 146: 152–92.
King, A.D. (1995) 'The times and spaces of modernity (or who needs postmodernism?)', in M. Featherstone, S. Lash and R. Robertson (eds) *Global Modernities*, London: Sage.
Ley, D. (2003) 'Forgetting postmodernism? Recuperating a social history of local knowledge', *Progress in Human Geography* 27(5): 537–60.
Lyotard, J.-F. (1984) *The Postmodern Condition: A Report on Knowledge*, Minneapolis: University of Minnesota Press.
Simon, D. (1998) 'Rethinking (post)modernism, postcolonialism and posttraditionalism: South–North perspectives', *Environment and Planning D: Society and Space*, 16(2): 219–45.
Simon, D. (1999) 'Development revisited: Thinking about, practising and teaching development after the cold war', in D. Simon and A. Närman (eds) *Development as Theory and Practice: Current Perspectives on Development and Development Co-operation*, Harlow: Longman.
Slater, D. (1992) 'Theories of development and politics of the post-modern – exploring a border zone', *Development and Change*, 23(3): 283–319.
Slater, D. (1997) 'Spatialities of power and postmodern ethics – rethinking geopolitical encounters', *Environment and Planning D: Society and Space*, 15(1): 55–72.
Soja, E. (1991) *Postmodern Geographies: The Reassertion of Space in Critical Social Theory*, London: Verso.
Watson, S. and Gibson, K. (eds) (1995) *Postmodern Cities and Spaces*, Oxford: Blackwell.

2.13 Post-colonialism

Cheryl McEwan

What is post-colonialism?

Post-colonialism is a difficult and contested term, not least because it is far from clear that colonialism has been relegated to the past. Its meaning is not limited to 'after-colonialism' or 'after-independence', but refers to ways of criticizing the material and discursive legacies of colonialism (Radcliffe 1999: 84). Broadly speaking, therefore, post-colonial perspectives can be said to be *anticolonial*. They have become increasingly important across a range of disciplines since the early 1980s.

A number of core issues underpin post-colonial approaches. First, they stress the need to destabilize the dominant discourses of imperial Europe (e.g. history, philosophy, linguistics and 'development'), which are unconsciously ethnocentric, rooted in European cultures and reflective of a dominant Western world view. Postcolonial studies problematize the very ways in which the world is known, challenging the unacknowledged and unexamined assumptions at the heart of European and American disciplines that are profoundly insensitive to the meanings, values and practices of other cultures.

Second, post-colonial critiques challenge the experiences of speaking and writing by which dominant discourses come into being. For example, a term such as 'the Third World' homogenizes peoples and countries and carries other associations – economic backwardness, the failure to develop economic and political order, and connotations of a binary contest between 'us' and 'them', 'self' and 'other' – which are often inscribed in development writings. These practices of naming are not innocent. Rather they are part of the process of 'worlding' (Spivak 1990), or setting apart certain parts of the world from others. Said (1978) has shown how knowledge is a form of power and, by implication, violence; it gives authority to the possessor of knowledge. Knowledge has been, and to a large extent still is, controlled and produced in 'the West'. The power to name, represent and theorize is still located here, a fact which post-colonialism seeks to disrupt.

Third, post-colonialism invokes an explicit critique of the spatial metaphors and temporality employed in Western discourses. Whereas previous designations of the Third World signalled both spatial and temporal distance – 'out there' and 'back there' – the post-colonial perspective insists that the 'other' world is 'in here'. The Third World is integral to what 'the West' refers to as 'modernity' and 'progress'. It contributes directly to the economic wealth of Western countries through its labour and economic exploitation. In addition, the modalities and aesthetics of the Third World have partially constituted Western languages and cultures. Post-colonialism, therefore, attempts to rewrite the hegemonic accounting of time (history) and the spatial distribution of knowledge (power) that constructs the Third World.

Finally, post-colonialism attempts to recover the lost historical and contemporary voices of the marginalized, the oppressed and the dominated, through a radical reconstruction of history and knowledge production. Post-colonial theory has developed this radical edge through the works of political and literary critics such as Spivak, Said and Bhabha, who, in various ways, have sought to recover the agency and resistance of peoples subjugated by both colonialism and neocolonialism.

These core issues form the fabric of the complex field of enquiry of post-colonial studies, based in the 'historical fact' of European colonialism and the diverse material effects to which this phenomenon has given rise.

Post-colonialism and development

The possibility of producing a truly decolonized, post-colonial knowledge in development studies became a subject of considerable debate during the 1990s, culminating in new dialogue between the two approaches that continues today. In theoretical terms, post-colonialism has been greatly influenced by Marxism and post-structuralism, drawing on the political-economy approaches of the former and the cultural and linguistic analyses of the latter. The politics of post-colonialism diverge sharply from other discourses and, although it shares similarities with dependency theories, its radicalism rejects established agendas and accustomed ways of seeing. This means that post-colonialism is a powerful critique of 'development' and an increasingly important challenge to dominant ways of apprehending North–South relations.

Critiquing discourses of development

Post-colonialism challenges the very meaning of development as rooted in colonial discourse depicting the North as advanced and progressive and the South as backward, degenerate and primitive. Early post-colonial writers, such as van der Post, challenged this assumption by referring to hunter-gatherers as the first affluent peoples. Post-colonialism has prompted questions about whether such indigenous systems of equity, reciprocity and communalism are more advantageous to peoples of the South than the pursuit of capitalism, with its emphasis on individual wealth and incorporation into the global economy. The superiority of modern industrialization and techno-logical progress is increasingly questioned, creating alternative knowledges to reshape perceptions of non-Western societies and their environments.

Critics argue that to subject development to post-colonial critique is a form of intellectual fad-dism; as long as there are pressing material issues such as poverty in the world, concerns with the *language* of development are esoteric. However, language is fundamental to the way we order, understand, intervene and justify those interventions (Escobar 1995). As Crush (1995) argues, post-colonialism offers new ways of understanding what development is and does, and why it is so difficult to think beyond it. The texts of development are written in a representational language – metaphors, images, allusion, fantasy and rhetoric – the imagined worlds bearing little resemblance to the real world. Development writing often produces and reproduces misrepresentation. Post-colonialism seeks to remove negative stereotypes about people and places from such discourses. It challenges us to rethink categories such as 'Third World' and 'Third World women', and to under-stand how location, economic role, social dimensions of identity and the global political economy differentiate between groups and their opportunities for development.

As Crush suggests, the texts of development are 'avowedly strategic and tactical', promoting and justifying certain interventions, and delegitimizing and excluding others. Power relations are clearly implied in this process; certain forms of knowledge are dominant and others are excluded. The texts of development contain silences. It is important to ask who is silenced, and why. Ideas about development are not produced in a social, institutional or literary vacuum. A post-colonial approach to development literature, therefore, can say a great deal about the apparatuses of power and domination within which those texts are produced, circulated and consumed. Development discourse promotes and justifies real interventions with material consequences. It is, therefore, imperative to explore the links between the words, practices and institutional expressions of devel-opment, and between the relations of power that order the world and the words and images that represent the world. By doing so, post-colonial approaches have possibilities for effecting change.

Agency in development

Post-colonialism challenges the notion of a single path to development and demands acknowl-edgement of a diversity of perspectives and priorities. The politics of defining and satisfying needs is a crucial dimension of current development thought, to which the concept of agency is central. Who voices the development concern? What power relations are played out? How do participants' identities and structural roles in local and global societies shape their priorities, and which voices are excluded as a result? Post-colonialism attempts to overcome inequality by opening up spaces for the agency of non-Western peoples. However, poverty and a lack of technology make this increasingly difficult; non-Western academics, for example, rarely have the same access to books and technologies of communication as their Western counterparts.

Despite this, the work of Third World academics has led to a questioning of authorization and authority. By what right and on whose authority does one claim to speak on behalf of oth-ers? On whose terms is space created in which they are allowed to speak? Are we merely trying to incorporate and subsume non-Western voices into our own canons? It is no longer feasible to represent the peoples of the Third World as passive, helpless victims. Their voices are now being heard, and their ideas are increasingly being incorporated into grass-roots development policies. Third World critics have also had impacts on development studies, particularly within gender and development. They have forced a move away from totalizing discourses and a singular fem-inism (based on the vantage point of white, middle-class Western feminists, which failed to acknowledge the differences between women) towards the creation of spaces where the voices of black women and women from the South can be heard (see, for example, Mohanty 1988). Post-colonial feminisms allow for competing and disparate voices among women, rather than reproducing colonialist power relations where knowledge is produced and received in the West, and white, middle-class women have the power to speak for their 'silenced sisters' in the South.

Critiques, advances and new dialogues

One of the major dilemmas for post-colonialism is the charge that it has become institutionalized, representing the interests of a Western-based intellectual elite who speak the language of the contemporary Western academy, perpetuating the exclusion of the colonized and oppressed (Loomba 1998). Moreover, critics suggest that greater theoretical sophistication has created greater obfuscation: post-colonialism is too theoretical and not rooted enough in material concerns; emphasis on discourse detracts from an assessment of material ways in which colonial power relations persist; consequently, post-colonialism is ignorant of the real problems characterizing everyday life in the Global South. Moreover, debates about post-colonialism and globalization have largely proceeded in relative isolation from one another, and to their mutual cost. Economic relations and their effects elude representation in much of post-colonial studies. Thus, despite attempts by a few authors (e.g. Crush 1995; McEwan 2001; see also *The Geographical Journal* 2006), development studies and post colonial studies remain stubbornly apart: 'development studies does not tend to listen to subalterns and postcolonial studies does not tend to concern itself with whether the subaltern is eating' (Sylvester 1999: 703).

Despite criticisms, post-colonialism is a significant advancement in development studies. It demonstrates how the production of Western knowledge forms is inseparable from the exercise of Western power. It also attempts to loosen the power of Western knowledge and reassert the value of alternative experiences and ways of knowing (Thiong'o 1986; Bhabha 1994). It articulates some difficult questions about writing the history of 'development', about imperialist representations and discourses surrounding 'the Third World', and about the institutional practices of development itself. It has the potential to turn critique of conventional development into productive 're learning to see and reassess the reality' of the Global South (Escobar 2001: 153). It has been an important stimulus to alternative formulations, such as 'indigenous' and 'alternative modernities', and rights-based approaches to development (Simon 2006). And, precisely because of their divergent traditions, increasing dialogue between post-colonialism and development studies offers new ways of conceptualizing development. For example, Sylvester (2006) demonstrates how post-colonial development might be imagined by linking the personal to the global through the articulation of lived experience in poetry and novels alongside more conventional development studies accounts.

Post-colonialism has an expansive understanding of the potentialities of agency. It shares a social optimism with other discourses, such as gender and sexuality in Western countries, and rethinking here has helped generate substantial changes in political practice. Emerging dialogues between post-colonialism and development studies have the potential to engage post-colonial theory in considering questions of inequality of power and control of resources, human rights, global exploitation of labour, child prostitution and genocide, helping to translate the theoretical insights of post-colonialism into action on the ground and a means of tackling the power imbalances between North and South. They might also inspire critical reshaping of post-colonial futures and counter new forms of orientalism that continue to disadvantage the developing world. The challenge now, as Simon (2006) contends, is to link post-colonialist concerns with local identities, practices and agendas to broader campaigns and projects for progressive and radical change that are substantively post-colonial and critically developmental. This is beginning to emerge with new North–South alliances, alternative and progressive trading structures, such as fair and ethical trade, and critical analysis of the role of agencies and institutions. Therefore, despite the seeming impossibility of transforming North–South relations by the politics of difference and agency alone, post-colonialism is a much-needed corrective to the Eurocentrism and conservatism of much writing on development. It is playing an important role in reimagining critical development studies and generating new dialogue and action.

GUIDE TO FURTHER READING

Bhavnani, K.-K., Forna, J. and Kurian, P. (eds) (2003) *Feminist Futures. Re-imagining Women, Culture and Development*, London: Zed Books. A collection of essays that challenge established approaches to development by proposing a new paradigm that puts women and culture at the centre and culture on a par with political economy; implicitly, if not explicitly, post-colonial in orientation.

Crush, J. (ed.) (1995) *Power of Development*, London: Routledge. A collection of essays exploring the language of development, its rhetoric and meaning within different political and institutional contexts.

Escobar, A. (1995) *Encountering Development: The Making and Unmaking of the Third World*, Princeton, NJ: Princeton University Press. A provocative analysis of development discourse and practice.

Schwarz, H. and Ray, S. (eds) (2005) *A Companion to Postcolonial Studies*, Oxford: Blackwell. A wide-ranging volume of essays by leading post-colonial scholars that cuts across themes, regions, theories and practices of post-colonial study.

The Geographical Journal (2006) 'Postcolonialism and development: New dialogues', special issue, 172(1): 6–77.

USEFUL WEBSITES

http://web.worldbank.org/WBSITE/EXTERNAL/COUNTRIES/AFRICAEXT/EXTINDKNOWLEDGE/0,,menuPK:825562~pagePK:64168427~piPK:64168435~theSitePK:825547,00.html The World Bank's website on Indigenous Knowledge and its role in the development process.

http://www.fairtrade.org.uk/ UK website of the Fairtrade Foundation, which aims to offer independent guarantees that disadvantaged producers in the developing world are getting a better deal.

http://us.oneworld.net/ US website that encourages people to discover their power to speak, connect and make a difference, by providing access to information, and enabling connections between thousands of organizations and millions of people around the world.

http://www.forumsocialmundial.org.br/ Website of the World Social Forum, where social movements, networks, NGOs and other civil society organizations opposed to neoliberalism and all forms of imperialism come together to share and debate ideas and to network for effective action.

REFERENCES

Bhabha, H. (1994) *The Location of Culture*, London: Routledge.

Crush, J. (ed.) (1995) *Power of Development*, London: Routledge.

Escobar, A. (1995) 'Imagining a post-development era', in J. Crush (ed.) *Power of Development*, London: Routledge, pp. 211–27.

Escobar, A. (2001) 'Culture sits in places: Reflections on globalism and subaltern strategies of localization', *Political Geography*, 20: 139–74.

Loomba, A. (1998) *Colonialism/Postcolonialism*, London: Routledge.

McEwan, C. (2001) 'Postcolonialism, feminism and development: Intersections and dilemmas', *Progress in Developing Studies*, 1(2): 93–111.

Mohanty, C. (1988) 'Under western eyes: Feminist scholarship and colonial discourses', *Feminist Review*, 30: 61–88.

Radcliffe, S. (1999) 'Re-thinking development', in P. Cloke, P. Crang and M. Goodwin (eds) *Introducing Human Geographies*, London: Hodder Arnold, pp. 84–91.

Said, E. (1978) *Orientalism*, London: Routledge and Kegan Paul.

Simon, D. (2006) 'Separated by common ground? Bringing (post)development and (post)colonialism together', *The Geographical Journal*, 172(1): 10–21.

Spivak, G. (1990) *The Postcolonial Critic: Interviews, Strategies, Dialogue*, London: Routledge.

Spivak, G. (1999) *A Critique of Postcolonial Reason*, Cambridge, MA: Harvard University Press.

Sylvester, C. (1999) 'Development studies and postcolonial studies: Disparate tales of the "Third World"', *Third World Quarterly*, 29: 703 21.

Sylvester, C. (2006) 'Bare life as a development/postcolonial problematic', *The Geographical Journal*, 172(1): 66–77.

The Geographical Journal (2006) 'Postcolonialism and development: New dialogues', special issue, 172(1): 6–77.

Thiong'o, Ngugi wa (1986) *Decolonising the Mind*, London: James Curry.

2.14 Responsibility to distant others

David M. Smith

Introduction

The question of responsibility to distant others is at the heart of the notion of development as the deliberate improvement of life in the world's deprived regions. It is implicitly a perspective of the more affluent ('North') towards the less developed ('South'), raising the role of beneficence in the transfer of resources from rich to poor. Beneficence is the process of active kindness or actually doing good, implied by the acceptance of a moral responsibility, as opposed to benevolence as merely charitable feelings or the desire to do good. A major ethical and practical issue is how benevolence can be turned into beneficence, requiring sacrifices on the part of those in affluent parts of the world for the sake of less fortunate persons elsewhere.

The use of the term 'others' is indicative of differences, with respect to culture or way of life, on the part of those for whom a responsibility may be thought to exist. The term 'strangers' is sometimes adopted in the literature, to emphasize lack of the familiarity which often provides a basis for beneficence. While 'distance' is usually thought of in a geographical sense, it can also signify emotional or psychological separation: hence the coupling of 'nearest and dearest' in some accounts of what might be regarded as the convention of favouring people who are close in both senses. Sentiments of localized partiality are challenged by those who deploy the moral power of impartiality and universality in support of the more spatially extensive or global reach of responsibility for others.

Some versions of the argument for responsibility to distant others include future generations. This adds intergenerational justice to the territorial social justice invoked by the case for promoting more even development by transfers of resources across geographical space. The time dimension raises issues of sustainable development, arising from the question of what natural resources and other production possibilities the present generation should bequeath to its successors.

The question of responsibility to distant others has been debated in moral and political philosophy, as well as in development ethics (see below). There have also been contributions from geographers working in development studies (Corbridge 1993), and by others interested in the spatial scope of caring or supportive relationships (Silk 1998; Smith 1998, 2000).

Theoretical issues

Responsibility to distant others raises important theoretical issues. The central question is that of how spatially extensive beneficence can be justified by moral argument, given what might appear to be the natural human tendency to favour our nearest and dearest over more needy strangers further away.

An influential early discussion was provided by Peter Singer (1972), who called for a change in the way people in relatively affluent countries react to a situation like famine elsewhere. He began with the proposition that, if it is in our power to prevent something bad from happening, without thereby sacrificing anything of comparable moral importance, we ought to do it. This takes no account of proximity or distance:

> The fact that a person is physically near to us, so that we have personal contact with him [sic], may make it more likely that we *shall* assist him, but this does not show that we *ought* to help him rather than another who happens to be further away. If we accept any principle of impartiality, universalizability, equality, or whatever, we cannot discriminate against someone merely because he is far away from us (Singer 1972: 24).

Thus, we ought to give as much as possible to famine relief, perhaps to the point at which, by giving more, we would cause ourselves more suffering than we would prevent.

This formulation reflects the general perspective of utilitarianism, under which greatest aggregate good can be achieved by satisfying the more intense needs of the poor at the expense of the less intensive needs of those better-off. Ideally, resources would continue to be transferred (from 'North' to 'South') until need, satisfaction or living standards were equalized. According to Singer (1972: 29), redistribution should not be constrained by ownership: 'From the moral point of view, the prevention of the starvation of millions of people outside our society must be considered at least as pressing as the upholding of property norms within our society.' Singer's contribution has been the subject of subsequent debate (e.g. Chatterjee 2004), including recognition that people cannot necessarily be blamed for favouring their nearest and dearest over distant strangers in greater need.

Another influential contribution was by James Sterba (1981). He suggested that, of the various moral grounds for justifying the welfare rights of distant peoples (and future generations), the most evident are those which appeal to either a right to life or a right to fair treatment. A right to life involves a positive right to the satisfaction of a person's basic needs: those which must be satisfied in order not to seriously endanger health or sanity, preserving life in the fullest sense (such as for food, shelter, medical care, protection, companionship and self-development). It also involves a negative right which requires persons not to interfere with attempts by others to meet their basic needs, which raises the question of whether persons with goods and resources surplus to basic needs are justified in keeping them if this prohibits others from satisfying their basic needs. He echoes Singer in concluding that, in the view of most people, 'their right to acquire the goods and resources necessary to satisfy their basic needs would have priority over any other person's property rights to surplus possessions' (Sterba 1981: 102). A right to fairness involves the argument that, from a position of disinterest (i.e. not knowing who or where they might be), people would endorse limitations to a right to accumulate goods and resources, so as to guarantee a minimum sufficient to provide each person with the requirements to satisfy their basic needs.

More recent years have seen the emergence of an ethic of care (e.g. Clement 1996), as a challenge or supplement to the prevailing ethic of justice, with its emphasis on human rights and on rules governing redistribution. It has been argued that all persons need care, from cradle to grave, and that the meaning and practice of care should be given greater moral priority. The ethic of care has become an important framework for discussion of responsibility to others, well beyond the feminist ethics within which it was initially promoted (Smith 1998, 2000).

Some proponents of an ethic of care stress the importance of knowing the other for whom we care. They may be sceptical about the possibility of caring for distant others, claiming that we cannot truly care for people we do not know. Feminist writers often applauded the special quality of caring that requires knowing people in their concrete particularity, rather than as representatives of such disadvantaged groups as the distant poor. However, there is a risk of over-prioritizing the mutuality of face-to-face relations. Critics of parochial interpretations of an ethic of care have argued for the construction of ever-widening circles of care, out to those far distant others in need. This is part of a process of increasing moral sensibility: 'we learn to care for distant others by first developing close relationships to nearby others, and then recognizing the similarities between close and distant others' (Clement 1996: 85).

Marilyn Friedman (1991) has drawn special attention to the unequal distribution of resources required for caring. If the better-off have greater capacity to care for their own nearest and dearest, and if the less well-off lack the means to care, inequality in need satisfaction will be perpetuated and even exacerbated. Thus, the ethics of care and justice have to be brought together, to combine the sympathy customarily expressed in partiality towards our nearest and dearest with the institutions required for impartiality in the (re)distribution of capacity to care according to need.

Stuart Corbridge (1993, 1998) grounds responsibility to distant others in recognition that our lives are entwined with those of distant strangers, through flows of capital and commodities, modern communications, and so on. Various processes subsumed under the concept of globalization are creating a more interdependent world, in ways largely beyond individual control. Our own position of advantage on what may be an increasingly uneven development surface is very much a matter of good fortune, rather than something we deserve. Thus 'the needs and rights of strangers could easily – and but for the "accident" of birth – be the needs and rights of ourselves' (Corbridge 1993: 464).

Practical issues

More practical issues may be considered briefly. It is obvious that some persons may be better placed than others (literally, in a geographical sense) to care for those in need, arising from an ongoing and necessarily local relationship. This was recognized by Singer (1972: 24):

> it is possible that we are in a better position to judge what needs to be done to help a person near to us than one far away, and perhaps also to provide the assistance we judge to be necessary. If this were the case, it would be a reason for helping those near to us first.

However, he went on to point out that instant communication and swift transportation enable aid to be disseminated, with the assistance of expert observers and supervisors, concluding: 'There would seem, therefore, to be no possible justification for discriminating on geographical grounds.' While everyday experience confirms that the needs of family or local community members may be first identified by those closest to them, and that some kinds of response may depend on such proximity, the diagnosis of need and the provision of effective care can seldom be so confined. However, the danger of outside agencies or professionals imposing inappropriate remedies suggests that some local, insider knowledge of the situation is helpful.

Both theory and practical experience suggest that, while benevolent sentiments may be a necessary condition for the recognition of responsibility for others, they are not in themselves sufficient to guarantee spatially extensive beneficence. And, like personal voluntarism, organized charity is an uncertain basis for ensuring the assistance required, on a scale likely to make a difference to large numbers of persons in great need. For justice to be done, in the sense of reliably meeting responsibilities to distant others, the process has to be institutionalized, at an international scale, and with a far greater commitment of resources than those currently deployed by individual or supposedly united nations.

GUIDE TO FURTHER READING

Responsibility to distant others, or strangers, is related to various issues at the interface of political philosophy and development studies in two important papers by Corbridge (1993, 1998). A general review of debates concerning the spatial scope of beneficence is provided by Smith (1998), and linked to other concerns about community, development and the environment in Smith (2000). More practical implications of the problem of caring at a distance are covered by Silk (1998) and Wenar (2003).

REFERENCES

Chatterjee, D.K. (ed.) (2004) *The Ethics of Assistance: Morality and the Distant Needy*, Cambridge: Cambridge University Press.
Clement, C. (1996) *Care, Autonomy, and Justice: Feminism and the Ethic of Care*, Oxford: Westview Press.
Corbridge, S. (1993) 'Marxisms, modernities and moralities: Development praxis and the claims of distant strangers', *Environment and Planning D: Society and Space*, 11: 449–72.
Corbridge, S. (1998) 'Development ethics: Distance, difference, plausibility', *Ethics, Place and Environment*, 1: 35–53.
Friedman, M. (1991) 'The practice of partiality', *Ethics*, 101: 818–35.
Silk, J. (1998) 'Caring at a distance', *Ethics, Place and Environment*, 1: 165–82.
Singer, P. (1972) 'Famine, affluence and morality', *Philosophy and Public Affairs*, 1: 229–43, reprinted in P. Laslett and J. Fishkin (eds) (1979) *Philosophy, Politics and Society*, 5th series, Oxford: Blackwell Publishers, pp. 21–35.
Smith, D.M. (1998) 'How far should we care? On the spatial scope of beneficence', *Progress in Human Geography*, 22: 15–38.
Smith, D.M. (2000) *Moral Geographies: Ethics in a World of Difference*, Edinburgh: Edinburgh University Press.
Sterba, J.P. (1981) 'The welfare rights of distant peoples and future generations: Moral side-constraints on social policy', *Social Theory and Practice*, 7: 99–119.
Wenar, L. (2003) 'What we owe to distant others', *Politics, Philosophy and Economics*, 2(3): 283–304.

2.15 Social capital and development

Anthony Bebbington

During the 1990s and into the current decade, 'social capital' became one of development's buzzwords. It gained traction not just in development policy and studies, but also in discussions of democracy and community in the USA, UK and other anglophone countries. This chapter considers what the term has been taken to mean, how and why it became popular, and several ways in which it has been incorporated into development studies. It closes with a brief reflection on criticisms of the concept.

Meanings of social capital

While the concept of social capital has been criticized for meaning too many things to too many people (Fine 2001), several core, recurring ideas seem to underpin its different uses. First, it is taken to refer to qualities inherent in or deriving from people's social relationships. Second is the notion that these qualities can have important implications for other dimensions of economic and socio-political life – at both the individual and collective levels. Third, a notion apparent in some more than other renditions, is the idea that there is no simple relationship between the structure of people's social networks and their broader class, socio-economic or otherwise structural positions in society.

Two distinctions help give some order to the meanings which have been given to the term. The first is Uphoff's (1999) differentiation between *cognitive* and *structural* social capital. Some literature on social capital has worked with attitudinal survey data which, among other things, records and gives quantitative measures to levels of trust in society. This research relates these levels of trust to other indicators, in particular ones of economic performance. It has taken 'trust' to be a measure of social capital, arguing that there is a close relationship between the quality of social relationships in any given population and the extent to which people trust both each other and social institutions. Uphoff refers to such trust as cognitive social capital – the domain of values and perceptions.

He distinguishes this cognitive dimension from what he calls structural social capital, which instead dwells within the structure of social relationships. A structural conception of social capital leads researchers to focus on social relations, networks, loose associations and formal organizations. In development studies this structural conception has gained more attention than has the cognitive. In this rendering, social capital refers to the resources – information, reputations, credit – that flow through a social network. These resources can be understood and approached in differing ways (Bebbington et al. 2006). For writers such as Bourdieu (1977), social capital is a resource just like any other (land, money, etc.). It can be used to enhance one's wealth and status, to marginalize others, or both. Conversely, for political scientists such as Putnam (1993), the primary focus is on the nature and extent of the network structure itself. Here the concern is more with understanding how and why particular networks are structured and the consequences for those who are and those who are not members of these networks. This approach also considers how social networks can be shaped so that they are conducive to building more democratic, supportive and inclusive communities. Notwithstanding these differences, each of these structural conceptions of social capital understands it in terms of the assets that reside within social actors' relationships. These assets are generally understood as constituting an important part of people's identities, aspirations, livelihood and political strategies.

Why did social capital become important in development?

Robert Putnam and development studies

While there are continuities between the concept of social capital and ideas at work in nineteenth-century classical sociology (Woolcock 1998), it was only with the publication of Putnam's (1993) study of regional government performance in Italy that the concept became popular and began to influence development studies. Putnam argued that, *ceteris paribus*, Italy's local governments were more effective and responsive to their citizens, and its sub-national economies more dynamic, in those regions exhibiting higher rates of participation in civic associations. Through their involvement in these associations, he argued that people learned citizenship and developed networks of civic engagement (*social capital*) that, in their aggregate, fostered greater levels of accountability and responsibility in society and more efficiency in the economy. He argued forcefully that this social capital was the independent variable in these relationships. The lesson for international development, he said, was that fostering such social capital was an important path towards enhancing government and economic performance.

The book was well reviewed in the press (for instance, in *The Economist*) and, importantly, Putnam argued his case in more popular outlets (such as *The American Prospect*), as well as academic ones. He also began to pursue the relevance of similar arguments to the USA, where he claimed to chart the steady demise of social capital. The visibility of his work drove collective debate of his argument in sociology and political science (especially in the USA). It also caught the attention of senior figures in the World Bank, where both the economic research and the social development communities began exploring the relevance of social capital for their own understandings of development (Bebbington et al. 2006). This passage through the World Bank is important because, while the concept was set to be widely debated within academic social science and North American community development, its passage into development studies was accelerated and amplified by its usage within the World Bank.

A language and concept for social development?

Economists and non-economists alike experimented with the concept of social capital. Economists used it as a way of describing the 'social something' (Hammer and Pritchett 2006) that their econometric tools could otherwise not handle: the social relationships through which information was exchanged, the social bases of collective action in community development, and so on. However, it was the non-economists in the Bank – or, more precisely, those who questioned the value of formal econometric approaches – who made most use of the concept. An early statement (Serageldin and Steer 1994) argued that the sustainability of development could be understood as a function of the mixes and trade-offs among produced capital, natural capital, human capital and social capital. It suggested that levels of sustainability could be conceptualized in terms of the rules governing the substitution among these different stocks of capital. A 'weak' concept of sustainability would consider development as sustainable as long as the overall capital stock increased, regardless of the substitutions occurring among different types of capital, while an 'absurdly strong' notion of sustainability would not allow drawdown in any of these forms of capital. In the middle ground, 'sensible' sustainability would hold total capital stock intact, and avoid depletion of any capital beyond critical levels, while 'strong' forms of sustainability would imply maintaining each component of capital intact at an aggregate level, meaning that were natural capital to be destroyed in one place, it would have to be replaced by cultivated natural capital in other places (as in carbon sequestration and trading arrangements and carbon offsets against air miles).

Two points merit comment here. First, this approach worked with a notion of 'forms of capital' that understood them as distinct from one another. Questions of distribution receive little attention, and structural relationships between the distribution of one form of capital and that of social capital are not considered (nor were they in the World Development Report 2000/2001, *Attacking Poverty*, in which the concept of social capital figured prominently). In this sense, the underlying influence on the use of the concept came from neoclassical economic approaches to production functions, and (to a lesser extent) ideas in ecological economics about stocks of natural capital. Notably absent was any influence of Bourdieu's (1977) notion that the distributions of forms of capital (economic, cultural, symbolic, social) have to be understood as interrelated and in large measure mutually reinforcing (i.e. social capital serves to consolidate control of economic capital and relationships of power).

The second point is that, even if the broader model at work here was underpinned by frameworks from economics rather than sociology, social development professionals latched on to the idea quickly. They saw in social capital – and these broader asset-based frameworks – a way of incorporating their commitments to participation and local organizations into a larger narrative on development, one that saw participatory processes and strong organizational fabrics as assets of equal importance to education, finance or infrastructure. Capital-based approaches to sustainable development offered the prospect of incorporating what had typically been local, idiographic and operational concerns, into wider theories of development in which (and here Putnam's 1993 argument was so important) the social was as important as the economic.

If national development was a function of capital mixes and substitutions, then it was only a few short steps to analyse poverty, welfare and livelihoods in similar terms. The second half of the 1990s thus saw various studies and frameworks that gave social capital an important (sometimes *primus inter pares*) position in asset-based notions of poverty and livelihood (Carney 1998; Moser 1998). These approaches took their scale of analysis to the individual and household and argued that social capital – understood, broadly, as the networks, organizations and relations to which the person or household had access – had an important effect on poverty and livelihood. This was so for various reasons. Social capital might facilitate access to other assets, or to the institutions providing those assets. A person's social networks might influence their access to schools, health care or institutions providing financial services. This social capital might also facilitate access by guaranteeing the person's reliability and accountability. This argument has been used in micro-financial services' literature and practice, in which social capital (in the form of group membership) is taken as a guarantee that loans will be repaid. Another strand in this writing has seen social capital as an important safety net, a means of reducing vulnerability. Here, social relationships (formal or informal) are valued for the role they can play in helping people recover from or cope with crisis, violence or other sources of risk and perturbation (Moser 1998).

Capital-based notions of livelihood and household welfare gained considerable traction in a number of development agencies. Most significantly perhaps, the UK Department for International Development adopted the sustainable livelihoods framework (see http://www.livelihoods.org) with considerable enthusiasm, and for some years it occupied a central place in their work on natural resources and (if less so) in social development. Similar frameworks were assumed by parts of the United Nations system[1] and non-governmental organizations. Following the path of all development fads, this enthusiasm has since waned, more in some (and some parts of) agencies than in others. However, it has left its mark, and the notion that livelihoods draw on a variety of assets, among which social relationships are particularly important, will be with us for many years to come.

Criticisms and concerns

Concepts that rise to prominence quickly generate antibodies, and social capital has been no exception. It has been subject to penetrating critique in both social and political science, as well as in development studies. These criticisms have been many and varied. The chapter has already hinted at some of them. Use of the concept has been (justifiably) criticized for being too loose, for allowing the term to refer to so many dimensions of social life that it becomes relatively meaningless. Its use has also been criticized for ignoring questions of political economy and social power, and, more generally, the rough and tumble of real-world politics. In considerable measure, this reflects the extent to which its early adoption was underlain by production-function approaches rather than approaches grounded in Bourdieu's social theory. Put another way, while social capital approaches have often ignored political economy, they do not necessarily have to. If social capital is understood as both constituted by and constitutive of wider relations of political and cultural economy – à la Bourdieu – then there is no reason why using the concept should necessarily preclude an awareness of politics and power. However, to date, much use of social capital in development studies has overstated the potential that social capital holds as a resource for poor people, and understated the extent to which structural relations at local, national and international levels constrain their ability to accumulate more assets and to get ahead.

In retrospect, many of those social development professionals and researchers who worked in the early formulations of (social) capital-based approaches to livelihoods, welfare and sustainabil-

---

1 For instance, the United Nations Development Programme, the UN Economic Commission on Latin America and the Caribbean, and the Food and Agricultural Organization.

ity were probably always uneasy about some of the conceptual leaps being made. Social capital proved notoriously difficult to operationalize in research in anything other than a qualitative way, and indicators always seemed partial and deficient. Like some of the economists who saw social capital as a way of talking about the 'social something' (Hammer and Pritchett 2006) that their models could not catch, these social scientists also saw it as a heuristic for talking about the 'social something' whose theoretical and political importance seemed understated by languages of participation and local organizations. It may well be, then, that social capital has far more heuristic and discursive value than it has analytical value. As among development economists (Hammer and Pritchett 2006), so also among social development researchers, there appears to be something of a move away from the term. With time, it may be that the fate of social capital ends up being similar to that of that other development buzzword, sustainability – an idea with great heuristic and political resonance, but limited usefulness for research. For the same reason, social capital's value as a 'keyword' will have a long shelf life, one that far outlasts its value as a 'key concept'.

GUIDE TO FURTHER READING AND REFERENCES

Bebbington, A., Woolcock, M., Guggenheim, S. and Olson, E. (eds) (2006) *The Search for Empowerment. Social Capital as Idea and Practice at the World Bank*, West Hartford, CT: Kumarian Press.

Bourdieu, P. (1977) *Outline of a Theory of Practice*, Cambridge: Cambridge University Press.

Carney, D. (ed.) (1998) *Sustainable Rural Livelihoods. What Contribution Can We Make?* London: Department for International Development.

Fine, B. (2001) *Social Capital Versus Social Theory. Political Economy and Social Science at the Turn of the Millennium*, London: Routledge.

Hammer, J. and Pritchett, L. (2006) 'Scenes from a marriage: World Bank economists and social capital', in A. Bebbington et al. (eds) *The Search for Empowerment. Social Capital as Idea and Practice at the World Bank*, West Hartford, CT: Kumarian Press, pp. 63–90.

Moser, C. (1998) 'The asset vulnerability framework: Reassessing urban poverty reduction strategies', *World Development*, 26(1): 1–19.

Putnam, R. (1993) *Making Democracy Work: Civic Traditions in Modern Italy*, Princeton, NJ: Princeton University Press.

Serageldin, I. and Steer, A. (eds) (1994) *Making Development Sustainable: From Concepts to Action*, Environmentally Sustainable Development, Occasional Paper Series No. 2, Washington, DC: World Bank.

Uphoff, N. (1999) 'Understanding social capital: Learning from the analysis and experience of participation', in P. Dasgupta and I. Serageldin (eds) *Social Capital: A Multifaceted Perspective*, Washington, DC: World Bank.

Woolcock, M. (1998) 'Social capital and economic development: towards a theoretical synthesis and policy framework', *Theory and Society*, 27(2): 151–208.

2.16 Social exclusion and development

Marina Della Giusta

What is social exclusion?

The definition of social exclusion is not fixed, but rather varies from context to context as each society defines what participation entails, and the conditions for individuals to be able to participate. Indeed, a widely used definition states explicitly that an individual is defined as socially excluded if he or she does not participate in key activities of the society in which he or she lives (Burchardt et al. 1998: 30), which clearly varies depending on what the key activities are. This is reflected in the presence of several indicators of social exclusion, rather than one unified index. Indicators include such things as economic circumstances (income, wealth, land, etc.), health (both physical and mental) and well-being (including emotional dimensions), access to education, training and work, access to services such as housing, transport, and so on. This means that not only are measures complex, but they vary from society to society, and if it is hard to compare poverty indicators, it is harder still to compare indicators of social exclusion across countries. General indices do exist, however, and they go beyond poverty indicators such as those included in the World Bank's World Development Report (http://www.worldbank.org/poverty) to include broader measures of human development, such as the human development index (HDI) employed in the United Nations Human Development Reports (http://hdr.undp.org), or more specific ones which aim to target the dimension of social exclusion, such as the gender-related human development index (GDI) devised by the United Nations Development Programme (UNDP) (www.undp-pogar.org/countries/morestats.asp?cid=4&gid=l&ind=4). Targets to improve countries' scores along many of these measures are at the centre of the Millennium Development Goals (www.un.org/millenniumgoals), which do not just aim to address poverty, but also to improve access to safe water and sanitation, reduce malnutrition and improve gender equality.

In order for an individual to be included, then, they need to have access to different forms of capital, from financial to human and social. Piachaud (2002) provides a useful checklist of the assets that an individual needs access to if he/she is to be able to participate fully in the activities of their society; these include financial assets (inherited, earned, won), other assets (such as land, other property), skills (abilities, education, training), public infrastructure (roads, schools, hospitals) and collective social resources, including networks and shared norms and values, which scholars including Bordieu, Loury, Coleman and Putnam (see, for a review, Dasgupta and Serageldin 2000) have all variously described as social capital. All these forms of capital are complementary, which means that they all need to be available in some form for an individual to flourish and develop. A good example of the consequences deriving from lacking access to many of these resources is provided in a study by Cleaver (2005), who illustrates the interlocking disadvantages (i.e. disadvantages that happen simultaneously and are interrelated) experienced by poor households in Tanzania. These include small family size, weak family networks, lack of assets – including labour power – which constrains their ability to engage in reciprocal collective activities and thereby build relations which they could then draw on for help, poor health, inability to articulate their issues in public fora, as well as the derogatory perceptions of other community members towards them. Many studies of poverty in both developing and developed countries observe that although poor people may have social links to others, these are weak links because the people they know more closely experience the same difficulties that they do, and therefore are not in a position to help them and spend most of their energies concentrating on their own survival. The implication of studies like this is that social capital cannot be understood as a ready substitute for other missing capitals (human, natural, financial), and the same issue has been found across a variety of contexts and countries, as illustrated in studies of youth disadvantage in the UK (Hobcraft 2003), social capital and micro-finance in Mexico (Casson and Della Giusta 2004), and the well-being of immigrant women in the UK (Della Giusta and Kambhampati 2006).

The generation and reproduction of social exclusion

Several processes contribute to creating and maintaining social exclusion, and this section provides some basic ideas regarding the ways in which such processes come about and interact with each other. Following Burden and Hamm (2000), we distinguish between economic, political and socio-cultural processes of exclusion, which we examine in turn below.

Economic processes include both the ways in which modes of production determine a division of labour between forms of work that are highly valued and from which status and income are derived, and those which are not. This is especially relevant when the division between paid and unpaid work is considered. Unpaid work includes subsistence activities and caring activities, which form the majority of the hours worked around the world, especially, but by no means exclusively, in developing countries (Waring 1988). The exclusion that derives from being assigned to those activities is a very significant factor in explaining observed poverty and vulnerability patterns (including violence). Economic processes also include consumption activities, which, again, are a cause of marginalization for those who do not have the necessary resources to participate in them, a problem felt at low as well as relatively higher levels of income in societies driven by consumption.

Turning now to political processes, these are, of course, very important as they define both the conditions for being part of a society (citizenship rights) and participating in activities such as voting (which include restrictions that can be based on age, gender, citizenship status, etc.), and the rules defining which behaviour is deemed antisocial or criminal. Political processes are also combining with cultural ones in determining the actual detection and conviction rates for crime, which themselves tend to differ widely according to the personal characteristics of the arrested. They also combine with economic processes, as, for example, criminal records are used to discriminate in employment and in social participation (stigmatization).

Cultural and social processes, finally, underlie many of the above processes as they help to define what 'the norm' is in terms of appropriate behaviour, and what inherited or constructed aspects of an individual's identity (ethnicity, age, bodily appearance, sexuality, wealth, education, etc.) are relevant to determine appropriate behaviour in each sphere of life. Indeed, according to institutional theory (see, for example, North 1990), it is precisely such informal institutions – that is, norms and customs regulating socio-economic life – which, over time, are becoming enshrined in formal institutions such as the law, and they then together determine each individual's positioning in relation to others, as well as their ability to access resources. Since these processes evolve over time, the power of each person can be said to depend on historically and culturally determined power relations, which are continuously changed by people pushing the boundaries of what is feasible (see Sen 1981).

The importance of social mechanisms for accessing resources

Social-structural resources – that is, the systems of social relations in which each of us is embedded – are therefore defining opportunities and constraints for individual agency, which is the reason for considering them as a capital asset to the individual that can be used as a productive resource. Sociologists of the rational action perspective, such as Coleman (1990), describe social relationships as systems that can be capable of establishing and maintaining effective norms among individuals belonging to them. If this happens, it means that everybody is bound to everybody else in these systems by the expectations and obligations that each has of the others. In this context, the social capital available to an individual is simply the sum of all the obligations running towards her from all other individuals. If each individual has some control over the others' actions, the more they are obliged and the higher such control will be: the power of an actor is a direct measure of the social capital available to the actor within that system.

As we said earlier, however, having strong ties with people who suffer from the same lack of resources as oneself may not be very helpful, and can even hinder individual inclusion. Some excluded actors are characterized by only having access to primary and non-cross-cutting social networks which limit their sphere of action (e.g. poor, low caste or women in some contexts).

Primary social groups are often not able to ensure the inclusion and participation of their members, as witnessed by the work on intra-household conflicts and unequal allocation which illustrates the difficulties experienced by women and children. Other examples are provided in the micro-finance literature which illustrates the exclusion at village level of the poorest from group-based micro-finance, and by the literature illustrating the costs and benefits associated with family- or ethnic-group-based businesses networks (Ben-Porath 1980).

Socially included actors can usually access both cross-cutting social networks, and through them have the ability to access institutional capital as well – that is, develop links with formal organizations such as local government which are providers of essential services and conduits for exercising political voice. Networks of secondary associations with more heterogeneous membership (within which ties may cut across ethnic, caste, class, wealth, religion, location or other characteristics) are thus key to accessing resources and opportunities, as well as being capable of complementing the role of the government and even providing a substitute in areas in which government policy is ineffective, as illustrated in the case of Indian villages by Krishna (2002), where different agents operate for economic development, for community peace and for political participation. Again, there can be downsides to bridging networks as well, as witnessed by the literature on exploitative and patronage-based relations. At the macro level, social or institutional capital describes the connection individuals have with institutions and their ability to avail themselves of their services; it thus involves local government institutions that both enable the scaling-up of micro-level social capital and actually contribute to creating social capital. Institutions can do this by creating conditions that are favourable to entering and maintaining social networks on the one hand, and through social policy and the attitude they promote in public officials, on the other. Thus, if government institutions are not supportive, it may be impossible for people belonging to certain social networks to scale up to macro-level social capital. The informal economy can in this sense be interpreted as a failure of scaling up from micro-level to institutional social capital, which can be motivated by institutional failure, as well as lack of connecting individuals helping to build bridges across networks.

GUIDE TO FURTHER READING AND REFERENCES

Ben-Porath, Y. (1980) 'The F-connection: Families, friends, and firms and the organisation of exchange', *Population and Development Review*, 6: 1–29.

Burchardt, T., Le Grand, J. and Piachaud, D. (1998) 'Social exclusion in Britain 1991–1995', *Social Policy and Administration*, 33(3): 227–44.

Burden, T. and Hamm, T. (2000) 'Responding to socially excluded groups', in J. Percy-Smith (ed.) *Policy Responses to Social Exclusion*, Buckingham: Open University Press.

Casson, M. and Della Giusta, M. (2004) 'The costly business of trust', *Development Policy Review*, 22(3): 319–40.

Cleaver, F. (2005) 'The inequality of social capital and the reproduction of chronic poverty', *World Development*, 33(6): 893–906.

Coleman, J.S. (1990) *Foundations of Social Theory*, Cambridge, MA: Harvard University Press.

Dasgupta, P. and Serageldin, I. (eds) (2000) *Social Capital: A Multifaceted Perspective*, Washington, DC: World Bank.

Della Giusta, M. and Kambhampati, U.S. (2006) 'Well being and social capital: Women migrant workers in the UK', *Journal of International Development*, special issue, 18(10).

Hobcraft, J. (2003) 'Continuity and change in pathways to young adult disadvantage: Results from a British birth cohort', CASE Paper 66, April.

Krishna, A. (2002) *Active Social Capital: Tracing the Roots of Development and Democracy*, New York: Columbia University Press.

North, D. (1990) *Institutions, Institutional Change and Economic Performance*, Cambridge: Cambridge University Press.

Piachaud, D. (2002) 'Capital and the determinants of poverty and social exclusion', CASE Paper 60, September.

Sen, A. (1981) *Poverty and Famines: An Essay on Entitlement and Deprivation*, Oxford: Clarendon Press.

Waring, M. (1988) *If Women Counted: A New Feminist Economics*, New York: Harper & Row.

Rural development

Editorial introduction

Rural poverty persists and remains a concern of many developing countries despite impressive advances in agricultural technology such as GM crops, which have led to an increase in agricultural productivity and successful agricultural systems. Different strategies and policies have been adopted in the last 50 years. The UN has taken initiatives in outlining the Millennium Development Goals in order to make reduction of poverty the most important goal in the twenty-first century. Agriculture is still the main source of income and employment in rural areas. Rural livelihoods are increasingly under stress and rural poverty has intensified in many regions. Rapid urbanization and improvements in communications and transport technology have resulted in a significant increase in mobility. Family life is increasingly individualized and many villages are experiencing erosion of community life.

In order to survive, many farmers are exploiting the land beyond its carrying capacity. For these reasons critics argue that yield benefits cannot be extended or even sustained. An alternative system advocates integrated management. Input use can be cut substantially if farmers substitute knowledge, labour and management skills. It is important to explore how different means have affected farmers' livelihoods and whether or not they are likely to deliver food security for hungry people.

Intensive agricultural methods such as agrochemicals and pesticides degrade agricultural resources. This leads to accelerated deforestation, soil degradation, damage to biodiversity, pollution and vulnerability to pest attacks, and contributes to environmental stresses and extreme weather conditions, leading to deteriorating food security. Food security in the developing countries must not come to be dependent on surpluses from the industrialized countries or, worse, food aid. Priority must be given to the future nutritional needs of their people and to ways and means of meeting those needs locally.

To understand environmental degradation, we need to consider people's livelihoods, for these establish the relationship between economic activity and local environment. Characteristically, forms of environmental degradation are generated by livelihoods based on primary commodity production, such as those of wage labourers in agriculture, or petty commodity producers, sometimes degraded to subsistence producers. The vulnerability of rural people, created by shifting seasonal constraints, short-term economic shocks, long-term trends of change (such as trade liberalization and globalization), the spread of AIDS, ethnic rivalry and conflicts influence institutional structures and processes which encourage them to pursue diverse livelihood strategies to combat rural poverty and vulnerability. All these reasons have led to modern famines, which are more complex and have challenged the role of governments, donors and humanitarian organizations in this respect.

Sustainable development and poverty alleviation in rural areas depend on effective common resources management and local governance which hinges on adaptations to local agro-ecological and social conditions. Varied types of cooperatives have helped people cope with various economic, social and environmental problems. A successful example of NGOs promoting cooperatives is the Fair Trade movement, which guarantees coffee producers a minimum price. There is a need to sustain natural systems and achieve greater equity (for example, providing more secure and affordable access to land for the poor and credit) in economic, social and political dimensions, to form part of a broader strategy of pro-poor growth.

3.1 Rural poverty

Joe Mullen

Introduction

Since the last edition of this chapter in 2002, a number of critical developments relating to rural poverty have taken place. The Millennium Development Goals (MDGs), sponsored by the United Nations, to which the member countries of the UN have committed themselves, have become an article of faith in relation to poverty reduction, particularly among the extreme poor. International attention has focused on poverty reduction, through 'making poverty history' campaigns, celebrity events and the G8. More importantly, there has been widespread involvement of civil society and non-state actors in establishing ownership over the process. Discussions of poverty reduction meet with a much more informed audience than was the case at the dawn of the millennium. However, we have to ask ourselves constantly, is it a matter of spin or politically correct rhetoric, rather than having a transformative effect on citizens in poor rural environments in the least developed countries?

Progress report on the MDGs

There has been a five-year review of the MDGs (see Millennium Development Report 2006), which disaggregates results by region. In all ten categories, results for sub-Saharan Africa are of serious concern. In extreme poverty reduction, for example, the proportion of people living on less than $1 per day declined marginally, from 44.6 per cent in 1990 to 44 per cent in 2002. (For south Asia the decline over the same period was from 39.4 per cent to 31.2 per cent). When taking the population growth into consideration, this represents a substantial increase in numbers of persons in poverty. Further modest declines in the case of sub-Saharan Africa are equally registered in areas such as hunger decline, clean water provision, universal primary education (UPE) and child mortality. There has been a major increase in the spread of AIDS and other contagious diseases such as TB. Progress has been registered mainly in south and east Asia. It is likely that state collapse, ethnic rivalry, violent conflict and warfare in African conflict zones has been a major contributory cause to the poor performance in achieving the interim MDG targets. Conversely, improving state stability and reducing conflict and poverty would contribute to improving MDG performance. However, sub-Saharan Africa appears to be the core geographical area of extreme poverty. This is further reinforced by the high level of involuntary flows of populations within Africa, either across international boundaries as refugees or within national borders as internally displaced persons (IDPs). The majority of transient populations are located in rural areas, often contributing to environmental stress due to intense water, land and energy usage, and forming pockets of extreme poverty and vulnerability, with a disproportionate representation of women and children (often as high as 80 per cent). IDPs outnumber refugees by 2 to 1, they fall under the responsibility of national governments for security and well-being. However, as weak states tend to generate the highest numbers, their capacity to fulfil their obligations is problematic. Africa is the most affected continent, generating an IDP population of 11.8 million across 21 countries.

The agreement by the G8 countries at Gleneagles, and their commitment to increasing overseas aid, particularly to Africa, should, in principle, reduce rural poverty. However, with the diversion of substantial sums originally committed to poverty reduction into debt relief, and prevarication among donors, the aid package appears less attractive than was first thought.

Climate change and conflict

Capital alone is seldom the answer to rural poverty reduction. The two factors that have had the most destructive impact on poor people's rural livelihoods have been climate change and conflict. The study by the Intergovernmental Panel on Climate Change (IPCC) has predicted differential impacts on rich and poor communities, urban and rural. The effects of increased drought, crop failures and extreme weather events, such as floods or tsunamis, are more likely to impact on struggling rural populations in Africa and Asia than on their peers in industrialized countries. The costs of adapting to these changes is estimated (by the IPCC) at between 5 and 10 per cent of GDP. The countries that have contributed most to creating greenhouse gases and consequent climate warming are least likely to feel the aggressive effects. The correlation between conflict and environmental degradation is also likely to exacerbate the negative impacts of global warming.

Floods and drought associated with tsunamis or the El Niño effect have made agricultural activities unpredictable. This has led to climate change having a much wider impact than in the immediate environment; it is becoming a humanitarian disaster, involving the erosion of land and water resources, the destruction of livelihoods and social capital, the breakdown of state governance, its loss of legitimacy and the exacerbation of conflict.

Similarly there is a persuasive case for a correlation between violent conflict and poverty. In rural environments, conflict leads to the destruction of basic food crops; the undermining of social capital; ethnic dissent and community disruption; the spread of AIDS, which debilitates the workforce and increases the dependent rates; and the rape and kidnap of young women. Wars tend to take place in the poorest countries, and generally the poorest in rural ennvironments become the frontline victims. In Participatory Poverty Assessments (2005/2006) carried out by the author among minority rural communities in Middle Shabelle and Hiran, Somalia, the participant farmers clearly identified conflict and clan tensions as a critical factor in clashes with pastoralists; roadblocks and predatory practices of militias, leading to higher costs of crop processing; kidnapping, leading to shortage of labour and the reintroduction of forced labour; and the lack of protection undermining confidence in the investment environment. While the displacement of the rural poor in situations of conflict is to be deplored, on the positive side, the remittances of the overseas diaspora have made a substantial contribution to the reduction of poverty among many vulnerable households. There is evidence of this in Bangladesh and in Somalia. The United Nations Development Programme (UNDP) in Somalia estimates annual remittances from the two million people who have left the country since 1991 to be in the region of $750 million, or more than three times the total sum of all development aid. Furthermore, it reaches poor families directly through the hawala system, without deductions or intermediaries. While a substantial proportion of the remittances are absorbed by pressing consumption needs, investment in local facilities and livelihoods also takes place.

External variables

External variables impacting on the rural poor have been structural reform, trade liberalization and globalization, particularly of commodity markets, which in turn has led to increased indebtedness. It is widely acknowledged that the poor – and particularly the rural poor – have been adversely affected in terms of their weaker purchasing power, removal of concessional credit schemes, lack of quality inputs, collapse of extension systems and risk aversion in relation to export cropping opportunities. There have been powerful vectors of rural differentiation, erosion of livelihood systems, marginalization, and disempowerment of men and women. Worsening socioeconomic profiles between rural and urban areas, particularly in terms of public goods such as health care and education, and income-earning opportunities, are in evidence.

Is more aid the answer?

International flows of aid, such as from the Gleneagles Agreement, do not necessarily reach the neediest among the rural poor. This fragility is characterized by weak mediating institutions, which often suffer from poor governance, centralization, political manipulation and lack of commitment. Poverty, as argued by the International Fund for Agricultural Development (IFAD 2001), is inefficient as well as being inequitable, as it makes people too poor to avail themselves of micro-credit systems, as they live in remote areas poorly connected to markets. There is also a weak correlation in the distribution of aid to poor and remote rural environments, with perhaps only 63 per cent of aid going to where 85 per cent of the rural poor live (IFAD 2001). The jury is still out on whether the magnitude of aid leads directly to rural poverty reduction or whether the key variable is transparency, stakeholder control, local management and good governance.

Evidence-based verification of rural poverty reduction: poverty auditing

Given the plethora of 'poverty' initiatives, a review of good practice at the level of governments and of aid agencies is an important component of public accountability. The poverty audit (or poverty impact assessment) is an important means of verifying that the investments made by governments or development agencies reach those for whom they are intended; that they are supported institutionally at the local level in order to achieve sustainability; that they are not isolated one-offs, but fit into a broader enabling governance framework; and that they provide information to national policymakers on the impact of macro-policy at the micro-level. The methodology of implementing poverty audits at the local level in remote rural communities requires setting up a local database on the incidence and depth of poverty at sub-district level, where a local poverty profile is established, vulnerable groups are identified, and a participatory poverty assessment determines the local architecture of poverty.

The next crucial step is linking problems to solutions within resource availability, and also within the local standards of service delivery throughout the region. The priority of resource allocation to bridging the gaps between regional averages and pockets of extreme poverty is often a difficult commitment for local authorities to make. A budgetary review would then be in order to trace the coherence between actual resource allocation patterns and the spatial and social incidence of extreme poverty. Finally, in a joint local government/civil society organization/community planning meeting, commitments are made to address the causal and symptomatic features of local poverty with a regional, equitable and transparent process. Concrete examples of this are in evidence in the Local Government Reform Programme of Tanzania, in regional authorities of northern Namibia and in the Romanian Social Development Fund. (A germane paradigm called poverty proofing has also been used by the Ministry of Finance in Ireland; the World Bank equivalent, Poverty and Social Impact Analysis (PSIA), has less of a strategic dimension for putting things right.)

A new rural paradigm to meet the challenges of poverty reduction

Given the pessimistic environmental scenario for the poor, and the debilitating events such as conflict and corruption that are beyond the immediate power of change of actors on the international and national scenes, any new scenarios are obviously limited.

Agriculture has been the mainstay of the rural poor in terms of food and sources of income and employment. The protectionism of EC and US agricultural markets seriously constrains growth in this sector. There is a very pessimistic prognosis for the sector emerging from the IPCC (2007) study on climate change. Agriculture and food production are likely to be seriously compromised by climate variability affecting the surface area suitable for agriculture, increasing deterioration between arid and semi-arid areas, decreasing yield potentials and reducing fish stocks, all leading to deteriorating food security, which is of vital importance to the rural poor. In this respect, Africa is considered to be one of the most vulnerable continents to climate variability and change because of multiple stresses and low adaptive capacity – up to 250 million people could be adversely affected.

Given the obvious constraints affecting the agriculture sector, can we look towards a viable future for the rural poor?

A coordinated sustainable livelihoods approach, which synchronizes market opportunities, governance, security concerns and the rule of law, a vibrant civil society, progress across all areas of the Millennium Development Goals, might appear utopian. However, in remote, poor, rural communities, access to income-generating opportunities, labour mobility and product market opportunities, both locally and further afield, Internet connectedness supplementing mobile phone technology, off-farm product development, micro-credit schemes, small rural enterprises and analysis of local competitive advantage can all be seen to have an impact. These community approaches would be underpinned by a transfer of administrative powers to local levels – an investment-based public expenditure approach, which would be based on partnerships with local organizations and local communities. Such interventions would be results-driven, with incentives designed to elicit good performance and, where appropriate, to correct market failures, which tend to be many in isolated poverty environments.

Stronger rural-urban linkages can contribute to creating a constructive synergy of labour market and product mobility, thus adding value to the production base in the rural area, improving competitiveness and generating employment opportunities. Enhanced infrastructure can stabilize the working population in rural areas, provided the correct enabling economic environment is created by the public sector.

GUIDE TO FURTHER READING AND REFERENCES

CPRC (Chronic Poverty Research Centre) (2004) *The Chronic Poverty Report, 2005–05*, Manchester: Institute for Development Policy and Management.

G8 (2005) *G8 Gleneagles 2005: Africa* (available at http://www.fco.gov.uk/Files/kfile/PostG8_Gleneagles_Africa,O.pdf).

IDMC (Internal Displacement Monitoring Centre) (2007) *Internal Displacement: Global Overview of Trends and Developments in 2006*, Geneva: Norwegian Refugee Council.

IFAD (2001) *Rural Poverty Report 2001: The Challenge of Ending Rural Poverty*, Rome: International Fund for Agricultural Development.

IPCC (Intergovernmental Panel on Climate Change) (2007) *Climate Change 2007: Impacts, Adaptation and Vulnerability*, Geneva: World Meteorological Organization/United Nations Environment Programme.

Local Government Reform Programme (2003) *Auditing Poverty in Tanzania*, Dar es Salaam: Department for International Development/BC/President's Office.

Mullen, J. (1999) *Rural Poverty, Empowerment and Sustainable Livelihoods*, Aldershot: Ashgate.

Mullen, J. (2002) *Training Compendium relating to Poverty Auditing*, Dar es Salaam: Urban Authorities Partnership Project and Department for International Development.

Mullen, J. (2005) 'Ten critical lessons on poverty and local governance', in B.S. Rao (ed.) *Guidelines for Good Governance*, Dhaka: Centre on Integrated Rural Development for Asia and the Pacific and Commonwealth Secretariat.

Narayan, D. and Petesch, P. (eds) (2002) *Voices of the Poor*, New York: Oxford University Press and World Bank.

OECD (2007) *Migration, Remittances and Development*, Paris: Organization for Economic Cooperation and Development.

Oxfam (2004) *The Rural Poverty Trap*, Briefing Paper 59, Oxford: Oxfam.

UN (2006) *Millennium Development Goals Report 2006*, New York: United Nations Department of Economic and Social Affairs.

UNDP (2007) *Human Development Report 2006*, New York: United Nations Development Programme.

3.2 Rural livelihoods

Annelies Zoomers

Introduction

During the final decades of the twentieth century and the first decade of the twenty-first, in many countries in Africa, Asia and Latin America, both agriculture and the rural sector rapidly lost ground. At the same time, however, more people now inhabit ecologically vulnerable zones, and the incidence of extreme poverty has become more prominent. Globally, three-quarters of the 1.2 billion people who are in 'extreme consumption poverty' work and live in rural areas (IFAD 2001).

To the extent that governments and NGOs have tried to improve the situation of the rural poor, we see a wide range of different strategies that have been implemented since the mid-twentieth century (see Table 1). Whereas for decades the policy goals were agricultural growth and regional development (e.g. the 'green revolution', land reform, agricultural colonization and integrated rural development), the focus is now on sustainable development and poverty alleviation (or, more explicitly, achieving the Millennium Development Goals, or MDGs). In spite of this long history of policy interventions rural livelihoods generally have not improved. Rural livelihoods are increasingly under stress, and today the rural poor are often described as 'chronically poor'. Increasing numbers see migration as the quickest way to move out of poverty.

Since the 1990s, efforts have been made to gain a better understanding of rural livelihoods and to bring rural development strategies more in line with the aspirations and priorities of rural people. This *livelihood approach* was a response to the disappointing results of former approaches in devising effective policies to encourage development and/or to alleviate poverty; the central objective was 'to search for more effective methods to support people and communities in ways that are more meaningful to their daily lives and needs, as opposed to ready made, interventionist instruments' (Appendini 2001).

There are many different approaches to sustainable livelihoods, but the most common definition is that given by Chambers and Conway (1991):

> A livelihood comprises the capabilities, assets (including both material and social resources) and activities required for a means of living. A livelihood is sustainable when it can cope with and recover from stresses and shocks and maintain or enhance its capabilities and assets both now and in the future, while not undermining the natural resource base.

The livelihood approach helped to uncover a number of dimensions of rural livelihood that previously had not been very clear. It also helped to achieve a more holistic understanding of livelihood, showing that livelihood does not concern material well-being, but rather that it also includes non-material well-being. According to Bebbington (1999: 2022):

> a person's assets, such as land, are not merely means with which he or she makes a living: they also give meaning to that person's world. Assets are not simply resources that people use in building livelihoods; they are assets that give them the capability to be and act. Assets should not be understood only as things that allow survival, adaptation and poverty alleviation, they are also the basis of agent's power to act and to reproduce, challenge or change the rules that govern the control, use and transformation of resources.

The livelihood approach represents a multidisciplinary view of poverty, acknowledging that poverty is not an economic problem, but that it involves political, cultural, social and ecological aspects as well (Kaag et al. 2004: 52).

In addition, most livelihood studies have in common that – in contrast to the earlier tendency to conceive poor people as passive victims – they highlight the active, and even proactive, role played by the (rural) poor. The emphasis is on seeing people as agents actively shaping their own future, focusing not on what poor people lack, but rather on what they have (their capitals) and on their capability (Sen 1981; Chambers and Conway 1991).

The livelihood approach is grounded in the idea that people's livelihood largely depends on the opportunity to access capitals which form the basis of their livelihood strategies. These capitals are human capital (skills, education), social capital (networks), financial capital (money), natural capital (land, water, minerals) and physical capital (houses, livestock, machinery). Sometimes a cultural capital is added; or the physical or financial capitals are replaced by produced capital (Bebbington 1999). Moser, in her vulnerability framework (1998), makes a distinction between labour and household relations – and housing – as additional assets. According to Bebbington, social capital is the most critical asset to rural people because it enables access, and access is necessary in order to diversify and expand their assets portfolio. Social capital enables people to widen access to resources and actors, to make living meaningful and to modify power structures and rules (Bebbington 1999).

In the livelihood approach, the emphasis is on the flexible combinations and trade-off between capitals (all capitals are linked to each other), that is, if a person does not have land to cultivate (natural capital), he will try to acquire a plot through his network of social relations (social capital). Somebody who decides to migrate will often be forced to spend more money on hiring labour for working his fields; after some time (due to his absence), people can no longer rely on the free help provided by neighbours and/or relatives (financial capital replacing social capital). 'A positive increase in access to one capital can mean a decrease in access to another capital; this is because the input of the one capital can mean a decrease in access to another capital' (Bebbington 1999). To the extent that rural livelihoods are described in terms of 'vulnerability', a distinction can be made between sensitivity (the magnitude of a system's response to an external event) and resilience (the ease and rapidity of a system's recovery from stress) (Moser 1998: 3).

A weakness of the livelihood approach is that poverty is sometimes romanticized, focusing on the ability, or flexibility, of people to cope with crisis. The emphasis is placed on whether or not the poor are able to keep their position rather than on the possibility of social upward mobility (and finding a way out of poverty).

Another important drawback of the livelihood approach is the relative neglect of structural limitations. The livelihood framework is centred on people's assets and capabilities, and by speaking about capitals, it seems that people have access to assets. While people might have access to land, for the majority this means only small plots of eroded land; it will not help people to find a way out of poverty, and many are not capable of using this to accumulate capital. The success of the rural poor may be related less to strategic actions than to structural, often locational, limitations. In the rural context, sustainability often means continuing poverty reduction, together with environmental, social and institutional sustainability.

An evaluation

The livelihood approach has enabled us to gain a better understanding of the realities of rural life and the dynamics of rural livelihoods. It made clear that rural livelihoods cannot be understood without opening the black box of the household. Within the family, members are selectively involved in decision making, and are occupied in different activities, each having their own negotiating power. Along with the growing complexity of labour division, the interests of a household's individual members will not always be consistent with the family goal (if there is one); variations in personal capacities and motivations affect the interrelationships among the various activities, as well as the degree of internal cohesion. Conflict and competition may arise between activities and among members of the household. In many rural areas, family life is increasingly individualized, and many villages are experiencing the erosion of community life. Village or community organizations no longer perform the traditional role of a safety valve.

Moreover, livelihood studies have ascertained that, since the mid-1990s, increasing numbers of people in rural areas have opted for a development path characterized by multitasking and income diversification (Bryceson 2000; Reardon, Berdegué and Escobar 2001). There is a tendency towards livelihood diversification, namely, 'a process by which…households construct an increasingly diverse portfolio of activities and assets in order to survive and to improve their standard of living' (Ellis 2000: 15). In many cases, the bulk of the income of the rural poor no longer originates from agriculture; people have multiple income sources. It has become increasingly difficult to make distinctions between rural and urban livelihoods: rural people live in cities during some months of the year, to work in construction, for example; and 'new poor' in the urban sphere start growing food crops in the cities; at the same time, the well-off invest their accumulated money in the purchase of rural lands; while the rural people buy parcels of land in the cities in order to give their children a better education (exit strategies). A considerable proportion of rural land belongs to non-farmers, some of whom are affluent urbanites who obtain the land by foreclosing on loans. Increasing land values have led them to consider land as an attractive commodity for investment purposes.

In addition to multitasking and the blurring of the rural-urban interface, there is another trend in which rural people increasingly develop multi-local livelihoods. In development geography, regions frequently have been conceived as demarcated areas, with people being rooted to localities. Concepts such as carrying capacity were applied to express a region's ability to support a certain population. But rapid urbanization and the improvement of communications and transport technology have resulted in a significant increase in mobility. Increasing numbers of rural poor now engage in urban and rural life, commuting from the countryside to urban centres on a daily basis. Poor people also supplement their incomes by travelling large distances to earn additional money as temporary migrants, and international migration (South–South and South–North) is rapidly increasing. Considerable numbers of rural poor are no longer rooted in one place; although they maintain relations with their home communities, they are also attached to other places and function in larger networks.

Conclusion

Livelihood research has made clear that policymakers and the rural populations do not always operate according to the same logic, which may be a major reason why many policy interventions had disappointing results. First, with respect to policymakers' persistent focus on the *via campesina*, the majority of the rural poor are no longer investing in agriculture, but have a broad range of different income sources, while their land is used mainly for subsistence farming, not for generating income. Policymakers often base their intervention on solving problems *in situ* (i.e. the area where poverty is concentrated – poverty mapping), whereas many of the poor search for outside solutions (such as migration); the majority of the rural poor have multi-local livelihoods. Rural life is in many cases no longer agricultural or village-based. The '*via campesina* of development is only a realistic option for a happy few in areas with good market access, especially those with sufficient land and capital (and knowledge of international markets. There are limited possibilities for campesino agriculture in a few accessible locations' (Bebbington 2000). The majority of the rural poor are now trapped in a multilocal livelihood and the possibilities for a better life are hard to find: low prices, environmental degradation, erosion and land fragmentation restrict the possibilities for locally based livelihood improvements, and there is no clear way out of this situation.

At the same time, however, it is not realistic to depict the rural poor as a homogeneous 'social category' of non-viables. Given the diversity and dynamics of livelihood strategies, problems cannot be resolved by a fixed selection of programmes or projects; priorities – and needs – will differ by socio-economic class, as well as by gender and age; moreover, needs change over time; instead of assuming that it is possible to reach different types of target groups with one and the same policy, it would be useful to adopt a more flexible 'supermarket approach', with an array of choices.

Table 1 An overview of dominant concepts related to rural development policies since the 1950s

Period	Dominant concepts	Dominant actor	Examples of interventions
1950s	Green revolution	National governments and private sector	Investments in agricultural extension, mechanization, irrigation, etc., stressing the need for introducing Western technology allowing for 'modernization'
1960s–1970s	Land reforms and/or agricultural colonization	National governments and international donors	Redistribution of the land/expansion of agricultural area; stressing the need to redistribute the land and/or providing the rural poor with more and better land ('growth with distribution')
1970s–1980s	Integrated rural development	International donors, national governments and NGOs	Area-based investment in infrastructure, agriculture, small-scale industry, irrigation schemes, etc., stressing the need for a bottom-up and integrated approach with sufficient participation ('basic needs, bottom-up development, appropriate development')
1980s–present	Sustainable development	International donors, NGOs and local governments	'[A] development that meets the needs of the present generation without compromising the ability of future generations to meet their needs' (WCED 1987), stressing the need to sustain the natural system and achieve greater equity in economic, social and political dimensions, with more emphasis put on the long-term environmental and distributional aspects of development
1990s–present	Pro-poor growth/ achievement of MDGs	Market forces/ international donors, local governments, private sector and NGOs	Stressing the need to create an enabling environment and facilitating market forces (e.g. helping smallholders to become involved in non-traditional agro-export; the creation of an active, free and transparent land market; micro-credit and saving systems; sustainable (rural) tourism
2000s	Migration as development strategy	Migrant networks and diaspora organizations, international donors and NGOs	Stressing the need to make productive use of remittances sent by migrants for developing (rural) areas of origin

GUIDE TO FURTHER READING AND REFERENCES

Appendini, K. (2001) 'Land and livelihood: What do we know, and what are the issues?', in A. Zoomers (ed.) *Land and Sustainable Livelihood in Latin America*, Amsterdam, Madrid and Frankfurt: KIT Publications and Iberoamericana/Vervuert Verlag, pp. 23–38.

Bebbington, A. (1999) 'Capital and capabilities: A framework for analysing peasant viability, rural livelihoods and poverty', *World Development*, 27(12): 2021–44.

Bebbington, A. (2000) 'Reencountering development: Livelihood transitions and place transformations in the Andes', *Annals of the Association of American Geographers*, 90(3): 495–520.

Bryceson, D., Kay, C. and Mooij, J. (eds) (2000) *Disappearing Peasantries? Rural Labour in Africa, Asia and Latin America*, London: Intermediate Technology Development Group Publishing.

Chambers, R. and Conway, G. (1991) 'Sustainable rural livelihoods: Practical concepts for the 21st century', Discussion Paper 296, Brighton: Institute of Development Studies.

de Haan, L. (2000) 'Globalization, localization and sustainable livelihood', *Sociologia Ruralis*, 40(3): 339–65.

de Haan, L. and Zoomers, A. (2003) 'Development geography at the crossroads of livelihood and globalisation', *Journal of Economic and Social Geography*, 94(3): 350–62.

de Haan, L. and Zoomers, A. (2005) 'Exploring the frontier of livelihood research', *Development and Change*, 36(1): 27–47.

Ellis, F. (2000) *Rural Livelihoods and Diversity in Developing Countries*, Oxford: Oxford University Press.

International Fund for Agricultural Development (IFAD) (2001) *Rural Poverty Report 2001 – The Challenge of Ending Rural Poverty*, http://www.ifad.org/poverty

Kaag, M. et al. (2004) 'Ways forward in livelihood research', in D. Kalb, W. Pansters and H. Siebers (eds) *Globalization and Development. Themes and Concepts in Current Research*, Dordrecht: Kluwer Publishers, pp. 49–74.

Moser, C. (1998) 'The asset vulnerability framework: Reassessing urban poverty reduction strategies', *World Development*, 26(1): 1–19.

Reardon, T., Berdegué, J. and Escobar, G. (2001) 'Rural non-farm employment and incomes in Latin America: Overview and policy implications', *World Development*, 29(3): 395–409.

Scoones, I. (1998) 'Sustainable rural livelihoods. A framework for analysis', Working Paper 72, Brighton: Institute of Development Studies

Sen, A. (1981) *Poverty and Famines. An Essay on Entitlements and Deprivation*, Oxford: Oxford University Press.

USEFUL WEBSITES

http://www.odi.org.uk
http://www.livelihoods.org
http://www.undp.org
http://www.ids.ac.uk/ids/bookshop
http://www.ifad.org/poverty

3.3 Food security

Rachel Slater, Kay Sharp and Steve Wiggins

Approaches to food security

> Food security exists when all people at all times have physical and economic access to suffi-
> cient, safe and nutritious food to meet their dietary needs and food preferences for an active
> and healthy life (FAO 1996).

This definition is now widely accepted, but it was not always the case. In the 1960s and 1970s, Malthusian fears that the rapid growth of the world population would outstrip food production and lead to widespread famine meant that food production and *availability*, rather than access, were the key concerns. Matters came to a head during the world food crisis of the early 1970s, when a combination of poor harvests and reduced food stocks led to rapid increases in the price of food. The price spike proved short-lived, as did the focus on food availability.

The 1980s saw a growing awareness of the importance of *access* to food, determined economi-
cally and socially. As Amartya Sen influentially observed, 'Starvation is the characteristic of some people not *having* enough food to eat. It is not the characteristic of there *being* not enough food to eat' (Sen 1981: 1).

Subsequently, analyses of famine mortality in Darfur in 1984–85 and insights from nutrition have added a third dimension to food security: the *utilization* of food for nourishment, in which health plays a major role. Approaches to food security have thus shifted from national and international concerns about food supply and self-sufficiency, to ensuring household and individual access to food, and that individuals are healthy enough to make full use of nutrients in their diet.

Progress towards food security targets

In 1996, the UN World Food Summit (WFS) agreed a target of halving the *number* of under-
nourished people in the world to 415 million, or 6 per cent of the population, by 2015. By the end of the decade it was already clear that this target would not be met. Consequently, the Millennium Development Goal (MDG) target for food security is the less ambitious one of halving the *proportion* of undernourished people over the same period, from 20 per cent to 10 per cent.

Progress towards these targets is shown in Table 1 and in the graph from the Food and Agriculture Organization (FAO). The latter shows that the overall number of undernourished people stagnated in the 1990s, after reductions of 37 million in the 1970s and 100 million in the 1980s. On current projections, the MDG target will be met at a global level: however, this masks considerable variation among regions (Table 1).

Asia and Latin America have made significant progress. Vietnam is a notable success story where the proportion of undernourished people has declined from 31 per cent to 17 per cent. In China, nearly 50 million people moved out of food insecurity in the 1990s, and the under-nutrition rate fell from 16 per cent to 12 per cent, largely due to strong economic and agricultural growth (FAO 2006). In Africa, on the other hand, although the proportion of undernourished peo-
ple has been falling since 1990/92, given population growth the absolute numbers have been ris-
ing, and are expected to continue to rise, so that there will probably be more people undernourished in 2015 than in 1990/92.

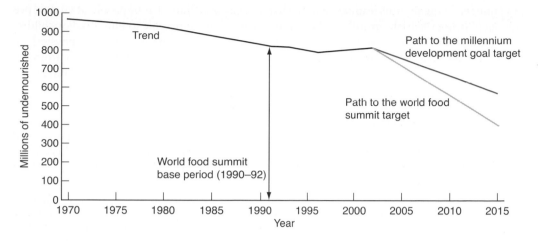

Progress towards MDG and World Food Summit targets
Source: FAO 2006

Table 1 Projected undernourishment in the developing world

	Number of undernourished people (millions)			Prevalence of undernourishment (percentage of population)		
	1990–92*	2015	WFS target	1990–92*	2015	MDG target
Developing countries	823	582	412	20.3	10.1	10.2
Sub-Saharan Africa	170	179	85	35.7	21.1	17.9
Near East and North Africa	24	36	12	7.6	7.0	3.8
Latin America and the Caribbean	60	41	30	13.4	6.6	6.7
South Asia	291	203	146	25.9	12.1	13.0
East Asia**	277	123	139	16.5	5.8	8.3

Source: FAO 2006

Notes:
The base period for projections is 1999–2001 and not 2001–03. Some small countries have also been excluded from the projections.
* Data for 1990–92 may differ slightly from numbers reported elsewhere in the report as the projections are based on undernourishment estimates that do not include the latest revisions.
** Includes South East Asia.

What should be done?

Food insecurity manifests itself in three ways. Acute crisis and, at worst, famine are the most dramatic form. Almost always temporary, food crises can affect large numbers of people who are not normally hungry, but who are generally poor and vulnerable to shocks, both natural, such as droughts, and human, as in the case of war or sudden increases in the price of food. Owing to the numbers involved and the likelihood of large-scale mortality – even if most people who die in famines succumb to disease rather than starvation – such crises attract much attention.

Chronic or persistent under-nutrition affects hundreds of millions of people who are essentially too poor to be able to eat sufficient food to satisfy their calorie and protein needs. Where agriculture is the main source of food and incomes, the problem is often seasonal, with people regularly going hungry in the months leading up to the harvest. Chronic hunger robs people of vitality, prevents them using their labour fully, and can leave them more vulnerable to illnesses. For children under the age of three, the effects are more damaging: under-nutrition can affect their physical and mental development, reducing their capabilities as adults, and so transmitting poverty from one generation to the next. For young mothers, under-nutrition causes low birth weights. Although the toll of chronic under-nutrition is high, it does not result in sudden mass death and thus attracts less attention than food crises and famines.

A third form of food insecurity is deficiency of micro-nutrients, principally iodine, iron and vitamin A, owing to inadequate and unvaried diets. As many as 2 billion people may be affected. The consequences are illness, disability and, for young children, failure to develop full physical and mental capabilities. These problems are so little appreciated that they are sometimes referred to as 'hidden hunger'.

While the three forms of food insecurity overlap, in that some people may be subject to all three at some time, the distinction is useful for policy purposes, since each problem calls for different measures.

Acute food crises

These can be prevented if poor people can maintain their entitlements to food. In practical terms, this means preventing the collapse of incomes and sharp rises in food prices, for example by providing public employment or cash transfers when crises arise. It may mean public management of reserve stocks of foods to contain price rises. If these measures fail, food distributions may be needed. Children are particularly vulnerable, and may need supplementary feeding and inoculation. Clean water, sanitation and medical supplies are often critical in averting famine deaths.

> Technically, the prevention and mitigation of famine are well understood: yet the threat of mass starvation persists in the modern world. Recent analysis of late-twentieth-century famines focuses on politics as central to understanding the causation of, and responses to, the 'new famines' (Devereux 2006).

Chronic malnutrition

The agenda for chronic malnutrition consists of helping people to escape extreme poverty, keeping the prices of basic foodstuffs low, and ensuring reasonable health and hygiene. A particular problem in poverty alleviation is the shocks that push people down towards destitution; safety nets and other forms of social protection can prevent this. Keeping food prices low is best done through increased farm output, rather than by price controls and subsidies. In Bangladesh, for example, increased output from the green revolution helped to halve real food prices between the 1980s and 2000. Young mothers and children under three are particularly vulnerable to the consequences of chronic hunger. Health programmes are needed to monitor their nutrition, immunize infants, provide oral rehydration to treat diarrhoea, combat malaria through measures such as bednets, and deliver safe water and sanitation.

Food aid and chronic hunger
Food aid is a vital last resort in crises where local food supplies have collapsed, but its appropriateness in other contexts, its costs, and its impact on local markets and livelihoods have long been questioned (see Barrett and Maxwell (2005) for a review of the issues).

In recent years, increased attention to chronic hunger has fostered a growing preference for cash transfers (Harvey 2007) and other approaches such as social protection, risk management and insurance.

Micro-nutrient deficiency

The hidden hunger of micro-nutrient deficiency can readily be tackled through fortifying staple foods where these are commonly processed (e.g. bread and salt); by providing supplements to young mothers and infants; and by encouraging dietary diversification through home gardens, raising chickens, fish ponds and the like.

In all three cases, most measures are not technically difficult, nor hard to implement, nor even that costly: the challenge is summoning the political will to make a difference.

Emerging challenges

HIV/AIDS

Recurrent food crises, particularly in southern Africa, where HIV prevalence rates are the highest in the world, have placed HIV/AIDS on the food security agenda. De Waal (in Devereux 2006) has warned that a different type of famine – 'new variant famine' – may emerge as HIV/AIDS increases household vulnerability and reduces production.

Rural households affected by HIV/AIDS tend to suffer falling assets and productivity. Time spent caring for the sick reduces labour time on productive activities such as agriculture, while money that would otherwise be spent on productive investments is diverted to pay for medicines and funerals. Similarly, urban households unable to work lose entitlements to food.

HIV/AIDS and nutrition are interlinked. People with poor diets are more vulnerable to HIV infection; once infected, they develop AIDS more quickly; once they have AIDS, their nutritional requirements increase; and antiretroviral drugs are effective only when coupled with an adequate diet (Gillespie 2006).

Climate change

Climate change is expected to affect both food supply and access. Even under scenarios with small amounts of climate change, agricultural yields may fall where crops are near their maximum temperature tolerance; decreased rainfall could affect agriculture regardless of latitude; and there may be significant negative effects for small farmers and pastoralists who are weakly integrated into markets (Parry, Rosenzweig and Livermore 2005).

Africa is considered most at risk of increased hunger, both acute and chronic: there will be more short-term shocks from unpredictable weather events, and changing temperature and water resources may result in longer-term declines in yields. As prospects worsen for national, regional and even continental self-sufficiency in cereals, and transportation of food is more heavily taxed, food *supply* may re-emerge as a focal point of food security policy.

Changing food systems

The character of global food systems is changing as urbanization, technology and industrialization change the way food is produced, marketed and consumed (Maxwell and Slater 2004). Food businesses, such as supermarkets, play new roles in moving food between countries and in establishing new kinds of supply chains within developing countries. Urbanization is changing dietary patterns and preferences, leading to a 'nutrition transition' towards increasing proportions of proteins and fats in people's diets. Town dwellers, especially poor people, are consuming more food outside the home.

These dietary changes are not unique to the developed world. As a direct result, non-communicable diseases such as diabetes, obesity, high blood pressure and heart disease are emerging in developing countries. Proportional obesity rates are as high in parts of Mexico and South Africa as they are in the USA, and diabetes is at epidemic levels in urban Ethiopia. Small farmers and producers are being squeezed out of supply chains by larger producers and supermarkets. Poor consumers may find themselves paying higher prices for less healthy food, or being socially excluded because they cannot afford a diet that society considers 'normal'.

In response, the 'new' food policy (see Table 2) requires a wider range of policies to tackle *mal*-nourishment, not only *under*-nourishment – from taxing unhealthy food to ensuring that poor producers can benefit from the new global food system. However, these policies are expensive and are likely to be weakest in poor countries.

Table 2 Food Policy – old and new

		Food policy 'old'	Food policy 'new'
1	Population	Mostly rural	Mostly urban
2	Rural jobs	Mostly agricultural	Mostly non-agricultural
3	Employment in the food sector	Mostly in food production and primary marketing	Mostly in food manufacturing and retail
4	Actors in food marketing	Grain traders	Food companies
5	Supply chains	Short – small number of food miles	Long – large number of food miles
6	Typical food preparation	Mostly food cooked at home	High proportion of pre-prepared meals, food eaten out
7	Typical food	Basic staples, unbranded	Processed food, branded products More animal products in the diet
8	Packaging	Low	High
9	Purchased food bought in	Local stall or shops, open markets	Supermarkets
10	Food safety issues	Pesticide poisoning of field workers Toxins associated with poor storage	Pesticide residues in food Adulteration Bio-safety issues in processed food (salmonella, listeriosis)
11	Nutrition problems	Under-nutrition	Chronic dietary diseases (obesity, heart disease, diabetes)
12	Nutrient issues	Calories, micro-nutrients	Fat; sugar; salt
13	Food-insecure	'Peasants'	Urban and rural poor
14	Main sources of national food shocks	Poor rainfall and other production shocks	International price and other trade problems
15	Main sources of household food shocks	Poor rainfall and other production shocks	Income shocks causing food poverty
16	Remedies for household food storage	Safety nets, food-based relief	Social protection, income transfers
17	Fora for food policy	Ministries of agriculture, relief/rehabilitation, health	Ministries of trade and industry, consumer affairs, finance Food activist groups, NGOs
18	Focus of food policy	Agricultural technology, parastatal reform, supplementary feeding, food for work	Competition and rent-seeking in the value chain, industrial structure in the retail sector, futures markets, waste management, advertising, health education, food safety
19	Key international institutions	FAO, WFP, UNICEF, WHO, CGIAR	FAO, UNIDO, ILO, WHO, WTO

Source: Maxwell and Slater 2004

GUIDE TO FURTHER READING

Devereux, S. (ed.) (2006) *The New Famines: Why Famines Persist in an Era of Globalization*, Abingdon: Routledge.

Devereux, D. and Maxwell, S. (eds) (2001) *Food Security in Sub-Saharan Africa*, London: Intermediate Technology Development Group Publishing.

Maxwell, S. and Frankenberger, T.R. (1993) *Household Food Security: Concepts, Indicators, Measurements*, Rome: UNICEF and IFAD.

Sen, A.K. (1981) *Poverty and Famines: An Essay on Entitlement and Deprivation*, Oxford: Clarendon Press.

USEFUL WEBSITES

http://www.eldis.org/food
http://www.fao.org/monitoringprogress
http://www.ifpri.org
http://www.odi.org.uk

REFERENCES

Barrett, C. and Maxwell, D. (2005) *Food Aid After Fifty Years: Recasting its Role,* Abingdon: Routledge.

FAO (1996) *Rome Declaration on World Food Security*, Rome: Food and Agriculture Organization.

FAO (2006) *The State of Food Insecurity in the World 2006*, Rome: Food and Agriculture Organization.

Gillespie, S. (ed.) (2006) *Aids, Poverty and Hunger: Challenges and Responses*, Washington, DC: IFPRI.

Harvey, P. (2007) 'Cash-based responses in emergencies', HPG Report 24, London: Overseas Development Institute.

Maxwell, S. and Slater, R. (eds) (2004) *Food Policy – Old and New*, Oxford: Blackwell.

Parry, M., Rosenzweig, C. and Livermore, M. (2005) 'Climate change, global food supply and risk of hunger', *Philosophical Transactions of the Royal Society, Series B*, 360: 2125–38.

Sen, A.K. (1981) *Poverty and Famines: An Essay on Entitlement and Deprivation*, Oxford: Clarendon Press.

3.4 Rural cooperatives

D.W. Attwood, B.S. Baviskar and D.R. Sick

Some development goals are best achieved by cooperatives or similar organizations, rather than private corporations or state bureaucracies. This chapter examines the role of cooperatives in rural development, starting with examples from India.

We discuss 'formal' cooperatives (established under official regulatory frameworks), 'informal' cooperation (customary methods of pooling labour, savings, etc.) and 'cooperative-friendly' organizations, such as NGOs promoting micro-credit, micro-thrift or fair trade. What factors cause these varied organizations to succeed or fail, and what benefits accrue to the rural poor if they succeed? Given the huge number and variety of such organizations, our examples are only suggestive.

Formal cooperatives in India

Formal cooperatives started under British administration, financed and administered by regional governments. After Independence (1947), more types of cooperatives were promoted for rural development. India now has over 500,000 cooperatives, reaching a majority of rural households.

However, these cooperatives suffer many weaknesses. Few become economically viable; many are moribund or defunct. Few operate under democratic control by their members; most are managed by government officials.

Success in sugar and milk processing

There are some genuine, member-controlled cooperatives. Notable examples include sugar factories in Maharashtra state and dairies in Gujarat.

India is the world's largest sugar producer; cooperatives in Maharashtra make up about 30 per cent of the total. Compared to private factories in other regions of India, these cooperatives are superior in efficiency, enabling them to pay higher prices for sugar cane – a vital benefit for their members, most of whom are small farmers.

These cooperatives were highly successful from the 1950s to the 1980s. Many expanded and diversified into ancillary enterprises. They built schools, colleges, clinics and hospitals in their local areas. Their success resulted from management by members and elected leaders, assisted by hired managers and technicians. More recently, many sugar cooperatives have declined (for reasons outlined below).

As Maharashtra led in sugar cooperatives, Gujarat led in dairies. The renowned Kheda District Cooperative Milk Producers' Union has an annual turnover of 3 billion rupees (roughly US$100 million). The Gujarat Cooperative Milk Marketing Federation has a distribution network all over India, with an annual turnover of 150 billion rupees (Candler and Kumar 1998). The main benefit for members, as dairy farmers, is access to distant urban markets. Because milk is perishable, such access is impossible without industrial processing and transport, as provided by the cooperatives.

Understanding patterns of success and failure

Institutional design analysis looks inside organizations for factors promoting efficiency or inefficiency (see Shah 1996). An example may be taken from our work on sugar factories. Because sugar cane is perishable, the efficiency of a modern sugar factory depends on a steady supply of freshly cut cane, harvested over several months from an area of several thousand hectares. India's high population density and land scarcity made big sugar plantations unfeasible in most areas. Thus, most private sugar factories had to buy cane from thousands of local farmers. This entailed high transaction costs and irregular cane supply, making private factories inefficient.

After Independence, this problem was overcome. In 1951, cane growers in western Maharashtra established a cooperative sugar factory. As co-investors and co-managers (via an elected board of directors), they acquired a stake in the efficient use of heavy industrial equipment and thus needed a centrally managed harvest system. The factory hired and coordinated teams of migrant harvest workers to obtain a carefully scheduled supply of fresh cane. Shareholders remained independent farmers; joint ownership meant tying each share to a contract to grow one half-acre of cane for the factory annually.

As the first such cooperative succeeded, others arose in Maharashtra. More efficient than nearby private factories, they drove most out of business. One must wonder, then, why cooperative sugar factories did not flourish in other regions, particularly northern India. This question mirrors a basic one in institutional economics: why does competition not compel all producers to adopt better innovations? Following North's (1990) example, we use a political economy approach to look for answers.

Political economy analysis looks beyond internal design to external context, helping explain patterns of success and failure among regions. For example, 'cooperative' sugar factories in northern India superficially resemble those in Maharashtra, yet they are highly inefficient. Their main problems stem from state management.

After Independence, India's industrialization policies promoted public-sector enterprises. Five-year plans, modelled on those of the Soviet Union, regulated the economy. In most regions, it seemed logical that 'cooperatives' should also be managed by state officials. However, state-managed 'cooperatives', like state-owned industries, were consistently inefficient. As such, they could not offer good cane prices, so many farmers in northern India looked elsewhere to market their crop. Thus these cooperatives could not obtain a steady supply of cane, making them even more inefficient. Those that managed to survive did so only with heavy subsidies from the government.

Political problems have now also infected sugar cooperatives in Maharashtra. Starting in the 1980s, shifts in party politics at the national and state levels encouraged massive corruption. In addition, abrupt changes in national sugar pricing policies created a black market which left the cooperatives swimming in undisclosed cash, an irresistible temptation to many leaders. Above all, too many new sugar cooperatives were licensed as a form of political patronage. Sugar cane is a thirsty crop, and in this semi-arid region, over-expansion put a crushing demand on irrigation sources, particularly in years of drought. Of 190 cooperative sugar factories in the state, only 70 now have revenues exceeding costs; 26 may be salvageable, but 17 are truly 'sick', and 77 have closed down. The state government finally plans to limit the number of sugar factories and cut the massive subsidies to non-viable cooperatives.[1]

Cooperatives and the state: Other regions

African cooperatives resemble India's in several respects. They were first established by colonial rulers and managed by bureaucrats. After Independence, new rulers expected cooperatives to promote development by harnessing customary patterns of informal cooperation for building modern enterprises.

Early hopes soon faded. The much-publicized *ujamaa* programme in Tanzania provides a classic example. National leaders thought state-mandated collectivization would promote equality and productivity. The programme failed due to simplistic assumptions about rural society, coupled with top-down management by state officials (Hyden 1988). The new African nations generally lacked established democratic traditions, making it hard for member-controlled cooperatives to emerge.

In Latin America, as in Africa, many regimes were hostile to organizations not under state control, yet member-controlled cooperatives can be found. In Costa Rica, member control is facilitated by democratic traditions. The state supports cooperatives (e.g. via tax concessions) without managing them directly. To better compete in the global market, members of one coffee-processing cooperative decided to improve the quality of their product by harvesting more carefully (Sick 1999). In doing so, they gained higher prices through the cooperative, putting pressure on private factories to raise their prices. As this example illustrates, cooperatives perform better with cautious government support; however, direct control or unlimited subsidization is lethal.

Informal cooperation and NGOs

Many people use small, 'informal' institutions to pursue common interests. Almost everywhere, rural producers cooperate by pooling or exchanging labour. Informal savings groups are found in villages and cities around the world, where savings are collected in small increments from members, with each member gaining access to the pool by rotation. In some areas of Kenya, women's groups have been quite effective at pooling both labour and savings (Thomas-Slayter and Rocheleau 1995).

NGOs sometimes try to fill the gap between informal savings groups and dysfunctional, state-run 'cooperative' credit systems. In 1976, the Grameen Bank, a new type of NGO, was established in Bangladesh. The bank makes only small loans to poor people, primarily women organized in small groups. As with informal savings groups, group discipline ensures loan repayment. Other

1 'Financial performance of co-operative sugar factories in Maharashtra, financial year 2004–2005', published by the Vasantdada Sugar Institute, Manjari (BK), Tal. Haveli, Dist. Pune, 2005, p. 137.

NGOs have established similar micro-credit programmes. This system seems effective in reducing poverty and promoting women's empowerment (Hashemi, Schuler and Riley 1996).

In India's Andhra Pradesh state, an experiment in women's thrift cooperatives (WTCs) was launched in 1990 under the auspices of a local NGO, the Cooperative Development Foundation. WTCs raise funds solely through small, regular contributions from their members, who earn interest on savings at 1 per cent per month. (For loans they pay 2 per cent.) A village WTC may consist of 200–500 women, divided into groups of 10–50. Group discipline ensures excellent rates of loan recovery. Loans are used for household maintenance, education, health care and investments in livestock or small businesses.

In less than a decade, over 33,000 women had formed 101 WTCs, and their combined savings totalled 26 million rupees, with no external grants or loans. The NGO provided advice and support in establishing WTCs, but the latter soon become self-sufficient and self-managing. About half the members and leaders come from landless households (Biswas and Mahajan 1997).

India has poured vast sums into formal, state-run credit 'cooperatives', whose assets never consist of members' savings. Their loans mostly go to landowners (mainly men), and many loans are never repaid. Thus, state-sponsored 'cooperative' credit is neither self-supporting nor beneficial to the poorest villagers, including women. Worldwide, micro-credit programmes appeal to NGOs and donor agencies for various reasons, including their focus on disciplined repayment and their targeting of poor people, especially women. Yet these programmes may have overlooked the potential of 'micro-thrift', which is less dependent on external donors. Micro-thrift more closely resembles age-old patterns of informal cooperation and group discipline.

Formal cooperatives and fair trade

A special case of NGOs promoting cooperatives is the expanding fair trade movement, which guarantees coffee producers (for example) a minimum price when world prices are low, plus an additional premium when prices rise. To promote equity and ensure that producers control production and marketing, fair trade organizations (FTOs) deal only with cooperatives or other producer associations. As in the 1960s, this revival of faith in cooperatives as inherently democratic and equitable raises questions regarding how well cooperatives linked to FTOs are meeting the needs of producer members.

In Costa Rica, a country with a long history of coffee and cooperatives, established co-operatives have been slow to form fair trade partnerships. The experience of Costa Rican cooperatives formed expressly for fair trade has been varied. While some find that fair trade provides access to new markets and higher prices, others feel they are no better off than with conventional markets. In a study of Tanzanian coffee farmers, Parrish, Luzadis and Bentley (2005) likewise found that farmers did not always benefit from selling to FTOs as opposed to other buyers; depending on market conditions, the two strategies were complementary.

While the benefits of fair trade for cooperatives have been many (Raynolds, Murray and Taylor 2004), a number of problems remain. As supplies of fair trade coffee continue to outstrip demand, fair trade cooperatives must sell a large proportion of their coffee to the conventional market. Moreover, while fair trade prices benefit farmers when world prices are low, when prices rise, farmers often want to sell in the open market (Rice 2001). In Costa Rica, farmers often sell their better-quality beans outside the cooperatives for higher prices, causing tension with the cooperatives and FTOs. Research elsewhere also indicates that fair trade regulations can be burdensome for producer cooperatives (Moberg 2005).

GUIDE TO FURTHER READING

Attwood, D.W. (1992) *Raising Cane: The Political Economy of Sugar in Western India*, Boulder, CO, and London: Westview Press. A social history of factors leading to successful sugar cooperatives in Maharashtra.

Baviskar, B.S. and Attwood, D.W. (1995) *Finding the Middle Path: The Political Economy of Cooperation in Rural India*, Boulder, CO, and London: Westview Press. Case studies of cooperatives in several regions; analysis of patterns of success and failure.

Shah, T. (1996) *Catalysing Co-operation: Design of Self-Governing Organizations*, New Delhi: Sage Publications. Institutional design analysis of why cooperatives succeed or fail.

Sick, D.R. (1999) *Farmers of the Golden Bean: Costa Rican Households and the Global Coffee Economy*, DeKalb, IL: Northern Illinois University Press. Case study of a coffee-processing cooperative competing with private firms.

REFERENCES

Biswas, A. and Mahajan, V. (1997) *Sustainable Banking with the Poor: A Case Study on Women's Thrift Co-operative System in Warangal and Karimnagar Districts of Andhra Pradesh*, Hyderabad: Co-operative Development Foundation.

Candler, W. and Kumar, N. (1998) *India: The Dairy Revolution: The Impact of Dairy Development in India and the World Bank's Contribution*, Washington, DC: World Bank.

Hashemi, S.M., Schuler, S.R. and Riley, A.P. (1996) 'Rural credit programs and women's empowerment in Bangladesh', *World Development*, 24(4): 635–53.

Hyden, G. (1988) 'Approaches to co-operative development: Blueprint versus greenhouse', in D.W. Attwood and B.S. Baviskar (eds) *Who Shares? Cooperatives and Rural Development*, Delhi: Oxford University Press.

Moberg, M. (2005) 'Fair trade and eastern Caribbean banana farmers: Rhetoric and reality in the anti-globalization movement', *Human Organization*, 64(1): 4–15.

North, D. (1990) *Institutions, Institutional Change, and Economic Performance*, Cambridge: Cambridge University Press.

Parrish, B.D., Luzadis, V.A. and Bentley, W.R. (2005) 'What Tanzania's coffee farmers can teach the world: A performance-based look at the fair trade–free trade debate', *Sustainable Development*, 13: 177–89.

Raynolds, L.T., Murray, D. and Taylor, P.L. (2004) 'Fair trade coffee: Building producer capacity via global networks', *Journal of International Development*, 16: 1109–21.

Rice, R.R. (2001) 'Noble goals and challenging terrain: Organic and fair trade coffee movements in the global marketplace', *Journal of Agricultural and Environmental Ethics*, 14: 39–66.

Shah, T. (1996) *Catalysing Co-operation: Design of Self-Governing Organizations*, New Delhi: Sage Publications.

Sick, D.R. (1999) *Farmers of the Golden Bean: Costa Rican Households and the Global Coffee Economy*, DeKalb, IL: Northern Illinois University Press.

Thomas-Slayter, B. and Rocheleau, D. (1995) *Gender, Environment, and Development in Kenya: A Grassroots Perspective*, London: Lynne Rienner.

3.5 Land reform

Martin Adams

Introduction

'Land reform' is generally understood to mean the redistribution of land for the benefit of the landless, tenants and farm labourers (Adams 1995). It has more recently been expanded to include the upgrading of land tenure arrangements for the benefit of the poor. While it is now used more broadly, its essence is land redistribution. Economists have long recognized the link between inequality of asset distribution and poor macroeconomic performance, and have argued that the surest way to poverty reduction in most societies is through the reform of the property system. Although there are other roads to poverty alleviation, all are subject to distortions induced by inequality, especially the skewed distribution of property ownership. Economic growth does not reduce poverty when the bulk of income and consumption is monopolized by a small landowning minority. Landless people are located mostly in rural areas and often survive as seasonal workers on large farms and plantations, returning to unemployment in depressed rural settlements in the off season. Not surprisingly, the demand for land reform resurfaces periodically, especially at election times. However, as argued below, for the majority of countries, land redistribution is an increasingly difficult process to carry through, especially in a world in which small farmers must compete in global markets.

Redistributive reform worldwide

In Europe, beginning with the French Revolution, land reform in the eighteenth and nineteenth centuries took various paths, some less violent than others. In Denmark, there was a peaceful transition from bondage to small independent farmers. Peasants obtained ownership of their tenancies with the help of state funds channelled through a land bank. Social reforms, particularly in education and farm cooperatives, were accompanied by agrarian change, stimulated by the collapse of grain prices due to cheap cereal imports from the New World. This in turn provoked a conversion from grain to dairy production on small family farms.

In the twentieth century, many large estates and plantations in South East Asia (Japan, Taiwan, South Korea, Philippines) and Latin America (e.g. Colombia, Mexico, Bolivia, Brazil, Peru and Chile) were transferred to tenants. The reform of landlord tenancies in the Middle East (e.g. Iran, Iraq and Egypt) and India (Kerala State) followed a similar pattern and resulted in the breakdown of long-established power relationships. The reforms were most successful when the transfer of ownership to sharecropping tenants did not involve the break-up of the peasants' operational holdings. The subdivision of large farms in Latin America and southern Africa, under which beneficiaries formerly had small plots for subsistence but worked principally on the landlord's estate, has been less successful.

Redistributive land reform has often followed in the train of major political changes. The circumstances have varied, depending on the political imperatives underlying the change. In Japan and Taiwan, soon after the Second World War, the purpose was the removal of the landed elite and former military class. More recent attempts to implement land-to-the-tiller reforms in South East Asia followed the 1988 transition to democracy in post-Marcos Philippines. Land reform has often been implemented only at a token scale, to release the pressure, and then quietly dropped.

In China, commencing in 1949, redistributive land reform took place initially as a result of peasant mobilization against landlords. Landless peasants subdivided large landed estates and organized cooperatives. Communes were then enforced in the mid-1950s, but in the late 1970s, households were assigned individual responsibility for marketing and were allowed to dispose of farm products in excess of the fixed quotas that had to be sold to the state. In 1988, China's constitution was amended to legalize private land-use rights and land transfers. The reforms increased both farm and non-farm rural employment and eliminated the rural landlessness of the pre-revolutionary era that still afflicts much of Asia, Africa and Latin America today. The most recent round of tenure changes has led to the concentration of landholdings and industrial urbanization, as peasants have left the countryside, either renting out or cashing in their rural property assets.

Land redistribution in post-colonial Africa

The repossession of land taken by European settlers has been a major agrarian issue in post-colonial Africa. Under the 'one million-acre scheme' in Kenya, more than a thousand white farms were transferred to Africans between 1962 and 1966, with Britain underwriting financial compensation. The plan was to transfer freehold land to three categories of African farmers: large-scale commercial farmers, small-scale commercial farmers and peasants. In the event, the demand for small-scale commercial farms was lower than expected, resulting in the resettlement of more smallholders. In the 1970s, small-scale African farmers greatly expanded dairy and cash crop production. The expansion was more a result of the waiving of restrictions and the opening up of markets for Africans than of land redistribution per se. Beneficiaries in the large-scale commercial category were less successful than small-scale producers. By the 1980s, large-scale African landowners had become a new class of absentee landlords, renting out their land to peasants. Though the government's land redistribution programme came to an end after ten years, most of the 10 million hectares of land formerly owned by whites has now been transferred to Africans through the operation of the land market.

As Zimbabwe's future leaders entered negotiations in 1979, they saw the UK-sponsored land redistribution in Kenya as a precedent. However, the independence constitution, which was binding for ten years, provided for the government compulsorily to acquire only 'underutilized' land for resettlement, and only then with the prompt payment of compensation in hard currency to the owner. The UK committed funds for physical infrastructure and settlement purposes, including funds for land purchase on the basis of a willing buyer, willing seller principle. In the period 1980–89, some 3.3 million hectares (about 25 per cent of the land occupied by whites at the time) were redistributed to some 52,000 families (Adams and Howell 2001: 3). An evaluation in 1988 found that the programme had made impressive strides towards achieving its principal objectives (Cusworth and Walker 1988). These findings were partly confirmed by the results of long-term research some 15 years later (Kinsey 1999; Hoogeveen and Kinsey 2001). Between 1996 and 2000, the UK and Zimbabwe failed to reach agreement on the refinancing of the land redistribution programme (Adams 2000: 45). Between 2000 and 2006, long-overdue 'fast-track' land redistribution occurred in an anarchic and violent manner. It has been followed by economic collapse, massive unemployment and an unprecedented humanitarian crisis.

In South Africa, the land reform debate has oscillated between those who believe that land reform must focus on the redistribution of land to the poor and those who wish it to focus on measures to raise agricultural production and black economic empowerment. However, in 1994, when the African National Congress (ANC) swept to power, the objective of increased agricultural production took second place to the need to redress past injustices. There was a strong desire for a peaceful transition to majority rule, devoid of conflict over land. The constitutional negotiations provided for land expropriation for the purpose of land reform and set the conditions for compensation. Under President Mandela (1994–99), land redistribution was to provide the disadvantaged and the poor with land for residential and productive purposes. The government provided grants to eligible applicants, assisting them to purchase land directly. People formed groups to purchase larger farms because small affordable parcels of land were not available on the market.

At the end of the Mandela presidency, some 54,000 households had received grants for a total of about 820,000 hectares, a mere 1 per cent of the total area of private farmland held by whites at the transition in 1994 (Adams and Howell 2001: 2). In addition to the redistribution programme, land was restored to those who could show that they had been dispossessed as a result of discriminatory laws or practices under the colonial and apartheid governments. Land restitution competed with land redistribution for scarce financial and human resources.

The land redistribution process was demand-led and market-based, in so far as land for redistribution was purchased on the land market. It did not involve the prior acquisition of land by the state for subsequent resettlement, as in Kenya and Zimbabwe, or, more recently, in neighbouring Namibia. The application-based land redistribution had high transaction costs. The process resulted in scattered projects, often without regard to people's needs, without infrastructure or provincial or municipal plans to provide it. The small size of the land reform grant encouraged people to form dysfunctional groups in order to raise the sum necessary to meet the cost of farm purchase. Under the first Mbeki government (1999–2004), changes were made to the land redistribution programme, which aimed to increase the size of the grant for black commercial farmers. However, there remain formidable barriers to entry into the white-dominated commercial agricultural sector, which had evolved with strong government support over some 70 years. By the end of 2005, 3 per cent of the total area of agricultural land had been redistributed through the government programme.

Conclusions relating to redistributive land reform

In each arena, the political circumstances have been different, but the main objective has been the same, namely a more efficient and equitable distribution of land and the political power emanating from it. Outcomes have rarely lived up to expectations. Processes have usually been complex and convoluted, although often less complicated where land redistribution has involved the reform of landlord tenancies, granting tenants full ownership. Where agrarian restructuring has required the subdivision of large farms, the process has been much slower. Land redistribution cannot run ahead of other services, particularly those for providing infrastructure (e.g. water, power and roads), credit, input supply and marketing to enable farmers to become competitive.

Agricultural economists have long argued that small farms operated by family labour are invariably more productive per unit of land than large farms in which labour has to be hired in. However, questions are now being raised about the commercial viability of family farms. The assumed efficiency of small family farms in the utilization of labour has not necessarily led to successful competition in increasingly dynamic and liberalized markets, where ready access to information and capital favour larger enterprises. Maintaining a competitive edge in global markets, particularly for fruit and other high-value exports, requires large inputs in herbicides, fertilizers and chemical pest control. The high cost of credit, and the risks involved, constitute enormous barriers to small family farms. Since the incorporation of agriculture into the WTO in 1996, several major international agreements now apply to agriculture. Their combined effect has been the shift of regulatory power over agriculture from the national to the global level, and the setting of standards unattainable by small enterprises (Fortin 2005). The result has been a growing exclusion of small family farms involved in export crop production, and an increasing gap between the rich and poor farmers. Land suitable for export crops is more valuable and the powerful are pushing the weak off what land they have (Berry 2002). Ironically, international economic policies are now reproducing their colonial precedents.

Bernstein (2002 and 2004) argues that the long wave of land reform, beginning with the French Revolution, came to an end in the 1970s, coinciding with the emergence of globalization and the development of both industrialization and more productive agriculture, based on capitalist relations. Industrial urbanization has since taken people off the land and provided new and expanding markets, as in China. The outcome is a globalized economy characterized by the search for ever cheaper and more exploitable seasonal workers.

In recent years, more attention has been paid to tenure reform as a means of providing more secure and affordable access to land for the poor, for women as well as men. While not redistributing new land, the aim is to provide more secure and well-defined land rights for the land actually used and occupied by the rural and urban poor. In most cases, however, the results have been disappointing, as the scope and scale of implementation has been constrained by insufficient resources, reflecting a lack of commitment on the part of governments and international donors.

GUIDE TO FURTHER READING

Deininger, K.W. (2003) *Land Policies for Growth and Development*, London and Washington, DC: Oxford University Press and World Bank.

Ntsibeza, L. and Hall, R. (eds) (2006) *The Land Question in South Africa: The Challenge of Transformation and Redistribution*, Cape Town: HSRC Press.

Putzel, J. (1992) *A Captive Land: The Politics of Agrarian Reform in the Philippines,* Manila and London: Ateneo de Manila University Press and the Catholic Institute for International Relations.

Toulmin, C. and Quan, J.F. (eds) (2000) *Evolving Land Rights, Policy and Tenure in Africa*, London: Department for International Development, with International Institute for Environment and Development and Natural Resources Institute.

Warriner, D. (1969) *Land Reform in Principle and Practice*, Oxford: Clarendon Press.

REFERENCES

Adams, M. (1995) 'Land reform: New seeds on old ground?' *Natural Resource Perspectives*, 6, London: Overseas Development Institute.

Adams, M. (2000) *Breaking Ground: Development Aid for Land Reform*, London: Overseas Development Institute.

Adams, M. and Howell, J. (2001) 'Redistributive land reform in southern Africa', *Natural Resource Perspectives*, 64, London: Overseas Development Institute.

Bernstein, H. (2002) 'Land reform: Taking a long(er) view', *Journal of Agrarian Change*, 2 (4): 433–63.

Bernstein, H. (2004) ' "Changing before our very eyes": Agrarian questions and the politics of land in capitalism today', *Journal of Agrarian Change*, 4(1/2): 190–225.

Berry, S. (2002) 'Debating the land question in Africa', *Comparative Studies in Society and History*, 44(4): 638–68.

Cusworth, J. and Walker, J. (1988) *Land Resettlement in Zimbabwe: A Preliminary Evaluation*, Evaluation Report EV434, Evaluation Department. London: Overseas Development Administration.

Fortin, E. (2005) 'Reforming land rights: The World Bank and globalization of Africa', *Social and Legal Studies*, 14(2): 147–77.

Hoogeveen, J.G.M. and Kinsey, B.H. (2001) 'Land reform, growth and equity: Emerging evidence from Zimbabwe's resettlement programme – A sequel', *Journal of Southern African Studies*, 27(1): 127–36.

Kinsey, B.H. (1999) 'Land reform, growth and equity: Emerging evidence from Zimbabwe's resettlement programme', *Journal of Southern African Studies*, 25(2): 173–96.

3.6 Agricultural sustainability

Jules Pretty

The scale of the challenge

Something is wrong with our agricultural and food systems. Despite great progress in increasing productivity in the last century, hundreds of millions of people remain hungry and malnourished. Further hundreds of millions eat too much, or the wrong sorts of food, and it is making them unwell. The health of the environment suffers too, as degradation seems to accompany many of the agricultural systems we have recently evolved. Can nothing be done, or is it time for the expansion of another sort of agriculture, founded more on ecological principles, and more in harmony with people, their societies and cultures?

Humans have been farming for some 600 generations, and for most of that time the production and consumption of food has been intimately connected to ecological, cultural and social systems. Yet over the last two or three generations, we have developed hugely successful agricultural systems based largely on industrial principles. These certainly produce more food per hectare and per worker than ever before, but only look so efficient if the harmful side effects are ignored – the loss of soils, the damage to biodiversity, the pollution of water, the harm to human health. Agricultural sustainability offers some new opportunities by emphasizing the productive values of natural, social and human capital – all assets that can be regenerated at relatively low financial cost. National policies, though, remain as yet largely unhelpful to these principles.

What is sustainable agriculture?

What, then, do we now understand by agricultural sustainability? Many different expressions have come to be used to imply greater sustainability in some agricultural systems over prevailing ones (both pre-industrial and industrialized). These include biodynamic, community-based, eco-agriculture, ecological, environmentally sensitive, extensive, farm-fresh, free-range, low-input, organic, permaculture, sustainable and wise-use (Pretty 1995, 2002; Conway 1997; McNeely and Scherr 2003; Clements and Shrestha 2004). There is continuing and intense debate about whether agricultural systems using some of these terms can qualify as sustainable.

Systems high in sustainability can be taken as those that aim to make the best use of environmental goods and services, while not damaging these assets (Altieri 1995; Pretty 1995, 2005; Conway 1997; Jackson and Jackson 2002; Uphoff 2002; Millennium Ecosystem Assessment 2005). The key principles for sustainability are to:

- integrate biological and ecological processes, such as nutrient cycling, nitrogen fixation, soil regeneration, allelopathy, competition, predation and parasitism, into food production processes;
- minimize the use of those non-renewable inputs that cause harm to the environment or to the health of farmers and consumers;
- make productive use of the knowledge and skills of farmers, so improving their self-reliance and substituting human capital for costly external inputs;
- make productive use of people's collective capacities to work together to solve common agricultural and natural resource problems, such as for pest, watershed, irrigation, forest and credit management.

The idea of agricultural sustainability, though, does not mean ruling out any technologies or practices on ideological grounds. If a technology works to improve productivity for farmers, and does not cause undue harm to the environment, then it is likely to have some sustainable benefits. Agricultural systems emphasizing these principles also tend to be multifunctional within landscapes and economies (Dobbs and Pretty 2004; Millennium Ecosystem Assessment 2005). They jointly produce food and other goods for farmers and markets, but also contribute to a range of valued public goods, such as clean water, wildlife and habitats, carbon sequestration, flood protection, groundwater recharge, landscape amenity value, and leisure/tourism. In this way, sustainability can be seen as both relative and case-dependent, and implies a balance between a range of agricultural and environmental goods and services.

Empirical evidence from the 1990s and early 2000s shows that successful agricultural sustainability initiatives and projects arise from shifts in the factors of agricultural production (e.g. from the use of fertilizers to nitrogen-fixing legumes; from pesticides to emphasis on natural enemies; from ploughing to zero-tillage). A better concept than extensive is one that centres on intensification of resources – making better use of existing resources (e.g. land, water, biodiversity) and technologies (Pretty et al. 2000; Tegtmeier and Duffy 2004). The critical question centres on the 'type of intensification'. Intensification using natural, social and human capital assets, combined with the use of best available technologies and inputs (best genotypes and best ecological management) that minimize or eliminate harm to the environment, can be termed 'sustainable intensification'.

Capital assets for agricultural systems

What makes agriculture unique as an economic sector is that it directly affects many of the very assets on which it relies for success. Agricultural systems at all levels rely on the value of services flowing from the total stock of assets that they influence and control, and five types of asset – natural, social, human, physical and financial capital – are now recognized as being important.

1   Natural capital produces environmental goods and services, and is the source of food (farmed and harvested or caught from the wild), wood and fibre; water supply and regulation; treatment, assimilation and decomposition of wastes; nutrient cycling and fixation; soil formation; biological control of pests; climate regulation; wildlife habitats; storm protection and flood control; carbon sequestration; pollination; and recreation and leisure (Millennium Ecosystem Assessment 2005).
2   Social capital yields a flow of mutually beneficial collective action, contributing to the cohesiveness of people in their societies. The social assets comprising social capital include norms, values and attitudes that predispose people to cooperate; relations of trust, reciprocity and obligations; and common rules and sanctions mutually agreed or handed down. These are connected and structured in networks and groups (Pretty 2003).
3   Human capital is the total capability residing in individuals, based on their stock of knowledge skills, health and nutrition (Orr 1992). It is enhanced by access to services that provide these, such as schools, medical services and adult training. People's productivity is increased by their capacity to interact with productive technologies and with other people. Leadership and organisational skills are particularly important in making other resources more valuable.
4   Physical capital is the store of human-made material resources, and comprises buildings, such as housing and factories, market infrastructure, irrigation works, roads and bridges, tools and tractors, communications, and energy and transportation systems, which make labour more productive.
5   Financial capital is more of an accounting concept, as it serves as a facilitating role rather than as a source of productivity in and of itself. It represents accumulated claims on goods and services, built up through financial systems that gather savings and issue credit, such as pensions, remittances, welfare payments, grants and subsidies.

Agriculture, therefore, is fundamentally multifunctional. It jointly produces many unique non-food functions that cannot be produced so efficiently by other economic sectors. Clearly, a key policy challenge, for both industrialized and developing countries, is to find ways to maintain and enhance food production. But a key question is: can this be done while seeking both to improve the positive side effects and to eliminate the negative ones? It will not be easy, as past agricultural development has tended to ignore both the multifunctionality of agriculture and the considerable external costs.

Improving natural capital for agro-ecosystems

Agricultural sustainability emphasizes the potential benefits that arise from making the best use of both genotypes of crops and animals and their agro-ecological management. Agricultural sustainability does not, therefore, mean ruling out any technologies or practices on ideological grounds (e.g. genetically modified or organic crops), provided they improve biological and/or economic productivity for farmers, and do not harm the environment. Agricultural sustainability, therefore, emphasizes the potential dividends that can come from making the best use of the genotypes of crops and animals and the ecological conditions under which they are grown or raised.

There are several types of resource-conserving technologies and practices that can be used to improve the stocks and use of natural capital in and around agro-ecosystems. These are:

- integrated pest management, which uses ecosystem resilience and diversity for pest, disease and weed control, and seeks only to use pesticides when other options are ineffective;
- integrated nutrient management, which seeks both to balance the need to fix nitrogen within farm systems with the need to import inorganic and organic sources of nutrients, and to reduce nutrient losses through erosion control;
- conservation tillage, which reduces the amount of tillage, sometimes to zero, so that soil can be conserved and available moisture used more efficiently;
- agroforestry, which incorporates multifunctional trees into agricultural systems, and collective management of nearby forest resources;
- aquaculture, which incorporates fish, shrimps and other aquatic resources into farm systems, such as irrigated rice fields and fish ponds, and so leads to increases in protein production;
- water harvesting in dryland areas, which can mean formerly abandoned and degraded lands can be cultivated, and additional crops grown on small patches of irrigated land, owing to better rainwater retention;
- livestock integration into farming systems, such as dairy cattle, pigs and poultry, including using zero-grazing cut-and-carry systems.

Many of these individual technologies are also multifunctional. This implies that their adoption should mean favourable changes in several components of the farming system at the same time. For example, hedgerows and alley crops encourage predators and act as windbreaks, so reducing soil erosion. Legumes introduced into rotations fix nitrogen, and also act as a break crop to prevent carry-over of pests and diseases. Grass contour strips slow surface water run-off, encourage percolation to groundwater, and can be a source of fodder for livestock. Catch crops prevent soil erosion and leaching during critical periods, and can also be ploughed in as a green manure. The incorporation of green manures not only provides a readily available source of nutrients for the growing crop, but also increases soil organic matter and hence water retentive capacity, further reducing susceptibility to erosion.

The wider policy context

Three things are now clear from evidence on the recent spread of agricultural sustainability.

1 Many technologies and social processes for local-scale adoption of more sustainable agricultural systems are increasingly well tested and established.
2 The social and institutional conditions for spread are less well understood, but have been established in several contexts, leading to more rapid spread during the 1990s to early 2000s.
3 The political conditions for the emergence of supportive policies are the least well established, with only a few examples of positive progress.

Agricultural sustainability can contribute to increased food production, as well as making a positive impact on environmental goods and services. Clearly much can be done with existing resources, but a wider transition towards a more sustainable agriculture will not occur without some external support and money. There are always transition costs in developing new or adapting old technologies, in learning to work together, and in breaking free from existing patterns of thought and practice. It also costs time and money to rebuild depleted natural and social capital.

Agricultural policies with both sustainability and poverty-reduction aims should adopt a multi-track approach that emphasises five components:

1 small farmer development linked to local markets;
2 agribusiness development – both small businesses and export-led;
3 agro-processing and value-added activities to ensure that returns are maximized in-country;
4 urban agriculture, as many urban people rely on small-scale urban food production that rarely appears in national statistics;
5 livestock development to meet local increases in demand for meat (predicted to increase as economies become richer).

In industrialized countries, however, it is perverse subsidies that still promote harm to the environment, though agricultural reforms are now putting into place systems that pay for the provision of environmental services and the development of multifunctional agriculture.

In this context, it is unclear whether progress towards more sustainable agricultural systems will result in enough food to meet the current food needs in developing countries, let alone the future needs after continued population growth and adoption of more urban and meat-rich diets. But what is occurring should be cause for cautious optimism, particularly as evidence indicates that productivity can grow over time, if natural, social and human assets are accumulated.

GUIDE TO FURTHER READING

Uphoff, N. (ed.) (2002) *Agroecological Innovations*, London: Earthscan.

REFERENCES

Alticri, M.A. (1995) *Agroecology: The Science of Sustainable Agriculture*, Boulder, CO: Westview Press.
Clements, D. and Shrestha, A. (2004) *New Dimensions in Agroecology*, Binghampton, NY: Food Products Press.
Conway, G.R. (1997) *The Doubly Green Revolution*, London: Penguin.
Dobbs, T. and Pretty, J.N. (2004) 'Agri-environmental stewardship schemes and "multifunctionality" ', *Review of Agricultural Economics*, 26(2): 220–37.
Jackson, D.L. and Jackson, D.L. (2002) *The Farm as Natural Habitat*, Washington, DC: Island Press.
McNeely, J.A. and Scherr, S.J. (2003) *Ecoagriculture*, Washington, DC: Island Press.
Millennium Ecosystem Assessment (2005) *Ecosystems and Well-being*, Washington, DC: Island Press.
Orr, D. (1992) *Ecological Literacy*, Albany, NY: State University of New York Press.
Pretty, J. (1995) *Regenerating Agriculture: Policies and Practice for Sustainability and Self-reliance*, London and Washington, DC: Earthscan and National Academy Press.
Pretty, J. (2002) *Agri-culture: Reconnecting People, Land and Nature*, London: Earthscan.
Pretty, J. (2003) 'Social capital and the collective management of resources', *Science*, 302: 1912–15.
Pretty, J. (ed.) (2005) *The Pesticide Detox*, London: Earthscan.
Pretty, J., Brett, C., Gee, D., Hine, R., Mason, C.F., Morison, J.I.L., Raven, H., Rayment, M. and van der Bijl, G. (2000) 'An assessment of the total external costs of UK agriculture', *Agricultural Systems*, 65(2): 113–36.
Tegtmeier, E.M. and Duffy, M.D. (2004) 'External costs of agricultural production in the United States', *International Journal of Agricultural Sustainability*, 2(1): 1–20.
Uphoff, N. (ed.) (2002) *Agroecological Innovations*, London: Earthscan.

3.7 GM crops and development

Stephen Morse

Introduction

Genetic modification (GM) is the insertion, transfer or deletion of a gene or genes in an organism's genome (its genetic material). It is typically visualized as the transfer of a gene/genes from one species to another by circumventing biological boundaries that prevent different species from exchanging their genetic material. In nature, the sharing of genetic material within eukaryotes (higher plants and animals) can take place only between members of the same species, or between closely related species. It should be noted that cross-species exchange can (and does) happen naturally. Bread wheat (*Triticum aestivum*), for example, is said to have originated in part from natural crosses between related grass species in the Fertile Crescent of the Middle East. The figure shown here is a highly simplified diagram of the origin of bread wheat. The shaded boxes and dashed lines indicate crossing with wild grasses (*Aegilops* species). As far as we can tell, there was no direct human intervention in the crosses, but it is likely that there was also a great deal of selection by farmers once crosses had occurred. The crosses involved the plants' own mechanisms for sexual reproduction.

With GM there is a circumvention of sexual reproduction as genes are inserted directly into plant cells which are nurtured into a full plant. There are various ways in which the genes can be inserted, including a 'shotgun' approach, involving the literal shooting of genes on particles of gold into the recipient cells, or the use of biological carriers such as the bacterium *Agrobacterium*

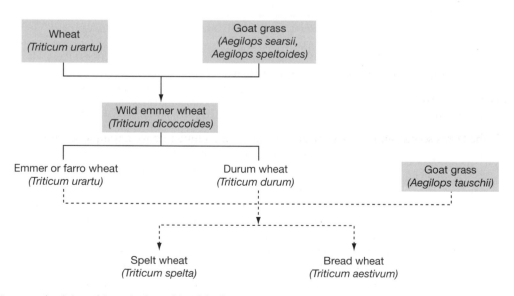

Presumed origins of bread wheat (simplified)

Note: Shaded boxes represent wild grass species and the dashed lines represent natural crosses (as far as it is possible to tell).

tumefaciens. The inserted genes can be from any source: other plant species or even animals and bacteria. Once the transformed cells have produced a full plant, it follows that every cell of the plant will have a copy of the inserted genes, and when the plant reproduces, the inserted genes will be passed to some offspring. Provided they can be made to express (to function) in their new environment, the inserted genes will confer a new characteristic.

GM crops: the promise

Why employ GM instead of traditional plant breeding techniques? There are various advantages, including the following.

- *GM allows access to a much wider range of genetic material.* Plant breeders are no longer restricted to looking for genetic variation within the same species or a close relative. Proponents argue that the technology will allow plants to have an almost limitless set of desired characteristics. These can include characters which help boost production and/or quality of plant products (seeds, fibre, tubers, etc.) or generate entirely new products in a much more cost-effective way. An example of the latter is to engineer crops to produce biofuels, pharmaceuticals or even vaccines to human and animal disease.
- *GM is more targeted and quicker.* With conventional approaches to plant improvement the breeder has to handle millions of genes, but may be interested in only a few. The consequence is a laborious and time-consuming process of crossing to transfer the required genes, selection for the required characteristic(s) and back-crossing to retain desired 'background' characteristics. With GM, the required genes can be isolated and inserted without disturbing the background. In addition, the required genes can be physically linked to 'marker' genes that can be tracked easily. The breeder knows that if a plant has the marker, then it also has the new genes. Some of the most popular markers are genes that code for antibiotic resistance in bacteria. The biology of antibiotic resistance is well understood, and testing is easy and cheap.

Given this potential, some proponents of GM herald it as the technology for the future with bullish promises that it will solve the problem of world hunger, facilitate sustainability and improve food security and profitability.

Examples of GM crops

Commercialization of GM crops to date has largely focused on:

- herbicide resistance;
- insect resistance.

While the terms sound similar, they are actually quite different and have a unique set of potential repercussions for farmers. The herbicide resistance trait involves the insertion of genes that provide resistance to a 'total' herbicide, such as glyphosate, which kills a broad spectrum of plants. Glyphosate is a very effective and relatively cheap herbicide, and hence farmers would be able to reduce their costs significantly, rather than having to use more expensive and selective herbicides that kill some weeds but not the crop. Glyphosate was sold for many years as a formulation called 'Roundup'; hence crops engineered for resistance to glyphosate are often referred to as 'Roundup Ready'.

Insect resistance represents another form of input substitution. In this case, the GM crop is able to resist attack from insect pests. As these are typically controlled by insecticides, or maybe not at all, farmers benefit from reducing costs and boosting yield and quality. In addition, they reduce the risk of accidental pesticide poisoning and damage to the environment. An example of such a trait is that provided by genes from a bacterium, *Bacillus thuringiensis* (abbreviated as Bt). Bt is a pathogen of many species of insect within the Lepidoptera (butterflies and moths) and Coleoptera (beetles) orders, some of which are economically important crop pests. The pathogen has genes which code for an endotoxin, a protein, which, when eaten by an insect, causes death.

Thus, while the two characteristics are substitutes for existing inputs, the forms of the inputs being replaced are quite different. Both substitute for labour. Weeding can account for a substantial drain on labour, especially among women and children, and all crops suffer from weed competition. Insect resistance substitutes in part for insecticide and would be of benefit only for crops that suffer significantly from insect damage, and even then may only tackle damage from a few pests, rather than all.

Evidence of benefit from GM crops

The hypothesized benefits of growing herbicide-resistant and insect-resistant GM crops have been tested in a number of countries and contexts. In developing countries, the GM crop which has received the greatest attention is insect-resistant (Bt) cotton (*Gossypium hirsutum*). Cotton is a crop which can suffer from serious pest damage, and farmers may have to apply insecticide up to 12 times in a growing season. It has been estimated (Abate, van Huis and Ampofo 2000) that, for Africa as a whole, cotton received some 13–15 per cent of all the pesticide used on the continent. Various studies have shown a significant drop in the need for insecticide with Bt cotton (Morse, Bennett and Ismael 2006), and while the Bt seed is more expensive than that of non-Bt, the increased yield of Bt cotton combined with less insecticide has been shown to increase gross margin (revenue – variable costs). Examples include:

- South Africa (Morse, Bennett and Ismael 2004; Bennett, Morse and Ismael 2006);
- Argentina (Qaim and De Janvry 2005);
- China (Pray et al. 2002);
- India (Qaim 2003; Qaim and Zilberman 2003).

An example is provided by the release of Bt cotton in the Makhathini flats, KwaZulu Natal, South Africa (see figure). Soon after commercial release of Bt cotton in the 1997/98 season, research generated the economic results summarized as Table 1. Columns represent three growing seasons, divided into non-Bt and Bt cotton plots and the difference (Bt – non Bt) between the two. The statistics in Table 1 are based on what farmers actually do with their cotton plots, not controlled trials, and, unusually for such studies, the sample represents the majority of cotton growers in Makhathini.

From Table 1 it can be seen that Bt plots have higher average yields and revenue on a per-hectare basis than do non-Bt plots. When it comes to costs, there is no marked overall difference between Bt and non-Bt; what is saved on insecticide with Bt is used to pay for the more expensive seed. But the higher revenue for Bt, combined with costs that are much the same, results in gross margins for Bt which are highly favourable compared to non-Bt. To put these figures into context, the gross margins in South African rand per hectare have also been expressed as US$ and as days of paid work (based on the average manual labour rate for South Africa). Gains of between 26 and 50 days paid work per hectare of cotton are substantial. Given these benefits, it is perhaps no surprise that, over the three seasons of the study, the proportion of Bt adopters in the sample increased from 7 to 49 per cent, and since the 2003/04 season, Bt adoption has levelled off at around 98 per cent of cotton farmers.

Problems of GM crops

While various GM traits have proved to be advantageous, they have not been without their problems. Some of these are postulated rather than proven and there is still much to learn. Ironically, some of these stem from success, and are not in themselves a result of GM, but could arise from

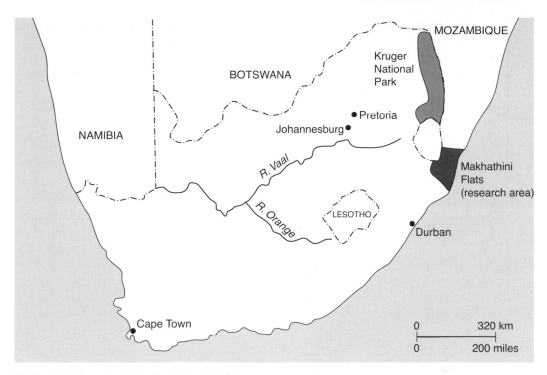

Makhathini Flats, KwaZulu Natal, South Africa
Source: Morse, Bennett and Ismael 2006

any technology that boosts production and/or quality, such as fertilizer or non-GM hybrid seeds. For example, it may be that as more farmers adopt GM crops, and production rises without any increase in demand, perhaps because of a limitation in processing facilities, prices may be depressed, resulting in less profit for farmers. Allied to this is the argument of dependency. Farmers growing GM may get 'locked' into purchasing their seed from relatively few suppliers and may be unable to save their own seed. The narrowing of the supply chain may be a result of licensing of GM products by patent holders. The suppliers would thereby have a great deal of power, but would this be any worse than what many farmers already face with other agricultural inputs?

Another problem often associated with GM that confers resistance to insect pests is that the resistance could break down – insects may become resistant to the resistance! The same breakdown has occurred with non-GM-based plant resistance, and much depends on selection pressure, which, in turn, is related to the effectiveness of the plant resistance, the extent of cultivation and the presence of alternative hosts. Given that genes allowing the insects to overcome Bt resistance are typically recessive, refugia (areas of non-resistant varieties) have been promoted as a means of reducing the onset of resistance breakdown. Indeed it may be argued that GM also provides a cure. For example, with Bt-based resistance there are a number of forms of the Bt endotoxin, and this allows breeders to 'stack' the genes in the plant, thereby widening the resistance and making it more durable.

There are other problems that are more specific to GM. There is the potential for gene escape from the crop to closely related species. In Africa, for example, there are wild *Gossypium* species and it is possible that genes will 'escape' from Bt or herbicide-resistant cotton to these wild relatives, thereby creating so-called 'super weeds'. Related to this point is the contamination of non-GM varieties with pollen from GM varieties. This is particularly an issue with organic production,

Table 1 Summary results of research designed to explore the economic impact of the adoption of Bt cotton by farmers in Makhathini Flats, South Africa, between the 1998/99 and 2000/01 growing seasons

	Units	1998/1999			1999/2000			2000/2001		
		Non-Bt	Bt	Bt − non-Bt	Non-Bt	Bt	Bt − non-Bt	Non-Bt	Bt	Bt − non-Bt
Output										
Yield (Y)	kg ha⁻¹	452 (96)	738 (118)	286	264 (23)	489 (68)	225	501 (81)	783 (93)	282
Total revenue (R) = Y * 2.18	SAR ha⁻¹	984 (57)	1605 (257)	621	574 (50)	1064 (148)	490	1090 (176)	1704 (202)	614
Costs										
Seed (S)	SAR ha⁻¹	138 (9)	278 (46)	140	190 (19)	413 (65)	223	176 (18)	260 (21)	84
Insecticide (I)	SAR ha⁻¹	153 (11)	72 (20)	−81	222 (15)	104 (19)	−118	305 (30)	113 (16)	−192
Spray labour (SL)	SAR ha⁻¹	77 (6)	38 (11)	−39	108 (7)	49 (9)	−59	135 (13)	45 (7)	−90
Harvest labour (HL)	SAR ha⁻¹	113 (7)	184 (30)	71	66 (6)	122 (17)	56	125 (20)	196 (23)	71
Gross margin = R − (S + I + SL + HL)	SAR ha⁻¹	502 (52)	1033 (207)	531	−11 (53)	376 (143)	387	348 (148)	1090 (166)	742
Gross margin	$US ha⁻¹			87			64			121
Gross margin	days work			36			26			50
Sample size		1196	87		329	112		254	245	
Number of adopters as % of sample		7			25			49		

Source: Adapted from Morse, Bennett and Ismael 2006

Notes: Figures are means and 95 per cent confidence limits in parentheses.
Revenue based on a price of SAR (South African rand) 2.18 for each kg of cotton.
Days work based on SAR 15/day (average wage for factory work in South Africa).
All adopter and non-adopter differences are significant at P < 0.001.

where GM is deemed unacceptable, and with some export markets for developing countries. Europe is a major market for many countries, but the European consumer is broadly antagonistic to GM, and retailers try to avoid sourcing material which may contain GM. Hence they demand segregation of GM from non-GM, and labelling. This places extra demands on exporters, as well as government monitoring agencies. Another issue is the reduction in biodiversity which can follow from the use of total herbicides combined with the herbicide-resistance trait.

Conclusion

GM crops are but a further extension of the modernization ethos in development, and thus are within the same family of agricultural technologies as artificial fertilizers, pesticides, conventionally bred crop varieties (including hybrids) and machinery. They may represent a powerful addition to these modernizing technologies, and arguably have a different set of associated problems, but fundamentally they are of the same ilk. For all its critics, modernization has been a remarkably resilient notion within development and, as with all the other modernizing technologies, GM crops are unlikely to disappear. There is also little doubt that some farmers will benefit from GM, and, given the high cost of seed, some will need to have access to affordable credit in order to gain from GM. While positive impacts from GM crops have occurred and will no doubt continue, the refrain that the technology will solve problems of poverty at a stroke has been heard many times before. Unfortunately, the hype will not happen; experience has long proven that magic bullets for poverty just do not exist.

GUIDE TO FURTHER READING

Halford, N.G. (2003) *Genetically Modified Crops*, London: Imperial College Press. More of an introduction to the technology of GM crops, but also covers the broad issues surrounding their introduction. Takes a global stance and is not specifically focused on developing countries.

Pinstrup-Andersen, P. and Schiøler, E. (2001) *Seeds of Contention: World Hunger and the Global Controversy over GM Crops*, Baltimore, MD: Johns Hopkins University Press. Somewhat dated, given that it was first published in 2001 and the GM crops arena has moved so fast, but still provides a good overview of many of the advantages and disadvantages of GM crops for developing countries.

Wu, F. and Butz, W.P. (2004) *Future of Genetically Modified Crops: Lessons from the Green Revolution*, Santa Monica, CA: Rand Corporation. Takes a pro-GM stance and discusses the circumstances and processes required to establish the new 'Green Revolution'.

USEFUL WEBSITES

http://www.agbioforum.org/ AgBioForum, *The Journal of Agrobiotechnology Management & Economics*, an online and open-source journal which publishes refereed papers on all aspects of GM crops and biotechnology. Readers are given the chance to comment on all articles published.

http://www.genewatch.org/ Genewatch UK, a not-for-profit group that monitors developments in genetic technologies from a public interest, environmental protection and animal welfare perspective. Genewatch takes a broadly negative stance towards GM crops.

http://www.isaaa.org/kc/ The Global Knowledge Center on Crop Biotechnology is a website maintained by a not-for-profit organization (ISAAA) which is funded in part by the biotechnology industry. By and large it provides a pro-GM perspective. Readers can also subscribe to a newsletter which provides regular updates for a general audience on advances in biotechnology.

REFERENCES

Abate, T., van Huis, A. and Ampofo, J.K.O. (2000) 'Pest management strategies in traditional agriculture: An African perspective', *Annual Review of Entomology*, 45: 631–59.
Bennett, R., Morse, S. and Ismael, Y. (2006) 'The economic impact of genetically modified cotton on South African smallholders: Yield, profit and health effects', *Journal of Development Studies*, 42(4): 662–77.
Morse, S., Bennett, R. and Ismael, Y. (2004) 'Bt cotton boosts the gross margin of small-scale cotton producers in South Africa', *Nature Biotechnology*, 22(4): 379–80.
Morse, S., Bennett, R. and Ismael, Y. (2006) 'Environmental impact of genetically modified cotton in South Africa', *Agriculture, Ecosystems and Environment*, 117: 277–89.
Pray, C., Rozelle, S., Huang, J. and Wang, Q. (2002) 'Plant biotechnology in China', *Science*, 295: 674–7.
Qaim, M. (2003) 'Bt cotton in India: Field trial results and economic projections', *World Development*, 31(12): 2115–27.
Qaim, M. and De Janvry, A. (2005) 'Bt cotton and pesticide use in Argentina: Economic and environmental effects', *Environment and Development Economics*, 10(2): 179–200.
Qaim, M. and Zilberman, D. (2003) 'Yield effects of genetically modified crops in developing countries', *Science*, 299: 900–02.

3.8 Famine

Stephen Devereux

Introduction

'Famine' can be defined as a widespread and protracted disruption in access to food, which will result in acute malnutrition and mass mortality unless alternative sources of food are available. An estimated 70 million people died in famines during the twentieth century (Devereux 2000). On the other hand, by the 1970s, famine was eradicated from historically famine-prone Europe (Russia) and most of Asia (China, India, Bangladesh). Nonetheless, since the 'Band Aid' famine in Ethiopia in 1984, a number of famines have occurred in Africa (Malawi, Niger, Somalia, Sudan) and Asia (North Korea). The persistence of famines into the twenty-first century is paradoxical, given recent impressive advances in agricultural technology, communications, early warning systems and international humanitarianism.

Historical famine trajectories

Pre-twentieth-century famines were often triggered by natural disasters that destroyed the subsistence basis of agrarian communities, whose vulnerability was exacerbated by underdevelopment – weak markets, undiversified livelihoods, no food aid system. Since the late nineteenth century, improvements in transport and communications integrated isolated communities into the wider economy, allowing governments and traders to respond promptly to food crises. Another factor that reduced famine vulnerability was the emergence of nation states, but this also exposed previously autarkic communities to potent global forces. During the colonial period in India, catastrophic famines occurred that cost millions of lives, until the British introduced the Famine Codes in the 1880s, to prevent further famines and legitimize their rule (Davis 2001). In parts of Africa, starvation was used as a way of crushing initial resistance to colonization. The penetration of colonial capitalism into subsistence-oriented economies – the commodification of food crops and expansion of 'cash crops' – was blamed for causing the 1970s famine in the West African Sahel (Meillassoux 1974).

After independence, historically famine-prone countries took one of two routes. Some, like India, made progress in reducing vulnerability factors, through strengthening political accountability for famine prevention, and through improvements in food production associated with 'Green Revolution' biotechnology. There has been no major famine in south Asia since Bangladesh in 1974. By contrast, independence in Africa was associated with increased political instability and the emergence of 'war famines', the first occurring in Biafra, Nigeria, in the 1960s. Subsequently, many African countries suffered food crises related to conflict and militarization, including Angola, Mozambique, Liberia, Sierra Leone and Uganda. In the Horn of Africa, the lethal combination of wars and droughts has contributed to the persistence of famine to the present (von Braun, Teklu and Webb 1998).

Theories of famine

Theoretical explanations for famine tend to reflect the disciplinary specialization of their authors. This section reviews the main theories by discipline: demography (Malthusianism), economics ('entitlements', market failure), politics (democracy, international relations) and conflict (war).

Malthusianism

The most famous theory of famine was conceived in the 1790s by an English priest, Thomas Malthus, who argued in his *Essay on the Principle of Population* (Malthus 1798) that population could not grow indefinitely in a world of limited natural resources. Eventually, the number of people needing food would exceed global production capacity, when famine would intervene to regulate population growth and balance the demand and supply of food. Although Malthusianism remains extremely influential, as a theory of famine it has many limitations (Dyson and Ó Gráda 2002). Malthus developed his theory before the Industrial Revolution moved vulnerable people out of agriculture and into urban centres, before advances in transport and communications allowed food surpluses to be shipped around the world, and before scientific advances in agricultural research dramatically increased crop yields.

Moreover, in no country has population growth ever been 'regulated' by famine. When 30 million Chinese died in the 'Great Leap Forward' famine around 1960, the population of China was 650 million; it now exceeds one billion. In poor countries, high fertility rates and 'dependency ratios' persist as a vulnerability factor, but it is economic growth that solves this problem, not food crises. In wealthy countries, a 'demographic transition' to zero population growth (when births equal deaths) has already occurred. Global population is projected to stabilize during the twenty-first century, at a total well within global food production capacity.

Economics and Sen's 'entitlement approach'

Amartya Sen's *Poverty and Famines* was published in 1981 (Sen 1981), and was immediately recognized as the most influential contribution to famine thinking since Malthus. Sen argued that a person's 'entitlement to food' derives from four sources – production, trade, labour and gifts – and that famine is not determined primarily by national food availability, but by failures of access to food at the level of groups or individuals. Even when a drought causes crop failure, only some groups suffer 'entitlement failure' and face starvation – wealthy families and urban residents are rarely affected. Paradoxically, farmers who produce food are often most vulnerable to famine; this is because their 'entitlement' derives from a single unreliable source – rain-fed agriculture.

The entitlement approach complements economic explanations for famines that are based on poverty and market failures. When food production or market supplies of food fall, prices rise and, because food is essential for survival, people who cannot afford to buy the food they need face starvation. In Bangladesh in 1974, rapid food price rises caused by expectations of harvest failure made rice unaffordable for landless labourers, because wealthy people and traders hoarded rice and created an artificial scarcity that caused 1.5 million deaths (Ravallion 1987).

Politics: Famine as 'act of man'

Famines have always been 'political', but the role of political factors in either creating or failing to prevent famine is increasingly recognized. First, famines affect people who are politically and economically marginalized. Most famines occur in countries that have little global economic or geopolitical significance – Ethiopia, Sudan, Malawi, North Korea. Within countries that suffer famine, the entire population is never at risk – invariably, minority ethnic groups and poor people living in remote rural districts with negligible political influence are most vulnerable.

Second, famines are related to lack of democracy. Apart from his 'entitlement approach', Sen made an invaluable contribution to the political analysis of famines. Sen argued that two features of democracies protect people against famine: a vigilant free press, so that emerging food crises are neither ignored nor covered up; and free and fair elections to ensure state accountability, because a failing government can be dismissed by the electorate (Drèze and Sen 1989). To illustrate this argument, Sen contrasted the experiences of India and China. Since achieving independence in 1947, India has effectively prevented famine, while China suffered the worst famine in history in 1958–62. Sen attributes India's success largely to its democratic institutions of campaigning journalism and active opposition politics, both of which were absent in Communist China, where lack of information meant the famine was not predicted, while lack of accountability allowed the state to escape unpunished.

Another famine theorist, Alex de Waal, adapted Rousseau's concept of the 'social contract' to argue that post-independence governments in India have upheld an 'antifamine contract' with the population (de Waal 1997). Conversely, the persistence of famine in other countries might be explained by the absence of such a 'contract'. If the state faces no pressure to prioritize the basic needs of its citizens, human rights abuses carry no political cost, and this explains why famines are more likely to occur in authoritarian regimes (Stalin's Soviet Union, Mao's China, Mengistu's Ethiopia, Kim Jong-Il's North Korea) or during wars, than in stable democracies. The famines in the Soviet Union were attributable to punitive government policies, such as forced collectivization and grain seizures. The 1984 famine in Ethiopia was concealed by the military government, which was fighting a civil war against drought-affected Tigray at the time, until it was exposed by the foreign media. The 1990s famine in North Korea occurred under a repressive regime that does not respect basic human rights and is not responsive to international pressure.

A third political factor in contemporary famines is the role of aid donors. The emergence since the Second World War of an international humanitarian community that assumes some responsibility for protecting lives across the world has played a significant role in reducing famine deaths, and has taken the pressure off governments for ensuring the food security of their citizens. When food aid is not delivered in time to prevent a food crisis, the national government blames the international donors, and the donors blame the government. Ultimately, no one is held accountable. Political tensions between aid donors and national governments have also played a role – food aid has even been used as a political weapon. During the 1974 famine in Bangladesh, the United States withheld food aid because Bangladesh was trading with Cuba, in violation of US trade sanctions; in 1984, the United States delayed sending food aid to Ethiopia in an attempt to undermine the Marxist Dergue regime; and in 2000 emergency food aid to the Somali region was delayed because the donors disapproved of Ethiopia's border war with Eritrea.

War and 'complex political emergencies'

Conflict has become a feature of many African famines, and in the 1990s the phrase 'complex political emergencies' was coined to characterize these famines. But the relationship between war and famine is not new. Famine has been used as a weapon of war at least since the Middle Ages, when cities were besieged until their inhabitants surrendered or starved. During the Second World War, parts of the Netherlands were blockaded by the German army, food stores were seized and all imports were prohibited into cities like The Hague and Leiden, where an estimated 10,000 people died. More recently, the town of Juba was subjected to similar starvation tactics during a civil war in Sudan.

Famine conditions can also be created as an unintended consequence of conflict, because of the devastating multiple impacts on food production, marketing systems and relief interventions. First, conflict disrupts agricultural production – farmers are displaced, conscripted, disabled or killed; food crops and granaries are destroyed; livestock are raided or slaughtered. Second, war undermines food marketing – trade routes are disrupted, markets are bombed, traders stop operating because they fear for their safety. Third, relief interventions are undermined by logistical constraints and security risks – governments often ban humanitarian agencies from operating in conflict zones, food convoys are attacked and aid agencies withdraw their staff. People in conflict areas become completely cut off from any source of food, and starvation follows (de Waal 1997; Duffield 2001).

Future famines

Modern famines are less widespread and less severe than historical famines: fewer countries are vulnerable and fewer people die. On the other hand, in the early twenty-first century, famines have been exacerbated by a number of new factors, including flawed processes of economic liberalization and political democratization, rising prevalence of HIV/AIDS, and problematic relationships between national governments and international donors. Modern famines are also more complex, being caused by multiple failures – of the weather, 'coping strategies', markets, local politics, national governments and the international community. The Malawi famine of 2002 is typical of these 'new famines' (Devereux 2007): though triggered by erratic rains, food subsidies and parastatal marketing outlets had been abolished under structural adjustment reforms, food prices spiralled as traders failed to respond, high HIV-prevalence had undermined community coping capacity, and donors intervened too late, trying to force the government to admit that it had corruptly sold the national strategic grain reserve.

All contemporary famines are fundamentally political. Decisions taken by governments, donors and humanitarian organizations either contribute to creating famine conditions, or are responsible for failures to prevent famine. It follows that political will to prevent famine is essential, at every level. The 'right to food' is enshrined in the Universal Declaration of Human Rights of 1948, but little progress has been made in enforcing this right. Some writers have argued that famine should be criminalized as a crime against humanity in international law (Edkins 2000). Until an 'anti-famine contract' is established at the global level, whether voluntarily or enforced under international law, future famines will continue to be tolerated, rather than eradicated.

GUIDE TO FURTHER READING

de Waal, A. (1997) *Famine Crimes: Politics and the Disaster Relief Industry in Africa*, Oxford: James Currey. Takes an explicitly political approach to explaining contemporary African famines, blaming African governments and failures of the international community.

Devereux, S. (1993) *Theories of Famine*, Hemel Hempstead: Harvester Wheatsheaf. This book summarizes the main theoretical explanations for famine causation, including climate shocks, Malthusianism, 'entitlement failure', market failure, government policy and war.

Devereux, S. (ed.) (2007) *The New Famines: Why Famines Persist in an Era of Globalisation*, London: Routledge. This edited collection critically reviews recent developments in famine theory and includes studies of recent famines in Ethiopia, Madagascar, Malawi, Sudan, Iraq and North Korea.

Sen, A. (1981) *Poverty and Famines: An Essay on Entitlement and Deprivation*, Oxford: Clarendon Press. The most influential book on famine since Malthus's *Essay on the Principle of Population*, in which Sen introduces his 'entitlement approach' to the analysis of poverty and famines.

REFERENCES

Davis, M. (2001) *Late Victorian Holocausts: El Niño Famines and the Making of the Third World*, London: Verso.

de Waal, A. (1997) *Famine Crimes: Politics and the Disaster Relief Industry in Africa*, Oxford: James Currey.

Devereux, S. (2000) 'Famine in the twentieth century', *IDS Working Paper*, 105, Brighton: Institute of Development Studies.

Devereux, S. (ed.) (2007) *The New Famines: Why Famines Persist in an Era of Globalization*, London: Routledge.

Drèze, J. and Sen, A. (1989) *Hunger and Public Action*, Oxford: Oxford University Press.

Duffield, M. (2001) *Global Governance and the New Wars*, London: Zed Books.

Dyson, T. and Ó Gráda, C. (eds) (2002) *Famine Demography: Perspectives from the Past and Present*, Oxford: Oxford University Press.

Edkins, J. (2000) *Whose Hunger? Concepts of Famine, Practices of Aid*, Minneapolis: University of Minnesota Press.

Malthus, T. (1798, 1976 edn) *An Essay on the Principle of Population*, New York: W.W. Norton.

Meillassoux, C. (1974) 'Development or exploitation: Is the Sahel famine good business?', *Review of African Political Economy*, 1: 27–33.

Ravallion, M. (1987) *Markets and Famines*, Oxford: Oxford University Press.

Sen, A. (1981) *Poverty and Famines: An Essay on Entitlement and Deprivation*, Oxford: Clarendon Press.

von Braun, J., Teklu, T. and Webb, P. (1998) *Famine in Africa: Causes, Responses, and Prevention*, Baltimore, MD: Johns Hopkins University Press.

PART 4 | Globalization, employment and development

Editorial introduction

We are living through an era that many maintain is characterized by globalization. This increasingly global remit seems to apply in the fields of industrialization and employment in particular. The sets of interrelated changes involved have often been referred to under the umbrella title 'global shifts'. On the one hand, there has been a shift whereby some parts of the so-called 'Third World' have become newly industrializing countries (NICs), although it is vital to stress that this is true of a very limited number of nations. On the other hand, there has been another shift that has witnessed the increasing globalization of production via the activities of transnational companies (TNCs), economic units which are to be found operating in more than one country.

The so-called new international division of labour (NIDL) has to be seen as a vital aspect of globalization, pinpointing shifts in production by world region, and affecting both manufacturing and producer services. At least three NIDLs can be recognized: at the time of European colonization, the industrial development of certain semi-developed areas at the end of the nineteenth century, and the present era, in which foreign direct investment (FDI) has expanded greatly.

But ideas concerning globalization have to be qualified. In the sphere of production, for example, the shifts that have occurred have only witnessed the incorporation of a limited number of new locations. Thus, commentators have referred to a process of 'divergence', which is leading to increasing differentiation between the places that make up the global economic system. Thus, the thesis of hyper-mobility can be overstretched, especially in respect of productive capital. Realities such as this have given rise to the growing appreciation, in certain quarters at least, that rather than becoming more uniform, the world is becoming more differentiated and unequal. Thus, while many governments continue to state their invariant faith in globalization as a macroeconomic policy, the protests of the antiglobalization movement have been increasingly heard, along with the call for policies that may be less detrimental to the poor and to poor regions. In contrast, key aspects of consumption and consumer tastes show signs of becoming ever more uniform at the global scale, and this process of relative homogenization is described as global 'convergence'.

These types of changes need to be seen in a context where perspectives on trade and industrial policy in developing countries have altered greatly since the early 1980s. Recent trends have seen the wholesale promotion of deregulation and liberalization, after an early platform which emphasized protectionism – hence the clarion call for fair trade policies as opposed to free trade policies. In the neoliberal approach, export-processing zones and free trade zones are important parts of the so-called new international division of labour, and represent what are seen as relatively easy paths to industrialization. By the end of the twentieth century, more than 90 countries had established export-processing zones as part of their economic strategies.

In the context of all of these market-oriented changes, the informal sector has generally responded by providing more jobs. In effect, the informal sector has compensated for public-sector cutbacks, recession and neoliberal programmes of economic restructuring. Questions of regulation loom large in this regard, and the high incidence of child labour in Africa, Asia and South America has been a notable point of debate in recent years. Other fundamental correlates of globalization are enhanced levels of transnationality and migration, including that of illegal as well as legal workers within the global economy.

4.1 Global shift: Industrialization and development

Ray Kiely

The last 30 years have seen a global shift in the international division of labour, in which some parts of the former 'Third World' have become newly industrializing countries (NICs). This is most visible in the case of East Asia, and particularly in China in the early twenty-first century, but can also be seen in other parts of the developing world. The old, colonial-based division of labour in which it was said that the 'advanced' capitalist countries produced the industrial goods and the 'Third World' produced the primary goods was always an oversimplification; now it is simply inaccurate. Thus, according to United Nations Development Programme (UNDP) figures, by the late 1990s, almost 50 per cent of manufacturing jobs were located in the developing world and over 60 per cent of developing-country exports to the so-called 'First World' were of manufactured goods, a 1200 per cent increase since 1960 (UNDP 1998: 17). The share of the developing world in global manufacturing exports has increased substantially, from 4.4 per cent in 1965, to 30.1 per cent in 2003 (Glyn 2006: 91).

One explanation for these changes can be found in the growing globalization of production. Transnational companies (TNCs), which operate in at least one country beyond that of origin, are major agents in this globalization process. They may invest beyond their own country to take advantage of market access, cheap labour, lack of regulation (such as rules concerning the environment) or access to raw materials. Apologists argue that TNCs are therefore developmental, providing host countries with income, employment, technology, and so on. Critics argue that TNCs are agents of exploitation, and that they distort the development of nation states. For instance, the use of cheap labour amounts to super-exploitation, and intra-firm trade and capital mobility allow these companies to evade tax payments.

This debate over the character of TNCs is also reflected in disputes over the nature of the changing international division of labour. Apologists such as neoliberals argue that the rise of some newly industrializing countries is evidence that the global economy is a level playing field on which any nation may develop as long as it follows the correct policies. In this way, more open investment, trade and financial policies allow developing countries to draw on the opportunities presented by globalization, thereby reducing global poverty (World Bank 2002).

While it is undoubtedly true that there have been enormous changes in the world economy since the 1970s, many advocates who claim a substantial global shift of industrial production overstate their case. In particular, one sometimes has the impression that *productive* capital is as hyper-mobile as *financial* capital (which itself is selective in terms of where it locates), and that its movement from one part of the globe to another is a relatively unproblematic task. However, capital continues to concentrate in certain areas. This is because capital faces a number of 'sunk costs' which constitute significant barriers to exit. These may include start-up costs, access to local suppliers, and the acquisition of local trust and acceptance. Once established, growth tends to be cumulative, as earlier developers tend to monopolize technology and skills, established markets and access to nearby suppliers.

Of course, these advantages are never absolute, and later developers may leapfrog earlier outmoded production techniques. So, for example, Korean steel and shipbuilding industries developed and ultimately became more competitive than those of Britain in these industrial sectors. This was not because of a hyper-mobile productive capital that relocated from high-cost Britain to low-cost Korea, but was instead the product of a successful alliance between the Korean state and local capital in developing these industries.

Similarly, the partial move away from Fordist mass production to smaller-batch post-Fordist niche production may give some potential to late developers. However, the key point is that these changes do not entail the end of capital's tendency to agglomerate in certain parts of the world and thereby marginalize others, thus maintaining uneven development. Indeed, global, 'post-Fordist' flexible accumulation may intensify this tendency as suppliers locate even more closely to final producers as their stock is delivered on a regular, just-in-time basis, as opposed to the old, irregular, just-in-case system.

In some sectors, the barriers to exit are less significant and so industrial capital is more mobile. This is especially the case in labour-intensive industries such as clothing, textiles and semiconductors. In these and other sectors, fixed costs are lower as technology is not so advanced. This provides former developing countries with potential competitive advantages over the 'advanced' capitalist countries, and is the source of growing concerns in the USA, particularly in relation to its growing trade deficit with China. But even this advantage is a mixed blessing, as employment (often of young women) may involve work for low wages in poor conditions. Employers in these factories are just as likely to be local capitalists as TNCs. Sometimes these employers may be suppliers to Western retailers, who focus their activities on design and marketing. It could be argued, as neoliberals contend, that this focus on low-cost, labour-intensive production is a necessity for poorer countries, and that upgrading to higher-value production will occur over time, just as it did for the now developed countries. The recent rapid growth of China is therefore good news, and it clearly shows the benefits of globalization in contrast to the closed policies of the Maoist era. One need not apologize for the Maoist period to question these upbeat claims. The key point is precisely that while low barriers to entry constitute a competitive advantage for developing countries over their more established competitors, precisely because the barriers are low, the chances are that many enter a highly competitive environment. The risk, then, is of a race to the bottom, whereby many developing countries compete on the basis of cost-cutting, to the detriment of the potentially developmental dynamic experienced by those countries who upgraded in an earlier era (and through protectionist policies – see Chang 2002). This problem is exacerbated by a global reserve army of labour which can keep wages low, and substantial global over-capacity in many sectors, which further drives down prices and leads competitors into yet another round of competitive cost-cutting (Kaplinsky 2005; Kiely 2007).

Industrial production can therefore be said to be increasingly globalized, but the networks of production processes which lead to a finished commodity remain hierarchically structured. Gereffi (1994: 219) distinguishes two kinds of production process or commodity chain, which, although perhaps oversimplified, remains useful for understanding the nature of continued global hierarchies. First, producer commodity chains exist where the site of production is relatively immobile and so production agglomerates in favoured locations. Second, buyer commodity chains exist where there is greater mobility and labour intensity of production. This may give so-called peripheral areas certain advantages in terms of low labour costs, but in these industries barriers to entry exist at the levels of brand name merchandising and retail. In the first case, marginalization occurs through absence of industrial investment; in the case of the latter, the value added by industrial production tends to be low, at least compared to the marketing and design stages.

The continued concentration of higher-value industrial production in selected areas is reflected in the figures on foreign investment. Most foreign direct investment (FDI) is located in the 'developed' world – the global FDI share of developing countries for the period from 2003 to 2005, was approximately 35 per cent, with Asia and Oceania's share standing at 21 per cent and South, South East and East Asia's share standing at 18.4 per cent, compared to Latin America and the Caribbean's 11.5 per cent and Africa's share of just 3 per cent (UNCTAD 2006: 6–7). Moreover, investment in the developing world is itself highly concentrated. While the global FDI share of the top five developing countries has increased substantially, from around 11 per cent in 2000, to around 18 per cent in 2005 (UNCTAD 2006: 4), the share for most other developing countries has declined.

Foreign investment figures alone do not tell the whole story, as TNCs may raise investment capital from a variety of sources (international money markets, equities, and so on), and production may involve cross-border production networks between formally independent firms – the buyer commodity chains discussed above, for example. However, the evidence suggests that in these areas there is also a high rate of concentration, not least in the trade in manufactured goods.

The above outline contrasts sharply with neoliberal and (some) dependency perspectives outlined earlier. Both neoliberal and dependency theories assume that productive capital is hyper-mobile, but each goes on to draw very different conclusions. For neoliberalism, this mobility means that capital will move from areas of abundance to areas of scarcity, in order to take advantage of lower costs in the latter. In the long run, so long as there is a global free market unhindered by the operations of interventionist nation states, this will lead to a system of perfect competition between free and equal producers each exercising their respective comparative advantages. For some versions of dependency theory, this mobility means that capital can move to areas of lower costs in order to increase the rate of exploitation without promoting national development. The exposition above suggests that such a scenario does exist in certain sectors, but it cannot be generalized across the board. The result is the continuation of a core–periphery division of the world, as peripheral industrializers suffer from new forms of dependence. Similarly, while neoliberals regard TNCs as modernizing agents, dependency-oriented writers regard them as agents of underdevelopment.

As we have seen, *both* positions exaggerate the degree of mobility of capital and this weakness leads to other problems. Clearly, given the tendency for capital to concentrate in certain regions and (relatively) marginalize others, neoliberal optimism concerning a level playing field in the global economy is seriously misplaced. On the other hand, the tendency of some dependency theorists to regard the newly industrializing countries as being simply peripheral industrializers is also inadequate. To conceptualize the world on the basis of a timeless core–periphery divide is ahistorical, and one is left with the feeling that whatever happens in the 'Third World' (for instance, industrialization or lack of industrialization), it occurs because of the will of an all-powerful core, simply pulling the strings of a passive periphery.

Similarly, the debate on the developmental effects of TNCs is too black and white, with one side (neoliberalism) assuming that the effects are unproblematically favourable, while the other (some dependency approaches) assumes that they are all bad. The impact of TNCs will depend on a number of specific factors, such as the particular sector in which the TNC operates, the role of the state in regulating TNC behaviour, and local resistance to the potentially bad effects of a particular transnational company. In a capitalist-dominated world, the question then moves away from a simple one of whether particular countries can or should open up or do without TNC investment, and instead becomes one of finding the best strategies for dealing with companies which may have different interests from those of the local population. However, given the global concentration of capital, the desperation of countries to attract foreign investment, and neoliberal hegemony in the international order, it is fair to say that the capacity (or perhaps even willingness) of states in the developing world to regulate (foreign and local) companies to behave in 'developmental' ways is seriously compromised.

The global economy therefore continues to be characterized by polarization, with some people and regions at the cutting edge of globalization, while others are marginalized. Transnational companies tend to be highly selective in their choice of investment location, concentrating in parts of the former First World or selected parts of the former periphery, and being highly selective in the kinds of economic activity within particular locations. There is no longer a clear division of the world between core and periphery (though, in fairness, this division may never have been as clear as some underdevelopment theorists implied), but at the same time, this does not mean the end of uneven and unequal development. The world is divided into many cores and peripheries, many of which can be located *within* nation states. At the same time, the rise of manufacturing in the developing world has not narrowed the gap between the developed and most developing countries.

GUIDE TO FURTHER READING

The following texts afford an introduction to global shifts in industrialization.

Dicken, P. (2007) *Global Shift: Mapping the Changing Contours of the World Economy*, fifth edition, London: Sage Publications.

Gereffi, G. and Korzeniewicz, M. (eds) (1994) *Commodity Chains and Global Capitalism*, Westport, CT: Greenwood Press.

Glyn, A. (2006) *Capitalism Unleashed*, Oxford: Oxford University Press.

Held, D., McGrew, A., Goldblatt, D. and Perraton, J. (1999) *Global Transformations*, Cambridge: Polity Press.

Hoogvelt, A. (2001) *Globalisation and the Postcolonial World*, London: Macmillan.

Kiely, R. (1998) *Industrialization and Development: A Comparative Analysis*, London: UCL Press.

REFERENCES

Chang, H.J. (2002) *Kicking Away the Ladder*, London: Anthem. Important analysis of how developed countries themselves industrialized through protectionist policies, and an examination of the implications for contempoary developing countries.

Gereffi, G. (1994) 'Capitalism, development and global commodity chains', in L. Sklair (ed.) *Capitalism and Development*, London: Routledge, pp. 211–31. A useful summary of the theory of global commodity chains.

Glyn, A. (2006) *Capitalism Unleashed*, Oxford: Oxford University Press.

Kaplinsky, R. (2005) *Globalization, Poverty and Inequality*, Cambridge: Polity Press. Very useful examination of the links between global commodity chains, uneven development and poverty and inequality.

Kiely, R. (2007) *The New Political Economy of Development*, Basingstoke: Palgrave Macmillan. Examination of the current state of the international political economy (and geopolitics) of development, challenging upbeat claims made for the links between globalization and development.

UNCTAD (2006) *World Investment Report 2006*, Geneva: United Nations. Annual report on investment flows in the global economy. Its generally upbeat nature becomes blurred after a close reading of the figures, and even at times the implicit argument.

UNDP (1998) *Globalization and Liberalization*, New York: United Nations Development Programme. Report on the social effects of development in the global economy.

World Bank (2002) *Globalization, Growth and Poverty*, Oxford: Oxford University Press. Well-known, if thinly argued, upbeat case for the claim that poverty reduction is a reality, which has been caused by pro-globalization policies.

4.2 The new international division of labour

Alan Gilbert

Since at least the mid-1990s, both the academic literature and the popular media have been obsessed with the process of globalization. This process has seemingly generated a new international division of labour (NIDL). Few writing about the NIDL and globalization mince their words. According to the World Bank (1995: 1), 'These are revolutionary times in the global economy.' According to the ILO (1995: 68–9), 'Globalization has triumphed.' While it is clear that the world has changed, it is less obvious what precisely has changed. And, if some parts of the world have been fully embraced by the NIDL, others still play a rather peripheral role. What few understand, although many claim to, is what effect the NIDL is having on our lives. Perhaps the only certain answer is that it depends on who you are and where you live; some people are doing very well in the NIDL, whereas others are most certainly not.

What is the NIDL?

According to Held and McGrew (2002: 1):

> Globalization, simply put, denotes the expanding scale, growing magnitude, speeding up and deepening impact of transcontinental flows and patterns of social interaction. It refers to a shift or transformation in the scale of human organization that links distant communities and expands the reach of power relations across the world's regions and continents.

This has produced an NIDL that is difficult to define precisely, but incorporates the following ingredients.

- Most areas of the world now constitute part of the global market. Increasingly, we all consume the same products and are bombarded with the same kinds of advertising. This has made the world more culturally homogeneous but has also produced local variations. As the World Bank (2002: 15) points out: 'as societies integrate, in many respects they become more diverse: Ikea has brought Swedish design to Russians, co-existing with Russian design; Indian immigrants and McDonald's have brought chicken tikka and hamburgers to Britain, co-existing with fish and chips'.
- Manufacturing production is no longer confined to a relative handful of industrialized countries. The production of clothes, shoes, bicycles and televisions has become global. Transnational companies produce their goods in an increasing number of countries. Many favour countries where labour is cheap and political conditions are stable. As a result, the trade in manufactured goods from poorer countries has increased greatly.
- NIDL has been characterized increasingly by the globalization of services and particularly producer services. US investment in Latin America, for example, grew by 3.7 times between 1970 and 1996, and much of that investment went into services. Investment in banking, finance and services rose from 32 per cent in 1980 to 54 per cent in 1996.
- The investment and portfolio capital flowing across the globe has grown immensely. 'In the mid-1980s some US$200 million per day flowed across the globe; by the late 1990s that figure had risen to a staggering US$1.5 trillion' (Munck 2005: 5). This has had both positive and negative effects on different countries, and has transformed some, such as Hong Kong and Singapore.
- People too have been moving in large numbers. Increasing numbers of skilled and unskilled workers have been crossing borders in search of work, and sometimes for protection. Although the relative importance of these flows is still less than those that took place in the nineteenth century (Held and McGrew 2002: 39), most countries have become ethnically more diverse (Bidwai 2006). Another consequence is that most migrants send money home, which is having a major impact on the sending communities.
- The transnational corporations have become more important players in the world economy. 'Multinational corporations now account, according to some estimates, for at least 25 percent of world production and 70 percent of world trade, while their sales are equivalent to almost 50 per cent of world GDP' (Held and McGrew 2002: 53). These corporations have not only changed the world, but have also changed themselves from production companies into the organizers and coordinators of production and services (Dicken 1994: 106). Today, most large companies operate transnationally and few retain a close allegiance to a single country. Ford cars are no longer made principally in Detroit; they are manufactured in different places all

over the globe. The transnational corporations are the new global brokers, responsible for most of the investment flows flushing around the world system.

The geography of the NIDL

The dramatic changes that have taken place have not affected every country equally or every region in each county in the same way. As Bidwai (2006: 31) puts it:

> Today's globalised world is deeply contradictory. On the one hand, there is growing interdependence, exchange and interaction between many different parts of the globe. On the other hand, there are huge swathes of land that are virtually excluded from any meaningful interaction with the rest of the world. They have experienced stagnation or decline, want and insecurity, mounting social chaos, and even outright economic and political devastation through war and famine. About two-fifths of the world's people live in such societies.

Even the World Bank (2002: 43) recognises the uneven geography of the NIDL. While

> some countries receive large inflows…other countries receive little. The top 12 emerging markets are receiving the overwhelming majority of the net inflows – countries such as Argentina, Brazil, China, India, Malaysia, Mexico and Thailand. Much the most successful developing countries in attracting FDI were Malaysia and Chile, both with stocks of FDI of about $2,000 per capita.

One of the great concerns about the NIDL is how it has supposedly marginalized substantial parts of the world. While many Africans occasionally buy global products, very few global products are made there. And, even when industry locates in poor countries, the benefits may be less than apparent. As Bidwai (2006: 38) points out, one recent shift has seen 'polluting, dirty and hazardous industry' moving from the Global North to the South.

Is NIDL new?

The technological innovations that have allowed the development of rapid transport links and instant electronic communication are definitely new. But many of the changes have a longer history; what is different is that they are occurring on a larger scale than before. Indeed, in some respects, the advocates of fundamental change exaggerate because the massive movement of capital, agricultural products, manufactures, people and ideas has been under way for centuries (Gilbert 1990). In this sense, NIDL is definitely not new. It is merely the latest in a series of major restructurings of the world economy. Walton (1985) has argued that at least two NIDLs have preceded the present one. NIDL mark one was brought about by Europe dividing the world into colonies and reorganizing production and markets in the new colonies. NIDL mark two occurred when previously semi-developed areas of the world began to industrialize from the end of the nineteenth century. The process of import-substituting industrialization created major industrial concentrations in countries such as Argentina, Brazil, China, India, Mexico and South Africa. Despite their continuing poverty, these countries contained some of the world's largest industrial economies in 1960.

The current NIDL, which perhaps we ought to call NIDL mark three, is highly significant, but so were these earlier shifts. NIDL mark one led to the decimation of aboriginal peoples in Latin America and Australasia, the slave trade across the Atlantic, the incorporation of new food products into the European diet and their production in the colonies, certainly these constitute as significant a change to the world as the events since the 1970s. Think of the diet of the average Briton before the potato, the banana, tobacco, sugar cane, tea and coffee reached these shores. Around 10 per cent of the world's population left one country for another between 1870 and 1914 (World Bank 2002: 3). NIDL mark two led to the growth of industry and major cities in the periphery of Europe, North and South Africa, India, China and much of Latin America. Again, this represented a major shift in the organization of world production.

What effect has NIDL mark three had on the world at large?

Some view the impact of NIDL mark three to be wholly positive; others view the process as being totally undesirable. The difference may be due to the fact that NIDL3's effects have been highly variable: whether you gain or lose depends on who you are and where you live. To its critics, and even to some of its advocates, the most worrying outcome of globalization is its impact on poverty and particularly inequality. Pogge (2001: 8) claims that global inequality ranks as 'by far the greatest source of human misery today'. For, if the world is becoming a richer place, dire poverty remains well entrenched, and in many places people are actually becoming poorer. The unleashing of fierce competition between nations has led to Western Europe, North America and parts of the Far East increasing their wealth, while most of Africa and parts of Asia and Latin America have been losing out (Held and McGrew 2002: 1).

In addition, there are major shifts in the distribution of income within countries. 'The owners of capital, along with some managerial and professional groups, have generally gained while the organized working class has lost out' (UNRISD 1995: 26). If poverty is not actually increasing in most places, there is no doubt that virtually every country in the world is becoming more unequal; 'life is marked by a deepening divide between rich and poor' (Mittelman 1996: 18). In the United States, chief executive officers made 431 times more than their workers in 2004, compared with 'only' 142 times more in 1994 (http://www.ips-dc.org). Access to the privileged elites is becoming increasingly difficult because 'the privileged top 20 per cent' are tightening their 'grip on the great institutions of upward mobility – the elite universities, the law and business schools' (Hutton 2002: 152).

The effect on the state

To some, a key feature of NIDL3 is the change it has brought in the role of the state. Power has shifted from the nation state to the transnational corporation.

> The world's 37,000 parent trans-national corporations and their 200,000 affiliates now control 75 per cent of all world trade in commodities, manufactured goods and services. One third of this trade is intrafirm – making it very difficult for governments and international trade organizations to exert any control (UNRISD 1995: 27).

> Globalization has weakened the ability of individual states to manage their economies. At the macroeconomic level, the mobility of finance capital has reduced government control over interest rates and the exchange rate; the flexibility of multinational enterprises has reduced the ability of government to affect the level of investment and its geographical location; and the international mobility of technical and skilled labour has made it more difficult for governments to impose progressive income and wealth taxes and to sustain high levels of public expenditure (ILO 1995: 69).

Some argue that:

> The decisions of private investors to move private capital across borders can threaten welfare budgets, taxation levels and other government policies. In effect, the autonomy of states is

compromised as governments find it increasingly difficult to pursue their domestic agendas without cooperating with other agencies, political and economic, and above and beyond the state (Held and McGrew 2002: 23).

Worse still is that in many places the state has simply lost control to new and often sinister groups, drug gangs, people traffickers and the mafia (Harvey 2005: 171).

In one sense, the role of the modern state has changed rather than diminished. The experience of the East Asian 'tigers' shows that global markets are entirely compatible with strong states (Held and McGrew 2002: 47). According to this interpretation, state power has not declined because transnational corporations cannot run the world alone, and rely on national governments to perform a series of important local tasks (Dicken 1994). The state is now concerned less with protecting its national citizens than with creating the conditions which will attract foreign investment.

Some argue that the increasing power of transnational corporations has forced states to reduce the level of taxation and that 'tax termites' have been eating away at national budgets through the use of offshore financial centres and dubious forms of 'transfer pricing'. Yet, Bhagwati (2004: 101) points out that 'the total tax burden of the members of the OECD has in fact increased over the last thirty years'; at 36 per cent of GDP in 2006, the UK tax yield is at a 15-year peak.

Is NIDL mark three stable?

According to the World Bank (1995: 55), 'Global markets are not only larger than any single domestic market but generally more stable as well – and still have room to accommodate newcomers.' As a result, national economies should be more stable within a globalized economy. One problem with this view is that the fortunes of individual countries are likely to ebb and flow. Colombia's position as the world's second largest exporter of cut flowers could disappear as competitors in Ecuador and Kenya increase their competitiveness. Chinese competitiveness could undermine industrial activity almost everywhere.

Capital flows are a still more problematic form of globalization which worry even the defenders of NIDL3 (Stiglitz 2005; Bhagwati 2004). Uncontrolled capital flows threaten to exaggerate rather than even business cycles and the deregulation of international trade leads to forced deflations and states adopting beggar-thy-neighbour policies. Certainly the economic crises that hit Mexico in 1994, the Far East in 1997–98 and Brazil in 1999 demonstrate that in an era of global financial markets, economic disaster always lurks just around the corner.

It is also possible that political discontent will spread under NIDL3. Since one of its key features is the growth of democracy, this could mean that governments are less stable because voters regularly remove them from power. Nowhere is this seen better than in the fall from grace of Mexico's PRI in 2000, the party that had held power constantly since 1928. But there is a greater danger still to national governments: that their populations will become more radical and hostile. According to this scenario, globalization will 'undermine state power and unleash subterranean cultural pluralism' (Mittelman 1996: 7–8). Arguably, the 'austerity riots' which greeted national governments' acceptance of IMF structural adjustment agreements are part of the result of a similar process (Walton 1998).

The need for multinational governance

During the twentieth century, the population in developed countries was increasingly protected by the construction of a welfare state. Keynesian economic management enabled national governments to control the worst excesses of economic instability. But now that the world economy is global, 'the role of "moderator" can no longer belong to the nation-state, but to international (global) actors. It is where the international financial institutions, such as the World Bank, enter' (Milanovic 2003: 679).

Unfortunately, some argue that these global actors do not act fairly. According to Stiglitz (2005: 231), 'Globalisation has been hijacked by the special interests in the North, often at the expense of the poor in developing countries.'

In order to protect the poor, and indeed the majority, from the unfavourable side of globalization, there is increasing agreement that it is vital to reform the nature of world government (ILO 1995; ODI 1999; Stiglitz 2005). To counter the power of the transnational corporations, new forms of multinational government must be created. The emergence of huge political alliances and trade blocs like the European Union and NAFTA is possibly a welcome step in this direction. But others would argue that we need world institutions that can control financial flows and tax capital movements. Only in this way will the undesirable face of NIDL be controlled. Without the creation of such a level of government, tax havens, drug flows, international crime, environmental devastation and labour exploitation will get wholly out of control. In this sense, the role of the state with respect to the market has not changed. It is just that in the NIDL, a powerful state is needed at the international level to help the disabled national state look after those who are less able to compete in the new competitive world.

GUIDE TO FURTHER READING AND REFERENCES

The following references provide the basis for further reading.

Bhagwati, J. (2004) *In Defense of Globalization*, New York: Oxford University Press.

Bidwai, P. (2006) 'From what now to what next: Reflections on three decades of international politics and development', *Development Dialogue*, 17, 29–64.

Dicken, P. (1994) *Global Shift: Transforming the World Economy*, London: Paul Chapman.

Gilbert, A.G. (1990) 'Urbanisation at the periphery: Reflections on the changing dynamics of housing and employment in Latin American cities', in D. Drakakis-Smith (ed.) *Economic Growth and Urbanisation in Developing Areas*, London: Routledge, pp. 73–124.

Harvey, D. (2005) *A Brief History of Neoliberalism*, Oxford: Oxford University Press.

Held, D. and McGrew, A. (2002) *Globalization/Anti-globalization*, London: Polity Press.

Hutton, W. (2002) *The World We're In*, London: Little, Brown.

ILO (International Labour Office) (1995) *World Employment: An ILO Report: 1995*, Geneva: ILO.

Milanovic, B. (2003) 'The two faces of globalization: Against globalization as we know it', *World Development*, 31(4): 667–83.

Mittelman, J.H. (ed.) (1996) *Globalization: Critical Reflections*, Boulder, CO: Lynne Rienner Publishers.

Munck, R. (2005) *Globalization and Social Exclusion: A transformative perspective*, Kumarian Press.

ODI (1999) 'Global governance: An agenda for the renewal of the United Nations?' ODI Briefing Paper, 2 July.

Pogge, T.W. (ed.) (2001) *Global Justice*, Oxford: Blackwell.

Stiglitz, J. (2005) 'The overselling of globalization', in M.M. Weinstein (ed.) *Globalization: What's new?* New York: Columbia University Press, pp. 228–61.

UNRISD (United Nations Research Institute for Social Development) (1995) *States of Disarray*, Geneva: UNRISD.

Walton, J. (ed.) (1985) *Capital and Labour in an Industrializing World*, London: Sage, Chapter 1.

Walton, J. (1998) 'Urban conflict and social movements in poor countries: Theory and evidence of collective action', *International Journal of Urban and Regional Research*, 22: 460–81.

World Bank (1995) *World Development Report 1995*, Oxford: Oxford University Press.

World Bank (2002) *Globalization, Growth, and Poverty: Building an Inclusive World Economy*, New York: World Bank and Oxford University Press.

4.3 Global convergence, divergence and development

Robert B. Potter

Introduction: Globalization and development

Globalization is customarily recognized as consisting of three principal strands: the economic, the cultural and the political. In respect of *economic globalization*, distance has become less important to economic activities, so that large corporations subcontract to branch-plants in far distant regions, effectively operating within a 'borderless' world. The stereotype of *cultural globalization* suggests that as Western forms of consumption and lifestyles spread across the globe, there is an increasing convergence of cultural styles on a global norm, with that norm being codified and defined by the global capitalist system. In addition, in the arena of *political globalization*, internationalization is regarded as leading to the erosion of the former role and powers of the nation state.

One of the most pressing issues, therefore, is what development means in a contemporary context which is dominated by processes of globalization and global change. One of the important questions to be addressed is whether globalization is, in fact, a new process in the first place. Does globalization mean the entire world is becoming more uniform? Does it also mean that there is a chance that the world will become progressively more equal over time? If not, is it the case that such a process of accelerated homogenization will come about in the near future? In short, does globalization mean that change and development will trickle down, and that this will occur more speedily than it has in the past?

In respect of homogenization–heterogenization, two generalized views have emerged concerning the relationships between globalization and patterns of development. The first is the familiar assertion that places around the world are fast becoming, if not exactly the same, certainly increasingly similar. This view dates from the 1960s belief in the process of modernization. Such a perspective tacitly accepts that the world will become progressively more 'Westernized', or more accurately, 'Americanized' (Massey and Jess 1995; Murray 2006). The approach stresses the likelihood of social and cultural homogenization, with key North American traits of consumption being exemplified by the 'coca-colonization' and the Hollywoodization, or Miamization, of the Third World, replete with McDonald's golden arches (see Potter et al. 2004).

The second and far more realistic stance presents almost the reverse view, that rather than uniformity, globalization is resulting in greater difference, flexibility, permeability, openness and hybridity, both between places and between cultures (Potter 1993; Massey and Jess 1995). Following on from this perspective, far from leading to a uniform world, globalization is viewed as being closely connected with the process of uneven development and the perpetuation and exacerbation of spatial inequalities.

This view of globalization argues that localities are being renewed afresh. This is particularly so in respect of economic change, where production, ownership and economic processes are highly place- and space-specific. Even in regard to cultural change, it may be argued that although the hallmarks of Western tastes, consumption and lifestyles, such as Coca-Cola, Disney, McDonald's and Hollywood, are available to all, such dominant worldwide cultural icons are reinterpreted locally, and take on different meanings in different places (Cochrane 1995). This view sees fragmentation and localization as key correlates of globalization.

Global convergence and divergence: Cultural and economic globalization

This leads to a major conceptualization of what is happening to the global system in the contemporary world, and what this means for growth and change in present-day developing countries. The basic argument is that the uneven development that has characterized much of the Third World during the mercantile and early capitalist periods has intensified post-1945, as a result of the operation of what may be referred to as the dual processes of global convergence and global divergence. These terms originate in the work of Armstrong and McGee (1985) (see also Potter 1990). Together these processes may be seen as characterizing globalization.

Divergence relates to the sphere of production and the observation that the places which make up the world system are becoming increasingly differentiated. Starting from the observation that the 1970s witnessed a number of fundamental shifts in the global economic system – not least the slowdown of the major capitalist economies and rapidly escalating oil prices – Armstrong and McGee (1985) stressed that such changes have had a notable effect on developing nations. Foremost among these changes has been the dispersion of manufacturing industries to low labour-cost locations, and the increasing control of trade and investment by TNCs. It is this trend which has witnessed the establishment of Fordist production-line systems in the newly industrializing countries (NICs), while smaller-scale, more specialized and responsive, or so-called flexible systems of both production and accumulation have become more typical of Western industrial nations. Productive capacity is being channelled into a limited number of countries and metropolitan centres. Thus, increasing international division of labour, and the increasing salience of TNCs are leading to enhanced heterogeneity or divergence between nations with respect to their patterns of production, capital accumulation and ownership. Thus, the industrializing export economies of Taiwan, Hong Kong and South Korea can be recognized, along with the larger, internally directed industrialized countries such as Mexico, raw material exporting nations like Nigeria, and low-income agricultural exporters such as Bangladesh.

In the contemporary world, such changes are highly likely to be non-hierarchic in the sense that they are focusing development on specific localities and settlements. Armstrong and McGee (1985: 41) state that 'Cities are...the crucial elements in accumulation at all levels,...and the *locus operandi* for transnationals, local oligopoly capital and the modernising state.' It is these features which gave rise to the title of their book, which characterized cities as 'theatres of accumulation'. Other commentators point to what seems, ostensibly, to be the reverse trend – that of the increasing similarity which appears to characterize world patterns of change and development. There is at least one major respect in which a predominant pattern of what may be referred to as global convergence is occurring. This is in the sphere of consumer preferences and habits. Of particular importance is the so-called 'demonstration effect', involving the rapid assimilation of North American and European tastes and consumption patterns (McElroy and Albuquerque 1986).

The influence of the mass media is likely to be especially critical in this respect. The televising of North American soap operas may well lead to a mismatch between extant lifestyles and aspirations (Miller 1992; Potter and Dann 1996). Such media systems became truly global in character in the 1990s. Potter and Dann (1996) show that the ownership of televisions and radio receivers is near universal, even among low-income households in Barbados in the eastern Caribbean. Even as early as 1990, some 43.24 per cent of households had a video recorder; video ownership was as high as 27.82 per cent for the occupants of all wood traditional houses, and 48.26 per cent for the denizens of combined wood and concrete houses, those which are generally in the process of being upgraded. Other aspects of the wider trend of convergence involve changes in dietary preferences and the rise of the 'industrial palate', whereby an increasing proportion of food is consumed by non-producers (Drakakis-Smith 1990).

Developing cities may be seen as the prime channels for the introduction of such emulatory and imitative lifestyles, which are sustained by imports from overseas, along with the internal activities of transnational corporations and their branch-plants. These, in turn, are frequently related to collective consumption, indebtedness and increasing social inequalities. These changes toward homogenization are ones which are particularly true of very large cities. Such a view sees globalization as a profoundly unsettling process both for cultures and for the identity of individuals, and it suggests that established traditions are dislocated by the invasion of foreign influences and images from global cultural industries. The implication is that such influences are pernicious and extremely difficult to reject or contain (Hall 1995). Following this line of argument, Hall (1995: 176) has observed that 'global consumerism, though limited by its uneven geography of power (Massey, 1991), spreads the same thin cultural film over everything – Big Macs, Coca-Cola and Nike trainers everywhere'.

However, the impact of standardized merchandising is likely to be highly uneven, especially when viewed in respect of social status. Thus, it is the elite and upper-income urban groups who are most able to adopt and sustain the 'goods' thereby provided – for example, health care facilities, mass media and communications technologies, improvements in transport and the like. It may be conjectured that the lower-income groups within society disproportionately receive the 'bads' – for example, formula baby milk and tobacco products. Thus, once again, forces of globalization may be seen to be etching out wider differences on the ground.

A direct and important outcome of this suggestion is a strong argument that the form of contemporary development that is to be found in particular areas of the developing world is the local manifestation and juxtaposition of these two seemingly contradictory processes of convergence and divergence at the global scale. In terms of examples, Armstrong and McGee (1985) look at the ways in which these trends are played out in Ecuador, Hong Kong and Malaysia. Potter (1993, 1995, 2000) has examined how well the framework fits in the examination of the Caribbean, in which context, it is argued, tourism has a direct effect in relation to trends of both convergence and divergence.

Conclusions

At this point, a number of important arguments can be reconciled. The first is that it can be posited that it is the key traits of Western consumption and demand that are potentially being spread in a hierarchical manner within the global system, from the metropolitan centres of the core world cities to the regional primate cities of the peripheries and semi-peripheries, and, subsequently, down and through the global capitalist system. But the actual impact of these will be highly locality-, class- and gender-specific. It is interesting to observe that the innovations cited by commentators in the 1960s and 1970s as having spread sequentially from the top to the bottom of the urban system of America were all consumption-oriented ones – for example, the diffusion of television stations and receivers (Potter and Lloyd-Evans 1998). Thus, it needs to be emphasized that the spread is one of potential, with many real differences evolving between places.

In contrast, aspects of production and ownership are becoming more unevenly spread, and are generally being concentrated into *specific nodes*. This process involves strong cumulative feedback loops. Hence considerable stability is likely to be maintained at selected points within the global system, frequently the largest world cities. Hence, entrepreneurial innovations will be concentrated in space, and are not likely to be spread through the urban system; an argument which has parallels with the view that dependency theory deals with the diffusion of underdevelopment, not development.

On the one hand, the culture and values of the West are potentially being diffused on a global scale. By such means, patterns of consumption are spread through time, and there is an evolving tendency for convergence on what may be described as the global norms of consumption. These aspects of global change are primarily expressed hierarchically, and are essentially top-down in nature. In contrast, cities appear to be accumulating and centralizing the ownership of capital, and this process is closely associated with differences in productive capabilities. The tendency towards divergence is expressed in a punctiform, sporadic manner, which stresses activities in area. Transnational companies and associated industrialization are the most important agents involved in this process. Thus, cities and urban systems have to be studied as important functioning parts of the world economy. In such a role, cities are agents of concentration and spread at one and the same time.

GUIDE TO FURTHER READING

Armstrong, W. and McGee, T. (1985) *Theatres of Accumulation: Studies in Asian and Latin American Urbanization*, London and New York: Methuen. Chapter 3 on 'Cities: theatres of accumulation, centres of diffusion' provides an introduction to the key concepts.

Murray, W. (2006) *Geographies of Globalization*, London and New York: Routledge. Provides a critical appraisal of globalization from a primarily geographical stance.

Potter, R.B. (1993) 'Urbanisation in the Caribbean and trends of global convergence–divergence', *Geographical Journal*, 159: 1–21. Considers the appropriateness of the convergence–divergence thesis in the regional context of the Caribbean.

Potter, R.B. (2000) *The Urban Caribbean in an Era of Global Change*, Aldershot, Burlington, VT, Singapore and Sydney: Ashgate. A monograph aiming to bring the Caribbean story of globalization and development up to date.

REFERENCES

Armstrong, W. and McGee, T. (1985) *Theatres of Accumulation: Studies in Asian and Latin American Urbanization*, London and New York: Methuen.

Cochrane, A. (1995) 'Global worlds and global worlds of difference', in J. Anderson, C. Brook and A. Cochrane (eds) *A Global World?* Oxford: Oxford University Press and Open University, pp. 249–90.

Drakakis-Smith, D. (1990) 'Food for thought or thought about food: Urban food distribution systems in the Third World', in R.B. Potter and A.T. Salau (eds) *Cities and Development*, London: Mansell, pp. 100–20.

Hall, S. (1995) 'New cultures for old', in D. Massey and P. Jess (eds) *A Place in the World?* Oxford: Oxford University Press, pp. 175–213.

McElroy, J. and Albuquerque, K. (1986) 'The tourism demonstration effect in the Caribbean', *Journal of Travel Research*, 25: 31–4.

Massey, D. (1991) 'A global sense of place', *Marxism Today*, June: 24–9.

Massey, D. and Jess, P. (1995) *A Place in the World? Places, Cultures and Globalization*, Oxford: Oxford University Press and the Open University.

Miller, D. (1992) 'The young and the restless in Trinidad: A case of the local and the global in mass consumption', in R. Silverstone and E. Hirsch (eds) *Consuming Technologies*, London: Routledge, pp. 16–82.

Murray, W. (2006) *Geographies of Globalization*, London and New York: Routledge.

Potter, R.B. (1990) 'Cities, convergence, divergence and Third World development', in R.B. Potter and A. Salau (eds) *Cities and Development in the Third World*, London: Mansell.

Potter, R.B. (1993) 'Urbanisation in the Caribbean and trends of global convergence–divergence', *Geographical Journal*, 159: 1–21.

Potter, R.B. (1995) 'Urbanisation and development in the Caribbean', *Geography*, 80: 334–41.

Potter, R.B. (2000) *The Urban Caribbean in an Era of Global Change*, Aldershot, Burlington, VT, Singapore and Sydney: Ashgate.

Potter, R.B. and Dann, G.M.S. (1996) 'Globalisation, postmodernity and development in the Commonwealth Caribbean', in Y.-M. Yeung (ed.) *Global Change and the Commonwealth*, Hong Kong: University of Hong Kong.

Potter, R.B. and Lloyd-Evans, S. (1998) *The City in the Developing World*, Harlow: Longman.
Potter, R.B., Binns, T., Elliott. J.A. and Smith, D. (2004) *Geographies of Development*, second edition, Harlow: Prentice Hall.

4.4 Trade and industrial policy in developing countries

David Greenaway and Chris Milner

Introduction

The last quarter of the twentieth century witnessed a substantial change of attitude in academic and policy circles about the appropriate form of trade and industrial policy for economic development. In this essay we consider the nature, extent and consequences of the resulting liberalization of trade policies in developing countries.

Recent liberalization in developing countries

Defining liberalization

In a stylized, two-sector world, defining liberalization is straightforward: removal of a tariff, or indeed any other intervention, which restores the free trade set of relative prices is unambiguously trade liberalization. However, in practice, things are more complicated and at least two other concepts are used: changes in policy which reduce anti-export bias and move the relative prices of tradables towards neutrality; and the substitution of more efficient forms of intervention. These are overlapping, but they do not map on to one another on a one-to-one basis. It is possible to engineer a more neutral set of relative prices by introducing an export subsidy with a pre-existing import tariff, or by lowering the tariff, but the resource allocation effects of the two may differ. Although trade theory points to some striking non-equivalences between tariffs and quotas, a theorist might not regard the replacement of the latter with the former as liberalization. Policy analysts do, and this particular reform is a standard ingredient of World Bank liberalization packages.

Rationale for liberalization

There are very powerful economic arguments in favour of free trade (Dornbusch 1992; Krueger 1997). It is not too difficult to show that, in the absence of imperfections, free trade is optimal for a small open economy, as most developing countries are. Of course, we do not live in a world free of imperfections, and there are a great many arguments for second-best intervention. However, trade policy is rarely the most efficient form of intervention, and even where it is, as the recent analysis of strategic trade policy has shown, the results are not easily generalizable. So the theoretical case for liberal trade policies appears to be a robust one. Why, then, in the early 1980s, did it suddenly become so much more persuasive and more acceptable to developing countries to adopt reform measures?

The accumulation of empirical evidence relating to the costs of protection/benefits of liberalization was a factor. Evidence on the former was certainly comprehensive and also fairly convincing. Several influential cross-country studies (Krueger 1981; Balassa 1982), together with a multitude of country-specific studies, emphasized the consequences of long-term reliance on import substitution regimes in the form of high and complex patterns of protection, high resource costs, pervasive rent-seeking behaviour, poor macroeconomic performance and stagnating growth (see Greenaway and Milner 1993).

More controversial was the evidence which appeared to suggest that liberal trade policies were also growth-enhancing – the key piece of data here being the export performance and growth of the so-called 'gang of four': Hong Kong, Taiwan, Korea and Singapore. Although placing great emphasis on the experience of these countries was a little disingenuous, given that only one (Hong Kong) followed a free trade policy, it was nevertheless influential, since the others did pursue explicit export promotion policies. Moreover, their growth performance may have had more to do with their ability to react to key macroeconomic shocks in the 1970s, than with their trade policies.

Role of the Bretton Woods agencies and other sources of liberalization

Policy conditionality is routinely applied by the International Monetary Fund (IMF) in connection with stabilization loans (SLs). World Bank policy conditionality dates from the launch of its structural adjustment programme (SAP) in 1980. This involves the disbursement of staged support in the form of structural adjustment loans (SALs) or sector adjustment loans (SECALs), typically on concessional terms, which are conditional upon reforms, often involving trade policy.

Post structural adjustment reform, there have been additional sources or expressions of commitment to trade liberalization in developing countries. Many countries have sought to anchor their early reforms through membership of the World Trade Organization (WTO), and to participate more actively in regional trading arrangements. The further evidence of successful opening up of domestic markets and export-led growth (e.g. by China and India) has increased the desire and need for developing countries to integrate further, both regionally and globally.

Ingredients of trade reform programmes

All episodes of trade policy reform typically include measures to reduce anti-export bias, whether they are import liberalization or export support measures. Tariff reductions, quota elimination, relaxation of import licensing, and so on, all figure prominently. Note also that measures designed to rationalize and improve the transparency of the protective structure are common: conflating shadow tariffs into actual tariffs; reducing tariff exemptions; and substituting tariffs for quotas.

Although the menu of reforms has been fairly standard, the manner of implementation has varied. This is partly due to the fact that the agreement of a package is the outcome of a bargaining process, and relative bargaining power differs from one case to another; and partly due to a growing recognition that initial conditions and infrastructural support (Milner and Zgovu 2006) are vital to the prospects for sustainability, and these vary from case to case (see Dean 1995).

Evaluating experience with liberalization

It is possible that, in the short run, liberalization has some undesirable, but inevitable, side effects. Specifically, during the transition, unemployment may rise and/or trade tax revenue may fall. Both are invariably fears on the part of liberalizing governments. A minority of analysts, most notably Michaely, Papageorgiou and Choksi (1991), claim that such fears are unfounded. In practice, however, they do occur in many cases: it all depends on initial circumstances and the sequencing of reform.

The evidence

There are some rather important complications associated with conducting an evaluation of a liberalization. First, what is the counterfactual? Should one just assume a continuation of pre-existing policies and performance? Second, how does one disentangle the effects of trade reforms from other effects? Third, supply responses will differ from economy to economy: how long should one wait before conducting an assessment? For a review of these issues, and of the evidence on outward orientation and performance, see Edwards (1998) and Greenaway (1998).

The evidence suggests that reform programmes tend to be associated with an improvement in the current account of the balance of payments and with an improvement in the growth rate of real exports. Some countries which have undergone adjustment show a subsequent improvement in investment, but some experienced a slump. Finally, on balance, the impact on growth may be positive, in the sense that there are more cases of a positive growth impact than a negative growth impact, although growth does sometimes deteriorate.

What can one say overall? There have certainly been notable adjustment successes and failures. Some adjustment programmes, where trade liberalization has figured prominently, have resulted in rapid adjustment, a rapid supply-side response and sustainable growth. In many others, especially in sub-Saharan Africa, stabilization has turned out to be a false dawn, as a significant supply response failed to materialize. Are there general lessons to be learned?

Design of trade policy reform

Timing and sequencing issues

Initial timing

A number of arguments have been put forward for conducting any required macroeconomic stabilization in advance of structural adjustment policies. The stabilization programme may, for example, reduce the burdens on the export sector of an overvalued exchange rate. Against these arguments, evidence suggests that the aggregate adjustment costs of trade reform are relatively small alongside those associated with stabilization. One might be able to reap efficiency gains from trade reform quickly and before political resistance builds up.

Sequencing

The general view is that liberalization of the capital account should be held back until well into the process of trade reform, and that the initial stages of trade reform should see import quota reform before tariff liberalization. The costs of rent-seeking and monopoly associated with quotas, and greater transparency and increased tariff revenue, are often cited in the ranking of tariffs over quotas. On export incentives, the general consensus appears to be in favour of giving exporters access to inputs at world prices, and against export subsidization.

Speed of liberalization

There are a number of general arguments for rapid reform. First, it gives strong signals to economic agents, demonstrates government commitment and thereby increases the effectiveness and credibility of reforms. Second, it restricts the time and opportunities for resistance from affected lobby groups. There are, however, arguments for gradualism. First, government revenue may decline too rapidly if trade taxes are eliminated in advance of non-trade tax reforms. Second, adjustment costs may justify gradualism on political economy grounds, especially if gradualism slows down the pace of income redistribution. Third, although rapid/radical reform may be viewed as a means of signalling commitment, overambitious reforms may also lack credibility if the government does not have a 'reputation' for good governance or sustaining policies. Finally, given limited foreign exchange reserves and the external creditworthiness of many developing countries, it is important that liberalizations are compatible with other policy changes. Abrupt liberalization may require abrupt exchange rate depreciation. If this is not politically feasible, then credibility may require gradual trade liberalization (see Falvey and Kim 1992, for discussion).

Sustainability and credibility issues

The private sector is likely to be sceptical about sustainability and credibility where governments are pressured into trade reform. Commitment is uncertain and external circumstances may change, or internal reaction to reform may undermine resolve. A lack of credibility both blunts the incentives to adjust (for example, deterring reallocation of factors to the export sector or deferring investment) and sets in motion forces that undermine sustainability. If consumers expect reforms to be reversed, they have an incentive to consume or speculatively accumulate more of the temporarily cheaper imports. This increases the current account deficit and the probability of policy reversal.

Mitigating strategies can be designed. The need for macroeconomic stability and consistency is obvious. It may also be inadvisable to remove capital controls until trade reforms are fully consolidated. Where lack of credibility is associated with fear of reversion to previous policies once the private sector has reacted to reform, governments need to design strategies to build reputation and demonstrate commitment (see Rodrik 1989).

Trade policy and macro-stability

Direct links between trade policy and macroeconomic stability are limited. Trade policy determines the functional openness of the economy (e.g. trade-to-GDP ratio), but the trade balance is determined by the balance between national income and expenditure. It is exchange rate overvaluation (and fiscal deficit) that is the important link between macroeconomic balances and stability. Although trade reform (if sufficiently radical) can signal government commitment to inflation control, it can also interfere with the prevention of real exchange rate appreciation. Countries liberalizing trade policies often devalue their currency to compensate for the liberalization impact on the balance of payments. The potential inflationary effects of depreciation are likely to constrain the use of nominal exchange rate policy; hence sustained trade liberalization is likely to involve some deterioration in the external balance until there is an export response.

Trade reform and stabilization are linked through trade taxes. Given the high dependence of many developing economies on trade taxes, and the slowness of any non-trade tax reforms, fiscal effects must be borne in mind. Replacement of quotas by tariffs, greater simplicity and uniformity in tariff structures which reduce tax evasion through smuggling and under-invoicing are likely to be fiscal-enhancing.

Conclusions

Economic perspectives on trade and industrial policy in developing countries have changed profoundly since the 1970s. The current consensus is that deregulation and liberalization can help in growth promotion, but are not in themselves a panacea. Trade policy reform may be necessary, but not sufficient, to reap the growth benefits of greater openness and outward orientation (see Milner 2006): the macroeconomic environment, the broader infrastructural and social context are all equally important to fashioning the outcome of reform.

GUIDE TO FURTHER READING

Greenaway, D. and Milner, C.R. (1993) *Trade and Industrial Policies in Developing Countries*, London: Macmillan. This book explains the analytical toolkit with which the economist measures and evaluates trade policies and their impacts, with evidence relating to trade policies and structural adjustment lending (SAL) reforms in the 1980s.

Michaely, M., Papageorgiou, D. and Choksi, A. (eds) (1991) *Liberalising Foreign Trade*, Oxford: Blackwell. This large, multi-country study, commissioned by the World Bank, evaluates the impact and success of trade liberalizations during structural adjustment programmes. Though arguably not wholly impartial, and using a methodology open to challenge (see Greenaway 1993), it remains a valuable source of information on pre- and post-reform trade regimes in many developing countries.

Morrissey, W.O. and McGillivray, M. (eds) (2000) *Evaluating Economic Liberalisation*, London: Macmillan. This collection of essays on economic liberalization issues from across the developing world includes essays on trade liberalization and on the linkages between wider policy reforms sponsored by the World Bank.

Rodrik, D. (1999) *The New Global Economy and Developing Countries: Making Openness Work*, Washington, DC: Overseas Development Council. This essay considers the set of domestic policies and institutions required to take advantage of the opportunities created by globalization and to reduce the costs associated with rapid economic and social change.

Santos-Paulino, A. (2005) 'Trade liberalisation and economic performance: theory and evidence for developing countries', *The World Economy*, 28: 783–821. This is a recent and comprehensive survey article on the theoretical and empirical literature on trade liberalization and economic performance in developing countries.

REFERENCES

Balassa, B. (1982) *Development Strategies in Semi-industrialised Economies*, Baltimore, MD: Johns Hopkins University Press.

Dean, J.M. (1995) 'The trade policy revolution in developing countries', *The World Economy*, special issue, *Global Trade Policy 1995* (eds S. Arndt and C. Milner): 173–90.

Dornbusch, R. (1992) 'The case for trade liberalisation in developing countries', *Journal of Economic Perspectives*, 6: 69–85.

Edwards, S. (1998) 'Openness, productivity and growth: What do we really know', *Economic Journal*, 108: 383–98.

Falvey, R. and Kim, C.D. (1992) 'Timing and sequencing issues in trade liberalisation', *Economic Journal*, 102: 908–24.

Greenaway, D. (1993) 'Liberalising foreign trade through rose tinted "glasses"', *Economic Journal*, 103: 208–22.

Greenaway, D. (1998) 'Does trade liberalisation promote economic development?' *Scottish Journal of Political Economy*, 45: 491–511.

Greenaway, D. and Milner, C.R. (1993) *Trade and Industrial Policies in Developing Countries*, London: Macmillan.

Krueger, A.O. (ed.) (1981) *Trade and Employment in Developing Countries*, Chicago, IL: University of Chicago Press.

Krueger, A.O. (1997) 'Trade policy and economic development: How we learned', *American Economic Review*, 87: 1–22.

Michaely, M., Papageorgiou, D. and Choksi, A. (eds) (1991) *Liberalising Foreign Trade*, Oxford: Blackwell.

Milner, C.R. (2006) 'Making NAMA work: Supporting adjustment and development', *The World Economy*, 29: 1409–22.

Milner, C.R. and Zgovu, E. (2006) 'A natural experiment for identifying the impact of "natural" trade barriers on exports', *Journal of Development Economics*, 80: 251–68.

Rodrik, D. (1989) 'Credibility of trade reform – A policy maker's guide', *The World Economy*, 12: 1–16.

4.5 Free trade and fair trade

Robert N. Gwynne

Introduction

In retrospect, the latter half of the twentieth century saw the gradual but uneven emergence of a more liberalized world trading system. Some have argued (Hirst and Thompson 1999) that this period was broadly comparable to the era of freer trade in the latter part of the nineteenth and early twentieth centuries. World trade growth has been higher than growth in production since 1950, and especially since 1985.

Freer trade was a key issue in the post-Second World War reconstruction of the world economy. The result was the General Agreement on Tariffs and Trade (GATT), a multilateral forum for tariff negotiations. GATT was set up in 1947 in order to reduce tariffs in international trade and to eliminate all other measures preventing free trade. The GATT regime was based on four main principles:

1 non-discrimination;
2 reciprocity – that tariff reductions in one country should be matched by reductions among its trading partners;
3 transparency – that the nature of trade measures should be clear;
4 fairness – so that practices like the dumping of goods at below market prices were deemed unfair and national governments were entitled to institute protection against them.

GATT formed the basis for the post-war trade regime and the framework for seven subsequent rounds of global tariff reduction negotiations. The number of countries involved rose steadily – from 30 in 1950 to around 120 in 1995. In 1995, GATT was replaced by the World Trade Organization (WTO). This is, theoretically, a more powerful institution, as its dispute panels have the authority to make binding judgments in cases where trade rules are subject to dispute (Held et al. 1999: 165). Along with the many multilateral trade agreements that have emerged 'underneath' it, the WTO promotes a neoliberal agenda of opening up markets on a global scale and encouraging export-oriented growth (Hughes 2006: 636). By the early twenty first century, tariffs on manufactured goods were at their lowest level and barriers to trade in services had been reduced significantly; non-tariff barriers may have attained a greater relative significance, particularly in agricultural trade. What is the theoretical framework that attempts to explain the advantages of free trade over trade protection or even autarky?

Theoretical arguments for freer trade

Trade has a strong geographical base. It is argued that on the geographical reality of a heterogeneous landscape, people find it advantageous to develop those resources with which they are best endowed and to work in those activities for which they are best suited. They can then trade in those products in which they have a comparative advantage and can exchange any surplus of these home-produced commodities which other people may be relatively more suited to produce. This process of trade and exchange can occur at a wide range of different geographical scales – from local rural spaces (with periodic markets) through to a huge variety of regional, national and global networks of exchange.

Principles of specialization and comparative advantage have long been applied by economic theorists to the exchange of goods between individual states in the form of international trade theory. In answer to the questions of what determines which goods are traded, and why some countries produce some things while others produce different things, economic theorists since the writings of David Ricardo in the early nineteenth century have sought the answer in terms of international differences in production costs and the prices of different products (Todaro 1994). According to this theory, the promotion of free international trade both maximizes global output and allows countries to escape from the confines of their resource endowments.

The later Heckscher-Ohlin model took into account the effect of differences in factor supplies (natural resources, labour and capital) on the international specialization of production. Their factor endowment theory rested on two crucial propositions (Todaro 1994). The first proposition stated that different products require productive factors in different relative proportions – for example, some manufacturing products (clothing, assembly of electronic products) require relatively greater proportions of labour per unit of capital than other goods (cars, aircraft).

The second proposition was that countries have different endowments of factors of production. If a country's relatively abundant factor is natural resources or labour, then that country will have a comparative advantage in exporting products based on natural resources or labour respectively. Examples of a country with abundant and varied natural resources would be Chile (Gwynne 2004: 60–4), while Chinese export growth since the 1980s has been founded on low labour costs combined with high labour productivity, particularly in coastal areas (Carter 2001).

These differences in relative factor endowments – with some countries being relatively abundant in natural resources, while others are relatively abundant in capital or labour – are sufficient to give differences in costs and prices, thereby forming a basis for international trade. Other differences also contribute to a country's comparative advantage – technology, the quality of factors of production, economies of scale and consumption patterns.

Dynamic comparative advantage

The Heckscher-Ohlin model allows one to discuss a more dynamic interpretation of comparative advantage, such as if firms within nations gain a lead in technology, thereby permitting the creation of new products. Vernon (1966) argued that firm innovations in both product and process technology can give a country a temporary monopoly position and easy access to foreign markets. However, the 'imitation lag' will not be long, and soon firms in other countries will be manufacturing a similar (or better) product and developing mass-production technologies which reduce the price of the product. If these mass-production technologies involve large amounts of labour, firms may be tempted to move production to developing countries with lower labour costs (Gwynne, Klak and Shaw 2003: 164–6). Meier (1995: 456) argues that a country that initially imported a product can subsequently become so efficient in its import-substitution production that it eventually acquires a comparative advantage for the mature product based on low labour costs (see figure). The historical trajectory of electronics production in Taiwan between the 1960s and 1980s (Gwynne, Klak and Shaw 2003: 166) and the shifting of apparel manufacture to and within Mexico during the 1980s and 1990s (Gereffi, Spener and Bair 2002) provide instructive examples. These examples demonstrate that global shifts in production, based on dynamic comparative advantage, continue to evolve.

Taiwan was regarded in the 1960s as one of the few relatively free trading spaces in the developing world. It demonstrated the potential benefits of increased production that a free trade space could generate. Subsequently, governments from a range of developing countries delimited free trading spaces within their own countries, often known as export-processing zones (EPZs).

Export-processing zones

In EPZ locations, there was normally an added bonus for the global firm, as developing country

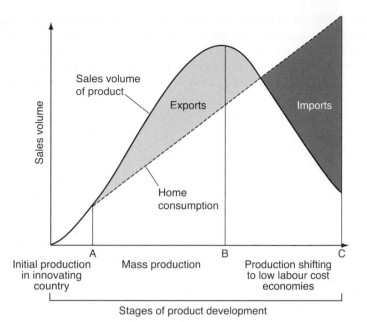

Product life cycle and trade in a country with initial innovating firms

governments offered them more favourable investment, trade, tax and labour conditions compared with locations in the remainder of the host country. Concessions included:

- trade – the elimination of customs duties on imports;
- investment – liberalization of capital flows in and out of the EPZs and, occasionally, access to special financial credits;
- EPZs have often been characterized by important investments in the provision of local infrastructure by central and/or local government of the host country;
- taxation – reduction or exemption from federal, state and local taxes;
- labour relations – limitations on labour legislation that apply in the rest of the country, such as the presence of trades unions and the adherence to minimum wage and working hours legislation.

EPZs tended to be spatial enclaves in which export-oriented manufacturing, organized largely through global firms, was concentrated. These enclaves were separated from neighbouring areas by the wide range of incentives and exemptions offered to capital within them. Links with surrounding areas were mainly through the attraction of local populations to work in the EPZs. Inputs came from international sources and EPZ production was by definition exported. Within developing countries, EPZs have been established in a wide range of environments – from border areas (as in north Mexico) to relatively undeveloped regions to locations adjacent to large cities. The most common location has been on the coast, as in China. The creation of EPZs has been a popular policy for governments of developing countries because they represent a relatively easy path to begin industrialization in a country. The global firm normally provides technology, capital, inputs and the export markets. Central and local government authorities have relatively few commitments apart from investing in local infrastructure.

Although the establishment of an EPZ could be seen as beneficial in the short term for the developing country, in the long term it provided a major problem as regards economic sustainability. The argument can be presented as follows. Global firms were normally attracted to locate a branch plant in an EPZ by trade and tax incentives, low labour costs and labour flexibility. However, these locational attractions did not necessarily last. Labour costs could rise if the demand for industrial labour began to increase rapidly. In these scenarios, the type of firm attracted to an EPZ (interested in reducing costs at a global scale for the manufacture of a labour-intensive product) moved on to a cheaper EPZ location. Thus, a reliance on simple export processing would at best perpetuate a reliance on low-skilled, labour-intensive assembly, and at worst see the premature end of this type of manufacturing activity within the developing country.

Brief critique of free trade theory

Free trade as a theoretical framework relies on the assumption of market-mediated transactions between different firms in different countries. However, the contemporary realities of trade between countries are becoming increasingly divorced from this theoretical image. In essence, more and more trade is becoming what could be termed non-market mediated. First of all, there is the growing amount of intra-firm trade – trade in products and services logistically 'organized' within global firms – already estimated at about 40 per cent of total world trade by the World Bank. Such firms have the opportunity to allocate prices of traded products and services between their subsidiaries in their own self-interest and not with reference to competition and the rigours of the market.

Second, there is an increasing amount of trade organized through value chains (Gereffi et al. 2001). Many value chains are buyer-driven chains in which retailers, designers and trading companies are fundamental to the development of decentralized production networks. Global firms, such as Nike and Reebok, design and market their own-brand products, but manufacturing is outsourced to large numbers of firms in other countries. These 'other' firms are tied by detailed contracts to the global buyer. Although the size of this type of value-chain trade is difficult to gauge, it is nevertheless increasing rapidly. Finally, there is increasing trade (notably export trade from China) between global firms and joint ventures (in which the global firm is linked with a local partner).

Furthermore, many economic theorists have argued that there are some serious problems with the theoretical logic of free trade. First of all, gains from trade can be biased in favour of the core economies of the world. Myrdal (1957) criticized the factor endowments model as he argued that economic development (through trade) is a process of circular and cumulative causation, which tended to favour those countries which were already well endowed, and thwarted the efforts of lagging or backward regions. Second, most developing countries have entered into international trade through specializing in exports of primary products. Fifty years ago Myrdal (1957: 52) emphasised that such exports can be faced by weak and inelastic demand in foreign markets and by 'excessive price fluctuations'. Little has changed since then if one takes out the special case of oil exporters from the analysis of primary product exporters.

Fair trade

The low prices for primary agricultural products in international markets have created an image in core economy markets that the benefits of free trade do not get down to the small-scale producers and workers. As a response to the perceived inequalities of trade and the low wages for workers and low prices for small-scale producers the concept of fair trade has developed some significance since the mid-1970s. Hughes (2005: 500) sees this as an alternative trading form, while noting that market coordination increasingly appears to underpin its organization through more mainstream distribution channels.

The fair trade model was developed in the 1970s by Oxfam and other European aid organizations involved in imports of handicrafts (Barrett-Brown 1993). Since then, regulation has become more formalized. Fairtrade Labelling Organizations International (FLO), established in 1997, had by November 2006 become an association of 20 Labelling Initiatives that promote and market the Fairtrade Certification Mark in their countries (FLO 2006).

The logic behind such international standards is to stimulate demand and promote consumer confidence in what fair trade is and means (Goodman 2004). The FLO fair trade system guarantees that producers receive fair terms of trade and fair prices (particularly compared to the conventional market) and creates extra resources (through participating firms) for 'producer organizations or worker bodies to enable them to invest in social, economic or environmental improvements' (FLO 2006). Thus the fair trade concept can actively link consumers in certain core economies (mainly in Europe) with producers in the developing world, with the guarantee that 'good prices' will be enjoyed by producers and that some of the proceeds will go to fund directly social projects in housing, education and health in the communities linked to the fair trade co-operatives in Asia, Africa and Latin America. 'Fair trade thus operates not only within the interstices of globalization through alternative economic means, but also parallel to the historical tracks of the trade in global commodities' (Goodman 2004: 897). Cook (2006) sees this in an optimistic way as reconnecting producers and consumers at a global scale, and draws attention to the geographical knowledges and imaginaries mobilized through fair trade.

GUIDE TO FURTHER READING

Gereffi, G. and Kaplinsky, R. (eds) (2001) 'The value of value chains: Spreading the gains from globalisation', *IDS Bulletin*, 32(3). This is a special edition (with 13 papers) from the journal of the Institute of Development Studies in Sussex, and focuses on globalization and value chains, which are providing a rapidly growing form of trade between firms in developing and core economies – as discussed in this chapter, such trade is not mediated by the market.

Goodman, M.K. (2004) 'Reading fair trade: Political ecological imaginary and the moral economy of fair trade foods', *Political Geography*, 23: 891–915. This is an article that not only provides an insightful argument into the contemporary nature of fair trade, but also has an impressive bibliography to assist further study.

Gwynne, R.N. and Kay, C. (eds) (2004) *Latin America Transformed: Globalization and Modernity*, second edition, London: Hodder Arnold. Through the analytical lens of political economy, this book examines the shift to more outward-oriented policies in Latin America and introduces the wider theoretical and empirical context behind the move to export growth.

Myrdal, G. (1957) *Economic Theory and Under-developed Regions*, London: Duckworth. The Swedish economist, Gunnar Myrdal, undoubtedly wrote the early classic relating economic theory to trade and space, back in the 1950s. His arguments on backwash and spread effects, on circular and cumulative causation and on uneven development still resonate through contemporary geographical analysis.

REFERENCES

Barrett-Brown, M. (1993) *Fair Trade: Reform and Realities in the International Trading System*, London: Zed Books.

Carter, C. (2001) *Globalizing South China*, Oxford: Blackwell.

Cook, I.J. (2006) 'Geographies of food: Following'. *Progress in Human Geography*, 30(5): 655–66.

FLO (Fairtrade Labelling Organizations International) (2006) http://www.fairtrade.net

Gereffi, G., Humphrey, J., Kaplinsky, R. and Sturgeon, T.J. (2001) 'Introduction: Globalization, value chains and development', *IDS Bulletin*, 32(3): 1–8.

Gereffi, G., Spener, D. and Bair, J. (2002) *Free Trade and Uneven Development: The North American Apparel Industry after NAFTA*, Philadelphia, PA: Temple University Press.

Goodman, M.K. (2004) 'Reading fair trade: Political ecological imaginary and the moral economy of fair trade foods', *Political Geography*, 23: 891–915.

Gwynne, R.N. (2004) 'Structural reform in South America and Mexico: Economic and regional perspectives', in R.N. Gwynne and C. Kay (eds) *Latin America Transformed: Globalization and Modernity*, second edition, London: Hodder Arnold, pp. 39–66.

Gwynne, R.N., Klak, T. and Shaw, D.J.B. (2003) *Alternative Capitalisms: Geographies of Emerging Regions*, London: Hodder Arnold.

Held, D., McGrew, A., Goldblatt, D. and Perraton, J. (1999) *Global Transformations: Politics, Economics and Culture*, Cambridge: Polity Press.

Hirst, P. and Thompson, G. (1999) *Globalization in Question*, second edition, Cambridge: Polity Press.

Hughes, A. (2005) 'Geographies of exchange and circulation: Alternative trading spaces', *Progress in Human Geography*, 29(4): 496–504.

Hughes, A. (2006) 'Geographies of exchange and circulation: Transnational trade and governance', *Progress in Human Geography*, 30(5): 635–43.

Meier, G.M. (1995) *Leading Issues in Economic Development*, sixth edition, Oxford: Oxford University Press.

Myrdal, G. (1957) *Economic Theory and Under-developed Regions*, London: Duckworth.

Todaro, M. (1994) *Economic Development*, fifth edition, London: Longman.

Vernon, R. (1966) 'International investment and international trade in the product cycle', *Quarterly Journal of Economics*, 80: 190–207.

4.6 Pro-poor globalization

Dirk Willem te Velde

This chapter discusses the concept of pro-poor globalization. It first defines the terms 'globalization' and 'pro-poor', and provides some examples of how far economic globalization has proceeded. We then turn to the debate on the links between globalization and poverty, and, finally, we discuss what types of actions might help to make globalization more pro-poor.

Defining 'globalization' and 'pro-poor'

Economic globalization is influenced by three features that increasingly link countries together. First, trade in goods and services has increased in importance over time. The share of trade in GDP has increased in all regions (see Table 1). Increased fragmentation and global value chains are two recent features of increasing trade.

Table 1 Trade (exports and imports) as a percentage of GDP

Region	1970	1975	1980	1985	1990	1995	2000	2004
World	26.6	33.2	38.6	38.0	38.4	42.2	49.5	..
Latin America & Caribbean	20.4	24.4	28.1	28.0	31.9	37.9	42.2	48.6
Middle East & North Africa	..	72.6	61.6	45.1	60.0	56.2	54.4	67.4
South Asia	12.1	16.5	20.8	17.5	20.2	27.1	31.1	41.4
Sub-Saharan Africa	47.8	55.8	62.7	54.0	53.5	59.7	64.1	65.6
East Asia & Pacific	15.8	21.1	33.8	33.2	47.3	58.7	67.9	82.4

Source: World Bank 2006

The *fragmentation of the production processes* is also called vertical specialization and is commonly referred to as the relocation of parts of the production process from one country to another (Feenstra 1998). Most of the attention used to focus on fragmentation in the goods chain, but around the turn of the twenty-first century attention also began to focus on fragmentation of services processes. There have been various measures of fragmentation (e.g. imported semi-finished products), and while they differ by level, all indicate that fragmentation has increased over recent decades.

Global value chains involve trade through rapidly growing networks of firms across borders. A value chain includes the full range of activities required to bring a product or service from conception, through the intermediary phases of production (transformation and producer services inputs), to delivery to final consumers and, ultimately, disposal after use. Examples include buyer-driven chains for garments, footwear and fresh fruits and vegetables, and supply-side-driven chains for automobiles (see, for example, Kaplinsky 2000).

Second, private cross-border finance has become increasingly important. The sources that have increased – more than net bank lending – include portfolio flows and remittances. The rise of foreign direct investment (FDI) has received most attention. Table 2 shows the rise from 1980 to 2005, both in developed and developing countries, though the absolute flows are concentrated in a few large developing countries. Some developing countries have also experienced significant capital outflows.

Table 2 Inward FDI stocks, as a percentage of GDP by region and country

	1980	1985	1990	1995	2000	2005
Developed countries	4.9	6.2	8.2	8.9	16.2	21.4
Developing countries	12.4	16.3	14.7	16.3	26.3	27.0
Africa	8.2	9.8	10.9	15.4	26.2	28.0
Sub-Saharan Africa	10.9	13.5	12.0	16.5	33.0	30.2
South/East Asia	27.4	24.6	20.8	20.8	30.5	25.8
Latin America and Caribbean	6.5	11.0	10.4	11.7	25.8	36.7

Source: UNCTAD 2006

Third, migratory flows have increased, but are relatively low (Table 3). Nonetheless, some developing countries have lost more than 50–100 per cent of their domestic tertiary-educated labour force. Some migratory flows (IT workers, nurses, teachers) get specific attention in South–North flows.

Table 3 World population and migrant stocks (million), 2000

	Total population	Migrant stocks	% of population
Asia	3672.3	49.7	1.4
Africa	793.6	16.2	2.1
Europe	727.3	56.1	7.7
Latin America/Caribbean	518.8	5.9	1.1
Northern America	313.1	40.8	13.0
Oceania	30.5	5.8	19.1
Global	6056.7	174.7	2.9

Source: IOM 2005

There are *other processes* related to globalization, such as the spread of communicable diseases, the rise in carbon dioxide emissions, the spread of IT, governance structures and the spread of information. These are related to knowledge, health and governance – global public goods.

Poverty can be defined in monetary and other terms, but, broadly speaking, there are three definitions of pro-poor growth:

1 growth that is good for the incomes of the poor in absolute terms;
2 growth that is proportionally better for the poor than the rich;
3 growth that is both good for the absolute incomes of the poor, and that improves the relative position of the poor, (1) and (2).

Some authors and agencies prefer option 1, while those concerned with equality prefer option 2. Option 3 seems desirable and is used by many. Son and Kakwani (2006) define pro-poor growth as growth that benefits the poor proportionally more than the non-poor.

The conceptual links between globalization and poverty

A framework to analyse globalization and pro-poor growth (PPG) can be structured in many ways. Global integration affects the movement of products and factors of production across borders – trade in goods and services and the movement of people and capital – which in turn affect poverty through various routes. Global integration can also affect poverty directly though special initiatives and programmes, including the provision of global public goods. The movements of products and factors of production will also be interrelated (horizontally). Finally, there will be feedback from economic variables to globalization processes.

Thus, there are four ways in which globalization processes affect PPG, as shown in the figure:

1 through changes in volume and poverty and focusing on trade;
2 through changes in volume and poverty and focusing on investment;
3 through changes in volume and poverty and focusing on migration;
4 through other routes (including the provision of global public goods).

Globalization allows countries to specialize according to their comparative advantages and initial endowments, and this static efficiency gain should lead to a one-off increase in GDP, which can be used to reduce poverty (following the Heckscher-Ohlin-Samuelson – HOS – model). Globalization also involves dynamic effects, increasing competition and reaping economies of scale and scope. Trade, investment and migration can all lead to gains and losses for different groups in society, as the initial growth gains for the poor are enhanced or mitigated by distributional effects.

The distributional effects depend on how globalization processes affect the demand and supply for the different groups in a country (see Borjas 2004, for migration; Wood 1997 for trade; and te Velde 2006, for FDI). For conceptual reasons, groups tend to be divided according to skills or occupation. The effects of FDI (migration and trade can be analysed in the same way) on inequality depend on:

• sector and location;
• introduction of technology biased towards a particular skill category;
• effects on the bargaining position of different skill categories;
• the effects on the supply side of various skill categories.

Nissanke and Thorbecke (2006) employ a similar framework to analyse the transmission mechanisms from globalization to poverty, which they argue work through:

• growth (the HOS and new trade effects, above);
• technology (skill-biased technological change, above);
• factor/labour mobility (effects of migration, above);

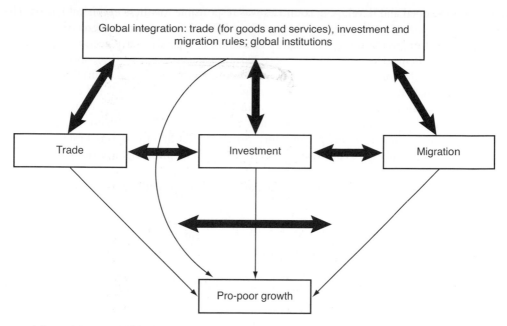

Global integration: trade (for goods and services), investment and migration rules; global institutions

Trade

Investment

Migration

Pro-poor growth

Source: Adapted from te Velde, 2006

- vulnerability (through greater uncertainty of global shocks);
- information diffusion (other, knowledge-related globalization processes);
- institutions (globalization can affect institutions and political economy structures, and institutions affect the outcome of globalization).

Globalization itself can be pro-poor

The evidence on the effects of globalization is generally favourable, although hotly contested by development practitioners looking at certain groups or (poor) individuals. Countries that are *more open* grow faster than those that are closed (see Dollar and Kraay 2001), although *trade policy* does not necessarily lead to poverty reduction (Rodriguez and Rodrik 1999). This strand of thought argues that trade *is* good for the poor because trade raises growth. In this way, globalization (trade, FDI, migration) can be pro-poor.

The new trade theory emphasizes the long-run productivity effects of trade (Grossman and Helpman 1991), in addition to one-off allocative efficiency gains. Productivity spillovers can occur via importing and exporting (Coe, Helpman and Hoffmeister 1997). Not only does a country's efficiency increase due to allocation effects, but trade helps actors to learn from each other and appropriate R&D spillovers. These learning effects turn into long-run efficiency gains.

Most macroeconomic studies find a positive relation between FDI and growth, although the models, methods and precise pathways involved increasingly face scrutiny (te Velde 2006). Studies have argued that the contribution of FDI to growth depends on the conditions in recipient countries (e.g. their trade policy stance (Balasubramanyam, Salisu and Sapsford 1996) or human resource policies). Borensztein, De Gregorio and Lee (1998) suggest that the effectiveness of FDI depends on the stock of human capital in the host country. Carkovic and Levine (2005) used more advanced econometric techniques and argued that FDI does not exert an independent effect on growth. Countering this view, Blonigen and Wang (2005) argued that inappropriate pooling of data from developed and developing countries was responsible for these empirical results. These opposing views show that the jury is still out on how FDI relates to aggregate growth.

The effects of migration on human capital formation and growth have been the focus of several studies (e.g. Beine, Docquier and Rapport 2001), suggesting that such prospects may in fact foster human capital formation and growth in sending countries. If the return to education is higher abroad than at home, the possibility of migration increases the expected return to human capital, thereby enhancing domestic enrolment in education. More people, therefore, invest in human capital as a result of increased migration opportunities. This acquisition can contribute positively to growth and economic performance. Some suggest that the optimal migration rate of a highly educated population is positive. However, there will be immediate capacity constraints in some areas.

FDI, trade and migration can also affect the pattern of growth with consequences for distribution and pro-poor growth. The effects will differ by country, period, sector and policy and institutional setting. There is no uniform impact of trade on inequality, and so it is difficult to say whether trade reduces poverty. However, there does seem to be a non-negative correlation between FDI and inequality (te Velde 2006), while there is very little evidence on the effects of migration. Skilled workers are more likely to migrate from developing countries to developed countries, though there is significant South–South migration, some of it of unrecorded unskilled workers.

It is also possible to identify specific groups that stand to gain or lose from globalization. For instance, if a country reduces its tariff, it will benefit consumers and importing industries, but will harm import-competing industries. Inward FDI can crowd out inefficient domestic investment. Unskilled workers will suffer from unskilled immigration.

Conclusion: What can make globalization more pro-poor?

While globalization could be pro-poor to some degree, many would argue that this misses the point. What is really important is how to make globalization *more* pro-poor than it already is, or how to turn globalization pro-poor if it is not so already.

There are two ways of thinking about this issue.

1 Use policy to influence the globalization processes directly (e.g. use trade, investment or migration policies, and tweak these directly so that the poor would be affected less negatively).
2 Use policies and create and improve institutions that are complementary to globalization, and which enhance the positive aspects and mitigate the negative ones for pro-poor growth; such complementary policies include education, infrastructure, entrepreneurship and other more specific policies (McCulloch, Winters and Cirera 2001; Nissanke and Thorbecke 2006; and te Velde 2006).

Economic theory suggests that it is more efficient to set optimal trade, migration and investment policies in order to raise growth, and that the use of other policies to influence the distributional effects is crucial. Some would counteract that globalization-induced growth never reaches the poor (i.e. assuming that growth was not produced by the poor in the first place), which leads us into a debate on growth plus distribution versus distribution with growth. There can also be new trade theory reasons as to why some protection might be helpful to reap economies of scale initially, though political economy arguments suggest that protection can often be abused.

Those advocating direct intervention (1) in trade may argue for incomplete tariff liberalization to protect certain industries, while those advocating a complementary approach (2) would make the case for tariff liberalization while encouraging the capabilities of domestic industries using normal development policies, including skill enhancements.

Debates on (1) focus on the need for a common set of trade and investment rules for all countries that are members of the World Trade Organization, and include special and differential treatment for poorer economies; while approach (2) would argue that it is more efficient to have a common set of transparent and stable investment rules, which could be enhanced, for instance, by aid for trade for the less well advanced economies, while the effects of FDI on PPG could be enhanced by education, appropriate skills and technology policy, competition policy and infrastructure targeted at activities that help the poor.

In the case of migration, countries have opted mostly for a very strict migration regime (approach 1), so that developing and developed countries are denied the opportunity to gain from a more efficient allocation of (labour) factors, thus failing to consider (2).

GUIDE TO FURTHER READING AND REFERENCES

Balasubramanyam, V.N., Salisu, M. and Sapsford, D. (1996) 'Foreign direct investment and growth in EP and IS countries', *Economic Journal*, 106: 92–105.

Beine, M.F., Docquier, F. and Rapport, H. (2001) 'Brain drain and economic growth: Theory and evidence', *Journal of Development Economics*, 64(1): 275–89.

Blonigen, B. and Wang, M.G. (2005) 'Inappropriate pooling of wealthy and poor countries in empirical studies?' in T.H. Moran, E. Graham and M. Blomstrom (eds) *Does Foreign Direct Investment Accelerate Economic Growth?*, Washington, DC: Institute for International Economics and Center for Global Development.

Borensztein, E., De Gregorio, J. and Lee, J.-W. (1998) 'How does foreign direct investment affect economic growth?', *Journal of International Economics*, 45: 115–35.

Borjas, G.J. (2004) 'The rise of low-skill immigration in the South', Harvard mimeo.

Carkovic, M. and Levine, R. (2005) 'Does foreign direct investment accelerate economic growth?' in T.H. Moran, E. Graham and M. Blomstrom (eds) *Does Foreign Direct Investment Accelerate Economic Growth?* Washington, DC: Institute for International Economics and Center for Global Development.

Coe, D.T., Helpman, E. and Hoffmeister, A.W. (1997) 'North–South R&D spillovers', *Economic Journal*, 107: 134–49.

Dollar, D. and Kraay, A. (2001) 'Trade, growth and poverty', *World Bank Policy Research Department Working Papers*, 2615, Washington, DC: World Bank.

Feenstra, R.C. (1998) 'Integration of trade and disintegration of production in the global economy', *Journal of Economic Perspectives*, 12(4): 31–50.

Grossman, G.M. and Helpman, E. (1991) *Innovation and Growth in the Global Economy*, Cambidge, MA: MIT Press.

IOM (International Organization for Migration) (2005) *World Migration Report 2005*, Geneva: IOM.

Kaplinsky, R. (2000) 'Spreading the gains from globalisation: What can be learned from value chain analysis', IDS Working Paper.

McCulloch, N., Winters, L.A. and Cirera, X. (2001) *Trade Liberalisation and Poverty: A Handbook*, London: Centre for Economic Policy Research.

Nissanke, M. and Thorbecke, E. (2006) 'A quest for pro-poor globalization', UNU-Wider, Research Paper 2006/46.

Rodriguez, F. and Rodrik, D. (1999) 'Trade policy and economic growth: A skeptic's guide to the cross-national evidence', *NBER Working Papers*, 7081, Cambridge, MA: National Bureau of Economic Research.

Son, H.H. and Kakwani, N. (2006) 'Global estimates of pro-poor growth', UNDP Poverty Centre, Working Paper 31.

UNCTAD (United Nations Conference on Trade and Development) (2006) *World Investment Report 2006*, Geneva: UNCTAD.

Velde, D.W. te (2006) *Regional Integration and Poverty*, Aldershot: Ashgate.

Wood, A. (1997) 'Openness and wage inequality in developing countries: The Latin American challenge to East Asian conventional wisdom', *The World Bank Economic Review*, 11: 33–57.

World Bank (2006) *World Development Indicators 2006*, Washington, DC: World Bank.

4.7 Migration and transnationalism

Katie D. Willis

Introduction

International migration has become one of the key characteristics of the increasingly intercon-nected world of the early twenty-first century (Castles and Miller 2003). While many of these migrants are fleeing persecution or natural disasters, economic migration is highly significant. Between 1970 and 2005, the number of international migrants more than doubled to 190.6 mil-lion. Although Europe had the largest share of the world's international migrants in 2005, largely as a result of movement within the European Union by citizens of EU member states, international migrants made up the largest percentage of the population in Northern America and Oceania (see Table 1).

Table 1 The world's international migrants, 1970–2005

	International migrants (millions)		International migrants as % of pop.	% of international migrants by region
	1970	2005	2005	2005
More developed countries	38.4	115.4	9.5	60.5
Less developed countries	43.0	75.2	1.4	39.5
Africa	9.9	17.1	1.9	9.0
Asia	27.8	53.3	1.4	28.0
Latin America & Caribbean	5.7	6.6	1.2	3.5
Northern America	13.0	44.5	13.5	23.3
Oceania	3.0	5.0	15.2	2.6
Europe	21.9	64.1	8.8	33.6
WORLD	81.4	190.6	3.0	100.0

Source: Compiled from data from United Nations (2006)

Because of improved communications technology and transport, links across national borders are easier than they were in the past. This means that many migrants now live what have been termed 'transnational lives'. According to Basch, Glick Schiller and Blanc-Szanton (1994: 6) 'transnationalism' in relation to migration is 'the process by which transmigrants, through their daily activities, forge and sustain multi-stranded social, economic, and political relations that link together their societies of origin and settlement, and through which they create transnational social fields that cross national borders'. This ability to live both 'here' and 'there' has implications for the construction of migrant identities, but the focus of this chapter will be on the role of transnational migration in development practices in the Global South.

Brain drain

While emigration may be a positive strategy for individuals and their families, for communities and countries in the Global South, such migration has often been represented as a loss of resources – a so-called brain drain. This is because more educated, skilled and dynamic individuals are over-represented within economic migrant flows. Within agricultural communities, this outmigration (to both national and international destinations) can leave insufficient labour to maintain agricultural production.

The medical sector has received particular attention in relation to the brain drain and international migration (Clark, Stewart and Clark 2006). Training doctors, nurses and other medical personnel is very expensive for governments, but it is viewed as a wise investment as these workers will contribute to a country's social and human development once they have been trained. However, as migration becomes more affordable and logistically possible, medical workers may choose to migrate overseas for better salaries and working conditions. Jobs are available due to shortages in hospitals in the Global North, or the unmet demand for care workers for the elderly, infirm and children. The impacts of the migration of medical personnel are particularly acute in sub-Saharan Africa, where formal health care resources were already limited due to insufficient funding for staff, infrastructure and medicines.

Remittances

Remittances are money and goods sent 'home' by migrants. This process has become much easier due to developments in the banking system and international money transfer services such as Western Union. Remittances may also be returned through less formal means, such as being sent with friends or relatives on a trip. The transnational connections, both virtual and real, help facilitate the flows of remittances.

Remittances can clearly be used by family members for personal consumption, such as home improvements and property, health or education expenditure. Such expenditure is often characterized as being 'economically non-productive', particularly if money is spent on imported goods. However, in some cases, money received from abroad may be invested in small businesses, so contributing to local-level economic development. While this benefits the recipients, it may lead to increasing inequalities within communities (de Haas 2006).

As the level of international migration and flow of money have increased, remittances have attracted greater attention from governments and development policymakers. While it is impossible to provide an exact figure for the level of remittances due to informal and illegal transfers, the World Bank estimates that global remittances reached US$233 billion in 2005, with US$167 billion of this going to developing countries (World Bank 2006). To put this into perspective, in 2005, Overseas Development Assistance (ODA) from the countries of the Development Assistance Committee (DAC) of the Organization for Economic Cooperation and Development (OECD) was US$106.48 billion (OECD 2006: Figure 1.1). This means that remittances far outweighed the amount of bilateral aid from the world's richest countries. The importance of the remittance flows to countries in the Global South can be crucial. For some countries, such as the Philippines, Morocco and Mexico, remittances represent one of the largest sources of foreign capital.

Given the size of these money flows, it is not surprising that governments in certain key labour-exporting countries have sought to encourage migrants to remit. This may be in the form of individuals remitting, or through community organizations investing in projects. International migrants from the same village or urban district often end up migrating to the same location overseas. Hometown associations or their equivalent may be set up to provide support for migrants overseas, but they may also raise money for projects at home. These can be crucial for local infrastructure developments such as schools or health clinics. In 2002, the Mexican government started the 3 × 1 Citizenship Initiative scheme, under which donations from hometown associations would be trebled by contributions from federal, state and municipal government funds (IOM 2005: 281).

The role of diasporas (both migrants and later generations born overseas) in providing development finance in this way has been highlighted by international development organizations such as the United States Agency for International Development (USAID) and the UK Department for International Development (DFID 2006). Such contributions are both a reflection and a constituent part of transnational processes.

Return migration

International migration can contribute to development processes of the 'home' country through more than just remittances. While the brain drain involves a loss of talent and human resources, skills and experiences gained during migration can provide very positive inputs if migrants return. The influx of social, cultural and human capital, as well as financial capital, can be an important trigger to economic development. This process has been represented as a 'brain gain'.

Of course, not all return migrants contribute in this way. For some, return may represent the end of their working lives, while in other cases, the reality of coming home fails to live up to their expectations, and further mobility follows as they cannot settle. Return migration may also be associated with the transference of potentially destructive practices, such as the development of US-linked criminal gangs in Mexico and Central America. However, there are many cases of positive outcomes for both individuals and communities, as return migrants invest in new businesses, provide an impetus in local politics or add to the pool of skilled labour (Conway and Potter 2006). In some cases, governments have been so keen to encourage certain kinds of return migration that they have offered tax incentives (IOM 2005: 290).

As with many forms of migration, it is impossible to identify return migration definitively, as a migrant may move away again in the future. In certain parts of the world, transnational connections have developed around businesses, thus creating migration circuits. These businesses often started by providing goods, such as food, for immigrant communities who are missing their home comforts (Alvarez 2005).

The state and transnational migration

Increasing international mobility and the intensification of transnational exchanges does not mean the end of the nation state; in fact without the continued presence of the nation state the concept of transnationalism would be redundant. However, processes of transnationalism and globalization have required national governments to change their development strategies and the relationships between states and citizens. As outlined above, international migration provides opportunities for development capital and expertise. This has meant governments paying increased attention to citizens living elsewhere and encouraging continued links. This is a break from past practices where governments focused almost completely on citizens living within the national boundaries.

Given the financial possibilities provided by remittances, governments are increasingly facilitating temporary labour outmigration through formal government-approved schemes. Such activities are not new – for example, thousands of Mexicans migrated to the USA as part of the Bracero Programme (1942–1964) – but the current scale of government involvement in such schemes is unprecedented in countries of the Global South. The government of the Philippines, for example, regulates the activities and fees of agencies recruiting workers through the Philippine Overseas Employment Administration (POEA). There is also a strong political rhetoric of the overseas Philippine workers being heroes and heroines of the nation, so encouraging these migrants to feel a continued attachment to the country.

Such attachment is also encouraged through the increased relaxation of dual nationality regulations. While some countries, such as India, do not allow dual citizenship, many others are allowing their nationals to take on passports of another country. There is also increased flexibility in relation to voting in elections and standing for political office. All these legal changes reflect national government attempts to seize the opportunities presented by transnational migration.

Conclusions

Migration is often viewed as a response to development failure, as individuals seek to find a better life for themselves and their families elsewhere. Increasing international migration flows and greater possibilities for transnational economic, social and political practices have meant that emigration does not mean the severing of ties with home that it often did in the past. Rather, international migration is increasingly being seen as a positive contributor to development, in both the sending and receiving countries. This perspective has meant national governments, international development organizations and donor agencies have begun to develop policies to maximize the benefits accruing from international migration. Of course, international mobility can involve great hardships for the people involved and those left behind, and it can exacerbate existing inequalities at a local, national and global scale, but there is also considerable potential for migration to contribute to improvements in the standard of living and quality of life.

GUIDE TO FURTHER READING

Conway, D. and Cohen, J.H. (1998) 'Consequences of migration and remittances for Mexican transnational communities', *Economic Geography*, 74(1): 26–44. Uses the case of Mexican migration to the USA to examine the role of remittances in community development.

de Haas, H. (2005) 'International migration, remittances and development: Myths and facts', *Third World Quarterly*, 26(8): 1269–84. A clear overview of the role of remittances in development in sending regions.

International Migration Review (2003) 'Transnational migration', theme issue, 37(3): 565–892. A wide-ranging collection of articles on economic, political and social dimensions to transnational migration.

Levitt, P. (2001) 'Transnational migration: Taking stock and future directions', *Global Networks*, 1(3): 195–216. A useful and accessible summary of debates around transnational migration.

USEFUL WEBSITES

http://www.migrationinformation.org Migration Information Source, run by the Migration Policy Institute, a think tank based in Washington, DC.

http://www.iom.int International Organization for Migration, an intergovernmental organization focusing on migration policies and the impacts of migration. *World Migration Reports* provide excellent overviews of policies and statistics.

http://esa.un.org/migration United Nations Department of Economic and Social Affairs, World Migrant Stock database.

REFERENCES

Alvarez Jr, R.R. (2005) *Mangos, Chiles and Truckers: The Business of Transnationalism*, Minneapolis: Minnesota University Press.

Basch, L.G., Glick Schiller, N. and Blanc-Szanton, C. (1994) *Nations Unbound: Transnational Projects, Post-Colonial Predicaments, and Deterritorialized Nation-States*, Longhorne, PA: Gordon and Breach.

Castles, S. and Miller, M. (2003) *The Age of Migration: International Population Movements in the Modern World*, third edition, Basingstoke: Palgrave-Macmillan.

Clark, P.F., Stewart, J.B. and Clark, D.A. (2006) 'The globalization of the labor market for health-care professionals', *International Labor Review*, 145(1–2): 37–64.

Conway, D. and Potter, R.B. (2006) 'Caribbean transnational return migrants as agents of change', *Geography Compass*, 1: 25–50.

de Haas, H. (2006) 'Migration, remittances and regional development in Southern Morocco', *Geoforum*, 37: 565–80.

Department for International Development (DFID) (2006) *Moving Out of Poverty – Making Migration Work Better for Poor People*, London: DFID, http://www.dfid.gov.uk

International Organization for Migration (IOM) (2005) *World Migration 2005*, Geneva: IOM, http://www.iom.int

Organization for Economic Cooperation and Development (OECD) (2006) *Development Aid at a Glance: Statistics by Region 2006*, http://www.oecd.org

United Nations (2006) *World Migrant Stock: The 2005 Revision Population Database*, http://esa.un.org/migration

World Bank (2006) *Global Economic Prospects 2006*, Washington, DC: World Bank.

4.8 The informal sector and employment

Sylvia Chant

What is the informal sector?

The 'informal sector' is often equated with precarious, low-productivity, poorly remunerated work in cities of the South, although in reality the sector is highly heterogeneous (Potter and Lloyd-Evans 1998). Informal employment usually prevails in commerce and services, but also occurs in manufacturing production (see Table 1). Moreover, although many people in the informal sector work on their own account in street-vending, the running of 'front room' eateries, stalls or shops, the operation of domestic-based industrial units, and the transport of passengers and goods (see figure), other informal workers are subcontracted by large firms, especially in labour-intensive industries, such as toys, footwear and clothing (McIlwaine, Chant and Lloyd-Evans 2002).

The term 'informal sector' first appeared in the academic and policy literature in the 1970s. It is usually associated with the work of the anthropologist Keith Hart, in Ghana, who classified informal employment as that which fell outside the boundaries of formal-sector enterprise (factories, public services, large-scale commerce, for example), and subdivided the sector into 'legitimate' and 'illegitimate' activities. The former comprised work which made a contribution to economic growth, albeit in small ways, such as petty commerce, personal services and home-based production. 'Illegitimate' informal activities described occupations which, if not necessarily 'criminal' in nature, were arguably of dubious worth to national development, such as prostitution, begging, pickpocketing and scavenging (Hart 1973).

Hart's work was embraced by the International Labour Organization (ILO), whose criteria distinguishing the formal and informal sectors comprised relative ease of entry, size, nature of enterprise ownership, type of production, and levels of skill, capital and technology (ILO 1972; see also Table 2). The single most important factor which persists in contemporary definitions of the informal sector, however, is regulation (Roberts 1994: 6).

Table 1 Percentage of production which is informal in different economic sectors for selected developing countries

	Percentage of production which is informal in:			
	manufacturing	transport	services	total
AFRICA				
Burundi (1990)	35	8	18	25
Congo (1984)	39	10	36	33
Egypt (1986)	21	29	15	18
Gambia (1983)	48	16	57	51
Mali (1990)	45	45	37	40
Zambia (1986)	41	7	48	39
LATIN AMERICA & THE CARIBBEAN				
Brazil (1990)	12	23	23	18
Costa Rica (1984)	14	9	16	15
Honduras (1990)	26	17	28	26
Jamaica (1988)	19	23	30	25
Mexico (1992)	9	20	20	16
Uruguay (1985)	16	10	16	16
Venezuela (1992)	16	46	22	23
ASIA & THE PACIFIC				
Indonesia (1985)	38	44	56	49
Iraq (1987)	15	33	7	12
Republic of Korea (1989)	17	34	44	30
Malaysia (1986)	13	20	23	19
Qatar (1986)	1	3	1	1
Syrian Arab Republic (1991)	21	38	22	24
Thailand (1990)	10	40	18	16
Fiji (1986)	14	21	12	13

Source: United Nations 1995: 135, Table 9

Pedal power: informal transport in Mexico City
Photo: Sylvia Chant

Table 2 Common characteristics used to define formal and informal employment

Formal sector	Informal sector
Large scale	Small scale
Modern	Traditional
Corporate ownership	Family/individual ownership
Capital-intensive	Labour-intensive
Profit-oriented	Subsistence-oriented
Imported technology/inputs	Indigenous technology/inputs
Protected markets (e.g. tariffs, quotas)	Unregulated/competitive markets
Difficult entry	Ease of entry
Formally acquired skills (e.g. school/college education)	Informally acquired skills (e.g. in home or craft apprenticeship)
Majority of workers protected by labour legislation and covered by social security	Minority of workers protected by labour legislation and covered by social security

Source: Chant 1999

Regulation and the informal sector

Regulation primarily implies legality, recognizing that legality has different dimensions, and that there are three which are particularly pertinent to the demarcation between formal- and informal-sector enterprises (Tokman 1991: 143):

1 legal recognition as a business activity (which involves registration, and possible subjection to health and security inspections);
2 legality concerning payment of taxes;
3 legality vis-à-vis labour matters, such as compliance with official guidelines on working hours, social security contributions and fringe benefits.

Social security tends to be the most costly aspect of legality, so while micro-enterprises may well register themselves as businesses with the relevant authorities, they may avoid paying social security contributions for themselves and their workers (ibid.).

Recent trends in informal employment

Time-series data on informal-sector activity need to be treated with caution, not only on account of the irregular and/or clandestine nature of informal work, but because of shifting classificatory schema by different governments and regional organizations (Thomas 1995). Acknowledging that this also makes international comparisons difficult, the informal sector seems to have grown in most parts of the world in recent decades. In Latin America, an estimated 7 out of 10 new jobs created during the 1990s were in the informal sector, and between 1990 and 2002, the share of the non-agricultural labour force employed in the informal sector rose from 43 per cent to 51 per cent (Chant 2004). In Asia, the share of the workforce who are informally employed is even higher, at 71 per cent in 2002, and in Sub-Saharan Africa, 72 per cent, with countries such as Benin and Chad reporting levels of 90 per cent (see Heintz 2006; also Figure 1).

From the 1980s onwards, most growth in informal employment has been forced by recession and neoliberal economic restructuring. People have been pushed into informal employment through cutbacks in public employment, the closure of private firms and the increased tendency for formal employers to resort to subcontracting arrangements. Another significant process has been for smaller firms to move wholesale into informality as a result of declining ability to pay registration, tax and labour overheads. As Thomas (1996: 99) summarizes, the 'top-down' informalization promoted by governments and employers has been matched by a 'bottom-up'

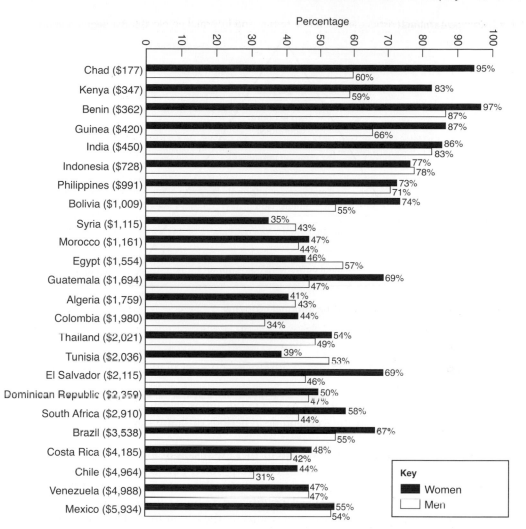

Figure 1 Estimated percentage of total non-agricultural employment in the informal sector by gender, 1994–2000

Source: Heintz 2006: 21, Figure 5

Note: GDP per capita in US$, 2000, in brackets.

informalization, stemming from the need for retrenched formal-sector workers and newcomers to the labour market to create their own sources of earnings, and/or to avoid the punitive costs attached to legal status.

The nature of the informal sector during recession and restructuring

In light of the above, it is hardly surprising that the informal sector has become increasingly competitive during the last two decades. Yet although ever more creative strategies to generate income can be found in cities in the South, competition is such that, according to ILO figures for Latin America and the Caribbean, there was a 42 per cent drop in income in the informal sector between 1980 and 1989 (Moghadam 1995: 122–3). In turn, although the informal sector has continued to expand during some of the hardest years of crisis and restructuring, it has not been able to absorb

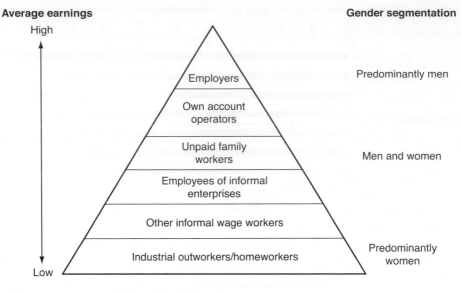

Figure 2 The gender segmentation of the informal economy

Source: Chen, Vanek and Carr 2004

all the job losses in the formal sector. This has led to the notion that growth of the informal sector may not be as much *counter-cyclical* – expanding in periods of slump – as *pro-cyclical*, and contingent upon health in the formal sector.

Whatever the case, it is likely that limits to further expansion of more lucrative and entrepreneurial activities in the informal sector are threatened by lower purchasing power among the population in general and greater numbers of people entering the workforce (Roberts 1991: 135). This looks set to continue given the legacy of high fertility and declining mortality during the 1960s and 1970s, and the steadily rising participation of women in the labour force. There are many reasons why more women are joining the labour force, but one of the most significant is economic necessity. In turn, the saturation of the informal sector is often argued to have hit women the hardest, because aside from their heavy representation in the sector (Figure 1), their limited skills and resources confine them to the lowest tiers of informal activity (see Figure 2).

Links between formal and informal sectors

The years of crisis and restructuring since the early 1980s have made ever more visible the interconnectedness of the formal and informal sectors, and, in particular, the dependence of the latter on the former for contracts, supplies and economic viability. Detailed empirical studies have revealed that the informal sector is linked to the formal sector in many ways (see Table 3), thereby rendering redundant previous notions of labour market dualism.

An early attempt to resist the construction of the formal and informal sectors as discrete and autonomous entities was Moser's seminal neo-Marxian exposition on 'petty commodity production'. Unlike the 'dualist model', this theorized urban labour markets as a continuum of productive activities in which large, formal-sector firms benefited from the existence of micro-entrepreneurs (Moser 1978). This provided fodder for a thesis of 'stucturalist articulation', which views urban labour markets as 'unified systems encompassing a dense network of relationships between formal

Table 3 Economic linkages between the formal and informal sectors of the urban economy

BACKWARD LINKAGES

a) Informal vendors sell products (e.g. soft drinks, cigarettes) obtained from manufacturers, wholesalers and retailers in the UFS.

b) Informally produced goods such as cooked foodstuffs, home-made clothing and embroidered items are likely to comprise raw materials supplied by the UFS.

FORWARD LINKAGES

a) The UIS may produce intermediate goods destined for final elaboration and distribution through the UFS. This may occur through sub-contracting or purchase on the part of the UFS.

Benefits for UFS of sub-contracting to UIS

   i) Informal employers may avoid paying legal minimum (or above-minimum) wage

  ii) Formal employers avoid obligations to provide social security contributions and fringe benefits to workers in informal enterprises

 iii) Formal employers can respond more flexibly (and at lower cost) to fluctuations in product demand

b) The (cheap) goods and services produced in the UIS, when consumed by UFS workers, arguably subsidise the wages of the UFS.

Source: Thomas 1996: 56–9
Notes: UFS = urban formal sector; UIS = urban informal sector.

and informal enterprises'. Although it is recognized that links between large- and small-scale firms are often exploitative, however, it is also acknowledged that some opportunities may be opened up for informal enterprises by globalization and neoliberal strategies of export promotion (Portes and Itzigsohn 1997: 240–1). In many respects, this has encouraged recommendations for more active and sympathetic policy stances towards the informal sector.

The informal sector in urban economic and employment policies

The fact that there was no explicit policy towards the informal sector in most developing countries until the 1980s was partly due to anticipation that labour surpluses would eventually be absorbed by formal industry and services (Tokman 1989: 1072). Another factor was the reluctance of economists and civil servants to acknowledge informal activities as anything other than a 'parasitic', 'unproductive' form of 'disguised unemployment' (Bromley 1997: 124). In effect, the informal sector was (and in many circles still is) viewed as an employer of 'last resort', or a fragile means of basic subsistence in situations where social welfare provision for those outside the formal labour force is minimal or non-existent (Cubitt 1995: 163; Gilbert 1998: 67).

Even where informal entrepreneurs may have wanted to 'become legal', prohibitive costs and convoluted bureaucratic procedures have usually dissuaded them from doing so (Tokman 1989: 1068). In addition to indirect discrimination resulting from state subsidies to the large-scale capital-intensive sector, informal entrepeneurs have often been subjected to harrassment or victimization (Thomas 1996: 56–7).

This scenario has been prone to change since the late 1980s, however, as government authorities, along with planners and social scientists, have come round to the notion that the informal sector is more of a seedbed of economic potential than a 'poverty trap' (Cubitt 1995: 175). With echoes of Keith Hart's 'popular entrepreneurship' concepts, these more positive constructions have been fuelled by a growing body of empirical research showing that some informal workers earn more than salaried workers; that self-employment can be a source of pride or prestige; that informality permits flexibility and ready adaptation to changing demand and family circumstances; and that people often acquire skills in the formal sector which can subsequently be used to advantage in their own businesses. Theoretical weight has been added to this shift in perspective by the Peruvian economist, Hernando de Soto, whose controversial book, *The Other Path* (1989), argues that the informal sector is a product of excessive and unjust regulation, created by governments in the interests of the society's powerful and dominant groups (Bromley 1997: 127). Emphasizing the ways in which the existence of the informal sector relieves unemployment, provides a gainful alternative to crime, and harnesses the entrepreneurial talent of the disaffected masses, de Soto asserts that 'illegality' is a perfectly justifiable response on the part of the urban poor. Governments should consider tolerating their 'nonconformity' more widely, and give them greater encouragement, protection and freedom (de Soto 1989).

These ideas have been hotly debated in the literature. One problem with de Soto's eulogization of informality is that it gives a misleading impression of a sector, which is perhaps better understood as '...a picture of survival rather than a sector full of entrepreneurial talent to be celebrated for its potential to create an economic miracle' (Thomas 1995: 130; see also Cubitt 1995). Another set of problems arises from the potentially perverse implications of proactive informal-sector policies. One outcome of advocating decontrol of economic enterprise is that a precedent is set for greater deregulation in the formal sector. This in turn contributes to broader processes promoted by multilaterals such as the International Monetary Fund (IMF) and the World Bank, to liberalize production and markets in developing regions, which have often been harmful to low-income groups.

Nonetheless, accepting that the informal sector is likely to persist for the foreseeable future, measures are arguably needed to help it operate more efficiently and with better conditions for its workers. With reference to the Caribbean, for example, Portes and Itzigsohn (1997: 241–3) suggest that much could be done to diminish the constraints faced by the informal sector. Prominent obstacles at present include lack of working capital through limited access to mainstream financial institutions, concentration in highly competitive low-income markets, the social atomization of informal entrepreneurs due to the irregular and/or chaotic nature of supplies, and the existence of a 'craftsman ethic', which prevents some informal entrepreneurs, particularly in artisanal production, from changing their traditional methods of production (ibid.).

While specific policy initiatives in different developing countries are discussed in detail elsewhere, a much-favoured intervention on the institutional/macroeconomic side of the labour market is the repeal of regulations and policies which obstruct entrepreneurship without serving any legitimate public regulatory purpose. There has also been advocacy for governments to consider simpler and diminished requirements and/or allow for progressive implementation (Tokman 1991: 155).

On the supply side of the labour market, there has been interest in, and/or support for, policies geared to education and training to promote the diversification of the informal sector, to enhance access to credit, to provide assistance in management, marketing and packaging, and to introduce measures to promote greater health and safety. These initiatives are particularly relevant for groups within the informal sector, such as ambulant traders and food vendors, where women often represent a large percentage of operatives (Tinker 1997; see also Chen, Vanek and Carr 2004). There has also been advocacy for orienting policies away from individual firms or workers, as a means of utilizing the social networks and social capital (reciprocity, trust, social obligations among kin, friends, neighbours, and so on) which so frequently fuel the operation of the informal sector (Portes and Itzigsohn 1997: 244–5).

Prospects for the informal sector

Regardless of policies which may be implemented by governments and agencies, it is likely that the informal sector will continue to be a significant feature of urban labour markets in the South in the twenty-first century (see Fernández-Kelly and Shefner 2006). One important reason for this is demographic pressure. The youthful age structure of most developing nations means that new entrants to the labour force will continue to rise at least until the year 2010. On top of this, the ageing of populations, coupled with exiguous state welfare and declining household incomes, will probably mean that older people will not be able to exit the labour force. The potential 'crowding-out' of the informal sector is likely to be exacerbated by ongoing increases in the number of women in employment.

On the demand side of the labour market, the current climate of deregulation is likely to provoke further contraction in public employment and to foster increasingly 'flexible' labour contracts in the formal sector, as firms face ever tougher global competition. In addition, increased capital intensity in the formal sector is likely to push more people into informal occupations over time.

Recognizing that policies to bolster the informal economy will have to address a wide range of concerns simultaneously, one key area is that of extending and enhancing systems of public education and training, so that people have greater choice and capabilities in their employment prospects, whether in the formal or informal sector. As such, education which encompasses commercial and managerial skills, alongside instruction in cutting-edge developments, such as information technology, could well bring about greater productivity and employment.

Policies geared to supporting people's efforts to sustain their livelihoods should also take due steps to consult the groups concerned. The fact that the informal sector has survived so well through the economic crisis and restructuring in developing regions since the early 1980s testifies to the fact that there are valuable lessons to be learned 'from below', and governments, not to mention multilateral institutions, would be well advised to heed them.

GUIDE TO FURTHER READING

Chen, M.A., Vanek, J. and Carr, M. (2004) *Mainstreaming Informal Employment and Gender in Poverty Reduction*, London: Commonwealth Secretariat. A comprehensive review of the role of informal employment in reducing poverty, including mainstream debates on the urban informal sector, and dedicated discussion on gender in the informal sector.

Fernández-Kelly, P. and Shefner, J. (eds) (2006) *Out of the Shadows: Political Action and the Informal Sector in Latin America*, Pennsylvania: Pennsylvania State University Press. The constituent chapters concentrate mainly on the political dimensions of the informal sector and what its existence means for the state in the twenty-first century. The emphasis is on Latin America, but many of the discussions have wider applicability.

Portes, A., Dore-Cabral, C. and Landoff, P. (eds) (1997) *The Urban Caribbean: Transition to a New Global Economy*, Baltimore, MD: Johns Hopkins University Press. This book combines discussion of debates on the informal sector, urbanization and globalization, with case studies from the capital cities of Costa Rica, Haiti, Guatemala, Jamaica and the Dominican Republic.

Thomas, J.J. (1995) *Surviving in the City: The Urban Informal Sector in Latin America*, London: Pluto Press. A thorough account of the nature and behaviour of the informal sector of employment in Latin American cities.

REFERENCES

Bromley, R. (1997) 'Working in the streets of Cali, Colombia: Survival strategy, necessity or unavoidable evil?', in J. Gugler (ed.) *Cities in the Developing World: Issues, Theory and Policy*, Oxford: Oxford University Press, pp. 124–38.

Chant, S. (2004) 'Urban livelihoods, employment and gender', in R. Gwynne and C. Kay (eds) *Latin America Transformed*, second edition, London: Hodder Arnold, pp. 210–31.

Chen, M.A., Vanek, J. and Carr, M. (2004) *Mainstreaming Informal Employment and Gender in Poverty Reduction*, London: Commonwealth Secretariat.

Cubitt, T. (1995) *Latin American Society*, second edition, London: Longman.

de Soto, H. (1989) *The Other Path: The Invisible Revolution in the Third World*, New York: Harper & Row.

Fernández-Kelly, P. and Shefner, J. (eds) (2006) *Out of the Shadows: Political Action and the Informal Sector in Latin America*, Pennsylvania: Pennsylvania State University Press.

Gilbert, A. (1998) *The Latin American City*, second edition, London: Latin America Bureau.

Hart, K. (1973) 'Informal income opportunities and urban employment in Ghana', in R. Jolly, E. de Kadt, H. Singer and F. Wilson (eds) *Third World Employment*, Harmondsworth: Penguin, pp. 66–70.

Heintz, J. (2006) *Globalisation, Economic Policy and Employment: Poverty and Gender Implications*, Geneva: International Labour Organization, Employment Policy Unit, Employment Strategy Department, Employment Strategy Paper 2006/3.

International Labour Organization (ILO) (1972) *Employment, Incomes and Inequality: A Strategy for Increasing Productive Employment in Kenya*, Geneva: International Labour Organization.

McIlwaine, C., Chant, S. and Lloyd Evans, S. (2002) 'Making a living: Employment, livelihoods and the informal sector', in C. McIlwaine and K. Willis (eds) *Challenges and Change in Middle America: Perspectives on Development in Mexico, Central America and the Caribbean*, Harlow: Pearson Education, pp. 110–35.

Moghadam, V. (1995) 'Gender aspects of employment and unemployment in global perspective', in M. Simai, with V. Moghadam and A. Kuddo (eds) *Global Employment: An International Investigation into the Future of Work*, London: Zed Books, in association with United National University, World Institute for Development Economics Research, pp. 111–39.

Moser, C. (1978) 'Informal sector or petty commodity production? Dualism or dependence in urban development', *World Development*, 6: 135–78.

Portes, A. and Itzigsohn, J. (1997) 'Coping with change: The politics and economics of urban poverty', in A. Portes, C. Dore-Cabral and P. Landoff (eds) *The Urban Caribbean: Transition to a New Global Economy*, Baltimore, MD: Johns Hopkins University Press, pp. 227–48.

Potter, R. and Lloyd-Evans, S. (1998) *The City in the Developing World*, London: Longman.

Roberts, B. (1991) 'The changing nature of informal employment: The case of Mexico', in G. Standing and V. Tokman (eds) *Towards Social Adjustment: Labour Market Issues in Structural Adjustment*, Geneva: International Labour Organization, pp. 115–40.

Roberts, B. (1994) 'Informal economy and family strategies', *International Journal of Urban and Regional Research*, 18(1): 6–23.

Thomas, J.J. (1995) *Surviving in the City: The Urban Informal Sector in Latin America*, London: Pluto Press.

Thomas, J.J. (1996) 'The new economic model and labour markets in Latin America', in V. Bulmer-Thomas (ed.) *The New Economic Model in Latin America and its Impact on Income Distribution and Poverty*, Basingstoke: Macmillan, in association with the Institute of Latin American Studies, University of London, pp. 79–102.

Tinker, I. (1997) *Street Foods: Urban Food and Employment in Developing Countries*, New York and Oxford: Oxford University Press.

Tokman, V. (1989) 'Policies for a heterogeneous informal sector in Latin America', *World Development*, 17(7): 1067–76.

Tokman, V. (1991) 'The informal sector in Latin America: From underground to legality', in G. Standing and V. Tokman (eds) *Towards Social Adjustment: Labour Market Issues in Structural Adjustment*, Geneva: International Labour Organization, pp. 141–57.

United Nations (UN) (1995) *The World's Women 1995: Trends and Statistics*, New York: United Nations.

4.9 Child labour

Sally Lloyd-Evans

Introduction: child labour as a global issue

One of the most hotly debated issues in the development agenda since the late 1980s has been the high incidence of child labour in Asia, Africa and Latin America (Alston 1994; Roberts 1998; Bartlett et al. 1999; White 2002). In the 1990s, heightened concern over the future welfare of millions of the world's poorer children largely developed from widespread media coverage of child-related issues, such as the murder of Brazilian street children by police death squads, and increased documentation on child work by non-governmental organizations (NGOs) and international institutions such as the United Nations Children's Fund (UNICEF), the World Bank and the International Labour Organization (ILO). Increased awareness has escalated child labour as a priority issue for global institutions concerned with human rights, equity and civil society in the twenty-first century. This movement has resulted in a more child-focused development agenda, which is linked to the focus of the Millennium Development Goals (MDGs) on the provision of 'decent work' for youth and universal primary education, and the promotion of the largest global programme against child labour (International Programme on the Elimination of Child Labour – IPEC) by the ILO since the 1990s. Furthermore, NGOs and new social movements, such as workers' organizations, have brought issues such as child trafficking and slavery to the attention of the general public across the globe, via new forms of media.

It has been estimated by the ILO (2006) that of the world's 317 million economically active children aged between five and seventeen, 218 million can be classified as child labourers, with the 5–14 age group constituting 166 million. These estimates present a significant decrease from the 250 million child labourers identified in the mid-1990s, and the ILO (2006) argues that the number of child labourers has fallen by 11 per cent between 2000 and 2004, as a result of global child labour elimination programmes. This decrease has occurred mainly in the numbers of children employed in hazardous industries, following the implementation of IPEC's Convention 182 on the elimination of the 'worst forms of child labour' in 1999. Despite the ILO's optimistic belief that 'the end of child labour is within reach', the fact remains that from as young as three or four years old, children from poor and vulnerable households are seen as potential income earners by their families, while numerous others in single-parent families undertake the sole responsibility of supporting the household financially.

Child labour is rooted in poverty, history, culture and global inequality (Potter and Lloyd-Evans 1998; Kielland and Tovo 2006). Although the fundamental reason why children work is poverty, there are other important factors which deserve consideration. While global institutions argue that the incidence of child labour will decline as a country's per-capita GDP rises, child labour is also seen to be a serious consequence of neoliberalism and unequal trade resulting from economic globalization. The negative consequences of globalization are centred around the exploitation of workers, including children, in the new international division of labour where developing countries are pressurized to compete in the global export economy. For example, in the 'successful' economies of South East Asia, increases in child prostitution are often linked to macroeconomic policies of governments which have promoted rapid industrialization at the expense of rural development and poverty alleviation. In Africa, Kielland and Tovo (2006: 6) argue that modern child labour is a result of the 'rapid and rather violent encounter between a rural farming society and a modern urban culture', where extended family survival strategies are disintegrating.

As a result, the debate over working children is marked by moral indignation and sympathy, which, although understandable, draws attention away from a more rational interpretation of the processes which draw children into the global labour market (Fyfe 1994; White 1994; Aitken 2001; Robson 2004). While the horrific stories of Latin America's street children have received the most attention in the media, little consideration is given to the far greater numbers of children who are 'invisibly' employed in the informal sector as agricultural or household workers (69 per cent of child labourers were estimated to be in the agricultural sector in 2004). Furthermore, prevailing perceptions of children as helpless 'victims' often serve to undervalue the essential contribution they make to household incomes, and denies them the 'right' to help their families in the struggle for a more equitable distribution of resources. Hence the question over whether child labour should be abolished or accepted within a broader, rights-based approach continues to be contested (Aitken 2001). As this chapter will highlight, child labour is an extremely complex and multifaceted subject, as 'work' can simultanously be seen as both harmful to a child's development and essential for providing for their basic needs.

Child labour and child work: Conceptual issues

What is child labour?

Child labour takes many forms, from paid work in factories and other forms of waged labour like street selling, which are particularly characteristic in cities, to unwaged labour in the household and predominantly rural areas, to bonded labour and trafficked labour, which are both forms of slavery. Industries, often export-oriented, which employ children have received the most attention, and include the production of carpets, glassware, matches, fireworks, gem-polishing and quarrying. 'Dollar Land' in Uttah Pradesh, India, so named due to its profitability, is a region geared to carpet production, where 150,000 children over ten years old work for 10–16 hours a day. Similarly, Nepal is famous for its 'kamaiya', bonded child labourers who have been sold into bondage in return for small sums or repayment of rural debts. Trafficked children and bonded labourers are seen to be the most severely exploited and vulnerable child workers, but their invisibility makes policy intervention difficult.

Major geographical differences in the incidence and nature of child labour can become blurred in the uniform category of 'child labour'. Of the estimated 218 million child labourers, the ILO (2006) estimates that 122.3 million are working in the Asia-Pacific region, 49.3 million in sub-Saharan Africa and 5.7 million in Latin America and the Caribbean. Geographical disparities also appear to be increasing, with Latin America and the Caribbean allegedly reducing the incidence of children in work by two-thirds, to just 5 per cent, while sub-Saharan Africa continues to have participation rates of over 26 per cent and rising (ILO 2006). In Africa, rising poverty and a diminishing adult labour force, due to the HIV/AIDS epidemic, have driven more children into the waged labour force (Robson 2004). Moreover, UNICEF (2006) has highlighted the plight of the world's invisible children, 8.4 million of whom are in slavery; and the organization still maintains that much child labour is hidden in household and agricultural sectors, which are not included in child labour statistics.

Although definitions of child labour vary, they are mainly centred on whether work has a 'detrimental impact' on a child's physical, mental or moral development. Current academic debates focus on whether there is a clear distinction between 'child labour' (usually waged) and 'child work' (unwaged), which is socialization undertaken in the course of everyday life (ILO 2006). Nieuwenhuys (1994) asks why unpaid household labour is considered to be morally 'neutral', compared to waged work in industry, when both are equally detrimental to the development of children. Here, issues of gender are salient, as girls rather than boys are usually expected to undertake a greater proportion of invisible household activities. While there is international condemnation of the employment of children in hazardous industrial activities, there is less agreement over whether household work should constitute 'child labour'. The understanding of children's work has been intertwined by such moral considerations throughout history and, as is highlighted below, it is important to deconstruct child labour in its appropriate social and cultural context.

Child labour and development: Contemporary thinking

'Western' perceptions of childhood

It has been suggested that the global preoccupation with Third World child workers is further evidence of the enforcement of Western codes of conduct in developing nations, as much of the recent literature on child labour stems from a Western, and predominantly middle-class, construction of 'childhood' (Fyfe 1994; Aitken 2001). The idea of 'working children' challenges traditional meanings of childhood, which are based predominantly on Western norms of behaviour. Definitions of childhood have considerable geographical, gendered and cultural implications, in relation to whether it is acceptable for children to make decisions about issues that govern their lives (White 1994; White 2002). New geographies and social studies of childhood have been important in highlighting the heterogeneity of childhood experiences in different parts of the world, and research on 'other childhoods' has sought to critique constructions of childhood which dominate understanding of child labour in the Global North (Holt and Holloway 2006).

Socio-spatial dimensions of child labour

There are socio-spatial dimensions to child labour which may explain why some categories of 'child work' are deemed to be more undesirable than others. In particular, many definitions of hazardous 'child labour' are defined by spatial parameters. As Jones (1997) argues, societal and public views on child labour and related issues will depend on the meanings people attach to public 'spaces' and what they see as appropriate places for children. In Latin America, millions of street children are perceived as 'criminal' and a 'threat' to family and social order. Such 'moral imaginations', which are fuelled by the media, led to public tolerance of the murder of street children in Brazilian cities. Across the world, city streets and industrial factories are seen as 'unnatural spaces' for child workers (Marquez 1999; Young 2003), while the private household space is deemed to be safe. Such conceptual dilemmas regarding children's spatial identities impact on the development and implementation of global policies which address child labour.

Towards a better future: Child labour and policy initiatives

In light of the above, it is not surprising that issues surrounding child labour have taken centre stage in the development campaigns of agencies and institutions around the world. Global institutions, such as the World Bank and the ILO, want to 'make child labour history', and they have largely adopted a 'paternalistic' approach to child workers, which regards them as passive victims of an unfair global system, and in need of protection (Jones 1997). Although the existence of child labour is a visible indication of the uneven development and poverty that exists worldwide today, most global institutions believe that hazardous child labour can be eliminated independently of poverty reduction. UNICEF (2006) has argued that real progress was made in 'realizing and protecting' children's rights in the 1990s, following the international adoption of the United Nations Convention on the Rights of the Child in 1989. The Convention (documented in Table 1) highlighted the need for child labour to be placed firmly on the international agenda, but the enforcement of child labour standards in many countries has been questioned.

Table 1 The United Nations Convention on the Rights of the Child, 1989

Children have the right to:

- enough food, clean water and health care
- an adequate standard of living
- be with their family or those who will care for them best
- protection from all exploitation, physical, mental and sexual abuse
- special protection when exposed to armed conflict
- be protected from all forms of discrimination
- be protected from work that threatens their education, health or development
- special care and training if disabled
- play
- education
- have their own opinions taken into account in decisions which affect their lives
- know what their rights are

Source: Potter and Lloyd-Evans 1998: 185

Internationally, the ILO wants to see programmes against child labour mainstreamed in national development and policy frameworks, mainly in the form of providing 'decent work' for parents, and the rehabilitation, education and training of child workers. While there is reticence by institutions and governments to abolish all forms of child work, the ILO's goal to eliminate the worst forms of child labour, such as bonded labour, by 2016 appears to be universally accepted. The ILO (2006) argues that a recent decrease in child workers is evidence that the global child labour movement is stronger than it was a decade ago, due to political commitment by governments to IPEC, and the rise of new partnerships with NGOs and workers' organizations.

Although a step in the right direction, international solutions to abolish child labour take the decision-making process away from child workers and are regarded by many as unfeasible (Robson 2004). By contrast, many NGOs and grass-roots organizations have attempted to implement small-scale programmes which aim to 'empower' children, by supporting their right to work. Ennew (1994) argues for the need to recognize children as rational individuals who can be empowered to take control of their own lives. Grass-roots initiatives, such as street drop-in centres, endeavour to give children the opportunity to work in safe environments, while also providing time for schooling and recreation. Kielland and Tovo (2006) have highlighted the use of 'conditional transfers' (food or fuel) to poor families, in exchange for removing their children from hazardous work in Africa.

There is still considerable scepticism over whether current policy initiatives will enhance children's quality of life, unless there are more fundamental changes to the unequal distribution of global wealth and trade. Although the ultimate goal of the United Nations remains the worldwide abolition of all child labour, there is now an understanding that progress will be slow, and that change must take into consideration the needs and rights of children and their families.

GUIDE TO FURTHER READING

Bartlett, S., Hart, R., Satterthwaite, D., de la Barra, X. and Missair, A. (1999) *Cities for Children: Children's Rights, Poverty and Urban Management*, London: Earthscan. This book discusses practical measures for meeting the rights of urban children in Africa, Asia and Latin America.

International Labour Organization (ILO) (2006) *The End of Child Labour: Within Reach*, Geneva: International Labour Organization. The latest report on the ILO's child labour policies, which includes conceptual debates and case study material.

Kielland, A. and Tovo, M. (2006) *Children at Work: Child Labour Practices in Africa*, London: Lynne Rienner. A contemporary and enlightened critique of conceptual and development issues relating to child labour in Africa.

Nieuwenhuys, O. (1994) *Children's Lifeworlds: Gender, Welfare and Labour in the Developing World*, London: Routledge. A detailed study of children's daily work in rural southern India, which examines how gender, class, household structure, education and state ideology combine to structure children's working lives.

Robson, E. (2004) 'Hidden child workers: Young carers in Zimbabwe', *Antipode*, 36(2): 227–48. A paper that explores children's right to work through a case study of carers of HIV/AIDS sufferers in Zimbabwe.

REFERENCES

Aitken, S. (2001) 'Global crises of childhood: Rights, justice and the unchildlike child', *Area*, 33: 119–27.

Alston, P. (ed.) (1994) *The Best Interests of the Child: Reconciling Culture and Human Rights*, Oxford: Clarendon Press and UNICEF.

Bartlett, S., Hart, R., Satterthwaite, D., de la Barra, X. and Missair, A. (1999) *Cities for Children: Children's Rights, Poverty and Urban Management*, London: Earthscan.

Ennew, J. (1994) *Street Children and Working Children: A Guide to Planning*, London: Save the Children.

Fyfe, A. (1994) *Child Labour*, Cambridge: Polity.

Holt, L. and Holloway, S. (2006) 'Childhoods in a globalised world', *Children's Geographies*, 4(2): 135–41.

Jones, G.A. (1997) 'Junto con los niños: Street children in Mexico', *Development in Practice*, 1(1): 39–49.

Kielland, A. and Tovo, M. (2006) *Children at Work: Child Labour Practices in Africa*, London: Lynne Rienner.

Marquez, P.C. (1999) *The Street is my Home: Youth and Violence in Caracas*, Stanford, CA: Stanford University Press.

Nieuwenhuys, O. (1994) *Children's Lifeworlds: Gender, Welfare and Labour in the Developing World*, London: Routledge.

Potter, R.B. and Lloyd-Evans, S. (1998) *The City in the Developing World*, Harlow: Longman.

Roberts, S.M. (1998) 'Commentary: What about the children?' *Environment and Planning A*, 30: 3–11.

Robson, E. (2004) 'Hidden child workers: Young carers in Zimbabwe', *Antipode*, 36(2): 227–48.

UNICEF (2006) *The State of the World's Children*, New York: UNICEF.

White, B. (1994) 'Children, work and "child labour": Changing responses to the employment of children', *Development and Change*, 25(4): 849–78.

White, S. (2002) 'From the politics of poverty to the politics of identity? Child rights and working children in Bangladesh', *Journal of International Development*, 14: 725–35.

Young, L. (2003) 'The place of street children in Kampala, Uganda: Marginalisation, resistance and acceptance in the urban environment', *Environment and Planning D: Society and Space*, 21(5): 607–28.

4.10 Irregular migrant workers

Dennis Conway

One particular characteristic of globalization's transformation of everyone's lives is its 'unruliness': in the widespread avoidance, or circumvention, of border regulatory mechanisms, its informal, underground economy associations, and in the growing complexity of global labour flows (Conway 2006). Consequently, *irregular worker migration* is affecting more and more nation states – as sources, destinations and transit countries. Concerns for irregular immigrants' human rights, as well as border security and regulatory concerns, fuel contemporary debates over the impacts and consequences of these volatile, unpredictable and difficult-to-estimate flows (Bogusz et al. 2004; Düvell 2006). In the first decade of the twenty-first century, both regulated and unregulated international migration are raising complex human rights and ethical issues, that challenge national and global regimes (Schindlmayr 2003; Taran 2000). Irregular migration from the perspective of the country of destination – as the host society – refers to non-nationals who have not complied with the required formalities of entry, staying and/or working. There can be *irregular entry* (with such 'clandestine migration' usually considered the most heinous/illegal); *irregular residence* (over-staying a visitor's visa being a common strategy, but less heinous); and *irregular activity* or *employment* (where non-nationals undertake unlawful activities, ranging from minor felonies to major criminal activities, or seek and undertake employment for which they do not have the required authorization or work permit). Irregular immigration – entry and residence – does not imply that irregular employment will occur, while all clandestine workers (employed in contravention of labour laws) are not necessarily illegal immigrants (Ghosh 1998).

The intertwining of these legal categories is further complicated by the institutional deficiencies in documentation procedures and monitoring practices of the sending and receiving countries. Inadequate documentation of entry and exit, or lack of employment verification, is not necessarily a deliberate intention of the migrant to circumvent the legal apparatus, but more a failure of information dissemination, unworkable governmental policies and ineffective institutional oversight (Düvell 2006).

Irregular migration's global reach

Usage of terms such as illegal immigrants, illegal aliens, clandestine or undocumented migrants is often imprecise, with the former 'illegal' label being purposely pejorative and/or discriminatory. Unauthorized entrants, visa overstayers, clandestine workers, underground workers, the illegally employed, are other terms used to characterize this stigmatized group of international migrants, many being critical of the informality or non-legal nature of these migrants' situation (Conway 2006). Characterizing such immigrant non-nationals as 'illegal' also implicitly places them outside the scope and protection of the host nation's legal systems (Taran 2000).

'Irregular migration', therefore, is a less prejudicial label, sanctioned by global institutions such as the International Labour Organization (ILO) and the International Organization for Migration (IOM). Although the magnitude of irregular immigration can never be known, estimates have suggested it may be around 30 million (Stalker 2000) or as high as 44 million (Düvell 2006). As will be shown later, irregular migration is more than a Global South-to-Global North cross-border phenomenon; it is a global search for gainful work.

While global capital now moves unfettered across boundaries, and global labour appears to have many more barriers and restrictions, irregular migrant labour – potential or actual – rarely views itself as undertaking a criminal act by crossing borders to seek employment in disregard of the destination's laws (Kyle and Siracusa 2005). These 'new immigrant' workers rarely compete with indigenous workers for their jobs, but their availability appears to encourage divisions of labour within lower-skilled markets which raise the productivity of the more skilled native workers. Many of the sectors in which irregular migrant workers are typically concentrated – agriculture, tourism, food processing, construction, some segments of the textile industry and the service sectors of hotel and catering, caring and domestic work (and the wide array of sex industry work, including prostitution, massage, strip-club dancing and escort services) – are industries that cannot be outsourced to countries with suitable low-wage labour regimes.

Entire industries in southern Europe – Italy and Spain, for example – rely on irregular migrant labour. In the USA, the availability of irregular migrant labour appears to be a prerequisite for the survival of otherwise uncompetitive industries. Entrepreneurial migrants revive abandoned industries, or create new informal businesses and industries in the domestic service, caregiving and textile and apparel production sectors. Small and family enterprises, as well as firms in the underground economy and declining or uncompetitive industries, commonly have a large share of irregular immigrant workers, in part because they are less visible to the regulatory authorities, and in part because their recruitment is conducted informally through social transnational networks (Ghosh 1998; Düvell 2006).

The USA has the largest estimated number of irregular immigrants (10.3 million in 2004). This is a considerable increase from previous estimates for 1990 of 4–4.5 million. Not only is this an unexpected rapid increase, but the diversity of source countries of irregular migrants in the USA, among the 50 per cent who are not from Mexico, is an enduring characteristic. Several are from Central America and the Caribbean, and Canada is also high on the list, together with several countries in Asia and Europe – notably, the Philippines, India and Poland (Passel 2005).

Estimates of the amount of irregular immigration into Europe are imprecise, in large part because the numbers who enter illegally, or who enter legally but work illegally, represent undocumented and unobservable events. Border apprehension data has been used, however, to derive estimates for the EU-15 and EU-25 groups of countries in 2001, and the resultant estimated annual 'illegal migration flows' are 650,000 for the EU-15 group, and 800,000 for the EU-25 group. Police authorities suggest that about half of all illegal migrants to the EU make use of smuggling organizations to cross borders.

China has become a global source for irregular, as well as managed emigration in today's globalization era, with trafficked nationals coming mainly from Fujian province. A considerable proportion of this country's illegal flow into North America and Europe is being organized by criminal syndicates (snakeheads), who channel flows along particular underground routes, and into 'target' cities where bridgehead communities serve as convenient shelters. Other Asian Pacific sources, such as the Philippines and Indonesia, have long-standing and deeper-embedded migration cultures, and for decades have sent appreciably larger irregular and sanctioned migrant volumes overseas to North America as well as to Malaysia, Thailand and Singapore. There are also an estimated two million irregular migrant workers from Myanmar (Burma), Cambodia and Lao PDR, who are working in Thailand's recovering economy (Conway 2006).

The 'commodification of migration'

International underground organizations and syndicates are the seamy underside of the world's migration facilitators, because they profit from irregular migrant trafficking and smuggling in which the migrants undertaking the highly risky journeys are often not much more than profitable, disposable commodities. Utilizing a flexibility of routes and strategic dynamism in responding to border enforcement and surveillance, these criminal syndicates are able to avoid detection by legal opposing forces, or use corruption and bribery to facilitate the cross-border shipments of their contracted human cargos. They organize irregular global migration networks and operate within informal, underground economies in sending, destination and transit countries (Williams 1999; Bales 2000). Migrants might be innocent, complicit or incidental parties to such criminal activities. And there is some circumstantial evidence to suggest that human smuggling is as lucrative as drug smuggling to organized crime.

Although estimates of such underground activity are always going to be questionable, a smaller proportion of these transnational organizations which organize cross-border entry, charge transit fees and serve as *coyotes*, or smugglers of irregular entrants, operate within family, community and kin-based social circles. As such, they are much less likely to dehumanize and 'commodify' their clients because they have been built around social contractual arrangements and the checks and balances within such transnational migration networks are socially determined as much as they are economically driven. A more neutral term for these informal transnational organizations is 'migrant-exporting schemes' (Kyle and Siracusa 2005). Therefore, the range of international organizations facilitating cross-border irregular migration will vary from the highly coercive and exploitative to the totally facilitative; some where the migrant's rights are fully honoured, some with operational restrictions and curtailment of freedoms, and others where she/he has no rights and little, if any freedom.

Forced irregular migration and human trafficking

Forced irregular migration

Many forced migrants are people fleeing for their lives either to protect themselves and their family from sustained physical harm and/or to escape dramatic-to-cataclysmic declines in their economic circumstances. As such, the urgency of flight inevitably prevents many of these unfortunates from having the time to complete the paperwork for border crossing, rendering them 'irregular' by default, rather than by design or criminal intent. In many cases, forced, irregular migrant flights are into neighbouring countries, which are often incapable of providing the logistic assistance necessary to harbour these influxes of desperate people. Many 'flights to safety' are anything but permanent, anything but successful, and often they have become long-term problems for the international community, as well as for the transit country or 'haven of first resort' (Papademetriou 2003).

Human trafficking – New slavery

Irregular migrants and other powerless people who are forced to leave their homeland or flee their destroyed home, community or land are prey to migration facilitators of a different breed: exploiters, rather than helpful intermediaries. Human trafficking is one form of forced, irregular migration that appears to be the most abusive of human rights, and the most inhumane of 'global businesses' (Bogusz et al. 2004).

The growing practice among international criminal groups, syndicates and organizations to profit from migration has become a 'new form of slavery', preying on young women, transsexuals and children by offering hope, while tricking, brutalizing and selling them into prostitution and sex working, sweatshop labour, and similar illicit, dehumanizing and/or dangerous occupations in which they have little autonomy or basic rights and human dignities (Williams 1999; Bales 2000).

The International Labour Office has recently estimated that at least 12.3 million people work as slaves or in other forms of forced labour, and as many as 2.5 million are 'enslaved' as a result of cross-border trafficking, with approximately half being employed in the sex trade (ILO 2005). In 2005, the ILO found that global profits from trafficking totalled $32 billion a year, or $13,000 per trafficked worker, while profits from forced commercial sexual exploitation totalled $27.8 billion annually, or $23,000 per worker (ILO 2005).

Before moving on from this discussion of the global sex trade, human trafficking and this dehumanizing global industry, one caveat is in order. Agustín (2006) exposes the delicacy with which sexual matters are examined in academic literature. She finds the criminological conceptualization – which brackets all women in the global sex industry as 'victims', and all, or most, as being coerced, tricked and abused, trafficked irregular migrants – highly questionable.

We should be mindful that many irregular migrant women who undertake domestic, care and sexual services for money qualify as transnationals in terms of the flexible work regimes they take up, in terms of the 'manner of migrating, arriving, finding sex jobs', and in terms of making contacts with employers. They deserve to be treated as decision-making agents in a conceptual framework which 'allows consideration of all conceivable aspects of people's lives and travels, locates them in periods of personal growth and risk-taking and does not force them to *identify* as "sex workers" or "victims" (Agustín 2006: 43).

Conclusion

From many an irregular migrant's perspective, their right to search for work across borders trumps any nation's categorization of them as illegal, or as a criminal. In similar fashion to their regular/legal counterparts, irregular migrant workers rationalize their decision 'on moral claims based on notions of social, economic and political (in)justice which help shape their decision to override the various legal routes to work abroad' (Kyle and Siracusa 2005: 157). Kyle and Siracusa continue:

> Illegal migrants often view themselves as a type of economic citizen of the political economic empire Western states and transnational corporations have created. This idea is relentlessly reinforced in the popular discourse of 'globalization' as a naturalized social reality promoted in a myriad of institutions, and it has led to the real blurring of state claims to sovereignty (Kyle and Siracusa 2005: 157).

Irregular migration, therefore, is going to remain unruly, difficult to legislate or manage, because it has become a deeply entrenched geo-economic feature of the 'newest age of migration' now under way (Papademetriou 2003). This means that irregular/illegal immigration will continue to be a major challenge for policymakers, citizenry and even for the new immigrants themselves, as they seek to regularize their irregular status in today's globalizing world of *Workers Without Frontiers* (Stalker 2000).

GUIDE TO FURTHER READING

Düvell, F. (2006) *Illegal Immigration in Europe: Beyond Control?* Basingstoke and New York: Palgrave Macmillan.

Ghosh, B. (1998) *Huddled Masses and Uncertain Shores: Insights into Irregular Migration*, The Hague, Boston, MA, and London: Martinus Nijhoff Publishers and International Organization for Migration.

Stalker, P. (2000) *Workers Without Frontiers: The Impact of Globalization on International Migration*, Boulder, CO: Lynn Rienner.

Williams, P. (1999) *Illegal Immigration and Commercial Sex: The New Slave Trade*, London and Portland, OR: Frank Cass.

REFERENCES

Agustín, L. (2006) 'The disappearing of a migration category: Migrants who sell sex', *Journal of Ethnic and Migration Studies*, 32(1): 29–47.

Bales, K. (2000) *Disposable People, New Slavery in the Global Economy*, Berkeley, CA: University of California Press.

Bogusz, B., Cholewinski, R., Cygan, A. and Szyszcak, E. (2004) *Irregular Migration and Human Rights: Theoretical, European and International Perspectives*, Leiden, Netherlands, and Boston, MA: Martinus Nijhoff Publishers.

Conway, D. (2006) 'Globalization of labor: Increasing complexity, more unruly', in D. Conway and N. Heynen (eds) *Globalization's Contradictions: Geographies of Discipline, Destruction and Transformation*, Abingdon: Routledge and Taylor & Francis, pp. 79–94.

Düvell, F. (2006) *Illegal Immigration in Europe: Beyond Control?* Basingstoke and New York: Palgrave Macmillan.

Ghosh, B. (1998) *Huddled Masses and Uncertain Shores: Insights into Irregular Migration*, The Hague, Boston, MA, and London: Martinus Nijhoff Publishers and International Organization for Migration.

ILO (2005) *A Global Alliance Against Forced Labour*, Geneva: Report of the Director General, International Labour Office.

Kyle, D.J. and Siracusa, C.A. (2005) 'Seeing the state like a migrant: Why so many non-criminals break immigration laws', in W. van Schendel and I. Abraham (eds) *Illicit Flows and Criminal Things: States, Borders, and the Other Side of Globalization*, Bloomington and Indianapolis: Indiana University Press, pp. 153–76.

Papademetriou, D.G. (2003) 'Managing rapid and deep change in the newest age of migration', *The Political Quarterly*, 74(s1): 39–58.

Passell, J. (2005) *Unauthorized Migrants: Numbers and Characteristics: Background Briefing Prepared for Task Force on Immigration and America's Future*, Pew Hispanic Center: A Pew Research Center Project (http://www.pewhispanic.org).

Schindlmayr, T. (2003) 'Sovereignty, legal regimes and international migration', *International Migration*, 41(2): 109–23.

Stalker, P. (2000) *Workers Without Frontiers: The Impact of Globalization on International Migration*, Boulder, CO: Lynn Rienner.

Taran, P.A. (2000) 'Human rights of migrants: Challenges of the new decade', *International Migration*, 38(6): 7–46.

Williams, P. (1999) *Illegal Immigration and Commercial Sex: The New Slave Trade*, London and Portland, OR: Frank Cass.

Urbanization

Editorial introduction

The Second United Nations Conference on Human Settlements, customarily referred to as 'Habitat II', held in Istanbul, Turkey, in 1996, attested to the continuing importance of the urbanization process in developing societies. In the period since 1950, rapid urbanization has become one of the principal hallmarks of developing nations. It is the magnitude of the changes that are occurring which underscores the salience of urban processes, for it is generally accepted that, on average, the conditions to be found in the rural areas of developing countries are much poorer than those that are to be encountered in the towns and cities.

It is now well established that in the contemporary world, for every urban dweller living in the affluent developed world, two exist in the poorer cities and towns of the developing world. In fact, by the end of the first quarter of the twenty-first century, this ratio will have risen to three to one in favour of urban residents in the developing world. This rapid rise in both urbanization (the proportion of the population living in urban places), and urban growth (the physical expansion of cities on the ground), is exemplified in a number of different ways. Globally, these include increases in the number of large cities, as well as increases in the size of the largest cities themselves. It is also associated with the ever-larger number of cities that have reached the million population mark. By 1990, the average population of the world's 100 largest cities was in excess of 5 million. In 1800, the equivalent statistic had stood at fewer than 200,000 inhabitants. Further, by 1990, there were 12 'mega-cities' with over 10 million inhabitants; most notably, seven were to be found in Asia, three in Latin America and two in the United States of America.

Since the mid-1980s, the concept of the 'world' or 'global' city has come to prominence. This approach stresses that cities have to be seen as key points in the articulation of the global economic system, and are dominated by transnational companies (TNCs) and transnational capital. However, recent research has pointed to the fact that in many regions – for example, in South America – it is medium-sized cities that are now showing the fastest overall rates of growth. In short, over the Third World as a whole, big and small cities are growing and exhibiting great dynamism.

Within these fast-growing urban settlements, poor housing is perhaps the most conspicuous manifestation of generalized poverty. Possibly the second most overt sign of the stresses and strains of rapid urban change are witnessed in the urgent need for sound and effective environmental management. While more urban residents die from preventable diseases than as the result of disasters, it is earthquakes, storms and floods that receive far greater media coverage on a day-to-day basis. Housing and environmental conditions are major areas calling for good governance in Third World cities, and perhaps more than anything else, the political will to improve matters on a broad social and economic front is pressingly required. This is a vital area when one considers that the very existence of urban areas is predicated on economies of scale, which should therefore allow environmental and health hazards to be tackled more effectively than in rural areas.

In the past, many analyses have treated the urban and the rural as being quite separate, although in reality they are, of course, functionally closely interrelated. For example, food is required for growing city populations, and is often produced at low procurement prices, giving rise to what is frequently described as urban bias in patterns and processes of national and international development.

5.1 Urbanization in low- and middle-income nations

David Satterthwaite

Urban trends

Urban areas in low- and middle-income nations now have more than a third of the world's total population and nearly three-quarters of its urban population. They contain most of the economic activities in these nations and most of the new jobs created since the 1980s. They are also likely to house most of the world's growth in population in the next one to two decades (United Nations 2006). Thus, how they are governed and what provisions are made to serve their expanding populations has very significant implications for economic and social development – and also for environmental quality and stability, as discussed in a later essay (see 5.6 Urbanization and environment in low- and middle-income nations).

In terms of regional distribution, by 2006, all independent nations in Africa and Latin America were within the low- and middle-income category. So too was most of the population of the Caribbean and Asia; the main exceptions in terms of population size were Puerto Rico for the Caribbean, and Japan, Republic of Korea, Saudi Arabia, Israel, Singapore and Hong Kong (China) for Asia. By 2000, 94 per cent of Asia's total population and 88 per cent of its urban population were in low- and middle-income nations.

Table 5.1 shows the scale of the growth in urban population in low- and middle-income nations – from 309 million in 1950 to over 2 billion at the end of the first decade of the twenty-first century; and also the shift from most of the world's urban population being in high-income nations to being in low and middle-income nations. Although Asia and Africa still have more rural than urban dwellers, they both have very large and rapidly growing urban populations. Asia alone has close to half the world's urban population and more than half of this is within just two countries, China and India. Africa now has a larger urban population than Northern America; so too does Latin America and the Caribbean – which also has more than three-quarters of its population living in urban centres.

Growth of large cities

Two aspects of this rapid growth in urban population have been the increase in the number of large cities and the historically unprecedented size of the largest cities (see Table 5.2). Just two centuries ago, there were only two 'million-cities' worldwide (i.e. cities with one million or more inhabitants): London and Beijing (Peking). By 2000 there were 380, three-quarters of which were in low- and middle-income nations. Many had populations that grew more than twentyfold between 1950 and 2000 – including Abidjan, Al-Khartum (Khartoum), Dar es Salaam, Dhaka, Goiânia, Kaduna, Karaj, Kinshasa, Lagos, Lomé, Lusaka, Sana'a, Santa Cruz, Shenzhen, Tijuana and Yaoundé. However, many of these had such rapid population growth rates because of such small populations in 1950, as a result of apartheid-like controls on the rights of indigenous populations to live and work in urban areas. Others, such as Shenzhen, Dhaka and Tijuana, were driven primarily by their economic success.

Table 5.2 also highlights how the size of the world's largest cities has grown dramatically over the last 200 years: in 1800, the average size of the world's 100 largest cities was less than 200,000 inhabitants, but by 2000 it was over six million. By 2000, there were 45 urban agglomerations within the world which had more than five million inhabitants, three-quarters of which were in low- and middle-income nations.

Table 1 The distribution of the world's urban population, 1950–2010

Region or country	1950	1970	1990	2000*	2010*
Urban populations (millions of inhabitants)					
WORLD	732	1329	2271	2845	3475
High-income nations	423	650	818	874	922
Low- and middle-income nations	309	678	1453	1971	2553
'Least developed nations'	15	41	110	166	247
Africa	33	85	203	294	408
Asia	234	485	1011	1363	1755
Europe	277	411	509	522	529
Latin America and the Caribbean	70	163	315	394	474
Northern America	110	171	214	249	284
Oceania	8	14	19	22	25
Urbanization level (percentage of population living in urban areas)					
WORLD	29.0	36.0	43.0	46.8	50.8
High-income nations	52.1	64.6	71.2	73.2	75.2
Low- and middle-income nations	18.1	25.2	35.2	40.3	45.5
'Least developed nations'	7.3	13.1	21.0	24.7	29.0
Africa	14.7	23.4	32.0	36.2	40.5
Asia	16.8	22.7	31.9	37.1	42.5
Europe	50.5	62.6	70.6	71.7	72.9
Latin America and the Caribbean	42.0	57.2	70.9	75.4	79.1
Northern America	63.9	73.8	75.4	79.1	82.2
Oceania	62.0	70.8	70.3	70.5	71.2
Percentage of the world's urban population living in:					
WORLD	100.0	100.0	100.0	100.0	100.0
High-income nations	57.8	49.0	36.0	30.7	26.5
Low- and middle-income nations	42.2	51.0	64.0	69.3	73.5
'Least developed nations'	2.0	3.1	4.8	5.8	7.1
Africa	4.5	6.4	8.9	10.3	11.7
Asia	32.0	36.5	44.5	47.9	50.5
Europe	37.8	30.9	22.4	18.4	15.2
Latin America and the Caribbean	9.6	12.3	13.9	13.9	13.6
Northern America	15.0	12.9	9.4	8.8	8.2
Oceania	1.1	1.0	0.8	0.8	0.7
Nations with largest urban populations (2000):					
China	9.9	10.9	13.9	16.0	17.5
India	8.3	8.3	9.6	9.9	10.3
USA	13.8	11.6	8.5	7.9	7.4
Brazil	2.7	4.0	4.9	5.0	4.9
Russian Federation	6.2	6.1	4.8	3.8	2.9

*The statistics for 2000 are an aggregation of national statistics, many of which draw on national censuses held in 1999, 2000 or 2001, but some are based on estimates or projections from statistics drawn from censuses held around 1990. There is also a group of countries (mostly in Africa) for which there are no census data since the 1970s or early 1980s, so all figures for their urban (and rural) populations are based on estimates and projections.

Source: Derived from statistics in United Nations 2006

Key characteristics of urban change

These statistics give the impression of very rapid urbanization that is focused on large cities. But some care is needed when making generalizations, because there is such diversity in the scale and

Table 2 The distribution of the world's largest cities by region over time

Region	1800	1900	1950	2000
Number of 'million cities'				
World	2	17	75	380
Africa	0	0	2	37
Asia	1	4	28	192
China	1	2	12	86
India	0	1	5	32
Europe	1	9	22	53
Latin America and the Caribbean	0	0*	7	51
Northern America	0	4	14	41
USA	0	4	12	37
Oceania	0	0	2	6
Regional distribution of the world's largest 100 cities				
World	100	100	100	100
Africa	5	2	3	8
Asia	63	22	42	49
China	23	13	18	17
India	18	4	6	8
Europe	28	53	26	10
Latin America and the Caribbean	3	5	8	16
Northern America	0	16	19	15
USA	0	15	17	13
Oceania	0	2	2	2
Average size of the world's 100 largest cities	187,520	726,350	2.0m	6.3m

* Some estimates suggest that Rio de Janeiro had reached one million inhabitants by 1900, while other sources suggest it had just under one million.

Source: Satterthwaite 2007; for 1950 and 2000, this drew primarily on United Nations 2006; for 1800 and 1900, the statistics are derived primarily from city populations given in Chandler 1987

Notes: Cities that have changed their country classifications and nations that have changed regions are considered to be in the country or region that they are currently in for this whole period. For instance, Hong Kong is counted as being in China for all the above years, while the Russian Federation is considered part of Europe.

nature of urban change between nations and, within each nation, over time. Also, for the larger and more populous nations, there is great diversity in urban trends between different regions. However, certain general points can be highlighted.

More than half the world's population does not live in cities

Although it is often stated that more than half the world's population lives in cities, this is not the case. According to the most recent UN statistics (United Nations 2006), the world's urban population will only come to exceed its rural population around 2008. The proportion of people living in cities is also considerably below the proportion living in urban centres, as a significant proportion of the urban population in low-, middle- and high-income nations lives in urban centres too small to be called cities (because they lack the size and the economic, administrative or political status that being a city implies). The economic and demographic importance of small urban centres is often overlooked; for instance, many nations have more than 10 per cent of their national population in urban centres with fewer than 20,000 inhabitants (Satterthwaite 2006).

Less urbanized populations, smaller cities

In all regions of the world, most of the urban population lives in urban areas with fewer than one million inhabitants. 'Mega-cities', with 10 million or more inhabitants, had 4 per cent of the world's population in 2000. Even in Latin America, with its unusually high concentration of population in large cities, four times as many people live in urban areas with fewer than one million inhabitants than in mega-cities.

Most of the world's mega-cities had slower population growth rates during the 1990s compared to the previous three or four decades. Several had more people moving out than in during the 1990s – for instance, in Kolkata, Buenos Aires, São Paulo, Rio de Janeiro and Mexico City. Mega-cities can only develop in countries with large, non-agricultural economies and large national populations; most nations have too small a population and too weak an urban-based economy to support a mega-city. In addition, the more decentralized patterns of urban development evident in the nations with large urban populations, including Brazil, China, India and Mexico, suggest that the number of mega-cities and the proportion of the world's population living in them will not increase much.

Although the size of the world's largest cities is unprecedented historically, most of the largest cities are significantly smaller than had been expected. For instance, Mexico City had 18 million people in 2000 – not the 31 million people predicted in 1980 (United Nations 1980). Kolkata had 13 million inhabitants in 2000, not the 40–50 million people that had been predicted during the 1970s (Brown 1974).

A range of factors helps explain this slowing of cities' population growth rates. For many cities, one reason was slow economic growth (or economic decline), so fewer people moved there; this helps explain slower population growth rates for many cities in Africa and Latin America during the 1980s and 1990s. A second factor was the capacity of cities outside the large metropolitan centres to attract a significant proportion of new investment. In various nations that have had effective decentralization, urban authorities in smaller cities have more resources and capacity to compete for new investment. Trade liberalization and a greater emphasis on exports from the 1980s also increased the comparative advantage of many smaller cities. Meanwhile, advances in transport and communications in many nations lessened the advantages for businesses of concentrating in the largest cities. A third factor, evident in many cities, was lower rates of natural increase, as fertility rates came down.

However, there are also large cities whose population growth rates remained high during the 1980s and 1990s – for instance, Dhaka (Bangladesh) and many cities in India, China, Mexico and Brazil – and strong economic performance by such cities is the most important factor in explaining this. In other regions, especially in sub-Saharan Africa, there are various cities whose population growth was much boosted by the movement there of people displaced by wars, civil strife or drought, but in many instances this is largely a temporary movement, not a permanent one.

The concentration of large cities in large economies

There is an economic logic to the location of most large cities. In 2000, the world's five largest economies (United States of America, China, Japan, India and Germany) had 8 of the world's 17 mega-cities (with more than ten million inhabitants) and more than two-fifths of its 'million-cities'. Within low- and middle-income countries, the largest cities were concentrated in the largest economies (which also tend to be among the most populous countries): Brazil, Mexico and Argentina in Latin America; China, India, Indonesia and the Republic of Korea in Asia. There is also a strong association between a nation's per-capita income and its level of urbanization. Most of the nations with the most rapid increase in their level of urbanization between 1960 and 2000 were also the nations with the most rapid economic growth (UNCHS 1996; Satterthwaite 2007).

Although much of the rapid growth in the major cities in low- and middle-income nations in the 1950s and 1960s was associated with political change – such as the achievement of political independence and the expansion in government – economic change is now a more powerful and important factor in where major cities grow (or decline) in most nations, and this is unlikely to change.

Beyond a rural–urban division

Perhaps too much emphasis is given to the fact that the world's population is to become more than half urban in 2007 or 2008, because of the imprecision in defining 'urban' and 'rural' populations, and the large differences between countries in the criteria used to define urban centres. These differences limit the validity of inter-country comparisons. For instance, it is not comparing like with like if we compare the 'level of urbanization' (the percentage of population in urban centres) of a nation that defines urban centres as all settlements with 20,000 or more inhabitants, with another that defines urban centres as all settlements with more than 1000 inhabitants. The comparison is particularly inaccurate if a large section of the population lives in settlements of between 1000 and 19,999 inhabitants (which is the case in most nations). The proportion of the world's population living in urban areas could be increased or decreased by several percentage points simply by China, India or a few of the other most populous nations changing their definition of what an urban centre is. Thus, the proportion of the world's population currently living in urban centres is best considered not as a precise percentage (i.e. 48.7 per cent in 2005), but as being between 45 and 55 per cent, depending on the criteria used to define an 'urban centre'. But what is beyond doubt is the fact that the world is becoming increasingly urban, as most of the world's economic production and most new investment is now concentrated in urban areas – as has been the case for many decades.

There is a tendency in the discussions of urban change to concentrate too much on changes in urban popualtions or on levels of urbanization, and too little on the economic and political transformations that have underpinned urbanization – at a global scale, the very large increase in the size of the world's economy and the changes in the relative importance of different sectors and of international trade – and how these transformations have changed the spatial distribution of economic activities, and the social and spatial distribution of incomes. The distinction between 'rural' and 'urban' populations has some utility in highlighting differences in economic structure, population concentration and political status (as virtually all local governments are located in urban centres), but it is not a precise distinction.

First of all, large sections of the 'rural' population work in non-agricultural activities or derive some of their income from such activities, or commute to urban areas. Many rural households also derive some of their income from remittances from family members working in urban areas. Distinctions between rural and urban areas are also becoming almost obsolete around many major cities as economic activity spreads outwards – for instance, around Jakarta (McGee 1987), around Bangkok and within Thailand's Eastern Seaboard, around Mumbai (and the corridor linking it to Pune), in the Pearl River Delta in China and in the Red River Delta in Vietnam (World Bank 1999).

Conversely, large sections of the 'urban' population work in agriculture or in urban enterprises that serve rural demand. In addition, discussing 'rural' and 'urban' areas separately can ignore the multiple flows between them in terms of migration movements and the flow of goods, income, capital and information (Tacoli 1998, 2006). Many low-income households draw goods or income from urban and rural sources.

An uncertain urban future

Most publications discussing urban change assume that all nations will continue to urbanize far into the future, until virtually all their economy and workforce are based in urban areas. Such assumptions should be viewed with caution. Given the historic association between economic growth and urbanization, a steady increase in the level of urbanization in any low-income nation is likely to take place only if it also has a steadily growing economy. While stronger and more buoyant economies for the world's lower-income nations should be a key development goal, the prospects for many such nations within the current world economic system are hardly encouraging. Many of the lowest-income nations have serious problems with political instability or civil war, and most have no obvious 'comparative advantage' on which to build an economy that prospers and thus urbanizes within the globalized economy.

There are also grounds for doubting whether a large proportion of the world's urban population will come to live in very large cities. As noted above, many of the largest cities have slow population growth rates and much new investment is going to particular medium-sized cities, well located in relation to the largest cities and to transport and communications systems. In addition, in prosperous regions with advanced transport and communications systems, rural inhabitants and enterprises can enjoy standards of infrastructure and services, and access to information, that historically have been available only in urban areas. Thus, both low-income and high-income nations may have smaller than expected increases in their urban populations, although for very different reasons.

GUIDE TO FURTHER READING

Bayat, A. and Denis, E. (2000) 'Who is afraid of Ashwaiyyat: Urban change and politics in Egypt', *Environment and Urbanization*, 12(2): 185–199.

Bryceson, D.F. and Potts, D. (eds) (2006) *African Urban Economies: Viability, Vitality or Vexation?* Basingstoke and New York: Palgrave Macmillan.

Douglass, M. (2002) 'From global intercity competition to cooperation for livable cities and economic resilience in Pacific Asia', *Environment and Urbanization*, 14(1): 53–68.

Montgomery, M.R., Stren, R., Cohen, B. and Reed, H.E. (eds) (2004) *Cities Transformed: Demographic Change and its Implications in the Developing World*, Washington, DC: The National Academies Press and London: Earthscan Publications.

Sassen, S. (2000) *Cities in a World Economy*, Thousand Oaks, CA: Pine Forge Press.

Satterthwaite, D. (2006) *Outside the Large Cities: The Demographic Importance of Small Urban Centres and Large Villages in Africa, Asia and Latin America*, Human Settlements Discussion Paper – Urban Change 3, London: International Institute for Environment and Development.

Satterthwaite, D. (2007) *The Transition to a Predominantly Urban World and its Underpinnings*, Human Settlements Discussion Paper, London: International Institute for Environment and Development.

Tacoli, C. (ed.) (2006) *The Earthscan Reader in Rural–Urban Linkages*, London: Earthscan Publications.

REFERENCES

This chapter draws on Satterthwaite, D. (2006), *Outside the Large Cities: The Demographic Importance of Small Urban Centres and Large Villages in Africa, Asia and Latin America*, Human Settlements Discussion Paper – Urban Change 3, London: International Institute for Environment and Development, and Satterthwaite, D. (2007) *The Transition to a Predominantly Urban World and its Underpinnings*, Human Settlements Discussion Paper, London: International Institute for Environment and Development. Both can be downloaded at no charge from http://www.iied.org/pubs/

Most of the urban statistics in this chapter are drawn from United Nations (2006) *World Urbanization Prospects: The 2005 Revision*, United Nations Population Division, Department of Economic and Social Affairs, CD-ROM edition – data in digital form (POP/DB/WUP/Rev.2005), New York: United Nations.

Brown, L. (1974) *In the Human Interest*, New York: W.W. Norton and Co.

Chandler, T. (1987) *Four Thousand Years of Urban Growth: An Historical Census*, Lampeter, UK: Edwin Mellen Press.

Chandler, T. and Fox, G. (1974) *3000 Years of Urban Growth*, New York and London: Academic Press.

McGee, T.G. (1987) 'Urbanization or Kotadesasi: The emergence of new regions of economic interaction in Asia', Working paper, Honolulu: East West Center, June.

Tacoli, C. (1998) *Bridging the Divide: Rural–Urban Interactions and Livelihood Strategies*, Gatekeeper Series No. 77, London: IIED Sustainable Agriculture and Rural Livelihoods Programme.

Tacoli, C. (ed.) (2006) *The Earthscan Reader in Rural–Urban Linkages*, London: Earthscan Publications.

UNCHS (United Nations Centre for Human Settlements) (Habitat) (1996) *An Urbanizing World: Global Report on Human Settlements, 1996*, Oxford and New York: Oxford University Press.

United Nations (1980) *Urban, Rural and City Population, 1950–2000, as assessed in 1978*, ESA/P/WP.66, June, New York: United Nations.

World Bank (1999) *Entering the 21st Century: World Development Report 1999/2000*, Oxford and New York: Oxford University Press.

5.2 Urban bias

Gareth A. Jones and Stuart Corbridge

Students of development and development practitioners have long concerned themselves with urban–rural relationships. A familiar assumption has been that ambitious people will move to urban areas to improve their lot. In the 1950s and 1960s an apparent bias in favour of urban-industrial models of development was justified by three key ideas. W. Arthur Lewis (1954) proposed that there is disguised unemployment or underemployment in rural areas of poorer countries, where the marginal productivity of labour is often very low. Men and women move to the city to find more productive work and to pull their families out of poverty. Hans Singer (1950) and Raoul Prebisch (1950) further argued that there is a long-run tendency for the terms of trade – the ratio of export commodity prices to import commodity prices – to move against primary commodities like foodstuffs and raw materials. Import substitution was commended partly on this basis. Urban planners, meanwhile, argued that goods and services would be diffused most efficiently from major cities to smaller cities and rural areas. Cities benefited from, and generated, economies of scale. This, after all, had been the experience of most Western countries.

All these arguments have been disputed. There is no reason why manufacturing or service-sector jobs must be based exclusively or even mainly in urban areas. China and Taiwan have each generated large numbers of industrial jobs in rural areas since the mid-1960s. In addition, countries like Norway and Canada became rich largely as exporters of food and raw materials. In practice, however, for both economic reasons (including the benefits of industrial clustering) and political reasons (including a disposition to think of the urban as modern), most non-agricultural jobs *have* been based in urban areas of developing countries. The question is whether this matters, and, if so, why and for whom, and in what terms?

One answer to this question is that concentrations of urban-industrial power damage the 'authenticity' of a country. Gandhi (1997 [1908]) believed that the soul of India was to be found in its villages. For him, large-scale industrialization was a form of social evil. Some deep ecologists also think in these terms, which, for the most part, are recognizably normative (that is, they advance a value judgement) (see Pepper 2004). In the 1960s Michael Lipton began to develop a more positive (or testable) account of urban bias in the process of world development. His urban bias thesis (UBT) was formally presented in his book *Why Poor People Stay Poor: A Study of Urban Bias in World Development* (1977). The UBT proposes that urban classes in poorer countries use their social power to bias (distort) a range of public policies against members of the rural classes. Lipton argued that urban bias 'involves (a) an allocation, to persons or organizations located in towns, of shares of resources so large as to be inefficient and inequitable, or (b) a disposition among the powerful [urban classes] to allocate resources in this way' (Lipton 2005: 724, summarizing Lipton 1977).

The urban bias thesis and its critics

In its first iteration, the UBT made five main claims, as follows.

1 Rural areas of developing countries suffer from too little spending on education and health care (relative to their population figures).
2 These inequalities, combined with excessively 'urban' forms of teaching and curriculum development, pull bright young people to the cities (when a more neutral incentive regime would keep them in the countryside).
3 People in rural areas are forced to pay a higher share of national taxes than is fair.
4 Urban bias is further and most damagingly evident in a series of government-imposed price twists, which cause inputs into rural areas to be overpriced when compared to a market norm, and cause outputs from rural areas to be correspondingly underpriced.
5 This combination of *distributional urban bias* (1, 2 and 3) and price-twisting is not only unfair, but inefficient: at the margin, Lipton maintained, a given sum of government money will earn higher returns in the small agriculture sector, or in rural off-farm employment creation, than it will in cities or large-scale urban-based industries.

Two principal critiques were levelled at this first iteration of Lipton's UBT. A first line of criticism was that the UBT lacked empirical validity and was overly generalized. The UBT failed to prove that the inter-sectoral terms of trade moved everywhere against rural areas. Critics also said that Lipton was inattentive to the issue of urban poverty; that most of the rural poor in south Asia were sellers of labour who benefited from cheap food; and that the UBT neglected the power of rural elites (see Byres 1979). A second line of critique was theoretical: it challenged Lipton's accounts of class, power and policy formation. Keith Griffin (1977) took exception to Lipton's attempt to account for intra-sectoral differences in wealth and power by counting members of the rural elite as members of the urban class, and members of the urban poor as part of the rural class. This seemed like sophistry to Griffin.

Early support for the UBT came from the political scientist Robert Bates, and from Elliott Berg at the World Bank. Bates (1981, 1988) argued that food production problems in sub-Saharan Africa were mainly the result of non-democratic governments using urban-biased policies to discriminate against smallholding agriculturalists. Governments used marketing boards and overvalued exchange rates to procure food cheaply from the countryside or overseas. They also made it difficult for farmers to sell food and other crops to private merchants, and spent large sums on industrial protection. Bates suggested that many ruling regimes in sub-Saharan Africa imposed urban-biased policies to keep the lid on unrest in towns and cities. The urban working class was bought off with cheap food, not least in nominally socialist countries. City-based bureaucrats also extracted large rents from systems of licences and quotas. In the medium term, however, rational farmers responded by producing less food for sale. This caused precisely those surges in food prices that triggered the urban food riots, or even coups, which Africa's ruling coalitions were keen to avoid.

Bates argued that international donors should exploit moments of political or economic crisis in sub-Saharan Africa to push more farmer-friendly policies. This view found support in the

World Bank's 1981 report on *Accelerated Development in Sub-Saharan Africa* (the so-called Berg report), and later became standard World Bank policy in sub-Saharan Africa when the debt crisis opened the way for structural adjustment loans and various forms of donor conditionality. Michael Lipton (2005), for his part, accepts that many structural adjustment programmes (SAPs) have improved the inter-sectoral terms of trade in sub-Saharan Africa: price twists are no longer so damaging to the countryside, although they remain significant at the global scale, given EU, Japanese and US farm-support policies. Lipton believes, however, that the World Bank's focus on price twists alone causes it to ignore the more deeply rooted inequalities in social and spatial power that promote urban bias. Rural collective action is hard to prosecute when population densities are low or where communication networks are poor.

The revised urban bias thesis and some new criticisms

Lipton's more recent argument, with Robert Eastwood, is that distributional urban bias has increased precisely at the same time as a series of successful neoliberal assaults on the urban–rural terms of trade. Eastwood and Lipton (2000) claim that:

- overall within-country inequality increased significantly after 1980–85, following adjustment policies;
- these increases have not been offset by declining rural-urban inequality;
- this absence of offset, save for a few countries in Latin America, must be accounted for by a rise in distributional urban bias at a time of reduced price twists against the countryside.

Urban bias still exists, and with it the case for offsetting measures to improve rural livelihoods.

There is considerable support for the view that urban/rural welfare ratios are not yet falling towards unity, and may even be diverging in some countries that are enjoying rapid economic growth (notably China). Nevertheless, we can identify at least four contemporary challenges to the UBT in its original and modified versions.

First, the UBT underestimates the scale and recent relative growth of urban poverty. It is now estimated that about 550 million people in the cities of the Global South live in absolute poverty, with nutritional and health conditions close to rural areas; and that over 920 million live in 'slums', with limited access to the resource allocations supposedly biased in favour of cities.

Second, the UBT is beset by definitional and measurement problems. Definitions of 'urban' and 'rural' are not stable. A large village in Bangladesh might count as a town in Peru. It is also difficult to carry out a detailed audit of all transfers of goods and services across the urban–rural divide. Many subsidies are hidden, as when developers are not required to pay the full costs of infrastructure provision, which might lead to an undercount of UBT. At the same time, many individual cities may appear hard done by from net allocations. Bogotá, for example, accounts for 52 per cent of Colombia's gross domestic product, yet receives only 9 per cent of national fiscal allocations.

Third, it has been a major contention of Frank Ellis and Nigel Harris (2004), among others, that the UBT overestimates the possibilities for *in situ* improvement in agricultural livelihoods in sub-Saharan Africa. In comparison to the arguments demonstrating the productivity of small-scale agrarian producers (see Schultz 1964), research on rural livelihoods has identified constraints to farmer productivity beyond price twists or the concentration of services in large towns. The thesis also underestimates (even ignores) the benefits of migration and ceaseless circulation, and the construction of livelihoods that move across the urban–rural divide. Boundaries are blurring, and where they are not blurring it is because of unhelpful government obstacles to mobility, notably in the case of pass laws or registration systems, such as the 'hukou' in China. Development agencies should be pushing hard for the removal or reduction of these restrictions (see World Bank 2005).

Fourth, there is a new challenge from a body of work called the 'new economic geography'. Research suggests that many non-primate cities in the developing world have grown, less because of rent-seeking and distorted patterns of political access (urban bias in Lipton's terms, in decline following SAPs) than because of the returns to scale and spillover effects that are associated with the clustering of innovative economic activities. In the case of many public goods, Overman and Venables (2005: 6) suggest that an '"urban bias" in public expenditure and provision may [also] be an efficient allocation of resources'. Biases in outcome are not always the result of wilful distortion (of markets by states), and even if 70 per cent of the world's poorest people reside in rural areas, it is not always and everywhere rational that at least 70 per cent of development spending should be spent in rural areas.

'Urban bias' and public policy

Where does all this leave us? It makes little sense to choose between the UBT and what might be called its opposite. There is much we still do not know, as Lipton readily concedes. Non-economic forms of urban bias are under-researched. Many rural people are stereotyped as backward or ignorant, and are treated by government officials on that basis. They might experience 'urban bias' in terms other than those set out in Lipton's UBT, but which are nonetheless consistent with his view that key development actors are disposed to equate the urban with the modern or developed (what he calls 'dispositional urban bias'). It is thus prudent to retain the provocation set out by Lipton's model (location matters for welfare), while avoiding reference to urban bias either as a social fact or as a pathology that always needs correction.

To the extent that the work of Lipton, Bates and Berg helped to authorize a change of policy within the World Bank and other development agencies in the 1980s, they rightly deserve acknowledgement, and even some applause. Whether some of these agencies and governments have since moved to an implicit or explicit anti-urban bias is not clear, although this has been the charge of some critics. What is clear is that the charge of distributional urban bias has been widely and often properly subjected to criticism. There are good reasons for thinking that many non-primate cities in developing countries are growing on the basis of a strong commitment to economic innovation and the production of dynamic growth clusters, and not by disadvantaging rural people or as a result of the activities of rent-seeking politicians. Not all 'bias' is bad, and many people in the countryside will rightly want to make their way to the city. In any case, many of the policies that Lipton and others want to see enacted – including better provision of primary education and health care in the countryside – can be argued for without resort to a generalized model of the exploitation of the countryside by the city. In this specific respect, the UBT can be unhelpful.

GUIDE TO FURTHER READING

Jones, G.A. and Corbridge, S.E. (2007) 'The continuing debate about urban bias: The thesis, its critics, its influence, and its implications for poverty reduction strategies', *Progress in Development Studies*, forthcoming. A broad-based critical review of the Urban Bias Thesis from inception to contemporary relevance.

Lipton, M. (1977) *Why Poor People Stay Poor: A Study of Urban Bias in World Development*, London: Temple Smith. The classic text, argued as both an eloquent narrative and through economic theory.

Tacoli, C. (ed.) (2006) *Rural–Urban Linkages*, London: Earthscan. Fifteen chapters, mostly based on original field research in South East Asia and sub-Saharan Africa, demonstrating the interdependence of livelihoods across the rural–urban divide.

REFERENCES

Bates, R.H. (1981) *Markets and States in Tropical Africa*, Berkeley, CA: University of California Press.

Bates, R.H. (1988) *Toward a Political Economy of Development*, Berkeley, CA: University of California Press.

Byres, T.J. (1979) 'Of neopulist pipe dreams', *Journal of Peasant Studies*, 6: 210–44.

Eastwood, R. and Lipton, M. (2000) 'Pro-poor growth and pro-growth poverty reduction: Meaning, evidence, and policy implications', *Asian Development Review*, 18(2): 22–58.

Ellis, F. and Harris, N. (2004) *New Thinking About Urban and Rural Development*, paper prepared for the government of the United Kingdom: Department for International Development (available at http://www.passlivelihoods.org.uk/site_files/files/2004%20Retreat%20Downloads/2004%20Sustainable%20Development%20Retreat_Ellis&Harris.doc).

Gandhi, M.K. (1997 [1908]) *Hind Swaraj*, with an editorial introduction by Anthony Parel, Cambridge: Cambridge University Press.

Griffin, K. (1977) 'Review of "Why Poor People Stay Poor"', *Journal of Development Studies*, 14: 108–9.

Lewis, W.A. (1954) 'Economic development with unlimited supplies of labour', *Manchester School of Economics and Social Studies*, 22: 139–91.

Lipton, M. (1977) *Why Poor People Stay Poor: A Study of Urban Bias in World Development*, London: Temple Smith.

Lipton, M. (2005) 'Urban bias', in T. Forsyth (ed.) *Encyclopedia of International Development*, London: Routledge.

Overman, H.G. and Venables, A.G. (2005) *Cities in the Developing World*, Centre for Economic Performance Discussion Paper No. 695, London School of Economics (available at http://cep.lse.ac.uk/pubs/download/dp0695.pdf).

Pepper, D. (2004) *Modern Environmentalism: An Introduction*, London: Routledge.

Prebisch, R. (1950) *The Economic Development of Latin America and its Principal Problems*, New York: United Nations Economic Commission for Latin America.

Schultz, T.W. (1964) *Transforming Traditional Agriculture*, New Haven, CT: Yale University Press.

Singer, H. (1950) 'The distribution of gains between investing and borrowing countries', *American Economic Review*, 40: 473–85.

World Bank (1981) *Accelerated Development in Sub-Saharan Africa*, Washington, DC: World Bank.

World Bank (2005) *Beyond the City: The Rural Contribution to Development*, Washington, DC: World Bank.

5.3 World cities and development

Robert B. Potter

Introduction

The dominant role that leading cities play in the process of global development in the early twenty-first century has been given explicit expression in the concept of the 'world city'. Although nebulous in size-definitional terms, the idea is that certain cities dominate world economic affairs and transactions. At one level, this is a very straightforward and obvious proposition, and indeed, Peter Hall drew attention to the significance of what he specifically referred to as world cities in the developed world in the mid-1960s (Hall 1966). However, the contemporary relevance of world cities has been elaborated by the American social scientist and academic planning and development analyst, John Friedmann (see Friedmann and Wolff 1982; Friedmann 1986, 1995). In the 20 years since Friedmann's original work served to make the term popular, a number of other writers have contributed to what Friedmann (1995) referred to as the 'world city paradigm' (see King 1990; Sassen 1991, 2002; Knox and Taylor 1995; Taylor 2004). However, both King and Sassen have written under the modified title, the 'global city'.

The basic ideas

As originally formulated, even Friedmann (1995) noted that there was an element of ambiguity attached to what at that juncture he referred to as 'the world city hypothesis'. Was it heuristic, providing a way of asking pertinent questions about cities in general, or was it a statement about a particular group or class of cities which displayed distinctive characteristics? In the paper Friedmann published in 1986 explaining 'the world city hypothesis', he started by noting that it was only in recent years that the study of cities had come to be connected directly with the disposition of the world economy. It was emphasized that certain cities had become the 'basing points' for international capitalism, and that the world city hypothesis was essentially about the spatial arrangements involved in the new international division of labour. In other words, world cities served to articulate regional, national and international economies into a global economic system. Of course, the argument is far from new and represents a central proposition of classical dependency theory according to Frank (1966).

In his early formulation, seven interrelated theses were put forward by Friedmann (1986), concerning what he saw as the nature of world cities.

1 The form and extent of a city's integration with the world economy, and its role in the new international division of labour, will be decisive for any structural changes within it.
2 Key cities throughout the world are used by global capital as 'basing points' in the spatial organization and articulation of production and markets. Thus, the resulting linkages make it possible to arrange world cities into a complex hierarchy.
3 The global control functions of world cities are reflected directly in the structure and dynamics of their production sectors and employment.
4 World cities are major sites for the concentration and accumulation of international capital.
5 World cities are points of destination for large numbers of both domestic and/or international migrants.
6 World city formation brings into focus the major contradictions of industrial capitalism, among them spatial and class polarization (giving rise to cores and peripheries and semi-peripheries at the global scale, and developed and less-developed regions at the national scale).
7 World city growth generates social costs at rates that tend to exceed the fiscal capacity of the state (e.g. those that arise from the rapid influx of poor workers into world cities and the massive need for housing, education and health that this generates).

The pattern of world cities identified by Friedmann

When Friedmann proceeded to actually identify what he regarded to be the system of world cities at the global scale, he distinguished between primary and secondary world cities in terms of their overall impact and influence. These two classes were not rigorously defined. He also distinguished between those occurring in what he referred to as 'core' and 'semi-peripheral' countries. While most of the primary world cities, such as London, Paris, Rotterdam, Frankfurt, Zurich, New York, Chicago, Los Angeles and Tokyo, were to be found located in the 'core' countries of the developed world, Singapore and São Paulo were recognized as primary world cities in the semi-periphery. In addition, Hong Kong, Bangkok, Taipei, Manila, Seoul, Mexico City, Caracas, Rio de Janeiro, Buenos Aires and Johannesburg were recognized as part of an emerging network of secondary world cities in the less developed world (Friedmann 1995). In short, world cities may be seen as points of articulation in a capitalist global system dominated by transnational companies (TNCs). Thus, Africa is the least developed continent, and it had the smallest number of world cities: just the one in the form of Johannesburg. African cities show relatively low numbers of international business and other headquarters (see Simon 1993).

Policy implications

As a descriptive statement, the world city hypothesis or paradigm seems little more than a statement of the obvious. In stressing that the salience of cities derives much more from their roles within the global capitalist system, rather than their size, the approach performs a more valuable function in a fast-globalizing world order. If one links the idea of world cities to the joint processes of global convergence and divergence, then clear policy implications start to emerge and the framework becomes a valuable tool for the analysis of development patterns and processes (see Potter and Lloyd-Evans 1998, in relation to this specific point).

There is the implication, for example, that uneven development is particularly likely to be associated with developing countries, and that their paths to development in the early twenty-first century will be infinitely more difficult than those that faced developed countries in former times. This argument has been reviewed in the case of poor countries by Lasuen (1973). He started from the premise that in the modern world, large cities are the principal adopters of innovations, so that natural growth poles become associated increasingly with the upper levels of the urban system. Lasuen also observed that the spatial spread of innovations is generally likely to be slower in developing countries, due to the frequent existence of single plant industries, the generally poorer levels of infrastructural provision and, in some instances, the lack of political will.

Thus, developing countries facing spatial inequalities have two policy alternatives. The first is to allow the major urban centres to adopt innovations before the previous ones have spread through the national settlement system. The second option is to attempt to hold and delay the adoption of further innovations at the top of the urban system, until the filtering-down of previous growth-inducing changes has occurred. This may sound theoretical, but these options represent the two major strategies which can be followed by developing nations. The former policy will result in increasing economic dualism, but also, some would argue, in the chance of a higher overall rate of economic growth. On the other hand, the latter option will lead to increasing regional equity, but potentially lower rates of national growth. Most developing countries have adopted policies close to the former alternative of unrestrained innovation adoption, seeking to maximize growth rather than equity. This all intimates the problems which are inherent in circular or cumulative growth in particular global urban places.

It is just this sort of patterning of entrained growth that was identified by Pred (1973, 1977) in his examination of the historical growth and development of the urban system of the United States. Pred noted that the growth of the mercantile city was based on circular or cumulative causation, linked to multiplier effects. Further, Pred argued that the growth of large cities was based on their interdependence, so that large city stability has been characteristic. However, Pred maintained that key innovation adoption sequences were not always hierarchic, frequently flowing from a medium-sized city up the urban hierarchy, or from one large city to another. Pred (1977) looked at the headquarters of TNCs in post-war America, and stressed the close correspondence with the uppermost levels of the urban system. Thus, growth within the contemporary urban system is increasingly linked to the locational decisions of multinational firms and government organizations. The recognition of global cities suggests that such patterns of uneven and non-hierarchical development are highly applicable at the international and global scales.

A modern expression of the value of the concept of the world city is provided by airline transport and the formation of airport hubs. The idea that transport is a key dimension in the development of world cities in the contemporary context is an interesting one which is relatively easy to exemplify, together with its developmental implications. The idea that globalized improvements in transport and communications are leading to the intensification of the functional importance of certain places or nodes is confirmed if we look at the evolution of airline networks in the 1990s. This has been considered by Keeling (1999), who produced a map showing the international air connections between the major cities. The map (see figure) shows the number of outward and

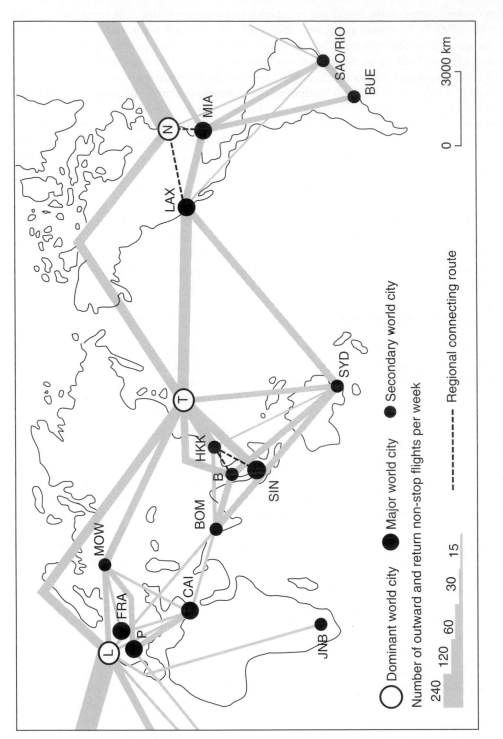

Dominant flows on the world airline network in the mid-1990s

Source: Potter *et al.*, 2004, Figure 4.3

return non-stop flights per week from various nodes. The outcome illustrates all too clearly the predominance of three global cities, namely London, New York and Tokyo, and the role these cities play as dominant global hubs. Together, these three cities receive 36.5 per cent of global non-stop flights to the world airline network's 20 dominant cities. Beyond these three cities, Paris, Cairo, Singapore, Los Angeles and Miami appear as secondary global hubs, and Johannesburg, Moscow, Bombay, Bangkok, Hong Kong, Sydney, São Paulo, Rio de Janeiro and Buenos Aires as secondary hubs. The flows mapped out in the figure show just how marked is the concentration. The essential similarity between this map of airline flows and a figure simply depicting world cities is highly apparent. This is a practical affirmation that increasing globalization is leading to strong local concentration within continents and that it can be seen as increasing the differences which exist between urban nodes. Thus, Johannesburg is the single airline hub in Africa south of the Sahara, and only Cairo stands out as a hub in the north of the continent.

Of course, such patterns are most certainly not fixed for all time. The pattern changes. Thus, Friedmann (1995) suggests that both Rio de Janeiro and Buenos Aires have both lost significant potential as world cities over recent years, and that they should no longer be listed among even the third rank of world cities. As with all aspects of modern capitalist development in a neoliberal world order, generally gradual and incremental changes are inbuilt to what otherwise appears to be a system based on inertia and stability. Interestingly in this context, Friedmann (1995) relates how he was co-opted by the government of Singapore, in an effort to find ways of specifically enhancing the city state's standing as a world city.

GUIDE TO FURTHER READING

Friedmann, J. (1986) 'The world city hypothesis', *Development and Change*, 17: 69–83. The article in which Friedmann promulgated, and made popular, the idea of the world city, arguing that only recently had the study of cities become directly linked to the examination of the world economy.

Friedmann, J. (1995) 'Where we stand: A decade of world city research', in P. Knox and P. Taylor (eds) *World Cities in a World-System*, Cambridge: Cambridge University Press, Chapter 2, pp. 21–47. An eclectic essay exploring the genesis and contemporary development of the global city hypothesis.

Keeling, D.J. (1995) 'Transport and the world city paradigm', in P. Knox and P. Taylor (eds) *World Cities in a World-System*, Cambridge: Cambridge University Press, Chapter 7, pp. 115–31. Argues that the role of transport linkages in the shaping of the world city system has been underexplored and, using contemporary data, looks at the current hierarchy of world airline network nodes.

Taylor, P.J. (2004) *World City Network: A Global Urban Analysis*, London: Routledge. A recent text exemplifying that cities represent the economic foci within transnational spaces of flow and movement.

REFERENCES

Frank, A.G. (1966) *Capitalism and Underdevelopment in Latin America*, New York: Monthly Review Press.

Friedmann, J. (1986) 'The world city hypothesis', *Development and Change*, 17: 69–83.

Friedmann, J. (1995) 'Where we stand: A decade of world city research', in P. Knox and P. Taylor (eds) *World Cities in a World-System*, Cambridge: Cambridge University Press, Chapter 2, pp. 21–47.

Friedmann, J. and Wolff, G. (1982) 'World city formation: An agenda for research and action', *International Journal of Urban and Regional Research*, 6: 309–43.

Hall, P. (1966) *The World Cities*, London: Weidenfeld and Nicolson.

Keeling, D.J. (1995) 'Transport and the world city paradigm', in P. Knox and P. Taylor (eds) *World Cities in a World-System*, Cambridge: Cambridge University Press, Chapter 7, pp. 115–31.

King, A.D. (1990) *Global Cities: Post-Imperialism and Internationalization of London*, London: Routledge and Kegan Paul.

Knox, P. and Taylor, P. (eds) (1995) *World Cities in a World-System*, Cambridge: Cambridge University Press.

Lasuen, J.R. (1973) 'Urbanisation and development: the temporal interaction between geographical and sectoral clusters', *Urban Studies*, 10: 163–88.

Potter, R.B. and Lloyd-Evans, S. (1998) *The City in the Developing World*, Harlow: Prentice Hall.

Potter, R.B., Binns, T., Elliott, J. and Smith, D. (2004) *Geographies of Development*, second edition, Harlow: Prentice Hall.

Pred, A. (1973) 'The growth and development of systems of cities in advanced economies', in A. Pred and G. Tornqvist (eds) *Systems of Cities and Information Flows: Two Essays*, Lund Studies in Geography, Series B, 38: 9–82.

Pred, A. (1977) *City-Systems in Advanced Economies*, London: Hutchinson.

Sassen, S. (1991) *The Global City*, Princeton, NJ: Princeton University Press.

Sassen, S. (2002) *Global Networks. Linked Cities*, New York: Routledge.

Simon, D. (1993) *Cities, Capital and Development: African Cities in the World Economy*, London: Belhaven.

Taylor, P.J. (2004) *World City Network: A Global Urban Analysis*, London: Routledge.

5.4 Prosperity or poverty? Wealth, inequality and deprivation in urban areas

Carole Rakodi

Cities and towns hold out great promise, but can also be unforgiving environments; opportunities abound, but the risks are great; the successful live well, but life for those who do not succeed is a struggle, marked by poverty, ill health and insecurity.

Prosperity or poverty?

The correlation between urbanization and economic development, statistics which show the disproportionate share of GDP generated in urban areas, and the modern buildings and ostentatious wealth of central business districts, industrial estates, shopping malls and high-income residential areas combine to reinforce a view of cities as 'engines of economic growth' and sites for wealth generation. Many do not regard urban poverty as a serious problem. In earlier models, the path to development was expected to be industrialization and urbanization. For a time, progress appeared to be promising. Protected industrialization and the expansion of public-sector activities resulted in increased formal-sector wage employment, mostly in urban areas.

Not all entrants to the urban labour force could obtain full-time employment or earn sufficient wages to support a family. However, the good prospects that were thought to encourage high rates of rural–urban migration, despite rising unemployment, led to a perception of urban areas as favoured environments. By the 1970s, it was clear that the basic needs of many, especially in Africa and South Asia, were not being met: trickle-down was not working as expected, especially for those living in rural areas. An influential explanation was Michael Lipton's 'urban bias' thesis. Lipton (1977) asserted that the major mistake in development policy was the 'urban bias' in expenditure and pricing policies. Failure to recognize the necessity of increased productivity in peasant agriculture for both sustained economic growth and increased prosperity for the majority of the population, he suggested, had led to a disproportionate emphasis on industrialization and thus concentration of investment in urban infrastructure. The political importance of concentrated urban populations reinforced this pattern and helped to explain the widespread adoption of cheap food policies. Subsidized food was paid for by low producer prices, which constrained the production and marketing of food crops and maintained small farmers in poverty, further fuelling outmigration.

The extent to which urban bias was a valid and sufficient explanation of development failure (especially persistent rural poverty) was questioned from the outset. It was noted that not all countries had an antirural policy bias; that other identities and political interests (ethnic, religious, class) cut across the rural–urban divide; and that rural/urban boundaries are arbitrary (Varshney 1993). Thus, although there was much truth in Lipton's analysis, which average income/expenditure figures for urban and rural areas appeared to bear out, the 'urban bias' thesis and the use of averages also served to conceal a more complex reality.

Wealth, inequality and poverty

While some urban residents were able to secure employment, housing and access to services, many were not. Increasingly, since the 1960s, wage employment, the formal housing development process and public provision of infrastructure have failed to keep up with population growth. An increasing proportion of workers was forced, in the absence of social security systems, to seek economic opportunities in the so-called informal sector. Residents unable to rent or buy in the formal housing sectors were forced to become house owners or tenants in informal settlements, with a variety of insecure tenure arrangements. Although physical infrastructure and social facilities were available, many poor households could not access them and had to rely on self-provision (wells, pit latrines), the purchase of relatively costly private-sector services (water from vendors) or illegal tapping of publicly provided services (electricity, water).

The urban bias thesis, which labelled urban areas as 'wealthy' and rural areas as 'poor', failed to recognize high degrees of urban inequality and the exclusion of a large proportion of residents from the wealth, opportunities and good living conditions supposedly typical of urban areas. Nevertheless, it was widely accepted, and the economic reforms of the 1980s had, as a result, a strong 'rural bias'. The need to address trade and budget deficits in countries subject to structural adjustment policies led to trade and financial liberalization, the abolition of price controls and subsidies, and the commercialization of physical and social services. The effect, deliberately, was to remove 'urban bias' and other economic 'distortions' in order to encourage agricultural production and exports of all kinds. The results, in urban areas, included falling real incomes and job losses from all formal employment sectors. Thus, much of the brunt of typical structural adjustment policies was borne by the urban poor, and the gap between average rural and urban incomes was more or less eliminated, undermining the continued validity of the 'urban bias' explanation for underdevelopment (Varshney 1993).

Before examining some evidence on the extent of inequality and poverty, and trends since the 1980s, a few methodological difficulties must be mentioned. The most common measure of poverty is household consumption or expenditure. An absolute poverty line represents the cost of a basket of necessities, including food (the food poverty line) and other needs. However, money-metric measures of poverty have limitations, many of which adversely affect comparisons of the incidence of poverty in urban and rural areas. In particular, prices and patterns of consumption vary between regions. However, some poverty assessments do not allow for differences in prices between urban and rural areas, and many fail to allow for differences in consumption bundles, especially the need for the urban poor to pay for housing and services which may not be monetized in rural areas, as well as the higher costs of transportation (especially for journeys to work). Further, the poorest urban residents often live in temporary accommodation or on the streets, and may not be captured in sample surveys. Lastly, changes in, and the arbitrary nature of, urban boundaries affect estimates of poverty incidence in urban and rural areas, either excluding large numbers of residents in informal settlements beyond urban boundaries or including rural households living within them (Rakodi 2002; Satterthwaite 2004; UN-Habitat 2006).

Inequality is generally greater in urban than rural areas and has increased over the last decades of the twentieth century. For example, in Sri Lanka the Gini coefficient for urban areas in 1985/86 was 0.62, compared to 0.55 for rural areas (Gunatilleke and Perera 1994). The incidence of poverty varies, but was at least a third higher in rural than in urban areas in most countries in the 1980s and 1990s (UNCHS 1996: 113). Trends often show urban poverty shadowing rural poverty. In countries where overall levels of poverty have decreased, such as India, the incidence of urban poverty has also decreased (Haddad, Ruel and Garrett 1999). Economic growth is associated with declines in both urban and rural poverty, while long-term economic decline and sudden economic crisis result in increases. For example, the economic crisis of the late 1990s in the industrializing countries of Asia precipitated a dramatic, if temporary, increase, especially in urban poverty, as formal-sector jobs were lost. In Indonesia, where there had been a steady decline in urban poverty, from 39 per cent in 1976 to 10 per cent in 1996, the level tripled to 30 per cent by mid-1998 (Firman 1999: 76). During Zambia's long economic decline since the 1970s, urban poverty has increased more rapidly than rural poverty. During Argentina's economic crisis between 1997 and 2002, the urban poverty rate almost doubled, from 24 per cent to 45 per cent (UN-Habitat 2004: 111).

The contribution of urban poverty to total poverty depends on both the incidence of poverty in urban and rural areas and the extent of urbanization. In the 1990s it varied from 8 per cent in Uganda (where only 11 per cent of the population was urban) to 57 per cent in Brazil (where 75 per cent of the population was urban). Although still small in many countries, the contribution of urban to overall poverty generally grew in the 1980s and early 1990s, and the World Bank estimates that by 2035 more poor people will live in urban than rural areas (Haddad, Ruel and Garrett 1999; Ravallion 2001). Average consumption figures and estimates of poverty incidence thus appear to show a lesser problem of poverty in urban than in rural areas, but high inequality and trends showing a shift in the locus of poverty demonstrate that these indicators conceal much of the reality.

Deprivation, vulnerability and insecurity

All headcount measures of poverty have been challenged on the basis that, even if refined, they do not recognize the life-cycle trajectories of households, and therefore do not distinguish between permanent and transient poverty. Moreover, a consumption-based conceptualization of poverty may not coincide with the perceptions of the poor themselves, who define poverty to encompass not merely low incomes, but also deprivation and insecurity.

In high-density urban environments, housing and utilities of adequate standard are critical to health. Their availability is an outcome of the interaction between private provision and public policy. In the monetized economies of towns and cities, access to housing, utilities and social services is determined not just by availability, however, but also by household financial resources. To the poor, good-quality accommodation, education and health care are unaffordable. Furthermore, their access to secure tenure, services and social facilities may be constrained by social and political discrimination, affecting groups differentially by gender, ethnicity, caste, religion, and so on.

Some basic health indicators, such as childhood mortality, are generally lower in urban areas. However, in some countries the reverse is true for other indicators, such as morbidity rates from infectious diseases (Haddad, Ruel and Garrett 1999). Higher population densities, combined with absent or inadequate piped water, drains, sanitation and refuse collection, mean that urban populations are more at risk from faecal contamination and other environmental hazards. HIV/AIDS prevalence rates are invariably higher in urban areas, affecting the poor disproportionately and exacerbating poverty and economic recession (UN-Habitat 2006). The high incidence of infectious diseases is associated with acute malnutrition, the absolute and relative incidence of which increased faster in urban than rural areas in many countries between the late 1980s and the mid-1990s. Thus, although the incidence of both poverty and under-nutrition remains lower in towns and cities, their locus is changing from rural to urban areas (Haddad, Ruel and Garrett 1999).

Moreover, there is greater variation in access to basic environmental services, rates of mortality and morbidity and nutritional status *among* urban than rural populations, consonant with the greater inequality referred to above. Estimates based on demographic and health surveys show that 46 per cent of the urban poor lack access to three or more of the key services, compared to 22 per cent of the non-poor (Montgomery et al. 2004: 175). Although overall levels of morbidity and mortality due to disease or injuries and accidents vary between cities, all are greater in poor areas, and in some cases as high, or higher, in slum as in rural areas (UN-Habitat 2006).

Insecurity is related to vulnerability: the sensitivity of well-being to a changing environment and households' ability to respond to negative changes. Households have assets that may be drawn down in times of need and built up in better times, to provide defences against shocks and stresses and to improve well-being. Assets of particular importance to urban households may be physical (housing, equipment for economic activities), human (labour power, skills, good health), financial (savings, credit), social (membership of formal or informal social organizations, which provide information, contacts and support) or political (channels of representation and influence) (Moser 1998; Rakodi 1999). Households which lack assets that they can mobilize in the face of hardship are more vulnerable to impoverishment. The assets available to households are determined in part by their characteristics and strategies. However, the potential for accessing and building up assets is also influenced by wider circumstances, including the operation of labour, land and housing markets; levels of crime and violence; arrangements for infrastructure and service provision; and the regulatory regimes governing urban activities, which may discriminate against self-help housing construction or informal-sector economic activities.

Access to labour market opportunities is a key element in the livelihood strategies of urban households. Wider economic circumstances, trade and industrial policies, availability of land and infrastructure, and the characteristics of the local labour market influence the opportunities available. Access to them depends on the resources available to and constraints on particular households: education and skills, dependency ratios, health status, relative location of affordable residential areas and employment centres, and access to public transport. Poor households with adults in work tend to depend on informal-sector activities, especially services, or on casual employment. They are, however, characterized by high unemployment rates among adults and also include households with limited labour resources: young households with children, especially single mothers; and those containing disabled, sick or elderly adults.

Much of the discussion so far has referred to households as though consumption is distributed equally among all their members, but there is extensive evidence to show that this is not the case: some individuals within households are disadvantaged in terms of access to resources, including the economically inactive (some elderly people, women and children) and unpaid family workers (especially domestic servants).

In times of wider economic difficulties, or in the face of household-level shocks, such as bereavement, illness or retrenchment, some households are better equipped than others to defend themselves against impoverishment. The key strategy seems to be diversification, so that households with multiple adults of working age, more than one source of income, an asset such as a house which can generate income, urban or rural land for food production, and urban or rural social networks that can be called on for support, cope better with economic crisis (Rakodi 1999). For some, impoverishment may be temporary, and improved well-being may follow national economic recovery or the development of alternative income sources. Others, however, may be forced to sell physical assets, move into inferior accommodation, send children out to work, reduce the quality and quantity of food consumed, postpone medical treatment, and/or withdraw from reciprocity arrangements, such as rotating savings and credit associations. The chronic poor are unable to take advantage of the opportunities offered in cities and become trapped in a vicious circle of poverty and deprivation.

Conclusion: Policy responses

The most powerful policies, with a direct or indirect impact on urban poverty, are national economic and social policies. Their effects are mediated through markets and through the activities of governments, which have varying capacity to adopt pro-poor policies, especially at the local level. The urban poor depend heavily on their assets of labour and human capital, tying them strongly into the money economy and labour markets. Access to housing and capital assets for informal economic activities is also important to their livelihoods. The role of social networks and the ways in which local political processes determine access by the poor to resources and assets are beginning to be better understood (Devas et al. 2004). Increased understanding of poverty, vulnerability and social exclusion, and identification of constraints on the ability of individuals, households and communities to access key assets and services, provide pointers to appropriate policy interventions.

GUIDE TO FURTHER READING

Relevant material published during the last ten years may be found in special issues of journals and edited or multi-authored books: *IDS Bulletin*, 28(3) (1997); *International Planning* Studies, 10(1) (2005); Jones, S. and Nelson, N. (eds) (1999) *Urban Poverty in Africa: From Understanding to Action*, London: IT Publications; Rakodi, C. with Lloyd-Jones, T. (eds) (2002) *Urban Livelihoods: A People-Centred Approach to Reducing Poverty*, London: Earthscan Publications; Devas et al. (2004); Montgomery et al. (2004). In addition, UN-Habitat's alternating annual flagship reports – the Global Reports on Human Settlements and the State of the World Cities reports – are both readable and empirically rich.

USEFUL WEBSITES

UN-Habitat's website (http://www.unhabitat.org) contains a wide range of information on urban characteristics and programmes, as well as publications, some of them downloadable.

Reports on the Demographic and Health Surveys in many countries can be obtained on http://www.measuredhs.com/aboutsurveys/dhs/start.cfm

The World Bank Urban Development website covers a variety of topics, including health, providing services to the poor and strategies for local economic development. It contains links to data and reports, many of them downloadable: http://web.worldbank.org/WBSITE/EXTERNAL/TOPICS/EXTURBANDEVELOPMENT/0,,menuPK:337184~pagePK:149018~piPK:149093~theSitePK:337178,00.html

The International Labour Organization site http://www.ilo.org/dyn/empent/empent.portal?p_prog=L&p_lang=EN also contains advice on Local Economic Development strategies as well as reports on urban employment and poverty; data on informal sector employment and informal sector survey methodologies can be obtained in machine-readable form through a clickable link: http://www.ilo.org/public/english/bureau/stat/info/dbases.htm

The International Institute for Environment and Development has a Human Settlements Programme, which focuses on rural–urban linkages and urban poverty. Reports and back issues of the journal *Environment and Urbanization* can be downloaded: http://www.iied.org/HS/themes/urbnpov.html

REFERENCES

Devas, N. with Amis, P., Beall, J., Grant, U., Mitlin, D., Nunan, F. and Rakodi, C. (2004) *Urban Governance, Voice and Poverty in the Developing World*, London: Earthscan Publications.

Firman, T. (1999) 'Indonesian cities under the "Krismon"', *Cities*, 16(2): 69–82.

Gunatilleke, G. and Perera, M. (1994) 'Urban poverty in Sri Lanka: Critical issues and policy measures', *Asian Development Review*, 12(1): 153–203.

Haddad, L., Ruel, M.T. and Garrett, J. (1999) 'Are urban poverty and undernutrition growing? Some newly assembled evidence', *World Development*, 27(11): 1891–904.

Lipton, M. (1977) *Why Poor People Stay Poor: Urban Bias in World Development*, London: Temple Smith.

Montgomery, M.R., Stren, R., Cohen, B. and Reed, H.E. (2004) *Cities Transformed: Demographic Change and its Implications in the Developing World*, London: Earthscan Publications.

Moser, C.O.N. (1998) 'The asset vulnerability framework: Reassessing urban poverty reduction strategies', *World Development*, (26)1: 1–19.

Rakodi, C. (1999) 'A capital assets framework for analysing household livelihood strategies', *Development Policy Review*, 17(3): 315–42.

Rakodi, C. (2002) 'Economic development, urbanization and poverty', in Rakodi C. with Lloyd-Jones T. (eds) *Urban Livelihoods: A People-Centred Approach to Reducing Poverty*, London: Earthscan Publications, 23–34.

Ravallion, M. (2001) *On the Urbanization of Poverty*, Washington, DC: World Bank Development Research Group, Policy Research Working Paper 2586.

Satterthwaite, D. (2004) *The Under-estimation of Urban Poverty in Low- and Middle-Income Nations*, London: International Institute for Environment and Development, Working Paper on Poverty Reduction in Urban Areas Series 14.

UNCHS (United Nations Centre for Human Settlements) (1996) *An Urbanizing World: Global Report on Human Settlements, 1996*, New York: Oxford University Press.

UN-Habitat (2004) *The State of the World's Cities 2004/2005: Globalization and Urban Culture*, London: Earthscan Publications.

UN-Habitat (2006) *The State of the World's Cities 2006/7: The Millennium Development Goals and Urban Sustainability – 30 Years of Shaping the Habitat Agenda*, London: Earthscan Publications.

Varshney, A. (1993) 'Introduction: Urban bias in perspective', in Varshney, A. (ed.) *Beyond Urban Bias*, London: Frank Cass, pp. 1–22.

5.5 Housing the urban poor

Alan Gilbert

Millions of families in the cities of the so-called Third World live in adequate accommodation, and some even live in luxury. Unfortunately, the majority do not. Most of the poor tend to live in homes without adequate sanitation, with an irregular electricity supply, built of flimsy materials and without sufficient security. Millions of others live in more solid and serviced accommodation, but in overcrowded conditions. Apart from the households living in shacks or overcrowded tenements, and those lacking adequate services, millions more would claim to have a housing problem. They live in houses that do not match their hopes and needs: they have difficulty paying their rent or mortgage, they have a long journey to work, their home is too small, they wish to own a house rather than rent. The Third World housing problem, therefore, is enormous (Gilbert 1998; Potter and Lloyd-Evans 1998; UN-Habitat 2003a).

If there can be little doubt about the severity of the difficulties to be tackled, it is important to recognize that there is no simple way of defining precisely what the housing problem is. In any society, the housing problem is defined socially and culturally. The kind of house that may be tolerated in one society may be damned in another; what may be regarded as desirable in one city may be anathema in another.

What constitutes poor housing is not just about physical standards. As John Turner (1968) demonstrated long ago, there is little point providing a poor family with a fully serviced, three-bedroom house if the family cannot afford the rent or mortgage payment. The most suitable shelter for such a family may be something rather flimsy. Adequate accommodation is that which fits the circumstances of the family rather than being determined on purely physical grounds. In the short term, at least, a poor family can survive in inadequate shelter; it cannot survive without food or water.

As such, the housing problem is not something that can be solved by architects and planners. It is a multifaceted problem that can only be helped through raising living standards, improving employment opportunities and applying sensible urban regulations. Unfortunately, policymakers and others in Third World countries often oversimplify diagnosis of how to 'solve' the problem. Politicians often put forward simplistic solutions; newspapers publish exposés of deplorable housing conditions and the public demands action. Unfortunately, as the housing problem is multifaceted, any simple solution is unlikely to help. Complex problems require complex responses.

The rest of this chapter considers some of the ideas that are held generally about Third World housing and shows how frequently reality diverges from our assumptions.

Homelessness

In general, homelessness is a major problem in relatively few Third World cities. According to the World Bank (1992: 14), only 0.8 per cent of Africans, 0.4 per cent of East Asians and 0.6 per cent of Latin Americans 'sleep outside dwelling units or in temporary shelter in charitable institutions'. It is only in South Asia where homelessness seems to be a significant issue, with 7.8 per cent of the population living on the streets. Beyond the Indian subcontinent, most people in Third World cities have homes. Indeed, the homelessness rate is lower than in industrialized countries (0.9 per cent). The problem in most Third World cities is not the lack of shelter, but the overcrowded, poorly serviced and flimsy accommodation that often constitutes a home (UN-Habitat 2003a).

Variations in the nature of the housing problem

The housing problem differs considerably between countries, both in form and in severity. In general, the poorer the country, the worse the urban housing situation: African and Indian shelter standards are far below those of Latin America. There are also major differences between housing conditions in different cities within the same country. The quality of housing between cities varies according to the nature of the land market, the state of the economy, the ability of governments to provide services, and local climate and topography. The principal housing problems facing one city may be of little significance in another. One city may have poor infrastructure and services, although its houses may provide families with plenty of space. In another city, families may suffer from severe overcrowding, but have plenty of services.

Most rural housing is worse than most urban housing

Public concern is often expressed about the state of housing in urban areas, particularly that in the largest cities. It is a reaction to the huge self-help areas that have developed and to fears about the likely political repercussions. In practice, urban housing conditions are generally far better than those in rural areas. In Colombia, for example, crowding in rural homes is far worse than in the urban areas; every room in the countryside contains an average of 2.3 persons, compared to 1.6 persons in urban homes. The differential is still worse when measured in terms of services; only 35 per cent of rural households in Colombia have electricity, compared with 97 per cent of urban homes.

Concern about illegality

Most urban governments are concerned about illegality. When land has been stolen, when green areas have been invaded, or when basic building standards are ignored, illegality can be a vital issue. In many cities, however, the problems of illegality are frequently exaggerated. In many places, housing is illegal only in the sense that it offends the planning regulations. The illegality consists of a lack of services, something that can easily be resolved by the provision of infrastructure. Elsewhere, perfectly decent and well-serviced homes simply lack properly registered title deeds; they are illegal only in a technical sense.

Even where illegality relates to more serious issues, such as the ownership of land, the real problem often lies elsewhere. More often than not, land has been invaded with the connivance of the authorities (Gilbert 1998). Some major cities of Latin America have a large proportion of the population living in illegal settlements, but the quality of that accommodation is actually superior to the housing found in other cities where there is little or no 'illegality'. The illegality of land and housing tenure, therefore, is only sometimes a problem. In general, most forms of illegality can be removed through the provision of title deeds, the supply of services or the modification of planning regulations.

Hernando de Soto (2000) has argued that giving families legal tenure will transform their lives. It will allow them to borrow money from banks and to develop the many enterprises that they already run from home. However, research suggests that his optimism is greatly exaggerated and that credit will remain scarce for poor families (Gilbert 2002; Bromley 2004). The problem of servicing will not be overcome because the authorities too often lack the capacity to supply poor neighbourhoods. De Soto also ignores the fact that the offer of a legal title does not come free and brings with it additional costs, like the need to pay city land taxes.

Concern about tenure

Many Third World governments consider that a key ingredient in housing improvement is to make ownership available to all. They do so because they think that this will win them votes, and they are not entirely wrong in this belief. Certainly, most families aspire to home ownership. They do so because they believe it is a good investment, that the house is something they can leave to their children, that it offers security in times of hardship and boosts their self-esteem (Gilbert 1999). Television and advertising have turned the desire for ownership across the globe into a cultural norm; it is where everyone expects to end up. In addition, home ownership also provides a series of alternative ways of generating incomes. Rooms can be let and small businesses operated from the premises (Kumar 1996; UN-Habitat 2003b).

Even if much of this is true, it does not mean that governments should strive to create universal home ownership. Indeed, there are good reasons why they should not. In particular, they should remember that there will always be some kinds of people who require rental accommodation, even when they have the resources to be homeowners. Among these are those planning short stays in the city, those who like living close to the city centre, those without family responsibilities and those who do not want the complications that home ownership brings. Table 1 shows how important renting is in many Third World cities, particularly in West Africa and parts of Asia.

There is also evidence that, although it is not an unproblematic tenure, renting has had a bad press. Conventional wisdom holds that tenants detest paying rent, that tenants are constantly being evicted, that they live in deplorable conditions and that landlords are grasping and vindictive (Mohamed 1997). However, survey results frequently provide a different picture. Landlords and tenants do not always see eye to eye, but strife is relatively infrequent (Rakodi 1995; Kumar 1996; UN-Habitat 2003b). If rental accommodation is often inadequate, tenants generally have better services than most families living in self-help settlements. Most landlords are neither exploitative nor grasping; indeed, rents in many cities are low relative to incomes. Nor is renting always an insecure tenure, for many tenants stay years in the same home, and the danger of eviction has been greatly exaggerated in most cities (Gilbert et al. 1993; UN-Habitat 2003b).

Table 1 Tenants as a proportion of total households by city, *c*.2000

City	% tenants	Year
Mexico City	16	2000
Quito	46	1998
Bogotá	40	2003
La Paz/El Alto	23	2001
Santiago	21	2003
Addis Ababa	60	1998
Cairo	63	1996
Port of Spain	52	1998
Lagos	49	1998
Kisumu, Kenya	82	1998
Bangkok	41	1998
Seoul	30	1995
Istanbul	32	1994

Source: Offical census figures and UN-Habitat 2003b

Government policy

Third World governments would not be able to solve their housing problems even if they were to try. The best they could be expected to do in an environment of generalized poverty is to improve living conditions. They should try to reduce numbers of people living at densities of more than 1.5 persons in each room; increase access to electricity and potable water; improve sanitary facilities; prevent families moving into areas that are physically unsafe; and encourage households to improve the quality of their accommodation (Buckley and Kalarickal 2005).

Past experience with building housing for the poor has rarely been a success, and today few governments attempt to do this. Some are offering housing subsidies to the poor as a means of stimulating the demand for private-sector housing. While this has generated a lot of additional housing in countries like Chile and South Africa, it has not been an unproblematic policy. All too often, the poor living in the new housing areas have been too poor to pay for services, some have been tempted to sell out for very little money, and the lack of employment opportunities has risked turning the new settlements into peripheral slums (Huchzermeyer 2003; Gilbert 2004).

A sensible approach is to destroy slums as seldom as possible, on the grounds that every displaced family needs to be rehoused and removing families is often disastrous. Governments should also avoid building formal housing for the very poor, because this housing tends to be expensive and the poor cannot afford to pay for the accommodation. Sensible governments attempt to upgrade inadequate accommodation by providing it with infrastructure and services of an appropriate standard. Where land prices permit, sites-and-services programmes should be developed which will provide space for low-income families and pre-empt the temptation to invade land. How far this kind of action will improve conditions, however, depends on other variables, like the efficiency of the servicing companies and the employment situation. It also depends on governments only intervening in areas where they can genuinely help (World Bank 1993).

There are no easy solutions to Third World housing problems because poor housing is merely one manifestation of generalized poverty. Decent shelter can never be provided while there is widespread poverty. Nor is the housing problem something that can be considered apart from the rest of the society, the type of economy and the nature of the state. At the same time, sensible policies can help mitigate shelter problems. We now know enough about the housing situation to be able to design sensible policies. Unfortunately, it has rarely been the lack of knowledge that has stopped us improving living standards. More often it has been the failure of governments to introduce the necessary policies that has constituted the critical barrier. Their inability and sometimes reluctance to adopt new legislation or to modify inappropriate policies have been determined by political realities. At root, therefore, the Third World housing problem is about politics and economics. Without appropriate political reforms and sustained economic growth, housing conditions will not get much better. Appropriate action will not cure the housing problem, but it could help a substantial minority of Third World citizens to improve their shelter situation.

GUIDE TO FURTHER READING AND REFERENCES

The following text references provide the basis for further reading.

Bromley, R. (2004) 'Power, property and poverty: Why de Soto's "Mystery of Capital" cannot be solved', in A. Roy and N. AlSayyad (eds) *Urban Informality in an Era of Liberalization: A Transnational Perspective*, Boulder, CO: Lexington Books, pp. 271–88.

Buckley, R.M. and Kalarickal, J. (2005) 'Housing policy in developing countries: Conjectures and refutations', *The World Bank Research Observer*, 20: 233–57.

Davis, M. (2004) 'Planet of slums', *New Left Review*, 26: 5–34.

de Soto, H. (2000) *The Mystery of Capital*, New York: Basic Books.

Gilbert, A.G. (1998) *The Latin American City*, London: Latin America Bureau, and New York: Monthly Review Press.

Gilbert, A.G. (1999) 'A home is for ever? Residential mobility and home ownership in self-help settlements', *Environment and Planning A*, 31: 1073–91.

Gilbert, A.G. (2002) 'On the mystery of capital and the myths of Hernando de Soto: What difference does legal title make?', *International Development Planning Review*, 24: 1–20.

Gilbert, A.G. (2004) 'Helping the poor through housing subsidies: Lessons from Chile, Colombia and South Africa', *Habitat International*, 28: 13–40.

Gilbert, A.G., Camacho, O.O., Coulomb, R. and Necochea, A. (1993) *In Search of a Home*, London: University College London Press.

Huchzermeyer, M. (2003) 'A legacy of control? The capital subsidy and informal settlement intervention in South Africa', *International Journal of Urban and Regional Research*, 27: 591–612.

Kumar, S. (1996) 'Landlordism in Third World urban low-income settlements: A case for further research', *Urban Studies*, 33: 735–82.

Mohamed, S.-I. (1997) 'Tenants and tenure in Durban', *Environment and Urbanization*, 9: 101–17.

Potter, R.B. and Lloyd-Evans, S. (1998) *The City in the Developing World*, Harlow: Longman.

Rakodi, C. (1995) 'Rental tenure in the cities of developing countries', *Urban Studies*, 32: 791–811.

Tipple, A.G., Korboe, D. and Garrod, G. (1997) 'Income and wealth in house ownership studies in urban Ghana', *Housing Studies*, 12: 111–26.

Turner, J.F.C. (1968) 'The squatter settlement: An architecure that works', *Architectural Design*, 38: 357–60.

UN-Habitat (2003a) *The Challenge of Slums: Global Report on Human Settlements 2003*, London: Earthscan Publications.

UN-Habitat (2003b) *Rental Housing: An Essential Option for the Urban Poor in Developing Countries*, Nairobi: UN-Habitat.

World Bank (1992) *The Housing Indicators Program: Volume II, Indicator Tables*, Washington, DC: World Bank.

World Bank (1993) *Housing: Enabling Markets to Work*, Policy Paper, Washingon, DC: World Bank.

5.6 Urbanization and environment in low- and middle-income nations

David Satterthwaite

Introduction

As described in Chapter 5.1 (Urbanization in low- and middle-income nations), in the first decade of the twenty-first century, most of the world's urban population and most of its large cities are in low- and middle-income nations in Latin America, Asia and Africa, and these are also likely to accommodate most of the growth in the world's population in the next one to two decades. The quality of environmental management in these urban centres (and of the governance structures within which this management occurs) has very significant implications for development. Despite great diversity in the size and economic base of urban centres, they all share certain characteristics. All combine concentrations of human populations and a range of economic activities. Their environment is much influenced by the scale and nature of these economic activities – both directly, in the resources they use and the pollution and wastes they generate, and indirectly, in the environmental impacts of their workforce and dependants and the other enterprises on which they draw. Urban environments are also greatly influenced by the quality and extent of provision for supplying fresh water and for collecting and disposing of solid and liquid wastes.

In most countries in Africa, Asia and Latin America, the expansion in the urban population has occurred without the needed expansion in the services and facilities essential to a healthy urban environment, especially provision for water, sanitation, drainage and solid waste management. It has often occurred with little or no effective pollution control. As well as these primarily local problems, there is the global problem of climate change. Cities are important in climate change because the businesses and wealthy populations that are concentrated in cities are the cause of most greenhouse gas emissions. Businesses and populations in Europe and North America are currently the greatest global threat, because they have contributed most to greenhouse gases already in the atmosphere and their populations remain the largest emitters per person. Emissions per person in cities in North America and Australia can be 25–50 times higher than those in cities in low-income nations. But urban centres in low- and middle-income nations in Africa, Asia and Latin America are likely to house most of the growth in the world's population, production and greenhouse gas emissions up to around 2030. In addition, they have a large and growing proportion of the world's population most at risk from climate-change-related impacts, including increased severity and frequency of extreme weather events and sea-level rise. Thus, what is done in their urban centres will influence strongly whether the current trend of increasing (and possibly escalating) risks for the whole planet from climate change will be reduced or stopped.

Urban opportunities and disadvantages

The fact that large urban centres have high concentrations of people, enterprises and motor vehicles – and their wastes – can make them very hazardous places in which to live and work. With inadequate or no environmental management, environmental hazards become the main causes of ill-health, injury and premature death. The urban poor face the greatest risks as their homes and neighbourhoods generally have the least adequate provision for water supplies, sanitation, drainage, garbage collection and health care. Within the tenements and informal settlements where much of the urban population lives, it is common for one-fifth of all children to die before the age of five, and for a high proportion of children to suffer from malnutrition.

Urban centres also provide many environmental opportunities. High densities and large population concentrations lower the costs per household and per enterprise for the provision of most kinds of infrastructure and services. The concentration of industries should reduce the unit cost of making regular checks on plant and equipment safety, as well as on occupational health and safety, pollution control and the management of hazardous wastes. There are also economies of scale or proximity for reducing risks from most disasters. There is generally a greater capacity among city dwellers to help pay for such measures, if they are made aware of the risks and all efforts are made to keep down costs. With good environmental management, cities can achieve life expectancies that compare favourably with those in Europe and North America – as demonstrated by well-governed cities such as Porto Alegre in Brazil (Menegat 1998, 2002).

Cities also have many potential advantages for reducing resource use and waste. For instance, the close proximity of so many water consumers provides greater scope for recycling or directly reusing waste waters. With regard to transport, cities have great potential for limiting the use of motor vehicles (and thus also the fossil fuels, air pollution and greenhouse gases that their use implies). This might sound contradictory, since most large cities have problems with congestion and motor-vehicle-generated air pollution, but compact cities allow many more trips to be made by walking or bicycling. Cities also make a greater use of public transport and a high-quality service more feasible (Kenworthy 2006).

Good environmental management can also limit the tendency for cities to transfer environmental costs to rural areas, for example, through:

- enforcing pollution control to protect water quality in nearby water bodies, safeguarding those who draw water from them, and also fisheries;
- an emphasis on waste reduction – reuse, recycle – to reduce the volume of wastes that are disposed of in the area around cities;
- comprehensive storm and surface drains, and refuse collection systems which reduce non-point sources of water pollution.

More resource-conserving, waste-minimizing cities can also contribute much to addressing global environmental problems, including de-linking a good quality of life from increased resource use, waste generation and greenhouse gas emissions. However, realizing these potential advantages of urban concentrations requires competent city governments that are accountable to their populations and guided by national urban policies, which ensure they also meet their regional and global environmental responsibilities.

The importance of governance

All urban areas require some form of government to ensure adequate-quality 'environments' for their inhabitants. Governments must also act to protect key resources and ecosystems in and around cities – for instance, to regulate land use, to protect watersheds, to control pollution and the disposal of wastes, and to ensure adequate provision of environmental infrastructure and services. Ensuring good-quality environments becomes increasingly complex, the larger the population (and the scale and range of their daily movements) and the more industrial the production base.

In all cities, environmental management is an intensely political task, as different interests compete for the most advantageous locations, for the ownership or use of resources and waste sinks, and for publicly provided infrastructure and services. The most serious environmental problems in urban areas are largely the result of inadequate governance and inadequate investment. Two concerns are particularly pressing:

1 reducing environmental hazards;
2 reducing the loss of natural resources and the damage to or disruption of ecosystems.

The emphasis on 'governance' rather than 'government' is because good environmental manage-ment needs city authorities and politicians to be accountable to their citizens and to work with them. The term governance is understood to include not only the political and administrative institutions of government, but also the relationships between government and civil society (McCarney 1996). Much of the innovation in urban environmental policies since the mid-1980s has been driven or much influenced by community-based organizations and local NGOs, and has taken place in nations where mayors and city governments are elected (see, for example, Velasquez 1998).

The scale and range of environmental problems

Infectious and parasitic diseases

Many of the most serious diseases in cities are 'environmental' because they are transmitted through disease-causing agents (pathogens) in the air, water, soil or food, or through insect or ani-mal disease vectors. Many diseases and disease vectors (for instance, the mosquitoes that transmit dengue fever or yellow fever) thrive when provision for water, sanitation, drainage, refuse collec-tion and health care is inadequate.

At any one time, around half the urban population in low- and middle-income nations is suf-fering from one or more of the diseases associated with inadequate provision for water and sani-tation (WHO 1999). Around half the urban population in Africa and Asia lacks provision for water and sanitation to a standard that is healthy and convenient. For Latin America and the Caribbean, more than a quarter lack such provision (UN-Habitat 2003, 2006). Tens of millions of urban dwellers have no toilet they can use, so they either defecate in the open or into waste materials or plastic bags. Improved provision for water and sanitation can bring great benefits in terms of improved health, reduced expenditures (on water vendors and on treatment from diseases) and much reduced physical effort (especially for those who collect and carry water from standpipes or other sources far from their shelters). In the early 1990s, many international agencies supported private-sector provision for water and sanitation, in the hope that this would increase efficiency, expand provision and bring in new capital, but the results have been very disappointing (Budds and McGranahan 2003; UN-Habitat 2003).

Airborne infections remain among the world's leading causes of premature death. For many, their transmission is aided by the overcrowding and inadequate ventilation that is common in the tenements, boarding houses or small shacks in which most low-income urban dwellers live. While improving housing and other environmental conditions can reduce their incidence (and, by reduc-ing other diseases, also strengthen people's defences against these), medical interventions such as immunization or rapid treatment are more important for reducing their health impact.

Chemical and physical hazards

The scale and severity of many chemical and physical hazards increases rapidly with urbanization and industrialization. While controlling infectious diseases centres on provision of infrastructure and services (whether through public, private, NGO or community provision), reducing chemical and physical hazards is largely achieved by regulation – for instance, of enterprises, builders and motor-vehicle users.

A great range of chemical pollutants affect human health. Controlling exposure to chemicals in the workplace ('occupational exposure') is particularly important, with action needed from large factories down to small, backstreet workshops. In most cities, there is an urgent need for measures to promote healthy and safe working practices and to penalize employers who contravene them. In many urban areas, domestic indoor air pollution, from open fires or poorly vented stoves that use coal or biomass fuels, has serious health impacts. Lower-income households are affected most, as people tend to move to cleaner, safer fuels when incomes rise.

There is also a growing need for more effective control of outdoor (ambient) air pollution from industries and motor vehicles. Worldwide, more than 1.5 billion urban dwellers are exposed to levels of ambient air pollution that are above the recommended maximum levels. Urban air pollution problems are particularly pressing in many Indian and Chinese cities.

Accidents in the home are often among the most serious causes of injury and premature death, especially where much of the population lives in overcrowded accommodation made from temporary materials, and uses open fires or unsafe stoves and candles or kerosene lights.

Traffic management which protects pedestrians and minimizes the risk of motor-vehicle accidents is also important. Motor-vehicle accidents have become an increasingly significant contributor to premature deaths and injuries in many cities. The number of fatalities and serious injuries per road vehicle is often much higher than in high-income countries.

Achieving a high-quality city environment

Attention should be given not only to reducing environmental hazards, but also to ensuring provision or protection of those facilities that make urban environments more pleasant, safe and valued by their inhabitants, including parks, public squares/plazas and provision for children's play and for sport/recreation. This should be integrated with a concern to protect each city's natural landscapes with important ecological and aesthetic value, for instance, wetland areas, river banks or coasts.

Managing wastes

Municipal agencies are generally responsible for providing waste collection services, although this is often contracted out to private businesses. Most urban governments lack the technical knowledge, institutional competence and funding base to ensure that these responsibilities are met. In many urban centres, more than a third of the solid wastes generated are not collected, and it is usually the low-income districts that have the least adequate collection service. This means that wastes accumulate on open spaces and streets, clogging drains and attracting disease vectors and pests (rats, mosquitoes, flies).

Many industrial and some institutional wastes (for instance, from hospitals) are categorized as 'hazardous' because of the special care needed to dispose of them – to ensure they are isolated from contact with humans and the natural environment. In most urban centres, governments do little to monitor their production, collection, treatment and disposal. Since managing hazardous wastes properly is expensive, businesses have large incentives to avoid meeting official regulations on how these wastes should be managed, and generally face little risk of prosecution.

Reducing the impact of disasters

Disasters are considered to be exceptional events which suddenly result in significant numbers of people being killed or injured, or in large economic losses. As such, they are distinguished from the environmental hazards discussed above. This distinction has its limitations, since far more urban dwellers die of easily prevented illnesses arising from environmental hazards in their food, water or air than from 'disasters', yet the death toll from disasters gets more media attention.

Cyclones/high winds/storms have probably caused more deaths in urban areas than other 'natural' disasters in recent decades. Earthquakes have caused many of the biggest urban disasters.

Flood disasters affect many more people than cyclones and earthquakes, but generally kill fewer people. Landslides, fires, epidemics and industrial accidents are among the other urban disasters that need attention. These may also take place as secondary disasters, after a flood, storm or earthquake.

Global warming will increase the frequency and severity of disasters in many urban areas. For instance, the rise in sea level will increase the risk of flooding for many port and tourist cities, and low- and middle-income nations have a higher proportion of their urban population in low-elevation coastal zones than do high-income nations (McGranahan, Balk and Anderson 2007). Sea-level rise will also disrupt sewers and drains, and may bring seawater intrusion into freshwater aquifers. Changes in rainfall regimes, caused by climate change, are likely to reduce the availability of freshwater resources in many nations or bring increased risk of floods in many cities.

Increasingly, urban authorities recognize the need to integrate 'disaster prevention' within 'environmental hazard prevention'. Even where disasters have natural triggers that cannot be prevented, their impact can generally be greatly reduced by understanding who within the city population is vulnerable, and acting to reduce this vulnerability before the disaster occurs. There are also important overlaps between 'the culture of prevention' for everyday hazards and for disasters.

Developing more sustainable interactions with nature

Cities transform natural landscapes both within and around them.

- The expansion of cities reshapes land surfaces and water flows. In the absence of effective land-use management, urbanization can have serious ecological impacts, such as soil erosion, deforestation, and the loss of agricultural land and sites with valuable ecological functions.
- The 'export' of solid, liquid and airborne pollutants and wastes often brings serious environmental impacts to regions around cities, including damage to fisheries by untreated liquid wastes, land and groundwater pollution from inadequately designed and managed solid waste dumps, and, for many of the larger and more industrial cities, acid rain.
- Freshwater resources are being depleted. Many cities have outgrown the capacity of their locality to provide fresh water, or have overused or mismanaged local sources so that these are no longer usable. Increasingly distant and costly water sources have to be used, often to the detriment of the regions from which these are drawn.

A focus only on such regional damages can obscure the fact that city consumers and enterprises provide the main market for rural produce, while rural inhabitants and enterprises draw on urban enterprises for goods and services. Urban markets can provide not only rural incomes, but also the basis for rural investments in better environmental management. Many low-income rural households also depend on urban markets, or one or more household members working in urban areas, for a significant part of their livelihood.

Global impacts

The demands concentrated in larger and wealthier cities for food, fuel and raw materials are increasingly being met by imports from distant ecosystems. They also avoid environmental costs by importing goods whose high environmental costs are generated at their point of production. This makes it easier to maintain high environmental standards within and around wealthy cities, including preserving natural landscapes, but this is transferring costs to people and ecosystems in other regions or countries. Other cost transfers are pushed into the future. For instance, air pollution may have been cut in some wealthy cities, but emissions of carbon dioxide (the main greenhouse gas) remain high in all wealthy cities and may continue to rise. This is transferring costs to the future through the human and ecological costs that atmospheric warming will bring.

All cities have to develop a more sustainable interaction with the ecocycles on whose continued functioning we all depend. But to promote a sustainable, development-oriented urban policy needs a coherent and supportive national policy. It is difficult for city governments to act on this because they are accountable to the populations living within their boundaries, not to those living in distant ecosystems on whose productivity the city producers or consumers may draw. It is also difficult for city authorities to take account of the needs and rights of future generations and of other species without a supportive, national, sustainable development framework.

There is also the issue of the profound unfairness globally in the likely impacts of global warming, since the people, cities and nations most at risk are not those that are responsible for most greenhouse gas emissions. The very survival of some small-island and low-income nations is in doubt, as much of their land area is at risk from sea-level rise (McGranahan, Balk and Anderson 2007), yet their contributions to global greenhouse emissions have been very small. There are also tens of millions of low-income urban dwellers in Asia and Africa, whose homes and livelihoods are at risk from sea-level rise, whose contributions to greenhouse gas emissions are similarly small. One wonders what will happen to global relations as the number and scale of urban disasters associated with climate change increases in low-income nations, against a backdrop of global recognition that this is driven by high-consumption lifestyles – mainly of people who live in high-income nations.

GUIDE TO FURTHER READING

This article draws on Hardoy, J.E., Mitlin, D. and Satterthwaite, D. (2001) *Environmental Problems in an Urbanizing World*, London: Earthscan Publications.

For discussions on the transfer of cities' environmental costs, see McGranahan, G., Jacobi, P., Songsore, J., Surjadi, C. and Kjellén, M. (2001) *Citizens at Risk: From Urban Sanitation to Sustainable Cities*, London: Earthscan Publications.

For a discussion of ecological urbanization, see two special issues of *Environment and Urbanization* (2006) on this topic: 18(1) and (2).

For a review of approaches to addressing urban environmental problems, see Leitmann, J. (1999) *Sustaining Cities: Environmental Planning and Management in Urban Design*, New York: McGraw-Hill.

For a discussion of sustainable development and cities, see Satterthwaite, D. (ed.) (1999) *The Earthscan Reader on Sustainable Cities*, London: Earthscan Publications.

For air pollution and cities, see Elsom, D. (1996) *Smog Alert: Managing Urban Air Quality*, London: Earthscan Publications; and McGranahan, G. and Murray, F. (2003) *Air Pollution and Health in Rapidly Developing Countries*, London: Earthscan Publications.

For discussions of climate change and cities in low- and middle-income nations, see the special issue of *Environment and Urbanization* (2007) on this topic: 19(1).

REFERENCES

Budds, J. and McGranahan, G. (2003) 'Are the debates on water privatization missing the point? Experiences from Africa, Asia and Latin America', *Environment and Urbanization*, 15(2): 87–114.

Hardoy, J.E., Mitlin, D. and Satterthwaite, D. (2001) *Environmentwal Problems in an Urbanizing World*, London: Earthscan Publications.

Kenworthy, J.R. (2006) 'The eco-city: Ten key transport and planning dimensions for sustainable city development', *Environment and Urbanization*, 18(1): 67–86.

McCarney, P.L. (ed.) (1996) *Cities and Governance: New Directions in Latin America, Asia and Africa*, Toronto: Centre for Urban and Community Studies, University of Toronto.

McGranahan, G., Balk, D. and Anderson, B. (2007) 'Populations at risk: The proportion of the world's population living on low-elevation coastal zones', *Environment and Urbanization*, 19(1).

Menegat, R. (main coordinator) (1998) *Atlas Ambiental de Porto Alegre*, Porto Alegre: Universidade Federal do Rio Grande do Sul, Prefeitura Municipal de Porto Alegre and Instituto Nacional de Pesquisas Espaciais.

Menegat, R. (2002) 'Participatory democracy and sustainable development: Integrated urban environmental management in Porto Alegre, Brazil', *Environment and Urbanization*, 14(2): 181–206.

Ruel, M.T. and Garrett, J.L. (2004) 'Features of urban food and nutrition security and considerations for successful urban programming', *The Electronic Journal of Agricultural and Development Economics*, 1(2): 242–71.

UN-Habitat (2003) *Water and Sanitation in the World's Cities; Local Action for Global Goals*, London: Earthscan Publications.

UN-Habitat (2006) *Meeting Development Goals in Small Urban Centres: Water and Sanitation in the World's Cities 2006*, London: Earthscan Publications.

Velasquez, L.S. (1998) 'Agenda 21: A form of joint environmental management in Manizales, Colombia', *Environment and Urbanization*, 10(2): 9–36.

WHO (World Health Organization) (1999) 'Creating healthy cities in the 21st century', in D. Satterthwaite (ed.) *The Earthscan Reader on Sustainable Cities*, London: Earthscan Publications, Chapter 6, pp. 137–72.

5.7 Rural-urban interaction

Kenneth Lynch

Introduction

Despite early development research including much work on the role of the interaction between cities and rural areas, most contemporary approaches in development studies – both theoretical and empirical – are based on the premise that there is a clear distinction between the urban and the rural (Lynch 2005). However, this distinction has also been challenged. There is research on urban activities, such as wage employment in rural spaces (Bryceson 2002); 'rural' activities, such as agriculture in 'urban' spaces (Lynch, Binns and Olofin 2001); understanding the interdependence between these two realms (Rigg 1998); and, finally, the livelihoods and resource management issues in the interface between the urban and the rural (Iaquinta and Drescher, 2000; McGregor, Simon and Thompson 2005). There is therefore a need to bring these disparate themes together.

Some of the earliest research on development focused on modernization diffusion, and the relations between city and country were a core part of the theorization. These were developed into spatial models that may be pessimistic, in the case of Friedmann's core-periphery model, or optimistic, in the case of Vance's mercantile model (Lynch 2005). These influential theories are focused primarily on settlement hierarchies, rather than the interaction between town and country, suggesting an urban focus. However, they are used to theorize about rural-urban interaction. A little later, Lipton (1977) made considerable impact on development studies, presenting the urban bias thesis on the ways in which urban-based industrialization policies can have an adverse impact on the development of rural areas. After Lipton, some research continued with this focus (see Lipton 1984 and Corbridge and Jones 2005), but, in the main, development studies moved on to examine development at a scale that focused more on local dimensions of development or on national and international dimensions, and the links between urban and rural change were largely left behind, as researchers tended towards *either* an urban *or* a rural focus, or on research at a scale where urban or rural issues were lost in a preoccupation with national and international change. Since the end of the twentieth century, however, the question of the distinction between urban and rural development has been questioned, particularly strongly in the field of demography and migration studies, but also in new research foci, such as the rurification of cities, the rise of non-farm income strategies, and the management of the peri-urban interface. The impact of the economic crises of the 1980s has also prompted research on the differentials between cities and rural areas, but this has not always provided insights into the links between rural and urban areas.

One interesting outcome of the research on peri-urban interfaces has been a move away from considering the physical interface between urban and rural, to conceiving of the relationships between them as more important. This is particularly evident in the work of Tacoli (1998) and the IIED (see the Livelihoods Connect website details at the end of the chapter). Even in the physical space where the urban and the rural meet, there is an emerging consensus that the physical location of these linkages is less important than the way they are constructed and structured.

The most recent research that elevates the urban-rural linkages to the main focus, centres on the challenge of fluidity and of fragmented identities that play a role in the lives of the people who communicate through, exchange across and travel between the links which bridge the rural-urban divide (for example, Rigg 1998). A key contention of this work is that this fluidity is often a deliberate strategy adopted by people living in rural and urban areas, in order to maximize their livelihood opportunities (Lynch 2005). This emphasis on flows and linkages is the key focus of this chapter. We will introduce the flows approach, explaining how it focuses on the flows that link the areas, rather than the structures or processes that separate them. The argument will be made that this provides a more useful and more powerful analysis of the relationship between city and countryside.

Rural-urban flows

Table 1 shows the categorization of rural-urban flows, illustrating the possibility that the flows can work in either direction. Under certain conditions, one-way flows may dominate, or the emphasis may change over time or from one context to the next. More detailed examples are discussed elsewhere (Lynch 2005).

Until the end of the twentieth century, much rural-urban research had focused on a single city and its hinterland. However, the increasing importance of international links and the process of globalization have had an impact on urban-rural relations. In addition, cities throughout the world are often caught between the pressure to be included in the world economy, on the one hand, and the need for links with their rural hinterlands, on the other. Such tensions raise issues that have not been considered until recently. This tension is paralleled in the competing processes of globalization and decentralization.

Table 1 Categorization of rural-urban flows and some characteristics in the literature

Flow	Rural to urban	Urban to rural	Intermediate
Food	Fruit, vegetables, staples	Processed foods, drinks	Urban and peri-urban agriculture
People	Migration in search of employment	Retirement migration, circular migration	Multi-locational households
Natural	Energy resources, water, raw materials for industry	Pollution, energy	Environmental footprint and the environmental 'affluence transition'
Capital	Rural savings to banks, hut taxes, sales duties, profits of large businesses	Investment, aid, credit, remittances, cash sales proceeds	Interdependent economies, generative or exploitative relationships
Ideas	Peasantization of cities, rural coping strategies	Development of non-farm employment, urbanization of rural lifestyles	Merging of 'urban' and 'rural' – ruralopolis, peri-urban, desakota

The role of 'urban' and 'rural' in the ideology of development in China

On coming to power in 1949, the revolutionary Chinese government was faced with one of the world's greatest urban-rural dilemmas. The government was made up largely of politicians from peasant backgrounds, with peasant support, but it took control of a country already struggling to cope with the demands of its many large cities. By 1950, Shanghai was already estimated to have a population of 5.3 million, Beijing, 3.9 million, and Tianjin, 2.4 million (UNHCS 2001). Some of the earliest government actions were to impose state-controlled marketing of agricultural goods and rationing of urban food consumption, and to control the movement of people – especially rural-to-urban migration. In addition, the level of land scarcity experienced by rural dwellers convinced the Chinese government that urban-based heavy industrialization was the only way the country would be able to support its population, which totalled 541 million in 1952, of which 57.7 million, or 10.6 per cent, were 'urban' (Knight and Song 2000). One of the issues that concerned the Chinese government was that, by 1964, the second census under communist rule, the urban population had grown to 129.3 million, or 18.4 per cent of the total population of 691.2 million. Such rapid growth, both nationally and in the cities, concerned the government. They decided that there was a need to control the population and to create employment for the urban population.

External hostility of global powers meant that foreign investment was unlikely: the only possibility of producing savings to invest in industrialization was to extract surplus from rural agricultural production, resulting in a bias of policy towards the urban areas over the rural areas. The result was that the State Purchase and Marketing Cooperative's main function was to 'extract as much of the harvest as possible from the peasants' (Knight and Song 2000: 11). In addition, the Cooperative supplied agricultural inputs, and the state also controlled the banking. The state therefore mediated all rural-urban flows of goods and capital, other than household remittances. This was compounded by the agricultural tax, which amounted to approximately 30 per cent of farm proceeds (Knight and Song 2000). The Chinese government therefore funded its industrialization by mobilizing the rural areas to produce and save more, in order to provide the capital and the tax revenue to invest.

Agricultural-industrial links

While the Chinese example illustrates a deliberate policy of exploiting rural areas, Hodder (2000) argues that, inevitably, rural agricultural sectors and urban industrial sectors play strategic roles in each other's development. He identifies six key reasons for these close links between the two sectors.

1 Agriculture depends on manufactured goods for the transformation of agriculture (such as farm tolls, machinery and inputs) and for consumer goods which are in demand as agricultural incomes rise (such as radios and bicycles).
2 As agriculture incorporates more technology in its activities, labour becomes a less significant factor. More technologically advanced agriculture releases capital and labour, which moves into the urban industrial sector.
3 Agriculture provides raw materials for some industries, such as tobacco, cotton and sisal.
4 Agriculture for export can earn foreign exchange, which is important for purchasing items that are vital to industrial processes. These include commodities such as petroleum, chemicals and technology, which are not produced locally.
5 There is an important balance to be struck in incomes, prices and taxation between urban and rural areas. For example, high food prices provide rewards to farmers and incentives to increase production, but may mean high prices in urban areas, which can lead to poverty and unrest. Taxation in the agricultural sector may be necessary to raise revenues to finance public expenditure, but this may act as a disincentive to farmers, particularly if much of the expenditure is urban- or industrial-focused.

6 In rapidly urbanizing countries, agriculture produces strategically important food for the growing number of urban residents in order to ensure food security at prices that are affordable (adapted from Hodder 2000: 80–2).

The FAO's report on the hallmarks of successful agricultural development (1995) indicated the strong positive relationship between agriculture and the rest of the economy, including, specifically, the urban and industrial economies. The argument rested on the evidence that there are positive feedback loops between the rural-agricultural sectors and the urban-industrial sectors which promote growth in both, but which can also hold each other back. The research approaches discussed in this chapter therefore suggest that approaches which focus on static spatial areas, such as 'urban' or 'rural', appear to be being superseded by approaches that adopt a more flexible approach, which emphasizes links, flows and opportunities as they arise. As Ellis and Harris (2004: iii) argue, 'poverty reduction is perhaps not so much to do with supporting spatially and temporally static and stagnating sub-sectors of national economies. Rather it is about running with growth where and when it occurs.' This suggests that a focus on the linkages between urban and rural areas may be as important as the focus on the areas themselves.

GUIDE TO FURTHER READING

Lynch, K. (2005) *Rural-Urban Interaction in the Developing World*, Oxford: Routledge. This is a textbook that attempts to integrate a wide range of academic and other material into a discussion which focuses on five main flows of interaction between city and countryside in the developing world. The flows are food, natural flows (resources and pollutions), people, ideas and finances.

Tacoli, C. (ed.) (2006) *The Earthscan Reader in Rural-Urban Linkages*, London: Earthscan. A collection of key writings on rural urban linkages, with a commentary from a leading researcher in the field.

USEFUL WEBSITES

Food and Agriculture Organization of the United Nations, Food for the Cities: http://www.fao.org/fcit/

Livelihoods Connect, Hot Topics: Urban and Rural Change: http://www.livelihoods.org/hot_topics/UrbanRural.html

Overseas Development Institute, *Rural-Urban Linkages*, Key Sheet No. 10: http://www.keysheets.org/red_10_ruralurban.html

UN-Habitat, *Habitat Debate*: http://www.unhabitat.org/pmss/getPage/asp?page=latestPeriods

REFERENCES

Bryceson, D.F. (2002) 'The scramble for Africa: Reorienting rural livelihoods', *World Development*, 30(5): 725–39.

Corbridge, D. and Jones, G. (2005) *The Continuing Debate About Urban Bias: The Thesis, its Critics, its Influence, and Implications for Poverty Reduction*, Research Papers in Environmental and Spatial Analysis, No. 99, Department of Geography and Environment, London School of Economics and Political Science (available at http://www.lse.ac.uk/collections/geographyAndEnvironment/research/Researchpapers/99%20corbridge%20jones.pdf).

Ellis, F. and Harris, N. (2004) *New Thinking About Urban and Rural Development*, paper prepared for the government of the United Kingdom: Department for International Development (available at http://www.passlivelihoods.org.uk/site_files/files/2004%20Retreat%20Downloads/2004%20Sustainable%20Development%20Retreat_Ellis&Harris.doc).

FAO (1995) *World Agriculture: Towards 2010. An FAO Study*, Rome and Chichester: Food and Agriculture Organization and John Wiley & Sons.

Hodder, R. (2000) *Development Geography*, London: Routledge.

Iaquinta, D. and Drescher, A. (2000) *Defining Periurban: Understanding Rural-Urban Linkages and Their Connection to Institutional Contexts*, paper presented at the Tenth World Congress, IRSA, Rio de Janeiro, 1 August 2000 (available at http://www.geographie.uni-freiburg.de/indigenoveg/Background1Periurban Typology.pdf).

Knight, J. and Song, L. (2000) *The Rural-Urban Divide: Economic Disparities and Interaction in China*, Oxford: Oxford University Press.

Lipton, M. (1977) *Why Poor People Stay Poor: Urban Bias and World Development*, London and Boston, MA: Temple Smith and Harvard University Press.

Lipton, M. (1984) 'Urban bias revisited', *Journal of Development Studies*, 20(3): 139–66.

Lynch, K. (2005) *Rural-Urban Interaction in the Developing World*, Oxford: Routledge.

Lynch, K., Binns, T. and Olofin, E.A. (2001) 'Urban agriculture under threat – The land security question in Kano, Nigeria', *Cities*, 18(3): 159–71.

McGregor, D., Simon, D. and Thompson, D. (2005) 'Contemporary perspectives on the peri-urban zones of cities in developing countries', in D. McGregor, D. Simon and D. Thompson (eds) *The Peri-Urban Interface: Approaches to Sustainable Natural and Human Resources Use*, London: Earthscan, pp. 3–17.

Rigg, J. (1998) 'Rural-urban interactions, agriculture and wealth: A Southeast Asian perspective', *Progress in Human Geography*, 22(4): 497–522.

Tacoli, C. (1998) *Bridging the Divide: Rural-Urban Interactions and Livelihood Strategies*, London: International Institute for Environment and Development, Gatekeeper Series, No. 77 (available at http://www.iied.org/pubs/pdf/full/6144IIED.pdf).

Tacoli, C. (2003) 'The links between urban and rural development', *Environment and Urbanization*, 15(3): 3–12 (available at http://eau.sagepub.com/cgi/reprint/15/1/3.pdf).

UNHCS (2001) *Cities in a Globalizing World. Global Report on Human Settlements 2001*, New York: United Nations Commission for Human Settlements.

5.8 Transport and urban development

Eduardo A. Vasconcellos

Introduction

In urban environments, transport is vital for social and economic life, and may be provided by several means. The specific modes used in a city are highly correlated to its size, to the quality and cost of available modes and to the economic and social characteristics of its inhabitants. As a general rule, in smaller cities, walking and cycling are the dominant modes, while in larger cities, motorized means become essential, be they public (bus, train, metro) or private (automobiles and motorcycles). As transport implies the consumption of natural resources and the generation of some negative impacts, such as accidents, pollution and congestion, the use of any particular mode and the overall balance of modes in a particular city have to be analysed carefully.

Transport modal choices

When we observe a large number of societies, encompassing all income and wealth variations, we find people using a large variety of transport means, from walking to motorized private means such as the car. The transport modes people choose to use are constrained by several social, cultural and economic factors. Family or individual income is the most important factor, since it determines the possibility of paying to have access to motorized means (including the bus). Age also influences mobility because it poses mental or physical limits using roads as a pedestrian and driving vehicles, as in the case of children, youngsters and elderly people. Gender imposes constraints that arise from the division of tasks among the household members, which vary according to different societies. Finally, cultural or religious beliefs may limit access to some sort of vehicles or place incentives on using others.

Mobility – measured as the number of trips per person per day – increases when income increases, and is higher among males and for those between 10 and 40 years old, who are either studying or working. Overall, the average individual mobility rates (trips/day) vary from one (for very poor people) to four (wealthy people). A parallel phenomenon is that of increasing use of motorized means with increasing incomes (either public or private), depending on the level of income and the availability of transport means. The figure summarizes data from São Paulo in 2002. It may be seen that as income increases, walking decreases and travel by public transport also decreases (for the higher income levels). In parallel, the use of private means increases across all income levels. The pattern revealed by the figure may change according to specific characteristics of every society and of transport alternatives. For instance, cycling is very important in Asia and in wealthy European cities, and it may replace trips made on public or motorized private modes; more importantly, the high quality of public transport may 'soften' the decrease in its use as income increases, as happens in Europe. The same effect may occur if the costs (fuel, parking) of using automobiles are high (such as in Europe and wealthy Asian cities).

Therefore, although the increase in the use of private motorized means is a worldwide phenomenon, the final pattern of modal share will be directly influenced by individual characteristics and by transport policies, concerning cost, availability and convenience of each transport mode.

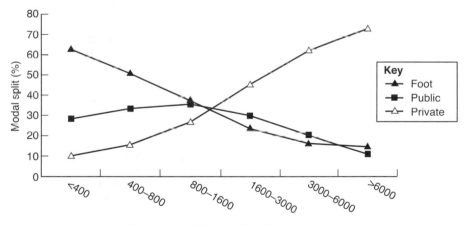

Modal split and income, São Paulo Metropolitan Region, 2002
Source: CMSP 2003

Characteristics of various transport modes

Accessibility

The first important outcome of a transport system is the accessibility it promotes so people may reach desired destinations. The essential difference in accessibility is that provided by non-motorized and motorized transport means. On the one hand, both walking and cycling are universal transport means. However, they have natural limits, related to the time and distance a person may cover with them. On the other hand, the use of any form of motorized transport overcomes the distance barrier, although it dramatically increases the consumption of money, energy and road space, and generates or increases negative externalities such as air pollution and accidents (Vasconcellos 2001).

The overall accessibility provided by any transport means depends on several components. The first is made of walking, waiting and transferring times while trying to use a vehicle. Another essential component is actual speed inside vehicles (fluidity conditions). In non-congested cities, automobile and motorcycle speeds may be triple that of buses (60 km/h as compared to 20 km/h), in more congested cities – as most large cities of contemporary developing countries are – speed of cars may still be the double that of buses. Finally, the comfort of using pavements and public transport vehicles is an issue.

Family and personal transport costs

As long as distances increase and more motorized means are used, people have to spend more money to travel. In developing economies, a large number of people have no money to pay for decent transport. The most pressing problems occur with those who cannot pay public transport fares, forcing some of them to change to slower modes or to stop travelling altogether.

Capacity

Transport modes have different characteristics concerning cost, capacity, fuel consumption, comfort and safety. Wright (1992) notes that no mode gets perfect grades on all proposed attributes: cycling may be too dangerous in some places, walking long distances is not feasible, transit may be inflexible and the car is highly polluting. The capacity of different transport modes is better translated by the quantity of people that can be transported per hour, per length of road (see Table 1).

Table 1 Transport mode carrying capacity (interrupted flow)

Mode	Speed range (km/hr)	Capacity range (passenger/hr/metre)
Walkway	3–4	3609
Bicycle	10–16	1000–1750
Cycle-rickshaw	6–12	500–1500
Motorcycle (1 person)	15–40	500–1000
Car (1.5 persons)	16–24	140–250
Regular bus	10–25	1000–6000 (busways)
Tram	10–30	1000–6000

Source: Wright 1992

The social and environmental impacts of different transport choices

Use of energy

Energy spent by a particular transport mode, per passenger, depends on vehicle and operating characteristics and on the number of people using the mode. Public transport means are always less energy-intensive than private means. Relations between buses and cars fall in the 1:5 range in most developing economies, although this may be even higher if bus occupancy is very high. On a city or country basis, the average (and total) energy consumption is highly dependent on the transport modal share. Considering that private vehicles consume much more energy per passenger-kilometre, the higher their share, the higher the energy spent.

Use of space

The first impact of transport is the land required to build roads and provide parking spaces. On a grid-type road system, with roads located 100 metres apart from each other, roads alone will occupy about 25 per cent of the city's area. If parking spaces are considered, this figure may grow to 30 per cent or more, as happens in sprawling US cities, such as Los Angeles and Houston. A second important issue is the road space required by any single method of transport. When we compare different modes, the most demanding is the automobile, which consumes 30 times more area per passenger than a bus, and about five times that of a two-wheeler. This also explains why the increase in the number of automobiles may rapidly exhaust existing road space and increase congestion.

Pollutant emissions

In most large cities, transport is the main source of pollution, especially private transport. Motor vehicles are responsible for most CO_2, almost all CO emissions, and most HC and NOx emissions. Diesel trucks and buses contribute to most of the PM, especially when low-quality diesel with a high percentage of sulphur is used. Two-stroke motorcycles are usually highly polluting. For policy analysis, the key factor is emission per passenger-kilometre, which depends on vehicle occupancies, favouring public modes. In a particular city or region, actual modal share will define the emission pattern. When comparing different motorized means, the environmental advantages of increasing the use of public transport are clear. In the case of São Paulo in 2002, motorcycles and automobiles emitted, respectively, 17 and 7.8 times more pollutants per passenger-kilometre than diesel buses.

Traffic accidents

It is estimated that every year there are 1.2 million road traffic deaths and about 50 million injured in the world, with costs varying from 1 to 2 per cent of the GNP of each country, adding up to about US$500 billion a year worldwide (WHO 2004). In developing economies, the same report estimates that the number of traffic fatalities in 2000 (613,000) will rise almost 100 per cent by 2020, amounting to 1.2 million fatalities. The severity of the problem is related to the mix of transport modes, with public transport modes being safer than private ones. Safety conditions may become critical where intense economic development occurs, with the corresponding change in the quantity of vehicles and the mix of transport modes. Negative results are more severe when 'soft' modes, such as walking and cycling are replaced with 'harder' modes, such as cars, trucks, buses and motorcycles.

The 'barrier effect' and urban disruption

Motorized traffic, especially cars, affects social relations by reducing social interaction and the use of public spaces (Appleyard 1981), and requiring people to redefine strategies for lowering the risk of accidents. Negative impacts may be attributed to all motorized means, according to their specific use. The most damaging effect, however, is that of automobiles, which can be seen clearly when we consider their number and their need to consume space to survive, often at the expense of the urban physical environment and its architectural and cultural heritage.

Congestion

The significance of congestion stems from two sorts of concerns. The first is equity, as people using the road cause delay to others. Environmental factors are also important. Congestion caused by motorized vehicles implies higher energy consumption and pollutant emissions. Contrary to auto-mobile-centred cities such as those of the USA, the analysis of congestion in developing economy cities has to consider other traffic conditions, especially the extensive use of non-motorized and public transport modes. A particular analysis of congestion that is relevant for developing countries is that of how bus traffic is affected by automobile traffic. If congestion lowers bus speed from 20 km/h to 12 km/h, every bus passenger will take an extra 20 minutes for a 10-kilometre trip.

Conclusions

The fundamental question for the future of cities in developing economies is how to accommodate and direct growth to ensure higher social equity and economic efficiency on the one hand, and more equitable transport conditions on the other. With the former, solutions lie mostly beyond the transport agenda – income distribution, better housing, educational and health conditions – although transport policies and social policies interact with one another. With respect to the latter, urban, transport and traffic policies may be worked out to change current conditions and help achieve the objectives. The variety of existing conditions requires a range of solutions, even considering that a few basic solutions may be devised to apply to a large number of cities. Three fundamental questions may be proposed, as follows.

1 What is the desirable balance between private motorized transport and public transport?
2 How can a shift from motorized means to more environmentally friendly ones be promoted? (This question poses others, relating to transferring trips to non-motorized or to public transport means.)
3 Even if private motorization is supported by public policies, how can the needs of the large number of people that will still be dependent on walking, cycling and using public modes be met?

The relevance of these questions relates directly to the environmental, economic and social consequences of urban and transport policy decisions. There are no reasons to believe that developing economies are condemned to automobile dominance, congestion and pollution. As Cervero (1998) and Newman and Kenworthy (1999) have pointed out, there are important lessons to be drawn from large cities that have managed to keep or create good public transport systems, despite tendencies of increasing use of private transport.

GUIDE TO FURTHER READING

Ilich, I. (1974) *Energy and Equity*, New York: Harper & Row.
Whitelegg, J. (1997) *Critical Mass: Transport, Environment and Society in the Twenty-first Century*, London: Pluto Press.

REFERENCES

Appleyard, D. (1981) *Livable Streets*, Berkeley, CA: University of California Press.
Cervero, R. (1998) *The Transit Metropolis: A Global Inquiry*, Washington, DC: Island Press.
CMSP (2003) *Pesquisa origem-destino na RMSP*, São Paulo: CMSP.
Newman, P. and Kenworthy, J. (1999) *Sustainability and Cities: Overcoming Automobile Dependence*, Washington, DC: Island Press.
Vasconcellos, E.A. (2001) *Urban Transport, Environment and Equity: The Case for Developing Countries*, London: Earthscan Publications.
WHO (World Health Organization) (2004) *World Report on Road Traffic Injury Prevention*, Geneva: WHO.
Wright, C. (1992) *Fast Wheels, Slow Traffic: Urban Transport Choices*, Philadelphia, PA: Temple University Press.

Environment and development

Editorial introduction

Since the mid-1980s, the environment has become a major dimension of development thinking. In the future, it is clear that it needs to become a major component of development practice. In the past, undoubtedly, too much attention has been paid to economics, and far too little emphasis has been placed on the environment–development interface. However, since the Brundtland Commission in 1987, attention has increasingly focused on the concept of sustainable development. Although there are many discourses on sustainability, reflecting the interests of many different groups, most adopt the Commission's working definition of sustainability as meeting the needs of the present, without compromising the ability of future generations to meet their needs. But it has to be recognized that the concept of sustainable development is complex and contradictory. For example, it is generally harder for the poor to operationalize, as it is tempting for them to 'discount' the future, in order to provide for the pressing needs of the present.

A major threat to the environment is posed by global climatic change, and it is now generally accepted that climate is changing, due at least in part to human activity. Once again, the concomitants of global warming, such as land degradation, desertification and flooding, appear to threaten to impact on the poor disproportionately. Such environmental circumstances are also expressed in terms of problems of food security. In this connection, urban environmental circumstances are also salient, not least as witnessed in waste dumping in watersheds, which causes major pollution problems downstream, where such waters may then be employed for irrigation and domestic purposes, thereby leading to a variety of health risks.

The United Nations Conference on Environment and Development (UNCED), held in Rio de Janeiro in 1992 and generally referred to as the Rio Earth Summit, was designed as a major effort to catalyse a more sustainable approach to development. However, some commentators have argued that the needs of national governments and business lobbies were too dominant in the various discussions that took place as part of the conference. Another major issue during the proceedings was that the nations broadly making up the North and the South seemed to adopt and stress different objectives. The nations of the North seemed intent to argue that environmental problems can be cured by the application of technology. In contrast, the governments of the South emphasized the need for real structural reforms in order to change the international economy, so as to impact directly on the effects of debt, structural adjustment programmes and the like.

It has frequently been maintained that not enough emphasis is being placed on brown agenda issues. These environmental problems, which are primarily encountered in urban environments, serve to put many millions of lives at risk. They are also expressed in the emergence of so-called 'pollution havens' in developing countries, where the pollutants of the North are effectively dumped in the South. Such circumstances make all too clear the need for international environmental regulations. Another major area of enquiry has re-examined the nature of disasters and vulnerability. Here views have been changing quite dramatically, in so far as there has been a move to recognize that even natural events need not turn into disasters, and that steps may be taken to avoid the harmful consequences of such events. The vulnerability and entitlement explanatory models are of particular salience in this connection. Other major foci have been on the developmental issues associated with reductions in biodiversity, water management issues, energy issues, forest management and the impact of tourism on the environment. Another increasingly important area of interest and concern is the complex interrelations between livelihood strategies and the environment.

6.1 Sustainable development

Michael Redclift

Discourses of 'sustainable development'

The expression 'sustainable development' has been used in a variety of ways, particularly within the context of development studies. In the early twenty-first century, we are confronted with several different discourses of 'sustainable development', some of which are mutually exclusive. For example, campaigners for greater global equality between nations, huge international corporations and local housing associations have all had recourse to the term 'sustainable development' to justify, or embellish, their actions.

We might begin our analysis of these different discourses by returning to essentials. Each scientific problem which is resolved by human intervention, using fossil fuels and manufactured materials, is usually viewed as a triumph of management and a contribution to economic good, when it might also represent a future threat to sustainability. In the 1970s, there was a fear that our major environmental problems would be associated with resource scarcities (Meadows et al. 1972). At the beginning of the twenty-first century, we are faced by another challenge: that the means we have used to overcome resource scarcity, including substitution of some natural resources, and 'cleaner' environmental products and services, may have contributed to the next generation of environmental problems. This realization provides an enormous challenge to conventional social science thinking, encapsulated in the term 'sustainable development', which has served as a concept, a policy prescription and a moral imperative.

Sustainable development was defined by the Brundtland Commission (1987) in the following way: 'development that meets the needs of the present without compromising the ability of future generations to meet their own needs'. This definition has been brought into service in the absence of agreement about a process which almost everybody thinks is desirable. However, the simplicity of this approach is deceptive, and obscures underlying complexities and contradictions. It is worth pausing to examine the apparent consensus that reigns over sustainable development.

First, following the Brundtland definition, it is clear that 'needs' themselves change, so it is unlikely (as the definition implies), that those of future generations will be the same as those of the present generation. The question, then, is where does 'development' come into the picture? Obviously development itself contributes to 'needs', helping to define them differently for each generation and for different cultures.

This raises the second question, not covered by the definition, of how needs are defined in different cultures. Most of the 'consensus' surrounding sustainable development has involved a syllogism: sustainable development is necessary for all of us, but it may be defined differently in terms of each and every culture. This is superficially convenient, until we begin to ask how these different definitions match up. If in one society it is agreed that fresh air and open spaces are necessary before development can be sustainable, it will be increasingly difficult to marry this definition of 'needs' with those of other societies seeking more material wealth, even at the cost of increased pollution. It is precisely this kind of trade-off which is apparent in developing countries today.

Furthermore, how do we establish which course of action is *more* sustainable? Recourse to the view that societies must decide for themselves is not very helpful. (Who decides? On what basis are the decisions made?) At the same time, there are problems in ignoring culturally specific definitions of what is sustainable in the interest of a more inclusive system of knowledge. There is also considerable confusion surrounding *what* is to be sustained. One of the reasons why there are so many contradictory approaches to sustainable development (although not the only reason) is that different people identify the objects of sustainability differently.

What is to be sustained?

For those whose primary interest is in ecological systems and the conservation of natural resources, it is the natural resource base which needs to be sustained. The key question usually posed is the following: how can development activities be designed which help to maintain ecological processes, such as soil fertility, the assimilation of wastes, and water and nutrient recycling? Another, related, issue is the conservation of genetic materials, both in themselves and (perhaps more importantly) as part of complex and vulnerable systems of biodiversity. The natural resource base needs to be conserved because of its intrinsic value.

There are other approaches, however. Some environmental economists argue that the natural stock of resources, or 'critical natural capital', needs to be given priority over the flows of income which depend on it (Pearce 1991). They make the point that human-made capital cannot be an effective substitute for natural capital. If our objective is the sustainable yield of renewable resources, then sustainable development implies the management of these resources in the interest of the natural capital stock. This raises a number of issues which are both political and distributive: who owns and controls genetic materials, and who manages the environment? At what point does the conservation of natural capital unnecessarily inhibit the sustainable flows of resources?

Second, according to what principles are the social institutions governing the use of resources organized? What systems of tenure dictate the ownership and management of the natural resource base? What institutions do we bequeath, together with the environment, to future generations? Far from taking us away from issues of distributive politics and political economy, a concern with sustainable development inevitably raises such issues more forcefully than ever (Redclift 1987; Redclift and Sage 1999).

The question 'What is to be sustained?' can also be answered in another way. Some writers argue that it is present (or future) levels of production (or consumption) that need to be sustained. The argument is that the growth of global population will lead to increased demands on the environment, and our definition of sustainable development should incorporate this fact. At the same time, the consumption practices of individuals will change too. Given the choice, most people in India or China might want a television or an automobile of their own, like households in the industrialized North. What prevents them from acquiring one is their poverty, their inability to consume and the relatively 'undeveloped' infrastructure of poor countries.

Is there anything inherently unsustainable in broadening the market for TV sets or cars? The different discourses of 'sustainable development' have different answers to this question. Many of those who favour the sustainable development of goods and services that we receive through the market, and businesses, would argue that we should broaden the basis of consumption. Others would argue that the production of most of these goods and services today is inherently unsustainable – that we need to 'downsize', or shift our patterns of consumption. In both developed and, increasingly, developing countries, it is frequently suggested that it is impossible to function effectively without computerized information or access to private transport.

The different ways in which 'sustainability' is approached, then, reflect quite different underlying 'social commitments', that is, the patterns of everyday behaviour that are seldom questioned. People define their 'needs' in ways which effectively exclude others from meeting theirs and, in the process, can increase the long-term risks for the sustainability of other people's livelihoods. Most importantly, however, the process through which we enlarge our choices, and reduce those of others, is largely invisible to people in their daily lives.

Unless these processes are made more visible, 'sustainable development' discourses beg the question of whether, or how, environmental costs are passed on from one group of people to another, both within societies and between them. The North dumps much of its toxic waste and 'dirty' technology on poorer countries, and sources many of its 'needs', for energy, food and minerals, from the South. At the same time, the elevated lifestyles of many rich and middle-class people in developing countries are dependent on the way in which natural resources are dedicated to meeting their needs. Finally, of course, the inequalities are also intergenerational, as well as intra-generational: we despoil the present at great cost to the future. Discounting the future (as economists call it), valuing the present above the future, is much easier to do in materially poor societies, where survival itself may be at stake for many people.

There are other forms of inheritance from the past. Economics developed, historically, around the idea of scarcity. The role of technology was principally that of raising output from scarce resources. Among other benefits of economic growth was the political legitimacy it conferred, within a dynamic economy, on those who could successfully overcome the obstacles to more spending, and wealth was usually regarded as a good thing in itself. This assumption of scarce resources and technological benefits sits uneasily with sustainability in the industrial North today, and underlines the difficulty in reconciling 'development' with 'sustainability'. It strikes at the legitimization of only one form of 'value', albeit the principal one, within capitalist, industrial societies. The German sociologist Habermas expressed his criticism of this view forcefully, in the following way:

> Can civilisation afford to surrender itself entirely to the...driving force of just one of its subsystems – namely, the pull of a dynamic...recursively closed, economic system which can only function and remain stable by taking all relevant information, translating it into, and processing it in, the language of economic value? (Habermas 1991: 33).

Human rights, democracy and sustainable development

Finally, since the various discourses of sustainable development began to flourish, it has become evident that another dimension to the problem of diminished sustainability needs to be considered. This is the extent to which, at the beginning of the twenty-first century, we need to refer to processes of democracy and governance in the context of sustainable development. The Brundtland Report took a highly normative view of both the environment and development, as did the Earth Summit deliberations in 1992. With the second Earth Summit in 2002 in mind, it may be useful to pause to consider whether we can ever achieve 'sustainable development' without increased democratization at all levels of society. Today, questions of sustainability are linked, intellectually and politically, to other issues, such as human rights and 'identity', with which they are connected. But notions of 'rights' and 'identity' are themselves changing. In the era of genetic engineering, the genetic modification of humans, as well as plants and animals, is shaping new senses of 'identity'. As individuals change, so do the groups to which they belong. In the era of globalization it is sometimes argued that 'sustainable development' may be more difficult to achieve, as economies converge towards shared economic objectives. At the same time, it may prove impossible to achieve 'sustainable development' (if it *is* achievable) without acknowledging quite distinctive accounts of human rights in nature, and even the rights *of* nature, which were previously ignored. The concept of 'sustainable development', as understood by different people, is contradictory, obscure and illuminating at the same time.

GUIDE TO FURTHER READING AND REFERENCES

Brundtland Commission (World Commission on Environment and Development) (1987) *Our Common Future*, Oxford: Oxford University Press. This report led directly to the term 'sustainable development' passing into common use. It was also the first overview of the globe which considered the environmental aspects of development from an economic, social and political perspective; cf. the UNESCO programme, Man and the Biosphere (MAB), launched almost a decade earlier. Among the principal omissions was detailed consideration of non-human species and their 'rights'. The 'Brundtland Report' (named after its chairperson, the Norwegian prime minister at the time) also opened the way for non-governmental organizations (NGOs) to be considered a serious element in environment and development issues.

Habermas, J. (1991) 'What does socialism mean today?' in R. Blackburn (ed.) *After the Fall*, London: Verso.

Meadows, D.H., Meadows, D.L., Randers, J. and Behrens, W. (1972) *The Limits to Growth*, London: Pan Books. This book was a milestone in thinking about the environment in the 1970s. It identified the main problem for development as the shortage of natural resources – these were the 'limits' to growth. This view changed in the 1970s and 1980s, largely because the price of oil rose very quickly and alternative substitutes for many natural resources were exploited in their place. In addition, of course, the 'Green Revolution' in staple cereal crops, which was largely undertaken in the 1970s and 1980s, appeared to show that the same land base could produce very much more food.

Pearce, D. (1991) *Blueprint 2: Greening the World Economy*, London: Earthscan Publications. Following on from Blueprint 1, David Pearce illustrated the applications of economic analysis to environmental problems, in a way that particularly interested policymakers.

Redclift, M.R. (1987) *Sustainable Development: Exploring the Contradictions*, London: Routledge. This was the first, and probably the best, treatment of 'sustainable development'. The case studies and ethnographic illustrations, combined with the accessible intellectual discussion, make this a 'classic'.

Redclift, M.R. and Sage, C.L. (1999) 'Resources, environmental degradation and inequality', in A. Hurrell and N. Woods (eds) *Inequality, Globalisation and World Politics*, Oxford: Oxford University Press. A good general overview of the relevance for development of inequality in resource endowments.

6.2 Climate change and development

Duncan McGregor

Introduction

That global climates are changing, due at least in part to human activity, is generally accepted by the scientific community, and the implications of this are potentially very important for the poorer of Earth's societies. Agriculture – subsistence and commercial – is still the most significant livelihood in developing areas, and will be the principal focus of this chapter.

Developing countries are located principally within the tropics and the subtropics, in areas ranging in climate from humid to arid, but predominantly hot, except at altitude. While natural vegetation in these areas is balanced with its environment, and the land has a balanced natural 'carrying capacity' (however loosely defined) of flora and fauna, interference through human activity almost invariably gives rise to problems, irrespective of any effects of changing climates. In the humid tropics, the combination of high temperatures and copious rainfall encourages high chemical weathering rates and the production of leached clay soils of low inherent fertility. Towards the drier zones, sandy soils support low biomass and are in general highly erodible. In both cases, where population or development pressures (or both) have led to the breakdown of traditional, adaptive forms of agriculture, such as shifting cultivation, deepening land degradation is a frequent consequence. It is against this background that the effects of contemporary climate change on agricultural livelihoods must be examined.

Scale and rate of contemporary climate change

The Intergovernmental Panel on Climate Change (IPCC) has recently firmed up its position on the anthropic contribution to climate change during the course of the twentieth century and into the twenty-first. It states that 'global atmospheric concentrations of carbon dioxide, methane and nitrous oxide have increased markedly as a result of human activities since 1750' (IPCC 2007: 2). Accompanying these significant changes in greenhouse gas concentrations have been a global surface-warming trend, averaging 0.13°C per decade since the mid-1950s; increases in atmospheric water vapour content since at least the 1980s; general increases in ocean temperatures in recent decades; and a rise in global average sea level, averaging 1.8 mm per year since 1961 (IPCC 2007). Precipitation changes have been highly variable temporally and spatially, but the IPCC (2007: 8) states that dessication has been observed in already dry lands such as the Sahel, the Mediterranean, southern Africa and parts of southern Asia. The Panel also notes that there is some evidence for an increase in tropical cyclone activity in the North Atlantic, consistent with rises in sea surface temperatures, though the data are equivocal.

Although these regional effects are now becoming better documented, prediction of their effects on agriculture remains a risky business! Global climate models (GCMs) still have typical discrimination levels of 100 km by 100 km, and their outputs cannot take account of significant meso-climatic and micro-climatic effects. Their effectiveness is reduced, for example, at the scale of small island states, which may occupy only a fraction of the largely sea-based GCM 'pixel', and where, for example, local topographic controls may cause significant changes in precipitation over short distances.

Climate change and environmental risk

Although it must be said that conclusive studies have yet to emerge, there is an increasing sense that we are dealing with an environment which is becoming progressively more 'risky', particularly for agriculture in the Global South. Though this must be set against a longer-term historical context, where extreme events have been reported with varying frequency in the past, the present-day ocean–atmosphere interaction appears to be one of progressive change. Among the effects cited are increased levels of El Niño/Southern Oscillation (ENSO) activity, increased hurricane activity and rising sea levels.

El Niño events in the Pacific region, where the 'normal' east-to-west ocean surface current and low-level airflow are reversed, appear to have become more frequent and stronger since the mid-1980s. As well as causing catastrophic decline in fish populations off the Peruvian coast, and unusually heavy rains inland in Peru and Ecuador, ENSO events have been associated in recent years with extreme weather events, such as drought in parts of Indonesia and Australia. Unusually heavy rains in parts of East Africa, from Mozambique to northern Kenya, and increased early season rainfall in the Caribbean, have been associated with the appearance of El Niño. Converse effects are frequently associated with the 'opposing' La Niña. Clear causal connections have not been established as yet (far less published), but the potential of using ENSO as a predictor of wetter and drought seasons has been recognized, and speculated upon.

Linked to global warming, rising sea surface temperatures have led to increased probabilities of the formation of tropical storms. A simple tabulation of recent activity in the Caribbean seems to bear this out (see Table 1). It can be seen that the average numbers of tropical storms, and of those which developed into hurricanes, was much higher in the five-year period from 2000 to 2004, than in the 50-year preceding period. This 50-year period included the relatively stormy 1930s and 1950s, but it may be further evidence of recently increasing storm activity that the 2005 season was the most active since the 1930s, with a modern record of 28 named storms, of which 15 developed into hurricane strength. It is worthy of note that the 1995 season was the previously most active

Table 1 Incidence of tropical storms and hurricanes in the Caribbean since the 1950s

	Tropical storms	Hurricanes	Intense hurricanes
Long-term average 1950–1999	9.3	5.9	2.3
2000	14	8	3
2001	15	9	4
2002	12	4	2
2003	17	8	3
2004	14	9	6
Average 2000–2004	14.4	7.6	3.6
2005	28	15	4
2006 NOAA prediction	13–16	6–8	
2006 actual	9	5	2

Source: http://www.caribwx.com/cyclone.html and http://www.srh.noaa.gov/tlh/climate/2005_
hurricaneseason_records.html (for 2005)

season since the 1930s, with 19 tropical storms recorded, 11 of which developed into hurricanes, but that this was significantly exceeded in 2005.

This table does, however, underline the uncertainty surrounding prediction. The National Oceanic and Atmospheric Administration's (NOAA) prediction for 2006 seems to have been based on a simple average of the period 2000–2004, yet the season was the quietest since the 1990s, and very close to the 1950–1999 average.

When allied to a situation where precipitation levels appear to be falling in parts of the Caribbean Basin (Walsh 1998; Taylor, Enfield and Chen 2002), a condition of increased storminess allied to generally drier conditions indicates more frequent drought conditions, and more intense land degradation through accelerated soil erosion on agricultural land at the start of the rainy season. The effects of this may be seen in the year-on-year performance of Jamaica's agricultural production in the face of severe climatic fluctuations in the period 2002–2005 (see Table 2).

Many primate cities in developing areas are situated in the coastal zone. In small islands, such as the coral islands of the Indian and Pacific Oceans, the entire land surface is within a few metres of sea level. In these conditions, peri-urban growth is frequently concentrated on reclaimed coastal lands at significant risk from rising sea levels and increasing storm surge. From current projections,

Table 2 Impact of hurricanes and drought on Jamaica's agriculture, 2002–2005

	Annual change: agricultural GDP	Annual change: domestic food production	Event	Damage to agricultural sector
2002	−8.3%	−11.3%	Heavy rainfall May/June & September	Flood damage J$1100 million
2003	+5.7%	+17.3%		
2004	−10.4%	−15.6%	Drought first half-year. Hurricanes Charley, Ivan	Charley: J$90 million Ivan: J$8500 million
2005	−7.3%	−3.4%	Drought Jan–April Hurricanes Dennis, Emily Tropical storm Wilma	Combined effects of storms: J$933 million

Source: Planning Institute of Jamaica, agricultural statistics for the years 2002–2005

sea levels may rise by between 8 and 13 cm by 2050, having already risen by around 8 cm since 1961, with about 3 cm of that occurring between 1993 and 2003 (IPCC 2007). In island groups such as the Maldives, such continuing rises in sea level, together with increasing storm surge, would inundate coastal land and tourism infrastructure, would flood valuable agricultural land, and would prejudice the limited groundwater aquifer through saline incursion. Densely populated coastal deltaic areas, such as the southern part of Bangladesh, present a particular hazard, since these are potentially at risk of flooding from both land and sea.

Principal among the human contributions to contemporary climate change are the burning of fossil fuels and deforestation by burning, both of which lead to increases in the main 'greenhouse gas', carbon dioxide. The nature and likely causes of contemporary climate change are reviewed elsewhere (see, for example, Houghton 2004; IPCC 2007), but two-way linkages between deforestation and regional-scale climate change seem increasingly likely. For example, in South America, Amazonian deforestation, estimated to have peaked at rates of around 5 million ha per annum through the 1980s (Grainger 1993: 131), appears to have led to subregional decreases in precipitation, increases in run-off, erosion and sediment delivery to rivers, and increased risk of flooding downstream.

Climate change, agricultural development and food security

Climate imposes direct constraints on agriculture, most critically in determining whether or not there is a sufficient growing season for a particular crop. Critical to this is the balance between precipitation and potential evapotranspiration, which largely defines the availability of water for plant growth. The combination of water availability and adequate temperature defines the plant growing period, as, for example, in the Food and Agriculture Organization of the United Nations' (FAO) Agro-ecological Zones project (FAO 1978). This applies to rain-fed agriculture – still the predominant form of agriculture in developing areas.

This moisture requirement for crop growth may be overridden by use of some form of irrigation, but at a risk of waterlogging, aquifer depletion and salinization. Salinization, in particular, is a major problem in arid and semi-arid lands, where net evaporative environments predominate (with potential evapotranspiration greater than precipitation for the major part of the year).

Changing rainfall patterns will lead to changing crop patterns. Short-term climatic fluctuations have occurred throughout history, and many farming societies have evolved a range of strategies to cope with this. In semi-arid lands, for example, vegetation is in a constant state of flux, responding to minor variations in local or regional climate. What may be perceived by the outsider as 'land degradation' may in fact be part of a normal, longer-term variability (Warren 1995; Sullivan 1996). Risk-spreading strategies have been evolved, including diversification of food production involving livestock, the use of varieties of seeds with a shorter growing season, a flexible, more opportunistic, approach to sowing, with the use of more drought-resistant seeds such as millet and sorghum, and grain storage.

Longer-term drought, sometimes classed as dessication, is more difficult to deal with, as has been seen in the case of the Sahel area of sub-Saharan Africa since the 1970s. Here, a number of years of above-average rainfall in the 1950s and 1960s, which encouraged intensification of agriculture and the northward displacement of nomadic pastoralism, were followed by an intense period of drought through the 1970s and into the 1980s, which led to widespread famine in the region, and the deaths of millions of animals and an estimated 50,000 to 250,000 people. The term 'desertification', originally coined in the late 1940s, has been used to describe the particular form of land degradation in arid and semi-arid lands due to human activities such as overgrazing, over-cultivation, mismanagement of irrigation systems and deforestation, exacerbated by the onset of drought conditions. The term was institutionalized by the United Nations Conference on Desertification, held in Nairobi in 1977. As Thomas and Middleton (1994) demonstrate, the institutionalized 'myth' of desertification, and the uncertainties surrounding it, can only be resolved through more sophisticated monitoring of climate and its effects on vegetation, through analysis of population trends, and through a better understanding of the social dynamics involved at the interface between climatic fluctuation, vegetational response to it, and traditional and introduced land use systems. The natural resilience of Sahelian ecosystems to short-term climatic fluctuations has been overprinted in a detrimental way by human activity.

A further issue to be confronted is the rise in atmospheric CO_2. As Slingo et al. (2005) note, recent research has downgraded the expected benefits of increasing CO_2 levels of the C3 crops (such as rice, wheat and soybean), while recent research confirms that the C4 crops (for example, maize, millet, sorghum) will either not benefit from or will be disadvantaged by increasing atmospheric CO_2. This has important implications for sub-Saharan Africa in particular.

With changing atmospheric composition and shifting climate patterns, there will inevitably be 'gainers' and 'losers'. Most at risk are those agricultural systems where already drought-marginal conditions will be exacerbated by the combination of rising temperatures and declining rainfall. The small farming sector is particularly at risk. Restricted access to land resources and financial assistance results in restriction of the potential for adaptation. There are many adaptation strategies which could be employed, and these have been implemented elsewhere (see, for example, Adger et al. 2003; Meadows and Hoffman 2003; Paavola 2004), but adaptations have to be appropriate and affordable. The difficulties in ensuring that equity and justice are appropriately applied to natural resource-dependent societies are rehearsed by Thomas and Twyman (2005). In the absence of equity and justice for the small farmer, increasing physical and economic vulnerability seems inevitable in a changing climate. Economic environments change with climate change, and though there will be 'gainers', who have the resources to seize opportunities, the livelihoods of those with least room for manoeuvre will inevitably be prejudiced.

Conclusion

Climate fluctuation and change have significant implications for food security, in terms of the sustainability of certain crops in particular climatic circumstances, the changing susceptibility of crops to pests and diseases, and the heightened susceptibility of intensely used land to degradation. At the heart of the problem in many developing areas is the uneven distribution of population and the mismatch with the availability of good-quality agricultural land (Greenland, Gregory and Nye 1998). Much of the presently cultivated land in developing areas is classed as marginal, either in climatic or pedological terms, and the pool of potentially cultivable land is unevenly distributed. Food security is therefore tenuous in many developing areas, though a change in climate may be a positive benefit to some, as well as a disbenefit to others.

It may be argued that, in the past, development has focused more on economics than on the environment. However, driving the response of the environment, the nature and scale of contemporary climatic change presents developing areas with a particular challenge. There is a critical disjuncture at present between the coarse scale of GCMs and the field or local scale of food crop information, which needs to be addressed. In many developing areas, there is a critical lack of data on basic physical processes, and on the likely effects of ongoing climate change which will impact on agriculture and living conditions. Proactive strategies are required to focus on food security in particular, and livelihoods in general. Such strategies must be underpinned by sound data on local-scale climate change and local environmental response. There will be 'gainers' as well as 'losers' in the environments of twenty-first-century developing areas, and the urgent research need is to identify both.

GUIDE TO FURTHER READING

Greenland, Gregory and Nye (1998) present a review of land and water resources in developing areas, with many useful data tables.

A most readable introduction to the causes and consequences of global warming is given by Houghton (2004).

The Intergovernmental Panel on Climate Change (IPCC) website (http://www.ipcc.ch/) is a key source of institutional activity and research on contemporary climate change.

Middleton (2003), although not focusing specifically on developing areas, covers a wide range of relevant material, and contains much useful data and follow-up reading.

For more information on climate and physical processes in the humid tropics, and for a good introduction to the problems of land management in that zone, Reading, Thompson and Millington (1995) is recommended, though certain sections require some background knowledge of physical geography.

The review paper by Slingo et al. (2005) will be useful in introducing the 16 contributions in the same volume to the debate on food crops in a changing climate. Many of the papers refer directly to developing areas.

REFERENCES

Adger, W.N., Huq, S., Brown, K., Conway, D. and Hulme, M. (2003) 'Adaptation to climate change in the developing world', *Progress in Development Studies*, 3: 179–95.

Food and Agriculture Organization of the United Nations (FAO) (1978) *Report of the Agro-ecological Zones Project: Volume 1. Methodology and Results for Africa*, World Soils Resources Report 48, Rome: FAO.

Grainger, A. (1993) *Controlling Tropical Deforestation*, London: Earthscan.

Greenland, D.J., Gregory, P.J. and Nye, P.H. (eds) (1998) *Land Resources: On the Edge of the Malthusian Precipice?* Wallingford, and London: CABI and the Royal Society.

Houghton, J. (2004) *Global Warming: The Complete Briefing*, third edition, Cambridge: Cambridge University Press.

Intergovernmental Panel on Climate Change (2007) *Climate Change 2007: The Physical Scientific Basis: Summary for Policymakers* (available at http://www.ipcc.ch/).

Meadows, M.E. and Hoffman, T.M. (2003) 'Land degradation and climate change in South Africa', *Geographical Journal*, 169: 168–77.

Middleton, N. (2003) *The Global Casino: An Introduction to Environmental Issues*, third edition, London: Edward Arnold.

Paavola, J. (2004) *Livelihoods, Vulnerability and Adaptation to Climate Change in the Morogoro Region, Tanzania*, CSERGE Working Paper EDM 04-12, Norwich: University of East Anglia.

Reading, A.J., Thompson, R.D. and Millington, A.C. (1995) *Humid Tropical Environments*, Oxford: Blackwell.

Slingo, J.M., Challinor, A.J., Hoskins, B.J. and Wheeler, T.R. (2005) 'Introduction: Food crops in a changing climate', *Philosophical Transactions of the Royal Society B*, 360: 1983–9.

Sullivan, S. (1996) 'Towards a non-equilibrium ecology: Perspectives from an arid land', *Journal of Biogeography*, 23: 1–5.

Taylor, M.A., Enfield, D.B. and Chen, A.A. (2002) 'Influence of the tropical Atlantic versus the tropical Pacific on Caribbean rainfall', *Journal of Geophysical Research*, 107 C9: 3127 (10-1 to 10-14).

Thomas, D.S.G. and Middleton, N.J. (1994) *Desertification: Exploding the Myth*, Chichester: Wiley.

Thomas, D.S.G. and Twyman, C. (2005) 'Equity and justice in climate change adaptation amongst natural-resource-dependent societies', *Global Environmental Change*, 15: 115–24.

Walsh, R.P.D. (1998) 'Climatic changes in the Eastern Caribbean over the past 150 years and some implications in planning sustainable development', in D.F.M. McGregor, D. Barker and S. Lloyd-Evans (eds) *Resource Sustainability and Caribbean Development*, Kingston, Jamaica: The Press, University of the West Indies, 24–48.

Warren, A. (1995) 'Changing understandings of African pastoralism and nature of environmental paradigms', *Transactions of the Institute of British Geographers*, NS20: 193–203.

6.3 The Rio Earth Summit

Mark Pelling

Introduction

The United Nations Conference on Environment and Development (UNCED), was held in 1992 in Rio de Janeiro, from which its more popular title, 'the Rio Earth Summit', was derived. The conference's aim was to formulate a number of voluntary frameworks and legally binding conventions for nation states to catalyse more sustainable global development. Most commentators agree that UNCED fell far short of this goal. The individual interests of national governments and business lobbies dominated negotiations, with the result that UNCED's prescription for confronting worldwide poverty and environmental degradation was based on the very policies that caused these problems in the first place (Thomas 1993). This chapter reviews the process of decision making as well as the outputs from Rio, and critically assesses their contribution to sustainable development discourse and policy.

The run-up to Rio

In 1989, the Canadian diplomat Maurice Strong was appointed Secretary General of UNCED, and over the following months, four preparatory committees, or PrepComms, were convened, by which the agenda for UNCED was set. At this stage it became clear that two very different approaches to sustainable development were being promoted. The Northern, industrialized nations held that environmental degradation was only a short-term problem, which could be tackled through the application of technological solutions (an approach called ecological modernization). In opposition to this, countries of the South argued that technological solutions could deal only with the symptoms and not the causes of the crisis; the real target for action should be the international economy, debt, structural adjustment programmes and the role of transnational companies (TNCs) (Connelly and Smith 1999).

UNCED

Delegations from 176 nations participated in the main conference, with over 30,000 NGOs taking part in the Global Forum. At the end of the conference, five agreements had been signed:

- the Rio Declaration
- the Biodiversity Convention
- the Framework Convention on Climate Change
- the Agreement of Forest Principles
- Agenda 21.

The Biodiversity Convention and the Framework Convention on Climate Change were both signed at Rio, although they had been negotiated beforehand outside the PrepComms system. Steps were also taken towards a Convention on Desertification.

The Rio Declaration

This is a statement of principles for sustainable development which framed the entire conference. It is a much watered-down version of an originally proposed 'Earth Charter'; the product of a compromise between Maurice Strong, who envisioned it as a pro-environment document, and the developmental priorities of the G77 (Group of 77, then representing 128 nations from the South). The influence of dominant neoliberal developmental philosophy underlies the declaration, which advances industrialization as the preferred path to development and nation states as the principal actors. Green and alternative development agendas are conspicuous by their absence. The Declaration has no binding authority, but presents 27 principles to guide national and international environmental behaviour in which the interdependence of the environment and development are recognized. In perhaps the most important statement of principle, the North acknowledges its special responsibility for the contemporary environmental crisis.

The Biodiversity Convention

This convention was conceived initially as a response to concerns for the ecological integrity of tropical rainforests, as voiced by Northern conservationist NGOs. In the latter stage of negotiations, the wider issue of biotechnology was introduced by G77, who feared the loss of rights over forest resources. The issue of biotechnology became contentious, with the USA finally refusing to sign, under pressure from the business lobby, which wanted open access to the genetic resources of tropical forests. Despite this setback, 156 countries did sign the Biodiversity Convention. Part of the reason for the Convention's success (and for its subsequent critique) was its simultaneous provision for the environmental and business concerns of governments from the North and South. However, in the process of negotiation, biodiversity was transformed into biotechnology, with no ownership rights for 'source' countries or communities. Moreover, the issue of ecological degradation through forest destruction – the original basis for the convention – was sidelined by the negotiation of biotechnology rights.

The Framework on Climate Change

The origins of this non-binding framework convention lie in the Intergovernmental Panel on Climate Change (IPCC) which stated in 1990 that growing rates of greenhouse gas emissions, principally from industry and transport, were linked to global climate change and sea-level rise, with consequences for 'natural' and human systems worldwide. Carbon dioxide was identified as a key agent in anthropocentric global warming, and the IPCC recommended that global emissions be cut by at least 60 per cent (as below). The industrialized nations of the North were the prime culprits in the production of carbon dioxide – the USA alone accounted for 23 per cent of global emissions (IPCC 1990). Negotiations in the run-up to Rio were blighted by the mutually incompatible positions of the industrialized and oil-producing states on the one hand, and the developing nations on the other (Elliott 1994).

During UNCED, talks were brought to a deadlock by the USA, which refused to set a target for stabilizing carbon dioxide emissions. The refusal to restrict emissions was first argued on the premise that the US economy would be hard hit by such a reduction, but later it became apparent that the USA believed that it could mitigate or adapt to the possible consequences of climate change and that this would give the country a strategic international advantage (Chatterjee and Finger 1994). Without the USA, any formal convention on climate change would be meaningless, and eventually the programme was scaled down to a framework convention without any legal commitments for industrialized countries to stabilize their carbon dioxide emissions. Debates about climate change go to the heart of the environment/development dilemma. There is a clear link between the products of fossil fuel-based industrialization and environmental change and risk to future development options. The framework convention offers in response a preference for facing the uncertainties of human and ecological adaptation to climate change, rather than stimulating any more fundamental movement away from fossil fuel-based industrial production as an engine for economic growth.

The Agreement on Forest Principles

This is a non-binding statement of principles for the management, conservation and sustainable development of forests. It is all that remains of a potential convention on forests. Conflict between the North and South (especially Malaysia and Indonesia, both major logging nations) was, again, the reason for this failure. Southern states claimed that moves by the North to promote the preservation of tropical forests threatened national sovereignty by removing the right to exploit their own forest resources. Most Northern nations had already benefited from the exploitation of their forests and it seemed unfair that these same Northern states should put pressure on the South, which would limit opportunities for macroeconomic development. The Agreement on Forest Principles is perhaps the greatest lost opportunity to come out of the Rio Earth Summit. No limits were placed on deforestation, and there was no regard for the need to preserve the biodiversity of forests (which, in any case, had been transformed into industrial resources of biotechnology in the Convention on Biodiversity).

Agenda 21

The most far-reaching and influential outcome of the Rio Earth Summit has been Agenda 21 – a guide towards a more sustainable future in the twenty-first century. The document is a non-binding framework for action. It was signed by all 176 nations participating in UNCED and incorporates the results of lobbying from NGOs and business interests. Given the breadth of participation, it is not surprising that the need to reach a consensus has led to contradictions within the text. Critical areas of contention were population control (opposed by the Vatican), reduction in fossil fuel use (opposed by the oil-producing states) and the renegotiation and cancellation of debt. The final document has 40 chapters, all dealing with substantive issues concerned with different sectors of, and actors involved in, development and the environment. The review here tackles the document by looking at its six main themes, as discerned by Chatterjee and Finger (1994): quality of life on Earth, efficient use of the Earth's natural resources, sustainable economic growth, protection of our global commons, management of human settlements, and chemicals and the management of waste.

The opening chapters of Agenda 21 contain a number of grand objectives that frame the goals of the subsequent chapters. These objectives, which outline a vision for quality of life on Earth, have long been at the heart of UN policy and include: the eradication of poverty, full employment, promoting good health and controlling population growth. The second theme for Agenda 21 is to promote the efficient use of the Earth's natural resources through the extension of economic valuation and decision-making frameworks. There are a number of philosophical problems with such an approach – such as whether it is appropriate or possible to put financial values on natural assets – which are not tackled. The emphasis on maintaining economic growth, which runs throughout the Earth Summit documents, is reiterated in the third theme on sustainable economic growth. The environmental crisis is seen as a problem to which ongoing economic activities must adapt, with no suggestion of a more radical departure.

The fourth theme, on oceans and the atmosphere, deals with common ownership of resources. There is a preference for exploitation over conservation or preservation, with a number of recommendations for regulation through international agreements. The theme of human settlements is dealt with in several chapters that seek to promote energy and resource efficiency. Given the deterioration of the urban environment, particularly in the world's mega-cities, it is unfortunate that UNCED did not put greater emphasis on critical brown agenda issues, such as polluted air, filthy water and inadequate sanitation, that affect a growing proportion of the world's population. The dangers and costs of waste, and the management of hazardous chemicals, are examined in the final thematic group of chapters, but there is no mention of the benefits of recycling, of reducing the production of waste or of the need to improve waste disposal techniques.

Unsaid at UNCED: A concluding assessment of the Earth Summit

Many argue that a great deal was left unsaid at Rio. The limits to the Rio agenda were constrained from the outset by its ecological modernist perspective, which placed emphasis on the need for continued economic growth, coupled with environmental regulation, rather than altering the basic relationship between development and the environment, as many NGOs lobbied for. There were no binding agreements on debt, structural adjustment programmes, population control, North–South technological and financial transfer, the role of TNCs and global militarism (Connelly and Smith 1999). This reflects the strong influence of international industrial and business interests (and the Vatican), which were effective in lobbying at the national levels during the PrepComms and within the UNCED process. The intransigence of the USA was a serious limiting factor; the USA was 'prepared to veto any initiative that could be viewed as redistributing economic power at the global level, that would create new institutions, or that would require additional budgetary resources, technology transfers, or changes in domestic US policies' (Porter and Brown 1996: 117–18). These problems raise two general issues of deeper concern for sustainable development: first, the tension between national sovereignty and international obligations; second, the erosion of government accountability to the electorate, and its replacement with interest politics – most clearly shown in the funding of presidential candidates in the USA.

Some positive movement was achieved. Public awareness of environmental issues was raised. The need to renew democracy through an increased stress on participation ran throughout the conference, and especially in Agenda 21. Governments and NGOs were forced to find ways to talk to each other, and a great many relationships were forged which have strengthened the network of contacts and alliances that have contributed to ongoing debates on sustainable development. Finally, two conventions were signed, and Agenda 21, with all its flaws, emerged as an important catalyst for further action towards a sustainable future (Grubb 1993).

The legacy of Rio has been no less contentious than the original conference. Meetings in New York in 1997 (Rio + 5) and Johannesburg in 2002 (Rio + 10) have continued to look for ways of reconciling economic development with environmental and social responsibility. While the UNCED process has failed to arrive at binding international targets for moving towards a more sustainable development path, it has simultaneously increased the role played by powerful business actors through the promotion of public-private partnerships in environmental management and, in particular, water management. The consequences of this private-sector incursion have yet to be seen, but critics are wary of negative social consequences that may come from a transfer of power from public to private sectors.

GUIDE TO FURTHER READING

For a concise and balanced critique of the UNCED process and its outputs, see International Institute for the Environment and Development (1994) *Earth Summit '92*, Wickford: Regency Press.

A spirited critique of Rio, from two environmentalists who witnessed the conference first-hand, is provided by Chatterjee, P. and Finger, M. (1994) *The Earth Brokers: Power, Politics and World Development*, London: Routledge.

For a view which contextualizes the Rio Earth Summit in the international political-economy of the time, see Thomas, C. (ed.) (1994) *Rio: Unravelling the Consequences*, Newbury: Frank Cass.

REFERENCES

Chatterjee, P. and Finger, M. (1994) *The Earth Brokers: Power, Politics and World Development*, London: Routledge.

Connelly, J. and Smith, G. (1999) *Politics and the Environment: From Theory to Practice*, London: Routledge.

Elliott, J.A. (2005) *An Introduction to Sustainable Development*, second edition, London: Routledge.
Grubb, M. (1993) *The 'Earth Summit' Agreements: A Guide and Assessment*, London: Earthscan Publications.
IPCC (Intergovernmental Panel on Climate Change) (1990) *The IPCC Scientific Assessment*, Cambridge: Cambridge University Press.
Middleton, N. and O'Keefe, P. (2003) *Rio Plus Ten: Politics, Poverty and the Environment*, London: Pluto Press.
Porter, G. and Brown, J. (1996) *Global Environmental Politics*, Boulder, CO: Westview Press.
Thomas, C. (1993) 'Beyond UNCED: An introduction', *Environmental Politics*, 2(4): 1–27.

6.4 International regulation and the environment

Giles Atkinson

Introduction

In late 2006, a comprehensive report on the economics of climate change concluded that, in terms of policy proposals to stabilize the stock of greenhouse gases (GHGs), such as carbon dioxide, in the global atmosphere: 'the benefits of strong and early action far outweigh the economic costs of not acting' (Stern et al. 2006: xiii). The most recent assessment of Working Group I of the Intergovernmental Panel on Climate Change (IPCC 2007) has continued to build on the scientific foundations that underpin current concerns about climate change. Nevertheless, while tentative steps have been taken, a robust political response in the face of this evidence base has been slow to evolve. This is only partly due to lingering uncertainties about the climate change problem and its likely future impacts. A more telling consideration is that a truly global problem is likely to require a global solution. This, in turn, necessitates genuine cooperation between numerous sovereign nations each with competing political and economic interests that might militate against the fulfilment of bold objectives. Yet where cooperation has been brokered, the formal 'glue' that holds it together is typically some form of international environmental agreement. This chapter provides a brief overview of some of the main issues that have characterized ongoing efforts to construct international responses, in particular, to global environmental problems.

International environmental problems

International environmental agreements (IEAs) – defined as a legal document between states to manage a natural or environmental resource (see Mitchell 2003 for a discussion of definitional issues) – are the outcomes of typically lengthy negotiation processes, and any single IEA may itself be one treaty within a framework of such agreements that characterize an 'environmental regime'. (The stages of an IEA are numerous (for a discussion see Barrett 2003). Initially, processes of agenda setting will evolve a negotiating text and subsequent deliberation. The end result is a final treaty which countries sign up to (or not). Nestling between a country becoming a signatory to and implementing an agreement is ratification by the country's national parliament. When there is significant disagreement within a country about the merits of what has been negotiated, ratification may not be a simple rubber-stamping of the earlier decision to sign (Froyn 2007).) For example, the Framework Convention on Climate Change (FCCC 1992) initially set out the broad aspiration: '(t)o achieve...stabilisation of greenhouse gas concentrations in the atmosphere at a level that would prevent dangerous anthropogenic interference with the climate system' (United Nations

1992: 4). However, it was the 1997 Kyoto Protocol (KP) that set out the first legally binding targets for GHGs across certain countries. Attention is now turning to what will succeed the KP, given its modest initial aims and even more modest outcomes, given the US withdrawal in 2001. However, international agreements now exist across a whole range of environmental issues, including transboundary air pollution, shared freshwater resources, trade in both hazardous substances and endangered species and the management of the international seas.

An increasing number of these problems, such as climate change, stratospheric ozone depletion, pollution of the oceans and biodiversity loss, can be viewed as global problems in terms of the sheer number of countries that can be affected, albeit to differing degrees (Pearce 1999). Many of these problems arise because the natural and environmental resources that are being depleted or degraded have no owner, that is, they are 'open access'. As such, they are prone to overuse. For example, the global atmosphere acts as a sink for many of the by-products of economic activity, including carbon dioxide (CO_2) and other GHGs. The fact of no ownership means that no one has an incentive to limit their contribution to the increasing stock of GHGs in the global atmosphere. An increasing mean global temperature, and associated adverse socio-economic impacts, is one consequence of this (for a discussion see Helm 2005). Other global resources have an owner in that they are located within a sovereign country. The world's tropical forests, which act as a significant store of biological diversity, would be one such example. The problem here is that the owner has little incentive to continue to provide these services when the value of alternative uses of the land, on which there is currently standing forest, 'out-competes' the conservation option (at least from the owner's standpoint).

In each of these cases, the incentives that countries face result in too little provision of globally valued resources. Changing these incentives is the foremost challenge facing the international community in seeking a collective response to shared environmental problems (Barrett 2003). Moreover, it is not enough that an agreement simply confers an overall 'global' gain; each state needs to perceive that it is better off being part of the agreement than remaining outside of it. The last notion has particular significance given that there is no 'global government' which can impose environmental objectives, no matter how worthy, on states. Matters are complicated further by the need to deter free-riders. This arises because in many cases those outside an agreement typically cannot be excluded from enjoying the benefits of the ocean, climate or stratospheric ozone protection efforts of those states contributing to an agreement.

Not surprisingly, significant attention has been devoted to questions about the enforcement of IEAs, both in terms of encouraging participation (i.e. being a party to an agreement) and compliance (i.e. fulfilling the obligations that one is party to). Enforcement methods might refer to rewards ('carrots') for becoming a party to or complying with an IEA, or punishments ('sticks') for 'antisocial' behaviour. Most famously of all, perhaps, the 1987 Montreal Protocol (MP) has within it the potential ban on trade in products which contain prohibited stratospheric ozone-depleting chemicals. Whether analogous provisions are needed or could be rolled out across new international environmental challenges is much debated. One anxiety is that IEAs, which make use of such mechanisms, may fall foul of international trade regime rules (Esty 2001) although this may well be clarified in due course given that this issue is now part of ongoing deliberations within the World Trade Organization (WTO). Yet if the credible threat of punishment such as trade restrictions exists, then there is a case, in principle, for it being available to negotiators. In practice, this depends on the ability to shape a consensus that any punishment is 'just' or (less grandly) politically acceptable, and this, in turn, may well depend on its being used in judicious combination with rewards, such as financial and technological inducements (Barrett 2003).

A related puzzle, however, is that there are numerous examples of IEAs which appear to operate with no tangible provisions for enforcing the obligations placed on countries. This has been interpreted by some as evidence that a change in country behaviour (given that there was an environmental problem in the first instance), and so meaningful cooperation, can be triggered without countries having to sign up to coercive provisions (see for example Young 1994; Chayes and Chayes 1995). This emphasis on meaningful cooperation is important; in reality, many IEAs obligate countries to do little more than they would have done in the absence of the agreement. In such cases, enforcement is largely superfluous. This is articulated by Barrett (2003: xii) in his assertion that 'most treaties...fail to alter state behaviour appreciably'. Which view is more correct is essentially a complex empirical question about the effectiveness of IEAs, not just in 'resolving' or 'significantly reducing' an international environmental problem, but also in achieving these ends relative to what would have happened without an agreement (for a review of evidence on IEA effectiveness see Mitchell 2003).

One mechanism whereby treaties might end up being watered down is when unanimity is central to the agreement. Froyn (2007), for example, notes the fact that the KP which was finally agreed in 2005 was a far softer version of what had been negotiated in 1997, primarily due to those countries favouring this lighter touch being able to 'exploit' the US withdrawal and the treaty's minimum country participation rule (i.e. if these remaining sceptical countries did not ratify, the KP would not enter into force). This 'law of the least ambitious programme' (Underdal 1980) has been observed in other environmental regimes as well. More broadly still, climate negotiations involve discussions between many nations on different stages along development paths. In this context, negotiations must reconcile debates about, among other things, responsibility for climate change and the economic wealth built on that environmental liability (see, for example, IPCC 1995), and considerations about what is within the art of the politically possible.

Financing international cooperation

The implementation of IEAs typically involves the introduction of domestic policies within participating countries. Increasingly, however, there is an international dimension to implementation, possibly involving substantial financial flows by creating markets in environmental services. The pre-eminent example of this – *carbon trading* – is concerned with cost-effectiveness in meeting climate change goals. The impetus for carbon trading is the KP. Under the KP, a number of countries (which include the Organization for Economic Cooperation and Development (OECD) countries and the 'economies in transition') have GHG targets defined with reference to 1990 levels of emissions. A feature of these targets is that, where this necessitates a reduction in a country's GHG emissions, these cuts do not necessarily all have to be achieved domestically. That is, a country, or more aptly an enterprise in that country, can purchase GHG reductions which have been achieved elsewhere in the world. The incentive for the buyer to make this trade occurs when mitigation carried out elsewhere is cheaper than that achieved domestically. Similarly, a seller will be willing to trade if it is adequately compensated. Most of these trades are currently being made via the European Union Emissions Trading Scheme (EUETS) and the Clean Development Mechanism (CDM) (Hepburn 2007). Interestingly, the CDM gives those countries with targets the opportunity to purchase certified emissions reductions in developing countries, subject to those countries satisfying a number of conditions such as contributing to 'sustainable development' in the latter.

In principle, carbon trading makes (reduction of) GHGs akin to any other internationally traded good. Yet clearly this is a novel exchange and challenges abound. Some of these are philosophical in flavour and reflect debates about whether buyers are 'buying' their way out of their domestic responsibilities and whether sellers, in turn, are getting a fair deal (Wiener 1999). Those discussions, however, are not entirely unrelated to equally important technical issues about monitoring and verification of how much *additional* GHGs are saved as a result of a trade (for a review see Tietenberg 2005). Hepburn (2007) notes that such concerns have served to circumscribe the type of GHG that can be traded, as well as the type of carbon-saving project that can be financed. All this and other factors have limited the extent of the market. Of course, carbon trading is very much a work in progress, and the relevant question is how these (and other evolving) challenges can be met in the future. The principle remains that in allowing options to reach GHG reduction targets in less costly ways, it is hoped that countries will be enticed into accepting meaningful targets. As such, carbon trading will almost certainly be a centrepiece of any future (post-KP) climate agreement.

Carbon trading involves a polluter paying for GHG reduction elsewhere. For other problems, however, it might be the 'polluter' who has a property right underpinning their current behaviour, perhaps because a threatened biological resource of international importance is sovereign property. For example, the 1992 Convention on Biodiversity (CBD) commits parties to the conservation and sustainable use of biological resources, but designates protection as an issue of national sovereignty to be determined within national boundaries. To the extent that others, elsewhere in the world, place a value on biodiversity conservation, and so would suffer if biological resources continued to be depleted, it is in the interests of the 'sufferer' (or beneficiary of conservation) to pay the polluter to change its behaviour. In Costa Rica, landowners are paid by the government for reforestation, forest protection and agroforestry under fixed-term contracts. Much of the finance for these payments has come from domestic sources. However, some resources have been transferred from other countries, for example, through the involvement of organizations such as the Global Environmental Facility (GEF) (for a detailed discussion of related schemes see Pearce 2004). By attracting money payments in excess of the cash flows associated with an alternative use, an opportunity arises for conservation to 'pay its way' and so be on a sustainable financial footing. Even so, Pearce (2004) notes that there are reasons to be cautious about this prospect, given that the flow of funds associated with these 'global bargains' are currently modest and it is still too early to make confident claims about their general effectiveness. This has not stopped ambitious proposals (e.g. UNEP 2005) for such schemes to generate funds for conservation objectives and to play a complementary role in poverty alleviation (although overshadowing much of that discussion is the fear that funding, in some cases, might simply be mirrored by cuts in existing aid flows).

Concluding remarks

A glance at the number of existing agreements across an array of international environmental issues might lend substantial encouragement about the prospects of facing new challenges in this way. Unfortunately, this is not the end of the story. Not all past agreements have been effective in changing countries' behaviour, despite giving every impression of having achieved that end. This is not to say that meaningful environmental agreement is not possible, rather that it cannot be assumed. Much of the international community's problem is one of balancing distributive considerations, for example, in terms of dividing the gains from cooperation among parties. And while the creation of environmental markets, through carbon trading for example, has emerged as an important bridge between competing interests, this does not deflect from deeper arguments about the distribution of the burdens of taking action to mitigate problems such as climate change.

GUIDE TO FURTHER READING AND REFERENCES

Barrett, S. (2003) *Environment and Statecraft*, Oxford: Oxford University Press.

Chayes, A. and Chayes, A. (1995) *The New Sovereignty*, Cambridge, MA: Harvard University Press.

Esty, D. (2001) 'Bridging the trade–environment divide', *Journal of Economic Perspectives*, 15(3): 113–30.

Froyn, C.B. (2007) 'International environmental cooperation: The role of political feasibility', in G. Atkinson, S. Dietz and E. Neumayer (eds) *Handbook of Sustainable Development*, Cheltenham: Edward Elgar.

Helm, D. (ed.) (2005) *Climate-Change Policy*, Oxford: Oxford University Press.

Hepburn, C. (2007) 'Carbon trading: A review of the Kyoto mechanisms', *Annual Review of Energy and Environment*, forthcoming.

IPCC (Intergovernmental Panel on Climate Change) (2007) *Climate Change 2007: The Physical Science Basis – Summary for Policymakers*, Geneva: IPCC.

IPCC (Intergovernmental Panel on Climate Change) (1995) *Climate Change 1995: Economic and Social Dimensions of Climate Change*, Cambridge: Cambridge University Press.

Mitchell, R.B. (2003) 'International environmental agreements: A survey of their features, formation and effects', *Annual Review of Energy and Environment*, 28: 429–61.

Pearce, D.W. (1999) 'Economic analysis of global environmental issues', in C.J.M. ven den Bergh (ed.) *Handbook of Environmental and Resource Economics*, Cheltenham: Edward Elgar.

Pearce, D.W. (2004) 'Market creation: Saviour or oversell?', *Portuguese Economic Journal*, Special Issue on Applied Environmental Economics.

Stern, N. et al. (2006) *Stern Review: The Economics of Climate Change*, Cambridge: Cambridge University Press.

Tietenberg, T. (2005) 'The tradable permits approach to protecting the commons: lessons for climate change', in D. Helm (ed.) *Climate-Change Policy*, Oxford: Oxford University Press.

Underdal, A. (1980) *The Politics of International Fisheries Management: The Case of the North-East Atlantic*, Olso: Scandinavian University Press.

UNEP (United Nations Environmental Programme) (2005) 'Creating pro-poor markets for ecosystem services', high-level brainstorming workshop, London School of Economics and Political Science, October 2005.

United Nations (1992) *United Nations Framework Convention on Climate Change*, New York: United Nations.

Wiener, J.B. (1999) 'Global trade in greenhouse gas control: Market merits and critics' concerns', in W. Oates (ed.) *The RFF Reader in Environmental and Resource Management*, Washington, DC: Resources for the Future Press.

Young, O.R. (1994) *International Governance: Protecting the Environment in a Stateless Society*, Ithaca, NY, and London: Cornell University Press.

6.5 The brown environmental agenda

Tim Forsyth

The 'brown' environmental agenda refers to environmental problems associated with urban and industrial areas, such as pollution, waste disposal, and the provision of safe housing and drinking water. The term is used in contrast to the 'green' environmental agenda, which describes environmental problems associated with vegetation and wildlife, such as biodiversity conservation or deforestation.

Brown environmental problems are becoming more important. According to United Nations statistics, in 1900, only 13 per cent of people lived in cities, yet by 2005 the proportion had risen to 49 per cent. Ninety per cent of global population growth occurs in cities. By 2030, the urban population will be 4.9 billion, of which 84 per cent will live in developing countries. By 1950, there were just two mega-cities, with 10 million or more inhabitants. By 2005, there were 20 mega-cities, and by 2015 there are projected to be 22, of which 17 will be in developing countries. Cities such as Lagos, Mexico City, Shanghai and Cairo are set to contain tens of millions of people by 2010. Moreover, many developing countries are undergoing rapid industrialization, bringing brown environmental problems to their cities and the populations living there (Bigio and Dahiya 2004).

These changes impact on the environment in a number of ways, at both the local and global scales. Again, according to the United Nations, about 1.2 billion people still have no access to safe drinking water, and 2.4 billion do not have adequate sanitation services. Some 2 million children die every year from water-related diseases. Local authorities often lack the infrastructure, training or funding to collect all urban and industrial waste created under rapid urbanization, leading to inadequate and dangerous dumping. Indeed, the World Bank has estimated that some 30–60 per cent of urban solid waste in developing countries is uncollected, and less than 50 per cent of the population has regular waste collection services. As a result, solid waste is simply taken to unsanitary waste dumps around settlements, or pumped untreated into lakes, rivers and coastal areas. Increasingly, the environmental impacts of urbanization and industrialization are now considered part of global concerns about anthropogenic climate change – although the brown environmental agenda is usually considered in terms of how it affects poor people locally, rather than the impact of pollution on the global environment.

Despite their importance, many analysts have claimed that insufficient attention has been paid to brown environmental problems as they are experienced within developing countries (Middleton and O'Keefe 2003). In part, this may be because of their relative newness and the difficulties of addressing problems when urbanization and industrialization are proceeding so quickly. But some critics have also claimed that most environmentalism has emerged contemporaneously with a middle-class urban elite, who have focused mainly on green concerns, such as threats to wilderness and wildlife (Nash 1982). Moreover, members of the middle classes may own factories, and therefore are likely to resist environmental regulations that might affect risk profits. The people most affected by brown environmental problems tend to be among the poorest inhabitants of developing countries, such as shanty-town dwellers or migrant workers, and therefore have little direct influence on the direction of environmental policy.

The role of politics is also important in explaining how brown environmental problems vary over time. For a number of years, some economists have argued that environmental pollution in developing countries may follow the so-called environmental Kuznets curve (based on the work of the economist Paul Kuznets), which proposed that pollution would first increase, and then gradually fall, as a country develops. The economic argument for this rise and fall in pollution was that pollution would be produced by rapid industrialization, but then greater wealth would allow investment in cleaner technologies, or enable governments to implement regulatory policies to reduce pollution (Stern 2004).

Against this, however, many political analysts have proposed that the environmental Kuznets curve has never been confirmed by empirical measurements, and, instead, that it is political factors which explain changes in pollution levels. For example, the decline in pollution may not result simply from increased wealth, but also from the rise of environmental social movements or NGOs that pressurize governments into taking action. Another possibility is that the spatial scale of assessing pollution may change. Investors or governments choose to relocate polluting industries to more remote locations, where governments or local people have less power to object. For example, this is claimed to have occurred when Japan relocated some of its shipbuilding and other industry to South Korea, or when polluting industries are moved to regions *around* cities, rather than *within* cities. Some have also alleged that this may happen with the relocation or trade in hazardous waste between developed and developing countries. In 1987, for example, two Italian firms sent almost 4000 tonnes of toxic waste, contaminated with polychlorinated biphenyl (PCB), to Koko, Nigeria, under the label of substances 'relating to the building trade', where they were stored in a farmer's backyard for a small fee. The waste eventually leaked, causing injury to local inhabitants and clean-up workers (Krueger 1999). More recently, developing countries have also become recipients of electronic waste (or e-waste), such as old computers from developed countries, which have a variety of metals and hazardous materials.

Pollution, and the identification of pollution, may also change over time. Commonly, theorists have argued that environmental problems in cities may pass through two main stages (Satterthwaite 2001). During the early stages of city growth, hazards include pathogens from human waste or bacteria- and insect-borne infections, such as dysentery and cholera, caused by poor sanitation, overcrowding and inadequate water management. But after the growth of manufacturing industry and the rise of car transport within cities, a second stage begins, characterized by hazards resulting from industrialization and technological advancement. This stage includes risks such as traffic fumes, heavy metal poisoning (such as from lead and cadmium) or threats inside factories, such as solvent poisoning (solvents are highly toxic fluids used for cleaning, and if inhaled in sufficient quantity can kill within seconds). In South East Asia, for example, Bangkok, Jakarta and Manila started this transition during the 1960s, when these countries began to industrialize. In Vietnam and China, these risks have been emerging since the 1990s.

But while these assessments of pollution refer to the physical presence of hazards, their impact also depends on the vulnerability of different people to them. For example, one of the most shocking causes of deaths among young children in developing nations is something that is not considered a major threat in developed countries: scalding from hot water. Scalding frequently occurs in shanty towns where few people have access to emergency health care, or where safety standards of cooking equipment are poorly regulated (McGranahan et al. 2001). Sometimes women are more at risk then men. In east Asia, for example, many electronics factories tend to employ more women than men, which means these workers may be more likely to experience solvent or lead poisoning (which are frequent hazards in the manufacture of electronics). Another, often unrecorded, cause of death is indoor air pollution resulting from dirty fuel sources, such as animal dung and charcoal. This often impacts on those who may spend more time indoors, such as older people. Moreover, indoor air pollution is difficult to monitor and is often overlooked by environmental legislation. Implementing safeguards is also challenging because it requires communicating with millions of people at the household level (Mitlin and Satterthwaite 2004).

In response to problems, international efforts to address the brown agenda are gradually increasing. In terms of toxic chemicals and waste, the Basel Convention of 1989 provided the first international restrictions on the transport of toxic waste. In 2001, the Convention on Persistent Organic Pollutants (POPs) placed restrictions on the manufacture and use of various toxic chemicals with serious health impacts, such as pesticides and industrial by-products. The Convention specifically aims for the halting of production of 12 chemicals known as the 'dirty dozen', including insecticides like DDT and chlordane, as well as PCBs, dioxins and furans.

In terms of urban development and housing, the United Nations created a Sustainable Cities programme in 1990, and urban environmental problems featured strongly in the United Nations Second Conference on Human Settlements (Habitat II) in 1996 and World Urban Forum (Habitat III) in 2006. The Sustainable Cities programme aims to develop more inclusive decision-making in cities, and to implement Agenda 21 at the local level (Agenda 21 is the list of guidelines for environmental management agreed at the Rio Earth Summit) (UN-Habitat 2006). The World Summit on Sustainable Development (the Rio + 10 meeting) at Johannesburg in 2002 also agreed that governments should work to halve the proportion of people without access to basic sanitation by 2015, and to use and produce chemicals that do not lead to significant adverse effects on human health and the environment by 2020. Critics, however, suggested that this meeting did not go far enough. For example, no hard targets were agreed for advancing renewable energy as a replacement for more polluting forms of energy, or for defining the crucial role of transport in cities (Marcotullio and Lee 2003).

These initiatives, however, are all state-led policies or programmes led by international organizations. In addition, some analysts are also optimistic that private investment, or economic globalization, will address brown environmental problems. Private investment may be able to provide cleaner technologies or environmental services and infrastructure, which are implemented more quickly and at higher standards than is possible under state-led activity alone. Some analysts have called this process 'leapfrogging' – the ability of rapidly industrializing countries to grow economically without undergoing the sudden rise in pollution associated with the environmental Kuznets curve.

Proponents of this view have claimed that international private investment can increase the supply of new technologies to developing countries, citing such examples as photovoltaics (technology that converts solar radiation into electricity) and highly advanced industrial waste treatment plants. Private investment may also implement large-scale technologies, such as integrated gasification combined cycles (IGCC), which are forms of power generation that can reduce emissions from dirty fuels such as coal, and hence can contribute to local air quality as well as global climate change policy.

Less optimistically, critics claim that private companies cannot achieve long-term technological upgrading of all facilities in developing countries, and that there will always be a role for the state in providing incentives or regulations that can harness private investment for technology transfer. For example, the Clean Development Mechanism of the Kyoto Protocol offers companies financial incentives for investing in climate-friendly activities in developing countries if they also contribute to local 'sustainable development'. But critics claim that there are insufficient incentives for this kind of investment to assist locally defined development objectives as well as the mitigation of greenhouse gases. For example, many companies have sought to win financial support under the Kyoto Protocol for flaring methane gas from landfills (methane has a global warming potential 23 times the value of carbon dioxide, so flaring may mitigate climate change by effectively converting methane to carbon dioxide). Against this, critics suggest that flaring methane misses the opportunity to use the gas for additional local benefits, such as heating or electricity generation. Under the Kyoto Protocol, however, there are no obvious incentives for investing in this way (Zetter and Watson 2006).

Privatization of environmental services may also provide unexpected impacts on poorer people in cities by reorganizing the ownership of environmental goods and services. For example, in Chennai (Madras), India, during the 1990s, a local NGO, Exnora, trained many Indians of low caste or from poor backgrounds to become 'street beautifiers'. These people earned a living and provided valuable environmental services by collecting the waste from middle-class streets in Chennai, and then either recycling metals, paper and plastic, or disposing of the remaining waste in clean ways. When the Chennai local government contracted an international investor to undertake waste disposal, many of these street beautifiers lost their livelihoods. Furthermore, critics claimed that waste disposal deteriorated (Anand 1999). Privatizing environmental service provision, or introducing new technologies, may therefore have various social impacts.

The brown environmental agenda, then, is not simply a matter of pollution or technological solutions. It also includes social and political factors underlying how different social groups are vulnerable to risks, and how they may be affected by proposed solutions. This is increasingly important, as much environmental policy to address pollution from industry or cities is now also addressed by global climate change policy rather than localized development agendas. Addressing the brown environmental agenda requires both states and investors to focus on how environmental risks are experienced by people who are less influential, and relatively underrepresented in policy processes (Bass et al. 2005).

GUIDE TO FURTHER READING

For readers seeking case studies and policy updates from the developing world, the most informative journal is *Environment and Urbanization*, which is published in the UK by the International Institute for Environment and Development (http://www.iied.org/eandu/index.html).

New and informative publications are also made available from the websites of international organizations, such as the World Bank (http://www.worldbank.org/) and the United Nations (http://www.un.org/), and specialist research institutes, such as the World Resources Institute (http://www.wri.org/) and the International Institute for Environment and Development (http://www.iied.org/). The reporting agency, the International Institute for Sustainable Development, also publishes information about recent policy discussions concerning the environment (www.iisd.org/).

For readers seeking a general introduction to the brown environmental agenda, there are two important text-books:

Hardoy, J., Mitlin, D. and Satterthwaite, D. (2001) *Environmental Problems in an Urbanizing World: Finding Solutions in Cities in Africa, Asia and Latin America*, London: Earthscan.

Satterthwaite, D. (ed.) (1999) *The Earthscan Reader in Sustainable Cities*, London: Earthscan.

REFERENCES

Anand, P.B. (1999) 'Waste management in Madras revisited,' *Environment and Urbanization*, 11(2): 161–76.

Bass, S., Reid, H., Satterthwaite, D. and Steele, P. (2005) *Reducing Poverty and Sustaining the Environment: The Politics of Local Engagement*, London: Earthscan.

Bigio, A. and Dahiya, B. (2004) *Urban Environment and Infrastructure: Toward Livable Cities*, Washington, DC: World Bank.

Krueger, J. (1999) *International Trade and the Basel Convention*, London: Earthscan.

McGranahan, G., Jacobi, P., Songsore, J., Suraidi, C. and Kiellen, M. (2001) *The Citizens at Risk: From Urban Sanitation to Sustainable Cities*, London: Earthscan.

Marcotullio, P. and Lee, Y.-S. (2003) 'Urban environmental transitions and urban transportation systems: A comparison of the North American and Asian experiences', *International Development Planning Review*, 25(4): 325–54.

Middleton, N. and O'Keefe, P. (2003) *Rio Plus Ten: Politics, Poverty and the Environment*, London: Pluto Press.

Mitlin, D. and Satterthwaite, D. (eds) (2004) *Empowering Squatter Citizen: Local Government, Civil Society and Urban Poverty Reduction*, London: Earthscan.

Nash, R. (1982) *Wilderness and the American Mind*, third revised edition, New Haven, CT: Yale University Press.

Satterthwaite, D. (2001) 'Environmental governance: A comparative analysis of nine city case studies', *Journal of International Development*, 13(7): 1009–14.

Stern, D. (2004) 'The rise and fall of the environmental Kuznets curve', *World Development*, 32(8): 1419–39.

UN-Habitat (2006) *Meeting Development Goals in Small Urban Centres: Water and Sanitation in the World's Cities 2006*, London: Earthscan.

Zetter, R. and Watson, G. (2006) *Designing Sustainable Cities in the Developing World*, Aldershot: Ashgate.

6.6 Vulnerability and disasters

Terry Cannon

Disasters and development

Astonishing as it may seem, it is only since the mid-1990s that donors and governments (of both rich and poor countries) have begun to accept that there are significant connections between disasters and development. Disasters triggered by natural hazards destroy and delay development: not only structures like schools, bridges and factories, but especially jobs and livelihoods. Worse still, many projects and other development activities are still carried out without the simple precaution of checking the potential impact of known risks in the area concerned. And there are no references to disasters in the Millennium Development Goals, either for the need to protect poverty reduction and development gains from hazards, or as a goal to prevent more people from becoming poor through the effects of disasters.

The situation should improve with the Hyogo Framework for Action (HFA) on disaster risk reduction, which aims to be 'Building the Resilience of Nations and Communities to Disasters'. The HFA 2005–2015 was supported by 168 governments and is the outcome of a UN-sponsored meeting held in January 2005 in Kobe, Japan, to follow up on international commitments ten years after the Kobe earthquake. The action plan mentions the need to reduce vulnerability, but does not have a strong development context and has little to say on poverty reduction or protection of livelihoods. It is also very doubtful that it would have been supported by so many governments if it had not been held, coincidentally, just a few weeks after the Indian Ocean tsunami disaster.

New thinking about disaster-development linkages has been a result of several factors. One is the devastating impact of a number of disasters since the mid-1990s that have highlighted their significance in creating poverty and undermining development. The Pakistan earthquake of 2005, for instance, is estimated to have led to $5 billion of damage, equivalent to the total of all development assistance in the previous three years (IEG 2006: xx). After Hurricane Mitch devastated several Central American countries in 1998, Carlos Flores (then President of Honduras) said: 'We lost in 72 hours what we have taken more than 50 years to build, bit by bit.'

Another factor has been the realization that by the end of the 1990–2000 UN International Decade for Natural Disaster Reduction (IDNDR), matters were worse than they had been at the beginning. The IDNDR was dominated by a view of disasters that emphasized the natural hazards rather than social vulnerability, and consequently tended to focus on technical fixes that could modify the hazards. By the end of the decade, there was much greater realization that disasters are social constructions, caused by the impact of a natural trigger on a vulnerable population. This has created a basis for treating disasters in the context of the social, economic and political processes that generate that vulnerability: in other words, disasters cannot be separated from problems of everyday life and livelihoods, and what is normally categorized as development.

Environment as risk and provider for production

Since the natural environment is crucial to many livelihoods, it can be analysed both in terms of the benefits it brings for human production systems, and the hazards inherent in environmental extremes. It is evident from situations everywhere in the world that people are often willing (or forced) to risk their exposure to the extreme in order to reap the everyday benefits of dangerous places. The environment involves many hazards that – depending on people's level of vulnerability – can threaten people and their livelihood systems. Many of the locations that are favourable to production are also prone to hazards: flood plains provide flat land for settlement, transport links and production activities; the slopes of volcanoes normally give rise to highly fertile soils for farmers; storm-prone coasts are often suited to agriculture, cities and trade; and even active geological faults that trigger earthquakes channel water to the surface and provide the basis for life in the desert, as in Bam, Iran, which was devastated by the earthquake of 2003.

In a sense, no disaster is 'natural' since hazards can be disastrous only when they affect people. Just as the environment can be considered a social construction (the environment consists of the characteristics of nature that both influence humans and are used by humans), disasters are the socially constructed outcome of environmental extremes visited on human systems. An earthquake in an unoccupied area is merely a natural phenomenon, and only becomes a hazard when it is capable of affecting humans: people get in its way. Disasters can happen only for socio-economic reasons: various factors encourage or compel people to 'get in their way'. This means that it is vital to understand disasters not only in terms of the environmental 'trigger', but, most importantly, in regard to the vulnerability of people.

At the simplest level, people can be vulnerable to the hazard impact itself simply because they have occupied parts of the Earth that are hazardous, as with the Indian Ocean tsunami of 2004. However, it is also evident that in many (probably most) disasters, the hazard's impact is socially constructed in a much more significant way: some groups of people seem to be affected far more than others. In this deeper sense, vulnerability is a characteristic not simply of being human and in a dangerous location, but of being part of a socio-economic system that allocates risk unequally between different social groups (such as those based on class, gender, ethnicity and age). This is often much more evident in developing countries, where there is a very high correlation between being affected in a disaster and being poor (though, logically, this effect would have to take account of the high proportion of poor people). But, as seemed evident in the aftermath of Hurricane Katrina in 2004, such socially constructed vulnerability is also a feature of rich countries. This suggests that it is valid to analyse disasters as being the result of vulnerability in this deeper sense.

Vulnerability analysis

The use of the concept of vulnerability in analysing disasters has become much more widespread since the mid-1980s. It has led to a serious challenge of the notion that disasters are 'natural', and has shifted the basis for dealing with disasters much more to issues of prevention (including precautions and reductions of vulnerability) rather than the more usual focus on emergency response or hazard mitigation (as in the IDNDR). While it may still be common for the media (and some politicians) to refer to 'natural disasters' (and there is still an overwhelming imbalance in spending on emergency relief as compared with preventive measures), there are signs of significant change. Key to this is the concept of vulnerability: if disasters are a consequence of vulnerability, if it is possible to reduce people's vulnerability, then disasters can be reduced or avoided. Since it is usually difficult or impossible to alter the impact of a hazard (mitigation), and it is only possible to issue warnings for some hazards, reducing people's vulnerability should be the main basis for disaster prevention. And because vulnerability is inherently connected to people's livelihoods, level of poverty and their ability to protect themselves (with the right type of house) or live in a safe place, it is also integral to development.

Some of the literature on disasters suggests that the incidence of disasters is growing. This means either that the number or intensity of hazards is rising, and/or that the number of vulnerable people is increasing, or that people's vulnerability is growing. It does not seem to be true that the number of geophysical events (mainly earthquakes, volcanic eruptions and tsunamis) has increased. There is evidence, though, for an increase in hydro-meteorological events (floods, drought, storms and hurricanes, heatwaves and related wildfires). It is highly likely that these are linked to global warming, and therefore that they will increase in frequency and intensity. Since floods and drought are responsible for the vast majority of deaths and disrupted lives, it is likely that the number of disasters related to such events will increase unless vulnerability can be reduced. So the reason for apparent worsening of disasters is a combination of increase in some hazards and the exposure of a growing population (e.g. in coastal zones, cities and flood plains), many of whom may also be made vulnerable by economic and social processes.

Prospects for applying vulnerability analysis to the reduction of disasters seem still to be remote. This is largely because the reduction of vulnerability requires changes in economic and political systems similar to those required to reduce poverty across the world. In other words, the barriers to reduction of disasters are similar to those that prevent or constrain the improvements in people's lives through development. But there is an additional layer to contend with in disasters:

even where poverty has been reduced, development is not a guarantee that people will be safe from hazards and disasters.

While it is true that there need to be significant changes in human behaviour (people are often willing to take risks, especially when the risk is from a sudden-onset hazard that is either infrequent or still in some indeterminate future – there is no shortage of people willing to live in earthquake zones in California and in hurricane-prone Florida), vulnerability analysis also typically finds economic and political causes of exposure to risks that are greater for some groups than for others. Remedies, therefore, by definition, are going to upset existing power structures that favour the status quo.

Vulnerability is not the same as poverty, marginalization or other conceptualizations that identify sections of the population who are deemed to be disadvantaged, at risk or needy in other ways. Poverty is a measure of current status: *vulnerability* should involve a *predictive* quality that is specifically related to the relevant hazards that may affect people. Precisely because it is predictive, the concept of vulnerability should be capable of directing disaster prevention, as well as the wider development interventions that can reduce vulnerability while also addressing poverty. It should do this by seeking ways to protect and enhance people's livelihoods, to assist vulnerable people in their own self-protection, and to support institutions in their role of disaster prevention (Cannon 2006). Unfortunately, the word vulnerability has been used in many different ways and has generated almost as much confusion as insight. Here is one definition, among many others, which may be identified as mainstream:

> the characteristics of a person or group and their situation that influences their capacity to anticipate, cope with, resist and recover from the impact of a natural hazard (Wisner et al. 2003: 11).

The vulnerability conditions are themselves determined by processes and factors that often involve the power relationships and institutional factors operating in the wider political and economic context. These conditions can be analysed as specific components of vulnerability that affect people's baseline status, their ability to protect themselves, and provide access to adequate social protection by other institutions (such as local government, NGOs, religious groups, and so on).

People's livelihood opportunities, and their related patterns of assets and incomes, are determined by wider political and economic processes. Their vulnerability to disasters is also a function of this wider political-economic environment. The causes of vulnerability are inherently connected with people's livelihoods (vulnerability is likely to be reduced when livelihoods are adequate and robust), and their position in society and its systems of power and governance (which determine access to livelihood resources and adequacy of social protection). Understanding livelihoods and power relations, and the pattern of assets, incomes and exchange opportunities which they involve, is therefore crucial to understanding much of how vulnerability differs between various groups of people.

It is therefore essential to put patterns of vulnerability in a wider social context. One attempt to do this is the pressure and release (PAR) model (see figure). This identifies a hierarchy of factors, from the international to the local, which can be identified as root causes and dynamic pressures, which lead to the unsafe conditions of people's vulnerability. In effect, this PAR model is a graphic representation of the commonly used equation: Risk = Vulnerability x Hazard. In the diagram, the risk of being harmed by a hazard is represented by the pressure between the hazard on one side and the vulnerability conditions on the other. To release people from risk involves reducing the hazard and/or reducing their vulnerability, turning the arrows around so that they release the pressure of risk.

Implications for policy

In spite of the new insights provided by political economic approaches, very little in the way of resources is going into vulnerability reduction. It is easier for national governments and the

Root causes	Dynamic pressures	Unsafe conditions		
International and national political economy	**Socio-economic and political factors**	**Vulnerability components**	**RISK= vulnerability × hazard**	**Hazard (natural)**
Power relations and property rights; distribution and control over assets, wealth	**Class:** Income distribution; assets; livelihood qualifications and opportunities	Livelihood and its resilience	D	Flood
			I	Cyclone
Civil security (war and conflict)		Initial well-being	S	Earthquake
	Gender: Women's status; nutrition; health		A	Volcanic eruption
Demographic shifts (growth, migration, urbanization)		Self-protection	S	Drought
	Ethnicity: Income; assets; livelihoods; discrimination		T	Landslide
Debt crises		Social protection	E	Biological
Environmental pressures; degradation and loss of assets, impacts on hazards	**State:** Institutional support; rights; security	Power, governance, civil society and institutional framework	R	etc.

Source: Adapted from Wisner et al. 2003

international disaster relief agencies to respond to an emergency than to tackle the structural (and politically sensitive) preconditions of vulnerability. There is also more political mileage to be made for governments from physical protection (bunds, flood shelters, sea defences) and conspicuous handouts of food and medical supplies, than from the reduction of vulnerability. Unfortunately, disaster relief is often inappropriate and brought by agencies that compete with each other, as was seen in the aftermath of the Indian Ocean tsunami.

It is also apparent that some of the organizations involved can undermine the most effective resource of all – local community self-help, local organizations and local networks. As yet, there is little understanding by the relief agencies, donors and governments that just as vulnerability needs to be reduced through an understanding of the links between disasters and development, so too must the relief and recovery process be rooted in actions that support, strengthen or replace livelihoods and enhance development. Once the emergency is over, the window of opportunity for structural reform to reduce vulnerability, and to integrate disaster relief and recovery into longer-term development policy is usually all too limited.

GUIDE TO FURTHER READING

Bankoff, G., Frerks, G. and Hilhorst, D. (eds) (2003) *Mapping Vulnerability: Disasters, Development and People*, London: Earthscan.

Department for International Development (DFID) (2004) *Disaster Risk Reduction: A Development Concern – A Scoping Study on Links between Disaster Risk Reduction, Poverty and Development,* London: DFID (available at http://www.dfid.gov.uk/pubs/files/drr-scoping-study.pdf).

Hewitt, K. (1997) *Regions of Risk: A Geographical Introduction to Disasters*, London: Longman.

Oliver-Smith, A. and Hoffman, S. (eds) (1999) *The Angry Earth: Disaster in Anthropological Perspective*, New York: Routledge.

Pelling, M. (2003) *The Vulnerability of Cities: Social Resilience and Natural Disaster*, London: Earthscan.

United Nations Development Programme (UNDP) (2004) *Reducing Disaster Risk: A Challenge for Development*, New York: UNDP Bureau for Crisis Prevention and Recovery.

Wisner, B., Blaikie, P.M., Cannon, T. and Davis, I. (2003) *At Risk: Natural Hazards, People's Vulnerability and Disasters*, second edition, London: Routledge.

REFERENCES

Cannon, T. (2006) 'Vulnerability analysis, livelihoods and disasters', in W. Ammann, S. Dannemann and L. Vulliet (eds) *Coping with Risks Due to Natural Hazards in the 21st Century*, Leiden, The Netherlands: Taylor & Francis/Balkema.

Independent Evaluation Group (IEG) (2006) *Hazards of Nature, Risks to Development: An IEG Evaluation of World Bank Assistance for Natural Disasters*, Washington, DC: World Bank (available at http://www.worldbank.org/ieg/naturaldisasters/report.html).

Wisner, B., Blaikie, P.M., Cannon, T. and Davis, I. (2003) *At Risk: Natural Hazards, People's Vulnerability and Disasters*, second edition, London: Routledge (the first three chapters are available free on the Internet at http://www.unisdr.org/eng/library/lib-select-literature.htm).

6.7 Development and biological diversity

Tim Swanson

Introduction

This chapter analyses the nature of the development process and its relationship to biodiversity decline. Here the focus is on development in one particular sense: as the rebalancing of the portfolio of societal assets (Solow 1974). Rapidly developing countries are precisely those countries engaging in rapid and substantial changes in the portfolio of societal assets on which they rely. In these countries, many of the natural assets which have provided natural flows of goods and services will be under substantial pressure for conversion into other forms. It is the conversion of lands to other uses that most affects the supply of global biodiversity, and it is development that drives this process.

Development as portfolio rebalancing

An important initial question concerns the economic nature of development. In the economic theory of growth and development, societies achieve higher levels of welfare by means of assembling and accumulating a capital structure from which they then receive an ongoing flow of goods and services. Societies develop (i.e. increase their per-capita consumption of their desired goods and services) by means of rebalancing their portfolios of capital. A 'more developed society' is one which has the capital portfolio that produces more of the flow of goods and services that it desires; a 'less developed society' is one which is further from this desired capital portfolio. In short, one very abstract way in which to view the process of development is that it is made up of the time and the choices that are required to move from a less desired to a more desired portfolio of societal capital.

Capital, of course, is any asset from which society receives a flow of goods and services. Natural resources may be conceived of as simply *naturally chosen capital stocks*: assets whose form was chosen initially by nature rather than society (Solow 1974). Societies may use the flows of goods and services from the capital forms initially chosen by nature, as much as any other form of capital stock.

The natural form of any asset is necessarily competitive with other forms in which humans might hold these same assets. Humans can remove forests for factories or fields, for example. If development is defined as the process by which a given set of assets is selected by society, then development must necessarily imply the decline of natural asset balances, simply because nature initially selected 100 per cent of the assets on which society depended. As humans become more actively engaged in the selection of the form that assets will take, this necessarily implies that the proportion of naturally chosen asset forms must fall.

Rebalancing portfolios of living resources

The key to the explanation for biodiversity decline probably lies in a technological change that occurred originally about 10,000 years ago; this was the realization of agriculture by human societies. Agriculture has consisted of the selection of a few prey species, and the expansion of their ranges. Prior to the occurrence of this idea, human societies preyed on species over their natural ranges (hunting and gathering); afterwards, human societies transported the species they used, displacing the naturally selected varieties. The discovery of this strategy (domestication and cultivation) and its implementation constituted a very important part of a technological shift that occurred in the late Pleistocene (about 10,000 years ago). This was a process that was important to the advancement and development of human society and civilization as we know it, but it is also a process that has generated biodiversity decline as a by-product.

Consider, for example, a hunter-gatherer society at the dawning of development. This would be a society that consumes only the flows from the natural capital stock (i.e. none of it was human-selected). This would be especially true with regard to the living resources: animals, vegetables, fruits. Everything that this society consumed would be acquired simply by stepping outside (the cave) and sampling whatever nature provided that day. The first step by that human society to choose its own capital stock (e.g. by domesticating a cow or shaping a tree limb) moves them away from a 100 per cent natural capital base and towards one that is now a mixture of natural and human-selected capital. The selection of a particular tree variety or grass variety (wheat) to plant, or animal to domesticate (cow) are all acts in moving that society away from the natural capital portfolio and towards a human-selected portfolio.

Biological portfolio rebalancing has taken the same form in most parts of the world. This is because human development has come through reliance on a small set of species and the expansion of their ranges (at the expense of most other species). The expansion of their ranges, and the consequent expansion of the human niche (so that population expansion has accompanied biological conversion throughout the development process: see Biraben 1979), has resulted in the global homogenization of the biosphere. It is this homogenization which, on the one hand, has generated human development, and, on the other, has generated the decline of diversity.

The earliest archaeological evidence of agriculture dates back only about 6000 or 10,000 years. This consists of the first signs in the fossil records that human societies were selecting individual species and translocating them with their culture. It is now the case that the biological production 'menu' for the bulk of all human society has converged on a relative handful of species. Of the thousands of species of plants which are deemed edible and adequate substitutes for human consumption, there are now only 20 species which produce the vast majority of the world's food (Vietmeyer 1986). In fact, the four big carbohydrate crops (wheat, rice, maize and potatoes) feed more people than the next 26 crops combined (Witt 1985). Although it is estimated that humans have utilized 100,000 edible plant species over their history, little more than 150 species are now under cultivation (Esquinas-Alcazar 1993). In short, humans have come to rely on a minute proportion of the world's species for their sustenance.

Development paths and diversity status

These portfolio changes, and the land use conversions on which they are based, are indicated by the impacts they have had on global land use changes. Estimates of aggregate natural habitat conversions over the past two centuries range from 25 to 50 per cent of the original land area (IIED and World Resources Institute 1989). More recently, 200 million hectares of forest land and 11 million hectares of natural grasslands were converted to agriculture between 1960 and 1980 alone, all of it in developing countries (Holdgate, Kassas and White 1982).

Table 1 Some rates of conversion of natural habitat to agriculture

	1960 (million ha)	1980 (million ha)	% change
Developing World			
Sub-Saharan Africa	161	222	37.8
Latin America	104	142	36.5
South Asia	153	210	37.2
South East Asia	40	55	37.5
Developed World			
North America	205	203	−1.0
Europe	151	137	−10.0
Former Soviet Union	225	233	0.4

Source: Repetto and Gillis 1988

Development and land use conversion have gone hand in hand. The entirety of the land conversions for purposes of agricultural development between 1960 and 1980 (see Table 1) occurred within the developing world. In the developed countries of Europe and the USA, there is little land conversion still taking place – the process is already complete. The proportion of Europe which is 'unmodified habitat' (of at least 4000 sq. km in area) is now certifiably zero, and it is about 5 per cent of the US land mass. This is to be contrasted with a global average of about 30 per cent (World Resources Institute 1990). This asymmetry in the holdings of natural habitat is the result of unevenly applied development. The land conversion process has worked its way across most of the developed world, and it is now proceeding in a similar manner in those countries now known as 'developing'.

It is important, of course, to recognize the benefits received from this development process. These conversions of land and species use have generated substantial worldwide productivity gains in terms of the human harvest from the living world. In agriculture, during the period of the massive land use change documented above (i.e. between 1960 and 1980), world cereal production grew at an average annual rate of 2.7 per cent (Hazell and Anderson 1989).

The general economic relationship between conversion and development is also indicated by the state of human development in the 'diversity-rich' states. Almost without exception, these are some of poorest nations on earth in terms of human wealth. They range between 1 and 7 per cent of the Organization for Economic Cooperation and Development's (OECD) average per-capita income (see Tables 2 and 3).

Development, therefore, has been driven, in part, by the process of conversion, and this has resulted in a remarkable asymmetry in the world. The states with high material wealth have low diversity wealth, and vice versa. This relative success at development acts as an incentive for the countries with high levels of biodiversity to choose to pursue the development paths selected by earlier developing countries. The increased agricultural yields and income levels in the developed world act as a persistent indicator to the less developed countries of the importance of portfolio rebalancing in the achievement of development. Rapid land use conversions are one of the responses of these countries to these inequalities – they wish to appear to be 'developing'.

Table 2 Countries with greatest 'species richness'

Mammals	Birds	Reptiles
Indonesia (515)	Colombia (1721)	Mexico (717)
Mexico (449)	Peru (1701)	Australia (686)
Brazil (428)	Brazil (1622)	Indonesia (600)
Zaire (409)	Indonesia (1519)	India (383)
China (394)	Ecuador (1447)	Colombia (383)
Peru (361)	Venezuela (1275)	Ecuador (345)
Colombia (359)	Bolivia (1250)	Peru (297)
India (350)	India (1200)	Malaysia (294)
Uganda (311)	Malaysia (1200)	Thailand (282)
Tanzania (310)	China (1195)	Papua New Guinea (282)

Source: McNeely et al. 1990

Table 3 GDP per capita in the diversity-rich states (in terms of purchasing power parity)

Country	2003 GDP per capita (PPP)	Country	2003 GDP per capita (PPP)
Tanzania	$600	Papua New Guinea	$2200
Uganda	$1400	Indonesia	$3200
India	$2900	Bolivia	$2400
Ecuador	$3300	Colombia	$7300
China	$5000	Brazil	$7600
World average	$8200		
OECD average	$26,300		

Source: World Bank 2006 and OECD 2006
(http://siteresources.worldbank.org/DATASTATISTICS/Resources/GDP_PPP.pdf)

Conclusion

Development is, in part, the result of portfolio rebalancing, as societies choose to rely on a very different capital stock from that with which they were initially endowed. This results in conversion of naturally existing forms of capital to other human-selected forms of capital. When this occurs within the biological realm, conversion results in the changing of natural habitats to other forms of human production and use. Agriculture has been portrayed as a bundle of species-specific technologies which have been handed on from one society to another, and which have displaced naturally existing living resources in many diverse habitats around the globe.

Biodiversity decline has been portrayed here as the outcome of uniformity within the development process when applied to the biosphere. Human societies realized the possibility of developing the biosphere about 10,000 years ago, with the advent of agriculture. Since that time, societies have chosen the portfolio of living assets on which they will rely, rather than using that which nature allocated to that territory. The chosen species have become a part of the overall method of production that humans use in biomass production. As this same development strategy has diffused within each society across the Earth, it has resulted in the homogenization of the biosphere, and the decline of diversity.

The fact that the diffusion of this development strategy has been a profound force for the removal of large amounts of biological diversity is indicated by the fact that there is a fairly obvious inverse relationship between diversity and development. Those states that retain large quantities of unconverted natural habitats are those with the last great quantities of diverse biological resources, and also those with the least developed capital portfolios in general (and so the lowest registered national incomes). As the push for portfolio rebalancing continues into these last great refugia for biological diversity, there are predictions of substantial proportionate losses of the Earth's remaining diversity.

GUIDE TO FURTHER READING AND REFERENCES

Biraben, J.-N. (1979) 'Essai sur l'évolution du nombre des hommes', *Population* (French edition), 34 Année, No. 1 (January–February): 13–25.

Boulding, K. (1981) *Ecodynamics*, London: Sage.

Esquinas-Alcazar, J. (1993) 'The global system on plant genetic resources', *Review of European Community and International Environmental Law*, 2(2): 151–7.

Futuyma, D. (1986) *Evolutionary Biology*, Sunderland, MA: Sinauer.

Hazell, P. and Anderson, J. (1989) *Variability in Grain Yields*, Washington, DC: Johns Hopkins University Press.

Holdgate, M., Kassas, M. and White, G. (eds) (1982) *The World Environment 1972–1982*, Nairobi: United Nations Environment Programme.

International Institute for Environment and Development (IIED) and World Resources Institute (1989) *World Resources 1988–89*, New York: Basic Books.

McNeely, J.A., Miller, K.R., Reid, W.V., Mittermeier, R.A. and Werner, I.B. (1990) *Conserving the World's Biological Diversity*, Gland, Switerland: International Union for the Conservation of Nature.

Repetto, R. and Gillis, M. (eds) (1988) *Public Policies and the Misuse of Forest Resources*, Cambridge: Cambridge University Press.

Romer, P. (1986) 'Increasing returns and long run growth', *Journal of Political Economy*, 94: 1002–37.

Romer, P. (1987) 'Growth based on increasing returns due to specialisation', *American Economic Review*, Papers and Proceedings, 77: 56–62.

Romer, P. (1990a) 'Endogenous technological change', *Journal of Political Economy*, 98: 245–75.

Romer, P. (1990b) 'Are nonconvexities important for understanding growth', *American Economic Review*, Papers and Proceedings, 80(2): 97–103.

Solow, R. (1974) 'The economics of resources or the resources of economics', *American Economic Review*, 64: 1–12.

Swanson, T. (1990) 'Conserving biological diversity', in D. Pearce (ed.) *Blueprint 2: Greening the World Economy,* London: Earthscan.

Swanson, T. (1994) *The International Regulation of Extinction*, London and New York: Macmillan and New York University Press.

Swanson, T., Pearce, D. and Cervigni, R. (1994) *The Appropriation of the Values of Plant Genetic Resources for Agriculture*, Rome: Commission on Plant Genetic Resources, Food and Agriculture Organization.

Vietmeyer, N.D. (1986) 'Lesser-known plants of potential use in agriculture and forestry', *Science*, 232(4756): 1379–84.

Witt, S. (1985) *Biotechnology and Genetic Diversity*, San Francisco, CA: California Agricultural Lands Project.

World Conservation Monitoring Centre (WCMC) (1992) *Global Biodiversity*, London: Chapman & Hall.

World Resources Institute (1990) *World Resources 1990–1991*, Oxford: Oxford University Press.

6.8 Water management and development

Phoebe Koundouri and Yiannis Kountouris

Water resource scarcity is one of the most pervasive natural resource allocation problems facing development planners throughout the world. Water resource scarcity can be a result of decreased water quantity following growing demand, or decreased quality resulting from degradation of freshwater resources, or both. By 2025, it is expected that the number of countries qualifying as 'water-scarce' will have increased to 35 from 20 in 1990 (UNEP 2003). To illustrate the magnitude of the problem, it has been estimated that, globally, 12 million deaths can be attributed to water scarcity in any given year (Shaw 2005). Water scarcity is widely perceived to be an important constraint on sustainable economic development, and has major environmental, social, economic and political repercussions. Furthermore, sustainable economic development, especially for developing countries, is threatened by flood events, stressing even more the need for appropriate policies for water resources management.

In this chapter, the market and government failures that affect water management are highlighted. We then provide a summary of valuation methods for water resources, and a typology of economic instruments considered and applied in providing incentives for the rationalization of common resources like surface and groundwater. Then we outline a methodology for integrated water resources management compatible with the goals of economic efficiency, equity and environmental sustainability. This emphasizes the importance of using declining social discount rates (DDR) for environmental management, and is illustrated by providing an example of flood-control investment in developing countries.

Market failures in water resources management and optimal use

Market and government failures

Water services are public goods, and a market failure will result in the misallocation of resources. Furthermore, some water services are characterized by economies of scale, resulting in monopolistic power and socially inefficient allocations. When considering groundwater resources, three externalities can be distinguished.

1 The finite stock of groundwater resources implies that each unit of groundwater extracted is no longer available for others to use, therefore there is little incentive to save water for future use, which in turn leads to overpumping. Provencher and Burt (1993) call this the stock externality.
2 In addition, there is a pumping cost externality: as the water table declines with increasing extraction, the pumping cost to the firm increases, as do the pumping costs of the other firms exploiting the resource. Since a firm does not take the other firms' costs into account, a second externality is generated.
3 Finally, there is the risk externality, which is caused by the inherent value of groundwater as a substitute source of water in times of surface water shortages.

Decreases in surface and groundwater quality are a result of environmental externalities in production. In these cases, the social costs of producing a good are ignored, leading to artificially low production costs and, hence, overproduction of the good that generates the externality. This situation is often enhanced by government failures that lead to misallocation of water resources. A key example is subsidies to agricultural production leading to over-exploitation of water resources for irrigation.

Optimal allocation of scarce water resources

As a result of the above failures, water supply and demand imbalances frequently occur, and water is not allocated efficiently among the resource users. Additionally, there are spatial and temporal considerations that need to be taken into account when valuing water, and these vary according to quality and its use, thus making water a more challenging resource to manage efficiently. In order to attain allocative efficiency, the marginal value of water should be the same for the last unit of water consumed by each water user, and should be equal to the social marginal cost of supplying water. For this to be achieved it is necessary that policymakers can properly value the water resource and then apply the appropriate policy instruments.

Non-market valuation techniques

In part, as a result of these market and government failures, degradation and loss of the environmental functions of water resources were prolific in the twentieth century. However, due to the observed loss of many ecological and hydrological services formerly provided (free of charge) by aquatic systems, and the consequent environmental and economic costs of this loss, aquatic system protection and conservation has become an internationally important political issue.

In economics, the basis of value is determined by individual preferences. Preferences reflect the utilities that are expected to be derived from the consumption of resources, given the needs, wants and wishes of consumers. In order to evaluate a given resource correctly, one needs to consider the *total economic value* (TEV) of the resource, that is, the whole class of values that have a basis in human preferences. Total economic value is composed of direct and indirect use values, as well as non-use values. Current use value derives from the utility gained by an individual from the consumption of a good or service, or from the consumption of others. *Current-use value* is composed of direct-use value (commercial and recreational) and indirect-use value (such as amenity value or general ecosystem support). *Option value* derives from retaining an option to a good or service for which future demand is uncertain. If we are not certain about either our future preferences or future availability, we may be willing to pay a premium (the option value) to keep the option of future use open. *Existence value* is derived from human preferences for the existence of resources as such and is unrelated to any use to which such resources may be put. Individual preferences may exist for maintaining resources in their present forms even where no actual or future 'use' is expected to be made of the resource.

Given that many of these components of value are not reflected in market prices of water, economists will attempt to estimate the true resource value through user *willingness to pay* for a given quantity and quality of supply. Valuation techniques are therefore necessary to assign appropriate prices that will enable water to be allocated in the most efficient manner. A variety of these techniques have been developed over the years to address this issue and are generally classified as revealed preference techniques and stated preference techniques. A comprehensive, state-of-the-art review of valuation techniques and relevant empirical applications from Europe and the rest of the world can be found in Koundouri (2004). Revealed preference techniques use data on goods or services that are marketed and do have observable prices, in order to value some environmental attribute, which is embodied in the marketed goods and services, but is not traded itself in any particular market.

Prominent revealed preference methods are the *residual value* method, the *hedonic pricing* method and the *travel cost* method. The residual value method values all inputs for the good produced at market price, except for the water resource itself. The residual value of the good is attributed to the water input. For example, one can value water as an input in the production of different crops. With the hedonic pricing method, the implicit prices of the characteristics that differentiate closely related goods can be estimated (Koundouri and Pashardes 2003). Travel cost models (also known as recreation demand models) represent an alternative revealed preference technique, which focuses on choice of trips or visits for recreational purposes, and looks at the level of satisfaction, time and money spent in relation to the activity. Patterns of travel to a particular site can be used to analyse how individuals value the site and, for example, the water quality of a river stretch.

In stated preference techniques, individuals are provided with a scenario in which they are asked how much they are willing to pay for changes in environmental quantity. The most widely applied stated preference method is the *contingent valuation* (Birol et al. forthcoming), while valuation practitioners are increasingly interested in alternative stated preference formats, such as *choice modelling* (Hanley, Mourato and Wright 2001). Choice modelling is a family of survey-based methodologies (including choice experiments, contingent ranking, contingent rating and paired comparisons) for modelling preferences for goods, which can be described in terms of their attributes and levels they take (Birol and Koundouri 2006; Birol et al. forthcoming).

Recent years have seen a growing interest in the application of meta-analysis for the estimation of use and non-use values generated by environmental resources. Meta-analysis is the statistical analysis of the summary of findings of empirical studies, that is, the statistical analysis of a large collection of results from individual studies for the purpose of integrating the findings. Brouwer et al. (2004) present such a meta-analysis for the use and non-use values generated by wetlands across Europe and North America.

Each of the valuation methods has advantages and disadvantages, and the appropriate method depends on the components of economic value one is trying to estimate. Once realistic estimates of surface and groundwater values are available, it is then necessary for governments to determine which policy measures are most suitable to achieve the desired outcomes.

Economic instruments for efficient surface and groundwater management

A number of economic instruments have been proposed for the efficient management of surface and groundwater resources (Karousakis and Koundouri 2006). In this section, a short description of the most common instruments is provided, and Table 1 summarizes the economic instruments proposed and their respective advantages and disadvantages.

Legal standards or quotas can be imposed to place restrictions on the quantity of water that can be extracted. Standards and quotas may also be used to prevent the deterioration of water quality below a certain level. An objection to the application of legal standards and quotas stems from the fact that they do not improve economic efficiency and, as such, they do not strictly qualify as economic instruments.

Taxes can be used to restrain water users from over-exploiting a water resource. The efficiency of taxes will depend on technical and institutional factors, while their effectiveness relies on the correct estimation of the marginal tax level and the risk aversion of farmers towards reduced water availability. Water pollution taxes can also be used to address water quality issues, when adopted to their optimal level.

Direct or indirect subsidies can provide incentives for water-saving measures. However, they are not economically efficient since they create distortions and provide counter-incentives for the adoption of new, environmentally friendly technologies.

In order to achieve efficient allocation of water resources, the creation of water markets, through the introduction of property rights to the common resource via tradable permit schemes, may be applied. The rationale behind tradable permit schemes is that in a competitive market, permits will flow to their higher value use. Their financial impact and their acceptability will be dependent on the initial allocation of property rights.

To minimize tensions between the stakeholders to the common water resource, voluntary agreements between farmers and government organizations can be implemented. Thus, efficiency is achieved since the agreements rely on the specialized knowledge of the agents directly concerned.

Environmental liability systems intend to internalize and recover the costs of environmental damage through legal action and to make polluters pay for the damage their pollution causes. If the penalties are sufficiently high, and enforcement is effective, liability for damage can provide incentives for taking preventative measures.

Table 1 Classification of economic instruments

Economic instrument	Advantages	Disadvantages
1 Standards and quotas		Not economically efficient
2 Water abstraction charges	Adjustment of price signals to reflect actual resource costs; encourage new technologies; flexibility; generation of revenues	Low charges will have minimal impact on user behaviour and will continue in resource overutilization
3 Pollution charges	Same as water abstraction charges; polluter-pays principle	Same as water abstraction charges
4 Subsidies	Readily acceptable	Not economically efficient
5 Tradable permits	Quantity-based targets that are able to attain least-cost outcome; allows flexibility	May entail high transaction costs
6 Voluntary agreements	Readily acceptable	
7 Liability legislation	Assess and recover damages *ex post*, but can also act as prevention incentives	Require an advanced legal system; high control costs; burden of proof

A methodology for implementing integrated water management in developing countries

Below, the problem of water resource allocation at the watershed level is addressed by providing a suggested methodology for integrated water management. The methodology can be seen in terms of two complementary stages, the first consisting of an objective approach to ascertaining economically efficient water allocations, and the second consisting of policy impact analysis. This two-stage methodology aims to present policymakers and resource managers with a procedure suitable to attain economic efficiency while simultaneously being compatible with the goals of equity and environmental sustainability.

In the first stage, water demands should be evaluated in order to derive the policy-relevant parameters, such as the *marginal value of water*, *price elasticities of demand*, *income elasticity of demand*, *marginal willingness to pay* and *risk parameters* for all relevant dimensions of demand. Then the economically efficient allocations – defined as those allocations where the *marginal social benefit* from consuming water is equated to the *marginal social cost* of supplying it – ought to be identified.

As the last step in this stage, the impacts of implementing the efficient allocations should be ascertained. This involves the identification of the impacts on society from applying economic instruments to implement the efficient allocation, thus leading to the second stage of the methodology.

In the second stage, a full policy impact analysis should be conducted. At first, the impact of the allocation of policy options on welfare needs to be evaluated and the distribution of costs and benefits to the society established. Next, possible externalities and market failures that may arise from the chosen allocation will have to be addressed, since ignoring them may lead eventually to suboptimal allocations. This is probable in cases where users are linked by the underlying hydrology of the aquifer. Overall, policymakers will consider the sectoral, spatial and temporal allocations. Finally, institutional and legislative analysis may be required in order to facilitate reallocation of water resources.

The issue of long-run discounting

The efficiency of a public investment project is determined by *social cost–benefit analysis*, where the total social benefit of the project is compared to its total social cost. In a competitive economy, the socially efficient level of investment is attained by investing in projects where the net present value determined by discounting cost and benefits at the *social discount rate* is positive. Then, the level of social discount rate is crucial in determining whether a public investment will pass the cost–benefit analysis test.

Discounting at a constant positive rate for policies seeking solutions to long-term environmental problems is considered problematic, since the net benefits accruing to generations in the distant future appear relatively negligible. Furthermore, constant discounting appears contrary to sustainable development.

In order to face these issues, the use of a discount rate that declines over time, following a predetermined trajectory (DDR), has been proposed (see, for example, Cropper, Ayded and Portney 1994, Cropper and Laibson 1999, providing experimental evidence revealing that people discount the future at declining rates roughly approximated by a hyperbolic function). In addition, Gollier (2002) has shown that when future consumption growth is uncertain, the appropriate discount rate falls over time. Finally, Weitzman (1998) shows that any uncertainty in the discount rate leads to a declining discount rate over time. Further arguments in favour of DDR can be found in Groom et al. (2005).

As an illustration, consider the case of applying different discount rates to flood-defences investment. In this case, declining discount rates may also have an effect on the economics of flood protection. Since the mid-1990s, flood-defence investment has been characterized by annual expenditure that has been assumed to offset significant damage – a cost–benefit ratio much greater than unity.

The figure shows the different cost–benefit ratios for various discount schemes. Employing a 6 per cent discount rate implies that flood-defence investment does not pass the cost–benefit analysis. However, a benefit–cost ratio of approximately 1.2 is obtained with a 3.5 per cent discount

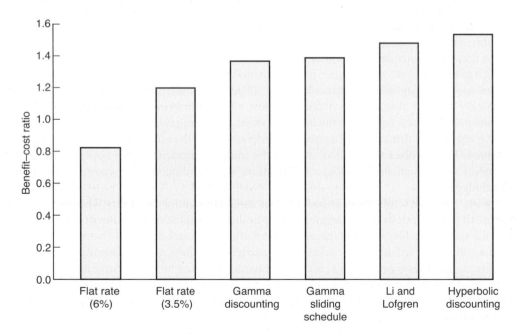

Figure 1 Benefit–cost ratio for flood defences

Source: Shrewsbury FAS project estimates and OXERA calculations. OXERA (Groom, B., Hepburn, C., Koundouri, P., David, P. and Smale, R.) (2002) *A Social Time Preference Rate for Use in Long-term Discounting*, Report to the Office of the Deputy Prime Minister and the Department for Environment, Food and Rural Affairs

rate. Furthermore, flood defences are more attractive under all declining rate regimes than under either a 6 per cent or 3.5 per cent fixed-rate regime. The benefit–cost ratio increases by about 17 per cent when the step schedule of discount rates is employed instead of a flat 3.5 per cent rate.

For short-term projects with time horizons of less than 30 years, declining discount rates have only minimal impact, as noted in Table 2. However, for projects with time horizons over 30 years, employing declining discount rates may have a significant impact on the preferred policy. In many such cases (such as road construction), shifting from a 3.5 per cent flat rate to the step schedule of rates could result in an increase in net present value from 8 per cent to 40 per cent.

When time horizons exceed 100 years, the potential impact is even greater. As Table 2 illustrates, it is estimated that the effect could be an increase or decrease of up to approximately ±100 per cent of net present value. For projects with costs and benefits accruing over a time horizon of 200–400 years (such as climate change mitigation), the step schedule of declining discount rates might have an impact of up to approximately ±150 per cent on net present value, relative to discounting at a 3.5 per cent constant rate.

Table 2 Effect of shift from flat 3.5 per cent to the step schedule of discount rates

Project time horizon	Potential effect on project net present value
0–30 years	Small, generally insignificant
30–100 years	Significant (± 50%)
100–200 years	Large impact (± 100%)
200–400 years	Major impact (± 150%)

Source: Shrewsbury FAS project estimates and OXERA calculations. OXERA (Groom, B., Hepburn, C., Koundouri, P., David, P. and Smale, R.) (2002) *A Social Time Preference Rate for Use in Long-term Discounting*, Report to the Office of the Deputy Prime Minister and the Department for Environment, Food and Rural Affairs

Conclusion

The importance of appropriate economic considerations in all aspects of water resources management is being recognized increasingly. This chapter has presented the necessary procedures for implementing an integrated approach from an economic perspective, and the identification of economic instruments and measures that are able to evaluate the true economic cost of water and to provide policymakers with the tools to allocate water in an efficient manner. The theory and applications of these valuation methods and the economic instruments have been described. Finally, a methodology for implementing a methodology that takes into consideration the efficiency aspects of water allocation, as well as the equity, environmental and sustainability issues, was presented. Together, these can help to provide policy prescriptions that endeavour to offer an integrated water resources management framework.

GUIDE TO FURTHER READING

Brouwer, R. and Pearce, D.W. (2004) *Cost–Benefit Analysis and Water Resources Management*, Cheltenham, UK, and Northampton, MA: Edward Elgar Publishing.

Koundouri, P. (2004) *Econometrics Informing Natural Resources Management: Selected Case Studies*, New Horizons in Environmental Economics Series, Cheltenham, UK, and Northampton, MA: Edward Elgar Publishing.

Koundouri, P. (forthcoming) 'Coping with water deficiency: From research to policy making', *Developments in Integrated Environmental Assessment (IDEA) Series*, Elsevier.

Koundouri, P., Karousakis, K., Assymakopoulos, D., Lagema, M. and Jeffrey, P. (2006) *Water Management in Arid and Semi-Arid Regions: Interdisciplinary Perspectives*, Cheltenham, UK, and Northampton, MA: Edward Elgar Publishing.

Koundouri, P., Pashardes, P., Swanson, T. and Xepapadeas, A. (2003) *Economics of Water Management in Developing Countries: Problems, Principles and Policies*, Cheltenham, UK, and Northampton, MA: Edward Elgar Publishing.

REFERENCES

Birol, E. and Koundouri, P. (2006) *Choice Experiments in Europe: Economic Theory and Applications*, New Horizons in Environmental Economics series, Edward-Elgar Publishing.

Birol, E., Karousakis, K. and Koundouri, P. (2006) 'Using a choice experiment to account for preference heterogeneity in wetland attributes: The case of Cheimaditida wetland in Greece', *Ecological Economics*, 60(1): 145–56.

Birol, E., Koundouri, P. and Kountouris, I. (forthcoming) 'Water resources management and wetland conservation: The case of Akrotiri Wetland in Cyprus', in *Water Policy Issues in Cyprus*, Washington, DC: Resources for the Future Press.

Brouwer, R., Langford, I.H., Bateman, I. and Turner, K. (2004) 'Meta-analysis of wetland contingent valuation studies', in Turner, R.K., Georgiou, S. and Bateman, I.J., *Environmental Decision Making and Risk Management: Selected Essays by Ian Langford*, Cheltenham: Edward Elgar Publishing.

Cropper, M. and Laibson, D. (1999) 'The implications of hyperbolic discounting for project evaluation', in *Discounting and Intergenerational Equity*, Washington, DC: Resources for the Future Press, pp. 163–72.

Cropper, M.L., Ayded, S.K. and Portney, P.R. (1994) 'Preferences for life-saving programs: How the public discounts time and age', *Journal of Risk and Uncertainty*, 8: 243–65.

Gollier, C. (2002) 'Discounting an uncertain future', *Journal of Public Economics*, 85: 149–66.

Groom, B., Hepburn, C., Koundouri, P. and Pearce, D. (2005) 'Declining discount rates: The long and the short of it', *Environmental and Resource Economics*, 32: 445–93.

Hanley, N., Mourato, S. and Wright, R. (2001) 'Choice modelling approaches: A superior alternative for environmental valuation?', *Journal of Economic Surveys*, 15(3): 435–62.

Karousakis, K. and Koundouri, P. (2006) 'A typology of economic instruments and methods for efficient water resources management in arid and semi-arid regions', in Koundouri, P. et al., *Strategic Water Management in Arid and Semi-Arid Regions: Interdisciplinary Perspectives*, Cheltenham, UK, and Northampton, MA: Edward-Elgar Publishing.

Koundouri, P. (2004) 'Current issues in the economics of groundwater resource management', *Journal of Economic Surveys*, 18(5): 703–40.

Koundouri, P. and Pashardes, P. (2003) 'Hedonic price analysis and selectivity bias: water salinity and demand for land', *Environmental and Resource Economics*, 26(1): 45–56.

Provenchur, B. and Burt, O. (1993) 'The externalities associated with common property resource exploitation of groundwater', *Journal of Environmental Economics and Management*, 24(2): 139–58.

Shaw W.D. (2005) *Water Resource Economics and Policy*, Cheltenham, UK, and Northampton, MA: Edward Elgar Publishing.

UNEP (United Nations Environment Programme) (2003) *Vital Water Graphics*, Nairobi: UNEP, www.unep.org/vitalwater

Weitzman, M. (1998) 'Why the far-distant future should be discounted at its lowest possible rate', *Journal of Environmental Economics and Management*, 36(3): 201–8.

6.9 Energy and development

B. Sudhakara Reddy

The need for energy

Energy is the fourth of the basic needs of human groups, along with food, clothing and shelter. It is of vital need to human civilization and an intense current concern. The demand for energy depends upon population growth, the rate of economic development, urbanization, changing lifestyles, availability of resources and the prices of various energy carriers. How are these demands met? Human groups are dynamic and hence are always exploring, experimenting and learning from the behaviour of their surroundings. Human groups are on the lookout for ways of getting energy in a useful form. They discover raw materials to use, search for them and invent methods of converting them to suitable forms to meet needs. In other words, the supply of energy depends on the ingenuity and strategy of humans' interaction with their environment. The energy issue is primarily a technological problem. An ideal source of energy, to be of some benefit to society and improve the quality of life, must be economically viable, environmentally sustainable and socially acceptable. Energy being the need of the day, it plays a significant role in the development of society. However, the development in energy utilization has been a highly uneven process. While in some countries the per-capita energy consumption is increasing exponentially, in others it has even shown a decrease. In India, we see fuel-wood stoves alongside nuclear devices; likewise, space vehicles coexist with bullock carts. The future of energy seems uncertain. At the beginning of the twentieth century, nuclear energy was unheard of. Today, the world abounds with nuclear reactors.

Similarly, the present-day person cannot imagine life without petroleum products. There is a distinct possibility of the exhaustion of these fuels by the end of this century. After reckless use of this scarce resource, modern society is now striving hard to avoid this situation.

Energy and development: looking back

Most thinking in developing countries on energy production and utilization is based on the pattern available in Europe and North America. India adapted virtually an identical path of energy development under the notion that it is unique, inevitable and unavoidable. However, despite five decades of adherence to this path, it has not met even the basic energy needs of the majority of its people. In such a scenario, a different paradigm of energy development needs to be evolved. This type of energy development goes beyond the traditional supply-side approach, which can contribute to the economically productive activities and improve the quality of life of the people. The main goal of this path is to use energy as a catalytic force to bring about both social and economic development. This type of development embraces the following principles:

- development-oriented;
- service-based;
- endogenous;
- self-reliant;
- environmentally sound;
- socially acceptable.

This chapter describes the relation between energy and development, looks at past experiences and suggests future directions. Taking an Indian example, the chapter provides a summary of the

Indian energy scenario, discusses the energy and development interactions and argues the need for more effective utilization of energy to make the system more sustainable.

Energy transformations: the backdrop

Energy can be classified broadly as commercial and non-commercial. Commercial energy (coal, oil, gas, etc.) is that which can be traded in the market. Non-commercial energy sources (which include fuel wood, dung, agricultural waste, etc.) are not traded in the market (even though fuel wood is traded in urban societies). The energy flow from source to end-use is shown in the figure. At the supply end, the primary energy is in the form found in nature – trees for wood, waterfalls, an oil well, and so on. This primary energy is converted into convenient energy carriers designated as secondary energy, for example, firewood logs, charcoal, kerosene, liquified petroleum gas, electricity. Secondary energy, after transportation/transmission and distribution, is delivered as final energy to consumers in the domestic, industrial, agricultural, commercial, transport and other sectors. The final energy delivered to consumers is converted through various end-use devices (stoves, lamps, furnaces, engines, etc.) into useful energy that provides energy services (such as cooking, illumination, process heating, shaft power) and satisfies basic needs. There are losses associated with the conversion of one form of energy into another. These losses are particularly significant in the conversion of final energy into useful energy. In many energy analyses, the efficiencies usually employed pertain only to the end-use of the devices. If we wish to study the energy requirement of a country, it is important to analyse the flow of energy from source to end-use service, taking into consideration all efficiencies.

The Indian energy scenario

The study of energy demand and its relation to development is of particular importance, in view of its extreme dependence on local energy resources and the way its exploitation affects the

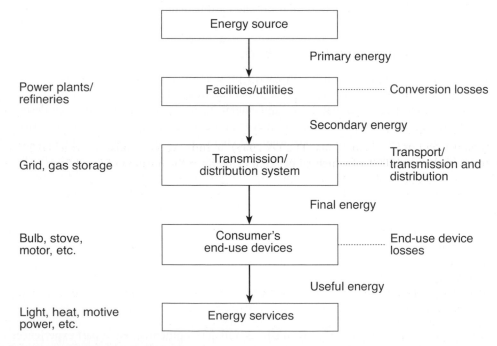

Flow of energy from source to end-use

economic growth of the country. The process of economic growth is traceable to the substitution of energy for human power in the performance of agriculture, industry and domestic services. Thus, economic development can be accelerated if we learn to use energy in new forms adaptable to a range of needs, which are diversified, based on the social and cultural environments of society. The two main forces that have an impact on energy demand are population growth and economic development. India has a population of 1 billion (2000 figures) accounting for 17 per cent of the world's population. India achieved its highest economic growth rate of 6 per cent per annum during the period 1981–95. With increasing population and economic growth, the need for energy also increases (TEDDY 2005).

Energy consumption: An overview

Commercial energy consumption
India consumes about 3 per cent of the total world commercial energy supplies and the per-capita energy consumption is only 5 per cent of that of developed countries (IEA 2000). In 1998, the total energy demand stood at 1.435 million terajoules (MTJ), of which 64 per cent originated from commercial sources. If sectoral energy consumption is considered, households consume nearly 45 per cent of the total, followed by industry, with 40 per cent, transportation, 10 per cent, and the commercial sector around 3 per cent (CMTE 2006). The share of the agricultural sector in total, though small (2 per cent), has increased at a faster rate than any other sector between 1980 and 1990, and has been responsible for the major advances in agricultural productivity which made India self-sufficient in food production.

Table 1 shows energy use by sector, from 1950 to 2005.

Non-commercial energy consumption
In most developing countries, including India, utilization of non-commercial energy is significant. Since the 1970s, there has been an increase in the consumption of various fuels in absolute terms, but their growth rates are declining significantly. Since non-renewable sources of energy, like petroleum, are limited and hence expensive, the vast potential of renewable energy sources merits serious and immediate consideration.

Environmental implications
In recent years, there has been growing concern about global warming due to the increased concentration of greenhouse gases (GHG) and the resulting socio-economic impact. These emissions are derived from a number of human activities, such as energy production and utilization, deforestation, agricultural practices, and so on. Of these, energy (production and use) contributes to nearly 50 per cent of GHG emissions (TEDDY 2005). In India, carbon emissions reached 238 million tones in the year 2000, of which 85 per cent came from the burning of fossil fuels (emission coefficients (tC/toe): coal – 1.08; oil – 0.86; gas – 0.62). Technological developments in energy demand and changes in fuel mix are therefore of the greatest significance in relation to environmental considerations.

Table 2 provides an overview of economic development, energy consumption and environmental implications for India.

Rural and urban household energy consumption
Households consume nearly 50 per cent of the total energy consumption and hence it is important to look at the pattern of utilization. The quantity and type of energy carriers used by households depend on household income and price. Another important consideration is the availability of commercial carriers, which is high in urban areas. The process of urbanization is traceable to the substitution of commercial energy for non-commercial energy in the industrial, commercial

Table 1 Energy use by sector (mtoe), 1950–2005

Year	Residential	% of total	Industry	% of total	Transport	% of total	Services	% of total	Agriculture	% of total	Total
1950	54	71.9	10	13.32	10	13.32	1	1.33	0.1	0.13	75.1
1960	66	69.99	14	14.85	12	12.73	1.5	1.59	0.8	0.85	94.3
1970	84	63.64	30	22.73	13	9.85	3	2.27	2	1.52	132
1980	96	55.17	52	29.89	16	9.2	5	2.87	5	2.87	174
1990	110	45.45	94	38.84	23	9.5	6	2.48	9	3.72	242
2000	132	38.15	138	39.88	55	15.90	9	2.60	12	3.47	346
2005	151	36.83	162	39.51	72	17.56	12	2.93	13	3.17	410
Growth rate (% p.a.)	1.7		2.8		1.1		0.2		2.4		

Source: CMIE 2006

Table 2 An overview of India's energy and economic development, 1998

Economic overview	Units	
Population	(million)	981
Urbanization	(%)	32
Per capita gross domestic product	(Rs in 1980–81 prices)	3177
Energy overview		
Reserves		
Coal	(billion tonnes)	82.3
Oil	(billion barrels)	4
Natural gas (Tcf)		19
Consumption		
Coal	(million tonnes)	342
Oil products	(million tonnes)	1.8
Natural gas	(Tcf)	0.7
Electricity	(Twh)	475
Fuel wood	(million tonnes)	280
Energy intensity	(Btu/US$)	31000
Environment overview		
Energy-related carbon emissions	(million tonnes)	238

Source: Economic Intelligence Service 1999

and domestic sectors (the share of consumption of commercial fuels by urban areas is about 80 per cent, with only 30 per cent of the total population living in urban areas, according to the 2000 census) (Sudhakara Reddy 1998). In the case of rural energy consumption, the main fuels are fuel wood, dung and agriculture wastes, which are used mainly for cooking and heating purposes, while kerosene and electricity are used for lighting (see Table 3).

Energy thresholds and the development path

After assessing the total energy consumption, it is important to find out whether the present pattern of consumption meets the minimum requirements of its people and whether sufficient energy will be available for increasing the pace of development. The per-capita minimum energy requirement is the one which supports daily life at a bare minimum and is necessary for human survival (Parikh 1980). After crossing this threshold, the country enters the phase of development. How can one arrive at these norms for services like cooking, lighting and transport? When can the country cross this threshold and embark on the path to development? The minimum energy requirements for urban and rural India are shown in Table 4.

Table 3 Utilization of various energy carriers in rural and urban households

	Per cent of households		
Energy carrier	Rural	Urban	Total
Cowdung	19.6	2.5	15.4
Fuel wood	75.7	30.2	60.5
Coal/charcoal	1.63	8.5	8.2
Biogas	0.43	0.5	0.5
Kerosene	1.34	23.6	7.2
LPG	1.1	26.6	7.9
Electricity	0.2	8.1	0.3
Total	100	100	100

Source: Based on estimates by Ramani et al. 1995

Table 4 Minimum energy requirements for rural and urban households

Energy requirements for a household per day (Kwh)

Service	Rural	Urban	Average
Cooking	1	2	1.3
Water heating	0.6	1	0.72
Lighting	0.6	1.2	0.78
Other services	0.3	1.8	0.75
Total	2.5	6	3.55
For total population (Gwh)	350	660	1010

Energy technology and economic development

The relation between energy technology and economic development is crucial for developing countries, since the process of substitution of energy for human power in the performance of industry, agriculture and households is taking place slowly. Here, the role of technology diffusion is very crucial. To increase productivity and develop economically, the energy inputs have to be increased significantly (between 1950 and 1990, energy consumption increased fourfold, from 86 to 350 mtoe). But this requires the raising of resources (the costs of power plants between 1950 and 2000 have gone up from 10,000 to 50,000 rupees per kW). Also, increasing energy consumption results in the consumption of precious non-renewable energy resources, like coal and petroleum products, and, more importantly, degrades the environment. The scale of problems created by this pattern of development suggests that a change in direction, without compromising growth, is essential. Efficient technologies and various demand-side management options (efficient lighting, motor drives, fans and pumps, cogeneration systems, etc.) induce consumers to use energy more effectively, so as to reduce demand without compromising services (Johanson et al. 1993). However, there exist many economic, environmental and social barriers for their effective penetration (Parikh, Sudhakara Reddy and Banerjee 1994). It is necessary, therefore, to study the relationship between the type of energy production with the natural resource system and the capital cost before adopting a particular technology. Table 5 provides data on various efficient technologies and the marginal cost of savings.

Sustainable energy systems

There is an urgent need to strive for a sustainable energy system. The modern world faces a choice: either to return to the austerity level of the pre-industrial period, or to opt for a development-oriented approach (using renewable energy sources, energy-efficient technologies, etc.) instead of the growth-oriented approach. The latter path is possible only if politicians, planners, equipment manufacturers, financial institutions and researchers begin, without delay, to re-channel the available human, technical and financial resources into mass production and marketing of efficient/renewable energy technologies. This path also has the potential to provide employment opportunities, as these energy technologies are more labour-intensive than the resource-intensive fossil fuel systems. The implementation of such a system requires the reorientation of energy planning and the priorities of governments and utilities; multiplying research efforts for clean, renewable energy systems; and changing the mindset of consumers. Efficiency measures are, on average, less capital-intensive per kilowatt than the supply-side options. Future energy projections should not be examined simply according to supply calculations, and planning should not be confined to energy experts. It is important that the consumers who are affected by the policy decisions should be consulted. The evolution of the needs of the people and the services that require energy (lighting, cooking, transport, motive power, etc.) have to be analysed along with demographic and social trends. Finally, for a sustainable energy strategy, policy and planning should be thought out as part of a global policy involving land use, infrastructure, urbanization and lifestyles, and not confined to a particular state or country.

Table 5 Efficient technologies and the marginal cost of savings

Option/service	Standard technology	Efficient technology	Marginal cost of savings (Rs/kWh)
Power generation		Combined cycle power plants	0.76
		Sugar co-generation	1.19
		Integrated gasifier combined cycle	1.15
Technologies	Standard motors	Efficient motors	0.66
	No variable-speed drive	Variable-speed drive	0.44
	Standard pumps/fans	Efficient pumps/fans	0.47
	Incandescent lamps	Compact fluorescent lamps	0.18
	Mercury lamps	High-power sodium vapour lamps	0.5
	Magnetic ballasts	Electronic ballasts	1.04
	Standard arc furnace	Efficient electric arc furnace	0.31
Process	No vapour absorption Refrigeration systems	Vapour absorption refrigeration systems	0.36
Residential cooking	Traditional wood stoves (10% efficiency)	Efficient stoves	–0.17
	Traditional wood stoves (10% efficiency)	Kerosene stove	–0.10
	Traditional wood stoves (10% efficiency)	LPG stove	0.10
Water heating	Traditional wood stoves (10% efficiency)	Solar water heater	0.48
	Electric water heater	Solar water heater	0.94
Commercial lighting	Incandescent lamp	Compact fluorescent lamp	0.56

Sources: for power generation, transmission technologies: ALCGAS 1999; for industrial, commercial and residential technologies: Parikh, Sudhakara Reddy and Banerjee 1994

Notes: All costs are in 1995 prices; the negative costs mean that the gains from these measures completely compensate the additional costs incurred; in addition they provide substantial returns to the investors.

REFERENCES

ALGAS (Asia Least-cost Greenhouse Gas Abatement Strategy) (1999) *Report of Phase I of the GEF Project*, New Delhi: TERI.

CMIE (Centre for Monitoring Indian Economy) (2006) *India's Energy Sector*, New Delhi: CMIE.

IEA (2000) *World Energy Outlook 2000*, Paris: International Energy Agency.

Johanson, T.B., Kelly, H., Reddy, A.K.N. and Williams, R.H. (1993) *Renewable Energy: Sources for Fuels and Electricity*, Washington, DC: Island Press.

Parikh, J.K. (1980) *Energy Systems and Development*, New Delhi: Oxford University Press.

Parikh, J.K., Sudhakara Reddy, B. and Banerjee, R. (1994) *Planning for Demand Side Management in the Electricity Sector*, New Delhi: Tata McGraw Hill Publishing House.

Ramani, K.V., Islam, M.N. and Reddy, A.K.N. (eds) (1995) *Rural Energy System in Asia-Pacific Region: A Survey of the Status, Planning and Management*, Kaula Lumpur: Asia-Pacific Development.

REP (1998) *Sectoral Energy Demand in India*, New Delhi: Regional Energy Demand Programme, Planning Commission, Government of India.

Sudhakara Reddy, B. (1998) *Urban Energy Systems*, New Delhi: Concept Publishers.

Sudhakara Reddy, B. and Balachandra, P. (2003) 'Integrated energy-environment-policy analysis', *Utilities Policy*, 11(2): 70.

Sudhakara Reddy, B. and Balachandra, P. (2005) *Energy, Environment and Development: A Technological Perspective*, New Delhi: Narosa Publishers.

TEDDY (2005) *Tata Energy Directory Yearbook (2003–2004)*, New Delhi: The Energy Research Institute.

6.10 Tropical moist forests and development

Alan Grainger

Introduction

The green girdle of tropical moist forests that circles the equator forms both a physical and a conceptual divide between the Global North and the Global South. For centuries, these forests were a dark, distant and mysterious 'other'. Mahogany, ebony and teak were miraculously translated from the steamy, dripping jungles into the urban jungle of the metropole. There then arose a colonial discourse of environmental crisis, in which the spread of deserts could be prevented only by managing forests with modern scientific tools. Colonial foresters were despatched from the metropole to play their parts in this drama, but by relying on local people to be proxy managers they created niches for resistance.

In the 1960s, the institutions that these 'scientific foresters' created were sustained as post-colonial memories when many countries achieved independence, and the colonial discourse of crisis was renewed by the neo-Malthusian, antimodernist horror story of planetary doom. Since then, television has shrunk the distance between tropical moist forests and people in the North, who now value the forests for their global contribution too. The texts of environmentalism have gradually become part of the official speech of governments in developed countries, provoking resistance from developing countries on a global scale. So tropical moist forests are now sites of contest between postmodern societies in the North, who favour retaining them to ensure sustainable development, and societies in the South in transition from traditionalism to modernity, who wish to exploit them to facilitate economic development. This chapter explores how this contest illuminates the meaning of development but leaves the forests themselves shrouded in an ambiguity that belies perceptions of proximity.

Tropical forest resources

Types of forest

Tropical forests can be divided into closed forest, which has a closed canopy and is more prevalent in the humid tropics nearest the equator, and open forest, which is more common in the drier and more seasonal tropics at higher latitudes, and has an open canopy because its trees are scattered. Tropical moist forest refers to all types of closed forest in the humid tropics, and has two main types: tropical rainforest, found in the permanently humid tropics, and tropical moist deciduous forest (or 'monsoon forest'), found where there is a distinct dry season.

Human impacts on forests

Human impacts on tropical moist forests may, from a positivist perspective, be divided into two main categories: deforestation and degradation. *Deforestation* is the temporary or permanent clearance of forest for agriculture or other purposes. If forest is not cleared, deforestation does not take place according to this definition.

Lesser impacts, which involve a temporary or permanent reduction in the density or structure of forest cover, or its species composition, are referred to as *degradation*. The dominant forestry practice in the humid tropics is not clear-felling, as in many temperate forests, but selective logging. As this usually removes only 2–10 trees per hectare (ha) out of a total of about 300 good-sized trees, it does not clear forest, and so does not cause deforestation as defined here. But it does degrade forest and can be an indirect cause of deforestation if farmers use logging roads to gain access to the forest after logging ends.

Environmentalist pressure groups, on the other hand, perceive logging to be the principal source of tropical forest destruction. In their eyes, logging occurs only to further capitalist interests. Smallholder farmers are victims of the latter, not forest destroyers, and so could never be upheld in the mass media as villains, whereas logging companies can. Such perceptions have inspired them to campaign, since the mid-1980s, to stop logging, or at least to make forest management more 'sustainable'. In doing so, however, they shrink time as well as space, claiming a cosmopolitan right to be stakeholders in forests of distant lands, and requiring tropical countries to abide by the values of the present when repeating the land transformations seen in developed countries centuries ago.

Extent and rate of change

Estimates of tropical forest areas and deforestation rates are still very inaccurate. In 1980, all natural forest (i.e. both closed and open) covered 1970 million ha, of which 1081 million ha was tropical moist forest. According to *Global Forest Resources Assessment 2005* (FRA 2005), published by the United Nations Food and Agriculture Organization (FAO), natural forest still covered 1949 million ha in 90 countries in 1990, declining to 1768 million ha in 2005. Tropical moist forest area was recently estimated as 1150 million ha in 1990, falling to 1116 million ha in 1997 (Table 1).

Table 1 Estimates of the area of all tropical forest and tropical moist forest (10^6 ha)

	All natural tropical forest				Tropical moist forest		
	1980	1990	2000	2005	1980	1990	1997
Africa	703	672	628	6070	205	198	193
Asia-Pacific	337	342	312	296	264	283	270
Latin America & Caribbean	931	934	889	865	613	669	653
Total	1970	1949	1829	1768	1081	1150	1116
No. of countries	76	90	90	90	63	52	52

Sources: Food and Agriculture Organization data in *Forest Resources Assessments 1980* and *2005*, interpreted by the author using a data set of 90 tropical countries published in *Forest Resources Assessment 1990*, and a modified version of Adrian Sommer's data set of 63 humid tropical countries. Estimates of tropical moist forest for 1990–97 are from Achard et al. 2002.

Notes: Totals may not match subtotals due to rounding.

In the late 1970s, all natural forest in the tropics was deforested at 11.1 million ha per annum, of which 6.1 million ha was in tropical moist forest. Another 4 million ha of tropical moist forest was logged every year for timber. The deforestation rate for the whole tropics rose by half in the 1980s, but from 2000–2005 was 11.4 million ha per annum. The rate for tropical moist forest was estimated as 5.8 million ha per annum in the 1990s, which is also similar to the 1970s rate (Table 2).

These figures convey a paradoxical message of change and continuity that keeps us at a distance from reality on the ground. While remote-sensing satellites have monitored the planet since 1972, FAO respects national sovereignty by still depending on its member states to submit the results of their latest national forest surveys. In FRA 2005, for the first time, governments even projected from these surveys to the reference years of 1990, 2000 and 2005 used for all countries. The FAO has admitted that the results often differed from estimates it made in the earlier FRA 2000. The

Table 2 Estimates of deforestation rates for all tropical forest and tropical moist forest (10^6 ha per annum)

	All natural forest			Tropical moist forest	
	1976–80	1981–90	2000–05	1976–80	1990–97
Africa	3.7	4.1	4.0	1.2	0.9
Asia-Pacific	2.0	3.9	2.7	1.6	2.5
Latin America & Caribbean	5.4	7.4	4.6	3.3	2.5
Total	11.1	15.4	11.4	6.1	5.8
No. of countries	76	90	90	63	52

Source: Food and Agriculture Organization data in *Forest Resources Assessments 1980* and *2005*, interpreted by the author using a data set of 90 tropical countries published in *Forest Resources Assessment 1990*, and a modified version of Adrian Sommer's data set of 63 humid tropical countries. The rate for all natural forest for 1976–80 uses data from a later summary of *Forest Resources Assessment 1980*. Estimates of tropical moist forest for 1990–97 are from Achard et al. 2002.

Notes: Totals may not match subtotals due to rounding.

latest tropical moist forest estimates were based on satellite images, but relied on a low-resolution sensor to estimate forest area. Deforestation rates were estimated using high-resolution images, but only of a sample of 'hot spot' areas where deforestation was thought most acute, and the accuracy of sampling in this context has been contested. So, owing to decisions made by government agencies, the FAO and scientists, we continue to 'look through a glass darkly' at tropical forests and receive only a blurred image of them. Fairhead and Leach (1996) demonstrated the limitations of gazing at forests from afar, showing that some areas of apparently 'virgin' forest in West Africa are growing on previously cleared land.

Causes of deforestation

The immediate causes of deforestation are the land uses that replace forest (Table 3). The underlying causes are socio-economic factors and government policies (Table 4) (Rudel 2005). Population growth and economic growth both increase demand for food, and poverty and landlessness cause poor people to flee from cities or other overpopulated areas to clear forest to feed themselves. Governments influence deforestation rates directly, by planning or promoting forest clearance, and indirectly through their social and economic policies.

Table 3 The immediate causes of deforestation

A   Shifting agriculture
    Traditional shifting cultivation
    Short-rotation shifting cultivation
    Encroaching cultivation

B   Permanent agriculture
    Permanent field-crop cultivation
    Government-sponsored resettlement schemes
    Commercial ranches
    Cash-crop plantations

C   Other land uses
    Mining
    Hydroelectric power schemes
    Narcotic plant cultivation

Source: Grainger 1993

Table 4 The underlying causes of deforestation

A	Socio-economic factors Population growth Economic growth Poverty and inequality
B	Facilitating factors Distribution and fragmentation of forests Proximity of rivers, roads and urban centres Topography Soil fertility
C	State intervention Agriculture policies Forestry policies Other policies
D	External factors Demand for exports Financing conditions

Source: Grainger 1993

During the 1980s and 1990s, various regression studies were undertaken to identify the causes of deforestation (Lambin 1997). Owing to a lack of long-term national time series for forest area, they used cross-sectional analysis of FAO's international data sets to simulate national trends. However, their reliability was brought into question when significant correlations found between rates of deforestation and population growth were linked to FAO's use of population growth rates to estimate deforestation rates (Rudel and Roper 1997). Despite their apparent scientific legitimacy, such studies still pay insufficient attention to data limitations.

Deforestation and national development

Statistical links between contemporary rates of deforestation and underlying causes shed little light on long-term trends in forest area, but if population density is taken as a proxy for economic development status, then international cross-sectional analysis suggests that percentage national forest cover should decline as a country develops, but then approach a lower limit. This, and evidence from national time series, has inspired various conceptual models. In one of these, all forested countries are expected to undergo a period of significant reduction in forest cover, called their *national land use transition* (see figure) (Grainger 1995). In another, the point where forest cover

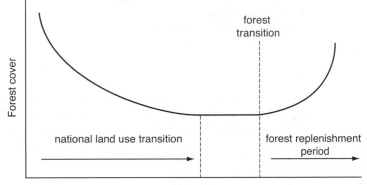

The national land use transition and forest transition

starts to rise again, as forest is replenished by plantations or natural regeneration on abandoned farmland, is called the *forest transition* (Mather 1992; Rudel et al. 2005). For example, according to FRA 2005, Cuba, Puerto Rico and Vietnam all sustained natural forest expansion between 1990 and 2005, and so seem to have passed through their forest transitions. India and Ivory Coast have done so too, if the trend in both natural forest and forest plantations is used.

Such models can be criticized for assuming deterministic relationships of the kind that underly all *unilinear development models*. They, and other U-shaped trends, also privilege economic factors at the expense of political change to which the latter are conducive. Experiences in the Philippines and elsewhere suggest that sustainable forest management shifts from being a stated policy used for symbolic purposes, to become the actual policy of government because *democratization* allows environmental groups to establish sufficient political spaces to challenge the hegemony of exploitative groups (Grainger and Malayang 2006).

Victims of remoteness

As remaining tropical forests are located in the peripheral regions of countries on the global periphery, events within them often go unnoticed by politicians in capital cities. Clearing them, however, helps to secure national borders and, as in the Indonesian Transmigration Programme and resettlement schemes in Brazilian Amazonia (Eden 1990), to redistribute population from overcrowded areas. Yet the ability of state forestry and conservation departments to monitor deforestation and the sustainability of forest management, and to protect forests against deforestation, is limited by physical distance, the inefficiencies of hierarchical institutions that link core and periphery through multiple organizational layers, and over-concentration of personnel in headquarters offices. Attempts to overcome these problems by *decentralizing* forest management have met with mixed success, as they threaten the power of national elites (Ribot 2004).

At the international level, tropical forests realized David Ricardo's predictions by becoming major peripheral sources of timber after the Second World War. Tropical hardwood exports grew fourteen-fold between 1950 and 1980, when temperate forests could not meet rising demand for timber in developed countries. By 1970, Asia provided 80 per cent of all supplies. *Dependency theory* and *world-systems theory*, two leading *structuralist* core-periphery theories, claim that the global core will continue to exploit the periphery's economic surplus and keep it underdeveloped. In the early structuralist discourse of *political ecology*, such relations also lead to environmental degradation (Blaikie and Brookfield 1987). However, while many developing countries still rely on primary commodity exports for income, with most of the value-added accruing to the developed countries that process them, the proportion of all tropical hardwood exported as logs fell from 63 per cent in 1980 to only 21 per cent in 2005.

A war between two worlds

Developing countries have increasingly asserted their sovereign rights in international relations. So tropical moist forests are now sites of conflict between two different worlds: the environmentally conscious, *postmodern* societies of the Global North and countries of the Global South in transition from traditional to modern societies. This war is fought with words and symbols, not guns, but is no less important for that. The *informal imperialism* that has dominated relationships between North and South since the Second World War has expanded to include what Deepak Lal (1990) calls *eco-imperialism*, as states and NGOs in developed countries press developing countries to improve environmental management 'for the good of all humanity'.

Developing countries have avoided or deflected coercion by the following means.

- Consenting only to non-binding and/or ambiguous international agreements. Spurred on by environmentalist groups, the governments of developed countries lobbied for a Forest Convention at the UN Conference on Environment and Development (UNCED) in Rio de Janeiro in 1992. By applying the same criteria to all countries, its protagonists believed this would improve tropical forest management. Yet the Group of 77 coalition of developing countries resisted this advance in *environmental globalization* (Grainger 2005), and only a weak, non-binding Statement of Forest Principles emerged. Agenda 21, supposedly a 'blueprint' for *sustainable development*, was approved only because it was ambiguous enough to be read by developing countries as supporting their pro-development discourse of sustainable development, and by developed countries as supporting their pro-environment discourse. The latest attempt to elaborate the global forests regime, the UN Forum on Forests (established in 2001), is not very effective (Humphreys 2006).
- Consenting only to non-ranking agreements. Cooperative mechanisms to improve tropical forest management, enshrined in the First International Tropical Timber Agreement (ITTA1), were replaced by a more coercive approach, in response to environmentalist pressures. A target was set for achieving sustainable management – 'the Year 2000 Objective' – and incorporated in 1994 into the successor agreement ITTA2. Yet the latter committed parties only to *introducing* policies on sustainable management by 2000, not implementing them. Criteria and indicators were devised, but, as these could not be used to rank the progress of particular countries (Poore 2003), they have become 'floating' symbols that cannot be attached to actual forests, though they are valid currency in diplomatic exchanges between governments. Annoyed by lack of progress through official channels, NGOs established their own forest certification schemes (Humphreys 2006), one of a number of *transnational networks* through which global civil society aims to substitute for underperforming international institutions.
- Symbolic resistance. Development is also constrained by conditions for aid and loan agreements, intended to minimize environmental impacts and further other new imperialist ambitions, such as democratizing and decentralizing governance. It was suggested above that the latter should facilitate the adoption and implementation of policies to promote sustainable forest management. However, the real aim of developed countries could be to strengthen the dependency of developing countries, who have perceived this symbolism and responded in kind. Their real centre of power is often not the modern institutional state, but a *shadow state* embedded in traditional interpersonal relationships (Richards 1996). The governments of developed countries seem satisfied with policy texts published by institutional states, even though, as experience in Sierra Leone shows (Grainger and Konteh 2007), they have little domestic meaning. Environmental groups have recently begun to campaign against 'illegal logging', that is, practices supposedly contrary to local laws. This effectively *simulates* (in Baudrillardian fashion) indigenous legal systems for cosmopolitan ends, just as, according to Cindy Weber (1995), the US Government simulated the sovereignty of Grenada and Panama to justify its invasions in 1983 and 1989, respectively. Not surprisingly, the governments of tropical countries are apparently supporting these campaigns!

Conclusions

The concept of development has, from its inception in the late 1940s, been mutually constituted by developed and developing countries, and relationships between them are not, from this reading, as one-sided as structuralist theories suggest. Times have changed. The emergence in developed countries of postmodern societies, in which symbols are often more important than substance, makes them vulnerable to manipulation by developing countries, which can avoid or deflect coercion by using symbolic skills that developed countries lost long ago. Even though technology and personal aspirations have made tropical forests less distant, the continued fuzziness of estimates of their areas, deforestation rates and management sustainability is unsettling. Whether this is a consequence of postmodernity in the Global North, or of the blend of visibility and invisibility in its contest with the Global South, is unclear. But it does ensure that the debate about the role of tropical moist forests in development will continue for decades to come.

GUIDE TO FURTHER READING

For extended overviews, consult Grainger, A. (1993) *Controlling Tropical Deforestation*, London: Earthscan Publications, and Rudel, T.K. (2005) *Tropical Forests: Regional Paths of Destruction and Regeneration in the Late Twentieth Century*, New York: Columbia University Press.

REFERENCES

Achard, F., Eva, H.D., Stibig, H.-J., Mayaux, P., Gallego, J., Richards, T. and Malingreau, J.-P. (2002) 'Determination of deforestation rates of the world's humid tropical forests', *Science*, 297: 999–1002.

Blaikie, P. and Brookfield, H. (1987) 'Approaches to the study of land degradation', in P. Blaikie and H. Brookfield (eds) *Land Degradation and Society*, London: Methuen, pp. 27–48.

Eden, M. (1990) *Ecology and Land Management in Amazonia*, London: Bellhaven Press.

Fairhead, J. and Leach, M. (1996) *Misreading the African Landscape: Society and Ecology in a Forest-Savanna Mosaic*, Cambridge: Cambridge University Press.

FAO (2006) *Global Forest Resources Assessment 2005*, FAO Forestry Paper No. 147, Rome: UN Food and Agriculture Organization.

Grainger, A. (1995) 'The forest transition: An alternative approach', *Area*, 27: 242–51.

Grainger, A. (2005) 'Environmental globalization and tropical forests', *Globalizations*, 2: 335–48.

Grainger, A. and Konteh, W. (2007) 'Ambiguity, autonomy and symbolism in African politics: The development of forest policy in Sierra Leone', *Land Use Policy*, 24: 42–61.

Grainger, A. and Malayang, B. (2006) 'A model of policy changes to secure sustainable forest management and control of deforestation in the Philippines', *Forest Policy and Economics*, 8: 67–80.

Humphreys, D. (2006) *Logjam: Deforestation and Global Governance*, London: Earthscan Publications.

Lal, D. (1990) 'The limits of international co-operation', *The Twentieth Wincott Memorial Lecture*, Occasional paper 83, London: Institute of Economic Affairs.

Lambin, E.F. (1997) 'Modelling and monitoring land-cover change processes in tropical regions', *Progress in Physical Geography*, 21: 375–93.

Mather, A.S. (1992) 'The forest transition', *Area*, 24: 367–79.

Poore, D. (2003) *Changing Landscapes*, London: Earthscan Publications.

Ribot, J. (2004) *Waiting for Democracy. The Politics of Choice in Natural Resource Decentralization*, Washington, DC: World Resources Institute.

Richards, P. (1996) *Fighting for the Rainforest: War, Youth and Resources in Sierra Leone*, Oxford: International African Institute in association with James Currey.

Rudel, T. and Roper, J. (1997) 'The paths to rainforest destruction: Crossnational patterns of tropical deforestation, 1975–90', *World Development*, 25, 53–65.

Rudel, T., Coomes, O.T., Moran, E., Achard, F., Angelsen, A., Xu, J. and Lambin, E. (2005) 'Forest transitions: Towards a global understanding of land use change', *Global Environmental Change*, 15, 23–31.

Rudel, T.K. (2005) *Tropical Forests: Regional Paths of Destruction and Regeneration in the Late Twentieth Century*, New York: Columbia University Press.

Weber, C. (1995) *Stimulating Sovereignty: Intervention, the State and Symbolic Exchange*, Cambridge: Cambridge University Press.

6.11 Tourism and the environment

Erlet Cater

The tourism/environment nexus

The short title to this chapter belies the complexities of the issues that are manifest in the tourism/environment interface. As Holden (2000: xv) suggests, the two simple words 'tourism' and 'environment' represent complicated concepts, and 'both can be interpreted as intricate systems, where actions taken in one part of the system have consequences for its other component parts'. Indeed, Hall (2000: 145) describes how tourism, like the environment, constitutes 'a meta-problem, characterised by highly interconnected planning and policy messes', cutting 'across fields of expertise and administrative boundaries and, seemingly…[being] connected with almost everything else'. This interconnectedness is, in fact, vitally important in terms of policy implications for two major reasons. On the one hand, it implies that tourism may have adverse environmental impacts, which not only affect tourism firms and tourists (for example, through marine pollution affecting the quality of bathing), but also non-tourism subjects (for example, hotel sewage piped into the sea, which can reduce fish catch). On the other hand, it suggests that tourism can be used in a positive way, to give both the impetus and the means for environmental conservation. While there are problems of commodifying nature by attaching a financial value to it (in particular because indigenous nature/culture relationships are often ignored), tourist revenue from nature tourism, especially wildlife viewing, provides a strong economic rationale for conservation. It has been estimated that, over its lifespan, a lion in Amboseli National Park in Kenya will draw US$515,000 in foreign exchange receipts from tourism; in Botswana, the gross contribution to GDP attributable to elephants from game-viewing tourism is estimated to be US$39 million.

The dilemma is not only to minimize the negative impacts of tourism on the environment, but also how to harness tourism as a development process which can have a symbiotic relationship with the environment as it can provide the financial incentive for conservation. Two major issues are therefore evident when we examine the interrelationship between tourism and the environment. The first concerns the ecological sustainability of tourism per se. The second, which heralds the shift from a singularly tourism-centric approach to recognition of the much wider context in which tourism is cast as a process, focuses on its potential contribution towards sustainable development.

The environmental impacts of tourism

Despite early perceptions of tourism as a 'smokeless industry', concerns over its potential environmental impacts mirrored the growth in environmental concern in Western societies during the 1970s and 1980s (see, for example, the seminal text by Mathieson and Wall 1982). Tourism may affect the composition and behaviour of floral and faunal species; cause or exacerbate various forms of pollution; precipitate erosion; contribute to depletion of natural resources; and have deleterious visual impact. Added to these direct impacts, however, indirect and induced environmental impacts arise from supporting activities such as those of the construction industry and quarrying (Cooper et al. 1998). For this reason, environmental auditing techniques, which monitor how the products and processes of tourism interact with the environment, should be a logical follow-up to an initial environmental impact analysis, but, like assessing environmental performance through certification and accreditation, they are not always feasible. There are a number of factors which militate against a cut-and-dried assessment and subsequent management of the environmental impacts of tourism.

First, as alluded to above, it is obvious that tourism does not operate in a vacuum. It is likely to be very difficult to separate out the net impact of tourism. As Southgate and Sharpley (2002: 256) declare, 'it is often difficult to differentiate between environmental changes caused by tourism from those associated with changing biophysical conditions or those related to other social or economic factors'. The latter, of course, takes account of environmental impacts from other activities, including those pursued by the host population. These activities may prejudice the sustainability, if not the very existence, of tourism in a locality. An example of this is furnished by the case of Bunaken National Park (BNP) in North Sulawesi, Indonesia, which suffered a slow, but continuous, degradation of its marine resources, attributable to anchor damage from the ever-increasing number of tourism boats visiting the park, as well as destructive fishing practices. Individual operators could not make an effective stand against the irresponsible practices threatening the viability of their operations, so collectively formed the North Sulawesi Watersports Association (NSWA). In mid-1998, NWSA succeeded in the official banning of anchoring in the park. As well as developing a self-reporting scheme, whereby violators of the ban faced the threat of being exposed in the local newspaper, they contributed fuel and boat time to local water police and park rangers, to help with patrol activities against reef-destructive practices. A daily entrance fee for divers to the National Park of US$5, or an annual fee of US$15, was formalized in 2003. Eighty per cent of this goes back to the BNP Management Board and is allocated to conservation programmes in the park, including environmentally friendly village development. An increase in live coral cover has resulted in increased diver satisfaction, and village fishers have reported increased fish catches since the bombing and cyaniding have stopped.

The second factor complicating an assessment of tourism's environmental impact concerns the absence of adequate baseline information, as well as the lack of a well-organized system of databases on potential and actual impacts of activities, inter alia tourism, in different types of ecosystems. Few areas are studied before tourism begins to make an impact.

Third, there are spatial and temporal discontinuities involved. The environmental impact will not be confined to individual species, but will extend to entire ecosystems. Also, because of spatial interconnectedness, particularly in the seas and oceans of the world, impacts may be felt hundreds of kilometres and even nations apart. For example, whale watching is now a popular pursuit in 87 countries and territories of the world. The migratory routes of cetaceans transcend national boundaries, so the same mammals could potentially be a prime attraction in several tourist destinations. This means that poor management practices in one location may subsequently affect viewing opportunities in another. Also, in terms of temporal discontinuities, certain environmental changes, such as the hunting patterns of wildlife, may take a considerable time to manifest (Butler 2000).

Fourth, there is a circular and cumulative relationship between tourism and the environment. This is particularly evident in the relationship between tourism and global environmental change (GEC): not only is tourism a factor in GEC (for example, through the contribution of air travel to carbon emissions), but it is also, in turn, affected by it (Gössling and Hall 2006). For example, while the reputation of the Maldives has been built around luxury resort development, it is heavily reliant on the health of its marine ecosystems as a large number of visitors engage in snorkelling and scuba-diving. Rising sea temperatures are therefore of concern as they jeopardize coral reefs: in 1997, the Maldives experienced a major bleaching event (whereby, due to stress, corals expel their symbiotic algae which give them colour, thus appearing white), when around 90 per cent of the reefs were affected. Tourists are therefore not only subjects, but also objects of natural impacts, as there may be significant impacts of natural phenomena and processes on tourism. The impact of the South Asian tsunami of 2004 on tourist destinations in Thailand and Sri Lanka is another pertinent, if poignant, case in point.

Finally, the impacts will vary over time and place. These variations are attributable to both the type of tourists (their motivations, modes of travel and behaviour) and the characteristics of place which both shape and are shaped by economic, sociocultural, political, ecological, institutional and technical forces that are exogenous and endogenous, as well as dynamic.

It is clear that the relationship between tourism and environmental change is far from simple. That it is a reflection of complex interrelationships indicates that, properly managed, including the utilization of adaptive carrying capacities, it may provide an escape route from the classic impasse of earning foreign exchange, without destroying the natural resource base at the same time. It is to this potential contribution to sustainable development that we now turn.

Sustainable development through tourism

It is somewhat ironic that, in the past, tourism development was seen as an inappropriate avenue for overseas development assistance, and yet from the mid-1990s there has been an explosion of interest in harnessing it as an agent of sustainable development. Sustainable tourism should result in a symbiotic, win-win scenario with environmental protection resulting both *from* and *in* improved local livelihoods; continued, and possibly even enhanced, profits for the tourism industry; sustained visitor attraction and satisfaction; and revenue as well as popular support for conservation (embracing the 'use it or lose it' philosophy: simultaneously making conservation pay and paying for conservation). Considerable attention has been focused on one form of sustainable tourism since the early 1990s, that of *ecotourism*. The very incorporation of the prefix 'eco' in the term indicates the close relationship between ecotourism and the environment. Indeed, three out of the five core principles of ecotourism outlined by Page and Dowling (2002) – that it is nature-based, ecologically sustainable and environmentally educative – emphasize this closeness and are regarded as essential attributes of ecotourism. The remaining two fundamental requisites, that it should be locally beneficial and generate tourist satisfaction, are viewed as being desirable for all forms of tourism.

There has been increasing recognition of the contribution that ecotourism can make towards sustainable development in general, as well as of the significance of 'pro-poor tourism' and of the relevance of tourism to the poverty agenda in general. International lending and bilateral development agencies, such as the World Bank, United States Agency for International Development (USAID), Department for International Development (DFID) (UK) and GTZ (Germany), have focused their attention on ecotourism as one of the few options open to rural communities to develop natural resource uses that are sustainable and, fundamentally, as a means of enhancing local livelihoods. The high ground claimed by ecotourism, in terms of its contribution to development, is that, in principle, it offers much enhanced prospects for local involvement compared with conventional tourism. Major international environmental non-governmental organizations, such as the World Wildlife Fund, Conservation International and The Nature Conservancy, often acting as the implementing agencies for the donor bodies, have placed ecotourism projects high on their agenda, but the dominance of Western ideology has not escaped criticism (Mowforth and Munt 2003).

Conclusion

It is obvious that the view of tourism as an environmentally degrading and exploitative industry positions it as a convenient scapegoat for more fundamental causal relationships. There is not only a need to adopt a more holistic approach, but also to 'rethink the relationship between tourism development, the environment and the communities dependent upon environmental resources' (Southgate and Sharpley 2002: 255–6). By situating tourism within a discourse embracing sustainable development and encompassing issues such as livelihood assets, traditional knowledge and biological diversity, the world's largest industry has the potential to actively promote both conservation and development. The challenge is to fulfil this promise.

GUIDE TO FURTHER READING

Hall, C.M. and Lew, A.A. (eds) (1998) *Sustainable Tourism: A Geographical Perspective*, Harlow: Addison Wesley Longman. In-depth debates on contemporary geographical approaches to sustainable tourism.

Roe, D., Leader-Williams, N. and Dalal-Clayton, B. (1997) *Take Only Photographs, Leave Only Footprints*, London: International Institute for Environment and Development. Examines the environmental impacts of wildlife tourism, with useful examples.

Scheyvens, R. (2002) *Tourism for Development*, Harlow: Pearson Education. A comprehensive analysis of the potential for tourism to work as a strategy for development.

USEFUL WEBSITES

http://www.propoortourism.org.uk Download a range of research reports and studies that focus on how tourism's contribution to poverty reduction can be increased.

http://www.tourismconcern.org.uk Works with communities in destination countries to reduce social and environmental problems connected to tourism, and with the outbound tourism industry in the UK to find ways of improving tourism so that local benefits are increased.

http://www.planeta.com Describes itself as a global journal of ecotourism: a lot of useful case studies and resources.

http://www.ecotourism.org The website of The International Ecotourism Society (TIES), which promotes responsible travel that unites conservation and communities. Its resources section is very useful.

REFERENCES

Butler, R. (2000) 'Tourism and the environment: A geographical perspective', *Tourism Geographies*, 2(3): 337–58.

Cooper, C., Fletcher, J., Gilbert, D. and Wanhill, S. (1998) *Tourism: Principles and Practice*, Harlow: Pearson Education.

Gössling, S. and Hall, C.M. (2006) 'Conclusion: Wake up…this is serious', in S. Gossling and C.M. Hall (eds) *Tourism and Global Environmental Change: Ecological, Social, Economic and Political Interrelationships*, London: Routledge, pp. 305–20.

Hall, C.M. (2000) 'Rethinking collaboration and partnership: a public policy perspective', in B. Bramwell and B. Lane, *Tourism Collaboration and Partnerships*, Clevedon: Channel View, pp. 143–58.

Holden, A. (2000) *Environment and Tourism*, London: Routledge.

Mathieson, A. and Wall, G. (1982) *Tourism: Economic, Physical and Social Impacts*, Harlow: Longman.

Mowforth, M. and Munt, I. (2003) *Tourism and Sustainability: Development and New Tourism in the Third World*, second edition, London: Routledge.

Page, S.J. and Dowling, R.K. (2002) *Ecotourism*, Harlow: Pearson Education.

Southgate, C. and Sharpley, R. (2002) 'Tourism, development and the environment', in R. Sharpley and D.J. Telfer (eds) *Tourism and Development*, Clevedon: Channel View, pp. 231–62.

6.12 Livelihood strategies and their environmental impacts

Susie Jacobs

Human livelihoods have always been formed and formulated in interaction with particular environments (Sahlins 1972). This is the case for both rural and urban peoples. However, urban centres as places with dense human settlement, appear to be more 'social' and 'further' from environmental concerns. In rural areas these concerns are more readily apparent.

Non-industrial societies

Many first nations or indigenous peoples have evolved ways of living that are in relative harmony with their environments, due mainly to production systems not based on accumulation. Some societies' belief systems revere nature and the environment. For instance, the Mbuti people of central Africa saw their forest environment as a 'mother', while North American native peoples shared a belief in a Great Spirit, present not only in human beings and animals but in plant life and inanimate natural objects. Such beliefs and religions tend to encourage actions that preserve the environment in which humans and other species live. There is a long history of seeing indigenous societies as 'pristine', and, recently, of admiration for the nature–society equilibrium achieved. However, these more positive views have emerged *after* the near-destruction of the peoples admired, as has happened in the USA, Australia and Mexico. Alternatively, they may be relegated to remote and usually inhospitable areas.

Non-industrial economies encompass different systems: hunting and gathering, pastoralism, swidden agriculture and permanent agriculture. Shifting cultivation allows for fallow periods and the partial regrowth of forests and vegetation. With the development of permanent, settled agriculture, it becomes necessary to clear forests; sometimes irrigation systems are also developed. These changes entail long-lasting impacts on the environment, but also permit population growth. As Marx (1954) hinted, there has always been a degree of tension between human livelihood needs, social change and 'nature' or the environment, as is being recognized dramatically today. Interlocking crises involving the economy, environment and security are emerging (Kirkby, O'Keefe and Timberlake 1999: 7).

North-South

Securing of livelihoods is a general human need, but many people, particularly in less-developed countries (LDCs), struggle to do so. Social groups are positioned differently in terms of their use of resources, their ability/ies to obtain livelihoods and their environmental impacts. These differences have spatial, national, social class, racialized and gender dimensions.

The living spaces of the poor are frequently the targets of exploitation by the more powerful in the 'international resource economy'. To use the most obvious example, many (although not all) people in the Global North are able to secure their own livelihoods, usually consume more and have greater environmental impacts in their use of resources. The majority of people in the Global South have more precarious livelihoods, use and consume fewer resources, but bear greater burdens of environmental deterioration. Yet Northern societies sometimes export waste to societies of the Global South, thereby creating pollution.

Urban environments

Cities are human constructions (in several senses) that create new environments, at once social and natural. Although it may appear as though the ('natural') environment is located elsewhere, urban-based peoples often have to contend with environmental degradation through pollution, lack of planning, unsafe housing and lack of potable water.

Many industrial processes are polluting. For instance, chromates produced in tanning and pigment processing are toxic to fish and cause kidney inflammation and skin ulcers; mercury produced in fungicides and pharmaceuticals causes damage to kidneys and the nervous system (Hardoy and Satterthwaite 1999: 185). Workers in factories that produce dangerous products which generate pollution may have little choice but to continue working in such environments as their livelihoods depend on this. Such factors are not specific to urban areas. For example, pesticides used in the cultivation of flowers for export often pose health threats to workers.

Cities depend almost entirely for their existence, on inputs from other areas – both within the same nation and, often, from other countries, indicating the interconnectedness of environmental impacts. The demands that urban dwellers make on the environment – for particular foodstuffs, for particular kinds of timber (e.g. hardwoods) or for coltan (used in the manufacture of mobile phones and computers) – may affect events in other parts of the world. Forests may be cut down, particular minerals extracted or land given over to export crops.

Social hierarchies are often expressed through differential situations with regard to environmental hazards and benefits. Famously, in Victorian Britain, the middle classes lived in more elevated areas to avoid the stench, crowding and pollution of working-class areas. In the early twenty-first century, in Rio de Janeiro, the wealthiest people live near the beaches, while the poor in *favelas* are much more exposed to environmental hazards. Differential positioning with regard to the environment also has racialized implications.

People considered of low status such as racialized 'others' and Harijan populations in south Asia are typically less advantaged in social class terms, and therefore in terms of housing and physical environments. Black and ethnic 'others' often have to contend not only with poor housing and transport, but also with pollution of their environments, for example, through siting of incinerators near their homes, as in New York City, or dumping of rubbish (Miller, Hallstein and Quass 1996). Such examples seem to confirm low social status in particularly graphic ways. Crime is another factor that many urban people experience as an aspect of 'environment'; this raises the question of the extent to which the environment should be viewed as 'natural' or socially constructed.

Rural areas

Although both rural and urban populations have environmental concerns, rural peoples can face environmental degradation in very immediate and concrete ways. These include loss of forest cover, depletion of soil fertility, loss of fishing stocks and pollution of water sources. One-third of humanity relies on direct access to fields, forest and pasture for their livelihoods (Sachs 2004). Conflicts over water in particular are increasing, and the livelihoods of the rural poor are the most at risk (UNDP 2006).

All types of states and governments have caused environmental damage, particularly during industrialization processes. For instance, environmentally blind 'socialist' industrialization under Stalin in the USSR caused serious air pollution and radioactive contamination. In China, great environmental damage has also taken place. High levels of cadmium and mercury concentration were found in rivers from the early 1980s, and much inland water has been polluted due to lack of treatment of industrial waste. Small-scale enterprises have been important in China's industrialization process and are usually thought of as 'appropriate' technologically. Local/village enterprises, or TVPEs, however, are often unregulated, and brickworks in many village enterprises emit large quantities of particulates, causing smog and lung diseases (Muldavin 1998, discussing Heilonjiang province).

Technological innovations have had both harmful and beneficial consequences. The building of dams is usually justified by the need to provide electricity and water supplies for urban populations, but – evidently – results in displacement of rural people and obliteration of their livelihoods. Dams may damage natural environments (e.g. down-river life is often affected). The application of irrigation and other inputs to farming systems often increases yields in the short term. In the medium term, consequences may include increased salinization of the water supply.

Commoditization and environment

The examples given above have taken place in different political systems. However, it is also the case that capitalist, market-based systems have heightened negative environmental impacts, with consequences for people's livelihood sources. Environmental problems in the Russian Federation stem from the Soviet era, but today these are exacerbated by lack of spending on environmental protection: less than one-tenth of that in the late 1980s (BBC 2002). The commoditization of natural resources poses a grave threat, as does agribusiness and the industrial 'farming' of the seas.

It is possible to cite cases that indicate the impact of commoditization on livelihoods and livelihood sources. For example, there are many examples of soil depletion from overuse, often in response to market forces. Agriculture in China was decollectivized from the late 1970s, and state policies emphasized increased production. Land use intensified and annual crop rotation was abandoned for monoculture (in the case of Heilonjiang, of corn). With the departure from sustainable practices, organic matter declined rapidly and groundwater became polluted. By the late 1990s, a rapid increase in desertification had occurred (Muldavin 1998).

In Veracruz, Mexico, environmental degradation has led to a reduction in river foods such as shrimp, which supplement local people's diets (Vázquez-García and Montes-Estrada 2006). The environment has been altered by deforestation, poisoning of fish with pesticides and the extraction of water for urban use. With economic changes such as liberalization and parcellization of many *ejidos* (farming collectives) after 1992, people now lack access to what had been communal resources. The processes here are gender-differentiated: women are mainly responsible for fishing, but their work – as happens commonly – is not acknowledged. Because they are not included in most local political processes, it is difficult to contribute when communities seek to confront negative impacts on the local environment.

The decline of forest cover is an environmental issue of great concern, due to the negative impact on biodiversity as well as on local ecosystems. Forests are crucial too, for the livelihoods of those who dwell in them. Sunderlin et al. (2005) indicate the extent to which the severely poor in LDC contexts tend to be forest dwellers. This is the case, for instance, in Vietnam and India. Forests have often been the last haven of indigenous peoples, and have become refuges for those fleeing conflicts. In the Democratic Republic of Congo, extraction of minerals such as diamonds and coltan fuels the war). Wars are increasingly recognized as environmental as well as livelihood hazards: disrupting production, destroying infrastructure and sometimes the environment, and creating refugees. In discussions of the need to preserve forest resources, the livelihoods of forest dwellers should also be taken into account.

The theme of 'conservation' vs 'livelihoods' is an old one. During the colonial and settler governments in southern Africa, black Africans often found themselves accused of 'destroying' the environment due to their 'cattle complex' (Beinart 1984) or their farming systems. Thus, the settler governments positioned themselves as 'guardians' of the environment, and even the land, which had been appropriated from African peoples.

Conflicts between peoples involved in different socio-economic and livelihood systems occur commonly. The classic example is in the Amazon. Economic refugees from the sugar latifundia of the north-east migrated to Amazonia from the 1960s and 1970s, when their own livelihoods were threatened. Some, encouraged by government colonization schemes, attempted to cultivate the land; however, underneath the forest canopy the soil was largely unsuitable and a number had to leave the area. Other in-migrants were rubber-tappers, often becoming ensnared in debt bondage. In-migrants potentially encroached on Indian peoples' lands, but were impoverished themselves. This example also indicates that the 'drivers' of such conflicts may be located, in part, in the wider political economy: in this case, in the concentration of Brazil's landholdings.

Conclusion

There exist numerous examples of people's resistance to degradation of the environment and ensuing threats to livelihoods. Environmentally oriented resistance can entail different types of action – and indeed, much 'resistance' does not involve organized movements at all. In a Veracruz *ejido* that retained collective control over land (see above), women still suffered discrimination, but were better able to access resources while working in groups. In urban areas, environmental actions frequently revolve around residence and the provision of services, partly because 'home' and (paid) 'work' tend to be separated. At work, trades unions are increasingly taking up environmental concerns as aspects of health and safety. Other movements are organized explicitly and may have a livelihoods focus (e.g. land reform movements) or environmental focus (conservation movements), or both (anti-GM crop movements in India; anti-dam movements).

Because livelihoods are always to some extent local and particular, as are environments, most actions and movements are, in the first instance, locality-specific. Environmental movements, however, were some of the first to use global networks (Keck and Sikkink 1998). For instance, farmers in Yunan, Shanxi province, who re-terrace land, plant trees and allow native scrub to re-establish (BBC World Service 2006) are acting 'locally', but they are also influenced by wider, global currents. 'Older' political and livelihood movements, such as those for land reform, now often take on board environmental concerns as an example of widening awareness of global issues; hence, the MST (Landless People's Movement) in Brazil advocates organic agriculture in its settlements.

Environmental justice and livelihoods movements demonstrate the ways that the 'local' and the 'global' are enmeshed. The scale of threats to livelihoods due to soil degradation, declining fish stocks, loss of forests, desertification and climate change is worldwide. Awareness is growing of the need for global environmental justice. This would recognize that everyone has the right to an environment which sustains shelter, health, nourishment and livelihoods – necessary for a degree of economic security. Environmental justice implies awareness of the interconnections of livelihoods with environment, of unequal North–South relations and of inequities *within* societies.

An international covenant already in existence is of importance for livelihood and economic rights: this is the ICESCR, or International Covenant on Economic, Social and Cultural Rights, adopted in 1966 (Elson and Gideon 2004). This deserves better publicity, due to its stipulation that economic and subsistence rights cannot be levelled 'down' – as happens, for instance, with structural adjustment policies. The ICESCR has radical implications. Reasserting rights to minimum economic security for all implies that affluent societies must change to avoid threatening the livelihoods of the poor (Sachs 2004). This also implies recognition that livelihoods, and lives, depend on environments.

GUIDE TO FURTHER READING

Jones, S. and Carswell, G. (eds) (2004) *The Earthscan Reader in Environment, Development and Rural Livelihoods*, London: Earthscan Publications.

Redclift, M. (ed.) (1999) *Sustainability: Life Chances and Livelihoods*, London: Routledge.

REFERENCES

BBC (2002) 'Report outlines Russia's deadly pollution', 25 November, http://news.bbc.co.uk/1/hi/world/europe/2512697.stm

BBC World Service (2006) 'One Planet – Counting the cost of Chinese development', 21 December, http://www.bbc.co.uk/pressoffice/proginfo/radio/wk51/thu.shtml

Beinart, W. (1984) 'Soil erosion, soil conservationism and ideas about development: a southern African perspective, 1900–1960', *Journal of Southern African Studies*, 11(1): 52–83.

Elson, D. and Gideon, J. (2004) 'Organising for women's economic and social rights', in S. Jacobs (ed.) *Feminist Organisations and Networks in a Globalising Age*, special issue, *Journal of Interdisciplinary Gender Studies*, 8(1–2): 133–52.

Hardoy, J. and Satterthwaite, D. (1999) 'Environmental problems', in J. Kirkby, P. O'Keefe and L. Timberlake (eds) *The Earthscan Reader in Sustainable Development*, London: Earthscan Publications, pp. 184–91.

Keck, M. and Sikkink, K. (1998) *Activists Beyond Borders: Advocacy Networks in International Politics*, Ithaca, NY: Cornell University Press.

Kirkby, J., O'Keefe, P. and Timberlake, L. (1999) 'Introduction', in J. Kirkby, P. O'Keefe and L. Timberlake (eds) *The Earthscan Reader in Sustainable Development*, London, Earthscan Publications, pp. 1–16.

Marx, K. (1954) *Capital: Volume I*, London: Lawrence and Wishart.

Miller, V., Hallstein, M. and Quass, S. (1996) 'Feminist politics and environmental justice: Women's community activism in West Harlem, New York', in D. Rocheleau, B. Thomas-Slayter and E. Wangari (eds) *Feminist Political Ecology*, London: Routledge, pp. 62–85.

Muldaʋin, J. (1998) 'Agrarian change in contemporary rural China', in I. Szelényi (ed.) *Privatising the Land*, London: Routledge, pp. 92–123.

Sachs, W. (2004) 'Environment and human rights', *Development*, 47(1): 42–9.

Sahlins, M. (1972) *Stone Age Economics*, New York: Aldine Transaction.

Sunderlin, W., Angelsen, A., Belcher, R., Burgers, P., Nasi, R., Santoso, W. and Wunder, S. (2005) 'Livelihoods, forests and conservation in developing countries: An overview', *World Development*, 33(9): 1382–402.

UNDP (United Nations Development Programme) (2006) *Human Development Report: Beyond Scarcity – Power, Poverty and the Global Water Crisis*, Geneva: United Nations.

Vázquez-García, V. and Montes-Estrada, M. (2006) 'Gender, subsistence fishing and economic change: A comparative study in southern Veracruz, Mexico', *International Journal of Sociology of Food and Agriculture*, 14: 1.

Gender, population and development

Editorial introduction

It is widely accepted that development must be informed by gender analysis. All major development agencies include a mandatory framework for all activities to check that gender is considered, even in neutral projects. Some might even argue that the way gender is integrated into development thinking and practice indicates a high degree of co-option or neutralization of feminist objectives, rather than their success in transforming the development agenda. Recent processes of globalization have questioned the state, institutional rules and processes to determine what open space is available to women to claim gender rights and justice. The important question is how do women engage the state in policymaking and hold it accountable. Increasingly, the political participation of women has become crucial to access the male-dominated world of policymaking. Empowerment involves challenging existing power relations and gaining greater control over sources of power, especially challenging patriarchy and inequality. It is a process by which women redefine and extend what is possible for them on an individual basis to bring about transformation. Women's interest can be served only when both the formal and informal spaces are brought together and negotiated by the women's movement.

This section argues that gender remains central to development and offers a lens through which to deconstruct gender-related processes and issues. It enhances understanding of women's lives and the gendered nature of economic, social and political processes.

UNICEF has identified women, or rather mothers and young children, as the groups most vulnerable to economic adjustment programmes. There has been a very rapid growth of women's employment, from which women have gained self-esteem and providing visible contribution to household income. Women's willingness to work is partly determined by the extent to which they have control over income generated in the household. This relates to gender bias in the household, and the gendered nature of negotiation and exchange within households. In addition, there is extensive evidence that women's income is almost exclusively used to meet household needs, whereas men tend to retain a considerable portion of their income for personal spending. Women with access to better education and employment opportunities rely less on their children for economic security and support in later life. Gender remains a problematic issue for post-structural adjustment policies as local constructions are not taken into account when deriving policies in developing countries.

Technological change and globalization raise many gender issues and have led to the disruption of cultural norms in households and traditional societies. Conflicts within households, within generations and between spouses have become quite prevalent. Female employment has led to the breakdown of joint families and nucleation of households; this has implications for the elderly, particularly in the context of demographic transition in relative numbers of children (due to falling fertility rates), working age population and older population (improvements in health, leading to higher life expectancy) in developing countries.

Today, as in the past, struggles and achievements in the domains of gender equality, reproductive autonomy and sexual pluralism are marked by tensions and deep controversies. By the 1990s a diverse and lively political agenda around sexual orientation and gender identity had also become globalized. Family planning programmes introduced over the past 40 years in many developing countries have implanted the value of a small family among people with aspirations to rise up the social ladder. But the mindset for a small family has not erased the deeper cultural roots of gender disparity.

7.1 Women and the state

Kathleen Staudt

Until the last two decades, the state had been relatively neglected in political studies. Analysts had long referred to the 'nation state', but were much more taken with the nation: the growth of nationalism, national and cultural values, political participation, popular attitudes towards government and society. The state, defined in its Weberian sense as the exercise of sovereign authority within territorial boundaries, was the empty box that structural-functional theorists drew in their political systems graphics, seemingly relegating that box to the sometimes tedious studies of public administration.

Even women and gender analysts succumbed to these tendencies. They studied 'inputs' to the box with research on social movements, revolutions, public opinion and political participation. They studied 'outputs' from the box in their analyses of public politics and laws that 'developed' women and men differently in various class, cultural and geographic contexts. In the 1970s, the fields of women in development and gender and development were born.

State analysis winds up

With the publication of *Bringing the State Back In* (Evans, Rueschemeyer and Skocpol 1985) comparative political theorists put the state on the analytic agenda. With historical and comparative perspectives, they ended the pretence (so common in studies of the USA) of an irrelevant or minimalist state, as in the classic liberal ideal. This focus led people to examine government institutions more carefully for the way they opened or closed doors to people and policy debates.

The study of institutions experienced some revival, with analysts attentive to the grand institutions and rules that enveloped the political scheme of legislative bodies, administrative agencies and electoral systems. As far back as 1955, Maurice Duverger compared the single-member and proportional representation electoral systems for their impacts on geographical or ideological politics and two- or multi-party systems. Soon analysts of female under-representation in high-level political decision-making positions would embrace these grand level approaches. Would proportional representation systems seat more elected women? What about parliamentary systems? And, most importantly, what difference would that make in the gendered decisions and outcomes of the political process? Policy analysts searched for ways to understand the connections between policies, institutions and decision makers for their resistance to gender justice and the persistence of deep inequalities.

These connections began to be made in relation to the state. Statist critique and analysis became attached to grand explanatory narratives, from pluralism to Marxism, but with attention to women and gender. States were conceptualized as historical and institutional shells that protected and advanced male privilege. Theorists challenged existing conceptions of the state as neutral umpire between competing interests (the pluralist view ingrained in US politics) or as the instrument of the dominant economic class (the Marxist view). The institutionalization of male interests reached beyond capitalist profiteering rationales. Moreover, although socialist models were few and flawed, gender inequality persisted in seemingly intractable ways.

During the 1980s, the wind-up period on women and the state analyses, the state and its ideology were tied to development policies. Debates existed among 'feminists': should feminists work with the state or against the state? The state was the foundation from which development policies operated. In contrast to the few states with a positive track record on women and gender justice, many states seemed doomed to perpetuate gender hierarchy.

Several collections emerged on the state–development–women connections in the 1980s. Charlton, Everett and Staudt (1989) reviewed literature on statism, calling for analysts to examine state officials and their gender ideologies, state policies and institutions, and state definitions of the parameters of politics. The area-studies chapters in their collection made theoretical use of the public–private divide that emerged in Western theories. Deere and León (1987) set their collection in terms that linked agricultural and land policies in Latin America to national economic policies and the global debt problem. Afshar's collection (1987) focused on nation-state case studies of policies in Asia and Africa. In their edited collection, Parpart and Staudt (1989) drew on critical theoretical perspectives of dependency and mode of production analysis to examine the origins of the state in Africa, women's access to the state and state management of resources. These collections traced state origins to Europe in centuries past, with the transnational spread of state structures and ideologies through world capitalism, colonization and imperialism. Yet even before the rise of the modern state, it appeared that men dominated women, drawing in part on public, institutional authority.

A proliferation of edited collections emerged using the nation state as a unit of analysis. It was refreshing and long overdue that country case studies appeared, for comparative politics had rarely integrated women and gender into analyses. Yet this flurry of country cases made it clear that analysts could not easily generalize about states in the nearly 200 countries worldwide.

State analysis winds down

Analysis on women and the state quickly wound down for a variety of reasons. Related analyses re-emerged with new conceptual language, such as democracy, governance, political representation and accountability. Why the wind-down? Some of the debates led to answers, pointing towards new analytic trends.

First, states began to be differentiated, not only in their strength and weakness as agents of control, authority and power, but also in the degrees to which they opened space to women's claims to be active and heard, for space within the state, and for justice in policy and legal terms. States were never all alike, and some of the most overdrawn feminist analyses treated them as monolithic, with men and women as monolithic inhabitants within them. All but the most simplistic research acknowledges the diversity among women and men by class, nationality, culture and geographic space, among other factors (Mohanty, Russo and Torres 1991). Further, international financial institutions began structural adjustment programmes in the 1980s that aimed to reduce the size of states, make them more efficient and expose more economic resources to market forces. It was an analytic mistake to assume that states were static.

Second, weak states and even some strong states never had full power, authority and agency to envelop the societies they claim (Midgal 1988). Important theorizing recognized that another part of power was the ability of inhabitants to resist, sabotage and ignore state machinery. In parallel fashion, women exercise power in resistance to men and to the state. It was an analytic mistake to accept theoretical or state claims of omnipotence.

Third, states are not monolithic, but rather bundles of contradictions that do not work in perfect harmony. Some of the most overdrawn statist analysis emanated from the USA, with over-generalized, almost biological notions of women as victims and men as sexual aggressors (MacKinnon 1989). The welfare state began to be viewed as a category worth analysis and engagement. Canada and the Scandinavian states emerged as models for ways that rights and justice agendas might be consolidated within (Vickers, Rankin and Appelle 1993; Gelb 1989; Hernes 1987).

States revisited: Democracy, governance and politics

With democratic space and process, along with healthy judicial systems, people make use of contradictions within the state to achieve gains. In the 1990s, with the so-called transitions to democracy beginning to appear, a new context led to greater analytic attention being paid to the kinds of institutions and democracies which permit democratic openings to women and to gender justice agendas. A mammoth collection, with 43 country case studies, focused on political institutions (Nelson and Chowdhury 1994). Collections on women engaging state and international bureaucracy institutions offered insights into openings for women-and-gender justice agendas (Staudt 1997). Goetz (1997) aptly titled a collection *Getting Institutions Right for Women in Development.*

With globalization increasing in full force, in a context lacking accountable global governance, claims for gender rights and justice are operable primarily in existing nation state governance and transnational organizations. Thus, analysts have put institutional rules and processes on the agenda in order to determine which open space to women and new policies (Rule and Zimmerman 1994; Goetz 1997). In the United Nations Development Programme's (UNDP) annual *Human Development Report*, readers can compare nation state 'human development index' rankings and how gender-disaggregated data reduce rankings.

At the World Conference on Women, in Beijing in 1995, participants resolved to follow up its elaborate Platform for Action. Accountability is now a key concept for organization and research. Currently, debates are less likely to be anti-state or pro-state, but rather: how do people engage the state and public affairs for accountability, not only on traditional women's policy issues, but also on mainstream policy issues (Staudt 1998)? One vehicle of engagement is transnational non-governmental organization (NGO) activism, whether analysed at global, well-established NGO levels (Keck and Sikkink 1998; Moghadam 2005) or at grass-roots levels (Staudt and Coronado 2002; Staudt forthcoming).

So analysts are back to institutions once again, but in ways focused more closely on strategies to increase women's representation, such as quotas that exist in 92 countries (Henderson and Jeydel 2007: 15, 2005 figures), or to strengthen policy responses on such issues as violence against women (Weldon 2002), reproductive health (Stetson 2001) and job training (Mazur 2001), among others.

Conclusions

The rise and fall of women-and-the-state analysis parallels the contemporary challenge to meta-analysis and grand narratives. The state as all-powerful agent of male control is one of those grand, but wobbly scaffolds which, with a critical eye, falls with its own flaws. Women-and-the-state analysts now pursue various paths that examine national and global governance with a wide variety of institutional rules and policies.

Debates on women and the state moved analysts beyond the pro- or anti-state stance, useful in applications to women's activism. Analysts also moved beyond the notions of states as static and the same. What emerged after statist analyses was a comparative approach that examined institutions and accountability strategies. Yet a common thread of male control lingers in the institutions, policies and laws in countries worldwide, part of a growing global economy. Hopefully, comparative studies of women in politics will not regress to a pluralist approach, worldwide, for the analysis convincingly demonstrated that few, if any, states have operated as neutral umpires in gender terms.

GUIDE TO FURTHER READING AND REFERENCES

Afshar, H. (ed.) (1987) *Women, State and Ideology: Studies from Africa and Asia*, Albany, NY: State University of New York and Albany Press.

Charlton, S.E.M., Everett, J. and Staudt, K. (eds) (1989) *Women, the State, and Development*, Albany, NY: State University of New York and Albany Press.

Deere, C.D. and León, M. (eds) (1987) *Rural Women and State Policy: Feminist Perspectives on Latin American Agricultural Development*, Boulder, CO: Westview Press.

Duverger, M. (1955) *The Political Role of Women*, Paris: UNESCO.

Evans, P.B., Rueschemeyer, D. and Skocpol, T. (eds) (1985) *Bringing the State Back In*, Cambridge: Cambridge University Press.

Gelb, J. (1989) *Feminism and Politics: A Comparative Perspective*, Berkeley, CA, and Los Angeles, CA: University of California Press.

Goetz, A.M. (ed.) (1997) *Getting Institutions Right for Women in Development*, London: Zed Books.

Henderson, S.L. and Jeydel, A.S. (2007) *Participation and Protest: Women and Politics in a Global World*, New York: Oxford University Press.

Hernes, H.M. (1987) *Welfare State and Woman Power*, Oslo: Norwegian University Press.

Keck, M. and Sikkink, K. (1998) *Activists Across Borders*. Ithaca, NY: Cornell University Press.

MacKinnon, C. (1989) *Toward a Feminist Theory of the State*, Cambridge, MA: Harvard University Press.

Mazur, A. (2001) *State Feminism, Women's Movements, and Job Training*, New York: Routledge.

Migdal, J.S. (1988) *Strong Societies and Weak States: State–Society Relations and State Capabilities in the Third World*, Princeton, NJ: Princeton University Press.

Moghadam, V.M. (2005) *Globalizing Women: Transnational Feminist Networks*, Baltimore, MD: Johns Hopkins University Press.

Mohanty, C.T., Russo, A. and Torres, L. (eds) (1991) *Third World Women and the Politics of Feminism*, Bloomington, IN: Indiana University Press.

Nelson, B. and Chowdhury, N. (eds) (1994) *Women and Politics Worldwide*, New Haven, CT: Yale University Press.

Parpart, J. and Staudt, K. (eds) (1989) *Women and the State in Africa*, Boulder, CO: Lynne Rienner Publishers.

Rule, W. and Zimmerman, J.F. (eds) (1994) *Electoral Systems in Comparative Perspective: Their Impact on Women and Minorities*, Westport, CT: Greenwood Publishing.

Staudt, K. (ed.) (1997) *Women, International Development and Politics: The Bureaucratic Mire*, second edition, Philadelphia, PA: Temple University Press.

Staudt, K. (1998) *Policy, Politics and Gender: Women Gaining Ground*, West Hartford, CT: Kumarian Press.

Staudt, K. (forthcoming 2008) *Violence and Activism at the Border: Gender, Fear and Everyday Life in Ciudad Juárez*, Austin, TX: University of Texas Press.

Staudt, K. and Coronado, I. (2002) *Fronteras no Más: Toward Social Justice at the US–Mexico Border*, New York: Palgrave USA.

Stetson, D.M. (2001) *Abortion Politics, Women's Movements, and the Democratic State*, New York: Oxford University Press.

United Nations Development Programme (UNDP) (annual) *Human Development Report*, New York: Oxford University Press.

Vickers, J., Rankin, P. and Appelle, C. (1993) *Politics as if Women Mattered: A Political Analysis of the National Action Committee on the Status of Women*, Toronto: University of Toronto Press.

Weldon, S. (2002) *Protest, Policy, and the Problem of Violence Against Women: A Cross-National Comparison*, Pittsburgh, PA: University of Pittsburgh Press.

7.2 Gender, families and households

Ann Varley

Family and household as cultural constructs

The distinction between 'The Family' and 'families' is a key fault line in contemporary social and political thought. Using the term 'families' signifies rejection of the nuclear family household as the universal norm. Insistence on the definite article signals support for an ideal family form or repudiation of 'Western' influences allegedly undermining local traditions. 'Family' is often used as a touchstone by which communities differentiate themselves from each other or gauge how they have changed over time. Changes in family life may therefore symbolize the effects of development or modernization processes, for better or for worse.

Debates about the family are often, in reality, debates about women's behaviour. The figure of the young woman leaving the family home to find work in the city has served as a symbol of modernity displacing tradition in many different societies. Women may be blamed for a range of social ills, while men's behaviour too often remains unquestioned. For example, to explain a rise in extra-marital pregnancies among unmarried teenagers, the main question may be why young *men* are refusing to marry. There is also a danger in isolating families as a subject for discussion. Families may be blamed for the consequences of structural forces because it is convenient for the state to individualize responsibility for poverty.

Families are clearly an emotive subject. The term 'household' is often seen as more neutral. Households are usually defined in functional terms as 'task-oriented residence units', whereas families are kinship units that 'need not be localized' (Netting, Wilk and Arnould 1984: xx). Confusion arises because household membership is also generally based on kinship. Although households may consist of single individuals, friends or homosexual partners, members are usually recruited through heterosexual partnerships, childbearing or the incorporation of other kin. Many discussions about 'the family' thus refer to the family household.

Household functions include co-residence, economic cooperation, reproductive activities such as food preparation and consumption, and socialization of children. It is mistaken, however, to regard 'household' as unproblematically descriptive by comparison with the value-laden 'family'. Households are also cultural constructs. We should not assume that our own society's understanding of 'household' is shared by others. For example, the functions mentioned above are often assumed to take place within the same unit, but in parts of sub-Saharan Africa, they may be spread across several residential units.

Functional accounts of the household unit run the risk of portraying it as isolated from the rest of society. In practice, members' survival and well-being is also influenced by connections with other households. The importance of social networks was demonstrated by Larissa Lomnitz's classic (1977) study of a Mexican 'shantytown'.

An emphasis on households as bounded units can also lead us to 'misconstrue them as social actors endowed with human consciousness' (Yanagisako 1984: 331), and it is then tempting to identify the group with one actual human actor. The 'head of household' concept has been much criticized. For one person to represent the household implies that there are no systematic conflicts of interest between members and that the head will act altruistically and equitably. Feminist scholars have challenged this assumption that family life is based on consensus and cooperation, arguing that households are characterized by inequality structured around the axes of gender, age and generation.

Gender, household headship and household relations

The theme of gender and households is often narrowly interpreted as referring to 'woman-headed households'. It is often assumed that the proportion of households headed by a woman is increasing dramatically, but the evidence is not clear-cut. Many countries show increases in recent years, but others report the opposite (United Nations 2000, 2006b). Some discussions of the subject are, however, seriously flawed, statistically and conceptually.

Statistically, problems of definition and meaning are daunting. An economic definition of headship may be preferred, but it is not practical for census purposes. Many census agencies ask respondents to say who heads their household or exclude the possibility of a woman being counted as head unless there is no adult male present. They may therefore 'considerably understate women's household responsibilities' (United Nations 2000: 42). Other agencies have replaced the head with a 'reference

Table 1 Percentage of household heads who are women, by region (1995–2003)

Region	Percentage		No. of countries for which data are available
Africa	23.8		37
Northern Africa		12.9	2
Southern Africa		42.2	3
Rest of sub-Saharan Africa		23.5	32
Asia and Oceania	13.4		27
Eastern Asia		20.0	5
Southeastern Asia		15.4	5
Southern Asia		9.6	5
Central Asia		27.6	5
Western Asia		10.8	5
Oceania		54.1	2
Latin America and the Caribbean	23.9		21
Caribbean		33.5	7
Central America		21.2	6
South America		24.2	8
Canada and United States	45.9		2
Europe	30.5		22
Eastern Europe		33.1	7
Western Europe		29.4	15
All	21.4		109
Excluding Canada, USA and Europe		16.4	85

Source: author's calculations, from United Nations (2006b) Table A6. Source of data mostly *Demographic Yearbook* database (as of January 2005), plus United Nations (1999), Topic 4.7.

Notes: no data available for China (other than Hong Kong and Macau), the Russian Federation, Ukraine, Thailand, or many smaller populations.

Weighted regional totals calculated using estimated number of households for each country obtained by dividing the population size (United Nations 2006a) by mean household size (United Nations 2006b, Table A6). For Germany and Jamaica, no figure was available for household size, so the number of households was taken from United Nations (1999), Topic 4.7.

For the need for caution in interpreting the meaning of these figures, see text and Varley (1996).

person', who may simply be the person who filled in the form. This may account, in part at least, for recent increases in countries such as the United States or New Zealand.[1] In other countries recording dramatic increases, such as Eritrea and Rwanda, very different explanations probably apply.[2]

Many authors nonetheless confidently assert that one-third of the world's households are headed by a woman. This figure comes from an 'educated guess' by participants in the 1975 International Women's Year conference (I. Tinker, personal communication 1995). It is not supported by census data (Varley 1996). We do not know how national data should be adjusted to counter male bias or to allow for married women taking responsibility for household maintenance. The available information, however flawed, is summarized in Table 1. Excluding Europe, the

1 The figure for New Zealand has recently risen from 37 to 55 per cent; that for the United States, from 36 to 47 per cent (United Nations 2000, 2006b). New Zealand uses as reference person the person who filled in the census form. The US census form describes 'person 1' as one of the household members who owns/rents/is buying the house; but if a married couple are doing so jointly, whoever fills in the form can choose who to name as person 1.

2 The figure for Eritrea has risen from 31 to 47 per cent in recent years; that for Rwanda, from 25 to 36 per cent (United Nations 2000, 2006b).

United States and Canada, this table suggests that one in six households is headed by a woman. Including all the countries reporting a figure, the proportion is around one in five.

Why has the 'one-third' figure proved so attractive? As Cecile Jackson (1996: 492) suggests, there has been an 'inclination...to "talk up" the numbers of women-headed households, and their poverty, to justify GAD [gender and development] in numerical terms'. 'One in three' grabs people's attention.

There are, however, dangers in prioritizing impact over accuracy. The evidence linking poverty and female headship is far from clear-cut; but this aspect of the 'feminization of poverty' debate can distract attention from other issues. Intra-household or 'secondary' poverty in households with both partners present – and, in particular, the denial to women and children of full access to men's income – has been described as a more important concern (Chant 2006).

The focus on woman-headed households has other dangers. First, there is a temptation to conflate households headed by women and those headed by men with, respectively, 'women' and 'men'. This renders women who are not heads of household invisible. The problems with such an approach can be seen, for example, in programmes providing security of tenure in self-built housing areas that seek to attain gender equity objectives by including women without a partner, but ignore those who do currently have a partner (Varley 2007). What will happen to such women should their relationship subsequently break down: will they be able to keep a roof over their heads? Second, there is a tendency to over- or underplay the agency of women who head their household. Portraying them as opting out of patriarchal relationships, for example, overlooks the question of widowhood. Table 2 shows that, in most regions, the highest proportion of woman-headed households occurs where the householder is aged 60 or over, pointing to the significance of widowhood in this context. Different life expectancies for men and women, together with a tendency for women to marry partners older than themselves, mean that demographic ageing may be increasing the percentage of woman-headed households.

Underplaying women's agency makes female household heads the victims of male desertion. Although it is more likely to be women who are left with the responsibility for raising children, it is not always men who leave. Recent interest in masculinities and development is helping to

Table 2 Percentage of household heads who are women, by region and age group, and percentage of household heads aged 60+, by region and sex of head (1985–1996)

Region	Where head is 24 or less	Where head is 25–44	Where head is 45–59	Where head is 60 or over	% of women heads aged 60+	% of men heads aged 60+	No. of countries
Africa	26	28	32	37	21	15	9
Latin America and Caribbean	15	14	22	32	31	15	10
Asia and Oceania	9	9	15	26	33	15	9
Europe	39	19	21	43	47	24	19
Other developed regions	43	27	25	40	30	20	5
All	28	20	23	38	34	19	52

Source: author's calculations, from United Nations (1999), Topic 4.7.

Note: No data available for China (other than Hong Kong and Macau), Pakistan, the Russian Federation, Nigeria, or many smaller populations. Data for India, Indonesia and Bangladesh are not disaggregated by age.

Regional headings as in United Nations (2000) Chart 2.25 (which presents unweighted averages). Weighted regional totals were calculated using either household totals from United Nations (1999), Topic 4.7, or the 1990 census round figure for total households (Topic 4.8) together with the percentage female headship for each country (Topic 4.7).

There is some variation in age categories (for instance, in a few cases, national figures cited as including ages 15 to 24 include ages 15 to 29).

counteract the stereotype of male 'irresponsibility' (Bannon and Correia 2006). In addition, intra-household conflict is not confined to conflict between spouses. There is a history of conflict between women in extended households, particularly in southern and eastern Asia and in Latin America. Where brides have traditionally moved in with their husband's parents, there has long been a problem of mothers-in-law teaching them to 'know their place', in a sometimes brutal fashion. Where greater prosperity and female employment has made young couples less dependent, the unhappiness created by sharing accommodation has encouraged household nucleation.

Down the line, such conflict has implications for the welfare of elderly women, who have been marginalized by the literature's emphasis on 'lone mother' households with dependent children (Varley 1996). What this means must be considered in the light of the observation that developing countries are currently ageing much faster than developed countries. Fertility decline implies that older people will have fewer children to support them, although it cannot be assumed that this means a decline in the availability of care, since not all children may have supported their parents in the past (Aboderin 2005). In addition, 'the growing number of young married couples who live on their own...means that care by a daughter-in-law is no longer automatic' (Wilson 2000: 120). We should not assume, therefore, that people living with younger relatives have been 'taken in' to be looked after. Intergenerational support does not necessarily flow 'upwards', especially when economic difficulties facing younger people make even the funds from meagre pensions attractive to other family members (Lloyd-Sherlock 2004). Old people can find themselves sharing their accommodation, pensions or limited incomes from informal employment with the younger generation far longer than they may have anticipated or desired (Skinner 2007).

Older people can find themselves in a vulnerable position – in extreme cases, as victims of abuse – when they live with relatives, particularly where the balance of power in the mother-in-law/daughter-in-law relationship is shifting towards the younger woman. Yet older women in need of accommodation may nonetheless be in a better position than their male counterparts. Women's association with housework and childcare means they can continue to 'make themselves useful'. By contrast, older men who have lost their breadwinner role risk being seen as 'useless' or being blamed for earlier failures to provide adequate financial or emotional support for their families (Varley and Blasco 2000).

The significance of gender in relation to families and households is, in short, far broader than the persistent emphasis on woman-headed households would suggest.

GUIDE TO FURTHER READING

Aboderin, I. (2005) 'Changing family relationships in developing nations', in M.L. Johnson, with V.L. Bengtson, P.G. Coleman and T.B.L. Kirkwood (eds) *The Cambridge Handbook of Age and Ageing*, Cambridge: Cambridge University Press, pp. 469–75. Succinct review of debates about family relationships and support for the elderly, and of the reasons for changing family systems.

Bannon, I. and Correia, M.C. (eds) (2006) *The Other Half of Gender: Men's Issues in Development*, Washington, DC: World Bank. Reviews the connections and contradictions between normative manhood and development in Latin America and Africa, with several chapters on men's family roles.

Chant, S. (2006) 'Re-thinking the "feminization of poverty" in relation to aggregate gender indices', *Journal of Human Development*, 7(2): 201–20. Questions the 'feminization of poverty' argument and proposes instead the existence of a 'feminization of responsibility and obligation'.

Lloyd-Sherlock, P. (ed.) (2004) *Living Longer: Ageing, Development and Social Protection*, London: Zed Books. Explores older people's well-being and family-based as well as formal provision of social protection across a range of different development contexts.

Wilson, G. (2000) *Understanding Old Age: Critical and Global Perspectives*, London: Sage. Chapter 9, 'Family and community in later life', pp. 115–30, offers a concise introduction to the role of families in caring for older people worldwide.

REFERENCES

Aboderin, I. (2005) 'Changing family relationships in developing nations', in M.L. Johnson, with V.L. Bengtson, P.G. Coleman and T.B.L. Kirkwood (eds) *The Cambridge Handbook of Age and Ageing*, Cambridge: Cambridge University Press, pp. 469–75.

Bannon, I. and Correia, M.C. (eds) (2006) *The Other Half of Gender: Men's Issues in Development*, Washington, DC: World Bank.

Chant, S. (2006) 'Re-thinking the "feminization of poverty" in relation to aggregate gender indices', *Journal of Human Development*, 7(2): 201–20.

Jackson, C. (1996) 'Rescuing gender from the poverty trap', *World Development*, 24(3): 489–504.

Lloyd-Sherlock, P. (ed.) (2004) *Living Longer: Ageing, Development and Social Protection*, London: Zed Books.

Lomnitz, L. (1977) *Networks and Marginality: Life in a Mexican Shanty Town*, London: Academic Press.

Netting, R.McC., Wilk, R.R. and Arnould, E.J. (1984) 'Introduction', in R.McC. Netting, R.R. Wilk and E.J. Arnould (eds) *Households: Comparative and Historical Studies of the Domestic Group*, Berkeley, CA: University of California Press, pp. xiii–xxxviii.

Skinner, E. (2007) 'Livelihood strategies in old age: Older people and poverty in urban Bolivia', PhD thesis, University College London.

United Nations (1999) *Women's Indicators and Statistics Database (Wistat)*, Version 4 CD-ROM, New York: United Nations.

United Nations (2000) *The World's Women 2000: Trends and Statistics*, New York: United Nations.

United Nations (2006a) *Demographic Yearbook 2003*, New York: United Nations.

United Nations (2006b) *The World's Women 2005: Progress in Statistics*, New York: United Nations.

Varley, A. (1996) 'Women heading households: Some more equal than others?' *World Development*, 24(3): 506–20.

Varley, A. 'Gender and property formalization: Conventional and alternative approaches', *World Development*, 35(10): 1739–53.

Varley, A. and M. Blasco (2000) 'Intact or in tatters? Family care of older women and men in urban Mexico', *Gender and Development*, 8(2): 47–55.

Wilson, G. (2000) *Understanding Old Age: Critical and Global Perspectives*, London: Sage.

Yanagisako, S.J. (1984) 'Explicating residence: A cultural analysis of changing households among Japanese-Americans', in R.McC. Netting, R.R. Wilk and E.J. Arnould (eds) *Households: Comparative and Historical Studies of the Domestic Group*, Berkeley, CA: University of California Press, pp. 330–52.

7.3 Feminism and feminist issues in the South*

D. Alissa Trotz

Is it possible to speak of 'feminist issues in the South' without reductions to stereotyping? Does such a title suggest that these are separate and distinct from what one might presume to be feminist issues in the North? Certainly any number of issues spring immediately to mind: women's human rights; access to equitably paid work and continuing non-recognition of unwaged work; violence; militarization; conflict resolution; reproductive health and rights; the effects of HIV/AIDS; migration; access to land, education, housing and other services; structural adjustment policies. This chapter is not, however, a 'list' of feminist issues (any list risks omissions and generalizations, and what is a pressing matter in one site will not be in another). Instead, it considers

* This is a revised version of an essay co-authored by Linda Peake and D. Alissa Trotz.

some of the epistemological questions at stake in such a discussion, since it is very much bound up in questions of representation.

It is important to begin by noting that 'the Global South' references a contingent community, one in which historic and contemporary patterns of global inequality have produced resonances across places that are quite specific in so many other ways. Women of the South may have had an engagement foisted upon them by colonialism and its enduring legacies, but their futures cannot be contained within a single script. This variability is often denied by a geopolitical arrangement that relies on discrete, seemingly stable, oppositional and ahistorical categorizations – of nations, of developed and un(der)developed countries, of First and Third World, of North and South – that are profoundly gendered.

A seminal essay by Chandra Talpade Mohanty (1991), drawing on Edward Said's work on Orientalism, explored the portrayal of 'Third World women' in a series of texts on gender and development, and suggested that they were unified by a set of analytical manoeuvres that converged on the depiction of Third World women as passive victims – of development, colonialism, family, violence and culture. Gatekeeping concepts mediated the apprehension of entire areas of the South, from Caribbean matriarchy to Latin American machismo, from sati in India to female genital mutilation in Africa. Such discursive practices set up a binary in which Western women emerge as liberated, true subjects of history; that is to say, their self-making practices are accomplished via the othering of their Third World counterparts. The consequences of this process are threefold: it ignores the historic and geographic variability in the ways in which masculinities and femininities are constituted across and within regions and countries in the global South; it reinforces ideas that North and South are neatly separable; and it anticipates any form of women's organizing as always proto-feminist and mapped on to a tradition–modernity divide that replicates the presumed hierarchical relationship between 'developing' and 'developed' countries. Moreover, responses to these post-colonial critiques have sometimes compounded the problem, as Uma Narayan (2000) shows in her careful exposition of how self-conscious feminist efforts to respond to charges of universalism and gender essentialism all too often result in cultural essentialisms and equally reified portraits of Third World women.

Nor are these discourses without material effects, as is evident in the rehearsal of narratives of victimhood to rationalize the US military occupation of Afghanistan, a campaign that drew partially – and with the support of the media and many feminist organizations in the West – on images of Afghan women uniformly oppressed under the Taliban in ways that efface both a problematic history of US involvement in the region as well as Afghan women's activities on the ground (Arat-Koc 2002). Current antitrafficking campaigns that have attained international visibility similarly recirculate gendered and racialized stereotypes to carve out anti-immigration policies that fortify the borders of the industrialized world and criminalize women from the South, obscuring the complex global factors that underpin the composition and direction of migrant flows (Kempadoo 2004).

Drawing attention to these hegemonic representational strategies has also underscored how they are partly related to the uneven circuits of knowledge production and dissemination which concentrate publishing resources and output in Europe and North America, and, in fact, there are now creative initiatives to circumvent this imbalance, such as the recent launching of two open-access online journals: *Feminist Africa*, published out of the African Gender Institute in South Africa, and the *Caribbean Review of Gender Studies*, from the Centre for Gender and Development on the Trinidad and Tobago campus of the University of the West Indies. There have also been earlier contributions that restore a sense of complex historical agency to women's lives in the global South, like Maria Mies's (1982) discussion of how the international division of labour resulting from a system of global capital accumulation framed the domestic and employment trajectories for women in India producing for the global market. Another central text in this regard is Kumari Jayawardena's (1986) examination of feminism and nationalism in the Third World, which showed that far from being merely symbolic of, or subject to, patriarchal constructions of nation, women were actively and variously invested in anticolonial and national liberation movements. This timely intervention highlighted the fact that feminism was neither a Western imposition (a view held by traditionalists in the South) nor a gift (the stance of liberal feminism in the North), but rather that situated 'historical circumstances produced important material and ideological changes that affected women' (Jayawardena 1986: 2), carving a space between the imperial gaze of Western feminism and a frequent local expectation that the 'gender question' be postponed or subordinated to a broader revolutionary struggle.

There is, of course, a wider context that frames these rebuttals. If in North America and Europe it relates to the contestation by those constituencies (queer, immigrant, women of colour and others) who found themselves excluded from the universal pretensions of mainstream feminism, tensions around the representation of 'feminist issues in the South' became clear in the first conferences following the Declaration of the United Nations Decade for Women in 1975. From the very start, women from the South (who also vary in the degree to which they use the term feminist as self-description) challenged what they saw as the hegemonic vision of Western feminism, raising questions about a global female sisterhood as well as the issue of who is defining a feminist agenda and from where. They refused to disengage from a materialist critique, insisting that highly skewed international political-economic arrangements needed foregrounding in any discussion of so-called 'women's issues'. While critiques of the liberalist growth models of development of the 1950s and 1960s had created a space through which issues of women and development could be inserted into mainstream development discourse, Southern-based groups, such as Development Alternatives with Women for a New Era (DAWN), argued that the question was not whether women were left out of development, but the skewed manner in which they were incorporated (Sen and Grown 1987).

DAWN's observations have become more prescient since the mid 1980s, during which time a comprehensive shift to neoliberal policies has resulted in the deepening of poverty and the widening of economic and social inequalities *across* the world. Ironically, one of the major challenges facing women's movements and activists in the Global South in a climate of economic liberalization has to do with the virtual explosion during this time of women's visibility in the global public arena. While this belated attention to 'women' on the part of supranational, regional and national regimes is partly the result of lobbying and mobilization of transnational feminist networks (Alvarez et al. 2002; Friedman 2003), the terms of inclusion have been far less promising. The visibility of women in survival strategies has put them on the radar of developmentalist agendas seeking to extend the reach of the market to everyone, raising questions about the ways in which the deployment of gender enables it to coexist with neoliberal projects (Obiora 2004). The instrumentalization of gender as a target of improvement via specific modes of intervention – micro-credit offers one excellent example – disarms the transformative agenda of women's movements in the South and turns women, and poor women in particular, into clients (Bergeron 2003; Rankin 2004). International funding, while offering opportunities for cash-strapped activist organizations, also presents new challenges related to the NGOization of the women's movement and the rearticulation of lines of accountability from the local to the international (Alvarez 1999; Ford-Smith 1997). Indeed, some activists have explicitly expressed the concern that the current gender dispensation highlights divisions among women, where grass-roots women are represented by a professional feminist class as requiring rescue, while dominant economic arrangements that marginalize most women in the Global South go unquestioned (Andaiye 2002).

In the face of these challenges, what has been significant is that the spaces in which women are predominantly located and which tend to be designated their main arenas of responsibility – the neighbourhood, the household – have become politicized and transformed into sites of struggle. In Latin America, for example, numerous studies have demonstrated the critical and ongoing contributions made by countless women to the transitions to democracy in the 1980s. That it is women in the South who are at the forefront of working to change the conditions under which they live is significant for what it says about the choices they are prepared to and have to make, in a world in which caring work does not come with a similar or equal set of obligations for everyone:

> Women stand at the crossroads between production and reproduction, between economic activity and the care of human beings, and therefore between economic growth and human development. They are the workers in both spheres – the most responsible, and therefore with most at stake, those who suffer the most when the two work at cross-purposes, and most sensitive to the need for better integration between the two (DAWN 1995: 21).

Centring women's lives is not just about rendering them visible in patterns of globalization, but rather seeks to reconfigure the terrain of what is possible to ask about the logic, effects and consequences of interconnected processes at a variety of scales. Viewing globalization not as an already done deal, but as the contingent – hence changeable – outcome of a confluence of factors permits a focus on how women are variously inserted into the global arena as complexly gendered *actors*, in ways that contest and reinforce patterns of subordination across shifting fields of power (Freeman 2001; Ramamurthy 2003). In these feminist discussions, it is no longer possible to sustain the fiction of compartmentalization: North–South; Third World producer–First World consumer; victim–actor; developed–developing. What is instead sought after is a relational approach and methodology (Katz 2001; Shohat 2002), one which can track 'historical and newly emergent forms of colonisation' (Alexander and Mohanty 1997) that unevenly connect and resonate across place (and here, an emblematic figure of this connectedness is the migrant female worker in advanced capitalist countries who confounds any effort to confine her spatially to the South). There is also a growing literature on efforts to organize women across borders, both within the Global South as well as across North and South (Basu with McGrory 1995; Alvarez et al. 2002; Naples and Desai 2002). Ultimately, we might conclude that the challenge is to craft inclusive and democratic practices, creating transnational feminist critiques while not losing sight of the specific and related spaces and inflected grammars (Nnaemeka 2004; Obiora 2004) through which diverse struggles for social justice are waged.

GUIDE TO FURTHER READING AND REFERENCES

Alexander, J. and Mohanty, C.T. (eds) (1997) *Feminist Genealogies, Colonial Legacies, Democratic Futures*, London: Routledge.

Alvarez, S. (1999) 'Advocating feminism: The Latin American feminist "boom"', *International Feminist Journal of Politics*, 1(2): 181–209.

Alvarez, S. et al. (2002) 'Encountering Latin American and Caribbean feminisms', *Signs*, 28(2): 537–79.

Andaiye (2002) 'The angle you look from determines what you see: Towards a critique of feminist politics in the Caribbean', Lucille Mathurin Mair Lecture, University of the West Indies, Kingston, Jamaica.

Arat-Koc, S. (2002) 'Imperial wars or benevolent interventions? Reflections on "global feminism" post September 11th', *Atlantis: A Women's Studies Journal*, 26(2): 53–65.

Basu, A. with McGrory, C.E. (eds) (1995) *The Challenge of Local Feminisms: Women's Movements in Global Perspective*, Boulder, CO: Westview Press.

Bergeron, S. (2003) 'Challenging the World Bank's narrative of inclusion', in A. Kumar (ed.) *World Bank Literature*, Minnesota: University of Minneapolis Press.

DAWN (Development Alternatives with Women for a New Era) (1995) *Markers on the Way: the Dawn Debates on Alternative Development*, Dawn's Platform for the Fourth World Conference on Women, Beijing.

Ford-Smith, H. (1997) 'Ring ding in a tight corner: Sistren, collective democracy, and the organization of cultural production', in M. Jacqui Alexander and Chandra Talpade Mohanty (eds) *Feminist Genealogies, Colonial Legacies, Democratic Futures*, London: Routledge, pp. 213–58.

Freeman, C. (2001) 'Is local:global as feminine:masculine? Rethinking the gender of globalization', *Signs*, 26(4): 1007–37.

Friedman, E.J. (2003) 'Gendering the agenda: The impact of the transnational women's rights movement at the UN Conferences of the 1990s', *Women's Studies International Forum*, 26(4): 313–31.

Jayawardena, K. (1986) *Feminism and Nationalism in the Third World*, London: Zed Books.

Katz, C. (2001) 'On the grounds of globalization: A topography for feminist political engagement', *Signs*, 26(4): 1213–34.

Kempadoo, K. (2004) 'Victims and agents: The new crusade against trafficking', in J. Sudbury (ed.) *Global Lockdown: Race, Gender and the Prison Industrial Complex*, New York: Routledge.

Mies, M. (1982) *The Lacemakers of Narsapur: Indian Housewives Produce for the World Market*, London: Zed Books.

Mohanty, C. (1991) 'Under Western eyes: Feminist scholarship and colonial discourses', in *Third World Women and the Politics of Feminism*, Bloomington, IN: Indiana University Press, pp. 51–80.

Naples, N. and Desai, M. (2002) *Women's Activism and Globalization: Linking Local Struggles and Transnational Politics*, New York and London: Routledge.

Narayan, U. (2000) 'Essence of culture and sense of history: A feminist critique of cultural essentialism', in U. Narayan and S. Harding (eds) *Decentering the Center: Philosophy for a Multicultural, Postcolonial, and Feminist World*, Bloomington, IN: Indiana University Press, pp. 80–100.

Nnaemeka, O. (2004) 'Nego-feminism: Theorizing, practicing, and pruning Africa's way', *Signs*, 29(2): 357–86.

Obiora, L. (2004) 'Supri, supri, supri Oyibo? An interrogation of gender mainstreaming deficits', *Signs*, 29(2): 649–62.

Ramamurthy, P. (2003) 'Material consumers, fabricating subjects: Perplexity, global connectivity discourses, and transnational feminist research', *Cultural Anthropology*, 18(4): 524–50.

Rankin, K. (2004) *The Cultural Politics of Markets: Economic Liberalization and Social Change in Nepal*, Toronto: University of Toronto Press.

Sen, G. and Grown, C. (1987) *Development Crises and Alternative Visions: Third World Women's Perspectives*, New York: Monthly Review Press.

Shohat, E. (2002) 'Area studies, gender studies, and the cartographies of knowledge', *Social Text*, 20(3): 67–78.

7.4 Rethinking gender and empowerment

Jane Parpart

Empowerment has become a largely unquestioned development goal of such diverse and contradictory development institutions as the World Bank, United Nations Development Programme (UNDP), Oxfam and many smaller non-governmental organizations (NGOs). Initially seen as a necessary ingredient for challenging and transforming unequal political, economic and social structures, empowerment was regarded as a weapon for the weak – best wielded through participatory, grass-roots, community-based NGOs. However, empowerment is a flexible concept, and by the mid-1990s mainstream development agencies had begun to adopt the term. While not abandoning their belief in liberal economic policies, the language of participation, partnership and empowerment increasingly entered mainstream development discourse (World Bank 1995; Elson and Keklik 2002). While the word might be the same, meanings varied, and mainstream institutions and their practitioners for the most part envisioned empowerment as a means for enhancing efficiency and productivity within the status quo rather than as a mechanism for social transformation (Parpart, Rai and Staudt 2002).

The issue of empowerment first surfaced in gender and development debates in the work of Caroline Moser (1993) and Gita Sen and Caren Grown (1987). These writings reflected a concern among feminists in the South and North that women would never develop unless they could become sufficiently empowered to challenge patriarchy and global inequality. Moser focused on self-reliance and internal strength, arguing that empowerment was best defined as the ability 'to determine choices in life and to influence the direction of change, through the ability to gain control over crucial material and non-material resources' (1993: 74–5). Sen and Grown emphasized collective action based on the lived experiences of women (and men) in the South, particularly the very poor. While rather utopian in tone, Sen and Grown (1987: 87) called for a collective vision, a set of strategies and new methods for mobilizing political will, empowering women (and poor men) and transforming society.

Writings on empowerment and gender have continued to emerge in the development literature, including important contributions from the South. In 1994, for example, Srilatha Batliwala warned that 'empowerment', which had virtually replaced terms such as poverty alleviation, welfare and community participation, was in danger of losing its transformative edge. She called for a more precise understanding of power and empowerment, one that sees power 'as control over material assets, intellectual resources, and ideology' (Batliwala 1994: 129). For Batliwala, empowerment is 'the process of challenging existing power relations and of gaining greater control over the sources of power' (ibid.: 130). It requires political action and collective assault on cultural as well as national and community power structures that oppress women and some men. Thus, while acknowledging the need to improve the lives of grass-roots women, Batliwala insists that women's empowerment requires transformative political action as well.

Naila Kabeer (1994) also insists on the centrality of empowerment for achieving gender equality. Drawing on Stephen Lukes (1974), she criticizes the liberal and Marxist emphasis on *power over* resources, institutions and decision making, and adds Lukes' focus on power as the ability to control discussions/discourses and agendas. She argues, however, for a more feminist analysis, one that emphasizes the transformative potential of *power within*. This power is rooted in self-understanding that can inspire women (and some men) to recognize and challenge gender inequality in the home and the community (Kabeer 1994: 224–9). Like Batliwala, Kabeer emphasizes collective, grass-roots participatory action – the *power to* work *with* others 'to control resources, determine agendas and to make decisions' (ibid.: 229). However, Kabeer is particularly concerned with enhancing the ability to exercise choice (associated with access and claims on resources, agency and achievements) (Kabeer 1999: 437).

Jo Rowlands argues that 'empowerment is more than participation in decision-making; it must also include the processes that lead people to perceive themselves as able and entitled to make decisions' (Rowlands 1997: 14). It is personal, relational and collective, and 'involves moving from insight to action' (ibid.: 15). Drawing on in-depth research in Honduras, she points to the crucial role played by social, political and economic contexts, warning that consciousness and agency are always context-specific. Sarah Mosedale, building on these debates, suggests that women's empowerment is best seen as both 'the process by which women redefine and extend what is possible for them to be and do in situations where they have been restricted compared to men', *and* 'the process in which women redefine gender roles in ways which extend their possibilities for being and doing' (Mosedale 2005: 252). For her the issue is not simply enhancing choice, it is the need to extend the limits of the possible.

Initially, mainstream development agencies ignored the language of empowerment, but as top-down development policies failed to alleviate poverty in the 1990s, especially among women, mainstream discourse began to change. Empowerment entered the lexicon of mainstream women's and development programmes. For example, the Beijing Platform stated unequivocally that women's empowerment is 'fundamental for the achievement of equality, development and peace' (United Nations 1995: para. 13). The Canadian International Development Agency's (CIDA) Policy on Gender Equality made women's empowerment one of the eight guiding principles for its policy goals (1999). While always hedged with concerns about improving women's productivity and efficiency within neoliberal economic systems and 'solutions' (World Bank 1995), development practitioners and policymakers from all perspectives increasingly agreed that empowerment is a necessary ingredient for women's development.

This seeming congruence of policy and approach obscures the difficulties faced by those trying to understand, implement and measure women's empowerment. While the instability of the term has its advantages – for empowerment varies by context and condition – that same fluidity can impede our understanding of the ways one might enhance both the process and outcomes of empowerment projects. Moser has expressed concerns about the transformative intentions of mainstream development agencies (1993: 74–5). Others, such as Naila Kabeer, point out that attempts to measure (and direct) empowerment have often been based on the assumption that 'we can somehow predict the nature and direction that change is going to assume. In actual fact, human agency is indeterminate and hence unpredictable in a way that is antithetical to requirements of measurement' (Kabeer 1999: 462). Mosedale (2005: 252–3) suggests a conceptual framework for establishing a baseline of power relations which is rooted in local contexts and can thus provide a basis for measuring movement towards or away from women's empowerment. No doubt others will enter the debate, as measuring empowerment continues to challenge those who wish to operationalize the term for development goals, particularly to enhance gender equality.

Despite different emphases and perspectives, discussions of empowerment have for the most part remained rooted in the local, in the needs of the 'poorest of the poor' – particularly women. While acknowledging the importance of the local and of grass-roots knowledge and activism, Parpart, Rai and Staudt (2002) argue that this focus on the local and the uncritical use of the term empowerment has constrained the transformative ability of the empowerment approach. They believe empowerment will only become an effective tool for challenging gender inequality when it moves beyond the local to address the four issues explored below.

First, critical approaches to power must be incorporated into all empowerment projects and plans. Empowerment must not be seen as *power over*, wherein women's empowerment means bringing women into the charmed circle of those wielding *power over* political and economic institutions. This approach ignores the internal blockages facing marginalized groups, and the subtle attitudinal and structural impediments to collective action (*power with*) and generative *power to*. Empowerment requires a nuanced, holistic approach that draws on feminist writings on power (Hekman 1996), as well as the scholars/activists mentioned above. It requires attention to language and meanings, identities and cultural practices, as well as the forces that enhance *power to* act *with* others to fight for change, often in hostile and difficult environments.

Second, while empowerment is often a local affair, we must remember that the local is embedded in the global and the national, and vice versa. Power (and empowerment) can only be understood within the interrelationships between and within these three levels. For example, global competitiveness affects job opportunities in even the smallest communities, drawing women and men into transnational migration networks and creating diasporas which can both help and hinder local and national gender practices. Global economic policies often define the limits of government policy and action at the national and regional level – witness the impact of structural adjustment policies on many Third World economies. Thus, understanding local processes requires understanding these larger forces as well.

Third, the empowerment literature needs to pay more attention to the ways institutional structures, material and discursive frameworks shape the possibilities and limits of individual and group agency and choices. This does not undercut the importance of local participation and consultation. It does, however, point to the need to situate individual and group action/agency within the material, political and discursive structures in which they operate. This requires careful, historically situated analyses of women's struggles to gain power in a world that is often neither of their own making or choosing.

Finally, empowerment is both a process and an outcome. At times the two are indistinguishable, at others they merge, and sometimes the process is the outcome. While recognizing that specific outcomes should (and often can) be measured, measuring empowerment remains elusive. Many subtle and often unexpected strategies have the potential, but not the certainty, of empowerment (Kabeer 1999). Others, such as international covenants and gender-sensitive laws, seem to guarantee empowerment, but fail due to patriarchal cultural practices and structures. Thus, while conceptual clarity demands some distinction between process and outcome, both are important. While attempts to measure outcomes can focus the mind and encourage new thinking, an obsession with outcomes and measurement can endanger the very processes most apt to nurture women's empowerment, even if not apparent at the time.

These critiques offer some guidelines for trying to ensure that women's empowerment is more than simply a 'motherhood' term for development agencies. They offer ways of making both the concept and practice of empowerment more rigorous, effective and nuanced. As we have seen, debates on empowerment, gender and development continue, in regard to both theory and practice. These debates are a welcome contribution to global efforts towards ensuring that empowerment can become a meaningful and effective tool for enhancing gender equity in an increasingly complex, global/local world.

GUIDE TO FURTHER READING AND REFERENCES

Batliwala, S. (1994) 'The meaning of women's empowerment: New concepts from action', in G. Sen, A. Germain and L.C. Chen (eds) *Population Policies Reconsidered: Health, Empowerment and Rights*, Boston, MA: Harvard University Press.

CIDA (1999) *Policy on Gender Equality*, Ottawa: Canadian International Development Agency.

Elson, D. and Keklik, H. (2002) *Progress of the World's Women: Gender Equality and the Millennium Development Goals*, New York: United Nations Development Fund for Women.

Hekman, S. (1996) *Feminist Interpretations of Michel Foucault*, University Park, PA: Pennsylvania State University Press.

Kabeer, N. (1994) *Reversed Realities: Gender Hierarchies in Development Thought*, London: Verso.

Kabeer, N. (1999) 'Resources, agency, achievements: Reflections on the measurement of women's empowerment', *Development and Change*, 30(3): 435–64.

Lukes, S. (1974) *Power: A Radical View*, London: Macmillan.

Mosedale, S. (2005) 'Assessing women's empowerment: Towards a conceptual framework', *Journal of International Development*, 17: 243–57.

Moser, C. (1993) *Gender Planning and Development: Theory, Practice and Training*, London: Routledge.

Parpart, J., Rai, S. and Staudt, K. (eds) (2002) *Rethinking Empowerment: Gender and Development in a Global/Local World*, London: Routledge.

Rowlands, J. (1997) *Questioning Empowerment: Working with Women in Honduras*, Oxford: Oxfam Publications.

Sen, G. and Grown, C. (1987) *Development, Crises, and Alternative Visions: Third World Women's Perspectives*, New York: Monthly Review Press.

United Nations (1995) *Beijing Platform for Action*, New York: United Nations.

World Bank (1995) *World Bank Participation Source Book*, Washington, DC: World Bank Environment Department Papers.

USEFUL WEBSITES

http://web.worldbank.org: see Alsop, R., Bertelsen, M. and Holland, J. (2005) *Empowerment in Practice*, World Bank.

http://www.undp.org/women; see the Resource Guide for Gender Theme Groups, January 2005.
http://www.unifem.org
http://www.jrf.org.uk/bookshop/eBooks/1859353185.pdf: see Seminars on Empowerment, Toronto Seminar
Group 2005.

7.5 Gender and globalization

Harriot Beazley and Vandana Desai

The impact of globalization on the lives of people of all nationalities, ages and ethnicities has accelerated in the past two decades. There has also been a growing acknowledgement that these processes of globalization have resulted in mixed consequences for men and women, but particularly for women in the developing world. This chapter examines some of the benefits and negative consequences afforded to women in the developing world as the result of new opportunities for economic empowerment presented to them by globalization. The analysis will begin with an overview of how production processes have sought to chase cheap and compliant labour in the export-oriented processing zones (EPZs) of different countries, resulting in new employment opportunities for women. Some of the negative consequences of neoliberal globalization, including the exploitation of women working in EPZs, and the threat of exploitation and abuse of women workers will then be explored. The chapter then considers how the international migration of women has rapidly increased as a result of these new opportunities, and how the feminization of labour has contributed to a shift in traditional gender relations within societies. Finally, the chapter describes some of the diverse and 'subtle strategies' employed by women as a response to the current challenges caused by neoliberal policies, and as a way of negotiating a sense of place within patriarchal societies which are slow to change. This includes a focus on how young women are developing new forms of feminism by drawing upon global images of young people reflected in the media. The chapter's main objective is to reveal how, even though women are taking a prominent role in the processes of globalization, they are not automatically benefiting from these endeavours.

Globalization

In recent years the term 'globalization' has gained escalating prevalence, with varied meanings. In the twenty-first century it is usually understood as the rapid international mobility of labour, goods, service-delivery and capital, facilitated by the liberalization of economies, privatization and the 'deregulation' of labour markets. In most developing countries, these neoliberal policies have often been adopted in the context of World Bank and International Monetary Fund (IMF)-supported rigid packages of structural adjustment programmes (SAPs) (Elson 1995). The aims of the SAPs were to strengthen the role of markets in these countries and to reduce the role of the state in trade and industry. These goals were considered critical for realizing economic growth and poverty reduction. Such programmes have led many governments and NGOs involved in development in the North and South to argue that globalization processes are consolidating a new kind of colonialism. Increasingly, power resources are being held by a relatively small number of global players who remain unaccountable to the vast population of people in poverty in the Global South (see Kerr and Sweetman 2003: 5).

For the past 25 years, owners of transnational corporations (TNCs) and multinational companies have been going offshore to build factories and produce their goods, where the labour is cheaper and the workers have no unions or rights. These investors are usually foreign (American, European, Australian or Japanese), and are able to make enormous profits through the employment and exploitation of cheap, predominantly female labour from developing countries. This practice has led to what is now known as 'the feminization of labour' in the majority world, particularly within the service and manufacturing industries. As the International Labour Organization has recently reported in a thorough analysis of gender and globalization: 'unequal gender relations have been shaped by and, in turn, shape globalisation' (Çağatay and Ertürk 2004: 1).

The feminization of labour

At face value, however, globalization has brought many new opportunities to young women in the developing world, and TNCs often promote women as the 'winners' in these new arrangements. In an effort to strive for economic development and industrialization most countries see private foreign investment from these corporations as the answer to their economic woes, and local employers are part of an international chain which links vast TNCs to individual women workers. As a result many countries focus on export-oriented industrialization (EOI), through the setting up of EPZs, where factories produce garments, shoes, sportswear, electronics, toys and other goods for production and export. These countries have to make sure that they have a 'comparative advantage', in order to appear attractive to foreign investors. Such 'comparative advantage' has been identified as existing in the abundant supply of low-paid 'flexible' female labour. There has also been an increasing trend for the setting up by multinational companies (including telecommunications companies, car rental companies and banks) of offshored services in these countries (e.g. India, Philippines and Indonesia). These call centres and data processing centres predominantly employ young female operators, and promote sexist and stereotypical images of women to the outside world.

A reliance on gender inequalities and low-waged female labour within host nations has been suggested as a fundamental component of structural adjustment and EOI (Elson 1995). The expansion of globalized industries has led to the migration of hundreds of thousands of young, usually single women, who the factories and service centres wish to employ. The reasons they want to employ young women is because they are considered to be more passive, flexible, acquiescent and more suited to mundane repetitive tasks (Elson 1995). Employers also believe that women are more likely to accept extremely low wages, precarious terms of employment and poor working conditions, as many are still living at home and do not yet have their own families to support, but are instead contributing to their parents' household income (Wolf 1992). In most patriarchal societies, if they are already married they are traditionally expected to be economically dependent on their husbands or to be secondary income earners, and so culturally their incomes are not considered as important as those of their husbands. It is these kinds of cultural beliefs and patriarchal gender-based hierarchies which the TNCs and factory employers are exploiting to their maximum advantage, and which are the basis of industrial capitalist development.

In her study of female factory workers in Java, Diane Wolf (1992) described the young women in her research as 'Factory Daughters', due to the patriarchal gender relations in the factories where they worked. In Wolf's research the young women were often poorly educated and were escaping poverty at home, as well as strict Muslim restrictions on young unmarried girls. Through their work experiences and their expendable incomes they had developed new-found freedoms, and were able to buy themselves small products of capitalism as the result of having their own income. This resulted in an improved status in the household, an increase in their position in society, as well as increased self-esteem.

The negative experiences of these young women, however, were exploitative working conditions, including shift work and over-long hours, and non-existent workers' rights. Wolf exposed patriarchal conditions within the factories, which were enforced by male managers, with strong discipline for those who complained. Wolf also documented the significant neglect of health and safety regulations in the factories, and how young women were dismissed if they got married, became pregnant or contracted work-related illnesses (Wolf 1992). Wolf found that in spite of multinational companies' and factory owners' claims that women were benefiting from their employment practices, in reality there was little hope for their long-term standard of living or their 'empowerment', as they were kept in low-paid positions and then dismissed when they got married, had children or became 'too old'. Factory owners and owners of multinational corporations are not interested in employing older female labour, as they are not considered to be so productive, and would prefer to employ young unmarried women.

The stories are similar elsewhere. In Saipan, within the territory of the USA, Philippine women are flown to the Pacific island to work in the garment factories, while living in appalling conditions in barrack accommodation, for which they have to pay an over-inflated rent. These women workers were drawn into poorly paid subcontracted work by agents who made false and glamorous promises to them that they would be working in mainland America. In some cases they were forced into bonded labour, as they had to repay their employers from their wages the cost of their recruitment and migration to Saipan from the Philippines (SBS 2002). If women try to demonstrate or speak out against appalling conditions they may lose their jobs, or worse: in 1993 in Java, a young female factory worker and activist called Marsinah was kidnapped and murdered. Her death was due to her participation in strike action at the factory where she worked (Weix 2002).

Gender and transnational migration

Transnational labour flows are a major result of economic globalization. With the rapid mobility of finance, capital and production, more than 120 million migrants have left their home countries in search of economic opportunities abroad (UN 2005). In South East Asia in 2000, the majority of migrant workers were women (Piper 2004). Since 2000, population mobility within and outside of South East Asian countries has escalated (UN 2005).

During the 1990s it was estimated that 4 million Indonesians were living abroad (Rahman 2002). Migrants from Indonesia are mostly overseas contract workers, working in Malaysia, Singapore, China, Hong Kong, South Korea and Taiwan. The Middle East, especially Saudi Arabia, has increasingly been a favoured destination for Indonesian and Indian women, who go to work as domestic workers or sex workers, with increased risk of HIV infection (Rahman 2002). Female migrants from the Philippines are mostly those who go to Hong Kong and Singapore to work as housemaids (Law 2002). For women from poor backgrounds, who are uneducated, migration can often take place only illegally, via a globalized network of human traffickers. In this way women take an extraordinary gamble to bridge the gap between poverty and gaining a livelihood leading to prosperity.

As with the growth of female factory workers, the escalation of female migrant labour is viewed by some as a positive indicator that women are benefiting from globalization and becoming 'empowered'. While the economic benefits of remittances from migration are well documented, many studies have also examined the social costs of migration on the migrants themselves, including their health concerns, labour conditions and treatment by employers (Rahman 2002; Piper 2004). As with women factory workers, women migrant labourers often come into adverse conditions once they enter into employment abroad. A combination of racial discrimination, employer abuse (including rape and sexual abuse), lack of health services, and vulnerable legal status confront women seeking low-paid jobs abroad (Piper 2004). Many cases have been reported of torture, rape, sexual assault, overwork and non-payment of wages (Silvey

2006). The increasing number of sexual harassment cases and human rights violations against female workers, particularly in Singapore, Hong Kong and the Middle East, have sparked major protests from labour unions and women's organizations globally (Law 2002).

Implications for gender relations

The sociocultural impacts of migration on the families of migrants who are left behind, including the impact of migration on the children of migrants, has also been documented (Beazley 2007a). Further, the migration of males has been a major factor leading to an increasing proportion of female-maintained households, the majority of which face extreme poverty. As a result, migration has led to the breakdown of extended family networks and a rise in divorce rates.

The breakdown of the extended family has been most evident in the cities where nuclear families are common, and they must manage work and home difficulties without extended family support networks. Pressure at work is compounded by calls for productivity and the achievement of quotas, with shift work and excessively long hours in the factories and call centres, particularly for female workers. These demands are impacting on the family, where there are daily struggles to catch up with the increasing cost of living and, as aspirations and attitudes change in the context of increasing opportunities, leading to exposure to fresh ideas and values, which oblige them to revaluate social identities, roles and undergo a process of psychological adjustment (see Desai 2006). Married women are also finding that they are unable to do their job and cope with traditional gender expectations at home. This is creating conflicts within families, between husband and wife, and between wives and mother-in-laws, resulting in an increased prevalence of familial breakdown, violence and divorce.

Traditionally there is a high expectation for girls in the developing world to take on family obligations at an early age and to stay close to the family home. In India and Indonesia, for example, young unmarried girls have restricted mobility, and are forbidden from going far from the house, where they are expected to be a 'good girl', perform domestic duties, and to be a good daughter. This trend is changing, however, as a result of the opportunity to work in the factories or overseas, to earn an income, and to escape the traditional expectations and gendered power relations in villages or in the cities.

Transnational migration has, therefore, become one way for girls to negotiate their circumscribed role in patriarchal societies, and to seek a new subjectivity. Going to work in the city in factories, or overseas as maids or domestic servants, offers them many more attractions and opportunities, and is increasingly perceived by them as a source of emancipation. In spite of stories of exploitation and abuse, the burning desire young women have to migrate for work, for the perceived benefits, continues to compel them to actively navigate such risks, in order that they may earn money, gain independence, and escape their restricted roles in the family and village (Silvey 2006; Beazley 2007a). These young women can be understood as active agents who are organizing their lives and negotiating the gendered power relations around them (Punch 2000).

Gender, cultural change and globalization

In most of the developing world, therefore, traditional patriarchal culture and religious ideas and upbringing have been a major influence on women's role in society. Social and technological change in these societies has, however, begun to replace stable identities based on familiar social class or caste hierarchies with multiple, fragmented and shifting identities, based on lifestyle and consumer choices. To compensate for their social and geographical exclusion, for example, young girls will avidly listen to the radio and watch TV. They are fascinated by soap operas and movies, and consume the media images of glamorous 'Western' lifestyles of free and independent women (see Ansell 2005). These are far more persuasive than the state or village community's construction of femininity, and much more appealing as an agent of socialization. Such circumstances have also given rise to fundamentalism, which is also connected to globalization, as politico-religious movements react to Western-imposed cultural domination. These emerging right-wing movements promote their own interpretations of 'tradition' and 'culture', at the expense of women's rights, and often their lives (Kerr and Sweetman 2003: 7).

Globalization, therefore, has not only influenced the identity construction of western women, but has resulted in increased media consumption, cultural production and identity formation among women in the developing world. These young women are not accepting their marginalized situation passively. Instead, they actively challenge and resist their situation through various psychological and spatial resistance strategies, and through the production of 'diverse and subtle strategies' (Beazley 2002; Desai 2006). New forms of feminism are emerging as women seek to negotiate traditional religious and cultural values and traditions, while embracing a more global culture. As a result of new-found opportunities, young women are creating their own gendered cultural spaces within strong patriarchal societies, which they use as sites of new-found autonomy and of resistance to prevailing values. Such spaces include the growing influence of the media on the changing identities and beliefs of women, and the use of new forms of virtual communication for women, giving them autonomy in how they run their lives (Holloway and Valentine 2003). For example, recent research has explored media consumption and cultural production among young women in Indonesia, India and Vietnam during a time of political transition and globalization, which has transformed and influenced the beliefs, values, spatial practices and identities of women in these countries (Thomas and Thuan, 2004; Beazley 2007b forthcoming; Chakraborty 2007 forthcoming). In these ways young women in the Global South have been able to construct 'geographies of resistance' to the dominant cultural models of femininity which persist in their societies (Pile and Keith 1997).

Conclusion

In conclusion, this chapter has demonstrated how although millions of women are playing a major role in the globalized networks of production and consumption in the developing world, they are not necessarily benefiting from this interaction. This is because, in many cases, globalization is compounding the poverty of women, causing increased marginalization and heightened gender inequalities. This trend follows rapid demographic change resulting from economic restructuring in many countries as a result of neoliberal policies, which has led to thousands of young women searching for new opportunities and identities. In particular, contemporary research into the gender impact of globalization in developing countries – via neoliberal economic policies including SAPs, and the rapid mobility of labour and capital – suggests that the benefits of globalization have not been equitably distributed, but have hampered efforts to improve the lives of women living in poverty. In fact, due to a relentless male bias in these global macroeconomics, women have been – and still are – the 'shock absorbers' of the global economic system (Elson 1995: 11).

In spite of this marginalization, however, women are not necessarily accepting their position passively. Mainstream modern Western culture has been influential in shaping a new form of feminism in the developing world, and this feminism is articulated through young women's involvement in global cultures. Young women are participating in a global society, by drawing upon international images of young people reflected in magazines and television, on the Internet, and in established youth cultures. The 'traditional' concept of women, and their role in developing countries – as promoted by the state and often a prerequisite for the investment of transnational corporations – is, in fact, being challenged by newly emerging identities and changing expectations of globally aware young women. It is implicit in all the above that action on the part of the international women's movement and gender and development policymakers and practitioners is needed more than ever (see Desai 2005). The key is how we turn the gender analysis of globalization into action for social change.

GUIDE TO FURTHER READING AND REFERENCES

Ansell, N. (2005) *Children, Youth and Development,* London: Routledge.

Beazley, H. (2002) 'Vagrants wearing makeup: Negotiating space on the streets of Yogyakarta, Indonesia', *Urban Studies*, 39(9): 1665–87.

Beazley, H. (2007a) 'The Malaysian orphans of Lombok: Children's livelihood responses to out-migration in Eastern Indonesia', in R. Panelli, R. Punch and E. Robson (eds) *Young Rural Lives: Global Perspectives on Rural Childhood and Youth,* London: Routledge, pp. 107–120.

Beazley, H. (2007b forthcoming) 'Chemical landscapes: Girls' resistance strategies through the Indonesian dance party scene', in L. Bennet and L. Parker (eds) Special Edition on *Indonesian Youth Today: Body, Sexuality and Gender* in *Intersections*.

Çağatay, N. and Ertürk K. (2004) 'Gender and globalization: A macroeconomic perspective', Working Paper No. 19, Policy Integration Department, World Commission on the Social Dimension of Globalization, International Labour Organization, Geneva.

Chakraborty, K. (2007 forthcoming) '*Pyaar, Ishq aur Mohabbat* – Love and risk in the *Bustees* [slums] of Kolkata', in D. Behara and R. Waterson (eds) *Ethnography of Asia Pacific Childhoods*, New Delhi: Sage.

Desai, V. (2005) 'NGOs, gender mainstreaming, and urban poor communities in Mumbai', *Gender and Development*, 13(2): 90–98.

Desai, V. (2006) 'Women's social transformation, NGOs and globalisation in urban India', in S. Raju, S. Kumar and S. Corbridge (eds) *Colonial and Postcolonial Geographies of India*, New Delhi, Thousand Oaks and London: Sage, pp. 120–140.

Elson, D. (1995) 'Male bias in macro-economics: the case of structural adjustment', in D. Elson, *Male Bias in the Development Process*, second edition, Manchester: Manchester University Press.

Holloway, S. and Valentine, G. (2003) *Cyberkids: Children in the Information Age*, London: Routledge.

Kerr, J. and Sweetman, C. (eds) (2003) *Women Reinventing Globalisation*, Oxford: Oxfam.

Law, L. (2002) 'Sites of transnational activism: Filipino non-government organisations in Hong Kong', in B.S.A. Yeoh, P. Teo and S. Huang (eds), *Gender Politics in the Asia-Pacific Region*, London: Routledge.

Pile, S. and Keith, M. (1997) (eds) *Geographies of Resistance*, London: Routledge.

Piper, N. (2004) 'Rights of foreign workers and the politics of migration in Southeast and East Asia', *International Migration*, 42(5): 71–97.

Punch, S. (2000) 'Children's strategies for creating playspaces: negotiating independence in rural Bolivia', in S. Holloway and G. Valentine (eds) *Children's Geographies: Living, Playing, Learning*, London: Routledge, pp. 48–62.

Rahman, N.A. (2002) 'Singapore girl? Indonesian housemaids want to be heard', *Inside Indonesia*, Jan–March. Online, available at http://www.insideindonesia.org/index.htm (accessed 20 January 2006).

SBS (Special Broadcasting Service) (Australia) (2002) 'Behind the labels: Garment workers in US Saipan', *Cutting Edge*, Sydney, NSW, 25th June (producer Tia Lessin).

Silvey, R. (2006) 'Consuming the transnational family: Indonesian migrant domestic workers to Saudi Arabia', *Global Networks*, 6(1): 23–40.

Thuan, N.B. and Thomas, M. (2004) 'Young women and emergent post-socialist sensibilities in contemporary Vietnam', *Asian Studies Review*, 28(2): 133–49.

UN (United Nations Economic and Social Council) (2005) 'Tackling emerging issues in international migration. International migration in the ESCAP region', 1–3 November 2005. Committee on Emerging Social Issues. Online, available at http://www.unescap.org/esid/committee2005/English/CESI2_2E.pdf (accessed June 2007).

Weix, G.G. (2002), 'Resisting history: Indonesian labour activism in the 1990s and the "Marsinah" case', in B. Yeoh, P. Teo and S. Huang (eds) *Gender Politics in the Asia-Pacific Region*. London: Routledge.

Wolf, D.L. (1992) *Factory Daughters: Gender, Household Dynamics, and Rural Industrialization in Java.* Berkeley, CA: University of California Press.

7.6 Gender and structural adjustment

Lynne Brydon

Introduction

This section focuses initially on structural adjustment programmes (SAPs), but concludes by locating SAPs within a broad range of economic policies trying, and largely failing, to target women. From the early 1980s, the International Monetary Fund (IMF) and the World Bank granted loans to the majority of states in the 'South' for the 'stabilization' and 'adjustment' of their economies. These loans were to be used to fund policies devised in accordance with the WB/IMF's dominant economic ideologies, broadly neoliberal, encouraging the shrinking of the state, the removal of subsidies and the growth of competition. Adjusting countries had to agree to implement measures calculated to restore their balances of payments and create entrepreneurially driven economies. There were incentives to produce 'tradable' goods (goods that could be traded for hard currency). The medium-term aim of adjustment was 'recovery with growth', the idea that Third World states could develop into middle-income countries by 2020.

Ideal outcomes of structural adjustment policies

SAPs derived from neoliberal economic theory and were supposed to create employment in new enterprises, competing in growing national, regional and global markets in a supposed level playing field (in short, economic theory and classical survey design do not provide 'level playing fields' with respect to gender – they are not gender-neutral). 'Recovery with growth' is a laudable aim, and the SAP policymakers assumed that efficient growth would involve the whole of a state's labour force, irrespective of gender: women's as well as men's labour would be included in the efficient workings of a state's economy, particularly those women who were educated and liable to be flexible in their approaches to work. But early empirical studies of the effects of SAPs indicated a range of hardships, apparently affecting women more than men: for example, declines in maternal and child health status (Cornia, Jolly and Stewart 1987), and cash shortages because of devaluation, removal of subsidies and increased competition in the informal sector (Afshar and Dennis 1992). Initial responses from the World Bank regarded the problems as temporary blips, but it did agree to monitor the situation. In the later 1980s, the World Bank set up Living Standards Measurement (LSM) surveys (large-scale statistical surveys done on a yearly basis, designed to monitor not only income spending, but also health indicators), to monitor the grass-roots effects of adjustment, and packages of short-term alleviatory policies, designed to target the worst-hit ('vulnerable') sectors of populations (for example, Ghana's PAMSCAD, the Programme of Actions to Mitigate the Social Costs of Adjustment; Brydon and Legge 1996).

Gender awareness?

At least some of the problems in achieving 'recovery with growth' can be blamed on gender-blindness. Informed by the neoliberalism of the World Bank, SAPs provide a prime example of the gender-blindness and 'male bias' (Elson 1995a) of supposedly gender-neutral theory. The LSM surveys built on economic theories incoporating specific household forms and power relations, resulting in outcomes that were male-biased, even if policy design were not. Only after serious criticisms of both SAPs and LSM surveys were serious attempts made to take gender into account, in the design and analysis of policies and surveys, and in the analysis of local labour market composition and divisions of labour.

Thus there were attempts at 'adding on' gender (Brydon and Legge 1996) to SAPs. Ghana's PAMSCAD, for example, targeted some policies specifically at women, but at women as 'reproducers' (nutrition and feeding programmes). Policies focused on income generation (loans for business or agricultural ventures) tended to favour men. Where women were the focus of loan policies, their prospective enterprises were confined within what is conventionally recognized as 'women's work'– for example, trading or food processing. Cultural assumptions of 'women's work' were not challenged. (Any attempt to disaggregate ostensibly gender-neutral survey data ran into difficulty as gender was not an integral axis in the LSM surveys.)

Empirical critiques

Contemporary critiques showed how women's lives were made more difficult as a result of SAPs (Afshar and Dennis 1992; Elson 1995a): increasing health problems for mothers (the implications being that mothers sacrifice their own nutrition and health for the sake of their children); women's household manager roles were made more difficult because of price rises (through devaluation and subsidy cuts); and opportunities for women's earning in formal and informal sectors declined. Cash shortages might mean switching to cheaper foods, either less nutritious (resulting in health risks) or, where pulses are introduced as protein, taking longer to prepare and cook (taking more of women's time and fuel).

Inefficient formal enterprises were rationalized (that is, wound up or seriously streamlined) with the introduction of SAPs, resulting in unemployment. Even though fewer women than men tended to be employed in these enterprises, disproportionately high numbers of women were laid off: whether this is because women were in low-level and unskilled positions (either through lack of education or connections/networks, or because of the gender division of labour within the market), or even because of blatant discrimination against women in downsizing the labour force, is a moot point. These points merit discussion in their own right, but the bottom line is that women were more likely to have been downsized than men.

But men were made redundant, and they too have to make a living, to survive and cope. The informal sector is the most obvious destination for the newly unemployed, so much so that it has become overcrowded. The practicalities of living are more difficult: there are only so many seamstresses, hairdressers, bakers and traders (women), and carpenters, electricians, plumbers and barbers (men) that a neighbourhood can support. The pool of SAP-created available labour is supposed to have been mopped up by new businesses, drawn by the availability of skilled labour and attractive conditions of production. Although a few new, locally owned companies have been founded, international capital has been shy of investing in adjusting countries, apart from under the favourable conditions of an export-processing zone (EPZ) or free trade area. But even where such zones exist, inward investment in many cases, and particularly in sub-Saharan Africa, has been minimal.

In EPZs most locally hired workers are women. The usually quoted rationale for this is their docility, because of women's 'natural' (sic) subordination to men (whether bosses or male relatives) and dexterity, because of the gendered training of women from childhood in 'nimble-fingered' tasks (Elson and Pearson 1981). This means that women can become family breadwinners, the power derived from their earnings at odds with 'traditional' household responsibilities (generally the outcome of gender stereotyping rather than any choice on the part of women themselves), where formerly they either had no or minimal control of cash (crudely summarizing, Asia, Latin America and the Middle East) or responsibility for specified areas of household expenditure (sub-Saharan Africa). Elson (1995a) has suggested that these changes lead to tension in domestic gender relations, and depression in the cases of husbands (resulting in stress for wives), as has happened with economic restructuring in the North.

These are the direct effects of SAPs on women, but there are also gendered, indirect consequences. Although the World Bank has denied that SAPs must necessarily mean cutbacks in social sector spending, particularly health and education, in practice, most adjusting countries have focused their revenues on the economy and balance of payments. While sectors like health and education have not been ignored under the dispensations of adjustment, neither have they been recipients of significantly increased central funding, and their overall share of GDP often declines, leaving women to pick up the burdens of providing education for children and health care for all family members at home. UNICEF reports: 'The region [sub-Saharan Africa] includes over 30 heavily indebted countries, and governments spend as much on debt repayment as on health and basic education combined – $12 billion in 1996, and per capita education spending is less than half that of 1980' (1999: 10). In addition, neoliberal thinking has been introduced into both health and education sectors in various ways.

Education

Although primary education remains nominally free in many adjusting states, cost-recovery principles have been introduced: costs such as uniform or books are borne by parents. Because there is still a bias towards educating sons rather than daughters, girls lose out where poor families have to pay. If fewer of today's girls have no or little education, there is less chance that their children will be educated and healthier (a mother's education level is positively correlated with nutrition and with her children's, especially daughters', education). In addition, overall economic growth of the country may be affected adversely: women's educational levels have been shown to be positively correlated with smaller family sizes.

Health

In the health sector, cost-recovery measures have been a strong feature, particularly with respect to drugs budgets. Prescribed drugs must now be paid for (at market rates), while costs of record-keeping, consultation and hospital care must also be borne by patients. Where sick people are too poor to pay for consultations or drugs, the costs of caring for the sick fall on women, who must both nurse and spend time looking for either cheaper patent or local herbal medicines.

In short, the empirical effects of adjustment for women were increases in their workloads, as the state sloughed off responsibility for a wide range of services. The burden of these services shifted from the public to the private, from the 'production'/visible account to the 'reproduction'/invisible account, and fell largely to the lot of women.

Gender, adjustment and economics

These empirical consequences of adjustment policies for women come about because the economic theory underpinning adjustment policies, although supposedly gender-neutral, is part of a set of discourses framed and operationalized in gender-biased contexts, and, in addition, the policies (again, ostensibly gender-neutral) they inform are put into practice in social environments which are emphatically not gender-neutral.

Work from the mid- to late 1990s on gender and adjustment moved away from the empirical and focused on the underlying assumptions of economic theories, particularly those of gender neutrality. Diane Elson (1993, 1995b, for example) has been at the forefront of this work, and has painstakingly deconstructed the assumptions underlying both neoliberal and structural economic theories. The problems with different varieties of economic theory stem mainly from three sources, as follows.

1 A failure to take into account (largely) women's unpaid 'work': social and biological reproduction.
2 A failure to recognize and address the manifestations of gender in a wide range of local contexts. The potential for gender disaggregation is not incorporated into models: there are women farmers and men farmers, women workers and men workers, and the parameters needed to describe their opportunities and constraints are different.
3 The notion of theorizing economic contributions of both men and women: the aggregation of their work per se is gendered. We have to question 'how priorities are established, and who gives way when agents' decisions do not add up to a coherent whole' (Elson 1995b: 1852). Thus we have to take on board issues of power and entitlements in domestic contexts.

Only by deconstructing economic theories in this way can distortions from the expected outcomes of SAPs (changes in divisions of labour, ambiguous gender relations within households, and more work for women through transferring tasks from public to private sectors), resulting in failure to achieve expected 'efficient' economic performance, be overcome.

Developments from this crucial work in the mid- to late 1990s have shown again and again that programmes and policies continue to be gender-biased, and that gender persistently fails to be mainstreamed. While the decade or so of the prominence and impacts of structural adjustment policies may have passed, the problems raised very visibly by the failure and mis-targeting of SAPs still remain: in the wake of the turn of the millennium, the over-strong identification between 'women' (gender) and poverty comes about at least partly because antipoverty agendas are written and are being foregrounded in terms of the Millennium Development Goals (MDGs). But gender, whether in economic theory or socio-economic policies and practices, remains problematic largely because local constructions are inadequately taken into account on the parts of the theoreticians, the policymakers and the policy-takers – the stakeholders themselves. In spite of almost 20 years of trying to deconstruct theories, as they apply to gendered issues, whether SAPs, MDGs or poverty, theoreticians, policymakers and policy-takers still tend to be both construed and constructed as uniform and male.

GUIDE TO FURTHER READING

Diane Elson's excellent edited collection, *Male Bias in the Development Process* (1995a), is a good introduction: Elson's own chapters for theoretical overviews, and empirical material by Dennis (Nigeria), MacEwen Scott (informal sector) and Pearson (Mexico).
Afshar and Dennis's edited *Women and Adjustment Policies in the Third World* (1992) is also a wide-ranging and clear collection.
More detail on the theoretical underpinnings of economic theories can be found in Elson (1993 and 1995b), and two special issues of *World Development* (Cagatay, Elson and Grown 1995 and 2000) bring advances in gender awareness in economics into the twenty-first century.
The focus on poverty is obvious in, for example, Curtin and Nelson (1999) and Sen (1999).
For more recent instances of gender bias in a range of policies, see, for example, the articles by N. Heyzer and N. Kabeer (2005) in *Gender and Development*, 13(1).

REFERENCES

Afshar, H. and Dennis, C. (eds) (1992) *Women and Adjustment Policies in the Third World*, Basingstoke: Macmillan.
Brydon, L. and Legge, K. (1996) *Adjusting Society: The World Bank, the IMF and Ghana*, London: I.B. Tauris.

Cagatay, N. (2003) 'Gender budgets and beyond: Feminist fiscal policy in the context of globalisation', *Gender and Development*, 11(1): 15–24.

Cagatay, N., Elson, D. and Grown, C. (1995) 'Introduction', *World Development*, 23(11): 1827–36, special issue, *Gender, Adjustment and Macroeconomics*.

Cornia, A., Jolly, R. and Stewart, F. (eds) (1987) *Adjustment With a Human Face* (2 vols), Oxford: Clarendon Press.

Curtin, T.R.C. and Nelson, E.A.S. (1999) 'Economic and health efficiency of education funding policy', in *Social Science and Medicine*, 48(11): 1599–611.

Elson, D. (1993) 'Gender aware analysis and development economics', *Journal of International Development*, 5(2): 237–47.

Elson, D. (1995a) *Male Bias in the Development Process*, Manchester: Manchester University Press.

Elson, D. (1995b) 'Gender awareness in modeling structural adjustment', *World Development*, 23(11): 1851–68, special issue, *Gender, Adjustment and Macroeconomics*.

Elson, D. and Pearson, R. (1981) 'Nimble fingers make cheap workers...', *Feminist Review*, 7: 87–107.

Grown, C., Elson, D. and Cagatay, N. (eds) (2000) *World Development*, 28(7), special issue, *Growth, Trade, Finance and Gender Inequality*.

Sen, G. (1999) 'Engendering poverty alleviation: Challenges and opportunities', *Development and Change*, 30(3): 685–92.

United Nations Children's (Emergency) Fund (UNICEF) (1999) *The State of the World's Children*, New York: UNICEF.

7.7 Gender, technology and livelihoods

Andrew Scott and Margaret Foster

(Maria Arce, a policy adviser for Practical Action, contributed to the revised version of this chapter.)

Introduction

Most of the world's poor are women. Of the 1.3 billion people living on less than $1 a day, 70 per cent are women (UNDP 1995). Women are at the forefront in meeting the basic needs of their families as well as being responsible for subsistence food production and income generation. At least 80 per cent of all food crops in sub-Saharan Africa, 70–80 per cent in South Asia, and 50 per cent in Latin America and the Caribbean are produced by women (UNDP 1995). Globally, women account for half of the world's food production in the early twenty-first century (60–80 per cent in developing countries), and are the main producers of staple food crops, rice, wheat and maize, according to the Food and Agriculture Organization of the United Nations. The majority of micro- and small-scale enterprise operators are women, and there are more women than men employed in the informal sector (Sethuraman 1998). Women more than men assume responsibility for the care of children, the sick, the incapacitated and the elderly, while also playing an important role in community organization, protection of natural resources and safeguarding of rights.

In this chapter, we describe the gendered nature of poor people's livelihoods and the holistic context of their lives and their technology, and we consider the factors that influence and are influenced by these gender differences. The chapter also describes ways that practitioners can take account of and address these differences in order to target very poor people.

Poverty

When targeting poverty the emphasis has to be on women's development needs and on building women's assets, reducing women's vulnerabilities, tackling those problems which women themselves identify, and empowering them. It must be possible

> to convince decision makers in governments and multi- and bilateral donors of the fact that many of the poorest people in the world depend for their survival on the innovatory technical skills of women, and that women's scientific and technical knowledge is too valuable to ignore (Appleton 1995: 304).

Such knowledge is undervalued by society and even by women 'technologists' themselves.

It is extremely difficult for prosperous 'outsiders' to understand the complex nature of poverty and to appreciate that 'the poor' are not a homogeneous group. With disaggregation it becomes clear that the effects of wealth or poverty, age, physical and mental abilities, ethnic group and religion, and so on, are all reinforced by the effects of gender. To understand the social context of development, therefore, we must take a gendered and disaggregated perspective of poor people's production.

Gender

Women and men absorb the norms and values of the society around them. They learn the roles and responsibilities, behaviour and expectations which relate to their sex and define for each their position in society. The skills and technology that they use, and the technical knowledge to which they have access are conditioned by this process, as are the options open to them to extend existing knowledge and skills in any direction and thus to increase their livelihood options.

In their daily activities women use their technical skills and knowledge, and they continually innovate and adapt technologies in response to the changing context of their lives. Although the popular notion of an inventor, farmer or artisan is male, it is frequently women who adapt and refine tools to fit their varying circumstances. Women, however, often claim that they only 'help out', when in fact they are supporting family businesses in essential ways, such as book-keeping, marketing or even light engineering (Foster 1999).

Women and men, living in the same place, may have different experiences of their economic, social, cultural, political and geographical environment. Women do not have the same access and control as men to the services, resources and opportunities within their communities. Exploiting available assets requires access to support mechanisms, credit, raw materials, transport, market information, and so on, yet all these are more difficult for women to secure. If they do manage to do so, they often lose control of their initiative to the men who made the services available to them.

The work of women and men can be perceived differently by development workers. They are often ignorant of women's contribution and depend on men to describe or 'translate' women's production processes to them. One study revealed that male extension workers in Africa think that women do not make significant contributions to agriculture, that they are tied down with household chores and children, shy and difficult to reach, and 'unprogressive' when considering innovations (Gill 1987).

Women often do not participate in community organizations, training courses or in representing their interests to decision makers because of gender bias in social structures and institutions, which can contribute to women's lack of self-confidence and social status. They are often invisible – literally, in some societies, where women avoid social interaction – and because of lack of representation they are voiceless. Their crucial role is frequently overlooked by outsiders, who may themselves be men. Few women are involved in extension work, research or technology development, with the result that information available about women technologists is scarce.

Women and livelihoods

As a result of their wide-ranging responsibilities, domestic, productive and community duties, women are generally involved in a broader range of tasks than men, and they will therefore frequently have a wider range of technical skills on which to draw for livelihood strategies.

Considering the livelihoods of very poor women helps us to appreciate the differential value and availability of their time. Women have more responsibilities during the day and less time available to learn about new techniques, attend meetings or undertake training. Many poor women in poor countries spend the majority of their productive lives either pregnant or lactating, with very young children to care for. As a result, they are frequently severely anaemic and always extremely tired. They cannot afford any risky investment of time or energy, which may or may not lead to an improvement of life in the future.

The pattern of women's daily activities is quite different from men's. Characteristically, women spend less time on a single activity and frequently carry out two or more tasks at the same time (e.g. cooking and child-minding). Men are more likely to be able to commit larger blocks of uninterrupted time to working with a particular technology or process. They are more likely to be available to participate in project interventions, and, as a result, tools are frequently designed for use by men rather than women.

Technology

Technology refers to the human skills, knowledge and organization, as well as the tools or 'hardware' involved in production. This definition highlights the separate and specific value of women's technology. Inherited knowledge, unique to location and culture, is often passed from mother to daughter, and is symbolized in many countries in Africa and South America by the traditional wedding present from mothers to daughters of trays of seeds or tubers. These enshrine the community's own biodiversity and the special responsibility women have to protect food crops for the future, illustrating how technical information passes by word of mouth between women.

Technical information and skills are communicated to women and between women using different channels (Appleton 1995). Women have different social networks and different access to education. Though women are more likely than men to be illiterate and/or uneducated, and to speak only a minority language, they are not ignorant, and if information is appropriate to their needs they will welcome and make use of it.

Technical change is influenced by access to resources, which can be allocated according to the perceptions and priorities of outsiders. Firewood is an example of such biased priorities. Biomass, the most common cooking fuel, accounts for 90 per cent of all the energy used in poor countries (World Bank 1996). It is a woman's task to ensure that cooked food is available, and to collect the fuel. It has been estimated that poor people spend up to a third of their income and their time on accessing this energy (Gamser, Appleton and Carter 1990).

Such a huge demand affects other decisions, including expenditure on heating and shelter, food choice, security and nutrition; and the effects of these on health and productivity imply that energy choice fundamentally affects other aspects of development. It is possible to trace energy scarcity to high fertility, low literacy rates, a lack of participation and decision-making ability at the local level, and a lack of empowerment.

Developing appropriate energy technologies is therefore central to the conservation of women's time and health, and the effective development of women's production. However, cooking fuel is mainly used by women and is perceived not to be linked to the generation of household income. This may account for the lack of technological innovation in cooking fuel technology, which could not only save time and effort, but might also increase food security and possibly have a positive effect on other development indicators (Gamser, Appleton and Carter 1990).

The distinction between 'reproductive' and 'productive' tasks is often meaningless when the producer is very poor. Activities involving the same tasks with the same technologies (e.g. processing food) are often used for both subsistence and income generation. Consequently, the technical innovations that women make are based on their own priorities and their understanding of the risks involved across the full range of their responsibilities (Appleton 1995: 10). Female micro-entrepreneurs, for example, often do not aim for growth of their enterprise to the same degree as male entrepreneurs. Women's micro-enterprises are generally more security-oriented than growth-oriented (Everts 1998: 25).

Lack of recognition of women's technical knowledge and of their contribution to family livelihoods has led to the neglect of important subsistence crops, usually grown by women, on which families and communities survive (Mpande and Mpofu 1995). Poor women's access to land where such crops can be produced has been restricted by developments favouring cash-cropping and involving irrigation, 'improved' seeds and chemical fertilizers.

The introduction of new technology to men in sectors previously controlled by women has brought about a loss of women's authority over activities from which they once gained an income. The evidence suggests that in 'the invention and development of technology, women's technical expertise has been displaced with particular efficacy' (Crewe and Harrison 1998: 34).

Participation and change

External support for improving technology for poor people should not be restricted to the perspective of an 'outsider' in terms of how the situation is understood. Successful intervention requires recognition of who the 'experts' are, who is doing what, and what their needs and priorities are. This should be the result of a rigorous gender analysis of the existing situation, and an analysis of interest groups that includes all stakeholders and does not allow one group to speak on behalf of another. 'Participation' will not by itself lead to technologies that serve the interests of all users (Appleton and Scott 1994), and some participative approaches have in fact marginalized women and benefits have gone to local elites (Mosse 1994). It depends on who participates, where, when and how.

The only effective way to work within such constraints is to involve poor women at every stage, to go at their pace and in their direction, working in their place and in their language. Involvement of poor women in this way, the sharing of means as well as ends, the sensitive appreciation of the uniqueness of place and time, helps not only to design more appropriate hardware and processes, but also builds on existing indigenous technical capacity, without threatening culture or traditional values.

Behaviour, social processes and concepts underlie the use of technical knowledge by women, and these deserve respect. New technological ideas will be accepted by poor women only if they are an obvious improvement, if they do not impose an extra burden and if they are culturally acceptable. Technology for human development should respond to women's technological needs, improve their access to useful information, and enable these invisible and often silent technologists to voice their interests and concerns.

Conclusion

For men and women, roles and responsibilities set by society and different life experiences impact differently on their livelihood capabilities and priorities, in relation to the use and development of technology. The implicit undervaluing of women's skills, knowledge and organization of technology use has had serious implications for the status of women as technology producers and users, and for their involvement in the development process.

Gender analysis is important in the assessment of the impact on poverty of technology-focused development projects. Employing gendered frameworks of technology use and capability allows disaggregation of areas of existing and potential technical expertise. Gender analysis also enables recognition of the gendered nature of livelihood activities within households and communities. Understanding of how such activities shape and are shaped by, this gendered technological context, enables a picture of the technological capabilities of women and men to be formed.

GUIDE TO FURTHER READING

Appleton, H. (ed.) (1995) *Do It Herself: Women and Technical Innovation*, London: IT Publications.
Everts, S. (1998) *Gender & Technology: Empowering Women, Engendering Development*, London: Zed Books.
Gender, Science and Technology Gateway: http://gstgateway.wigsat.org/gw.html
Gender, Technology and Development (journal), Sage Publications.
ITDG (Intermediate Technology Development Group) (2001) *Discovering Technologists: Women's and Men's Work at Village Level*, London and Colombo, Sri Lanka: ITDG Publishing and ITDG South Asia.

REFERENCES

Appleton, H. (ed.) (1995) *Do It Herself: Women and Technical Innovation*, London: IT Publications.
Appleton, H. and Scott, A. (1994) 'Gender issues in agricultural technology development', paper presented at Agricultural Engineers' Conference, Food and Agriculture Organization of the United Nations.
Crewe, E. and Harrison, E. (1998) *Whose Development? An Ethnography of Aid*, London: Zed Books.
Everts, S. (1998) *Gender & Technology: Empowering Women, Engendering Development*, London: Zed Books.
Foster, M. (1999) 'Supporting the invisible technologists: The Intermediate Technology Development Group', *Gender and Development*, 7(2): 17–24.
Gamser, M., Appleton, H. and Carter, N. (eds) (1990) *Tinker, Tiller, Technical Change*, London: IT Publications.
Gill, D.S. (1987) 'Effectiveness of rural extension services in reaching rural women: A synthesis of studies from five African countries', paper presented at Food and Agriculture Organization Workshop on Improving the Effectiveness of Agricultural Extension Services in Reaching Rural Women, Harare, Zimbabwe.
Mosse, D. (1994) 'Authority, gender and knowledge: Theoretical reflections on the practice of participatory rural appraisal', *Development and Change*, 25(3): 497–525.
Mpande, R. and Mpofu, N. (1995) 'Survival skills of Tonga women in Zimbabwe', in H. Appleton (ed.) *Do It Herself: Women and Technical Innovation*, pp. 188–93.
Sethuraman, S.V. (1998) *Gender, Informality and Poverty: A Global Review*, Cambridge, MA: WIEGO (Women in Informal Employment Globalizing and Organizing).
UNDP (United Nations Development Programme) (1995) *Human Development Report, 1995*, New York: UNDP.
World Bank (1996) *Rural Energy and Development: Improving Energy Supplies for Two Billion People*, Development in Practice Series, Washington, DC: World Bank.

7.8 Women and political representation

Shirin M. Rai

Why is representation an important issue for development? Development policies are highly politically charged trade-offs between diverse interests and value choices. 'The political nature of these policies is frequently made behind the closed door of bureaucracy or among tiny groups of men in a non-transparent political structure' (Staudt 1991: 65). In 2002, 94.5 per cent of the World Bank Board of Governors was made up of men, as was 91.7 per cent of its Board of Directors. The figures for the International Monetary Fund (IMF) were 97.8 per cent and 100 per cent (see WEDO under 'Useful websites' at the end of this chapter). The question then arises, how are women to access this world of policymaking so dominated by men? The answers that have been explored within women's movements have been diverse – political mobilization of women, lobbying political parties, moving the courts and legal establishments, constitutional reform, mobilization and participation in social movements such as the environmental movement, and civil liberties campaigns at local and global levels.

Representation has been the focus of reformist, inclusionary strategies in public policy in many political systems. Of itself, the concept is not such that it can bear the burden of close scrutiny – there are too many caveats that have to be taken on board for it to work. It is attractive largely in contrast to other political arrangements. Lack of representation is perceived as a problem, and citizens largely accept democratic institutions as important to the expansion of possibilities of political participation. Further, exclusion generates political resentment, adversely affecting not only the political system but also social relations within a polity; no individual or group likes being regarded as part of an excluded, and therefore disempowered, group.

Representation as a concept makes certain assumptions that are problematic. These affect the policymaking and functioning of political institutions. The first set of assumptions are related to representation of interests – that there are identifiable (women's) interests, that women can represent. For women, this raises issues about what women's interests are when they are being constantly disturbed by categories of race, ethnicity and class, and whether women can be homogenized in terms of their sex/gender without regard to their race, ethnic and class positionings. Martha Nussbaum has emphasized the importance of equality and human rights as the irreducible minimum rights for women in the development of their capabilities (Nussbaum 1995). Iris M. Young has addressed these issues through her exploration of the idea of group interests (1990). She suggests that group interests can be formulated by the meeting of groups supported by public resources; that the interests thus formulated would be more reflective of group concerns, securing greater legitimacy within the group. As such, these interests should be made part of policy, and policymakers asked to justify their exclusion from processes of policymaking. As a final protection of interests, Young suggests that these more cohesive groups should have power of veto over policy affecting them. This analysis would presumably take account of class-based groups such as trades unions, though most research which has taken on board Young's framework has focused on issues of race, ethnicity, sexuality and gender.

A second set of assumptions regarding representation is about appropriate forms of representative politics, and the levels of government and policymaking. Despite an enduring interest in direct participatory politics, representative government operates largely through a party political system. Political parties thus form an important constraint for individual representatives, especially if the representative seeks to support certain group interests. Group interests have often been regarded as too particularistic; 'general interests', or more often 'national interests', take precedence in party political rhetoric. Political parties also perform 'gatekeeping' functions – interests are given recognition through the agenda-setting of political parties. My study of Indian women parliamentarians suggests that institutional constraints, and systems of organizational incentives and disincentives are important explanations of the limited role that women can play in advancing the agenda of gender justice through party-based political work (Rai 1996, 1997).

Representation is a key concept in liberal understandings of governance – it focuses on institutions, organization and practices. Representation is also central to the concept of citizenship, both in its normative sense – participation in politics as a prerequisite for the subjective public self – and in the practical – the inclusion within state boundaries where particular development agendas take shape. The framework of citizenship has recently been used by corporate-sector engagements with the policy world, and civil society organizations – 'corporate citizenship' is an emergent field of enquiry in development studies as well as business studies. Representation is also important in terms of accountability – of public and private organizations alike. Increasingly, we see a critique not only of state-based institutions, but also of international non-governmental organizations (INGOs) and non-governmental organizations (NGOs), in terms of an accountability deficit and how this might influence interest articulations and formulations and implementation of policy. As it signifies consent, representation is also an essential element of good and therefore legitimate government, which is increasingly becoming the focus of the delivery network institutions of development (World Bank 1992: 6; 2000). Representation, however, is used as a universal and undifferentiated concept which does not take into account particular positionings, needs and claims of groups constituting a particular civil and political society.

Women in political institutions

A headcount of the officers of the state in all sectors – legislature, executive and the judiciary – in most countries of the world reveals an overwhelming male bias, despite many mobilizations furthering women's presence at both national and global levels. An Inter-Parliamentary Union Study found that the number of sovereign states with a parliament increased sevenfold between 1945 and 1995, while the percentage of women MPs worldwide increased fourfold (Karam 1998: 163). Seventeen per cent of parliamentarians are women, with the Nordic states leading the way with 40.8 per cent, and the Arab states with 8.8 per cent (see IPU under 'Useful websites' at the end of this chapter). Furthermore, data show that there is no easy positive correlation between economic indicators and the presence of women in public bodies. While in Europe (without the Nordic countries) women comprised 17.6 per cent of the total number of MPs, the figure in sub-Saharan Africa was 17 per cent. In recognition of the slow improvement in women's representation in national parliaments, enhancing women's presence within state bodies is now being pursued as a goal by women's movements and by international institutions. This suggests that an engagement with state structures is now considered an appropriate means of bringing about shifts in public policy.

Feminist debates on representation

Why are debates on women's representation important? First, women have recognized that interests need to be articulated through participation and then represented in the arena of politics. Within women's movements there was a significant shift in the 1980s towards engaging positively with state feminism as a strategy that could be effective in furthering the cause(s) of women. The argument about women's presence in representative politics, as Anna Jonasdottir (1988) has pointed out, concerns both the *form* of politics and its *content*. The question of form includes the demand to be among the decision makers, the demand for participation and a share in control over public affairs. In terms of content, it includes being able to articulate the needs, wishes and demands of various groups of women. The interest in citizenship has also been prompted by the shift in women's movements, in the 1980s, from the earlier insistence on direct participation to a recognition of the importance of representative politics and the consequences of women's exclusion from it (Lovenduski and Norris 1993; McBride Stetson and Mazur 1995; Rai 2000; Lovenduski 2006). It is here that politics – public and private, practical and strategic – begins to formalize within the contours of the state.

Gender and representation is also an important issue in the international sphere. Good governance has become important to the political discourses of world aid agencies and financial institutions. Having concentrated attention on the processes and practices of structural adjustment programmes (SAPs) in the Third World countries during the 1970s and 1980s, the World Bank and other aid agencies are faced with decelerating growth in many countries, accompanied by a rise in social tensions, in many cases as a consequence of SAPs. Issues of governance have therefore become important and the focus has shifted to supporting processes of institution building that would help manage the social and political fallout of economic policies supported by international aid agencies and Western governments (World Bank 2000). The UN has also played an important role in placing the issue of women's exclusion from political processes on the international agenda. The Platform for Action agreed in Beijing in September 1995 emphasized the need to increase the levels of women's participation in politics, and also the need for the development of national machineries for the advancement of women (Rai 2001).

While we cannot assume that more women in public offices would mean a better deal for women in general, there are important reasons for demanding greater representation of women in political life. First is the intuitive one – the greater the number of women in public office, articulating interests and seen to be wielding power, the more disrupted the gender hierarchy in public life could become. Without a sufficiently visible, if not proportionate, presence in the political system – 'threshold representation' (Kymlicka 1995) – a group's ability to influence either policy-making or, indeed, the political culture framing the representative system is limited. Further, the fact that these women are largely elite women might mean that the impact they have on public consciousness might be disproportionately larger than their numbers would suggest.

Second, and more important, we could explore the strategies that women employ to access the public sphere in the context of a patriarchal socio-political system. These women have been successful in subverting the boundaries of gender, and in operating in a very aggressive, male-dominated sphere. Could other women learn from this cohort? The problem here, of course, is precisely that these women are an elite. The class from which most of these women come is perhaps the most important factor in their successful inclusion in the political system. We can, however, examine whether socio-political movements provide opportunities for women to use certain strategies that might be able to subvert the gender hierarchy in politics. Finally, we can explore the dynamic between institutional and grass-roots politics. The 'politicization of gender' in the Indian political system, for example, is due largely to the success of the women's movement. Women representatives have thus benefited from this success of the women's movement. There has been limited interaction between women representatives and the women's movement, however. This, perhaps, is the issue that the women's movement needs to address as part of its expanding agenda for the 1990s.

Strategies for increasing women's representation

Many strategies have been discussed for increasing women's representation in politics – party lists in South Africa and the UK, and quotas at the local governance levels in India are two important experiments. There has also been discussion of parity representation for women and men, especially in the Nordic states (Karam 1998; Dahlerup 2005). All three are contested strategies, as the following discussion of quotas demonstrates. The arguments for quotas for women in representative institutions are fairly well rehearsed. Women's groups are now arguing that quotas for women are needed to compensate for the social barriers that have prevented women from participating in politics and thus making their voices heard: that in order for women to be more than 'tokens' in political institutions, a level of presence that cannot be overlooked by political parties is required, hence the demand for a 33 per cent quota: the quota system acknowledges that it is the recruitment process, organized through political parties and supported by a framework of patriarchal values, that needs to carry the burden of change, rather than individual women. The alternative, then, is that there should be an acknowledgement of the historical social exclusion of women from politics, a compensatory regime (quotas) established and 'institutionalized...for the explicit recognition and representation of oppressed groups' (Young 1990: 183–91). However, there is some unease felt by many women's groups with elite politics and elite women, and the role that quotas might play in consolidating rather than shifting power relationships.

Conclusions

While political representation is crucial to women's empowerment, there are also some critical issues that we need to reflect on. State institutions cannot be the only focus of women's political struggles. Both spaces – the informal and formalized networks of power – need to be negotiated by women's movements in order to best serve women's interests (Rai 1996). This would include the work of civil society associations, increased representation of women in state and political bodies to permit a wide-ranging set of interests to be represented by women, and also a discursive shift in the way in which politics is thought about, to enable women to function effectively in that field. Women's participation in representative institutions can be effective only in the context of such continuing negotiations and struggles.

GUIDE TO FURTHER READING AND REFERENCES

Dahlerup, D. (2005) *Women Quotas and Politics*, London: Routledge.

Goetz, A.M. (ed.) (1997) *Getting Institutions Right for Women in Development*, London: Zed Books.

Jonasdottir, A.G. (1988) *The Political Interests of Gender: Developing Theory and Research with a Feminist Face*, London: Sage.

Karam, A. (ed.) (1998) *Beyond Numbers: Women in Parliaments*, Stockholm: IDEA.

Kymlicka, W. (1995) *Multicultural Citizenship*, Oxford: Oxford University Press.

Lovenduski, J. and Norris, P. (1993) *Gender and Party Politics*, London: Sage.

Lovenduski, J. (2006) *Feminising Politics*, Cambridge: Polity Press.

McBride Stetson, D. and Mazur, A. (1995) *Comparative State Feminism*, London: Sage.

Nussbaum, M. (1995) 'Human capabilities, female human beings', in M. Nussbaum and J. Glover, *Women, Culture and Development*, Oxford: Clarendon Press.

Rai, S.M. (ed.) (1996) 'Women and the state: Some issues for debate', in S.M. Rai and G. Lievesley (eds) *Women and the State: International Perspectives*, London: Taylor and Francis.

Rai, S.M. (ed.) (1997) 'Women in the Indian Parliament', in A.M. Goetz (ed.) *Getting Institutions Right for Women in Development*, London: Zed Books.

Rai, S.M. (ed.) (2000) *International Perspectives on Gender and Democratisation*, Basingstoke: Macmillan.

Rai, S.M. (ed.) (2001) *Mainstreaming Gender, Democratizing the State? National Machineries for the Advancement of Women*, Manchester: Manchester University Press.

Staudt, K. (1991) *Managing Development*, London: Sage.

World Bank (1992) *Good Governance*, Washington, DC: World Bank.

World Bank (2000) *World Development Report 2000/2001: Attacking Poverty*, Washington, DC: World Bank.

Young, I.M. (1990) *Justice and the Politics of Difference*, Princeton, NJ: Princeton University Press.

USEFUL WEBSITES

IPU (Inter-Parliamentary Union), Women in National Parliaments, http://www.ipu.org/wmn-e/world.htm

WEDO (Women's Environment and Development Organization), 'The numbers speak for themselves', http://www.wedo.org/files/numbersspeak_factshl.pdf

7.9 Population trends in developing countries

Tiziana Leone

At the beginning of the twenty-first century, the global population had exceeded 6 billion; it took just 12 years for the population to increase from 5 to 6 billion. Developing countries (Africa, Latin America and the Caribbean, Asia (excluding Japan) and Melanesia, Micronesia and Polynesia) currently make up 80 per cent of the world's population, and 61 per cent of the global total is accounted for by Asia alone, driven by the population giants China and India. The global annual rate of population increase peaked at 2.04 per cent per year in the late 1960s, and had declined to 1.37 per cent per year by 2005. Developing region population is currently growing at a rate of 1.44 per cent per year (see figure), and growth rates in Africa still exceed 2.3 per cent per year, the highest growth rate of any major area.

The absolute annual increase in global population peaked at 88 million people per year in the late 1980s, and is currently 78 million people per year (at the time of writing, 2006). Ninety-five per cent of this population increase takes place in the less developed regions. Behind these 'statements of account' of global population lies a multitude of regional and individual country population trends. In the following discussion, the approach will be descriptive, focusing on the three demographic variables of fertility, mortality and migration.

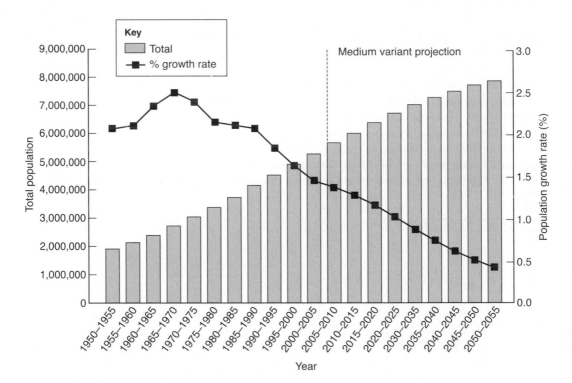

Population trends in less developed regions, 1950–2050
Source: UN *World Population Prospects* (2006 revision)

Data sources

A consideration of detailed population trends in developing countries must take into account the data available for analysis. There are three main sources of demographic data: censuses, vital registration (e.g. birth and death registration) and surveys (e.g. World Fertility Survey (WFS), Demographic and Health Surveys (DHS)). Cleland (1996: 433) states that, pre-1945, 'studies of the demography of less developed countries hardly existed'. Since the mid-1950s, considerable advances have been made in the collection of demographic data in developing countries, although vital registration continues to be very deficient (in terms of both coverage and quality). For some countries, particularly those with recent or ongoing conflicts, estimates of population data continue to be little more than educated guesswork. Publications such as the United Nations *World Population Prospects* and *Demographic Yearbook* provide country-level comparable data sets with which to work, although there are still concerns about data validity and reliability for some countries. This overview of population trends will use the most recent *World Population Prospects* (2006 revision), a source which is readily available on the Internet (http://esa.un.org/unpp/).

Age and sex structure

Many developing countries are experiencing very rapid changes in the relative numbers of children, working-age population and older persons. Less developed countries have tended to be characterized by relatively youthful age structures. For example, children under the age of 15 currently account for one-third of less developed region populations, and 41.5 per cent of least developed populations. (The grouping least developed uses the framework as defined by the United Nations General Assembly in 1998 and includes 48 countries, of which 33 are in Africa, 9 in Asia, 1 in Latin America and the Caribbean, and 5 in Oceania. They are included in the less developed regions.) Mainly as a result of declining fertility, these proportions have declined significantly since the mid-1960s (see Table 1). By 2050 it is estimated that children will account for only 20 per cent of less developed populations (UN medium variant projections).

Table 1 Percentage of population aged under 15 years, 1950–2005

Year	World	Major region		Geographical region		
		Less developed	Least developed	Africa	Asia	Latin America & Caribbean
1950	34.3	37.8	41.3	42.5	36.6	40.0
1955	35.6	39.3	41.8	42.8	38.1	41.0
1960	36.9	40.7	42.7	43.5	39.4	42.2
1965	37.7	41.8	43.4	44.2	40.4	42.8
1970	37.4	41.8	44.3	44.7	40.3	42.4
1975	36.9	41.3	44.9	45.0	39.9	41.3
1980	35.2	39.3	44.9	44.8	37.7	39.6
1985	33.5	37.1	45.0	44.6	34.9	37.9
1990	32.4	35.6	44.5	44.3	33.2	36.0
1995	31.2	34.3	43.4	43.6	31.8	33.7
2000	29.7	32.5	42.1	42.5	29.9	31.6
2005	28.3	30.9	41.5	41.4	28.0	29.8

As the proportions accounted for by children decline, there has been an accompanying increase in the proportions of elderly persons (aged 60 years and above) (see Table 2). People aged 60 and above currently account for just over 8 per cent of the population in less developed regions. In reality, this means that 33 million of the world's oldest old people (aged 80 years and above) are estimated to be living in less developed countries (Mirkin and Weinberger 2000).

Table 2 Percentage of population aged 60 years and older, 1950–2005

Year	World	Major region		Geographical region		
		Less developed	Least developed	Africa	Asia	Latin America & Caribbean
1950	8.1	6.4	5.4	5.1	6.7	5.9
1955	8.1	6.3	5.2	5.0	6.7	6.1
1960	8.1	6.2	5.1	4.9	6.5	6.2
1965	8.2	6.1	5.0	4.9	6.4	6.3
1970	8.4	6.1	5.1	5.0	6.5	6.4
1975	8.5	6.1	5.0	4.9	6.6	6.5
1980	8.6	6.3	5.0	5.0	6.8	6.6
1985	8.8	6.6	4.9	4.9	7.2	6.8
1990	9.2	6.9	4.9	4.9	7.6	7.3
1995	9.6	7.3	4.8	4.9	8.2	7.7
2000	10.0	7.7	4.9	5.0	8.8	8.3
2005	10.3	8.1	5.1	5.2	9.2	9.0

The proportions of elderly are predicted to continue to increase, and by 2050 it is estimated that 3.6 per cent of the population in less developed regions will be aged 80 years or older. The speed of the ageing of the populations in these areas is more rapid than has occurred in developed regions, mainly due to the rapidity of the fertility decline. Improvements in post-childhood mortality have also added to the process of population ageing in less developed countries.

There are profound implications for the care and support of the elderly, particularly in contexts where resources and civil institutions are already limited. Because women tend to live longer than men, issues of long-term care and support are especially acute for women. Demographic dependency ratios provide a simple measure of the relative sizes of the economically active and inactive populations. (Net dependency ratio = number of children aged below 15 years and adults aged 65 years or older per 100 people of working age; child dependency ratio = number of children aged below 15 years per 100 people of working age; elderly dependency ratio = number of people aged 65 years or older per 100 people of working age.) With increasing ageing in developing regions, the elderly dependency ratio is projected to increase by almost three times between 2000 and 2050. However, this trend must be placed against a background of declining child dependency ratios. The overall effect, therefore, is one of declining net dependency ratios in developing regions up to 2050.

Mortality

Life expectancy at birth is one of the benchmark indicators of development, and in developing countries it increased from 40.9 years in 1950 to 64.1 years by 2005, a remarkable and rapid achievement. The difference in longevity between the more and the less developed regions also decreased over this period, from 25.7 years to 11.5 years. There are still major regional disparities in life expectancy at birth, from 51.6 years in sub-Saharan Africa to 72 years in Latin America and the Caribbean. Sierra Leone, following nearly two decades of conflict, has the dubious honour of being the country with the lowest life expectancy, at 41 years. (The calculation of life expectancy at birth is heavily biased by levels of infant mortality. In populations with high levels of infant mortality, life expectancy at birth provides a very poor representation of the age at which people are likely to die.)

Livi-Bacci (1992: 152) states that 'Reduced mortality and establishment of the chronological age-linked succession of death are prerequisites to development.' Improvements in mortality generally occur first at younger ages, particularly in the first 12 months of life. The infant mortality rate (IMR: the number of deaths per year of live-born infants before their first birthday, divided by the number of live births in the year, usually expressed per 1000) in less developed regions is seven times higher than that recorded for more developed regions, at 59 per 1000 and 7.5 per 1000, respectively. Improvements in early-age mortality were achieved throughout the developing world (see Table 3) during the second half of the twentieth century due to a combination of health interventions (including disease control, immunization and oral rehydration therapy) and broader socio-economic development (including nutrition and parental education). Sub-Saharan Africa still continues to lag behind other major world regions, with an IMR of 99.8 per 1000.

Table 3 Trends in infant mortality rates (per 1000 live births), 1950–2005

Year	World	Major region		Geographical region		
		Less developed	Least developed	Africa	Asia	Latin America & Caribbean
1950–1955	155	178	194	180	176	126
1955–1960	139	160	179	168	160	113
1960–1965	117	134	166	156	130	101
1965–1970	102	115	154	145	106	91
1970–1975	93	104	146	133	94	80
1975–1980	87	98	138	122	86	69
1980–1985	78	87	128	113	74	57
1985–1990	69	76	116	107	64	47
1990–1995	62	68	108	103	59	38
1995–2000	57	63	99	99	54	32
2000–2005	54	59	95	93	49	25

The impact of improvements in early-age mortality extends far beyond a contribution to an increase in life expectancy; it has profound implications for fertility through a range of mechanisms (including the 'insurance' effect (the hypothetical result of parents choosing to have more births than their desired number of children due to a fear that some children will die), interruption of lactation, the 'replacement' effect (the replacement of dead children by subsequent births) and societal supports for fertility) (Preston 1978).

Maternal mortality (defined as a death during pregnancy, childbirth or six weeks post-partum, including deaths attributable to induced abortion) continues to be a major issue for teenage and adult women in developing countries, despite initiatives such as Safe Motherhood (1987) and the ICPD Programme of Action (International Conference on Population and Development, Cairo, 1994). It is estimated that, globally, a woman dies of maternal causes every minute, with an estimated 529,000 maternal deaths annually. Ninety-nine per cent of these deaths are in developing countries (Ganges and Long 1998), with concomitant negative implications for the survival of any existing children.

Mention must be made of the HIV/AIDS epidemic, with an estimated 39.5 million infected individuals at the end of 2006 (UNAIDS 2006). Ninety-five per cent of infected people live in developing countries, and it is likely that this proportion will continue to rise. The region most severely affected by HIV/AIDS is sub-Saharan Africa, which accounts for approximately 70 per cent of global HIV/AIDS cases. The demographic impacts of the HIV/AIDS epidemic are many and complex. Twentieth-century increases in life expectancy are predicted to reverse as a direct result of HIV/AIDS. For example, life expectancy at birth in Botswana rose from 42.5 years in 1950 to 60.4 years in 1990, but is predicted to decline to 46.6 years by 2005. HIV/AIDS will also have an indirect effect on morbidity and mortality through the spread of 'opportunistic' diseases such as tuberculosis (UNAIDS 2006).

Future trends in adult mortality will depend on changes in health technology and expenditure, lifestyle, disease patterns and economic development (and reversal). For example, the recent rapid rise of tobacco smoking in many developing countries will have an impact on adult mortality patterns. (Cigarette consumption per adult increased by 60 per cent between 1970–72 and 1990–92 in all developing countries (UNDP 1999).) Garenne's (1996) study of mortality trends in Africa includes changing diets (leading to obesity and diabetes), chemical-resistant disease development, migration (and its role in communicable disease spread), road traffic accidents, HIV/AIDS (and associated opportunistic diseases such as tuberculosis), conflict and urbanization (through its effect on disease ecology) as important future influences on developing country mortality levels.

Fertility

Pre-1960, there was little evidence of any fertility decline in developing countries, and the total fertility rate (TFR) was estimated at 6.16 children per woman for all developing regions (1950–55). (TFR is the most commonly used indicator of fertility and will be used throughout this discussion, representing the number of children a woman would have during her lifetime if she were to experience the fertility rates of the period at each age.) Countries such as Argentina and Uruguay, which had TFRs of less than 3.5 children per woman by 1950, were the exception rather than the rule. The TFR for all developing regions was estimated at 3 at the end of the twentieth century, representing a decline of more than 50 per cent since the 1950s (see Table 4). It must be remembered, however, that much of the decline in fertility in the developing world can be accounted for by the dramatic decline in fertility in China alone.

Table 4 Trends in total fertility rates, 1950–2005

| Year | World | Major region | | Geographical region | | |
		Less developed	Least developed	Africa	Asia	Latin America & Caribbean
1950–1955	5.02	6.15	6.67	6.75	5.87	5.88
1955–1960	4.96	6.01	6.7	6.82	5.63	5.93
1960–1965	4.98	6.04	6.76	6.87	5.65	5.97
1965–1970	4.9	6	6.73	6.8	5.67	5.54
1970–1975	4.47	5.41	6.61	6.72	5.04	5.04
1975–1980	3.92	4.65	6.39	6.61	4.19	4.48
1980–1985	3.58	4.15	6.28	6.45	3.67	3.92
1985–1990	3.38	3.84	6	6.13	3.4	3.41
1990–1995	3.05	3.42	5.68	5.68	2.97	3.03
1995–2000	2.8	3.11	5.29	5.28	2.67	2.73
2000–2005	2.65	2.9	4.95	4.98	2.47	2.52

Extreme heterogeneity in fertility levels and trends, between and within regions and countries, cannot be ignored. Sub-Saharan Africa is the world region with the highest overall levels of fertility, with little evidence of sustained fertility declines beyond Kenya, Botswana and Zimbabwe. In some countries, substantial fertility decline has not yet been recorded. For example, TFRs in Yemen remained virtually unchanged, at 7.6 children per woman, from the 1950s to the mid-1990s, although a decline in fertility was recorded in the 1997 Yemen Demographic and Health Survey, with a TFR of 6.5. In contrast, rapid and marked fertility declines have occurred elsewhere, particularly in Asia. For example, between 1970 and 2005, the TFR in Bangladesh fell from 7.02 to 3.22 children per woman.

Explanations for the decline in fertility in developing countries cannot rely on single-variable explanations. In terms of the proximate determinants of fertility (Bongaarts and Potter 1984), increased contraceptive prevalence is generally agreed to be the main cause of the fertility decline. The proportion of couples using modern contraception has increased dramatically, from approximately 1 in every 10 couples in the 1960s to 1 in 2 couples by 1999 (Black 1999). Other contributory proximate determinants include rising age at marriage for women and increased rates of induced abortion. Broader socio-economic changes such as rising levels of female education and employment and increased urbanization, have contributed to the fertility decline in developing countries.

Migration

Migration is very important in determining population (size and composition) at the local level. (Migration refers here to population movements involving a permanent or semi-permanent change of usual residence. Mobility refers to 'All phenomena involving the displacement of individuals' (Pressat 1985: 148).) The speed and scale with which population movements can take place means that net migration can far outweigh fertility and mortality changes in sub-national areas. Much of the rapid urbanization of many developing country populations may be accounted for by rural–urban migration. Migration flow data (both international and national) are notoriously difficult to obtain (Bilsborrow et al. 1997). Globally, it is estimated that developing countries contribute just over half of the international migrant population (Zlotnik 1998). The greatest outmigration flows are reported in Asia (see Table 5), with a net emigration rate of 0.3 migrants per 1000, while Latin America and the Caribbean report the highest net emigration rate of 1.5 per 1000. At a global level, developing countries have negative internal population movements (both voluntary and involuntary), with profound implications for populations. For example, refugees and internally displaced persons tend to have little or no access to health care provision, and the result can be increased morbidity and mortality (Gardner and Blackburn 1996). Conflict-related population migration continues to be a major contributor to national population levels in many developing countries (see http://www.unhcr.org for up-to-date information).

Table 5 Trends in net migration in less developed regions (medium variant), 1950–2050

Year	Major region		Geographical region		
	Less developed	Least developed	Africa	Asia	Latin America & Caribbean
1950–1960	−5	−95	−116	165	−58
1960–1970	−431	−140	−220	77	−64
1970–1980	−1104	−462	−293	−416	−388
1980–1990	−1512	−766	−244	−595	−649
1990–2000	−2569	9	−269	−1434	−798
2000–2010	−2462	81	−410	−1244	−740
2040–2050	−2158	−270	−322	−1204	−567

Conclusion

The twentieth century witnessed unprecedented change in population dynamics and the implications for future generations are uncertain. Demographers can make population projections from current population figures, along with assumptions about mortality and fertility. These projections serve as a useful planning tool, but they do not tell the whole story. Rapid fluctuations in population movements will be caused by unpredictable internal instability, natural disasters and conflict. Migration within countries has already changed the composition of many developing countries, driving rapid urbanization. The future ability of developing countries to cope with increasingly aged populations also remains to be seen, especially in combination with increasingly unpredictable economic futures.

GUIDE TO FURTHER READING

Demeny, P. and McNicoll, G. (1998) *The Earthscan Reader in Population and Development*, London: Earthscan.

Livi-Bacci, M. (1992) *A Concise History of World Population*, Oxford: Blackwell.

Livi-Bacci, M. (1997) *A Concise History of World Population*, second edition, Cambridge, MA: Blackwell.

Lutz, W. (1996) *Future Population of the World: What Can We Assume Today?* London: Earthscan.

Population Division, Department of Economic and Social Affairs of the United Nations Secretariat, *World Population Prospects: The 1998 Revision*, New York: United Nations.

Lutz, W. and Sanderson W. (eds) (2004) *The End of World Population Growth: Human Capital and Sustainable Development in the 21st Century*, London: Earthscan.

REFERENCES

Bilsborrow, R.E. et al. (1997) *International Migration Statistics: Guidelines for Improving Data Collection Systems*, Geneva: International Labour Office.

Black, T. (1999) 'Impediments to effective fertility reduction', *British Medical Journal*, 319: 932–3.

Bongaarts, J. and Potter, R.G. (1984) *Fertility, Biology, and Behaviour: An Analysis of the Proximate Determinants*, New York: Academic Press.

Cleland, J. (1996) 'Demographic data collection in less developed countries 1946–1996', *Population Studies*, 50(3): 433–50.

Ganges, F. and Long, P. (1998) 'Safe motherhood: Successes and challenges', *Outlook*, 16, special issue.

Gardner, R. and Blackburn, R. (1996) 'People who move: New reproductive health focus', *Population Reports*, Series J, No. 45.

Garenne, M. (1996) 'Mortality in sub-Saharan Africa: Trends and prospects', in W. Lutz (ed.) *The Future Population of the World: What Can We Assume Today?* London: Earthscan.

Livi-Bacci, M. (1992) *A Concise History of World Population*, Oxford: Blackwell.

Mirkin, B. and Weinberger, M.B. (2000) 'The demography of population ageing', paper presented at the Technical Meeting on Population Ageing and Living Arrangement of Older Persons: Critical Issues and Policy Responses, Population Division, United Nations, New York, 8–10 February.

Population Division, Department of Economic and Social Affairs of the United Nations Secretariat (1998) *World Population Prospects: The 1998 Revision*, New York: United Nations.

Pressat, R. (1985) *The Dictionary of Demography*, Oxford: Basil Blackwell.

Preston, S.H. (1978) *The Effects of Infant and Child Mortality on Fertility*, New York: Academic Press.

UNAIDS (2006) *AIDS Epidemic*, Geneva: UNAIDS.

UNDP (United Nations Development Programme) (1999) *Human Development Report 1999*, Oxford: Oxford University Press.

Zlotnik, H. (1998) 'International migration 1965–96: An overview', *Population and Development Review*, 24(3): 429–68.

7.10 Reproductive and sexual rights

Sonia Corrêa

Historical threads

Gender and sexuality have been and remain central to all human cultures. Across history, societies have regulated procreation and, more often than not, exercised varied forms of fertility regulation. Gender, reproduction and sexuality are constructed and enacted as discourses and practices in distinct spheres of personal and social interactions and institutional regulation. The analysis and exercise of reproductive and sexual rights, therefore, requires attention to be paid to their varying meanings and practices. Moreover it is crucial to recognize that the crafting and legitimizing of these rights in the early twenty-first century is deeply connected with the peculiar trajectory of the West in its transition to modernity.

Since the 1970s, starting with the French philosopher Michel Foucault, scholars have critically examined the reconfiguration of state–society relations in terms of sex, gender and reproduction, which first came about in Europe in the seventeenth century. Their critiques recall that sexuality is reconfigured in the same web of power and societal control in development and population policies. For the Foucauldian historicity of sexuality, modernity entails the development of technologies of life to which sex is central. Since sex is a means of access to the life of the body and the species, it offers a means of regulation of both individual bodies and the behaviour of 'population' (Weeks 1996).

Since the late eighteenth century, starting with Malthus, the statistical measurement of population became a regular state procedure. Concurrently, women's status and sex would be increasingly politicized. In the early nineteenth century, utopian socialists imagined a revolution combining the end of capitalist exploitation and sexual freedom. Then mass-produced condoms became available and were promoted by neo-Malthusians, liberal thinkers and feminists. Inspired by Friedrich Engels' *Origin of the Family, Private Property and the State* (1884), socialists and feminists articulated women's reproductive freedom and ideas for broader social and economic transformation.

By the early twentieth century, Margaret Sanger had coined the term 'birth control', Emma Goldman had further expanded the socialist agenda on abortion and sex education, and by the 1930s, radical theories of sexuality formulated by the SexPol group sprouted from central Europe. But from there on, progressive approaches to population-related matters lost ground to medical, health and eugenic approaches to fertility control, and race-based arguments of hygiene and societal cleansing.

Contemporary trends

By the 1950s, population control had the contours of a 'grand ideology'. The United Nations, multilateral and bilateral donors and private foundations argued that rapid demographic growth *would* curtail economic development in the South. But at the UN World Population Conference in Bucharest in 1974, developing countries contested the pressures to adopt family planning programmes and advocated 'development as the best contraceptive'. Ironically enough, a few years later, China and India – who had been the leaders of this reaction – adopted population control policies.

In the late 1970s, however, a distinctive critique of fertility control developed north and south of the equator, instigated by women's organizations claiming gender equality and citizenship rights in relation to sexual and reproductive self-determination. Feminists perceived that neither 'developmentalist' approaches nor population control programmes would address women's needs and aspirations. In 1984, in Amsterdam, the first International Reproductive Rights Conference legitimized 'reproductive rights' as a global feminist concept. Concurrently, the World Health Organization (WHO), mobilized by critiques of population control and the surge of HIV/AIDS, crafted the terms reproductive and sexual health.

The end of the cold war marked the threshold of globalization as we know it today, leading to US geopolitical dominance, neoliberal hegemony and increasing inequalities. But the 1990s also brought deepening democracy, the strengthening of multilateralism and greater connectivity among civil societies. In 1990, the United Nations launched the Human Development Agenda, which was followed by the UN cycle of social conferences and growing legitimacy of human rights. This climate favoured the legitimizing of gender equality and reproductive and sexual autonomy at the UN Conferences on Human Rights (Vienna, 1993), Population and Development (Cairo, 1994) and Women (Beijing, 1995). Concurrently, the increase of HIV/AIDS called for an agenda of the rights of the body, encompassing both sexual autonomy and entitlements to health care, food and nutrition, and access to treatment.

But religious extremism – openly antagonizing gender equality, reproductive autonomy and sexual plurality – had also been on the rise since the 1970s. In the 1980s, the Ronald Reagan administration, with support from US-based religious right groups, made abortion a major controversy, pre-empting the International Population Conference of Mexico City in 1984. These forces gained further strength from the the mid-1990s, and when the Cairo and Beijing programmes of action were reviewed five years later (Cairo and Beijing +5), the Vatican, Islamic nations and a few other countries attempted to erode previous agreements on gender-sensitive policies, abortion as a public health problem, and sexual and reproductive health and rights. This climate became yet more virulent after the election of George Bush in 2000, as illustrated by the harsh controversies created by the US delegation in the General Assembly Special Session on HIV/AIDS of 2001.

Since then, the USA and its conservative allies have systematically dislocated the new focus on health and rights towards a moralizing approach to reproduction and sexuality. In 2005, the Millennium Summit Review failed to retain reproductive rights, sexual health and sexual rights language in its final document. This climate has also favoured the revival of arguments, affirming that population growth is an obstacle to achieving the Millennium Development Goals. It must be said, however, that regressive policies and conservative speech acts are not exclusive to the USA. The application of sharia law and related punishments for adultery, prostitution and sodomy illuminates the politicization of gender and 'sex' biases in religion, and the regressive shifts in legislation which have taken place in many Southern states, as exemplified by the two cases below.

1 2006: The therapeutic abortion clause under the Penal Code of Nicaragua, which had existed since the nineteenth century, was abolished under pressure from the Catholic Church.
2 2007: The Nigerian Congress proposed to include the condemnation and punishment of public expression of non-heterosexual affection and the registration of gay organizations.

Despite such a regressive landscape, feminists, human rights defenders and some progressive states continue to struggle to preserve gains made during the 1980s–1990s, and to further advance the agendas of gender equality, reproductive justice and sexual plurality.

Relevant international and regional human rights definitions

• 1993: The International Conference on Human Rights, Vienna, acknowledged that human rights are universal, indivisible and interrelated, and that women's human rights must be respected in both the public and private spheres.

- 1994: The Programme of Action of the International Conference of Population and Development (ICPD, Cairo, 1994) defined reproductive rights as:

  [Embracing] certain human rights that are already recognized in national laws, international human rights documents and other consensus documents. These rights rest on the recognition of the basic right of all couples and individuals to decide freely and responsibly the number, spacing and timing of their children and to have the information and means to do so, and the right to attain the highest standard of sexual and reproductive health. It also includes their right to make decisions concerning reproduction free of discrimination, coercion and violence. (Paragraph 7.3)

- 1995: Platform of Action of the IV World Women Conference, Beijing, reaffirmed ICPD principles and spelt out the substantive content of women's sexual rights as follows:

  The human rights of women include their right to have control over and decide freely and responsibly on matters related to their sexuality, including sexual and reproductive health, free of coercion, discrimination and violence. Equal relationships between women and men in matters of sexual relations and reproduction, including full respect for the integrity of the person, require mutual respect, consent and shared responsibility for sexual behavior and its consequences. (Paragraph 96)

- 1997: The Treaty of Amsterdam, which amended the Treaty of the European Union, considered sexual orientation an unjustifiable basis for discrimination.
- 2000: The Council of Europe requested the inclusion of sexual orientation in the list of unjustified grounds for discrimination in the European Convention on Human Rights.
- 2000: The Declaration and Programme of Action of the Conference of the Americas in Preparation for the International Conference Against Racism, Racial Discrimination, Xenophobia and Related Discrimination recognized sexual orientation as a condition aggravating race-related infringements of human rights:

  We call States and the international community to recognize that some victims of the racism, racial discrimination, xenophobia and connected forms of intolerance are further more marginalized because of their age, gender, sexual orientation, disability or social or economic situation. (Paragraph 140)

- 2001: The final declaration of United Nations General Assembly Special Session on HIV/AIDS called for the promotion and protection of human rights as non-negotiable components of policy responses to the epidemics by:

  Recognizing that the full realization of human rights and fundamental freedoms for all is an essential element in a global response to the HIV/AIDS pandemic, including in the areas of prevention, care, support and treatment, and that it reduces vulnerability to HIV/AIDS and prevents stigma and related discrimination against people living with or at risk of HIV/AIDS. (Paragraph 16)

- 2003: The African Union adopted a Protocol to the African Charter on Human and Peoples' Rights on the Rights of Women in Africa that enshrines a series of principles concerning reproductive self-determination:

  States Parties shall ensure that the right to health of women, including sexual and reproductive health is respected and promoted… States Parties shall take all appropriate measures to [among others] protect the reproductive rights of women by authorising medical abortion in cases of sexual assault, rape, incest, and where the continued pregnancy endangers the mental and physical health of the mother or the life of the mother or the foetus. (Paragraph 14)

Human rights treaty bodies

In addition to these key international agreements, United Nations Human Rights Treaty bodies and reports of Special Procedures have also adopted relevant decisions, recommendations and resolutions with respect to reproductive and sexual rights in the most diverse domains: sterilization and abortion, female genital mutilation, medical abuses through contraception, discrimination and punishment of homosexual conducts, torture and extra-judicial execution of persons because of their sexual orientation and gender identity (Saiz 2004). In 2003, at the 59th session of the UN Commission on Human Rights (CHR), the government of Brazil presented a resolution addressing human rights violations occurring on grounds of sexual orientation. But a year later, pressured by fierce opposition on the part of Islamic states, the Vatican and a few other governments, it retreated from redrafting the text (Pazello 2005).

Even so, debates on sexual orientation and gender identity continue at CHR. This investment is sustained in the Human Rights Council, the new normative body with higher status that has substituted the Commission. In December 2006, in the Third Session of the Council, Norway presented a Statement to Council on Human Rights and 54 countries supported Sexual Orientation. In the Fourth Session of March 2007, acknowledged human specialist and LGBTQ (lesbian, gay, bisexual, transgender, queer) organizations launched the Yogyakarta Principles, which include the application of international human rights law in relation to sexual orientation and gender identity. The Principles affirm binding international legal standards with which all states must comply.

Conceptual controversies

The reproductive and sexual rights field is, inevitably, marked by ongoing conceptual controversies. During the 1980s and 1990s, one main debate concerned the individual woman's ownership of her body and women's autonomy in general, which were considered inappropriate in Southern settings. This perspective converged with the broader critique of human rights that is framed around cultural relativism. A related point of view considered the disjunction between the individual and social dimensions of sexual and reproductive rights, claiming that autonomy or choice in matters relating to reproduction and sexuality may be meaningless where livelihood is endangered, public health and education systems are inadequate, and cultural diversity is not respected.

During the 1990s, these critiques were addressed with an ethical frame based on four principles: equality, diversity, personhood and bodily integrity. This perspective argued that the language of sexual and reproductive rights must be placed firmly within a larger framework which includes adequate nutrition and access to health care, education, housing, jobs and social assistance. The sexual and reproductive rights framework implies both positive rights, such as reproductive health care and employment, and negative rights, such as protection against rape and discrimination, regardless of sexual orientation or marital status.

Nevertheless, unresolved tensions and problems persist. One of them concerns the complex articulation between gender equality, reproductive rights and sexual rights. These normative principles relate to realms of human life that are both connected and distinctive. This means that sexual rights cannot be automatically subsumed under reproductive rights. A related debate regards the dominant negative use of sexual rights as a tool to protect persons from disease, violence and other forms of abuse. Many authors have criticized the appeal to victimization that informs mainstream rights work in relation to sexuality, affirming that it is also necessary to emphasize the positive dimensions of sexual rights, addressing eroticism, pleasure and well-being (Petchesky 2003; Miller and Vance 2004, among others).

More importantly, conceptual enquiries have constantly called attention to the fact that framing and applying 'universal' rights to sexuality is an exceedingly complex task. A theoretical perspective that emphasizes the socially constructed nature and plasticity of sexuality is necessarily in tension with rights claims that are strongly based on fixed criteria of 'good' and 'bad'. In addition, efforts that inscribe 'sex' into rights frameworks must constantly bear in mind that identities, meanings and practices do not constitute a unified domain of human experience. Human rights language has the potential to sustain claims for sexual rights based on agency, accountability and indivisibility, although due attention must be paid to claims that are based exclusively on fixed identities such as gay, lesbian, transgender and youth (Saiz 2004; Samelius and Wagberg 2005).

Policy and political challenges

A human rights approach to reproductive politics and sexuality is also confronted with major technical and political difficulties, including non-binding provisions in United Nations documents. Even if these new principles are made legally binding, effective enforcement requires a rigid and continuing distinction between the public and private in international human rights law and national legal systems. This is particularly important for women, whose lives in many cultures are still locked within the domestic domain in which most abuses such as sexual coercion, marital rape, female genital mutilation and virginity codes occur.

In contrast to mainstream economic and demographic theories, feminists focus on women's rights and gender inequality, maintaining that women should be the subjects, not the objects, of any related policy. Similarly, scholars and activists engaged with LGBTQ and HIV/AIDS issues systematically interrogate biomedical and legal discourses that impose heterosexuality as a norm in research and public health interventions. The legitimizing of reproductive and sexual rights in international documents in the 1990s did not mean the end of moral controversies about gender, abortion and sexuality in societal contexts. In fact, the early twenty-first century is witnessing nationalism, ethnic hatred and, in particular, religious extremism and state security concerns as factors that have intensified the threats to gender equality, reproductive self-determination and sexual pluralism.

Greater challenges also emerge when reproductive and sexual rights discourses and practical claims are placed against the paradoxical landscape of globalization that implies increasing uncertainties and inequalities. In such circumstances, women, children and those whose sexual identity or conduct does not conform to dominant norms are particularly vulnerable to exclusion, stigmatization and abuse.

GUIDE TO FURTHER READING AND REFERENCES

Center for Reproductive Rights (2006) *Gaining Ground: A Tool for Advancing Reproductive Rights*, New York: Center for Reproductive Rights.

Corrêa, S. and Parker, R. (2004) 'Sexuality, human rights, and demographic thinking: Connections and disjunctions in a changing world', *Sexuality Research and Social Policy*, 1(1): 15–38.

Ilkkaracan, P. (ed.) (2000) *Women and Sexuality in Muslim Societies*, Istanbul: Women for Women's Human Rights, pp. 187–96.

IPPF (1995) *IPPF Charter on Sexual and Reproductive Rights*, London: International Planned Parenthood Federation.

Miller, A.M. and Vance, C.S. (2004) 'Sexuality, human rights, and health', *Health and Human Rights*, 7(2): 5–15.

Parker, R.G. and Aggleton, P. (eds) (1999) *Culture, Society and Sexuality: A Reader*, London: University College London Press.

Pazello, M. (2005) 'Sexual rights and trade', *Peace Review*, 17(2–3): 155–62(8).

Petchesky, R. (2003) *Global Prescriptions: Gendering Health and Human Rights*, London: Zed Books.

Rubin, G. (1984) 'Thinking sex: Notes for a radical theory of the politics of sexuality', in C.S. Vance (ed.) *Pleasure and Danger: Exploring Female Sexuality*, Boston, MA: Routledge and Kegan Paul, pp. 267–319.

Saiz, I. (2004) 'Bracketing sexuality: Human rights and sexual orientation – A decade of development and denial at the United Nations', *Health and Human Rights*, 7(2): 48–51.

Samelius, L. and Wagberg, E. (2005) *Sexual Orientation and Gender Identity Issues in Development: A Study of Swedish Policy and Administration of Lesbian, Gay, Bisexual and Transgender Issues in International Development Cooperation*, Swedish International Development Cooperation Agency, Health Division Document (available at http://www.ilga-europe.org/europe/guide/country_by_country/sweden/sexual_orientation_and_gender_identity_issues_in_development).

Sen, G. (2005) *Neolibs, Neocons and Gender Justice: Lessons from Global Negotiations*, UNRISD Occasional Paper 9, Geneva: United Nations Research Institute for Social Development.

United Nations (1994a) *Programme of Action of the International Conference on Population and Development*, New York: United Nations.

United Nations (1994b) *Report of the International Conference on Population and Development, Cairo, 5–13 September*, Sales E.95.XIII.18, New York: United Nations

United Nations (1995) *Report of the Fourth World Conference on Women, Beijing, 6–15 September*, A/CONF.177/20, 7, New York: United Nations.

United Nations (1996) *Beijing Declaration and Platform for Action*, adopted by the Fourth World Conference on Women, New York: United Nations.

Weeks, J. (1985) *Sexuality and Its Discontents: Meanings, Myths and Modern Sexualities*, London: Routledge and Kegan Paul.

Weeks, J. (1996) 'Sexuality and the body', in S. Hall et al. (eds) *Modernity: An Introduction to Modern Societies*, London: Blackwell, pp. 363–94.

7.11 Indigenous fertility control

Tulsi Patel

Introduction

Demographic studies have generally seen the world as divided into two broad parts. The less developed societies, because of their proclivity for high fertility, are seen to be under the spell of religious superstition and tradition, while the developed world is seen as capable of rational choice. Anthropological (Handwerker 1990; Patel 1994; Greenhalgh 1995) and historical (Harris and Ross 1987; Hufton 1995) studies situate population and fertility amidst cultural and political-economic considerations. It is evident that though barrenness was regarded as a curse, an over-abundance of living children was seen as something less than a blessing.

This chapter focuses on indigenous fertility control in two ways: mortality control on the one hand, and fertility on the other. Though many of the indigenous practices and techniques may not be of proven effectivity, they are not totally ineffective.

Social mechanisms and population regulation

The prevalence of indigenous population control (fertility) is reported in many societies. Heer (1964) reports for Indian-speaking communities in parts of Andean countries, Freebeme (1964) for traditional China, Smith (1977: 142–3) for Japan, Bledsoe (1997) for Gambia, Harris and Ross

(1987) for societies ranging from Paleolithic times to the present, Patel (1994 and 1998) for rural North Indian peasant and tribal society, and Ram and Jolly (1998) for Asia and the Pacific during colonial times.

Limiting fertility within marriage

Matters related to marriage and fertility are intimate, gendered, and elicit intense interest from surrounding kin, community and state (cf. MacCormack 1982; Patel 1994). The German ethnologist Felix Speiser (1990) attributes low birth rates to the pre-colonial sexual economy – the way in which older, less virile men monopolized women, and sterility in women ensuing from being 'used' for sexual purposes at a very early age.

Celibacy

Prayer to have self-control is emphasized so heavily in Christianity that virginity symbolizes bridehood with Christ. Hindu sadhus and sadhvis, and some wrestlers in India remain celibate for life, with a strict and elaborate regimen prescribed to control semen loss (Alter 1992: 133).

Unwelcome babies

Infanticide, especially female infanticide, has for centuries depressed the number of surviving children, with fewer girls to replace their mothers as reproducers. Vishwanath (2000) provides figures for the reduced population of Patidars during the 1820s and 1890s in Gujarat. In twentieth-century India and China, millions of girls were not allowed to survive. Douglas (1966) describes the customary beliefs and practices of eliminating babies among a few primitive communities. The neglect of female children is customary in south Asia and son preference is characteristic.

Colonial discourses have denounced as pathological infanticide other indigenous practices, such as abortion, neglect, widow strangulation and denial of remarriage, protracted periods of sexual abstinence, and so on, and decrease of population (see Ram and Jolly 1998). Though it is impossible to quantify them, accounts of female infanticide are available from autobiographical accounts (Dureau 1998).

Eugenics politics

Many colonizers encouraged breeding among the middle and upper classes. The colonies however, did not always respond to the desires of the colonial masters or missionaries (see Ram and Jolly 1998). Speiser (1990: 50) evokes this clearly from a mother: 'Why should we go on having children? Since the white man came they all die' (cf. Rivers 1922: 104).

Scheper-Hughes (1984), in her study of north-east Brazil, talks of ethno-eugenics. Mothers expressed a belief in a child's innate constitution relating to 'readiness or fitness for life', as opposed to traits displayed by a child 'who wanted to die'. The lifeboat ethics explains the absence of grief over such deaths, and is also excused by the widespread folk belief in Latin America that such infants are not affected by original sin and rise immediately to heaven to become little angels. Fijian mothers were under strict surveillance to increase the population of Fiji, and were often accused of procuring abortions and were liable to inquests.

In the last quarter of the twentieth century in south Asia, ultrasound technology and legalized abortion provided an effective handle to curtail the birth of too many daughters. Sex-selective abortion, an illegal act since 1994, has become prevalent among the educated, middle class and wealthy in northern and western India (Patel 2007). While the means are new, the goals to regulate the number and sex composition of one's children are not so new.

Abortion

In the early stages of pregnancy, abortion was widely tolerated all over the world for centuries as one of the only dependable methods of fertility control. Even the Catholic Church took the conveniently loose view that the foetus became animated by the rational soul, and abortion therefore became a serious crime at 40 days after conception for a boy and 80 days for a girl.

Among the Javanese (Alexander 1986) there are occasional reports of the occurrence of abortion. Treating delayed menstruation with herbs and massage is evidently common (see also the theme issue of *Social Science and Medicine* (1996), under 'Guide to further reading' at the end of this chapter). Herbs purchased at fairs and/or prepared from garden plants to bring on 'women's courses' before the pregnancy was far advanced are also reported for fifteenth- to seventeenth-century European society, and their knowledge passed on from one generation of women to another. Midwives were thought to be well versed in preparing these concoctions, as were whores. Dureau (1998: 248) reports the use of abortifacients by women in the Solomon Islands during the colonial period (cf. Fortes 1949: 167; Patel 1994). Some of the herbal preparations are also used as contraception (cf. Patel 1994).

Mechanisms of fertility regulation

Some of the practices of fertility control are related directly to the belief and value structures of a given society, while others might be related to the political and economic structures.

Abstinence

Abstinence within marriage has been used effectively for centuries in most cultures. Handwerker (1986: 103) refers to an old Liberian farmwoman stating that the foolproof method of contraception was to avoid your husband. A Rajasthani woman in her eighties confided that she had borne only two children because she had sternly kept her husband at arm's length. Besides institutional practices prescribing avoidance, women have used their ingenuity as well. They are known to introduce a barrier to reduce or prevent the possibility of sex. A demographer from the Philippines corroborated Patel's (1997) observation of enticing children to sleep in one's bed, with the specific aim of deterring sexual advances from one's husband.

> Madame de Sevigne, in seventeenth-century France, urged upon her daughter after three pregnancies in quick succession, the desirability of having her maid sleep in the same room to depress the sexual urges of the Comte de Grigan. Lower down the social scale, keeping children in the marital bed may have been used by women to lessen the prospects of pregnancy (Hufton 1995: 178).

An Indian village elder eulogized the much-reduced possibility of undesirable self-indulgence and sin when surrounded by people in a joint family (Wadley 1994).

Sleeping arrangements

The architecture of housing provides for only one, or at the most two, proper rooms. The rest of the large house space is either open or consists of half-covered structures that allow rather generous ventilation and disallow privacy (see Patel 1994: 173, 188–9; Wadley 1994: 13). Except for very young couples, closed rooms are not used for sleeping. The middle-aged and elderly sleep in common open spaces like the courtyard. Streets are lined with cots at night and men talk themselves to sleep. Sex relations of the elderly do not remain a secret for long and become a subject for gossip (cf. Dureau 1998: 244).

Even among the younger couples who are expected to be sexually active, mothers, mothers-in-law and grandmothers often intervene to restrict sexual intercourse. Sleeping close to the daughter-in-law restrains her man from making sexual advances. The Kusasi of Savanna in Ghana (Cleveland 1986) would report the matter to a mother or father and reprimand the man if he were observed not to be abstaining from sex or making advances without his wife's desire (cf. Patel 1994).

Social onomastics

The pattern of nomenclature signals the uncalled-for births after parents have had the socially optimum number of children of both sexes. The names indicating the parents' unwelcome attitude to their later children are Madi (one who has barged in), Aichuki (enough of coming), Santi (peace/quiet), Santos (satisfaction/complacency) and Dhapuri (satisfied/full/complete).

Pregnant grandmother syndrome

In Mogra (the village of Patel's 1994 study), a grandmother ceases to bear children. The norms prescribe the time when a couple should opt out of having a baby once their children are married. If elderly couples (parents of married children) display undue concern over sensual enjoyment they risk criticism and ridicule (cf. Vatuk 1990: 75 for Uttar Pradesh, Caldwell 1982 for the Yoruba of Nigeria).

Lactation practices

Prolonged breastfeeding is widely reported. Among the Asia-Pacific communities (Ram and Jolly 1998), children are ideally suckled for about four years. Studies from Java in Indonesia and from Africa (Handwerker 1986) report at least two years of post-partum breastfeeding *sans* coitus.

There exists ethnographic evidence of the association between lactation and anovulation. In Mogra, mothers breastfeed their infants on demand and consider mother's milk as the only vital nutrient for the infant. It is believed that mother's milk is the only feed that produces neither diarrhoea nor malodorous stools (cf. Hufton 1995). MacCormack reports for Sierra Leone: 'Sande women, with their secret knowledge, public laws, legitimate sanctions and hierarchical organization, bring women's biology under the most careful cultural control' (1977: 94). Also, in rural Rajasthan, if an infant dies, the older sibling is put to the breast with the clear purpose of avoiding an early conception.

Political and ritual considerations

Some African and Pacific tribes prolong breastfeeding and abstinence with the explicit purpose of having only one or two children per woman. The Bhils in Rajasthan (Patel 1998) practise abstinence for a month during the Gavari worship festivities, and once or twice a week when either spouse is fasting. A good fraction of men wear the ritually processed copper ring (called a *gole*) as part of a ritual which expects them to abstain on still more occasions.

Besides, the popular practice of *pomanchar*, literally 'guesting', involves frequent reciprocal visits of kin, relatives and even caste members. Sleeping is especially gender-segregated. During guesting, except for very young couples, sexual activity is inhibited.

Contraception

Coitus interruptus, or withdrawal, has been practised and passed on from generation to generation. Though the semiology varies from culture to culture, the seed and soil (*beej–kshetra*) for sperm and womb respectively is the most common metaphor in many parts of the world (Patel 1994). The preference for the right kind of field/soil for a seed is a widespread concern in most societies. Hufton records a case, 'When Isabella de Moerloose of the region of Ghent married a pastor in 1689, he tried by coitus interruptus and oral sex to avoid making Isabella pregnant' (1995: 174), as he did not want children from Isabella (who came from lower social stock) to claim his descent and inherit his property.

Conclusion

Both cultural and political aspects to fertility regulation are integral to people and vary over their life cycle. And economic considerations are at once cultural considerations, and the same applies to fertility. Conflicts between the reproductive desires of a society's fecund women and other individuals, groups and political elite are present. Differential access to power determines how conflicts over reproduction are conducted and resolved (if they are resolved). State/colonial power and also family and community (Patel 2007) exercise surveillance and intervene for eugenic change in stock of populations.

The use of intentionality in power dynamics relates with real-life situations where fertility decisions like sexual intercourse, conception, positions to retain or expel the seed, abort, kill, throw away, and so on, are taken. All household members are rarely likely to have a total consensus. Nor are macro-level results merely aggregates of the micro-level fertility decisions.

GUIDE TO FURTHER READING

Freebeme, M. (1964) 'Birth control in China', *Population Studies*, 18(1): 5–16.
Harris, M. and Ross, E. (1987) *Death, Sex, and Fertility: Population Regulation in Preindustrial and Developing Societies*, New York: Columbia University Press.
Heer, D.M. (1964) 'Fertility differentials between Indian and Spanish speaking parts in Andean countries', *Population Studies*, 18(1): 71–84.
Hufton, O. (1995) *The Prospect Before Her, Vol. 1: 1500–1800*, London: HarperCollins.
Patel, T. (1994) *Fertility Behaviour: Population and Society in a Rajasthan Village*, Delhi: Oxford University Press.
Scheper-Hughes, N. (1984) 'Infant mortality and infant care: Cultural and economic constraints in nursing in Northeast Brazil', *Social Science and Medicine*, 19: 535–46.
Social Science and Medicine (1996) 42(4): for several articles in the special issue on abortion.

REFERENCES

Alexander, P. (1986) 'Labour expropriation and fertility: population growth in nineteenth century Java', in W.P. Handwerker (ed.) *Births and Power: Social Change and Politics of Reproduction*, Boulder, CO: Westview Press.
Alter, J. (1992) *The Wrestler's Body*, Berkeley, CA: University of California Press.
Bledsoe, C. (1997) 'Reproduction and aging in rural Gambia: African empirical challenges for the culture of Western science', unpublished manuscript.
Caldwell, J.C. (1982) *Theory of Fertility Decline*, London: Academic Press.
Cleveland, D.A. (1986) 'The political economy of fertility regulation: the Kusasi of Savanna West Africa (Ghana)', in W.P. Handwerker (ed.) *Births and Power: Social Change and Politics of Reproduction*, Boulder, CO: Westview Press, pp. 263–93.
Douglas, M. (1966) *Purity and Danger: An Analysis of the Concepts of Pollution and Taboo*, London: Routledge and Kegan Paul.

Dureau, C. (1998) 'From sisters to wives: Changing contexts of maternity on Simbo, Western Solomon Islands', in K. Ram and M. Jolly (eds) *Maternities and Modernities: Colonial and Postcolonial Experiences in Asia and the Pacific*, Cambridge: Cambridge University Press.

Fortes, M. (1949) *The Web of Kinship Among the Tallensi*, London: Oxford University Press.

Freeberne, M. (1964) 'Birth control in China', *Population Studies*, 18(1): 5–16.

Greenhalgh, S. (ed.) (1995) *Situating Fertility: Anthropology and Demographic Inquiry*, Cambridge: Cambridge University Press.

Handwerker, W.P. (ed.) (1986) *Births and Power: Social Change and Politics of Reproduction*, Boulder, CO: Westview Press.

Handwerker, W.P. (1990) *Culture and Reproduction*, Boulder, CO: Westview Press.

Harris, M. and Ross, E. (1987) *Death, Sex and Fertility: Population Regulation in Preindustrial and Developing Societies*, New York: Columbia University Press.

Heer, D.M. (1964) 'Fertility differentials between Indian and Spanish speaking parts in Andean countries', *Population Studies*, 18(1): 71–84.

Hufton, O. (1995) *The Prospect Before Her, Vol. 1: 1550–1800*, London: HarperCollins.

MacCormack, C.P. (1977) 'Biological events and cultural control', *Signs*, 3(1): 93–100.

MacCormack, C.P. (ed.) (1982) *Ethnography of Fertility and Birth*, New York: Academic Press.

Patel, T. (1994) *Fertility Behaviour: Population and Society in a Rajasthan Village*, Delhi: Oxford University Press.

Patel, T. (1997) 'The fit between sterilization and traditional fertility in rural India', paper presented at the East–West Center Alumni Association International Conference, New Delhi, 23–26 November 1997.

Patel, T. (1998) 'Reproduction and tribal society: A study in Southern Rajasthan', project report submitted to the ICSSR, Delhi.

Patel, T. (ed.) (2007) *Sex-Selective Abortion in India: Gender, Society and New Reproductive Technologies*, New Delhi: Sage.

Ram, K. and Jolly, M. (eds) (1998) *Maternities and Modernities: Colonial and Postcolonial Experiences in Asia and the Pacific*, Cambridge: Cambridge University Press.

Rivers, W.H.R. (ed.) (1922) *Essays on the Depopulation of Melanesia*, Cambridge: Cambridge University Press.

Scheper-Hughes, N. (1984) 'Infant mortality and infant care: Cultural and economic constraints in nursing in northeast Brazil', *Social Science and Medicine*, 19: 535–46.

Smith, T.C. (1977) *Nakahara: Family Planning and Population in a Japanese Village, 1717–1830*, Stanford, CA: Stanford University Press.

Speiser, F. (1990 [1923]) *The Ethnology of Vanuatu: An Early Twentieth Century Study*, Bathurst: Crawford House.

Vatuk, S. (1990) '"To be a burden on others": Dependency anxiety among the elderly in India', in O.M. Lynch (ed.) *Divine Passions: The Social Construction of Emotion in India*, Berkeley, CA: University of California Press.

Vishwanath, L.S. (2000) *Female Infanticide and Social Structure*, Delhi: Hindustan.

Wadley, S. (1994) *Struggling with Destiny in Karimpur, 1925–1984*, Delhi: Vistar.

PART 8 | Health and education

Editorial introduction

Should poor countries be concerned about the implications for human welfare when they cannot afford to provide health and educational needs and when their economic resources are heavily constrained? There are three reasons for concern. First, the basic health, nutritional and educational needs of the most vulnerable groups – the under-fives, pregnant women and nursing mothers – are urgent and compelling. If these groups are neglected, they can set back the health and welfare of the whole future generation of a country, in addition to adding to present human and economic miseries. Second, there is considerable evidence that there are positive economic returns to interventions supporting basic nutrition, health and education; and third, human welfare and progress is the ultimate end of all development policy and so many of the UN Millennium Development Goals (MDGs) are related to health and education.

Levels of child malnutrition have fallen only slowly during the 1990s despite significant economic growth and considerable expenditure on various programmes. The poor and the very young in low-income countries seem particularly vulnerable to disease and there is evidence to suggest that, in many countries, the position of women in society relative to that of men makes them more prone to disease. Women's nutritional status influences children's nutritional status in a variety of ways both during pregnancy and early childhood. Women who are malnourished are more likely to deliver smaller babies, who, in turn, are at increased risk of poor growth and development. Additionally, malnourished women may be less successful at breastfeeding their children, have lower energy levels, and have reduced cognitive abilities, all of which hamper their ability to adequately care for their young child.

Two of the most critical caring practices for women that may affect child nutritional status are prenatal and birthing care. Prenatal care provides an opportunity for a number of preventative interventions, including various immunizations, prevention and treatment of anaemia and infections, and detection of high-risk pregnancies needing special delivery care. Many of those concerned with women's reproductive health argue that family planning services should be available not for population control but for birth control, and only as part of comprehensive health and welfare provisions. Preventative and curative measures to control infectious diseases in young children are also crucial to their nutritional status. Infectious diseases, many of which are relatively easy to cure, remain the major killers in low-income countries (e.g. malaria). Poverty is clearly connected with vulnerability to these infections, and undernutrition is often a major contributing factor. Lack of access to safe water and poor environmental sanitation due to unsanitary waste disposal are considered to be important causes of infectious diseases. These issues raise serious problems with the prevalent approaches to primary healthcare and accessibility for the poor to the health services. Over the last three decades there has been great concern about the transmission of HIV/AIDS, and its impact on communities, households, livelihoods and access to treatment. Studies are now highlighting that, as countries are becoming developed, health inequalities are widening between the rich and poor. This has implications for the ageing population as demographic transition takes place to an increasingly older population generated by a rise in life expectancy and falling fertility rates.

Adult literacy is a huge problem for human resource development, especially among women. Education greatly strengthens women's ability to perform their vital role in creating healthy households. Much emphasis has been placed on the role of female education in promoting good health. It increases their ability to benefit from health information and to make good use of health services; it increases their access to income and enables them to live healthier lives.

Globalisation has resulted in the growth in size and proportion of the informal economy, as well as the fragmentation of the service and commodity chains in developing countries resulting in children entering the world of work in large numbers, in the service sector and as unpaid family labour. Children out of school and in work should be targeted to secure long-term development goals. The right to education is a fundamental universal human right, and managing education systems at all levels and creating accessibility has become very crucial.

8.1 Malnutrition and nutrition policies in developing countries

Prakash Shetty

Introduction

A critical examination of the principal causes of mortality and morbidity worldwide indicates that malnutrition and infectious diseases continue to be significant contributors to the health burden in the developing world. Although reduction in the prevalence of under-nutrition is evident in most parts of the developing world, the numbers of individuals affected remain much the same or have even increased, largely the result of increases in the population in these countries. What is striking, however, is that the health burden due to non-communicable diseases, such as heart disease and cancer, is increasing dramatically in some of these developing countries with modest per-capita GNPs, particularly those that appear to be in some stage of rapid developmental transition. It would appear that even modest increases in prosperity which accompany economic development seem to be associated with marked increases in the mortality and morbidity attributable to non-communicable diseases related to diet and nutrition. These dramatic changes in the disease burden of the population are probably mediated by changes in the dietary patterns and lifestyles which typify the acquisition of an urbanized and affluent lifestyle. Countries in rapid developmental transition, like China, India and Brazil, seem to bear a double burden of poverty and under-nutrition, coupled with problems acquired due to urbanization and affluence.

What is malnutrition?

The term malnutrition refers to all deviations from adequate nutrition, including under- and over-nutrition, and encompasses both inadequacy of food or excess of food relative to need. Under-nutrition is defined as being the result of insufficient food, caused primarily by an inadequate intake of dietary energy, whether or not any specific nutrient is an additional limiting factor. This emphasis on dietary energy as a general measure of food adequacy seems justified, since an increase in food energy, if derived from normal staple foods, brings with it most other nutrients. Thus, in most situations, increased dietary energy is a necessary condition for nutritional improvement, even if it is not always sufficient in itself.

Malnutrition also encompasses specific deficiencies of essential nutrients such as vitamins and minerals. Thus malnutrition may arise from deficiencies of specific nutrients from diets based on wrong kinds, quantities or proportions of foods. Goitre, scurvy, anaemia and xerophthalmia are forms of malnutrition, caused by inadequate intake of iodine, vitamin C, iron and vitamin A respectively. Conditions such as obesity, though not the result of inadequacy of food, also constitute malnutrition. The terms 'malnutrition' and 'under-nutrition' are often used loosely and interchangeably, although a distinction exists and may need to be made.

Malnutrition refers to nutritional situations characteristic of relatively poorer socio-economic populations of 'low-income' developing countries. Although it is possible to arrive at the prevalence and the numbers of individuals within a population manifesting signs of specific nutrient deficiency, for instance anaemia as a result of iron deficiency, they are almost always associated with marginal or low food energy intakes. Thus the term 'malnutrition' is often used in the broader sense, referring to any physical condition implying ill health or the inability to maintain adequate growth or appropriate body weight, or to sustain acceptable levels of economically necessary and socially desirable physical activities, brought about by an inadequacy in food – both quantity and quality.

The causes of malnutrition

To develop policies related to food and nutrition that affect the health of populations in developing countries, it is helpful to review the factors that determine malnutrition. The causes of malnutrition are multidimensional and its determinants include both food- and non-food-related factors, which often interact to form a complex web of biological, socio-economic, cultural and environmental deprivations. Establishing a relationship between these variables and the indicators of malnutrition does not necessarily imply causality, but does demonstrate that, in addition to food availability, many social, cultural, health and environmental factors influence the prevalence of malnutrition. Although people suffering from inadequacy of food are poor, not all the poor are undernourished. Even in households that are food-secure, some members may be undernourished. Income fluctuations, seasonal disparities in food availability and demand for high levels of physical activity, and proximity and access to marketing facilities may singly or in combination influence the nutritional status of an individual or a household. For example, the transition from subsistence farming to commercial agriculture and cash crops may help improve nutrition in the long run; however, this may result in negative impacts over the short term unless accompanied by improvements in access to health services, environmental sanitation and other social investments. Rapid urbanization and rural-to-urban migration may lead to nutritional deprivation of segments of society. Cultural attitudes reflected in food preferences and food preparation practices, and women's time constraints, including that available for child-rearing practices, influence the nutrition of the most vulnerable in societies. Inadequate housing and overcrowding, poor sanitation and lack of access to a protected water supply, through their links with infectious diseases and infestations, are potent environmental factors that influence biological food utilization and nutrition. Inadequate access to food, limited access to health care and a clean environment, and insufficient access to educational opportunities, in turn, are determined by the economic and institutional structures, as well as the political and ideological superstructures within society.

Poor nutritional status of populations affects the physical growth, intelligence, behaviour and learning abilities of children and adolescents. It impacts on their physical and work performance and has been linked to impaired economic work productivity during adulthood. Inadequate nutrition predisposes them to infections and contributes to the negative downward spiral of malnutrition and infection. Good nutritional status, on the other hand, promotes optimal growth and development of children and adolescents. It contributes to better physiological work performance, enhances adult economic productivity, increases levels of socially desirable activities and promotes better maternal birth outcomes. Good nutrition of a population reflects on the nutritional status of the individual in the community and contributes to an upward positive spiral that reflects improvement in the resources and human capital of societies.

Economic growth and prosperity can also contribute to the problem of malnutrition in a population by creating conditions that are conducive to the development of chronic diseases of adulthood which include heart disease, diabetes and cancer. Urbanization, which characterizes economic development of developing societies, alters several environmental factors, including the pattern of diet and changes in lifestyles of individuals. It is well recognized that economic prosperity helps attain adequacy of food in quantitative terms for much of the population. This improvement, however, is accompanied by a qualitative change in the diet, with increased dietary energy being provided by fat in the daily diet replacing the carbohydrates from staples or cereals. There is an increase in the consumption of food from animal sources which has other ecological consequences. Consumption of salt and sugars also increases. Lifestyle changes, particularly with relation to the level of occupational and leisure time activities, predisposes populations to an increasingly sedentary lifestyle, which consequently leads to the occurrence of obesity. These developmental changes in largely rural societies break down social support systems and networks, favour inequalities in societies and increase stress levels of individuals. In addition, the deterioration of the physical environment, particularly the increase in levels of environmental pollution, contributes to the health burden of societies in transition.

Policies and programmes to promote good nutrition in developing countries

A recognition and proper understanding of the range, complexity and interplay of the factors that sustain the problem of malnutrition in developing societies is essential to help develop policies and programmes that meet the nutritional needs of the populations and to reduce the burden of all forms of malnutrition in these countries.

Improving household food security is one of the stated objectives of all democratic societies and constitutes an important element of the human rights to adequate food now endorsed by the international community. *Food security* is defined as the access by all people at all times to the food they need for an active and healthy life. The inclusion of the term household ensures that the dietary needs of all the members of the household are met throughout the year. The achievement of household food security requires an adequate supply of food to all members of the household, ensuring stability of supply all year round, and the access, both physical and economic, which underlines the importance of the entitlement to produce and procure food. The links between food security and malnutrition are evident as nutritional status is the outcome indicator. The presence of under-nutrition is not only causally related to food insecurity at the household or individual level, but is also determined by other health-related factors, such as access to safe water, good sanitation and health care, as well as the care practices that include proper breastfeeding and complementary feeding, and ensuring fair and appropriate intra-household food distribution.

The pre-eminent determinant of household food insecurity is poverty in societies. Several policy measures undertaken by governments in developing countries are aimed at ensuring food supply and household food security. These include the following:

- macroeconomic policies and economic development strategies that ensure both public-sector and private-sector investment in agriculture and food production;
- appropriate policies to promote expansion and diversification of food availability and agricultural production in a stable and sustainable manner, and to regulate the import or export of foods and agricultural products to ensure food security;
- policies that help create adequate employment opportunities for the rural poor, and improving market efficiencies and opportunities;
- policies that improve distribution and access to land, and to other resources such as credit, as well as other agricultural inputs;
- legislating for policies that deter discrimination and ensure equal status for women, and ensuring their effective implementation;
- identification of good and culturally appropriate caring practices and policies that protect, support and promote good care and nutrition practices for children;
- policies that enable public health measures to reduce the burden of infectious diseases and to ensure access to primary health care.

Several programmes have been initiated in developing countries in order to intervene to improve the current situation with regard to nutrition of their population. These intervention programmes have been aimed at the immediate or short-term amelioration of the nutritional situation. Strategies used include the following.

- *Supplementation* of food or specific nutrients to meet the immediate deficits. Examples include food supplementation during acute food shortages such as famines or disasters, and the mandatory provision of iron and folate supplements to all pregnant mothers attending antenatal clinics in primary health care centres.
- *Fortification* of food items in the daily diet is another successful strategy that has been adopted to deal with specific nutritional problems or nutrient deficiencies. A good example is the fortification of common salt with iodine (iodized salt) to tackle the problem of iodine deficiency and goitres – one of the most successful strategies that has helped reduce the burden of iodine deficiency disorders globally.
- *Food-based approaches* include attempts to improve the nutrition of households by promoting kitchen gardens to enable families to produce and consume a diversified diet rich in vitamins. This has been promoted as a programme to reduce vitamin A deficiency in developing countries.

Preventing malnutrition is just as important as solving the problem, and both goals require the need to assess the severity of the problem as well as the ability to predict its occurrence to make prevention a realistic goal. *Nutritional surveillance* plays an important role in assembling information to assist the development of policy and programme decisions and involves the regular and timely collection of nutrition-relevant data, as well as its analysis and dissemination. There are obvious advantages in the collection of nutrition-relevant information, since the nutrition of a population is the outcome of social, economic and other factors, and is hence a good indicator of the overall development, and often a better indicator of the equitable development of societies. Nutritional surveillance systems may vary, depending on the immediate objective for which they have been set up, and some developing countries have more than one system in place. National governments of developing countries are also involved in *improving food quality* and *ensuring food safety*. Most countries have legislation to help ensure safety and quality of foods from production to retail sale. They also have established institutions or ministries to oversee food safety and quality.

Economic growth and development should reduce the burden of under-nutrition even if the reduction is slow and many people continue to suffer needlessly. There is thus a need for well-conceived policies for sustainable economic growth and social development that will benefit the poor and the undernourished. The deleterious consequences of rapid growth and development need to be guarded against, and policies need to be in place to prevent one problem of malnutrition replacing another in these societies. Given the complexity of factors that determine malnutrition of all forms, it is important that appropriate food and agricultural policies are developed to ensure household food security, and that nutritional objectives are incorporated into development policies and programmes at national and local levels in developing countries.

GUIDE TO FURTHER READING

ACC/SCN (2000) *Nutrition Through the Life Cycle, Fourth Report on the World Nutrition Situation*, Geneva: UN Administrative Committee on Coordination Sub-Committee on Nutrition, with the International Food Policy Research Institute.

Berg, A. (1987) *Malnutrition: What Can be Done?* Baltimore, MD: Johns Hopkins University Press.

Brun, T.A. and Latham, M.C. (1990) *Maldevelopment and Malnutrition*, World Food Issues 2, Ithaca, NY: Cornell University.

FAO (1993) *Developing National Plans of Action for Nutrition*, Rome: Food and Agriculture Organization.

Gopalan, C. (1992) *Nutrition in Developmental Transition in South-East Asia*, New Delhi: World Health Organization, South-East Asia Regional Office (SEARO).

Gopalan, C. and Kaur, H. (1993) *Towards Better Nutrition: Problems and Policies*, New Delhi: Nutrition Foundation of India.

Latham, M.C. (1997) *Human Nutrition in the Developing World*, Rome: Food and Agriculture Organization.

Sen, A. (1981) *Poverty and Famines: An Essay on Entitlement and Deprivation*, Oxford: Clarendon Press.

Shetty, P.S. (2006) The Boyd Orr Lecture: Achieving the Goal of Halving Global Hunger by 2015, *Proceedings of the Nutrition Society*, 65: 7–18.

World Bank (1994) *Enriching Lives: Overcoming Vitamin and Mineral Malnutrition in Developing Countries*, Washington, DC: World Bank.

8.2 Quality of maternal health care and development

Maya Unnithan-Kumar

Most developing countries in south Asia and sub-Saharan Africa are high-mortality settings, which are defined, in particular, in terms of maternal and infant deaths. In 2003, it was estimated that there were 540 maternal deaths per 100,000 live births in India, compared to 350 in low- and middle-income countries. The overall figure for the infant mortality rate in India is in the region of 72 deaths per 1000 births, although some states in India compare with countries in sub-Saharan Africa, with much higher figures, between 80 and 90 deaths per 1000 live births. Other states, such as Kerala, have much lower figures, comparable to those of developed countries (Government of India 2001; Misra, Chatterjee and Rao 2003). While maternal mortality is perhaps the most visible manifestation of the ill health of women, it is maternal morbidity (or reproductive conditions, ranging from anaemia to reproductive tract infections, which can translate into life-threatening conditions) which is a better indication of the widespread and deep-rooted nature of the risks associated with childbearing and motherhood. Maternal and child well-being is a product of a complex set of interrelated social, biological and environmental factors. Poverty, as embodied in the lack of adequate food and nutrition, absence of clean water and good sanitation, and the poor quality of the public health services, are some of the main factors which underlie the high levels of maternal morbidity in developing countries. An obvious means of addressing maternal health has been for governments to focus on building up health infrastructure in terms of equipment and personnel. Such an approach has been limited, especially in high-population contexts, where public health programmes and delivery have been guided by the objectives of population control and, in particular, the control of women's fertility.

Since the late 1990s, the 'quality of care' perspective has arisen in health policy and planning circles as the need to reframe health service delivery in terms of the experiences and life circumstances of the users rather than in relation to the objectives of population management. Increasingly, health care users are seen as having their own agency rather than as subjects who receive health care services uncritically (Unnithan-Kumar 2001, 2004a). In recognition of this fact, quality of care in terms of maternal health has been defined as 'the degree to which maternal health services for individuals and populations increase the likelihood of timely and appropriate treatment for the purpose of achieving desired outcomes that are both consistent with current professional knowledge and uphold basic reproductive rights' (Hulton, Mathews and Stones 1999: 4). The quality of care approach outlined here also departs from previous approaches to maternal health in that it views all pregnant women, not just those who experience problems during pregnancy (the focus of previous health care programmes), as being at risk of obstetric complications due to the unpredictable nature of childbearing. (In the area of maternal health, the quality of care approach is influenced by the concept of reproductive health, which, following the International

Conference on Population and Development in Cairo in 1994, emphasizes the provision of safe and consumer-driven services.)

When motherhood is unsafe

Six months before this article was written, Munga lived in a village on the outskirts of Jaipur, the capital city of Rajasthan in north-west India. She was 20 years old and expecting her third child. She already had a daughter and a son. When her labour pains started, she called for Samina (her father's younger brother's wife) and Munaan (an elderly relative), both known in the local area for their expertise in birthing babies. A boy was born at 6 p.m. that day. Samina and Munaan left shortly after this. Munga continued to bleed profusely and twice vomited the milk she was given to drink. Six hours later, at 1 a.m., she died.

Why did Munga die? It could have been for any one or all of the following reasons. Munga's parents were poor and she had little nutrition as a child and later suffered from tuberculosis. When she married, her husband earned enough but never gave her any money. As a result, she could not afford to pay for doctors or medicines, or for transport to the government centres – these were far away and, in any case, it was uncertain that the doctors would be there. She relied on the local midwives. The midwives, competent in delivering normal babies, were anxious as Munga was weak and could not push hard enough during her contractions. They exerted abdominal pressure during the last stages of her labour contractions (a risky procedure because of the danger of rupture to the uterus). Munga also received an injection by a local doctor to speed up her labour (the unassessed provision of intramuscular oxytocin also greatly enhances the risk of rupture to the uterus). For Munga, as for a number of other young women in her village, childbearing and birthing carries with it the potential of a serious risk to one's life.

Given the poverty-related nutritional deficiencies, scarcity of water for washing and sheer physical work that frame the contexts of their continuous biological reproduction, it is not surprising that childbearing is a physically debilitating and unsafe period for rural and urban poor women. There is a strong and often pragmatic tendency in these contexts to avoid the use of contraceptives, which means for most of their childbearing life, from menarche to the menopause, Munga and women like her are in continuous cycles of bearing, birthing and breastfeeding their children.

High and closely spaced fertility, along with poor nutrition and poor health care, are the primary reasons for the high mortality and morbidity figures for women and children in India (Patel 1994; Jejeebhoy 1998). The risks associated with closely spaced deliveries and an early initiation into childbearing are also among the factors identified in East Africa, where mothers with pregnancy intervals of less than a year and aged either below 15 years (first birth) or above 35 years (in their seventh or eighth pregnancy), were regarded as at high risk (McDonagh 1996). As a result, some of the important effective interventions which address the risks associated with motherhood are considered to be the distribution of contraceptives to space pregnancies, and the provision of iron, folate and malarial prophylaxes to strengthen women and enhance their immunity. However, empirical observations of health-seeking behaviour show that the provision of contraceptive devices and nutritional supplements will not in itself ensure a reduction in maternal morbidity. There are both cultural reasons for this (gender ideologies make it difficult to discuss sexual matters across the sexes; the cultural expectations and value placed on women's reproduction make childbearing a social imperative; women's subservience to men in decisions relating to childbearing) and physiological reasons (the low-cost contraceptive technologies available are not sustainable by weak, anaemic and nutritionally deficient women). Moreover, the supply of contraceptives is often misplaced as it ignores more pressing local demands, such as for reducing high levels of reproductive tract infections and related conditions of secondary infertility. There is thus a disjunction between the contraceptive-oriented health services provided and the demands for assisting conception, fertility and safer birthing environments. This dissonance is reflected in the local perceptions of health services as being of poor quality.

Enhancing the quality of maternal health services

The provision of a high quality of maternal health care is related to an understanding of what constitutes good quality of care, on the one hand, and a commitment on the part of the state to invest resources towards this end. In their framework for assessing the delivery of institutional maternal care, Hulton, Mathews and Stones (1999) suggest two basic levels which must be addressed. First, are the elements of the provision of care, such as the use and quality of the personnel employed and the infrastructure available to provide the essential obstetric care, as laid down by World Health Organization (WHO) regulations; an efficient referral system; universal emergency provisioning; the use of appropriate technologies; and an awareness of internationally recognized good practice. Second, come the elements of the experience of care (dealing with the patient's cognition of the services, the respect received and emotional support during care).

In her review of the effectiveness of antenatal services in reducing maternal morbidity and mortality, McDonagh (1996) suggests there is more rather than less evidence to cast doubt on the positive effects of antenatal care where it exists. She finds the greatest impact made by antenatal care in places like Gambia, Lesotho and Tanzania, is where a domiciliary midwifery service is supported by local efficient obstetric services. Such findings support my observations on antenatal care in rural India as well.

It is the trained auxiliary nurse midwife (ANM) who acts as the first point of professional contact with the public health sector for women in developing countries. The training in midwifery is critical in a situation such as in rural India, where most births take place at home rather than in institutional settings. Yet it is common to find that the ANM who is trained in delivering children is very rarely called on to do so. When her assistance is sought, it is in emergency situations for which she has neither the qualifications nor the resources to act effectively. As most women and families seek institutional assistance only in crisis conditions, and there is no culture of antenatal check-ups, the inability of ANMs to deal with emergencies immediately curtails their importance as health providers in local perceptions.

A lack of accountability on the part of health care personnel is among the factors identified which are responsible for the ineffectiveness of public health programmes in resource-poor countries. This failing would be addressed if health workers' perceptions of their social worth were taken into account. Health care workers often suffer from a lack of institutional, infrastructural and technical support, which, if addressed, would enhance their engagement and rapport with the community.

As the ANMs are not trained or equipped to deal with obstetric complications, it becomes vital for the routes of referral through the system to the appropriate institution to be efficient and failsafe, to ensure the quality of health service provision. Referral services are of particular importance in child delivery complications as these are usually emergency cases with late presentation. There is little cognizance of the vital significance of providing good referral services in healthplanning circles, mainly because there has been a focus on increasing the infrastructural facilities available as compared to the other elements of the quality of care approach, and because little attention has been paid to the functioning of maternal health services as a whole. In the absence of good and timely referral services, as I have argued elsewhere (Unnithan-Kumar 2004b), it may be more appropriate to provide gynaecological expertise, rather than general information on health and hygiene, to women at their first point of institutional contact. ANMs could then either be 'skilled up' or provided with close contact with the technical expertise to consult in emergencies. This would allow for obstetric and gynaecological professional care to be provided at the level of a local health centre itself, where emergency care is most needed. The role of NGOs in providing timely maternal health care services has been crucial in this respect (such as the pioneering effort of SEARCH in Maharashtra, India) who train local midwives and also provide local gynae-cological expertise, has proved to be very effective (Mavlankar, Bang and Bang 1999).

The quality of public health service provision is significantly linked to the state financial allo-cations for the health sector. The economic reforms brought in by structural adjustment pro-grammes have often led to a constriction in public spending on health. In India, it is noted, there has been a deceleration in the real capital revenue and capital expenditure on health since the mid-1980s (Seeta Prabhu 1999), which is a trend in accordance with the World Bank's recom-mendations to confine the role of the public sector to providing preventive rather than curative health services. (From 1989 to 1995, the Union government's revenue expenditure on the social sector, which includes expenditure on medical, public health and family welfare, fell from 3.04 per cent of the total revenue expenditure to 3.01 per cent of the same (Seeta Prabhu 1999: 121).) Given such constraints on public spending on health, it is unlikely that there will be any change in the quality of maternal services provided in countries like India. This is unfortunate as I believe the problem of the unsafe initiation of poor women into motherhood in Rajasthan is not because they desire domestic rather than institutional antenatal care. (The preference for home deliveries is an often cited argument which traces the problem of the poor access to health services to 'traditional' patterns of health-seeking behaviour rather than to the poor quality of services. To the contrary, I argue that a traditional resort to home births is more a result of an unequal access to health services, as well as the poor nature of the services.) Rather, they are caught in a bind, between the poor quality of public health service delivery, on the one hand, and the lack of indigenous expertise to cope with obstetric complications, on the other. The most effective solution seems to lie in the participation of locally trained midwives working alongside gynaecological experts. In the absence of appropriate antenatal expertise at the local level of the health service structure, and where there exist exacting cultural expectations which devalue the health risks of motherhood, the reproductive phase will continue to be a period in which poor women in developing countries face high health risks. More generally, a rights-based commitment to good health care (Unnithan-Kumar 2003) needs to develop within the service sector and in the community, so that women receive adequate support and understanding dur-ing, before and after their childbearing years.

GUIDE TO FURTHER READING

Inhorn, M. (2006) 'Defining woman's health: A dozen messages from more than 150 ethnographies', *Medical Anthropology Quarterly*, 20(3): 345–78.

McDonagh, M. (1996) 'Is antenatal care effective in reducing maternal morbidity and mortality?', *Health, Policy and Planning*, 11(1): 1–15.

Ramasubban, R. and Jejeebhoy, S. (2001) *Women's Reproductive Health in India*, Jaipur: Rawat.

Thaddeus, S. and Maine, D. (1994) 'Too far to walk: Maternal mortality in context', *Social Science and Medicine*, 38(8): 1091–110.

REFERENCES

Government of India (2001) *National Family Health Survey 1998–1999*, Mumbai: International Institute for Population Sciences.

Hulton, L., Mathews, Z. and Stones, R. (1999) *A Framework for the Evaluation of the Quality of Care in Maternity Services*, University of Southhampton: Department of Social Statistics publication.

Jejeebhoy, S. and Rama Rao, S. (1998) 'Unsafe motherhood: A review of reproductive health', in M. Dasgupta, L. Chen and T.N. Krishnan (eds) *Women's Health in India: Risk and Vulnerability*, Oxford: Oxford University Press.

McDonagh, M. (1996) 'Is antenatal care effective in reducing maternal morbidity and mortality?', *Health, Policy and Planning*, 11(1): 1–15.

Mavlankar, D., Bang, A. and Bang, R. (1999) 'Quality reproductive health services in rural India: The SEARCH experience', *Upscaling Innovations in Reproductive Health in Asia*, No. 2: India, Selangor, Malaysia: The International Council on the Management of Population Programmes.

Misra, R., Chatterjee, R. and Rao, S. (2003) *India Health Report*, Oxford: Oxford University Press.

Patel, T. (1994) *Fertility Behaviour: Population and Society in Rajasthan*, Delhi: Oxford University Press.

Seeta Prabhu, K. (1999) 'Structural adjustment and the health sector in India', in M. Rao (ed.) *Disinvesting in Health*, New Delhi: Sage, pp. 120–9.

Sinha, A. (2006) *India: Democracy and Well-Being*, Delhi: Rupa Publishers.

Unnithan-Kumar, M. (2001) 'Emotion, agency and access to healthcare: Women's experiences of reproduction in Jaipur', in S. Tremayne (ed.) *Managing Reproductive Life: Cross-Cultural Themes in Fertility and Sexuality*, Oxford: Berghahn Books.

Unnithan-Kumar, M. (2002) 'Midwives among others: Knowledges of healing and the politics of emotions', in S. Rozario and G. Samuels (eds) *Daughters of Hariti: Birth and Female Healers in South and Southeast Asia*, London: Routledge.

Unnithan-Kumar, M. (2003) 'Reproduction, health, rights: Connections and disconnections', in J. Mitchell and R. Wilson (eds) *Human Rights in Global Perspective: Anthropology of Rights, Claims and Entitlements*, London: Routledge.

Unnithan-Kumar, M. (ed.) (2004a) *Reproductive Agency, Medicine and the State: Cultural Transformations in Childbearing*, Oxford: Berghahn Books.

Unnithan-Kumar, M. (2004b) 'Medical pluralism and reproductive health: Forward-looking strategies', in S. Singh and V. Joshi (eds) *Human Values and Social Change in India*, Jaipur: Rawat.

8.3 The development impacts of HIV/AIDS

Lora Sabin and Candace Miller

HIV and AIDS

The human immunodeficiency virus (HIV) is a disease that attacks the human immune system. Once infected, a person's immune system deteriorates over a number of years, until it is incapable of resisting infections. At this stage, clinically defined by a low CD4 cell count (below 200 cells/mm) or by an AIDS-defining illness, the person has AIDS (acquired immune deficiency syndrome). HIV infection is transmitted through the exchange of body fluids, including semen, vaginal secretions, blood and breast milk. Worldwide, most people contract HIV from sexual contact, although needle-sharing, blood transfusions and breastfeeding are also responsible for large numbers of infections.

HIV infection was once a virtual death sentence, due to the lack of effective treatment. Without treatment, people living with HIV/AIDS (PLWHA) typically experience a range of symptoms and illnesses, including weight loss, declining energy and infections such as pneumonia, active tuberculosis and meningitis. In addition to failing health, PLWHA often experience AIDS-related stigma, as well as the pain of leaving children and parents who may need them for economic and caregiving support.

Since the late 1980s, however, antiretroviral therapy (ART) has been used to boost the immune system and suppress the HIV virus. Although ART has become available in most developing countries only since the mid-1990s, the global response to the HIV/AIDS epidemic has helped to increase access to ART worldwide, so that many PLWHA can expect to live ten years or more after beginning therapy. Still, throughout the developing world, human resource and drug shortages limit access to treatment. In 2006, only 23 per cent of the 4.6 million HIV patients needing treatment in sub-Saharan Africa (SSA) received medicine (UNAIDS and WHO 2006). Patients on ART usually experience dramatic improvements in their health within one to six months, though some only seek treatment so late that it is ineffective, while others suffer serious side effects.

Global trends in HIV and AIDS

The total estimated number of PLWHA in 2006 was 39.5 million, up 5.2 million from 1999 estimates. In 2006 alone, 4.3 million adults and children were newly infected, while 2.9 million persons died from AIDS-related causes, including about 400,000 children below the age of 15 years. In 2006, 40 per cent of all new infections in adults occurred in young people aged 15–24; in some regions, such as eastern Europe and southern Africa, HIV infections were concentrated in this population (UNAIDS and WHO 2006)

While the number of PLWHA has risen in every region in the world over the last decade, sub-Saharan Africa, home to nearly two-thirds of infected persons worldwide (63 per cent), continues to bear the greatest burden of AIDS. Southern Africa – where one in three HIV-positive persons lives, and where 34 per cent of all AIDS deaths occurred in 2006 – is the global epicentre of HIV/AIDS.

Worldwide, an evolving trend is the rising proportion of infections in women. In 1996, 42 per cent of HIV infections were among women. By 2006, 48 per cent (17.7 million) of adults living with HIV/AIDS were women. In sub-Saharan Africa, there are currently 14 infected adult women for every 10 infected men.

HIV/AIDS and development

HIV/AIDS has particularly devastating impacts on development because it attacks society's most productive members. The virus is mainly transmitted through sexual contact, typically infecting and killing people in the prime of their lives, when they are working on farms, in factories, as teachers or in other positions; when they are raising their children and caring for elderly parents; and when they are active in their communities. This contrasts with most other diseases, which usually strike those who are physically the most vulnerable, such as the very young and the very old.

HIV/AIDS can change population structures, negatively impact the supply and productivity of labour, and reduce household income and business earnings. At the household, community and national levels, it shifts resources from productive uses, such as investment in education, infrastructure and other forms of health care, to care and treatment for PLWHA. Additionally, as children are orphaned, and subjected to income, social and psychosocial impacts, HIV/AIDS lowers a society's future development potential.

Different impacts may occur separately or simultaneously at varying levels (see figure showing the radiating effects of an HIV infection). As individuals carry out various functions in society, each of these is affected by an illness or death. The PLWHA may be less helpful as a family and community member, produce less through lost labour, and change his or her consumption patterns. As this scenario is multiplied throughout a community, country or region, the macro-level impacts may be devastating.

The timing and visibility of development impacts

Development impacts may be felt as immediate and severe shocks or as complex, gradual and long-term changes. It may help to think of impacts as falling along a continuum between sharp shocks

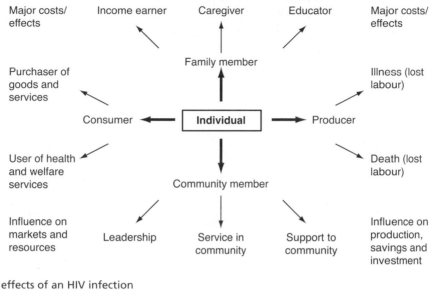

Radiating effects of an HIV infection

Radiating effects of an HIV infection

Source: Adapted from Barnett and Whiteside 2002: 184

and slow, but profound changes. These impacts emerge as the number of cumulative infections rise and AIDS deaths occur, and they may continue long after (see figure showing the timing of impacts).

Problems with information and measurement

Over two decades into the AIDS epidemic, we still cannot adequately identify and measure the myriad ways in which the epidemic impacts society. Prior to the epidemic, few developing countries had data collection systems that allowed a full assessment of the situation of individuals, households and communities. While the magnitude of the AIDS epidemic creates an even greater need for information, governments, NGOs and universities still lack the human, financial and/or technical resources needed to collect, analyse and share relevant data on the epidemic's many impacts.

Obtaining information from affected populations may be difficult because of AIDS-related stigma, denial and geographical barriers. Gaining access to the elderly, children and people living in rural areas is also challenging. Finally, assessing development impacts may be impossible because individuals, households and firms, especially in hard-hit communities, can virtually disappear, leaving little evidence of impacts, despite profound societal changes.

Impacts at different levels: What we do know

Despite significant data collection limitations, researchers have established a growing body of evidence on the impact of HIV/AIDS at various levels, from children and households up to communities and countries. What follows is a brief summary of confirmed impacts.

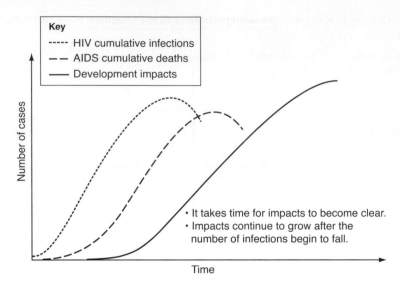

Key
----- HIV cumulative infections
-- AIDS cumulative deaths
—— Development impacts

Number of cases (y-axis)

Time (x-axis)

• It takes time for impacts to become clear.
• Impacts continue to grow after the number of infections begin to fall.

The timing of impacts
Source: UNAIDS 2002

Households affected by AIDS

In many households, the death of the main breadwinner plunges families into poverty. Given the limited infrastructure of health care services in developing countries, caregiving for the sick and dying usually takes place at home, rather than in hospitals or hospices. The most vulnerable children usually also remain in the home. Consequently, family members absorb the greatest burden of HIV/AIDS, caring for children, earning an income and holding the family together, often with few resources and while coping with social, psychosocial and health issues. Most caregiving responsibilities fall to women. The care of one PLWHA can take five or more hours per day – this is usually in addition to regular tasks. Families report having to borrow money, sell assets, send children to work and reduce spending on food in order to survive. Compromised food security is common in poor regions, which, in turn, may trigger long-lasting health, nutrition and productivity impacts.

Children orphaned by AIDS

An escalating orphan crisis is trailing the 32 million AIDS deaths that have occurred globally since the pandemic began (UNAIDS and WHO 2006). The sheer number of orphans (children who have lost one or both parents) is higher in Asia (80.1 million) than in sub-Saharan Africa (43.4 million); however, the number of children orphaned by AIDS has grown far faster in sub-Saharan Africa, from 3 million in 1995 to over 12.3 million by 2003 (UNICEF, UNAIDS and USAID 2004). Children with sick or deceased parents may confront increased vulnerability due to social and economic impacts, psychological trauma and their care circumstances following a parental death. Available data indicate the following.

• Nearly 20 per cent of children are orphaned in Botswana, Lesotho, Swaziland, Zambia and Zimbabwe (UNICEF, UNAIDS and USAID 2004).
• Throughout sub-Saharan Africa, households with orphans tend to be female-headed, have higher dependency ratios or fewer adults to care for children, have fewer assets, and be headed by older persons than heads of households without orphans (Monasch and Boerma 2004).

- In sub-Saharan Africa, orphaned children are less likely to attend school and have their basic needs met than non-orphaned children (UNICEF 2006).
- Orphans have elevated rates of depression and post-traumatic stress disorder compared to non-orphans (UNICEF 2006).

Community impacts

Not surprisingly, in the hardest-hit countries, the social fabric that once held communities together has unravelled due to heavy AIDS-related economic and caregiving burdens. Although community members once sustained vulnerable households, in many places they can no longer play this role. In fact, families throughout eastern and southern Africa report receiving no community-based support. In addition, illness and death may force individuals or families to migrate in search of care, work or support, transforming traditional villages and urban centres.

Sectors

AIDS impacts businesses and the public sector through direct and indirect costs, particularly when HIV prevalence rates are high. Businesses and government offices may be forced to pay for medical care and the costs of recruiting replacement workers, as well as experiencing reduced productivity, increased absenteeism and vacancies. When businesses have many employees with HIV/AIDS, they may face higher insurance premiums, litigation over dismissals, lost senior management time, production disruptions, and a decline in morale, experience and institutional memory.

AIDS also causes a reduction in human resources, killing teachers, health care professionals and other workers critical to communities. These deaths place an enormous strain on health care facilities, medical services and schools. In many countries in sub-Saharan Africa, AIDS has also decreased agricultural productivity, leading to lower food production for survivors.

National impacts

The presidents and top leaders of many countries, including Botswana, Malawi, Uganda and Lesotho, acknowledge the great threat that AIDS has posed to the development of their nations, due to the heavy and wide scope of impacts. For example, HIV/AIDS causes severe demographic changes and has lowered life expectancy by one to several decades throughout southern Africa, eliminating 50 years of gains in some countries.

Global response

While the global response to HIV/AIDS was slow to mobilize, by the twenty-first century the world community had developed international goals and targets for responding to the epidemic. For example, The *United Nations Millennium Declaration* (UN General Assembly 2000) establishes goals to combat HIV/AIDS. The *UN Declaration of Commitment on HIV/AIDS* (United Nations 2001) set targets for implementing effective policies and strategies, while the *Political Declaration on HIV/AIDS* (United Nations 2006), drafted at the 2006 United Nations General Assembly Special Session on HIV/AIDS, further articulates these goals. Also, the World Health Organization's 2003 '3x5 Initiative' called for 3 million patients on ART by 2005. While many goals have yet to be reached, there is positive momentum due to greater attention by national governments, and resources made available by the Global Fund for AIDS, Tuberculosis and Malaria, as well as bilateral donors, including the USA and the UK, and private foundations, such as the Bill and Melinda Gates Foundation and the Clinton Foundation. In addition, businesses, the private sector, non-governmental, faith-based and community-based organizations contribute to the AIDS response.

Remaining challenges

Funding for the AIDS response in developing countries grew from US$300 million to US$8.3 billion between 1996 and 2005. Although it is unclear how exactly these funds are used, the majority are directed to treatment, while impact mitigation garners a small percentage of overall funding. Consequently, impact mitigation efforts, such as support for AIDS-affected households, are lagging. Non-governmental organizations are often the main bodies working to mitigate the impact of AIDS, though their efforts often lack consistency, funding and an evidence base to guide activities.

Many obstacles to an effective AIDS response still exist, including HIV/AIDS-related stigmatization, which undermines HIV testing, prevention, treatment and impact mitigation efforts; uncoordinated responses; and insufficient commitment among governments. Furthermore, UNAIDS estimates that US$22.1 billion is needed for an effective global AIDS response, in 2008 alone.

Despite many uncertainties about the future, one lesson that AIDS has already taught is that the development impacts of the epidemic will continue to expand in the absence of an effective response.

GUIDE TO FURTHER READING

For the latest updates on the HIV/AIDS epidemic globally, see the most recent report of the Joint United Nations Programme on HIV/AIDS (UNAIDS) and the World Health Organization (WHO) (2006) *AIDS Epidemic Update – December 2006*, Geneva: UNAIDS and WHO (available at http://www.who.int/entity/hiv/mediacentre/2006_EpiUpdate_en.pdf).

For information on the impact of HIV/AIDS on work, see the International Labour Organization (ILO) (2006) *HIV/AIDS and Work: Global Estimates, Impact on Children and Youth, and Response*, Geneva: ILO (available at http://www.ilo.org/public/english/protection/trav/aids/publ/global_est06/global_estimates_report06.pdf).

For a comprehensive textbook on the epidemiology of AIDS, prevention, treatment, vaccine development and the impact of AIDS, see Essex, M., Mboup, S., Kanki, P.J., Marlink, R.G. and Tlou, S.D. (2002) *AIDS in Africa*, second edition, New York: Kluwer Academic/Plenum Publishers.

For more information on the situation of orphaned children, see the United Nations Children's (Emergency) Fund (UNICEF) (2006) *Africa's Orphaned Generations: Children Affected by AIDS*, New York, UNICEF (available at http://www.unicef.org/publications/index_35645.html?lpos=main&lid=unicef).

For more information on data collection, measurement and analysis, to measure the impact of HIV/AIDS on affected households, see Help Age International (2006) *Counting Carers: How to Improve Data Collection and Information on Households Affected by AIDS and Reduce the Poverty of Carers, People Living with HIV and Vulnerable Children*, London: HelpAge International (available at http://www.helpage.org/ResearchandpolicyHIVAIDS/Resources#eSg0).

For a broad variety of information on HIV/AIDS, including history, response, information about regions and populations, antiretroviral treatment and more, visit AIDS Education & Research Trust (http://www.avert.org).

An informative overview of the medical facts, conceptual issues and available data on the socio-economic impacts of HIV/AIDS is in Barnett, T. and Whiteside, A. (2002) *AIDS in the Twenty-First Century: Disease and Globalization*, second edition, New York: Palgrave Macmillan.

The World Bank's publications on the AIDS pandemic remain among the best. Though somewhat dated, this book is still relevant and useful: World Bank (1999) *Confronting AIDS: Public Priorities in a Global Epidemic*, revised edition, New York and Oxford: Oxford University Press for the World Bank.

To learn more about the US response to HIV, see *Action Today, A Foundation for Tomorrow: The President's Emergency Plan for AIDS Relief. Second Annual Report to Congress* (2006) (available at http://www.state.gov/documents/organization/60950.pdf).

REFERENCES

Barnett, T. and Whiteside, A. (2002) *AIDS in the Twenty-First Century: Disease and Globalization*, second edition, New York: Palgrave Macmillan.

Monasch, R. and Boerma, J. (2004) 'Orphanhood and childcare patterns in sub-Saharan Africa: An analysis of national surveys from 40 countries', *AIDS*, 18(2): S55–65.

UNAIDS (Joint United Nations Programme on HIV/AIDS) (2002) *Report on the Global HIV/AIDS Epidemic*, Geneva: UNAIDS.

UNAIDS and WHO (2006) *AIDS Epidemic Update: December 2006*, Geneva: UNAIDS.

UNICEF, UNAIDS and United States Agency for International Development (USAID) (2004) *Children on the Brink 2004: A Joint Report of New Orphan Estimates and a Framework for Action*, New York: UNICEF, UNAIDS and USAID.

United Nations (2001) *UN Declaration of Commitment on HIV/AIDS 2001*, United Nations General Assembly Special Session on HIV/AIDS, 25–27 June, New York: United Nations.

United Nations (2006) *Political Declaration on HIV/AIDS*, draft resolution submitted by the President of the General Assembly at the 2006 high-level meeting on AIDS, Uniting the World Against AIDS, 31 May–2 June, New York: United Nations.

United Nations Children's (Emergency) Fund (UNICEF) (2006) *Africa's Orphaned and Vulnerable Generations: Children Affected by AIDS*, New York: UNICEF.

United Nations General Assembly (2000) *55/2 United Nations Millennium Declaration*, General Assembly Resolution 55/2, 8 September, New York: United Nations.

World Health Organization (WHO) and UNAIDS (2005) *Progress on Global Access to HIV Antiretroviral Therapy: An Update on '3 by 5'*, Geneva: World Health Organization.

8.4 Managing health and disease in developing countries

Stephen J. Connor

Despite calls for 'Health for All by the Year 2000' (WHO 1978), entry to the new millennium saw many of the world's poorer communities suffering health status decline. The reasons for this are many-faceted and contextually diverse. To understand this situation it is useful to begin with a few basic questions. What is health? How is it measured? What are the major health problems? Who is responsible for health care provision? Why is it not provided adequately? Here, differing definitions of health, some aspects of ill health and development, and a focus on one particular health problem are used to explore some of the issues surrounding the management of disease in developing countries.

Defining health

While health is an integral component of development (Sen 1999), it is a condition which is beguilingly difficult to define (Phillips and Verhasselt 1994). The 'medical model' views health as 'the absence of disease'. Attempts to include a more human-ecological approach are apparent in disease ecology (Learmonth 1988) and public health (Turshen 1989). Recognition of health as a broad social construct is reflected in the World Health Organization's (WHO) definition: 'a state of complete physical, mental and social well-being and not merely the absence of disease or infirmity' (WHO 1992). Health care studies among rural communities support this broad perspective. Respondents in a study in Zaire included parents living, cultivated land and windows in their house within their definition of healthy. They included crime among health problems, and social reconciliation as a health intervention. These broad global and community definitions confirm health as an integral aspect of development, and demonstrate the significance of development as a major public health issue.

Health problems in developing countries

Clearly one would expect the health problems facing rural communities in Africa to be different from those facing urban populations in Europe. One aid to understanding these differences is the 'epidemiological transition', which links changing disease patterns over time with changes in the prevailing social, economic, demographic and ecological conditions. For example:

- First phase: subsistence agriculture; high fertility; high infant death rate; low life expectancy; infectious disease and periodic famine are the main causes of death.
- Second phase: gradual improvements in agriculture, nutrition and sanitation reduce crude death rate.
- Third phase: intensive agriculture/industrialization; lower fertility; longer life expectancy; non-communicable degenerative diseases become the main cause of death.

This somewhat oversimplistic (Smith and Ezzati 2005), 'one-way' process has clear parallels with the modernization theories of development and the demographic transition. The model is based on historical assessment of 200 years in Europe and the USA (Omran 1971). Japan, Taiwan and the Eastern European countries underwent the transition more quickly, while Eastern Europe challenges the one-way nature of the process.

Diseases affecting the elderly may be less of a constraint to development prospects than those of the young and middle years. However, beyond such a generalization we ought not to lose sight of the fact that health problems are not homogeneous in any country, at any time, regardless of its stage of development, and disparities occur with social class, gender and region, with the poorest at greatest risk (Phillips and Verhasselt 1994).

Responsibility for health care

That each individual has a basic responsibility to value their own health may be unequivocal. Beyond that, responsibilities for health become more complex and may include employers, family, health workers, hospitals, insurers, local or national government, international legislative/advisory bodies, and so on. Likewise, there is the equally complex issue of cost of health care provision. Is an individual's health something they alone benefit from, and should pay for, or is there a wider community benefit? Where are the community boundaries? Communicable, or infectious, diseases clearly pose a threat to others. Malaria, one example of a communicable disease, may serve as a focus to explore these issues further.

Malaria as a 'global' health problem

Malaria is considered a 'tropical disease', that is, geographically determined. This is not strictly accurate; malaria has occurred at the Arctic Circle, and poverty and social conditions play an important role in the distribution and persistence of the disease. Currently it is in African countries that malaria poses the greatest public health problem, accounting for 80 per cent of the world's malaria and 90 per cent of its estimated 1.7–3.4 million deaths annually (Bremen 2001).

Malaria results from a complex interaction between parasite, mosquito vector, human host and the broader environment (social and ecological). Control may focus on any, or all, of these components. In 1948 the World Health Organization was established and malaria quickly became its highest priority.

The global malaria control strategy, 1946–1954

The world had seen the mobilization of huge forces during the Second World War and it was felt that concerted efforts could now be made, as a major international humanitarian initiative, against one of the world's major public health problems. Intervention relied primarily on spraying the interior walls of dwellings with the insecticide DDT to kill resting mosquito vectors, and any malaria cases were treated with chloroquine to reduce the parasite pool. In the USA, Europe, North Africa and the Middle East malaria control campaigns were so successful that global eradication was seen as a realistic possibility.

The global malaria eradication campaign, 1955–1969

Fears over growing resistance to these cheap and effective control tools, and the costs of maintaining recurrent control measures, spurred the drive for eradication. While eradication in the developed nations of Europe and the USA was expected, India and Sri Lanka looked as if they too might succeed (Kondrachine and Trigg 1997). In India, prevalence levels of 70 million per year declined to about 100,000 cases by 1967, and Sri Lanka had just 17 cases in 1963 (Learmonth 1988).

Eradication efforts did not include most sub-Saharan African countries. There were two basic schools of thought on control in that region. The interventionists, with their strong commitment to eradication, were convinced of the need to vanquish malaria from every continent (Macdonald 1951). The conservationists argued that the equilibrium reached between humans and parasites under intense malaria transmission offered a high degree of adult protection and should not be interfered with (Wilson, Granham and Swellengrebel 1950). Ultimately, vector-control campaigns were not considered feasible in sub-Saharan Africa, due to the technical difficulties of intense malaria transmission, requiring extensive control efforts in countries which had very limited health infrastructure (Bradley 1992). However, Ethiopia, South Africa and the former Rhodesia did carry out effective malaria control campaigns. Major research experiments which included vector control, in Kenya, Tanzania and Nigeria, also produced significant reductions in infant and child mortality.

During the later part of this phase, the considerable gains made began to lose ground. Donors saw that eradication was going to be a long process. While prepared to invest significant funding for limited-term intervention, they were reluctant to maintain recurrent vector-control operations. They argued that further improvement in the malaria situation could be achieved only through greater national commitment and improved public health infrastructure. In recognition of this, along with the devastating epidemics in Sri Lanka during 1968 and the widescale re-emergence of malaria in Asia, the 1969 World Health Assembly radically re-examined the malaria eradication strategy. This was followed by an immediate reduction in bilateral and international financial support to antimalarial campaigns.

Malaria control with the ultimate goal of eradication, 1970–1978

During this period, the capability of many endemic countries to continue antimalarial operations, especially those involving vector control, were further reduced, and many countries, including India, experienced a dramatic resurgence of malaria. While antimalarial programmes were in decline, the efforts to establish basic health care services in the more peripheral areas of endemic countries met with little success. Extensive resurgence of malaria in south Asia and Latin America led to calls to develop malaria control programmes appropriate to the infrastructure existing in endemic countries.

Malaria control as part of primary health care (after 1978)

This approach was formulated at Alma-Ata, Russia, in September 1978. It centred on an actively participating community working closely with health services. Its aims were to ensure that malaria control activities would be integrated into the priority setting of the general health services, to reflect the prevailing infrastructure and level of service delivery possible, and to be able to maintain the gains achieved. It was argued that the fundamental element of the new approach reflected recognition of the variability of epidemiological situations, the feasibility of their modification and the availability of resources.

A decade after Alma-Ata, progress towards 'Health for All by the Year 2000' remained slow and disappointing. Only China had made significant inroads against malaria; elsewhere the situation was stagnant or deteriorating, especially in sub-Saharan Africa (Kondrachine and Trigg 1997). Financial resources available for health care in developing countries continued to decline. To support primary health care provision, UNICEF launched the Bamako Initiative in 1987, to encourage financing through cost recovery. In many countries, malaria control had been carried out as a public health measure; people were now expected to meet the cost of treatment themselves. By the end of the 1980s, the global malaria control strategy was in crisis.

The 1990s – a decade of hope?

In view of the increasing prominence of malaria as a major public health problem, the Executive Board of the WHO and the World Health Assembly adopted resolutions in 1989, asserting that control of malaria must again become a global priority. Malaria was seen as an excessive drain on limited health resources, a major constraint on child survival programmes, and as maintaining poverty through low productivity and impaired economic growth. International meetings in Brazzaville, New Delhi and Brasilia during 1991 and 1992, followed by consultation with experts at national and regional levels, led to the formulation of a new strategy, which was adopted by the Ministerial Conference on Malaria in October 1992. The New Global Malaria Control Strategy recognizes that malaria has no single formula for its control, but is a disease of differing epidemiological types, determined by a diversity of social, ecological and economic settings.

Strong political support for concerted action against malaria, especially in Africa, grew throughout the 1990s. In 1996, an Accelerated Strategy for Malaria Control in the Africa Region was approved by the WHO, and in 1997, the Meeting of Heads of State of the Organization of African Unity made its declaration on malaria control. Further international support came in 1997, with the Multilateral Initiative on Malaria, and in 1998, with the 'Roll Back Malaria' Global Partnership, which includes the WHO, United Nations Children's (Emergency) Fund (UNICEF), United Nations Development Programme (UNDP) and the World Bank. Roll Back Malaria aims to identify stakeholders, consolidate research and deliver concerted support to malaria control through strengthened health systems development. It aims to draw more commitment from the private sector in a drive for new control tools, through its Medicines for Malaria Venture, and the Malaria Vaccine Fund, which is supported by the Bill and Melinda Gates Foundation.

Into the new millennium

The malaria parasite respects few boundaries, and with increased international mobility comes an increased threat to all. The new momentum for tackling malaria comes at a time when the old control tools have lost much of their acceptability and effectiveness. While the pressure for a worldwide ban on DDT seems to have been halted, chloroquine resistance is now so widespread as to make the drug virtually useless. Hopes for an effective vaccine remain just that. However, there are promising new treatments and preventative measures in the Chinese herbal derivative Artemether, and the insecticide-treated 'bednet'. The latter is seen as an appropriate tool for many rural African situations, and widespread trials have shown it to be very effective in reducing malaria mortality (Lengeler and Snow 1996).

Recent macroeconomic analysis of the burden of malaria suggests a loss of GDP to sub-Saharan African countries of US$3–12 billion per year due to malaria, and argues that the required financial inputs into malaria control would pay for themselves many times over. Malaria figures highly in the UN Millennium Development Goals and, through Roll Back Malaria and the Global Fund for AIDS, Tuberculosis and Malaria, calls have been made for commitments of at least US$1 billion per year, and commitments have been made to ensure prompt treatment with effective drugs and that within five years every African child should sleep under the protection of a treated bednet.

Through this brief discourse we have seen perspectives of the malaria problem and responsibilities for its control shift from that of a global problem, to a national health problem, a community problem, an individual's problem and, finally, a regionalized health issue, involving multiple stakeholders recognizing common interests and requiring concerted action at all levels. The political will to tackle malaria is more promising than it has been at any time since the mid-1960s. Malaria is curable and preventable, and an estimated one-third of the world's population, living in previously malarious regions, are now free from the disease. The challenge to health and development agencies remains to extend this achievement to the poorer countries of the world.

GUIDE TO FURTHER READING

Desowitz, R.S. (1991) *The Malaria Capers*, London: W.W. Norton.

Learmonth, A. (1988) *Disease Ecology*, Oxford: Basil Blackwell.

Phillips, D. and Verhasselt, Y. (1994) *Health and Development*, London: Routledge.

Turshen, M. (1989) *The Politics of Public Health*, London: Zed Books.

WHO (1992) *Our Planet, Our Health: Report of the WHO Commission on Health and Environment*, Geneva: World Health Organization.

REFERENCES

Bradley, D.J. (1992) 'Malaria: Old infections, changing epidemiology', *Health Transition Review*, 2: 137–53.

Bremen, J.G. (2001) 'The ears of the hippopotamus: Manifestations, determinants, and estimates of the malaria burden', *American Journal of Tropical Medicine and Hygiene*, 64(1–2 S): 1–11.

Kondrachine, A. and Trigg, P.I. (1997) 'Control of malaria in the world', *Indian Journal of Malariology*, 34: 92–110.

Learmonth, A. (1988) *Disease Ecology*, Oxford: Basil Blackwell.

Lengeler, C. and Snow, R.W. (1996) 'From efficacy to effectiveness: Insecticide-treated bednets in Africa', *Bulletin of the World Health Organization*, 74: 325–32.

Macdonald, G. (1951) 'Community aspects of immunity to malaria', *British Medical Bulletin*, 8: 33–6.

Omran, A.R. (1971) 'The epidemiologic transition: A theory of the epidemiology of population change', *Milbank Memorial Fund Quarterly*, 4: 509–38.

Phillips, D. and Verhasselt, Y. (1994) *Health and Development*, London: Routledge.

Sen, A. (1999) 'Health in development', *Bulletin of the World Health Organization*, 77: 619–23.

Smith, K.R. and Ezzati, M. (2005) 'How environmental health risks change with development: The epidemiologic and environmental risk transitions revisited', *Annual Review of Environment and Resources*, 30: 291–333.

Turshen, M. (1989) *The Politics of Public Health*, London: Zed Books.

WHO (1978) *Alma-Ata 1978: Primary Health Care*, Report of the International Conference on Primary Health Care (Alma-Ata, USSR, 6–12 September), Geneva: World Health Organization.

WHO (1992) *Our Planet, Our Health: Report of the WHO Commission on Health and Environment*, Geneva: World Health Organization.

Wilson, D.B., Graham, P.C.C. and Swellengrebel, N.H. (1950) 'A review of hyperendemic malaria', *Tropical Diseases Bulletin*, 47: 677–98.

8.5 Ageing

Isabella Aboderin

Introduction

The ageing of populations worldwide has been likened to a 'silent revolution' that will have far-reaching implications for the future development of both industrialized and developing nations. This short essay outlines the global patterns of this phenomenon, and discusses key perspectives and current debates on its implications for development.

'Population ageing' – What is it?

'Population ageing' refers to the progressive increase in the numbers, and thus the proportion, of older people, compared to working-age adults and children in a total population. The formal definition of 'old age' used by the United Nations is 60+ years. Working-age adults are defined as those aged 15–59 years (or sometimes 15–64 years), and children as those aged 0–14 years. This definition of old age is becoming increasingly entrenched in the international discourse – among other things to facilitate international comparisons. However, many questions exist about the appropriateness, in different cultures and societies, of such a chronological definition of 'old age', or the specific age of 60 itself.

Population ageing is a global phenomenon, which has become increasingly manifest in recent decades. From 1950 to 2005, the number of older people worldwide grew from 205 million (8 per cent of the total global population) to 672 million (10 per cent). By 2050, it is expected to reach almost 2 billion, 21 per cent of the world total (see Table 1). This is a more rapid increase than for any other age group, and for the first time in history there will be more older persons than children in the world (United Nations 2006a).

The 'demographic' transition from a young to an older population is typically driven by two factors. The first is rising life expectancy, mainly due to improvements in health and consequent reductions in mortality. Globally, the expectancy of life at birth (LEB) rose from 46.6 years in 1950 to 66 years in 2005, and is projected to reach 75.1 years in 2050. The further life

Table 1 Projected population ageing, major world regions, 2005–2050

	Size of major age groups, millions (% of total population)			Size of major age groups, millions (% of total population)		
	2005			**2050**		
	0–14	**15–59**	**60+**	**0–14**	**15–59**	**60+**
World	1821 (28.2%)	3971.3 (61.4%)	672.4 (10.4%)	1832.6 (20.2%)	5275.2 (58.1%)	1968.2 (21.7%)
More developed regions	205.9 (17%)	761.3 (62.9%)	244.1 (20.2%)	193.4 (15.6%)	642.8 (52%)	400.0 (32.4%)
Less developed regions	1615.2 (30.7%)	3210 (61.1%)	428.3 (8.2%)	1639.2 (20.9%)	4632.4 (59.1%)	1568.1 (20.1%)

Source: United Nations 2006a

expectancy of those who have already reached the age of 60 (LE60), meanwhile, has already risen to 17 years for men and 21 years for women (United Nations 2006a; Kalache, Barreto and Keller 2005).

Second is falling fertility rates, due most immediately to the increased use of effective contraception. Worldwide fertility decreased from 5.02 in 1950 to 2.55 in 2005, and is projected to fall further, to 2.05 by 2050 (United Nations 2006a). Fertility is typically measured in terms of the total fertility rate (TFR), which denotes the average number of children a hypothetical cohort of women would have at the end of their reproductive period if they were subject during their whole lives to the fertility rates of a given period, and if they were not subject to mortality. It is expressed as children per woman (United Nations 2006a).

Developed and developing world trends and contexts

Although *all* societies worldwide are ageing, there are key differences between the developed and the developing world in terms of the pace and stage of the demographic transition, and the context within which it occurs.

In industrialized societies, such as in Europe, Japan or North America, the transition typically began in the late nineteenth or early twentieth century. Consequently, as Table 1 shows, the proportion of older people in these populations (20 per cent) is already higher than that of children (17 per cent). By 2050, these figures will be 32 per cent and 15 per cent, respectively. In general, population ageing in industrialized countries has unfolded against a backdrop of increasing employment, rising living standards of families, and an overall expansion of state resources.

Developing world populations typically began to age only in the second half of the twentieth century. They will, therefore, remain younger than those in the developed world: the 8 per cent share of older people in the first decade of the twenty-first century will rise to 'only' 20 per cent by 2050. Yet the *pace* of population ageing, and the *sheer numbers* of older persons in the developing world, far outstrip those in the developed world. There are, however, some major regional variations. Africa (especially sub-Saharan), where fertility and mortality remain high, will age much more slowly than Asia (especially east Asia) and Latin America, where these indicators have declined sharply in recent decades.

In all developing world regions, in contrast to the industrialized world, the ageing of populations is typically unfolding within a context of poverty, economic strain and constricted public resources (Kalache, Barreto and Keller 2005; United Nations 2005).

Table 2 Projected population ageing, major developing world regions, 2005–2050

	Size of major age groups, millions (% of total population)			Size of major age groups, millions (% of total population)		
	2005			**2050**		
	0–14	**15–59**	**60+**	**0–14**	**15–59**	**60+**
Africa	375.6 (41.5%)	482.9 (53.3%)	47.4 (5.2%)	555.7 (28.7%)	1188.4 (61.4%)	192.9 (10%)
Asia	1086 (27.8%)	2454.6 (62.9%)	364.9 (9.3%)	953.9 (18.3%)	3032.1 (58.1%)	1231.2 (23.6%)
Latin America & Caribbean	168.1 (30%)	343.9 (61.3%)	49.3 (8.8%)	141.4 (18.1%)	452.8 (57.8%)	188.7 (24.1%)

Source: United Nations 2006a

Ageing as a 'development' issue

In recent decades, population ageing has received increasing research and policy attention as an issue with key implications for social and economic 'development' in the industrialized and the developing world (e.g. United Nations 2005, 2006b).

At the heart of the debates lies the notion that older people, as a result of their old age, come to have a diminished capacity to engage in productive work and to care for and support themselves. The question, however, of how far the diminished capacity is due to 'inevitable' biological processes of ageing, as opposed to social constraints or constructs, is subject to much debate, and indeed is critical to thinking about the implications of ageing for development (see Baars et al. 2006, introduction by Phillipson).

The relevance of ageing for development is typically considered on two distinct levels (though the literature often does not distinguish clearly between them). The first is the *position and well-being of older people as a 'social group' (at present or in future)*. At issue here are broad questions of:

- how social and economic change and forces have affected or will affect the well-being and support situation of present or future older people;
- how, in turn, older people's position (and addressing their needs) relates to perspectives for societal 'development';
- the consequences for policy.

The second level is *the changing age structure of populations*. Here the focus is on:

- how the growing proportion of older people in populations will impact on societies' economic performance and social structures;
- the consequences for policy.

Such assessments build on a broader, long-established recognition of links between a population's size or age structure and its economic development, and certain ideas about the benefits or disadvantages of different population scenarios (United Nations 2006b).

Thus far, developed and developing world discussions on ageing and 'development' have clearly differed in:

- the extent and ways in which they have considered each of the above two levels;
- the degree to which they have connected to mainstream development debates.

This disparity largely reflects the differences in the stage, pace and context of the demographic transition in the two world regions. The latter signifies the dominance of neoliberal perspectives, espoused by major intergovernmental bodies such as the World Bank, International Monetary Fund (IMF) or Organization for Economic Cooperation and Development (OECD) in mainstream development agendas. These focus on economic growth as the most immediate development task, and stress the need for liberalized markets and a reduced role of the state (Deacon 2007). These contrast with perspectives that emphasize the attainment of human welfare, rights and social justice as the most pressing task, and are encapsulated, for example, in the United Nations notion of 'social development' (United Nations 1995).

'Ageing' and development in industrialized countries

The 'ageing' (i.e. the changing age structure) of populations has become a (if not *the*) central development concern in industrialized (and some rapidly industrializing east Asian) countries. The CIA (2001: 10), for example, argues that 'Ageing presents the greatest challenge to US and global economic prosperity. Capital markets, investments, and trade will be most affected.' The perceived challenge arises from the looming demographic deficit – too few younger people compared to older people – in two interrelated ways:

1 The falling potential support ratio (PSR) raises questions of where the wealth will come from to support the current retired generation – especially in social security systems (e.g. pensions, health, long-term care) where ever fewer current workers (taxpayers) pay for the benefits of ever more retirees. Attendant pressures on public spending to sustain such systems are expected to impact negatively on economic growth. (PSR denotes the number of working-age adults (15–64 years) per number of older persons (aged 65+ years) and is taken to indicate the dependency burden on potential workers (United Nations 2006a).)
2 The ageing and shrinking of workforces nurtures concerns about the general capacity of economies to sustain the growth rates that underpin their prosperity. As 'old' workers retire (and with them their expertise), the supply of young labour falls and the average age of workers rises (given assumptions about older workers' productivity), doubts arise about the continued performance of businesses and the economy as a whole.

Mainstream perspectives on these issues (which variously see ageing as a 'crisis', 'challenge', or 'opportunity') have argued for the need to reform social security arrangements (especially limiting state welfare) and to extend working lives (e.g. IMF 2004; Nyce and Schieber 2005; Razan and Sadka 2005). The perceived need to reduce state provision is in line with the notion of the potential 'second demographic dividend', which is said to arise as societies' populations begin to age and which can be harnessed to increase economic growth – but only if private asset-based programmes (rather than public transfers) for older people are put in place.

In doing so, they intersect with a more specialized 'critical' gerontological discourse that queries the impacts of such dominant policy approaches on the well-being of the aged and is inspired (explicitly or implicitly) by a concern with reducing age-based inequalities and honouring older persons' rights (Baars et al. 2006). So far, however, this discourse has drawn little on general normative debates on development and rights.

This discourse itself is part of the wider Western social-gerontological debate, which has focused on understanding the nature and determinants of older people's situation and is driven, in the broadest sense, by the goal of elucidating ways for 'a good but affordable old age' (Johnson 2005).

Ageing and development in poor countries

A similar aim essentially defines current considerations of ageing and development in poor countries. The developing world debate on ageing effectively began with the first UN World Assembly on Ageing in Vienna (1982), and was driven by a 'humanitarian' concern, underpinned by modernization theory assumptions, about the fate of older people in developing nations as these became progressively modernized and, in the process, traditional family support systems were eroded (Aboderin 2005). While the projected change in societies' age structures is taken as a broad frame, its implications per se have – in contrast to the developed world – not been much discussed.

Rather, the debate (mainly conducted by a number of NGO and UN actors – notably HelpAge International, the United Nations Department of Economic and Social Affairs, the World Health Organization and United Nations Population Fund – and a small but growing corpus of researchers) has concentrated on the status of older people as a group, and in this regard put forward three key notions (e.g. Randel, German and Ewing 1999; Barrientos and Lloyd-Sherlock 2002; Lloyd-Sherlock 2004), as follows.

1 Older people's well-being and support situation is being undermined by social change, economic strain, HIV/AIDS, and dominant development agendas which, together, weaken customary informal support and care systems and employment opportunities, and militate against formal security and social service provision for the old.

2 Older people are therefore assumed to be particularly vulnerable to poverty, ill health and exclusion.
3 As a result, and as a matter of human rights and social justice, there is an urgent need for government policy action to fashion arrangements to ensure the well-being of present and future older people.

These arguments are expressed in the UN Madrid Plan of Action on Ageing 2002, which is squarely framed within the United Nations' social development paradigm (United Nations 2002). The Madrid Plan was ratified at the Second UN World Assembly on Ageing, 2002, in Madrid. Though it refers to older people globally, its emphasis is on mapping desired directions for policies on ageing in the developing world.

Nonetheless, 'ageing' remains virtually absent from mainstream development agendas. These centre, instead, on the achievement of the Millennium Development Goals (MDGs) and/or World Bank/IMF-driven poverty reduction aims, and focus almost exclusively on policy priorities related to the 'young' – namely, education, HIV/AIDS, other infectious diseases, and maternal health.

This situation exposes, on the one hand, the lack of evidence that shows authoritatively a greater vulnerability of older compared to younger age groups. On the other hand, and more importantly, it again reflects the dominance of neoliberal agendas, coupled with assumptions about the lack of productivity in older age. Policies to improve education and health for the young are meant, eventually, to raise human capital, productivity and economic growth (United Nations 2005) – especially if they are implemented (together with measures to utilize and deploy the enhanced human capital) in the expected 'window of opportunity', as fertility falls and there is a 'surplus' of the population at 'productive' ages (20–64 years) (World Bank 2006).

In response to this dominant perspective (and in a bid to get older people onto the development agenda), NGOs and scholars working on ageing have, in an additional strand of argumentation, sought to highlight older people's important 'productive' contributions to families and communities, and thus to development itself, and the potential economic 'costs' of failing to cater for older people now, before their numbers and proportion become much larger. A particularly potent example of the former is older people's contributions in the context of HIV/AIDS as carers of orphans or sick children (HAI 2003).

GUIDE TO FURTHER READING

Baars, J., Dannefer, D., Phillipson, C. and Walker, A. (2006) *Aging, Globalization and Inequality*, New York: Baywood.
HAI (2002) *State of the World's Older People 2002*, London: HelpAge International.
IMF (2004) *The Global Demographic Transition. World Economic Outlook 2004*, Washington, DC: International Monetary Fund.
Kalache, A., Barreto, S.M. and Keller, I. (2005) 'Global ageing: The demographic revolution in all cultures and societies', in M.L. Johnson (ed.) *The Cambridge Handbook of Age and Ageing*, Cambridge: Cambridge University Press, pp. 30–46.
Lloyd-Sherlock, P. (ed.) (2004) *Living Longer: Ageing, Development and Social Protection*, London: Zed Books.
Randel, J., German, T. and Ewing, D. (eds) (1999) *The Ageing and Development Report: Poverty, Independence and the World's Older People*, London: Earthscan.
United Nations (2002) *Report of the Second World Assembly on Ageing*, New York: United Nations.

REFERENCES

Aboderin, I. (2005) 'Changing family relationships in developing nations', in M.L. Johnson (ed.) *The Cambridge Handbook of Age and Ageing*, Cambridge: Cambridge University Press, pp. 469–75.

Baars, J., Danneer, D., Phillipson, C. and Walker, A. (2006) *Aging, Globalization and Inequality*, New York: Baywood.

Barrientos, A. and Lloyd-Sherlock, P. (2002) 'Older and poorer? Ageing and poverty in the South', *Journal of International Development*, 14: 1129–31.

CIA (2001) *Long-Term Global Demographic Trends: Reshaping the Geopolitical Landscape*, Washington, DC: Central Intelligence Agency.

Deacon, B. (2007) *Global Social Policy and Governance*, London: Sage.

HAI (2003) *Forgotten Families: Older People Caring for Orphans or Vulnerable Children Affected by HIV/AIDS*, London: HelpAge International.

IMF (2004) *The Global Demographic Transition. World Economic Outlook 2004*, Washington, DC: International Monetary Fund.

Johnson, M.L. (2005) 'General editor's preface', in M.L. Johnson (ed.) *The Cambridge Handbook of Age and Ageing*, Cambridge: Cambridge University Press, pp. xxi–xxvi.

Kalache, A., Barreto, S.M. and Keller, I. (2005) 'Global ageing: The demographic revolution in all cultures and societies', in M.L. Johnson (ed.) *The Cambridge Handbook of Age and Ageing*, Cambridge: Cambridge University Press, pp. 30–46.

Lloyd-Sherlock, P. (ed.) (2004) *Living Longer: Ageing, Development and Social Protection*, London: Zed Books.

Nyce, S. and Schieber, S. (2005) *Economic Implications of Ageing Societies: The Costs of Living Happily Ever After*, Cambridge: Cambridge University Press.

Randel, J., German, T. and Ewing, D. (eds) (1999) *The Ageing and Development Report: Poverty, Independence and the World's Older People*, London: Earthscan.

Razan, A. and Sadka, E. (2005) *The Decline of the Welfare State: Demography and Globalization*, Boston, MA: MIT Press.

United Nations (1995) *Report of the World Summit for Social Development*, New York: United Nations.

United Nations (2002) *Report of the Second World Assembly on Ageing*, New York: United Nations.

United Nations Millennium Project (2005) *Investing in Development: A Practical Plan to Achieve the Millennium Development Goals*, New York (available at http://www.unmillenniumproject.org/reports/index.htm).

United Nations Population Division (2006a) *World Population Prospects. The 2004 Revision* (available at http://esa.un.org/unpp/).

United Nations Population Division (2006b) *World Population Policies 2005*, New York: United Nations.

World Bank (2006) *World Development Report 2007: Development and the Next Generation*, Washington, DC: World Bank.

8.6 Health inequalities

Hazel R. Barrett

Introduction

Over the past 15 years the pivotal role played by good health in the development process has been acknowledged. The shift to the human development paradigm which followed the publication of the first *Human Development Report* in 1990, has been enshrined in the UN Millennium Development Goals (MDGs), agreed by 189 countries in September 2000. Of the eight MDGs, three directly address health challenges: reducing child mortality (Goal 4); improving maternal health (Goal 5); and combating HIV/AIDS, malaria and other diseases (Goal 6). The other five MDGs all indirectly impact on health: eradicating extreme poverty and hunger (Goal 1); achieving universal primary education (Goal 2); promoting gender equality and empowering women (Goal 3); ensuring environmental sustainability (Goal 7); and developing a global partnership for development (Goal 8).

The acceptance that good health is an essential element of the development process has stimulated much debate amongst academics and policymakers as to how to achieve the MDGs. It is now accepted that average health achievements, such as those stated in the MDGs is not a sufficient indicator of a country's performance in health, rather the distribution of health and health ineqality is paramount (Gakidou et al. 2000). The January 2000 special issue of the *Bulletin of the World Health Organization* focused on the theme of inequalities in health. This stimulated much debate on the definitions of health inequality and how it should be measured, as well as the impact of poverty on health outcomes. The arguments have focused on the health of the poor and vulnerable as well as how to target those with most need (Gwatkin 2000, 2002; Wagstaff 2002; Marmot 2005, 2006; WHO various). Questions are being asked as to why in 2004 life expectancy was 82.2 years in Japan but only 31.3 years in Swaziland (UNDP 2006). Why is it that in 2004 in every country in the world apart from Botswana, Kenya, Malawi, Maldives, Zambia and Zimbabwe, women lived on average longer then men (UNDP 2006)? Why is it that under-five mortality is 300 per cent higher amongst the poorest 20 per cent of Brazil's population than the richest 20 per cent, whilst in Chad, a much poorer country, the rates are the same for both rich and poor alike (UNDP 2006)? Why are there differences in life expectancy between rural and urban areas and social groupings? These are key questions for those with an interest in health inequality.

Definitions and measures of 'health inequality'

Whilst there is much evidence to demonstrate the differences in health achievements between countries and the social gradients of health within countries (Leon and Walt 2001; WHO annual) there is no internationally accepted definition of 'health inequality'. Gakidou et al. (2000) define health inequality as 'variations in health status across individuals in a population' (p. 42), which allows cross-country comparisons to be made as well the study of the determinants of health inequality. According to Shaw et al. (2002) 'where the chances of good or bad health are not evenly distributed among groups of people (defined by the area in which they live or work or some other common characteristic), we say that there is *health inequality*' (p. 126). Gwatkin (2000) states that when referring to health inequalities 'the principal objective is the reduction of poor–rich health differences' (p. 6). Feacham (2000) expands this definition suggesting that health 'inequalities refer to relative health status – between rich and poor, men and women, ethnic groups, regions or simply between the most healthy and the least healthy' (p. 1). All these definitions acknowledge that health varies between countries and amongst different groups of people within countries. It is these differences that are known as health inequalities.

According to Gwatkin (2002) there is not only a lack of a standard definition of health inequality there is also a dearth of measurement strategies and indicators. The traditional measures of health inequality, the Gini Coefficient and Concentration Index, are both taken from the field of economics. The Gini Coefficient ranges from 0, which represents perfect equality, to 100, which is perfect inequality. In 2004 Sweden had a Gini Coefficient of 25, which was the closest to equality, whilst Nambia had the worst at 74.4 (UNDP 2006). This is often represented diagrammatically as a Lorenz curve. The Gini Coefficient is often supplemented with the Concentration Index which indicates the extent to which a health outcome is unequally distributed across groups with ranges between −1 and +1. Interestingly the concentration index for sub-Saharan Africa is lower than the global mean and lower than for Latin America (Gwatkins 2002). These two measures focus on health status as measured by morbidity and mortality. Due to sparse and unreliable data for adult mortality and social status in developing countries, infant and under-five mortality rates are usually used, often derived from demographic and health surveys.

But health inequalities can also be measured according to need, access, efficacy and the effectiveness of health systems. In 2000, *The World Health Report* (WHO 2000) unveiled a new measure called the Health Inequality Index. Based on the child mortality data of 191 countries, this index measures the performance of different national health systems, based on fairness and achievement. This index identified that 35 of the 50 worst global health systems were in sub-Saharan Africa. The index, which is not based on any preconceptions about the dimensions along which mortality is unequally distributed, has been robustly criticized as it 'bears little relationship to socio-economic inequalities in mortality' (Houweling et al. 2001: 1672; Wolfson and Rowe 2001). Whilst there is much merit in a measure of health inequality that focuses on health delivery systems, it tells us little about the health risk environment and the socio-economic factors that result in health inequality.

The Gini Coefficient is still the most commonly used measure of health inequality, but its usefulness is being questioned and 'its position is slipping' (Gwatkin 2000: 8). But whilst several other indicators of health disparity are under consideration, such as the Health Inequality Index, there is no clear consensus of what should replace it.

Poverty and health inequality

Poverty has traditionally been accepted as an important determinant of health, with levels of income seen to be closely related to health outcomes (Wagstaff 2002; Curtis 2004). Empirical studies have often worked within this framework. For example Stillwagon's (1998) study of health in Argentina was based on the premise that 'health is primarily an economic, not a medical, problem' (p. 8). Not surprisingly her main conclusion was that health inequalities require an economic solution. Statistically based studies of health inequalities, such as that reported by Wagstaff (2002), which used Demographic and Health Survey data on child mortality from 42 developing countries, also conclude that there is a strong positive correlation between health inequality and average income. However the study also showed that, as countries get richer, health inequalities widen. Marmot (2006) suggests that the relationship between national income and life expectancy is strong up to a per-capita income of US$5000; after that there is little relationship between income and life expectancy. This irony demonstrates that the links between income and health are not straightforward or well understood.

Sen (2001), whilst recognising that there is a close connection between economic progress and health achievement, suggests the association depends on how the income generated by economic growth is used and if major health improvements can be achieved using available resources in a socially productive way. As he states: 'There is much merit in economic progress, but there is also an overwhelming role for intelligent and equitable social policies' (pp. 343–344).

The simplistic analysis that suggests income and health are directly linked has become problematic as the issue of poverty has been reconceptualised within the human development framework. Poor health is no longer regarded as the outcome or cause of poverty, instead poor health is now recognised as a component of poverty (Feacham 2000; Wagstaff 2002). Wagstaff (2002) asks, how can poverty be the driving force of poor health, when poor health is part of the factor? It is now recognised that researchers and policymakers need to go beyond the explanation that material deprivation is responsible for poor health and inequality (Marmot 2006; Whitehead and Bird 2006).

Over the past five years the concept of health inequality and its link to poverty has been contested. A recent study on intra-country socio-economic inequalities in infant and child mortality shows that inequalities appear to be smaller in sub-Saharan Africa than other parts of the world, with Latin America having the largest inequalities (Gwatkin 2002). Yet many would argue that the health situation and needs of sub-Saharan Africa are more serious than those in Latin America. Also reductions in health inequality do not always mean that the health situation of the most disadvantaged has been enhanced, instead it could mean that improvements in health amongst advantaged groups has slowed, stopped or been reversed (Gwatkin 2000). The debates have thus moved on to health inequity and issues of social justice.

Health inequality or health inequity?

Many would argue that any inequality in health is unjust or unfair if it is economically or socially determined. As Gwatkin (2000) states, 'those concerned with health inequalities are concerned with righting the injustice represented by inequalities or poor health conditions among the disadvantaged' (p. 6). The debate is thus moving from a focus on health inequality to the issue of health inequity. Fotso (2006) explains the difference between the two terms: '*health inequality* is a generic term used to designate differences and disparities in the health achievements of individuals and groups, whereas the term *health inequities* refers to inequalities that are unjust or unfair' (p. 9).

Whilst the term 'health inequalities' has become widely used, it is being confused with and used interchangeably with 'health inequities'. However, the distinction is an important one. Gatrell (2002) explains: 'Inevitably, there will be unevenness of variation in health outcome, whether from place to place or along some other dimension. But what really matters, and what 'inequity' implies, is the fact that these differentials may be avoidable, and should be capable of being narrowed; their existence is, in a sense, unethical' (p. 91). Thus all factors, including economic determinants, that contribute to health inequity must be addressed. If poor health is a component of poverty we need to determine the factors responsible for poverty and hence identify those contributing to health inequity.

Marmot (2005, 2006), building upon the work of Sen and Stern, suggests that health inequalities and inequities can be explained by two factors. The first is the material conditions for good health, which includes a nutritionally balanced diet, clean water, sanitation and the provision of medical and public health services. The second factor is empowerment, which includes community social cohesion, depth of social capital and systems of governance, as well as individual empowerment with respect to social networks, community engagement, lifestyle preferences, health perceptions and personal stresses. What Marmot suggests is that health inequalities can be explained by a lack of material conditions for good health, with health inequity the result of a lack of community and individual empowerment. For him health inequalities and inequities are a clear outcome of social injustice.

The arguments and empirical evidence that social action can improve health resulted in 2005 in the WHO setting up a Commission on Social Determinants of Health. The Commission is chaired by Marmot. The driving principle of the Commission 'is social justice: to reduce unfair differences in health between social groups within a country and between countries' (Marmot 2006: 2091). Using evidence-based policy the Commission is due to report in 2008 with recommendations on what can be done to reduce health inequalities and inequities. In line with the human development paradigm, the Commission hopes to change social conditions to 'ensure that people have the freedom to lead lives they have reason to value' and which will 'lead to marked reductions in health inequalities' (Marmot 2006: 2082). This philosophical position draws attention to the central role played by human freedoms in health and calls for social action to achieve the MDGs and reduce both inter- and intra-country health inequity. Based on the premise that inequalities in health between and within countries are avoidable and are the result of social injustice (Marmot 2005) the Commission will contribute to the ongoing debate as to how best to reduce inequalities and inequities in health.

GUIDE TO FURTHER READING

Gakidou, E.E., Murray, C.J. and Frenk, J. (2000) 'Defining and measuring health inequality: An approach based on the distribution of health expectancy', *Bulletin of the World Health Organization*, 78(1): 42–54. A seminal paper which raises pertinent issues about defining and measuring health inequalities.

Gwatkin, D.R. (2002) 'Reducing health inequalities in developing countries', *Oxford Textbook of Public Health*, fourth edition. Chapter which traces the history of concern about health inequalities, explores the main concepts associated with poverty and inequality, and discusses policies for reducing inequality.

Leon, D. and Walt, G. (2001) *Poverty, Inequality and Health: An International Perspective*, Oxford: Oxford University Press. This book contains 17 chapters written by leading experts, and covers issues of measurement, economic and social determinants of health inequality, life-course approaches through to health care systems and their roles in health inequality.

Marmot, M. (2006) 'Health in an unequal world', *The Lancet*, 368: 2081–94. This paper makes the case for understanding the socio-economic determinants of health inequality and inequity. It particularly stresses the importance of social justice in reducing health inequalities. Examples are taken from both the developed and developing world.

World Health Organization (annual) *The World Health Report*, Geneva: WHO. Gives an annual review of the global health situation. Each report focuses on a different health issue.

REFERENCES

Curtis, S. (2004) *Health and Inequality*, London: Sage Publications.

Feacham, R.G.A. (2000) 'Poverty and inequity: A proper focus for the new century', *Bulletin of the World Health Organization*, 78(1): 1–2.

Fotso, J. (2006) 'Child health inequities in developing countries: Differences across urban and rural areas', *International Journal for Equity in Health*, 5(9). Accessed at http://www.equityhealthj.com/contents/5/1/9

Gakidou, E.E., Murray, C.J. and Frenk, J. (2000) 'Defining and measuring health inequality: An approach based on the distribution of health expectancy', *Bulletin of the World Health Organization*, 78(1): 42–54.

Gatrell, A.C. (2002) *Geographies of Health: An Introduction*, Oxford: Blackwell Publishers.

Gwatkin, D.R. (2000) 'Health inequalities and the health of the poor: What do we know? What can we do?', *Bulletin of the World Health Organization*, 78(1): 3–18.

Gwatkin, D.R. (2002) 'Reducing health inequalities in developing countries', *Oxford Textbook of Public Health*, fourth edition.

Houweling, T.A.J., Kunst, A.E. and Mackenbach, J.P. (2001) 'World Health Report 2000: Inequality index and socioeconomic inequalities in mortality', *The Lancet*, 357: 1671–2.

Leon, D. and Walt, G. (2001) *Poverty, Inequality and Health: An International Perspective*, Oxford: Oxford University Press.

Marmot, M. (2005) 'Social determinants of health inequalities', *The Lancet*, 365: 1099–104.

Marmot, M. (2006) 'Health in an unequal world', *The Lancet*, 368: 2081–94.

Sen, A. (2001) 'Economic progress and health', in D. Leon and G. Walt, *Poverty, Inequality and Health: An International Perspective*, Oxford: Oxford University Press, pp. 333–45.

Shaw, M., Dorling, D. and Mitchell, R. (2002) *Health, Place and Society*, London: Pearson Education.

Stillwagon, E. (1998) *Stunted Lives, Stagnant Economies: Poverty, Disease, and Underdevelopment*, London: Rutgers University Press.

UNDP (2006) *Human Development Report 2006*, Basingstoke: Palgrave Macmillan.

Wagstaff, A. (2002) *Inequalities in health in developing countries*, World Bank Policy Research Working Paper 2795, Washington, DC: The World Bank.

Whitehead, M. and Bird, P. (2006) 'Breaking the poor health–poverty link in the 21st century: Do health systems help or hinder?' *Annals of Tropical Medicine and Parasitology*, 100(5&6): 389–99.

Wolfson, M. and Rowe, G. (2001) 'On measuring inequalities in health', *Bulletin of the World Health Organization*, 79(6): 553–60.

World Health Organization (annual) *The World Health Report*, Geneva: WHO.

World Health Organization (2000) *The World Health Report*, Geneva: WHO.

8.7 Children's work and schooling

V. Gayathri and T.T. Sreekumar

Introduction

Children's engagement in economic activity has been a contentious issue since the Industrial Revolution in the West. Guided by standards adopted by the International Labour Organization (ILO), a majority of countries have adopted legislation to prohibit or place severe restrictions on the employment of children. The process of globalization and the development of modern means of communication have made the plight of working children a major issue on the agenda of the international community. In this chapter we will look at the various perspectives that guide policy on child labour, and then examine the intersections between child work and schooling, and end with a discussion on what could be the way forward.

Child work: issues and positions

Since the mid-1980s there has been an intensification and polarization of viewpoints, especially with regard to the effect of child work on children's levels of learning achievements and on their overall health and well-being. It is generally believed that some work, especially light work, which does not affect health and personal development, or interfere with schooling, is positive and actually beneficial to the child's well-rounded development. Child labour, which is work that is mentally, physically, socially or morally dangerous and harmful to children, or which interferes with schooling, is considered harmful. The key point of debate and contention is that it is difficult to draw a line between acceptable and unacceptable forms of work by children, as a morally determined definition of labour may impinge on children's rights and obligation vis-à-vis their household.

Views on childhood, and what constitutes an appropriate childhood, vary widely between cultures. Many in developing nations believe in the poverty argument where children's work is viewed as inevitable. Socially too, there is widespread acceptance of children's work, as it is often viewed as an intrinsic part of the family structure, and a mark that the child is able to contribute appropriately to the well-being of his/her family. However, poverty-based explanations often lack substantiation due to the weak correlation between incidence of poverty and magnitude of child labour (Gayathri and Chaudhri 2002). There is thus an opinion that poverty may be necessary, but does not constitute a sufficient condition to explain children's presence in wage employment.

In developed countries today, almost any kind of work for children under the age of 16 is often considered exploitation, and childhood is considered a time when children should be protected and shielded from the harshness of the working world. Advocates of the 'education school' argue from the standpoint of child rights, which is articulated on the basis of various protections demanded by childhood. This 'rights' position has had an extensive influence on both international and national policymaking. While there is a nuanced understanding that a simplistic notion of children's participation in work will not lead to a practical and operational social policy, the notion of doing justice to children and protecting their rights often forms the guiding principle for policy.

Although the explicit notion that childhood is for schooling/education is enshrined in the Indian Constitution, the policy towards children's participation in work is not without ambiguity. It is only since the mid-1980s that there has been a burgeoning movement towards the universalization of education. The educational thrust has resulted in a recognition of causal factors, which impede achievement of the objective of schooling for all. Linkages between children's work and education have become obvious. Advocates of the education school state that a large number of children are not going to school because of their involvement in some form of work. Work hampers learning, which for individual children soon translates into poor learning outcomes and, later, dropping out and joining full-time work. The need to establish the norm that work should never be an impediment to full-time education is thus vocally stated.

According to the 2001 census, around 12.6 million children participate in paid work in India today. At the same time, an even larger number of children of primary school age have never attended school, while a still larger number drop out before they reach 14 years of age. Although they are often treated as separate problems, these are not seen as such by pro-educationists. Work prevents children from fully enjoying the benefits of education. Discussion on the right to education, in fact, has often been held without consideration of the fact that children's work is an impediment to the realization of this right.

However, the fact remains that in spite of the lively debate on the issue of children's work, and its causal relationship between poverty and the utility of children by poor households, on the one hand, and the presence of out-of-school children and educational delivery failures, on the other, the result has been largely inconclusive. It is a fact that in the poorer regions, a high proportion of children remain outside the formal educational system and this, in turn, increases their susceptibility to wage employment.

Policy approaches: Rights and obligations

Two competing perspectives on the question of child labour in the manufacturing industry may be identified as utilitarian and consequentialist viewpoints. The utilitarian argument focuses on the economic benefits of the abolition of child labour, which will maximize welfare in the long run by readjusting labour market parameters in favour of increased adult wages, while the dislocations caused by the resulting loss of income for specific groups due to abolition can be managed by short-term prescriptive policy interventions aimed to ameliorate their condition. This approach would not look at the work done by children in domestic or familial contexts as exploitative. The latter view, on the other hand, questions the reasoning underlying this approach, and warns that the emotional considerations of filial love and parental affection are embedded in the logic of the market, and hence cannot be disentangled from the realm of economic circulation. It is further argued that the elimination of child labour outside the family can obstruct goals of maximizing benefits or minimizing harm, by arbitrarily denying earning opportunities for children on the mistaken assumption that family labour is non-exploitative. Education of working children should be seen as part of the social and customary responsibilities that are shared with parents.

The fundamental rights to education and healthy living are not undermined in this perspective. Rather, an appeal to universal education and care is simply not seen as an attempt to undermine the moral economy of working children. It may be noted that these approaches also point to the futility of an appeal to fundamental rights as a possible political solution to the problem of child labour in general.

O'Neill (1989: 201) has argued that the discourse of rights neglects one crucial aspect of children's lives. According to him, rights would remain 'manifesto rights', 'which cannot be claimed unless or until practices and institutions are established that determine against whom claims on behalf of a particular child may be lodged' (ibid.: 201–2). As an alternative, he provides a typology of obligations of adults to children that may or may not have a corresponding claim to a 'right'. The inventory of obligations that he proposes includes perfect and imperfect obligations. The first is an obligation to all others, irrespective of the agent's relationship to any particular child or children. Hence it is a universal, perfect obligation and probably corresponds to a fundamental right. The second is an obligation to specified children by specified agents. Hence it is not a universal obligation, but is most certainly a perfect one. These special obligations will have special rights as their counterparts. However, they are not, by definition, fundamental. The third is a fundamental obligation that agents may be capable of discharging only in well-defined contexts to any particular child. This is neither universal nor perfect, but does not have any corresponding rights. Nonetheless, as O'Neill (ibid.: 191) points out:

> Although *imperfect* obligations lack corresponding rights, their fulfillment has not traditionally been thought of as optional: The very term *imperfect obligations* tells us that what is left optional by a fundamental imperfect obligation is selection not merely of a specific way of enacting the obligation but of those for whom the obligation is to be performed.

Imperfect obligations need to be institutionalized, and an institutionalization of the ways that specify for whom the obligation is to be performed is perhaps the only route through which these can be claimed.

An approach based on obligations rather than rights has both ethical and political significance. Moreover, the rights-based approach is flawed in believing that children are an oppressed group whose problems can be resolved if they have a claim to fundamental rights. Civil society interventions on behalf of children have highlighted the need for an approach based on social obligations rather than purely on children's rights. Children in the developing world have an array of manifesto rights, like those enshrined in the constitutions of their respective countries or international organizations. O'Neill gives the example of the United Nations Declaration of the Rights of the Child, which includes 'the right to grow and develop in health', the right to receive an atmosphere of affection and of moral and material security, and the right to an education which will promote general culture. For O'Neill, 'none of these rights is well formed as an enforceable claim; but can be seen as ideals that should inform the construction of institutions that secure enforceable claims' (ibid.: 201).

While the problem of children who are commercially and sexually exploited and trafficked, as well as those who are not trafficked but face situations of similar abuse, are different from the position of children who are placed in work situations/locations that make them vulnerable to abuse, the nature of psychological and ethical pressure on these three different groups would be similar and painful. The problem of providing education has become acute, and civil society intervention in this area has become correspondingly intense and focused. Many of the civil society organizations in developing countries attempt to create institutional as well as informal arrangements to help working children attain education.

Intersections between work and schooling

The incidence of child labour is only a small fraction of the proportion of child population that is stifled in India. A large subset of these deprived children are neither in school nor involved in 'productive' and 'economic' work. It has been observed that they are often engaged in forms of productive work that are not counted as economic activity by formal data collection efforts, or in socially stigmatized forms of occupation which tend to go unreported. Observations on various dimensions of poverty and its relationship with employment, as well as the implications for children's schooling, can be summarized as follows:

- children belonging to poorer households have higher probabilities for engaging in wage work;
- children belonging to disadvantaged and discriminated social and ethnic groups, like scheduled castes and tribes, are more likely to remain out of school;
- fewer girls are enrolled in school and more girls drop out.

One of the significant insights offered by these findings is that of the intersection of poverty with other types of disadvantages (e.g. caste and gender), which complicates its effect on the incidence of child labour.

For poor households, child labour and education are not polarized choices. Children often work *in order* to attend school (Nieuwenhuys 1994) and to free up household resources from investment in their education. The ability to contribute towards household livelihoods also contributes to their self-esteem. Further, the combination of school and work can be seen as a strategic choice for parents who wish to balance the benefits of minimum education with the discipline of economic activity, in contexts where employment opportunities are scarce or demand prior investment of social or financial capital.

However, recognizing that children may be engaged in both schooling and work does not resolve the debate on how to address their well-being. While seasonally adjusted school calendars and flexible schooling are ways to address the immediate constraints facing children who would otherwise be deprived of schooling, the physical costs for children who do both are high (Subrahmanian 2005)

The blockade and the way ahead

The dichotomy of child work/child labour can guide the priority of short-term objectives, but beyond this dichotomy there exists a large section of children who are deprived of their basic rights. The change that is witnessed in the realm of human rights towards more progressive values needs to be called on in pre-empting this dichotomy. Instead of getting stranded in competing explanations about the causes of child labour, it is important to acknowledge that child labour needs to be understood in terms of its linkages with other social processes, mostly guided by the pattern of development rather than the rate of growth. And beyond the apparently parallel arguments on poverty and education and/or demand and supply models, one can gather mutually reinforcing rather than mutually exclusive factors, operating with inseparable interdependence, ensuring an unrelenting supply of child labour.

In other words, two inferences are unmistakeable from a policy perspective: poverty, high fertility and non-participation in school education are mutually reinforcing and, consequently, need to be addressed by three separate but complementary instruments. One such instrument is raising per-child expenditure in primary and middle schools. Second is the major overhaul of primary and middle school facilities, and improving the content and delivery of quality education. This can be achieved by reducing the cost of school attendance for children, and improving supply-side facilities to increase retention rates in primary and middle schools. At the same time, as most of the child labourers in India hail from the disadvantaged social groups which also constitute the bulk of the country's poor, their differential engagement with mainstream development, and experience with formal education and return to education, need to be addressed as part of the various community development programmes, along with efforts to improve their income levels through the implementation of adult minimum wages and the promotion of occupational diversification. An action plan which addresses the links between education, poverty, and demand and supply, through a well-orchestrated policy and programmes is urgently required.

GUIDE TO FURTHER READING

Kabeer, N., Nambissan, B.G. and Subrahmanian, R. (eds) (2003) *Child Labour and the Right to Education in South Asia: Needs Versus Rights*, New Delhi: Sage.

Lieten, K., Karan, A.K. and Satpathy, A. (eds) (2005) *Children, School and Work: Glimpses from India*, New Delhi and Amsterdam: Institute for Human Development and IREWOC (Foundation for International Research on Working Children).

Lieten, K., Srivastava, R. and Thorat, S. (2004) *Small Hands in South Asia: Child Labour in Perspective*, New Delhi: IDPAD (Indo-Dutch Programme on Alternatives in Development) and Manohar Publications.

Nieuwenhhuys, O. (2000) 'The household economy and the commercial exploitation of children's work: The case of Kerala', in B. Schelmmer, *The Exploited Child*, London and New York: Zed Books.
Weiner, M. (1991) *The Child and the State in India*, Oxford University Press.

USEFUL WEBSITES

http://www.childlabour.net
http://www.ilo.org/ipec/index.htm
http://www.ucw-project.org

REFERENCES

Gayathri, V. and Chaudhri, D.P. (2002) 'Introduction', *The Indian Journal of Labour Economics*, 45(3), July–September.
Nieuwenhhuys, O. (1994) *Children's Lifeworlds: Gender, Welfare and Labour in the Developing World*, London and New York: Routledge.
O'Neill, O. (1989) *Constructions of Reason: Explorations of Kant's Practical Philosophy*, Cambridge: Cambridge University Press.
Subrahmanian, R. (2005) 'Education exclusion and the developmental state', in Chopa, R. and Jeffery, P. (eds) *Educational Regimes in Contemporary India*, New Delhi: Sage.

8.8 Adult literacy and development

Raff Carmen

'Literacy for all': from ILY90 to MDG2015

There has never been much doubt that the number of adults who have some sort of problem with reading and writing – from functional illiterates or semi-literates to those who have never attended a school or an adult education class in their lives – has never have strayed far from the 1 billion mark worldwide (Hinzen 2004: 3). This is in spite of the fact that, over half a century ago (1948), the human right to learn and the right to an education had been ranked among the most fundamental and inalienable human rights.

Since those early days, the 'enormous bow-wave' (Hinzen 2006) of children and young people who never go to school, and the even larger number of illiterate and semi-literate adults in countries most seriously affected, has remained virtually constant, regardless of the resolve to 'eradicate illiteracy' (UNESCO 1990a), or, at the very least, to cut their number by half 'by the turn of the century' (UNESCO, 1990b).

The long-awaited year 2000 came and went, with the unmet targets firmly in place. A second UNESCO Literacy Decade (2003–12) was declared, with the education goals now attuned to the overall 'Eradication of Hunger' Millennium Development Goals (MDGs): universal primary education (UPE) and literacy objectives are now to be achieved 'by the year 2015'. However, while Goal 2 does refer to education, there is no mention any more of adults – the great majority of whom are women – and their continued adult basic education (ABE) needs – leading one Dakar participant to muse whether EFA (Education For All), in the new century, stands for 'Except For Adults' (Almazan-Khan 2001).

Although never explicit, the argument in favour of educating children over adults, or for putting all the eggs, as it were, in the UPE basket, is hardly more convincing than the preceding ones, not only because it rather crudely relies on adults having to 'die off' for the illiteracy problem to solve itself, but also because education, previously provided, matter-of-factly, for free, has increasingly become a privilege that needs to be paid for – which means that millions simply will have to do without, or continue to do without.

By 2003, for example, 115 million children, 60 per cent of them girls, were still missing out on primary education (Action Aid 2003), while many of those lucky enough to receive formal education will drop out early and/or will have to make do with double-streamed, severely overcrowded classes, with a besieged, often untrained teacher in charge.

The debt write-off for the 18 poorest nations – 14 of them in Africa – agreed by the rich nations in 2005, will be, at best, a temporary respite: while it would allow a country like Zambia, for example, to hire 7000 new teachers, sub-Saharan Africa still needs 1.6 million extra teachers by 2015. Countries like Chad will need almost four times as many primary teachers, up from 16,000 in 2005 to 61,000 by 2015, while Ethiopia must double its stock to achieve UPE (UNESCO 2006).

Adult literacy and development myths

The view of educational economists and planners that a 40 per cent literacy rate constitutes the threshold for a development 'take-off' (Atkinson 1983: 60) has been among the driving forces behind the international push for UPE and literacy. Had not traditional society first to 'pass away' (Lerner 1964; Rogers 1969), while the 'savage mind' needed 'domesticating' (Goody 1984) for modernity and, hence, 'development' to take root?

Sociocultural and educational anthropologists, prominent among them Brian Street, managed to counter this economistic, 'autonomous' view of literacy as a single, monocultural technical skill, to highlight the rich cultural diversity of a whole raft of socially and culturally embedded literacy practices – or 'literacies' (and 'numeracies') (Street 1984), forming part of the 'ideological' model.

'Literacy', indeed, takes many forms: on paper, on the computer screen, on TV, on posters and signs. In an age where the monopoly of the printed word and reverence for the book are increasingly eroded by the onslaught of omnipresent digital, electronic and virtual modes of communication, it is salutary to remember that knowing how to use the alphabet (or equivalent symbols or characters in other cultures) is just one form of human communication among many.

The term 'illiterate', on the other hand (or 'analfabete', as it is more commonly known in other languages), defines individuals negatively by 'what-they-are-not' and 'what-they-know-not', reducing them to nobodies and ignoramuses. The fascinating encyclopaedic knowledge of the West African griot's (bard) orality and oratory, transmitted from father to son, as described in Alex Haley's book *Roots*, for example, should put paid to such types of disempowering condescendence. After all, 'was not literacy invented by illiterates?' (Enzensberger 1987).

Putting his finger on one of the prime reasons for decades of frustrated alphabetization efforts, Street concludes that 'unless the cultural complexity of "literacy-in-practice" is taken into account, UNESCO and other international aid agencies will continue to register high dropout rates' (Street 1990: 33).

Approaches and methods

Laubach and Laubach's (1960) phonically based 'Each One Teach One' (EOTO) method (also known as the 'missionary' approach because of the close links to proselytizing Bible reading – Hutton 1992: 30) is clearly part of the narrow pedagogical (as compared to andragogical/

liberating) transmission-of-skills approaches to literacy teaching and training. This in no way detracts from the Laubach school's claim to have made 100 million people literate.

'Functional' literacy, an idea originally developed by and for the US military, and tried out by UNESCO in the 1970s under its Experimental World Literacy Programme (EWLP), started from the belief that literacy ought to be 'the first step in the creation of qualified manpower' (UNESCO 1988, in Hutton 1992: 32). In practice, EWLP literacy, implemented in environments largely devoid of (formal) jobs, such as 1970s Tanzania, was fated, unsurprisingly, to remain 'dysfunctional'.

These and other inconsistencies may well have been behind a widely quoted poem by a group of poor West Bengali illiterate peasants, 'Why should we become literate?'

> What kind of people are we?
> We are poor
> but we are not stupid.
> That is why, despite our illiteracy, we still exist.
> But we have to know why we should become literate.
> We joined the literacy classes before.
> But after some time, we got wise.
> We felt cheated. So we left the classes (*Adult Education and Development* 1988)

'Liberating' literacy, popularized by the work of the Brazilian adult educator, Paulo Freire, has long ranked among the more prominent alternative approaches. Literacy learning, or learning to 'read the Word', above all in situations of poverty, exclusion and oppression, becomes the entry point for an overall 'conscientized' literacy (from the Portuguese 'conscientização') and capacity for 'reading the World' (Freire and Macedo 1985).

Freire's method was effective (for example, 'literate within 30 hours', Brown 1975), although he never set out to create 'a method' in the first place. Adult learners themselves, rather than being spoon-fed by infantilizing Janet-and-John-type literacy primers, are quite capable of generating, within a grown-up dialogue, their own 'codifications' and 'generative words', and positively feed them back into their own life-worlds ('praxis'). 'Learners must see the need for writing one's life and reading one's reality' (Freire 1985).

Cutting the umbilical cord with the primer, however, always proved difficult, including for Freire himself. Contrary to his own educational principles, primer-type instructions are handed down: 'The first generative word should be trisyllabic... Having chosen seventeen generative words, the next step...', and so on (Brown 1975: 8).

REFLECT, launched by Action Aid (London) in the mid-1990s, claims finally to have broken this 'stranglehold of the primer'. While taking on board Freire's andragogical principles, it complements them with learner-driven, 'bottom-up' (rapid) participatory rural appraisal methods (PRA), borrowed from agronomy and social anthropology (e.g. Chambers 1997), adapted to literacy work. Community members, working in groups, record their own knowledge in the form of diagrams, maps of their own natural resources, or calendars recording seasonal changes in income or food availability, matrices, and the like, which are originally drawn in the sand, to be transferred later to flip charts, using visual symbol cards and, eventually, letters. This allows the participants to meaningfully make the transition from the three-dimensional world of orality to the two-dimensional world of the alphabet (Archer 1995; Archer and Cottingham 1996).

Conclusion: Beyond the alphabet – the 'other' literacy

Measured against forever optimistic forecasts, literacy programmes, whether spearheaded by UNESCO, governments or NGOs, have been an uphill struggle, if not altogether a Sisyphean task.

One key factor which has been overlooked, ignored or, more probably, remains unrecognized in the literacy for development debate, is that 'development' is not just about knowing how to communicate in a new, complex media environment, but also, and above all, in a new, complex, increasingly globalized economic environment, the rules of which, quite obviously, *also* need to be learned.

If (alphabetic) literacy stands for the cross-cultural transition from a three-dimensional mode of communicating (orality, oracy, gesture, song, dance) to the two-dimensional, abstract world of the alphabetic symbol and computer digit, then the cross-cultural transition from the 'simple' world of the artisan/small producer to the complex world of the 'worker' (involving the division of labour – the process of becoming entrepreneurially and organizationally competent) can be said to be a genuine, albeit another, form of 'literacy'.

One way of facilitating this transition (the traditional one, practised for over half a century now) is to start with the alphabet and, from that bridgehead, find ways and means to make those new skills, in the words of Easton (2006), 'dovetail with other local development initiatives that create uses for it and that require it'.

Another way is to start from the economic reality, which, for illiterates, more often than not, is steeped in poverty and joblessness, so that the 'need' for the alphabet, and numbers too, will 'learn to know itself: it becomes a motive' (Leont'ev 1978: 118). People are not poor (and do not remain illiterate) because they do not work, and even less because they do not want to work, but 'because they have no jobs' (Campos 1997). Inside the very process of acquiring, in solidarity, the organizational and entrepreneurial skills allowing them to create jobs (sustainable livelihoods) for themselves, they will discover the genuine 'need' for literacy, and numeracy skills too.

A theory and a methodology, allowing precisely this type of 'dovetailing', does exist, albeit largely unrecognized, and therefore unappreciated for its powerful literacy and development potential. An example is the capacitating large group Organization Workshop (OW) theory and methodology of the Brazilian sociologist, Clodomir Santos de Morais. Like conscientization, 'capacitation' (from the Portuguese 'capacitação') represents a generically different adult educational concept and practice, in that, quite uniquely in the OW, it is not the teacher/trainer, but the 'object that teaches' – 'Objective/ised Activity' (Andersson, 2006). It has been successfully implemented since the 1970s on three continents (see, for example, Carmen and Sobrado 2000; Andersson 2006) and is being trialed, for the first time in a post-industrial context, at Marsh Farm Council Estate, Luton, UK, as part of the New Deal for Communities (NDC) regeneration effort (Jenkins and Potts 2006; Dobson 2007).

GUIDE TO FURTHER READING AND REFERENCES

ActionAid International (2003) *Worldwide Review 2003*, Johannesburg: ActionAid International (available at http://www.actionaid.org/docs/annualreport03.pdf).

Adult Education and Development (1988) 'Why should we become literate?', 31: 115–17.

Almazan-Khan, M. (2001) 'Does EFA stand for "Except For Adults"?', *Adult Education and Development*, 55: 171 (available at http://www.iiz-dvv.de/englisch/Publikationen/Ewb_ausgaben/55_2001/eng_Khan.html).

Andersson, G. (2006) 'Unbounded governance: A study of popular development organization', PhD thesis, Oxford University.

Archer, D. (1995) 'Using PRA for a radical new approach to adult literacy', *PLA Notes*, 23: 51–5, London: International Institute for Environment and Development.

Archer, D. and Cottingham, S. (1996) *The REFLECT Mother Manual*, London: Action Aid.

Atkinson, G.B. (1983) *The Economics of Education*, London: Hodder & Stoughton.

Brown, C. (1975) *Literacy in 30 Hours*, London: Readers and Writers Co-op.

Campos, M. (1997) 'Domador de la miseria – Clodomir Santos de Morais lleva sa voz y solaciones para la pro-breza (Conqueror of poverty: Clodomir Santos de Morais raises his voice and offers his solutions to poverty)', *Rumbo*, 658: 17.

Carmen, R. and Sobrado, M. (2000) *A Future for the Excluded*, London: Zed Books.

Chambers, R. (1997) *Whose Reality Counts?* London: IT Publications.

Dobson, J. (2007) 'Can a run-down housing estate become birthplace of dozens of businesses?', *New Start*, 7th December: 16–17.

Easton, P. (2006) *Education by All: A Brief for Literacy Investment*, keynote speech at the Biennale on Education in Africa (Libreville, Gabon, 27–31 March).

Enzensberger, H.M. (1987) 'In praise of the illiterate', *Adult Education and Development*, 28: 96–105.

Freire, P. and Macedo, A. (1985) *Reading the Word and the World*, London: Routledge.

Goody, J. (1984) *The Domestication of the Savage Mind*, Cambridge: Cambridge University Press.

Hinzen, H. (2004) 'Editorial', *Adult Education and Development*, 61: 3.

Hinzen, H. (2006) 'Editorial', *Adult Education and Development*, 66: 3.

Hutton, B. (ed.) (1992) *Adult Basic Education (ABE) in South Africa*, Oxford: Oxford University Press.

Jenkins, G. and Potts, R. (2006) 'Talking about regeneration', *Third Sector*, 20th September: 19–20.

Laubach, F.C. and Laubach, R.S. (1960) *Toward World Literacy*, Syracuse, NY: Syracuse University Press.

Leont'ev, A.N. (1978) *Activity, Consciousness and Personality*, New York: Prentice Hall.

Lerner, D. (1964) *The Passing of Traditional Society*, New York: Free Press.

Rogers, E. (1969) *Modernization Among Peasants*, New York: Holt.

Street, B. (1984) *Literacy in Theory and Practice*, Cambridge: Cambridge University Press.

Street, B. (ed.) (1990) *Literacy in Development: People, Language Power*, London: Education for Development.

UNESCO (United Nations Educational, Scientific and Cultural Organization) (1990a) *International Literacy Year*, Report No. ED/ILY/88.10, Paris: United Nations International Literacy Year Secretariat.

UNESCO (1990b) *World Conference on EFA – World Declaration on Education For All and Framework for Action to Meet Basic Learning Needs*, Paris: UNESCO (available at http://unesdoc.unesco.org/images/0012/001275/127583e.pdf).

UNESCO (2006) *Teachers and Educational Quality: Monitoring Global Needs for 2015*, Montreal: UNESCO Institute for Statistics (available at http://www.uis.unesco.org/ev_en.php?ID=6509_201&ID2=DO_TOPIC).

8.9 Management challenges in achieving Education For All: South Asian perspectives

Caroline Dyer

Achieving Education for All: The challenges

Education and development

Although education was accorded the status of a basic human right by the United Nations in 1948, much remains to be done to ensure universal enjoyment of that right. It is generally held that education (i.e. formal schooling) is positively associated with human development: it has long been seen as an engine to drive economic growth; create a productive labour force, improved health and controlled fertility. Education's expected role in nation building is also reflected in the way many developing countries, once liberated from colonial rule, pledged to provide universal primary education. Commitments to providing Education For All (EFA) were made at the World Conference on Education For All in Jomtien, 1990, and reaffirmed in Dakar in 2000. They have become headline news with the incorporation of universal primary education as the second Millennium Development Goal, to be achieved by 2015.

This goal can be seen as a reductionist agenda, which in its focus on primary education fails to capture the breadth and diversity of the idea of Education For All, which included provision for early childhood and adult education, and is set to an impossible timeframe. But it can also be argued that it has already been useful in highlighting both the widespread internal under-financing of public schooling systems and the inadequacy of aid support. It has also achieved high-profile political commitment to internationally agreed targets, and fuelled a drive to improve measures by which progress can be judged. Policies are gaining sophistication and shifting away from the simplistic, quantitative cause-effect thinking of earlier days – when lack of physical access to a school was seen as a key barrier to universal primary education and met with a response of expanding the network of schools and numbers of teachers, without much consideration of the quality of educational processes in those schools. Questions of quality, for many years neglected, are now being foregrounded in agency, academic and policy discourses, although quality itself remains notoriously difficult to define, as can be seen from the 2007 *Global Monitoring Report* (GMR 2007: 5):

Quality of education: the poor relation of education policies

While increasing children's access to primary education is a crucial step towards UPE, attention must also be paid to their progression once enrolled:

- In half the countries in South and West Asia with 2004 data, the percentage of primary school repeaters (9.2%) is above the median for all developing countries (6.7%), and it has been increasing in recent years in most countries in the region.
- Grade repetition is a particularly significant problem in Nepal (23%) and Bhutan (13%).
- In most regions boys repeat grade levels more often than girls, a pattern that holds true in each country of South and West Asia except Nepal.
- Repetition rates vary by grade; for example, in Nepal, 43% of pupils repeat grade 1, compared with 11% for grade 5. Such high repetition rates raise the issue of school transition and readiness, and a link can be made between these rates and low participation levels in pre-primary education.

Source: GMR 2007: 5

It is usually read via indicators that include rates of school enrolment, retention, achievement of learning outcomes and national literacy (e.g. UNESCO 1998; GMR 2005). Quantitative measures such as these have prompted concerns over the rates of return to investment, and highlighted a lack of internal efficiency, for example, relatively low levels of participation in primary schooling, early dropout and low levels of student achievement (see figure).

Schools: Sustaining or breaking down social inequality?

Read differently, these indicators reflect how schools are contextually situated within unequal socio-economic power relations. Non- or low participation, wastage and lower achievements are more pronounced among minority/low-caste/economically weaker/special needs groups, and among women. Existing educational provision may reinforce long-standing social stratification rather than promote social equity (Subrahmanian 2003). These more nuanced aspects of universalizing primary education are much more significant for longer-term social development than the achievement of numerical targets within a specified timeframe.

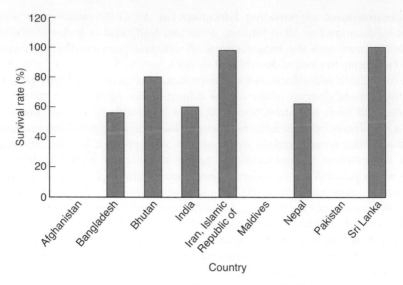

Survival rate to last grade of primary education (%) in south Asia (2001–02)
Source: Fennell 2006

Historically, educational systems of former colonies have been centralized, with formal deci-sion-making powers concentrated in the hands of a small elite at the top, and orders passed from the top down to teachers at the bottom (Dyer 2000). Bureaucrats have adhered to rigid operating principles embedded in the bureaucracy during colonial times, which lack the flexibility needed to be responsive to contemporary contexts. Teachers' autonomy and creativity are not much encour-aged, leading to widespread disaffection; and community involvement in the management and processes of education is insufficiently meaningful. Wide discrepancies between the knowledge that children gain from school, and its relevance or usefulness in their daily lives, are part of this pat-tern of schooling (e.g. PROBE 1999; Govinda 2002). The nature of curricular content and limited school success in attracting and retaining children (particularly girls) from minority groups are reflections of the need to search for ways of providing education that is equitable, inclusive and of good quality (Subrahmanian 2003). Focusing reform efforts on making this happen is a key chal-lenge for public educational systems. This challenge is exacerbated by competition from a rapidly expanding private sector, which, by enrolling children of families who can afford to pay fees, leaves the poorest of the poor (particularly girls) to be absorbed by the public system.

Management challenges at the primary school level

Promoting cultures of learning

Equity concerns over the lower enrolment and achievements of disadvantaged groups strongly imply the need to bring about radical shifts in the culture of teaching and learning (Alexander 2000). Centrally devised curricula and textbooks have tended to assume that all children are homogeneous. The focus has been on what is to be taught, rather than on children's learning, assuming that if the teacher teaches, children will learn. But if schools are to promote greater social equity, they need to operate in more democratic, participatory ways, with greater emphasis on learning, so that children's own knowledge and experiences are valued and validated.

A crucial policy shift is to encourage the one-way traffic of 'teacher as expert', transmitting a predetermined body of knowledge, to give way to two-way interactions, with a teacher as the facilitator of children's discovery (Kumar 2005). Individual difference needs to be valued and encouraged, and all children given opportunities to progress comfortably at their own speeds. But this role demands a different approach to teaching, classroom management and ideas about knowledge itself. Teachers may experience the demands of the new approach as a loss of control, subversion of their power in the classroom, and a challenge to their traditional standing as the gatekeeper of knowledge. If classrooms are to become more democratic, substantial changes need to be made to the way teachers are both managed and trained. Teachers are still seen as implementers of ideas generated by 'experts' elsewhere – as classroom technicians rather than creative education practitioners (McNiff 1991).

Releasing the creative potential of teachers is a challenge for educational managers, and unless progress is made in this respect, policy aspirations towards better-quality education may remain unrealized. Reform efforts need to have a core concern with shifting the balance of teacher accountability to the children in their care, and to ensuring learning outcomes, rather than accountability to an impersonal bureaucracy. This places an onus on management too, to improve their commitments to ensuring sound operating conditions, including appropriate and good-quality teaching/learning materials, so that all teachers, and all children, are assured the best possible chances of success. Decentralization, aiming to improve local accountability, by drawing parents into the life and management of schools, and making management more responsive to teachers, communities and children, is rapidly emerging as the dominant policy response.

The contribution of non-governmental organizations

Non-governmental organizations (NGOs) are significant educational actors, often pioneering innovative approaches or reaching communities which are omitted from other educational provision. Relations between government and NGOs are intrinsically complex: NGOs can be more flexible, more rapidly responsive and innovative, but their sphere of operation is limited unless they can work in partnership with government. These partnerships may take various forms: Eklaviya in Madhya Pradesh State, central India, was able to mainstream some of its curricular innovations; in Bangladesh the Bangladesh Rural Advancement Committee (BRAC) operates some 30,000 non-formal primary schools in areas where there is insufficient or no government provision; the Aga Khan Foundation has undertaken a significant School Improvement Programme in Pakistan. In contexts of changing structures of educational management, an important NGO role is the ability to support communities in developing the local understandings and capacity they need to make use of the new structures and powers that decentralization offers. Using the potential of NGOs constructively, and developing effective partnerships with civil society, is an important, if less visible, part of improving the quality and responsiveness of educational management.

Decentralization as a democratic response

Globally, the reform of management in the educational sector is increasingly seen as an essential component of enhancing relevance and promoting social justice. Decentralization is advocated as a means of improving public participation in decision-making, redistributing political power, and enhancing the efficiency, quality and stability of educational systems. Ironically, although its aim is to provide a foundation for greater political representation and participation of marginalized groups, there is no evidence that it is a response to civil society pressures.

Decentralization can be defined in many ways, but broadly requires a shift in the location of those who govern: 'a willingness to broaden or change the distribution of educational power...a transfer of decision-making power from the nation-state' (Davies 1990: 11). Its advocates argue that efficiency improves because local units of government can make more locally sensitive decisions about how and where to allocate resources. Quality is enhanced because nationally devised curricula or learning outcomes can be adapted to accommodate local cultural variations. Greater institutional and political stability should result because more is known about local or regional conditions, and there will be better support for national development policies if they are better understood and local support for them is mobilized. But since ownership of power and finances is inevitably hotly contested, decentralization may create more opportunities for political agendas of elected officials or powerful bureaucrats to undermine measures intended to improve the efficiency of the education system. It may also increase power tussles, and provide more opportunities for corruption. Defining a local community is difficult, and disparate groups may not combine appropriately to represent 'community' interests.

Three main forms of decentralization have been identified (see discussion in Dyer and Rose 2005): *deconcentration*, where a limited amount of decision-making authority is passed on to local agencies of central administrative units – this may result in greater central control; *delegation*, where decision-making responsibility is assigned to the elected officials of local agencies – but this power can be withdrawn again; and *devolution*, where local bodies with legal status are created. Many reforms bear the label of decentralization, and there is emerging evidence that, in its various guises, it is changing processes of decision making; shifting balances between the authority and responsibilities of different levels of government; encouraging new roles for schools, parents and communities; increasing devolution of financial and staff management; and encouraging more localized planning initiatives (Fiske 1996; Dyer and Rose 2005). Despite progress on these fronts, the United Nations Educational, Scientific and Cultural Organization (UNESCO) (GMR 2003: 214) argues: 'These are primarily shifts in the locus of management of responsibility... It is also difficult to gauge the relationship between decentralisation and learning outcomes, even though this is the real test.'

It is also widely argued that decentralization has a fourth form: *privatization*. However, unlike the other forms of planned decentralization noted above, this is a de facto shift, where market forces determine the operation of educational institutions. In south Asia, one response to unsatisfactory public-sector schooling is a rapid, under-regulated mushrooming of private schools. These also cater to the high demand for English language education, which is connected with access to better-paid jobs locally, and entry into the international sector. Advocates of marketization argue that it not only promotes efficiency and accountability, but also advances the democratic principles of free choice. The poorest, however, cannot afford private education of any variety, so marketization does not enhance choices for those who still depend on state facilities; indeed, private-sector expansion has failed to generate healthy competition and has labelled state education even more clearly as the preserve of those without choice. Furthermore, because education is widely seen as a public good, marketization does not lead to the retreat of the state, which still has a duty to provide education, and to invest in education for the collective social good. This form of decentralization suggests the need for a strong central role in regulating the private sector, to protect the quality of the education it offers.

The democratic impulse behind decentralization – the notion that all are equal, and equally entitled to success, is a powerful ideology. It implies that there is no rationing of social and economic goods, and that everyone is entitled to an equal share. Yet, historically, schools have played a major role in apportioning privilege. Through examinations, for instance, schools regulate who becomes 'successful'. The explosion of the private sector underlines the potential for education to maintain the privileges of the richer and more powerful, even in contexts where everyone is relatively poor. In terms of social equity, appropriate financial measures, proactive policies and innovative structures must underpin management reform, but they are not enough in themselves. Educational systems also need managers whose horizons stretch beyond technicist concerns with efficiency to question the role of schooling in upholding or breaking down unjust social structures, and who engage with the wider discourse of privilege and the structural inequalities in which schools are situated.

GUIDE TO FURTHER READING

Bruns, B., Mingat A. and Rakotomalala, R. (2003) *Achieving Universal Primary Education by 2015: A Chance for Every Child*, Washington DC: World Bank Publication. Available at http://www1.workdbank.org/education/pdf/achieving_efa/frontmatter.pdf

Fennell, S. (2006) *Future Policy Choices for the Education Sector in Asia*, paper presented to the Asia 2015 conference (available at http://www.asia2015conference.org/pdfs/fennell.pdf).

Fullan, M. (2001) *The New Meaning of Educational Change*, 3rd ed. Teachers College Press.

Harber, C. and Davies, L. (1997) *School Management and Effectiveness in Developing Countries*, London: Cassell.

Jansen, J. (2005) 'Targeting education: the politics of performance and the prospects of Education For All', *International Journal of Educational Development* 25(4), 368–380.

UNESCO (1998) *World Education Report: Teachers and Teaching in a Changing World*, Paris: United Nations Educational, Scientific and Cultural Organization.

REFERENCES

Alexander, R. (2000) *Culture and Pedagogy: International Comparisons in Primary Education*, Oxford: Blackwell.

Davies, L. (1990) *Equity and Efficiency? School Management in an International Context*, Lewes: Falmer Press.

Dyer, C. (2000) *Operation Blackboard: Policy Implementation in India's Federal Polity*, Oxford: Symposium Books.

Dyer, C. and Rose, P. (2005) 'Decentralisation for educational development? Editorial introduction', *Compare*, 35(2): 105–14.

Fennell, S. (2006) *Future Policy Choices for the Education Sector in Asia*, paper presented to the Asia 2015 conference (available at http://www.asia2015conference.org/pdfs/fennell.pdf).

Fiske, E. (1996) *Decentralisation of Education: Politics and Consensus*, Washington, DC: World Bank.

GMR (2003) *The Leap to Equality. EFA Global Monitoring Report*, Paris: United Nations Educational, Scientific and Cultural Organization.

GMR (2005) *The Quality Imperative. EFA Global Monitoring Report*, Paris: United Nations Educational, Scientific and Cultural Organization.

GMR (2007) *Early Childhood Education: EFA Global Monitoring Report*, Paris: United Nations Educational, Scientific and Cultural Organization.

Govinda, N. (2002) (ed.) *India Education Report: A Profile of Basic Education*, New Delhi: Oxford University Press.

Kumar, K. (2005) *Political Agenda of Education: A Study of Colonialist and Nationalist Ideals*, second edition, New Delhi: Sage Publications.

PROBE (1999) *Public Report on Basic Education in India*, the PROBE team, New Delhi: Oxford University Press.

Subrahmanian, R. (2003) 'Introduction: Exploring Processes of Marginalisation and Inclusion in Education', *IDS Bulletin* 34: 1–8.

UNESCO (1998) *World Education Report: Teachers and Teaching in a Changing World*, Paris: United Nations Educational, Scientific and Cultural Organization.

Political economy of violence and insecurity

Editorial introduction

For many people concerned about development, the most disturbing aspects are political instability, conflicts, and war, particularly civil war, as illustrated by images of turbulence, and distraught and destitute fleeing people. Some states are in 'complex emergency', characterized by protracted crisis and the collapse of state structures. Human rights violations resulting from current conflicts and rising violence are unprecedented. The costs are to be measured in deaths, broken lives, destroyed livelihoods, lost homes and increased vulnerability.

Total numbers of official refugees are difficult to measure, with official data on refugee flows never consistently collated and some very large displaced groups never formally registered as refugees. Many governments are increasingly unwilling to recognize and take responsibility for displaced populations. Rich countries attempt concertedly to restrict the arrival of asylum seekers on their territory and their exit from war zones.

Displacement operations have not only grown considerably but have also been handled disastrously, generating unprecedented resistance and high international visibility – for example, the Narmada dam in India. Population densities keep increasing, and every new major infrastructural programme requires 'space' that is often inhabited or already otherwise used. Development-induced forced displacement has been on the rise in many countries in the last decade. 'Displacement' is not just an economic transaction, substituting property with monetary compensation; it also involves 'resettlement' and requires true 'rehabilitation'.

In civil wars civilians tend to be the object of fighting and bear most consequences. Material resources and social networks, which made daily life possible, are destroyed. Long-standing arrangements of exchange between groups are often forcibly broken down. Levels of violence are less regulated in civil wars. It is important to recognize that contemporary internal conflicts have beneficiaries as well as victims. They include young men whose livelihoods become bound up with ongoing violence, and 'war lords' powerful because no authority can impose the rule of law. In some places, such as parts of Afghanistan and Sudan, civil wars are so prolonged that they have become the norm. Much of the population has had no experience of peace.

The international arms trade increased the availability of modern military equipment, strongly affecting the way in which civil wars break out and escalate. It is well known that industrialized countries compete with each other to secure lucrative export contracts for military hardware and know-how. Increased access to highly effective military equipment has been a major catalyst. Small arms have become profitable for powerful organizations and commercial companies prepared to engage in illegal trade. The availability of these modern weapons has indubitably facilitated escalating violence. Similarly, violence against women and children increasingly concerns development agencies as women challenge structures and practices of subordination. It is also nowadays used as a political tool of war. Most of the gender- and age-based violence occurs in private spaces and remains invisible in many societies of the South, as it is viewed as acceptable. Most of the age-based violence is against children and the elderly.

Economic deprivation is both cause and consequence of war. Social stratification linked to highly inequitable distributions of income is not new, and has often caused violent conflict.

Recently, however, the exclusion of populations from the benefits of economic growth has assumed a more overtly structured conflicts of interest and has regional dimension.

Corruption is a feature of state/society relations that undermines the legitimacy of the state, leads to wasteful public policies, and begs for increased transparency and accountability. Corruption can lead to the inefficient and unfair distribution of scarce benefits. It undermines the purpose of public programmes, encourages officials to create red tape, increases the cost of doing business and lowers state legitimacy.

Many commentators have suggested that the end of the cold war allowed scores of ethnic groups to compete ferociously for power and influence, encouraging demands for greater autonomy for populations within states and the restricting of central government controls. Development policies have become intertwined with group aspirations, and shaped nationalism and multiple identities. These identities are subject to interpretations, change over time, interact, oppose and complement each other. National identities based around religion and ethnicities are always viewed with suspicion. It is important to understand the relationship between religion and society and faith traditions and development and its implications for poverty reduction in developing countries and how beliefs, practices and organizations change over a period of time, especially in the context of economic development and globalization. Multilateral organizations such as the World Bank and the Department for International Development (UK) are keen to explore the potential of faith-based groups as agents of development.

The first Article of the United Nations Charter committed governments to maintain international peace and security, to take effective collective measures to prevent and remove threats to peace, and to suppress acts of aggression. Yet international response to conflict appears ever more inadequate. The United Nations' operations have proved very costly, in terms both of the funding required and of political credibility.

International NGOs have gained considerable experience of providing relief aid to traumatized populations. Interventions not intended to be sustainable have created aid dependency (for example, in Mozambique). The possibilities of providing for human security do not seem to have been enhanced. Embarrassing failures have resulted; the effectiveness of humanitarian aid has been questioned, especially in the context of the increase in natural disasters and a change in the nature of emergencies leading to a substantial increase in humanitarian assistance. The 'War on Terror' and the subsequent interventions in Iraq and Afghanistan post 11 September 2001 have created new challenges for the implementation of humanitarian assistance, human security, peacekeeping roles, partnership for post-conflict reconstruction, and the promotion of peace and good governance.

9.1 Gender- and age-based violence

Cathy McIlwaine

Violence is firmly established as an important development issue. This is due to global increases in everyday violence, the globalization of crime and violence, and the recognition that violence undermines sustainable development (Moser and McIlwaine 2006). An important dimension of these debates is gender- and age-based violence, usually involving violence against women and children, but less frequently involving men and the elderly. While these types of violence are now widely recognized as restricting women's and young people's freedom of participation in society, impeding the efficiency of development interventions and eroding their human rights, the international community has been slow to respond. Indeed, only in 1989 were the rights of children to protection from various forms of violence recognized in the United Nations Convention on the Rights of the Child. Similarly, the elimination of violence against women was only formally called for in 1993 through a United Nations declaration. This relates to the invisible nature of much gender- and age-based violence, the fact that it is often accepted as 'traditional', occurs in the private sphere, and is associated with high levels of fear and stigma.

Identifying gender-based violence

While definitions of violence are highly contested, it usually involves the use of physical force that causes hurt to others in order to impose a wish or desire. The primary motivating factor behind perpetration, either conscious or unconscious, is the gain and maintenance of power, which may be political, economic and/or social (Moser and McIlwaine 2006). In the case of gender, one of the main definitional issues recently has been the shift from the term 'violence against women' to 'gender-based violence'. Although some conflate these, strictly speaking violence against women is one type of gender-based violence, together with violence against men, boys and transgendered. Some argue that using the term gender-based violence depoliticizes it and diverts attention from the reality that women and girls suffer disproportionately from violence at the hands of men.

Definitions of gender-based violence have been contested. The benchmark is usually the 1993 United Nations Declaration of the Elimination of Violence against Women in Article 1:

> Any act of gender-based violence that results in, or is likely to result in, physical, sexual or psychological harm or suffering to women, including threats of such acts, coercion or arbitrary deprivations of liberty, whether occurring in public or in private life.

Article 2 continues that it may occur in the 'family, community, perpetrated or condoned by the State, wherever it occurs', and may refer to assault, sexual abuse, rape, female genital mutilation and other 'traditional' practices, as well as sexual harassment, trafficking in women and forced prostitution (UN 1993). It is important that this recognizes the private sphere, thus challenging the invisibility of gender-based violence and its associated impunity.

There is a huge diversity in types of gender-based violence, especially against women. However, some women are more likely to be vulnerable to such violence, according to occupation, residence, ethnicity, class and educational position. Some types are also specific to particular cultures and countries. These may include acid-throwing in Bangladesh, involving men throwing acid on women's faces as a form of attack (Zaman 1999), female genital mutilation, which is concentrated in Northern African and Middle Eastern societies (Rahman and Toubia 2006), and the recent 'femicides' in Mexico and Central America (Prieto-Carrón, Thomson and Macdonald 2007).

Although gender-based violence has been integral to armed conflict for centuries, it has only recently been recognized as a political tool of war, especially rape (Moser and Clark 2001). This was enshrined in the UN Security Council Resolution 1325 (available at http://www.un.org/events/res_1325e.pdf) in 2000, when, for the first time, sexual violence against women was recognized not as an individual act of soldiers, but as an act of conflict, with women being valued as peace-builders. The resolution also highlights the huge levels of violence against women during wars, by official armies, armies of national liberation and peacekeeping forces.

The dynamics of armed conflict also highlight how women can be perpetrators of violence as combatants and soldiers. But, most commonly, men can be victims of male-on-male violence, and especially male rape, as detainees and prisoners of war. Men are also more susceptible to homophobic violence. However, women are probably most likely to commit or collude with gender-based violence against other women in the role of mother-in-law, noted widely in south Asian societies.

Trends in gender-based violence

Under-reporting of violence against women is widespread, despite calls to improve data collection. This is mainly due to the taboo attached to it in many cultures, as well as the sensitivity surrounding data collection. Yet data sources on gender-based violence have improved dramatically in recent years, although data remain inconsistent.

Despite this, there is a consensus that violence against women is more prevalent than first thought. As many as 71 per cent of women experienced physical or sexual assault by an intimate partner in the case of rural Ethiopia (see Table 1), although the prevalence of non-partner violence was higher in urban areas (see Table 2). Anecdotally, it has also been shown that violence against women has increased over time (Pickup 2001). While even less is known about the prevalence of violence against men, the World Health Organization (WHO 2005: 20) study found that only in Thailand did more than 15 per cent of physically assaulted women report having initiated violence against their male partner more than twice in their life.

Table 1 Prevalence of violence against women by an intimate male partner

Country	Percentage of adult women ever experienced physical violence	Percentage of adult women ever experienced sexual violence	Percentage of adult women ever experienced physical or sexual violence, or both
Bangladesh (province)	42	50	62
Brazil (province)	34	14	37
Brazil (city)	27	10	29
Ethiopia (province)	49	59	71
Namibia (city)	31	16	36
Peru (province)	61	47	69
Peru (city)	49	23	51
Tanzania (province)	47	31	56
Tanzania (city)	33	23	41
Thailand (province)	34	29	47
Thailand (city)	23	30	41

Source: WHO 2005: 6

Table 2 Prevalence of sexual or physical violence against women by a non-partner

Country	Percentage of adult women ever experienced physical or sexual violence, or both
Bangladesh (province)	10
Brazil (province)	23
Brazil (city)	40
Ethiopia (province)	5
Namibia (city)	23
Peru (province)	18
Peru (city)	31
Tanzania (province)	19
Tanzania (city)	34
Thailand (province)	14
Thailand (city)	20

Source: WHO 2005: 13

Causes of gender-based violence

There are multiple and complex causes of gender-based violence. In general, it is rooted in ideological differences between women and men, usually related to the concentration of power in men's hands. Thus, gender-based violence is closely associated with the construction of gender identities, especially hegemonic masculinities (Barker 2005).

One set of explanations focuses on accepting male violence as 'natural' and rooted in biological differences, making it difficult to change. The second, shaped by feminist scholarship, relates male violence to social constructions of patriarchal forces, which, in theory, may be prevented (O'Toole and Schiffman 1997). It may also be linked with psychological factors in that men with 'impaired masculinity' may abuse women, influenced by socialization processes that involved witnessing violence as the norm. Socio-economic factors, such as increased poverty, may exacerbate violence, especially when masculinity is undermined. Ultimately, violence is the expression of power of one gender over the other, and it is aggravated or ameliorated depending on a range of risk factors at different levels (Pickup 2001). It may also be 'triggered' by issues such as infidelity, and exacerbated by alcohol or drugs (WHO 2005).

Identifying age-based violence

Age-based violence involves the abuse of those who are vulnerable in terms of their age, because they are young or old. This may 'involve physical or mental violence, injury and abuse, neglect or negligent treatment, maltreatment or exploitation, including sexual abuse' (Pinheiro 2006: 4; this is based on the UN Convention on the Rights of the Child, Article 1, but can be applied equally to elderly people). Most analysis of age-based violence in the South relates to violence involving children and youth, rather than elder abuse. Pinheiro (2006) usefully identifies the main places where violence against children occurs as the home and family, schools, care and justice systems, workplaces and communities. Although the home and family is where children can be protected against violence, it is also where they can suffer most, especially children aged under one year. Here, physical and sexual assault occur, together with traditional practices such as female infanticide, psychological abuse and neglect. In schools, physical and psychological violence against children may be perpetrated by teachers or by other children, through bullying, playground fighting and gangs. Abused and neglected children may end up in care homes, where their situation is likely to worsen; this particularly affects AIDS orphans (globally there were 15 million in 2006). The workplace can be dangerous for children who may suffer at the hands of employers, as well as co-workers, customers and, in the case of sexual exploitation, pimps. Child slavery is also widespread, especially among domestic and sex workers (Pinheiro 2006).

Most is known about violence against children in the community because of its visibility. Street children have received the most attention in this sphere, and are associated with petty theft. This is reflected in some of the slang words used for street children, such as 'the plague' (Colombia), 'vermin' (Ethiopia) and 'mosquitoes' (Cameroon). Because of their association with crime, they are often targeted and killed or harmed. In Guatemala, street children have been targets of 'social cleansing' (targeted killing of 'undesirables'). Gang activity is also important and growing. Largely urban-based, there is a huge diversity of types of gangs, most being male-dominated. They have different generic names, such as *maras* in Central America, as well as names such as the Area Boys of Lagos, Nigeria. Gang membership often reflects an attempt by young men to assert their identity within dysfunctional families, as well as in response to factors such as high rates of unemployment (Moser and McIlwaine 2004). Children also suffer severe psychosocial effects as witnesses of war, as well as committing violence as child soldiers. As of 2005, an estimated 250,000 children have been recruited in wars around the world (UN 2005).

Trends and causes of violence against young people

Although it is often assumed that young women and girls are more likely to experience abuse, recently there has been a steep increase in rates of victimization and perpetration among boys aged 15 and over. Indeed, globally, 77 per cent of all homicides are male, with most aged 15–29 (Krug et al. 2002: 10). Non-fatal violence is also higher among boys than girls. However, girls are more likely to experience sexual violence; an estimated 150 million girls and 73 million boys have experienced sexual violence (Pinheiro 2006).

The reasons for aged-based violence intersect with those underlying gender-based violence and also revolve around power. Their unequal position in the home and society makes children (and the elderly) vulnerable targets for those stronger than they are. Economic development is also important, in that the rate of child homicide in 2002 in low-income countries was twice that of high-income countries (Krug et al. 2002). Power relations are also central to why children perpetrate violence; besides those who are forced to do so, children may commit violence to empower themselves. There is often a continuum of causality that runs over generations, in that those experiencing or witnessing violence in the home may also become perpetrators in later life (Moser and McIlwaine 2004).

In terms of looking to the future and reducing rates of gender- and age-based violence, its scale must be recognized, as well as the fact that it undermines sustainable development. The Millennium Development Goals highlight both gender- and age-based inequalities, and recognize that these groups must be protected. Yet concrete policies and campaigns must be developed. The groundwork has already been laid by organizations such as the United Nations Development Fund for Women (UNIFEM) and United Nations Children's (Emergency) Fund (UNICEF), but much remains to be done in harnessing the potential of women and young people in resisting violence and in preventing them from perpetrating violence against others.

GUIDE TO FURTHER READING

Gender and Development (2007) special issue on *Gender-Based Violence*, 15(1). This collection considers gender-based violence as a development issue. It includes case studies from a range of countries, as well as thematic papers.

Krug, E.G., Dahlberg, L.L, Mercy, J.A., Zwi, A.B. and Lozano, R. (eds) (2002) *World Report on Violence and Health*, Geneva: World Health Organization. This is the first global report on violence from a health perspective, and includes discussion of the nature, causes and effects of violence.

O'Toole, L.L. and Schiffman, J.R. (eds) (1997) *Gender Violence: Interdisciplinary Perspectives*, New York and London: New York University Press. This text adopts an interdisciplinary approach to gender-based violence, examining the causes and consequences of different types of violence.

Pickup, F., with Williams, S. and Sweetman, C. (2001) *Ending Violence Against Women: A Challenge for Development and Humanitarian Work*, Oxford: Oxfam. This presents a summary of violence against women from research and policy perspectives.

Pinheiro, P.S. (2006) *World Report on Violence Against Children*, United Nations Secretary General's Study on Violence Against Children, Geneva: United Nations. This provides an overview of the incidence, causes and consequences of violence against children, as well as outlining policy recommendations.

UNIFEM (2003) *Not a Minute More: Ending Violence against Women*, New York: United Nations Development Fund for Women. This report describes a series of practical initiatives to eliminate violence against women.

REFERENCES

Barker, G.T. (2005) *Dying to be Men: Youth and Masculinity and Social Exclusion*, London: Routledge.

Krug, E.G., Dahlberg, L.L., Mercy, J.A., Zwi, A.B. and Lozano, R. (eds) (2002) *World Report on Violence and Health*, Geneva: World Health Organization.

Moser, C. and McIlwaine, C. (2004) *Encounters with Violence in Latin America: Urban Poor Perceptions from Columbia and Guatemala*, Routledge: London.

Moser, C. and McIlwaine, C. (2006) 'Latin American urban violence as a development concern: Towards a framework for violence reduction', *World Development*, 34(1): 89–111.

Moser, C.O.N. and Clark, F. (eds) (2001) *Victims, Perpetrators or Actors? Gender, Armed Conflict and Political Violence*, London: Zed Books.

O'Toole, L.L. and Schiffman, J.R. (eds) (1997) *Gender Violence: Interdisciplinary Perspectives*, New York and London: New York University Press.

Pickup, F. with Williams, S. and Sweetman, C. (2001) *Ending Violence Against Women: A Challenge for Development and Humanitarian Work*, Oxford: Oxfam.

Pinheiro, P.S. (2006) *World Report on Violence Against Children*, United Nations Secretary General's Study on Violence Against Children, Geneva: United Nations.

Prieto-Carrón, M., Thomson, M. and Macdonald, M. (2007) 'No more killings! Women respond to femicides in Central America', *Gender and Development*, 15(1): 25–40.

Rahman, A. and Toubia, N. (eds) (2006) *Female Genital Mutilation: A Guide to Laws and Policies Worldwide*, London: Zed Books.

UN (1993) *48/104: Declaration on the Elimination of Violence Against Women* (A/RES/48/104), Geneva: United Nations (available at http://www.un.org/documents/ga/res/48/a48r104.htm).

UN (2005) *Report of the Special Representative of the Secretary General for Children and Armed Conflict* (A/60/335), Geneva: United Nations (available at http://www.unicef.org/emerg/files/report_SRSG_cac.pdf).

WHO (2005) *Multi-Country Study on Women's Health and Domestic Violence Against Women*, Geneva: World Health Organization.

Zaman, H. (1999) 'Violence against women in Bangladesh: Issues and responses', *Women's Studies International Forum*, 22(1): 37–48.

9.2 Conflict, development and aid

Tim Unwin

As I write, US-led military forces continue to seek to impose the will of their governments on the people of Iraq, at an estimated cost to the USA alone of some US$318 billion since 2001 (http://www.infoplease.com/ipa/A0933935.html, accessed 9 October 2006). The 31,000 UK-led NATO forces that comprise the International Security Assistance Force do likewise in Afghanistan as they try to improve the capacity of President Hamid Karzai's government to rule, and thus to enable reconstruction and development to take place. In Sudan, it is estimated that more than 400,000 people have been killed and 2.5 million have been displaced in the genocide in Darfur (http://www.genocideintervention.net, accessed 9 October 2006).

War and conflict are commonplace. They always have been. They are one of the central features of human existence. Yet until recently they have all too often been ignored in academic discourses on development (although see for example Middleton and O'Keefe 1998). One of the central arguments of this contribution is that we need to understand the human horrors of war and conflict if we are truly to grapple with the complexity of 'development'. For millions of people across the world, conflict and violence are as much parts of daily life as are going to school, shopping in the supermarket, or surfing the World Wide Web for people in Western Europe or North America (Unwin 1994).

War is a notoriously difficult notion to define. At its most basic, the idea of war implies conflict and the acceptance of people being killed. But conflict of what kind? Does it have to be armed conflict? Do certain numbers of people have to be involved? Do people always have to be killed in war? Furthermore, even when more precise definitions of warfare are adopted, it is difficult to reach general agreement on what any one particular kind of conflict actually is. As the ongoing military interventions in Iraq and Afghanistan so clearly indicate, a peacekeeping operation in one person's mind is often seen as a repressive act of violence to somebody else. One of the most widely accepted classifications of armed conflicts in the 1990s was that adopted by the Stockholm International Peace Research Institute (SIPRI) (see also Craft 1999). As Williams (1994) emphasized, SIPRI subdivided the majority of post-1945 conflicts other than those associated with de-colonization into three categories. First, there were inter-state conflicts, which have generally been relatively rare phenomena, but which have, for example, included the Gulf War (1990–91) between the US-led coalition and Iraq following the latter's invasion of Kuwait, and the conflict between Pakistan and India in 1998. Second, there were internal conflicts. These have been the most frequent category of conflict in the post-1945 period, and involve disputes over control of government by an armed opposition, often with the intervention of external powers. Third, there were state formation conflicts, involving non-government forces seeking to secede or change the constitutional status of territory, with recent examples including the violence that came to a peak in East Timor in 1999, as well as the conflicts in Chechnya during the late 1990s and the beginning of the twenty-first century. Interestingly, SIPRI (2006) has highlighted that non-state actors have recently become increasingly prominent in conflicts, and notes that the international community has had only limited success in dealing with these, thereby giving rise to serious concern.

Another recent attempt to grapple with the complexity of warfare and political instability in the contemporary world has been the introduction of the term 'complex political emergencies', or CPEs. These have been described as a shorthand expression of conflicts which combine some or all of the following: conflict within and across state boundaries, political origins, protracted duration, social cleavages and predatory social formations (Goodhand and Hulme 1999; see also Cliffe and Luckham 1999). As Goodhand and Hulme (1999: 23) emphasize, 'Contemporary conflicts are not events with clear beginnings and ends, but are an element of a broader process of social change which is turbulent, discontinuous and the result of combinations of contingent factors.' As such, their resolutions can never be easy, and must lie largely within the societies in which they occur.

However we choose to define warfare and conflict, it is evident that it is something that is endemic to human society. The naive optimism with which some world leaders acclaimed the end of the cold war during the late 1980s, was short-lived. Economists such as Clements, Gupta and Schiff (1997) were swift to cite evidence for a real peace dividend in the early 1990s, with world-wide military expenditure falling from 3.6 per cent of world GDP in 1990 to 2.4 per cent in 1995, thereby giving a total saving of some US$720 billion since 1985. However, the peaceful expectations that surrounded the dawn of a new millennium were swiftly shattered, in large part as a direct result of US global interventionist policy. In the wake of the attacks on the USA by suicide bombers affiliated with Al-Qaeda on 11 September 2001, President Bush thus identified Iraq, Iran and North Korea as an 'axis of evil' in his January 2002 State of the Union address, in which he also vowed that the USA 'will not permit the world's most dangerous regimes to threaten us with the world's most destructive weapons' (http://www.whitehouse.gov/news/releases/2002/01/20020129-11.html, accessed 9 October 2006). As Bush claimed at the beginning of his address, 'As we gather tonight, our nation is at war, our economy is in recession, and the civilized world faces unprecedented dangers.' In 2005, world military expenditure rose 3.4 per cent over the previous year, and totalled some US$1118 billion, 47 per cent of which was accounted for by the USA (SIPRI 2006). Far from there being a 'peace dividend', the 1990s and early 2000s therefore witnessed increasing political instability and fragmentation across many areas of the world, with little sign of their abatement. Alongside tendencies towards an increasingly global economy and a new world order (for contrasting views of this see Fukuyama 1992; Huntington 1996), violence, death and all the horrors associated with conflict continue to dominate the lives of millions of people across the globe. SIPRI (2006) thus reported that there were 17 major internal armed conflicts across the world in 2005, and although this figure has steadily declined from a high of 25 in 1998, it still emphasizes that the rhetoric of peace and the reality of war remain very far apart in international diplomacy. Such conflicts are no respecters of persons, and at least six million children were killed or maimed in armed conflicts during the 1990s (for a wider discussion of child soldiers see Goodwin-Gill and Cohn 1994; for the linkages between war and hunger see Macrae and Zwi 1994; Messer et al. 1998).

The increased attention that has been paid to governance agendas in the first decade of the twenty-first century gives rise to some hope that these issues are indeed being addressed both by the governments of poor countries and also by the international 'development' community of donors, civil society organizations and global organizations (Trivedy 2001; de Zeeuw and Kumar 2006). The World Bank has thus placed considerable emphasis on responding to conflict, particularly in Africa, where it notes that one-fifth of Africans now live in countries severely disrupted by conflict, and that 15 million Africans were internally displaced in 2005, with another 4.5 million having sought refuge in neighbouring countries (http://web.worldbank.org/WBSITE/EXTERNAL/COUNTRIES/AFRICAEXT/0,,contentMDK:20266621~menuPK:537816~pagePK:146736~piPK:226340~theSitePK:258644,00.html, accessed 9 October 2006). The UK's latest White Paper on International Development, published in 2006, likewise focuses explicitly on ways in which better governance can be used to help the world's poor (http://www.dfid.gov.uk/wp2006/default.asp, accessed 9 October 2006). However, it is often very difficult to respond to the needs of poor people in conflict zones. Governments at war frequently do not want external agencies, be they civil society organizations or donors, to get involved in supporting those who are suffering (see Willett 2001), especially when they might take up arms once more. The continuing crisis in Darfur is but one example of this. It is also evident that aid interventions, especially when they are associated with so-called peacekeeping operations, can have unintended consequences, leading to increased immiseration among those for whom the aid is actually intended (see Aoi et al. 2007). This is typified by problems with the so-called three-block war model recently adopted by the USA (Farhoumand-Sims 2007), which seeks to combine the delivery of humanitarian aid with peace support operations and high-intensity fighting. As Farhoumand-Sims (2007) comments, this model is deeply flawed because of the impossibility of combining peace building while conducting violent warfare, the lack of engagement of local actors in peace building, and the increasing exclusion of women.

The role of the World Food Programme (WFP) in providing aid on the ground in conflict zones typifies many of the issues that need to be addressed at the interface between conflict and aid (Gelsdorf et al. 2007). The WFP began providing aid in Sudan in 1963, and since then both the needs of the people and the amount of food delivered has grown dramatically. Whereas in 1998 some 200,000 tonnes of food aid was supplied to Sudan, this figure had grown to 900,000 tonnes in 2005, more than three-quarters of which was provided by the WFP. However, as Gelsdorf et al. (2007: S2) highlight, 'In many cases food aid is not even the factor most central to the survival of crisis-affected groups. Competing demands on the available relief assistance – combined with poor road infrastructure, the long distances involved and the inhospitable climate – mean that food aid often has a relatively small impact on the ability of disaster-affected people to access food.' This realization is now forcing such agencies to turn their attention as much to trying to protect livelihoods in conflict zones as it is to providing life-saving food. However, it is extremely difficult to prevent the destruction of crops and other means of livelihood in conflict zones. As Messer et al. (1998) emphasised a decade ago, 'Conflict destroys land, water, biological, and social resources for food production, while military expenditures lower investments in health, education, agriculture, and environmental protection'. Once conflict has ceased, there is also a pressing need to ensure that the bases for enabling people to restore their livelihoods are put in place as soon as possible. De Zeeuw and Kumar (2006) thus emphasize the importance of institutional rebuilding, particularly with respect to elections, free media and human rights, in ensuring that this can occur. Nevertheless, as Muggah (2006: 267) reminds us, 'The post-conflict environment – whether ushered in by a significant reduction in direct mortality, the signing of a peace agreement, the deployment of a peacekeeping force, an arbitrary period of time, or the holding of national elections – is unstable.' He therefore concludes that the introduction of disarmament, demobilization and reintegration (DDR) alongside weapons reduction is essential to any reconstruction policy, whether or not this is supported by international donors.

Much academic research on governance agendas tends to be on the negative impacts that conflicts have on economic growth, the dominant contemporary leitmotiv of development practice, instead of on the moral arguments against violence and war that this chapter has sought to emphasize. It is likely that violence and war will always be with us, but rather than fuelling these conflicts, there is a powerful argument that arms-producing countries should make much greater efforts than they are already doing to limit their production of weapons of all kinds, and likewise to restrict their distribution. Instead of being seen as something extraordinary, we need to incorporate an understanding of conflict and violence as being commonplace to the changes taking place in the world today. Rather than ignoring war, we need to confront it. Only then will we be able to devise mechanisms which can effectively reduce the levels of deprivation, misery and psychological anguish that are caused by its practice.

GUIDE TO FURTHER READING

The following texts and source books provide useful material for exploring further the issues highlighted in this chapter.

Cliffe, L. (ed.) (1999) *Complex Political Emergencies*, special issue of *Third World Quarterly*, 20(1). This special issue provides very useful case study material of conflicts in Central America, Sri Lanka, the Horn of Africa, Sierra Leone, Liberia and Mozambique, as well as theoretical accounts of complex political emergencies.

Craft, C. (1999) *Weapons for Peace, Weapons for War: The Effect of Arms Transfers on War Outbreak, Involvement, and Outcomes*, New York: Routledge. This provides a useful account of the various trade-offs between weapons sales and the probability of conflict.

SIPRI (Stockholm International Peace Research Institute) (annual) *SIPRI Yearbook*, Oxford: Oxford University Press (summaries available at http://www.sipri.org). These yearbooks provide a wealth of useful data on armaments, disarmament and international society, as well as comprehensive essays on key issues relating to conflict and arms control.

REFERENCES

Aoi, C., de Coning, C. and Thakur, R. (eds) (2007) *Unintended Consequences of Peacekeeping Operations*, Tokyo: United Nations University Press.

Clements, B., Gupta, S. and Schiff, J. (1997) 'What happened to the Peace Dividend?', *Finance and Development*, March: 17–19.

Cliffe, L. and Luckham, R. (1999) 'Complex political emergencies and the state: failure and the fate of the state', *Third World Quarterly*, 20(1): 27–50.

Craft, C. (1999) *Weapons for Peace, Weapons for War: The Effect of Arms Transfers on War Outbreak, Involvement, and Outcomes*, New York: Routledge.

De Zeeuw, J. and Kumar, K. (eds) (2006) *Promoting Democracy in Postconflict Societies*, Boulder, CO: Rienner.

Farhoumand-Sims, C. (2007) 'The negative face of the militarization of aid', *Human Security Bulletin*, 5(1): unpaginated (www.humansecurity.info/page448.htm).

Fukuyama, F. (1992) *The End of History and the Last Man*, New York: Free Press.

Gelsdorf, K., Walker, P. and Maxwell, D. (2007) 'Editorial: the future of WFP programming in Sudan', *Disasters*, 31: S1–S8.

Goodhand, J. and Hulme, D. (1999) 'From wars to complex political emergencies: understanding conflict and peace building in the new world disorder', *Third World Quarterly*, 20(1): 13–26.

Goodwin-Gill, G. and Cohn, I. (1994) *Child Soldiers: The Role of Children in Armed Conflicts*, Oxford: Clarendon Press.

Huntington, S. (1996) *The Clash of Civilizations and the Remaking of World Order*, New York: Simon and Schuster.

Keegan, J. (1993) *A History of Warfare*, New York: Vintage Books.

Macrae, J. and Zwi, A. (eds) (1994) *War and Hunger: Rethinking International Responses to Complex Emergencies*, London: Zed Books.

Messer, E., Cohen, M.J. and D'Costa, J. (1998) 'Food from peace: Breaking the links between conflict and hunger', Washington, DC: IFPRI (IFPRI 2020 Brief, No. 50).

Middleton, N. and O'Keefe, P. (1998) *Disaster and Development: the Politics of Humanitarian Aid*, London: Pluto Press.

Muggah, R. (2005) 'Managing "post-conflict" zones', in *Small Arms Survey Yearbook 2005: Weapons at War*, Geneva: Small Arms Survey, pp. 267–301.

SIPRI (Stockholm International Peace Research Institute) (2006) *SIPRI Yearbook 2006: Armaments, Disarmament and International Security*, Oxford: Oxford University Press.

Trivedy, R. (2001) 'Conflict prevention, resolution and management – Improving coordination for more elective action', *IDS Bulletin*, 32(2): 79–88.

Unwin, T. (1994) 'States, wars and elections: the political structure of development', in T. Unwin (ed.) *Atlas of World Development*, Chichester: Wiley, pp. 239–40.

Willett, S. (ed.) (2001) *Structural Conflict in the New Global Order: Insecurity and Development*, Brighton: IDS (*IDS Bulletin*, 32(2), alumni issue).

Williams, S.W. (1994) 'Warfare', in T. Unwin (ed.) *Atlas of World Development*, Chichester: Wiley, pp. 252–3.

9.3 Refugees

Richard Black

Introduction

The relevance of a chapter on refugees in a compendium on development may not be immediately obvious. The plight of refugees might be seen, at best, as irrelevant to the goals of international development agencies. Instead, specialized international institutions are concerned with refugees, notably the United Nations High Commission for Refugees (UNHCR). At worst, the production of refugees might be seen as the *opposite* of development, especially as development has come to be defined more in terms of human rights, democracy and the rule of law.

Yet refugees are more than simply symptoms of the absence of development. Analysis of refugee flows both within the developing world and from 'South' to 'North' throws up discourses, policies and socio-economic processes that directly parallel wider development issues. In this context, interesting opportunities exist for enhanced learning and understanding in both directions between 'refugee studies' and 'development studies'.

Defining refugees

Refugees exist in both North and South. In the North, they are commonly defined (by states) according to the 1951 Geneva Convention on refugees, as those who have a well-founded fear of being persecuted for reasons of race, religion, nationality, membership of a particular social group or political opinion. In contrast, in many Southern countries a wider definition is often employed, as in Africa where 'victims of war or external aggression' are included, and accordingly far greater numbers proportionally are held to fall within the purview of 'refugee policy'. Based mainly on government figures, which involve a mixture of these two definitions, the UNHCR estimated that at the end of 2005 there were some 8.4 million refugees worldwide. Of these, 31 per cent were in Africa and 36 per cent in Asia. There were also a further 688,000 asylum seekers, mostly in Europe and North America – those who had claimed refugee status but whose claims were not yet recognized (UNHCR 2006).

Such geographical variations in the definition of who is a refugee stand as an initial warning of the lack of robustness of the category, and the potential for confusion. Indeed, there have been attempts both to narrow and to widen the definition of refugees. States in both the North and, increasingly, the South, have sought to justify more restrictive immigration policies, by cracking down on those they label as 'bogus' asylum seekers. The result has been a progressive narrowing of practical applications of the refugee definition, with a parallel reduction in the number of refugees reported by UNHCR. Refugees are emphatically not seen as those left behind by 'development' even if ongoing wars have prevented the return of some who fail to meet the narrow interpretation of the refugee definition employed by Northern states.

At the same time, though, moves have come from both academic and policy quarters to widen the refugee definition – or at least to focus on the broader issue of 'forced migration' rather than a narrow definition of 'refugees'. As a result, terms such as 'internally displaced person' (IDP), 'environmental refugee', 'relocatee' and even 'economic refugee' have entered the literature. For example, some 6.6 million IDPs were either protected or assisted by the UNHCR in 2005 – in effect, treated as if they were refugees – while the Internal Displacement Monitoring Centre estimated that 23.7 million IDPs existed worldwide in 2005. Estimates of the number of 'environmental refugees' range from 10 to 25 million, though such estimates – and indeed the concept itself – have been criticized widely. Although far from unproblematic in themselves, these additional categories of forced migration testify to the overlapping causes and consequences of migration. These range from situations of forced displacement across international borders as a result of essentially political events, to instances where state borders are not crossed, or environmental degradation, large-scale development schemes or economic crisis play a significant role in producing migration.

A major part of this difficulty in defining refugees is the dual context in which the term is used. In the policy world, the term 'refugee' is first and foremost a legal category. It confers rights to protection, but also to assistance, and possibly the right to stay in a country that offers far better conditions in terms of its economic opportunities or human rights record (Shacknove 1985). Yet the transplanting of the term to social science as a term with any explanatory power or analytical worth requires at the very least a consistent application of the term by policymakers, and preferably a conceptual basis that remains independent of its policy implementation. It is far from clear that either exists. Even a simple division of migration into 'forced' (refugees) and 'voluntary' (not refugees) is problematic, as people who are displaced have varying degrees of choice over when, where and how to move, even in conditions of extreme crisis.

Explaining forced migration

If the term 'refugee' itself is not self-explanatory, the next step is to explore different explanations of forced migration, to see whether any more consistency can be found. One view is that increasing numbers of refugees and forced migrants are the result of a breakdown of order in a post-cold war world. During the cold war, there was a perception in the West that refugees were mainly those fleeing persecution under communist regimes, even if some observers recognized that proxy wars being fought between the USA and the Soviet bloc had also produced mass flows of refugees in Africa and Asia. In contrast, in the post-cold war world, the 'security' of superpower rivalry is argued to have given way to a much more localized and bloody series of wars and internal conflicts. In these new wars, 'tribal' or 'ethnic' hatreds are seen as driving an ever-expanding number of refugees out of their homes. This is linked to environmental degradation caused by poverty, conflicts over increasingly scarce natural resources and a declining commitment to development aid among the world's leading donor nations.

Such a perspective, at the very least, suggests that moves to draw up typologies of refugees and forced migrants, and to identify the distinguishing features of different categories, may be misplaced. From this standpoint, the wars that cause displacement increasingly mix political, economic, social and environmental factors. The result is a new vicious circle of poverty, violence and displacement that makes a rigid categorization of refugees as 'political', 'economic' or 'environmental' highly problematic. Meanwhile, as poverty, violence and displacement are interlinked, the promotion of development – especially a pro-poor, pro-human rights and pro-good governance version of development – might be seen as a potential solution to the world's 'refugee crisis'. Yet much as it is compelling, such a perspective arguably misses both the main causes of forced migration and the importance of the links between refugees and development.

A first clue is provided by the one form of forced migration that does not fit neatly into the downward spiral hypothesis of poverty, violence and displacement – namely, so-called 'development-induced displacement'. Those who have been displaced by dams and other major public works bear many of the hallmarks of the refugee – they are forced to leave their homes and land, often at short notice and with little or no compensation. Yet by definition their flight is caused not by a lack of development, but by 'development' itself, albeit a particular vision of what development should be.

A number of major wars that have produced refugees in the last decade can be seen not as conflicts of poverty, but as wars driven by political elites seeking power over resources, territory or the state (or all three). In Bosnia, the war was between nationalist leaders, fighting for control of territory and access to lucrative business opportunities in the post-communist era. In Rwanda, the genocide can be seen as rooted in colonial oppression and state-sponsored violence. In both cases, ethnic rivalries were deliberately inflamed by leaders intent on gaining and/or maintaining power. Where environmental factors are relevant, it is often an abundance, rather than a lack of natural resources that leads to conflict. Thus in the Congo, Angola, Sierra Leone and Liberia, access to major deposits of diamonds, oil and other minerals has both caused and sustained long-running conflicts which have displaced millions of people. Meanwhile, external intervention has often been neither absent nor benign, as Western companies (and even, in some cases, aid agencies and 'peace-keeping' forces) have played a partisan role in bolstering the position of one or more of the warring factions.

Refugees and the discourse of development

The above discussion suggests that there are links between development and the production of forced migration, even if the latter is not the simple consequence of the former, or its absence or failure. Meanwhile, such links do not stop at the causes of refugee flight. In their responses to the humanitarian crises created by massive refugee flows, international aid agencies and donor governments have mirrored the policy shifts that have occurred in the development field. They have also used similar representations of the 'other' as they try to promote what Silk has described as 'caring at a distance' (Silk 1997). This leads us to probe further the connections between refugee and development discourse.

In the 1980s, discussion of the need to promote a 'relief to development continuum' was laudable in principle. Yet it led to grandiose projects for refugee resettlement based on development ideas that were already well out of date. In a review of over 100 such schemes in Africa since 1962, Kibreab (1989) found that just nine had reached the point of self-sufficiency by 1982. In the 1990s, in refugee assistance, attention shifted to the basic needs of refugees – food, water, shelter and health care – before moving on to a growing concern with environmental awareness and ensuring the sustainability of emergency interventions (Black 1998). Yet, at each stage, external interventions have been dogged by bureaucratic, technical and political problems, linked in grand part to a failure to heed the warnings derived from development experience.

Yet another, and arguably more important, element of these problems of refugee (and development) assistance has been the characterization of both the intended recipients of aid (passive, powerless, poor) and the problem itself (technical, unicausal, easily defined). Although development and refugee agencies have grappled with how to promote the participation of 'beneficiaries' in assistance programmes, it has proven difficult to break a pattern that Harrell-Bond (1986) describes as simply 'imposing aid'. Indeed, international humanitarian agencies have their own political and bureaucratic motives for involvement in refugee assistance, which may be far from benign or disinterested.

In this sense, refugee situations provide us with similar dilemmas and challenges to the broader development scene – how to deal with complex situations, in which poverty and need are not simply technical issues, but also political ones. Humanitarian aid may be driven as much by supply (excess food stocks, defence of strategic interests, guilt) as by demand (i.e. hunger or poverty). Increasing amounts of aid are provided by non-governmental organizations (NGOs), whose numbers have mushroomed. Around 250 NGOs are estimated to have operated in Albania and FYR Macedonia at the time of the Kosovo crisis in the late 1990s, causing immense coordination problems. The proliferation of agencies is encouraged by donor policies that favour the channelling of funds through NGOs.

It is important to hold up to scrutiny the role and motivations of these aid givers, as much as those who receive assistance. For example, while there has been some progress towards the definition of minimum standards for humanitarian assistance agencies, there is little to prevent NGOs from moving into refugee emergencies, whatever their objectives or capabilities. The results can be disastrous, as was seen in the 1994–96 emergency in eastern Zaire, when uncontrolled international agency activity may well have contributed to suffering, rather than relieving it. At the same time, whether we are concerned with emergencies or not, the task of engaging with recipients of aid requires us to understand people's own strategies and constraints, and resist the temptation to categorize and stereotype.

GUIDE TO FURTHER READING

Ager, A. (ed.) (1999) *Refugees: Perspectives on the Experience of Forced Migration*, London: Cassell Academic. This edited collection contains papers from a range of anthropological, sociological and psychosocial perspectives.

Black, R. (1998) *Refugees, Environment and Development*, London: Longman. Provides a critical analysis of both the growing literature on environmental causes of migration and attempts to make refugee assistance more closely linked to sustainable development priorities.

Harrell-Bond, B.H. (1986) *Imposing Aid: Emergency Assistance to Refugees*, Oxford: Oxford University Press. A classic study, which had a major impact across the field of refugee studies. It provides a detailed anthropological account of the situation of Ugandan refugees in southern Sudan in the mid-1980s.

Hyndman, J. (2000) *Managing Displacement: Refugees and the Politics of Humanitarianism*, Minneapolis: University of Minnesota Press. An in-depth account of humanitarian issues, informed by field research among refugees in Kenya in the 1990s.

UNHCR (2006) *The State of the World's Refugees – Humanitarian Displacement in the New Millennium*, Oxford: Oxford University Press. Sets out basic facts and figures about refugees worldwide, and looks back on the organization's history.

Zolberg, A. and Benda, P. (2001) *Global Migrants, Global Refugees: Problems and Solutions*, Oxford: Berghahn Books. This edited collection places the study of refugees within the wider context of international migration.

USEFUL WEBSITES

Forced migration online: http://www.forcedmigration.org
UNHCR: http://www.unhcr.org
Relief Web: http://www.reliefweb.int

REFERENCES

Black, R. (1998) *Refugees, Environment and Development*, Harlow: Longman.

Cohen, R. and Deng, F. (1998) *Masses in Flight: The Global Crisis of Internal Displacement*, Washington, DC: Brookings Institution Press.

Harrell-Bond, B.H. (1986) *Imposing Aid: Emergency Assistance to Refugees*, Oxford: Oxford University Press.

Kibreab, G. (1989) 'Local settlements in Africa: A misconceived option?', *Journal of Refugee Studies*, 2(4): 468–90.

Shacknove, A. (1985) 'Who is a refugee?', *Ethics*, 95(2): 274–84.

Silk, J. (1997) *The Roles of Place, Interaction and Community in Caring for Distant Others*, Geographical Papers No. 121, University of Reading, Department of Geography.

UNHCR (2006) *2005 Global Refugee Trends*, Geneva: United Nations High Commission for Refugees (available at http://www.unhcr.org/statistics/STATISTICS/4486ceb12.pdf).

United Nations Development Programme (2000) *Human Development Report 2000*, Oxford: Oxford University Press.

9.4 Humanitarian aid

Phil O'Keefe and Joanne Rose

Background

Humanitarian aid is the assistance given to people in distress, by individuals, organizations or governments, with the core purpose of preventing and alleviating human suffering.

The principles of humanitarian intervention are impartiality, neutrality and independence. Impartiality means no discrimination on the basis of nationality, race, religious beliefs, class, gender or political opinions: humanitarian interventions are guided by needs. Neutrality demands that humanitarian agencies do not take sides in either hostilities or ideological controversy. Independence requires that humanitarian agencies retain their autonomy of action. These principles, originally drawn up for war, and consolidated in humanitarian law expressed in the Geneva Convention of 1949, underlie response to conflict-related and natural disasters.

The international humanitarian system consists, principally, of four sets of actors: donor governments, including the European Commission Humanitarian Office (ECHO); the United Nations; the International Red Cross and Red Crescent Movement (ICRC); and international non-governmental organizations (INGOs). Local NGOs and beneficiaries have little voice in the system.

Since the early 1990s, there has been both an increase in the number of disasters and a change in the nature of emergencies, leading to a substantial increase in humanitarian assistance. Natural disasters have grown in number, largely due to increased climate variability. Complex emergencies (conflict) have increased, particularly since the end of the cold war, and these are now characterized by high levels of civilian casualty, deliberate destruction of livelihoods and welfare systems, collapse of the rule of law and large numbers of displaced people (8.4 million refugees and 23.7 million internally displaced persons (IDPs) as of December 2005 (UNHCR 2006).

Emergencies have changed in nature from predominantly natural disasters, dominated by flood and drought, to complex emergencies and technological disasters. The war on terror, following events on 11 September 2001, and the subsequent interventions in Afghanistan and Iraq, have created new challenges for the implementation of humanitarian assistance.

The increasing frequency and changing face of emergencies has caused humanitarian expenditures to soar. Total humanitarian assistance reached an all-time high in 2003, at US$7.8 billion – a rise of over US$2 billion compared with the previous year. In real terms, humanitarian aid from the Organization for Economic Cooperation and Development's (OECD) Development Assistance Committee (DAC) rose by 23 per cent in 2003 (Development Initiatives 2005). (DAC is a forum of major bilateral donors with 23 members, including the Commission of the European Communities and the USA.) These figures do not account for charitable donations from individuals or groups, such as churches, and they do not capture non-Western assistance, such as that provided by Islamic entities.

The United Nations, as lead agency, has an effective division of labour that sees the Office for the Coordination of Humanitarian Assistance (OCHA) in charge of the policy and planning framework; the World Food Programme (WFP) responsible for emergency food delivery and logistics; the United Nations High Commission for Refugees (UNHCR) responsible for shelter; the United Nations Children's (Emergency) Fund (UNICEF) responsible for nutrition, water and sanitation; and the Food and Agriculture Organization (FAO) responsible for emergency agriculture, which, if successful, should mark the end of the emergency and the diminution of the role of WFP. Medical interventions are largely left to international NGOs and the Red Cross.

Four key challenges to humanitarian assistance since the cold war

Four challenges dominate discussions of humanitarian assistance. These are explored below.

Where does global leadership in the planning and implementation of humanitarian assistance lie?

The short answer is with the United Nations system, through the OCHA. In 1991, the United Nations General Assembly adopted Resolution 46/182, which led to the establishment of the Department of Humanitarian Affairs; OCHA had its origins in this system, which is designed for the 'prompt and smooth delivery of relief assistance'. The two critical mechanisms for this coordination are the sharing of a Common Humanitarian Action Plan (CHAP) by all humanitarian actors, including those such as ICRC, which are not under the United Nations humanitarian effort, and the Consolidated Appeals Process (CAP). The latter is the critical fund-raising effort for humanitarian aid, although donor response, particularly in protracted African crises, tends to be poor, undermining delivery according to need.

The Central Emergency Response Fund was officially launched by the United Nations in March 2006. It is hoped this fund will address problems associated with the CAP, but will not detract from voluntary contributions to humanitarian programmes, nor replace the consolidated appeals process or additional funding channels. Rather, it is meant to mitigate the unevenness and delays of voluntary contributions and provide funding to under-supported operations.

Although OCHA, on behalf of the United Nations, provides leadership, it is leadership as a coordinating function, and not as a 'command-and-control' structure, as in most emergency situations. To do this requires building shared platforms of information from the different parts of the humanitarian system (evidence of these platforms can be sourced through www.reliefweb.int). The figure outlines these shared platforms and, by implication, maps the flow of funds. While the United Nations, as the lead global humanitarian actor, is frequently heavily criticized for poor performance, there is no doubt that for global reach it remains the key player. If it did not exist, it would have to be invented.

How does humanitarian assistance link across the broader issues of development?

The transition from relief to development, also known as the 'gap issue' or 'grey area', has been debated internationally since around 1990, initially in the hope that a smooth 'continuum', linking the three phases of relief, rehabilitation and development, could be achieved. By the mid-1990s, it was widely accepted that no such continuum was feasible and that elements of all three phases could best be implemented simultaneously.

Humanitarian aid remains organized around short-term, largely project-based, funding cycles, and the concept that emergencies are temporary interruptions of normal processes. It is true that humanitarian aid has been provided for long periods to populations of countries characterized by chronic conflicts (such as Afghanistan, Angola, Burundi, Liberia, Mozambique, Sierra Leone, Somalia and Sudan); however, the humanitarian system is essentially ill-equipped to engage with long-term crises, which can continue for decades and whose effects may stretch across an entire country and/or countries within a region. The humanitarian system is arguably already fully stretched.

In striving to close the gap between relief, rehabilitation and development assistance, several donors, like Sweden, have taken the view that the distinction between development and humanitarian relief obstructs recovery. More widely, the view is that careful coordination at and among all levels is the appropriate framework. One workable version came to become accepted from the late 1990s, and is referred to as 'humanitarian aid plus'.

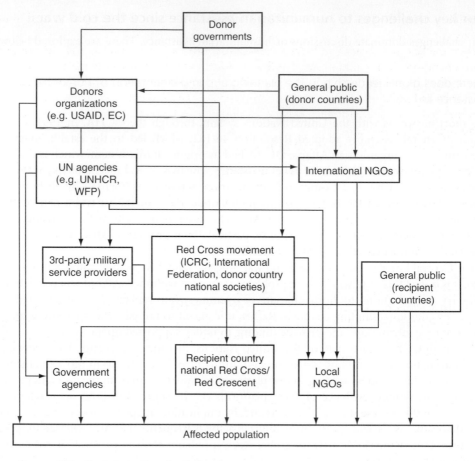

Resource flows within the international relief system
Source: Hallam 1998

Humanitarian aid plus was developed through the realization that basic needs alone were not sufficient to secure a durable, beneficial outcome from an emergency. It seeks to support progress to more developmental activities. It was hoped that, through linking relief to rehabilitation and development, the likelihood of further humanitarian need would be reduced: development would prevent conflict and humanitarian need. Humanitarian agencies looked to 'developmental relief' as a route towards this aim. This was obstructed by four obstacles:

1 humanitarian agencies have little influence;
2 there was little commitment to a radical redesign of the development and humanitarian assistance components of organizations;
3 protracted emergencies became even more intractable;
4 donors sometimes used humanitarian aid to avoid engagement with repressive or undemocratic states (Macrae and Harmer 2005).

How does humanitarian action, especially in complex emergencies, relate to military intervention?

The most significant development in humanitarian action since the cold war has been the increase in violent conflict. The *World Disasters Report* (IFRC 2001) estimated that, between 1991 and 2000,

2.3 million people lost their lives in conflict situations, compared to 665,598 who died in natural disasters.

Over the last two decades, military interventions have become commonplace within humanitarian operations. This encroachment of 'humanitarian space' led to significant questions of principle and policy, and subsequently resulted in the *Oslo Guidelines* (OCHA 1994), outlining the use of civilian and military assets in natural and technological disasters. The problem remains, however, that military intervention threatens the neutrality of humanitarian action and the humanitarian workers themselves.

Key principles for military involvement are:

- complementarity, which implies that the military will not be used if civilian assets are available;
- control of the military in support of humanitarian action must be the responsibility of civil authority;
- no costs associated with the military can be charged to the affected population;
- the military must withdraw at the earliest possible moment.

The use of the military raises wider issues in humanitarian aid, especially whether humanitarian assistance is independent of foreign policy. It is how humanitarian practice unfolds that allows a typology of donors and agencies. Broadly speaking, they are classified as Wilsonian (after Woodrow Wilson) and Dunantist (after Jean Henri Dunant). The former are dependent on, and cooperative with, government, while the latter are more independent of, and oppositional towards, government: the former emphasize delivery, the latter advocacy (ODI 2003).

How can humanitarian performance, and consequent accountability, be measured?

The increasing number of emergencies since the mid-1980s, and ever-inflating aid budgets, have been joined by a growth in international awareness of humanitarian emergencies. The media became capable of propelling complex emergencies and human suffering into the public spotlight. Consequently, many questions were raised, and aid agencies suffered mounting pressure to improve performance and be accountable for their actions.

In response, the ICRC developed the 'Code of Conduct for the International Red Cross and Red Crescent Movement and NGOs in Disaster Relief' in 1991. This document provides guiding principles for non-governmental interventions in humanitarian response. Adhesion to the Code is voluntary; however, it was agreed on by eight of the world's largest disaster response agencies in 1994, and currently has 381 signatories. Following this was the publication of the Steering Committee of the Joint Evaluation of Emergency Assistance to Rwanda (1996), which marked a turning point for the accountability and quality agenda, as all humanitarian actors acknowledge that they failed in delivering appropriate interventions; this is not dissimilar to the more recent multi-agency tsunami evaluation (Telford, Cosgrave and Houghton 2006), which comes to a similar conclusion.

Since 1996, the humanitarian sector has undertaken a range of initiatives, aimed at improving accountability and performance. The initiatives in the humanitarian field were also driven by wider changes in Western politics and public-sector management, whereby attention shifted to questions of the effectiveness of and accountability for public expenditure. Starting in the 1990s, Western democracies aimed to counter declining trust in government and public administration, by applying new management techniques, including the introduction of elaborate systems to monitor publicly funded activities, and to ensure quality output. The initiatives undertaken were:

- ALNAP, the Active Learning Network for Accountability and Performance in Humanitarian Action (1997), whose aim is to improve performance in the humanitarian sector and share best practice;

- HAPI, the Humanitarian Accountability Partnership International (2003), which is striving to improve the accountability of members to the beneficiaries of humanitarian assistance (it is a culmination of earlier accountability initiatives, including the Humanitarian Ombudsman Project, established in Kosovo in 1997, and the Humanitarian Accountability Project, which began in 2000);
- the Sphere Project (1997), a Humanitarian Charter and Handbook which outlines a humanitarian charter relating to the basic requirements needed to sustain life and dignity, and a Handbook of Minimum Standards which quantified these basic requirements;
- People in Aid Code (1997, revised 2003), which provides humanitarian agencies with a framework for assessing and improving their human resource management.

Until recently, there was no consensus about how donors should use their procedures to improve humanitarian response. Donor policy and approaches were often driven by political interest rather than according to need, and, overall, accountability mechanisms and transparency were weak (Harmer, Cotterrell and Stoddard 2004).

The Good Humanitarian Donorship initiative (GHDi), which was endorsed by 16 donor governments and a number of humanitarian agencies (Stockholm, June 2003), hopes to enhance donor accountability, by ensuring that the responses of donors are effective, equitable and consistent with the humanitarian principles of humanity, impartiality, neutrality and independence. *Principles and Good Practice of Humanitarian Donorship* were endorsed by Australia, Belgium, Canada, the European Commission, Finland, France, Germany, Ireland, Japan, Luxembourg, The Netherlands, Norway, Sweden, Switzerland, the UK and the USA. Others involved in creating the initiative included the DAC, UN agencies, the ICRC, INGOs and a number of academics.

Recurrent themes

Beyond the four key challenges, a number of recurrent themes exist throughout humanitarian assistance, including the impact of HIV/AIDS on humanitarian action, delivery of aid to internally displaced persons (IDPs), and the ability and right to protection. These themes highlight the difficulties in delivering appropriate humanitarian response despite good intentions.

HIV/AIDS

In 2003, 3 million people died of HIV/AIDS and the pandemic is turning into a large-scale chronic disaster. Rehabilitating agriculture marks the end of emergency aid and a return to development. The advancing HIV/AIDS epidemic has produced 'new variant famine', where lack of labour retards that transition and creates food insecurity (Waal and Tumushabe 2003).

The spread of HIV/AIDS is also of concern in complex emergencies (situations of armed conflict). The risk of HIV infection is exacerbated by the high incidence of sexual violence and sexual exploitation in conflict situations. Humanitarian interventions must recognize the importance of providing aid appropriate to, and which protects the rights of, people living with HIV/AIDS. The Inter-Agency Standing Committee (ISAC, a forum involving key UN and non-UN humanitarian partners) has produced the *Guidelines for HIV/AIDS Interventions in Emergency Settings* (revised 2003), which aims to integrate HIV/AIDS components into all relevant programming areas.

Internally displaced persons

Internally displaced persons (IDPs) are people who have been forced from their homes as a result of armed conflict or violence. Unlike refugees, whose movement across national borders provides them with special status in international law, with rights specific to their situation, IDPs have no such entitlement (Deng 1998) (the legal position of IDPs in terms of existing human rights and humanitarian law was established in the United Nations Guiding Principles on Internal Displacement). Humanitarian assistance is thus limited, in principle, to supportive actions undertaken with the consent of the country in question. Where governments are unable or unwilling, however, to provide protection to IDPs, humanitarian organizations have sought to assist these groups, grounding their right to provide assistance on existing provisions of international humanitarian law to war victims and on human rights treaties.

Identification of IDPs, the different groups of displaced persons and the varying needs of these groups are all further issues in the delivery of humanitarian assistance. A special category of IDPs generating extreme concern to the humanitarian community is that of demobilized soldiers, as their displacement is not only from their homes, but also from their livelihoods. Humanitarian aid must address all these issues, while upholding the principles of impartiality, neutrality and independence.

Protection

Since the early 1990s, military forces have become increasingly involved in humanitarian activities, which raises significant issues in respect of the humanitarian principles, as well as policy and operational questions. In parallel, the military protection of civilians and aid workers in complex emergencies, and the need to obtain unhindered and sustained access to populations in need, are vital to ensuring effective humanitarian assistance. The rise of terrorism and the range of counterterrorism initiatives by governments have also generated new protection issues.

Humanitarian interventions must address all aspects of protection, while maintaining accordance with the principles of international humanitarian law and human rights law. This necessitates strong coordination on a range of issues, including the proliferation of small arms and landmines, reintegration of combatants, security, sexual exploitation of women and children in conflict, and the restorative justice issues of impunity and property rights.

Conclusion

Despite progress, there are still well-known problematic areas in the delivery of humanitarian assistance, especially over coordination of interventions and connectedness to development activities once the emergency period has passed. There remains a lack of attention to preparedness and pre-disaster planning in general, and there is limited attention to indigenous coping strategies. Targeting of humanitarian assistance, particularly around issues of gender, remains problematic. It seems that these problems are somewhat intractable because, ultimately, no one has responsibility for the management of humanitarian assistance, and since, essentially, it is seen to be doing good.

GUIDE TO FURTHER READING

Sphere Project (2004) *Sphere Handbook*, Geneva: Sphere Project.
United Nations Central Emergency Response Fund (CERF) *What is the CERF?* (http://ochaonline2.un.org/Default.aspx?tabid=7480).
UNHCR (2000) *Handbook for Emergencies*, Geneva: United Nations High Commission for Refugees.
UNHCR (2006) *2005 Global Refugee Trends*, Geneva: United Nations High Commission for Refugees.

REFERENCES

Deng, F. (1998) *Guiding Principles on Internal Displacement*, New York: United Nations.
Development Initiatives (2005) *Global Humanitarian Assistance Update 2004–2005*, Evercreech, Somerset: Development Initiatives and Global Humanitarian Assistance and Good Humanitarian Donorship Project.

Hallam, A. (1998) 'Evaluating humanitarian assistance programmes in complex emergencies', *Good Practice Review*, 7: 102.

Harmer, A., Cotterrell, L. and Stoddard, A. (2004) 'From Stockholm to Ottawa: A progress review of the Good Humanitarian Donorship initiative', *Humanitarian Policy Group Research Briefing*, 18 (October).

IFRC (2001) *World Disasters Report*, Geneva: International Federation of Red Cross and Red Crescent Societies.

ISAC (2003) *Guidelines for HIV/AIDS Interventions in Emergency Situations,* Geneva: Inter-Agency Standing Committee.

Macrae, J. and Harmer, A. (2005) 'Re-thinking aid policy in protracted crises', *Opinions*, September, London: Overseas Development Institute.

OCHA (1994) *Oslo Guidelines*, New York: United Nations Office for the Coordination of Humanitarian Affairs.

ODI (2003) *Humanitarian NGOs: Challenges and Trends*, Humanitarian Policy Group, Briefing Paper 12 (July), London: Overseas Development Institute.

Steering Committee of the Joint Evaluation of Emergency Assistance to Rwanda (1996) *The International Response to Conflict and Genocide: The Rwanda Experience*, Copenhagen: Steering Committee of the Joint Evaluation of Emergency Assistance to Rwanda.

Telford, J., Cosgrave, J. and Houghton, R. (2006) *Joint Evaluation of the International Response to the Indian Ocean Tsunami: Synthesis Report*, London: Tsunami Evaluation Coalition (TEC).

UNHCR (2006) *2005 Global Refugee Trends*, Geneva: United Nations High Commission for Refugees.

Waal, A. and Tumushabe, J. (2003) *HIV/AIDS and Food Security in Africa: A Report for DFID*, London: Department for International Development.

9.5 Complex political emergencies in the war on terror era

Barry Munslow and Tim O'Dempsey

Complex political emergencies (CPE) is a concept which refers to intra-country conflict involving economic, political and social destabilization, often combined with a 'natural' trigger mechanism, such as a drought, flood or earthquake (Weiss and Collins 2000: 204). Humanitarian emergencies involving massive population displacements, hunger, disease and human suffering have long existed, and the international community has developed mechanisms to respond to these. What is different with the concept of complex political emergencies is the additional element of internal conflict.

Emergencies have always had political dimensions, so it is not just the presence of politics that makes CPEs different, it is the armed conflict form that the political struggles take. During the cold war, from the end of Second World War until the fall of the Berlin Wall in 1989, the communist and capitalist groupings internationally kept internal conflicts within their allied states in check. The end of cold war certainties unleashed a massive explosion of CPEs in the Balkans, the former Soviet Union, Africa and parts of Asia in particular. UN involvement in peacekeeping missions gives a good indication of the changes taking place internationally. Between 1948 and 1988, only 13 peacekeeping operations were established. Over the next 20 years, the number jumped to 47 missions. In 2006, there were 16 active peacekeeping missions, two political missions and no fewer than 92,300 UN people in the field, in Western Sahara, Georgia, Kosovo, Democratic Republic of Congo, Ethiopia/Eritrea, Afghanistan, Liberia, Ivory Coast, Haiti, Burundi, Sudan, Sierra Leone and East Timor. This list does not cover the very many more CPEs that did not have UN interventions, including, for example, northern Uganda, Sri Lanka, Somalia.

From cold war to war on terror

The post-cold war period of CPEs divides into two. The first was 1989 to 11 September 2001, a period which began with a belief in benign intervention on occasions for humanitarian reasons, as in Somalia and the Balkans, followed by a return to great caution after the deaths of 18 US Army Rangers and 78 other US military casualties in Mogadishu in October 1993. US Presidential Decision Directive-25 was produced, listing a raft of conditions to be fulfilled if the USA were to support peacekeeping initiatives in the UN Security Council (Power 2001). The dramatic and catastrophic effect of this was the fateful neglect by the international community of the genocide of 800,000 Tutsi and moderate Hutu in Rwanda in 1994, because the West did not have strategic interests in the country.

The big debates in this period concerned the need to bridge the great divide between humanitarian institutions, their role and funding mechanisms, and the development institutions and funding mechanisms which, on the whole, were entirely separate. While on the ground the idea was that there would be a seamless transition from emergency relief to rehabilitation and then reconstruction, the reality was that the institutional complexities of funding and restricted mandates prevented any such easy transition. Institutional complexities proved to be a significant part of the problem in complex emergencies. In other words, the proposed solution became, in reality, a major part of the problem itself (Munslow and Brown 1997).

War on terror and constraints on humanitarian space

The next phase, from 11 September 2001 to the present, was to have extensive and long-lasting ramifications for humanitarian operations in multiple ways. Al-Qaeda's attack on the USA, at the time when President George W. Bush and his neoconservative elite were leading the Republican Party and had won the US presidential election, would have catastrophic consequences for generations to come. President Bush designated a new war on terror era, in response to the terrorist attacks on America. In so doing, he was to create the clash of civilizations that Huntington (2002) had warned of as the new post-cold war conflict fault lines in international relations. Huntington (2002: 21) was clear that avoiding a global war of civilizations required world leaders to maintain the multi-civilizational characteristics of global politics.

What President Bush undertook was a crusade to establish Western ideas of democracy through force of invasion, first in Afghanistan and then in Iraq. Not only was this policy defeated in both countries, but there was a setback worldwide to the spread of human rights and the values of democracy, because of the manner in which the USA and its UK ally, in the form of the Blair government, formulated and pursued its strategy. Imposing liberal values by force is perceived as a contradiction in terms by those who are invaded, and by other countries and peoples who have different cultural values or who are affronted by stronger powers imposing their will by force. In his farewell speech as UN Secretary General, Kofi Annan said: 'No nation can make itself secure by seeking supremacy over others. We all share responsibility for each other's security, and only by working to make each other secure can we hope to achieve lasting security for ourselves' (the *Independent*, 12 December 2006).

To understand why US policy went so dramatically wrong, we need to examine the key tensions underlying effective possibilities for meaningful humanitarian interventions. The motivations behind the Bush administration's decisions were perceived to be strategic and material (oil), and taken unilaterally, rather than being altruistic and multilateral. Achcar (2006: 117) argues that this policy pushed a general resentment of US interference in Muslim countries towards a greater adherence to terrorism by significant numbers of Muslims in their countries of origin, as well as among those who have migrated to Western countries, with the barbarism of Washington fuelling an opposite barbarism of Muslim religious fanaticism.

National sovereignty versus international humanitarian laws and rights

The entire architecture of international relations is built on the notion that the world is composed of a distinct and discrete number of well-functioning nation states. These are the principal actors that exist on the world stage, and they take all the decisions over their citizens inside their own country, and act on behalf of all their citizens in relation to the international community. This is a giant lie, as many so-called nation states do not exist in reality. They were artificial constructs of colonial rule and of a decolonization process that never gave these geographically designated territorial entities the least chance of success. Hence Basil Davidson, the father figure of African studies, entitled his last book, *The Black Man's Burden: Africa and the Curse of the Nation-State* (1992). The curse remains in the form of adherence to the primacy of national sovereignty, when all kinds of crimes can be committed by governments against their own people, leaving the international community impotent to intervene to uphold the values of International Humanitarian Law and International Human Rights Law, which the international community has been developing patiently over time, with the International Committee of the Red Cross in the forefront of championing these principles (Bouchet-Saulnier 2002).

Because national sovereignty is paramount in determining international affairs, humanitarian interventions depend on the willingness of the major powers to intervene or to deny the option of intervention in complex humanitarian political emergencies. Objective humanitarian need, on the basis of the extent of human suffering, is never the criteria used to determine whether or not the international community will act. Power and money determine the workings of international politics, tempered, to a variable degree, by the humanitarian impulse, which is influenced by the media and electoral sentiment. What happened between 1989 and the US casualties in Mogadishu, Somalia, in 1993, resulted in significant gains in humanitarian principles and institutions. After the US military casualties this momentum turned to inertia, and the Rwandan genocide ensued. Heart-searching by the international community led to public apologies by the UN and US President Clinton to the people of Rwanda. But the realities of power politics were not to be overtaken by remorse concerning the genocide. Hence, in spite of multiple warnings, the massive devastation in Darfur unfolded from 2003 onwards, orchestrated by the government of Sudan (Prunier 2005).

A failure of US global leadership

The humanitarian gains in law, institutions and political will were to be compromised, with devastating effect, by President George W. Bush putting in place the war on terror policies. Unilateralism replaced Security Council consensus; America's respect for human rights was compromised; and commitments to global poverty alleviation were sacrificed at the altar of the war on terror ideology. Whatever the political shade of all subsequent governments worldwide, everyone has to live with the consequences of this mistake.

Essentially, the neoconservative agenda was based on expanding the US empire, but on the cheap, with minimum armed force commitments. Nation building was specifically off the Bush first election agenda, hence the post-9/11 response was to invade Afghanistan, and then Iraq, with no policy, institutional memory or coherent strategy of what to do afterwards. Afghanistan demonstrates how low inputs produce low outputs, with the lowest per-capita resourcing of any US nation-building exercise in six decades. As Dobbins (2006: 221), a seasoned US expert, concludes: 'As a result, terrorists, insurgents, bandits, drug lords, and warlords vie for control over much of the Afghan countryside.' In Iraq, massive quantities of funds were employed, but in an ineffective and counterproductive manner. The US Defense Department was given total responsibility for handling the aftermath of the invasion, not the State Department, where the experience of state building resided. It failed to establish security as a priority, disbanding the Iraqi army with no demobilization and reintegration strategy, creating a power vacuum filled by various insurgent forces. It also imposed military occupation rather than peace enforcement under the UN Charter. For the proud Arab world, the occupation invoked the same alienation and hostility as the Israeli occupation of Palestine, and this injustice holds the key to resolving the problem of instability in the Middle East. The USA had a war-fighting machine, trained to take power, it did not have the institutional capacity to maintain power, and hence lost in both Afghanistan and Iraq. Nation building is not primarily a military exercise, yet nearly all the money went on the military.

Beyond these catastrophic errors was the typical arrogance of power of empires who have peaked, are in decline and are also in self-denial as to the changing balance of power in the evolving new global order.

Constricted humanitarian space: The new challenges

President Bush's policies have had the following impact on the space for humanitarian interventions. First, they have provoked a clash of civilizations, between the Western and the Muslim world – hence the armed confrontations and CPEs will continue through the first half of the twenty-first century. Second, they have removed the vital neutrality of humanitarian space, by creating a Muslim versus Western Christian civilizational fault line. All humanitarian workers are now targets in civilizational confrontations. The symbols of the red cross and red crescent have become so politicized that a new symbol of a diamond has been introduced. The neoconservative US policy of massively prioritizing the use of hard military power has been extremely counterproductive. In Palestine and Lebanon, Hamas and Hezbollah have used soft power in the form of social welfare benefits to win mass popular support. In contrast, the vast sums of US taxpayers' money spent by America have filled the pockets of Republican Party supporters, as Democrat-led investigations and those of the media have revealed.

The realist interpretation of international politics explains the reluctance of both developed and developing countries to accept an early warning system for complex emergencies in the UN. The developed countries did not want to be obliged to intervene if there was a humanitarian emergency that did not warrant intervention on the criteria of their own strategic interests, and the developing countries did not want an excuse being given to powerful countries for them to intervene because of an early warning alert.

Diverting funds from areas of real need

There is a massive opportunity cost for the war on terror – money spent here leaves less for other causes. Climate change is a far greater threat to humanity than the ridiculously designated war on terror. CPEs as a result of drought, floods and disease in the poorest countries will create immense human suffering and chronic instability in certain areas of the globe, which inevitably impact on the rich countries, with asylum seekers, drugs, people trafficking, global crime networks and many more chickens coming home to roost (O'Dempsey and Munslow 2006).

GUIDE TO FURTHER READING

O'Dempsey, T. and Munslow, B. (2006) 'Globalisation, complex humanitarian emergencies and health', *Annals of Tropical Medicine and Parasitology*, 100(5&6): 501–16.

Terry, F. (2002) *Condemned to Repeat. The Paradox of Humanitarian Action*, London: Cornell University Press.

Weiss, G. and Collins, C. (2000) *Humanitarian Challenges and Intervention*, Oxford: Westview Press.

Weissman, F. (ed.) (2004) *In the Shadow of 'Just Wars'*, London: C. Hurst & Co.

REFERENCES

Achcar, A. (2006) *The Clash of Barbarisms. The Making of the New World Disorder*, London: Saqi.

Bouchet-Saulnier, F. (2002) *The Practical Guide to Humanitarian Law*, Oxford: Rowman & Littlefield.

Davidson, B. (1992) *The Black Man's Burden: Africa and the Curse of the Nation-State*, New York: Times Books.

Dobbins, J. (2006) 'Learning the lessons of Iraq', in F. Fukuyama (ed.) *Nation-Building Beyond Afghanistan and Iraq*, Baltimore, MD: Johns Hopkins University Press, pp. 218–30.

Huntington, S. (2002) *The Clash of Civilizations*, London: Free Press.

Munslow, B. and Brown, C. (1997) 'Complex emergencies and the institutional impasse', *Third World Quarterly*, 20(3): 551–68.

O'Dempsey, T. and Munslow, B. (2006) 'Globalisation, complex humanitarian emergencies and health', *Annals of Tropical Medicine and Parasitology*, 100(5&6): 501–16.

Power, S. (2001) 'Bystanders to genocide', *Atlantic Monthly*, September.

Prunier, G. (2005) *Darfur. The Ambiguous Genocide*, London: C. Hurst & Co.

Weiss, G. and Collins, C. (2000) *Humanitarian Challenges and Intervention*, Oxford: Westview Press.

9.6 Peace-building partnerships and human security

Timothy M. Shaw

'Human security' as concept and practice privileges personal economic and social rather than 'national' strategic concerns, including ecological, educational, food, habitat and health priorities (UNDP 1994: 22–40). But despite its relatively recent post-cold war definition and advocacy, human or individual security, along with human development, has become more problematic in the twenty-first century. In turn, debates about its definitions and elusiveness have proliferated and intensified, as indicated later in this chapter.

Any post-bipolar 'peace dividend' was shattered after a short decade by the 'global' shocks of 9/11 in the USA in 2001, then 7/7 in the UK in 2005. Subsequent 'wars on terrorism' and interventions in Iraq and Afghanistan have complicated previously rather simplistic or idealistic notions of peacekeeping roles and partnerships for post-conflict reconstruction, as articulated in the *Report of the International Commission on Intervention and State Sovereignty* (ICISS 2001).

This essay has been completely rewritten since the first edition of this book was published, because the interrelated worlds of human security and peace building are quite different towards the end of the first decade of the twenty-first century to what they were at the beginning. These shifts are reflected in revisionist UN (2003, 2004) and donor (DFID 2005) deliberations. But they remain as important as ever for 'development studies', and for state and non-state policies, as suggested in the first edition of this book (Shaw 2002). Further, as indicated later in this chapter, there is growing anxiety within international non-governmental organizations (INGOs) and related circles about the tendency towards the conflagration of development and security post-9/11.

This contribution has two interrelated themes. The first is that human security, however defined, remains as relevant as ever to global development, even if it was displaced momentarily by an apparent return to the hegemony of 'national security' after 9/11. And the second is that peace building is likewise vital, but it has now become much more dangerous, or robust, than at the end of the twentieth century. In short, development and security are more intertwined and inseparable than ever, leading to controversial notions like the securitization of development, as well as the privatization of security (as indicated below), and even the militarization of refugee communities and camps (Muggah 2006).

Human security before and after 9/11 and 7/7

Human security was articulated in the post-bipolar world as an antidote to established notions of national security and balance of power: the privileging of individual rather than collective security against the threat and practice of violence as the principal referent of security. Symptomatic of contemporary policy development, like parallel discourses on human development and human rights, human security has been defined by international agencies and think tanks. Such public diplomacy reflects growing 'contracting-out' by national regimes to combinations of non-governmental organizations, multinational corporations and international institutions: the bases of new multilateralisms of global, mixed-actor coalitions around 'new' security issues, like landmines and blood diamonds, small arms and child soldiers. The apex of the first period of human security deliberations was the late 1990s Ottawa Process around landmines, advanced by the 1400-member International Campaign to Ban Landmines (ICBL) and spearheaded by Lloyd Axworthy as Canadian foreign minister.

As conceived and advocated in the mid-1990s by the United Nations Development Programme (UNDP) (1994: 22–40), human security includes interrelated community, economic, environmental, food, health, personal and political securities. But by the middle of the first decade of the new century, uneven globalization has served to proliferate security issues, especially around the latest generation of 'new' states, which has led towards +/–200 today. Any lingering idealism was shattered by the shocks of 9/11 and the US unilateralist response: its declaration of a 'war on terrorism'.

Symbolically, the development of a human security doctrine, and the elaboration of the related 'responsibility to protect' (R2P) those communities and countries where it was threatened, was in process when 9/11 diverted attention. So the December 2001 report of the blue-ribbon Canadian-supported International Commission on Intervention and State Sovereignty (ICISS 2001) was overshadowed by the new preoccupation with international terrorism. Thus, while the notion of human security is over a decade old at the time of writing (2006), its definition and realization are more problematic than ever (MacLean, Black and Shaw 2006). The ICISS (2001: xi) intended to extend the notion of international law for the new millennium, from state sovereignty to the protection of people:

> Where a population is suffering serious harm, as a result of internal war, insurgency, repression or state failure, and the state in question is unwilling or unable to halt or avert it, the principle of non-intervention yields to the international responsibility to protect.

However, as the war on terrorism has dragged on, and its costs – human, financial, regional, and so on – have become ever more apparent, so analysts have begun to rediscover human rather than national, regional or even global security. Thus the 2003 report of the UN Commission on Human Security, and subsequent reports on new security threats and responses around the millennium summit in 2004–05, served to both rehabilitate and refine the concept. The post-bipolar and post-9/11 pre-summit panel report on *A More Secure World: Our Shared Responsibility* recognized that 'The threats are from non-State actors as well as States, and to human security as well as State security...The central challenge for the twenty-first century is to fashion a new and broader understanding...of what collective security means' (UN 2004: 11). Among the half-dozen clusters of threats identified by the UN (2004: 12) panel were: 'Economic and social threats, including poverty, infectious diseases and environmental degradation... Internal conflict, including civil war, genocide and other large-scale atrocities... Transnational organized crime.'

I conclude this section by noting the emergence of an intense debate around human security as the second decade of the twenty-first century approaches. This revolves around narrower versus broader conceptualizations: freedom from fear versus freedom from want (MacLean, Black and Shaw 2006). Initial formulations arising from the human development genre around the UNDP favoured the latter. By contrast, more cautious or conservative analysts, oriented towards traditional international relations (IR) favoured the former. Reflecting on such revisionist inclinations, Neil MacFarlane and Yuen Foong Khong (2006: 228) lament the 'conceptual overstretch' around 'freedom from want', preferring to limit such security threats to those 'against their physical integrity' or 'organised violence'. This standoff was previewed by 21 analysts in a special section of *Security Dialogue* (Burgess and Owen 2004). As indicated below, it entails more than conceptual disagreement; it profoundly affects data and policy.

Threats to human security in theory and policy

The second part of this chapter juxtaposes a set of overlapping discourses which increasingly have an impact on both the definition and implementation of human security towards the end of the first decade of the new century. In addition to freedom from fear/want, these include: uneven globalization, 'African' international relations (IR), and redefinitions of both development and security. Taken together, these debates have profoundly complicated the conceptual and empirical relationships between development and security.

First, globalization has clearly become more uneven than ever, leading towards a new trio of 'worlds':

- the Organization for Economic Cooperation and Development (OECD) states;
- the emerging economies of BRIC countries (Brazil, Russia, India and China) and newly industrializing countries (NICs);
- the approximately 50 fragile states.

Such inequalities are both intra- and inter-state, encouraging transnational alliances among the rich and the poor to either defend or challenge the status quo. Hence the privatization of security on the one hand, and the tendency towards political and/or religious radicalization on the other.

Second, a pair of transatlantic review articles on African IR by William Brown (2006) and Douglas Lemke (2003) has raised the issue of whether such relations can be limited to inter- rather than intra-state relations of cooperation and conflict. This 'academic' discussion poses profound implications for security policy: for example, do only deaths from classical inter-state wars count? The latter puts such African issues into a broader, comparative context:

> ...African international relations constitute the developing world activity most likely to be excluded from international relations research...
> ...standard international relations research describes the interactions of official states... In contrast, Africanist international relations scholars describe interactions between and among a variety of types of international actors...in the developing world, international relations are more varied than standard international research recognizes (Lemke 2003: 116, 138).

Reflecting conservative, traditional inter-state definitions, the first *Human Security Report 2005* from the University of British Columbia (UBC 2005) can claim an optimistic picture of a decline in conflicts and related deaths at the century's turn. By contrast, data on internal or intra-state wars and body-counts would be much less sanguine.

Third, as regional conflicts have continued in, say, Central Asia, the Great Lakes, the Horn (from Darfur to Somalia) and West Africa (Muggah 2006; Boas and Dunn 2007), two divergent responses can be identified. The first is an extended version of the optimistic perspective on new multilateralisms around new security issues like landmines, blood diamonds, child soldiers and small arms (GIIS 2006): further Ottawa and Kimberley Processes augmented by more robust peace building, as in Sierra Leone, for example, along with longer-term developmental innovations like the Diamond

Development Initiative. The second is a more critical or sceptical response, based on the recognition of greed rather than grievance: the political economy of conflict. This cautions that peacekeeping per se cannot be efficacious as conflict is over resources and revenues rather than principles, notwithstanding efforts around corporate codes of conduct, the Extractive Industries Transparency Initiative (EITI), and so on (Böge 2006): the 'new' extended peacekeeping partnerships.

Growing scepticism about the feasibility of a 'liberal peace' is reinforced by the trend towards the securitization of development and/or militarization of security. INGO policy analysts are increasingly apprehensive about this direction as it erodes the boundary between development and security, enabling national and private security organizations to claim to qualify for development funds under the Development Assistance Committee (DAC) of the OECD.

Futures for peace building and human security?

Given the above analytic and empirical trends and debates, optimism about the future of peace-building partnerships and human security is a scarce commodity. While the world of peace building continues to expand given demand and supply, post-9/11 and -7/7 conflicts have eroded and compromised its niche. Continued enlightened new multilateralisms and informed public diplomacy around the human development/security nexus are to be encouraged (MacLean, Black and Shaw 2006). But the context is now complicated by improved prospects for the securitization of development and the militarization of security (Muggah 2006).

GUIDE TO FURTHER READING

MacFarlane, S.N. and Khong, Y.F. (2006) *Human Security and the UN: A Critical History*, Bloomington, IN: Indiana University Press for the United Nations Intellectual History Project (UNIHP). A comprehensive, informed but sceptical overview of the evolution of human security, which advocates narrower freedom from fear rather than broader freedom from want.

MacLean, S.M., Black, D.R. and Shaw, T.M. (eds) (2006) *A Decade of Human Security: Prospects for Global Governance and New Multilateralisms*, Aldershot: Ashgate Publishing. A reflective, somewhat revisionist history of ten years of human security, informed by Canadian perspectives.

REFERENCES

Boas, M. and Dunn, K.C. (eds) (2007) *African Guerrillas: Raging Against the Machine*, Boulder, CO: Lynne Rienner Publishers.

Böge, V., Fitzpatrick, C., Jaspers, W. and Paes, W.-C. (2006) *Who's Minding the Store? The Business of Private, Public and Civil Actors in Zones of Conflict*, brief 32, Bonn: Bonn International Center for Conversion (BICC).

Brown, W. (2006) 'Africa and international relations: A comment on IR theory, anarchy and statehood', *Review of International Studies*, 32(1), January: 119–43.

Burgess, J.P. and Owen, T. (2004) 'Special section: what is "human security"?', *Security Dialogue*, 35(3), September: 345–87.

DFID (2005) *Why We Need to Work More Effectively in Fragile States*, London: Department for International Development.

GIIS (Graduate Institute of International Studies) (2006) *Small Arms Survey 2006: Unfinished Business*, Oxford: Oxford University Press.

ICISS (2001) *The Responsibility to Protect: Report of the International Commission on Intervention and State Sovereignty*, Ottawa: International Development Research Centre.

Lemke, D. (2003) 'African lessons for international relations research', *World Politics*, 56(1), October: 114–38.

MacFarlane, S.N. and Khong, Y.F. (2006) *Human Security and the UN: A Critical History*, Bloomington, IN: Indiana University Press for the United Nations Intellectual History Project (UNIHP).

MacLean, S.M., Black, D.R. and Shaw, T.M. (eds) (2006) *A Decade of Human Security: Prospects for Global Governance and New Multilateralisms*, Aldershot: Ashgate Publishing.

Muggah, R. (ed.) (2006) *No Refuge: The Crisis of Refugee Militarization in Africa*, London: Zed Books for Bonn International Center for Conversion and Small Arms Survey.

Shaw, T.M. (2002) 'Peace-building partnerships and human security', in V. Desai and R. Potter (eds) *The Companion to Development Studies*, first edition, London: Arnold, pp. 449–53.

UBC (University of British Columbia) (2005) *Human Security Report 2005*, Oxford: Oxford University Press.

UN (2003) *Human Security – Now. Report of the Commission on Human Security*, New York: United Nations.

UN (2004) *A More Secure World: Our Shared Responsibility. Report of the High-Level Panel on Threats, Challenges and Change*, New York: United Nations.

UNDP (United Nations Development Programme) (1994) *Human Development Report 1994*, New York: Oxford University Press.

9.7 Arms control and disarmament in the context of developing countries

Paul Rogers

Although the East–West confrontation of the cold war years did not lead to a world war, or even to a direct conflict between NATO and Warsaw Pact forces, one of its main consequences was a series of proxy wars fought throughout the Third World. These, together with many regional conflicts, meant that the period from 1945 to 2000 saw substantial losses of life and serious injuries, with 25 million people killed and 75 million seriously injured, and repeated disruption to local and regional economies, mostly in the Third World (Sivard 1996; IISS 2006).

The latter part of the twentieth century was a period in which intensive efforts were made to control armaments through a series of negotiated agreements. Most of the arms control activity until the 1990s involved nuclear armaments, together with the other weapons of mass destruction, and chemical and biological agents, whereas most of the casualties of war were caused by conventional weapons, especially light arms. Even so, Third World states have been significant participants in many aspects of arms control.

When the Bush administration came to power in the United States in 2001, there was a substantial change in US policy on arms control, with a move to a more unilateralist stance and opposition to a number of negotiated and prospective treaties. The 9/11 attacks further hardened the US perception of new threats. This was to lead to the termination of the Saddam Hussein regime in Iraq in 2003, principally on the charge that it was developing weapons of mass destruction, a charge that was subsequently proved to be unfounded.

Nuclear arms control

Serious nuclear arms control negotiations began in 1963 following the dangerous Cuban missile crisis of 1962. A Limited Nuclear Test Ban Treaty (LTBT) was agreed between the USA, the USSR and the UK in 1963, and has since been signed by more than 100 countries. It has the effect of banning atmospheric testing of nuclear weapons, bringing under control the dangerous effects of radioactive fallout that was prone to affect countries across the world.

From 1969 to 1992, a series of bilateral Soviet/US agreements brought limited control to the strategic nuclear arms race, but these had little direct effect on the race. In terms of global developments of direct relevance to developing countries, three areas of arms control were significant. The LTBT was the starting point for protracted negotiations towards a Comprehensive Test Ban Treaty (CTBT), an intended multilateral agreement promoted, in particular in the 1990s, by a number of Southern states, including South Africa and Mexico. Although finally opened for signature towards the end of the decade, it was dealt a severe blow by the refusal of the United States to ratify the Treaty in 1990, a move confirmed by the Bush administration in 2001.

The second area of global concern related to the development of nuclear-free zones. For 35 years from the mid-1960s, there was a series of regional negotiations to establish such zones, beginning with the Latin American nuclear-free zone, the Treaty of Tlatelolco of 1967. This established the whole of Latin America as a nuclear-free zone, and was further boosted by the significant, if largely overlooked, disengagement of Argentina and Brazil from a potential nuclear arms race in the 1980s. Further nuclear-free zone treaties were later agreed for Africa, the Pacific and much of South East Asia. Furthermore, in the early 1990s, three former Soviet republics, Ukraine, Belarus and Kazakhstan, returned to Russia the nuclear weapons deployed on their territories during the cold war, and South Africa dismantled its small nuclear arsenal.

Finally, the Non-Proliferation Treaty (NPT) was agreed in 1968, came into force in 1970 and was subject to regular review at five-yearly intervals. The NPT bans the possession of nuclear weapons by signatories, in return for the potential transfer of civil nuclear technologies to non-nuclear weapons states. Article 6 allows certain existing nuclear states to be parties to the Treaty, provided they engage in serious nuclear armament measures.

There are two distinct Southern views of the NPT. Some countries, notably India, regard it as a device by which powerful nuclear states control the spread of nuclear weapons without having to give up their own arsenals, essentially an exercise in political hypocrisy. A much larger number of states recognize this aspect of the Treaty, but regard progress towards a nuclear-free world as being of overriding importance.

The refusal of the United States to ratify the CTBT did damage to prospects for further developing the NPT, not least because there had been a tacit agreement at the time of the 1995 NPT Review Conference to extend the Treaty indefinitely in return for progress on the CTBT negotiations and a renewed commitment by nuclear weapons states to disarmament. At the 2000 NPT Review Conference in New York, the nuclear weapons states came under surprisingly heavy pressure to accept a commitment to a nuclear-free world. This they were prepared to do, in some cases with some reluctance, but a timetable was not established and the 2005 Review made no further progress, not least because of the attitude of the United States.

In 2006, North Korea was reported to have tested a small nuclear device, making it the ninth nuclear weapon state, and there were prospects for a crisis with Iran as that country energetically pursued its programme to develop civil nuclear power. While this was allowed under the terms of the NPT, the Bush administration believed that Iran was intent on using its civil programme as a front for developing a weapons capability. In spite of little evidence for this, the United States was insistent that Iran should not be allowed even to develop civil nuclear power, with the prospect of this confrontation having the potential to damage the non-proliferation regime.

Chemical weapons

Attempts to negotiate a Chemical Weapons Convention (CWC) banning all chemical weapons were made over several decades, but were boosted by the experience of the 1991 Gulf War and the ending of the cold war. As a result, a Convention was agreed and opened for signature in 1993 and entered into force in 1997, with 181 countries signing by 2006.

As the term 'convention' implies, the CWC imposes a complete ban on the development, production, acquisition, stockpiling or transfer of chemical weapons, and obliges parties to the CWC to destroy all their chemical weapons stocks and the production facilities. It is thus a complete treaty, widely welcomed by most states across the world, and includes an Organization for the Prohibition of Chemical Weapons (OPCW), with a professional inspectorate empowered to undertake a range of inspections of states that are party to the Treaty (Kenyon 2000).

A key aspect of the Treaty is the requirement for states to destroy their stocks, but only 19 per cent of the 71,331 tons of chemical weapons declared to the OPCW had been destroyed by 2006, far less than had been hoped for. A number of states, including Syria and North Korea, have not joined the Treaty.

Biological weapons

A convention banning biological weapons was one of the early multilateral arms control successes, the Biological and Toxin Weapons Convention (BTWC) being negotiated in 1972. It was, though, an agreement without any effective verification procedures, and there was evidence that the Soviet Union, South Africa and Iraq were among a number of countries pursuing active biological weapons programmes in the subsequent decades. Furthermore, developments in genetic manipulation and biotechnology were making it technically possible to develop very much more potent biological weapons agents (Dando 1996).

After the end of the cold war and the completion of the Chemical Weapons Convention, negotiations intended to refine the BTWC in a much more strengthened format commenced in Geneva. While good progress had been made by 2000, substantial problems remained, including the concern of major biotechnology companies that an intrusive inspection regime would breach issues of commercial secrecy. While many Southern states were strongly committed to a strengthened treaty, negotiations effectively broke down by 2004, not least because of opposition from the United States to the verification and inspection procedures that were likely to be developed.

Conventional weapons

Most wars since 1945 have taken place in developing countries, and almost all casualties are caused by conventional weapons. Furthermore, at the end of the cold war, major conflicts in Africa and central Asia resulted in huge quantities of small arms and light weapons being shipped to areas in conflict, many of them later entering the 'grey' market, leading to what has been termed a Kalashnikov culture in some regions.

Efforts to control the spread of conventional weapons were limited until the early 1990s, although some countries had legislation that controlled arms exports to regimes unacceptable to them, and there were some multilateral agreements, such as the Missile Technology Control Regime (MTCR), which involved a number of Western states.

There have been a number of regional developments, some involving Western state groups such as the European Union, and others relating to Third World regions. The EU adopted a Programme for Preventing and Combating Illicit Trafficking in Conventional Arms which has three aims: to strengthen collective efforts to prevent illicit arms transfers; to assist affected countries in controlling arms movements; and to promote light arms reduction by buy-back and other programmes (Benson 1998).

The Organization of American States agreed an inter-state convention on illicit manufacturing and trafficking; the Africa Union (which replaced the Organization for African Unity in 2000) has undertaken some limited work on the issue; and a group of West African states has sought to develop a regional agreement on arms transfers. There has also been an increasing interest in arms transfers control by the Southern African Development Community, including cooperation with the European Union.

At a global level, three developments are relevant. First, the Wassenaar Agreement, signed in 1996, has developed from collaborative Western restrictions on arms transfers to Warsaw Pact countries during the cold war, and involves a number of Southern and former Soviet-bloc countries, with 40 signatories by 2006. Second, Interpol has two systems relating to the tracking of firearms. The Orange Notice, which started in 2004, aims to alert police forces to unusual firearms issues, including parcel bombs. The International Weapons Electronic Tracking System (IWeTS) is a longer-term project concerned with firearms tracking. Finally, the UN established a Panel of Government Experts on Small Arms in 1995 which has sought to promote a range of measures (Benson 1998). One significant arms control success has been the intensive campaign, principally by citizen groups, to ban anti-personnel landmines, leading to a 1997 agreement signed by over 100 countries.

While there has been some modest success in seeking controls over conventional arms in recent years, it is still very small in relation to the overall problem. In particular, there is no process for controlling most kinds of area-impact munitions, including cluster bombs, thermobaric (fuel-air) explosives and multiple-launch rocket systems dispensing anti-personnel sub-munitions. Some of these systems are as damaging as small tactical nuclear weapons, yet they are proliferating to many countries. Towards the end of the Lebanon war in August 2006, Israel fired over a million cluster sub-munitions into southern Lebanon, many of them failing to explode, continuing to cause casualties long after the war had ended.

Conclusion

Overall, the role of developing countries in arms control has had two significant elements. First, many countries have played an important, if largely unrecognized, role in advocating the control of weapons of mass destruction, most notably with the Non-Proliferation Treaty. Second, they are playing an increasing role in seeking to control conventional weapons. Given that these are the weapons responsible for almost all casualties in wars across the developing world, this is an area of arms control that is ripe for much greater attention and effort in the future.

GUIDE TO FURTHER READING

Alternative Nuclear Futures, edited by John Bayliss and Robert O'Neill (Oxford University Press, 2000), is a multi-author analysis of trends in nuclear weapons and strategy.

The development of the Chemical Weapons Convention is summarized succinctly in *Controlling Chemical Weapons*, by Ian R. Kenyon (International Security Information Service, 2000).

Biological weapons and their control are dealt with by Malcolm Dando in *Preventing Biological Warfare: The Failure of American Leadership* (Palgrave, 2002).

A wide-ranging analysis of light arms issues is in William Benson's *Light Weapons Controls and Security Assistance: A Review of Current Practice* (joint report by Saferworld and International Alert, 1998).

The most useful journal is *Disarmament Diplomacy*, published by the Acronym Institute, which also has a good website.

Wider issues of international security in the context of North–South relations are covered by *Global Security and the War on Terror: Elite Power and the Illusion of Control*, by Paul Rogers (Routledge, 2007).

USEFUL WEBSITES

Acronym Institute: http://www.acronym.org.uk

Oxford Research Group, working particularly on North/South security issues: http://www.oxfordresearchgroup.org.uk

US Arms Control Association, with extensive resources on arms control and disarmament: http://www.arms control.org

REFERENCES

Benson, W. (1998) *Light Weapons Controls and Security Assistance: A Review of Current Practice,* London: Saferworld and International Alert (joint report).

Dando, M. (1996) *Biological Weapons in the 21st Century,* London: Brasseys.

IISS (2006) 'The 2006 chart of conflict', in *The Military Balance 2006,* London: International Institute for Strategic Studies.

Kenyon, I. (2000) *Controlling Chemical Weapons*, London: International Security Information Service.

Sivard, R.L. (1996) *World Military and Social Expenditure,* Washington, DC: World Priorities Inc.

9.8 Risks analysis and risk reduction: IRR – A theoretical and operational model for population resettlement

Michael M. Cernea

This paper describes concisely a theoretical model of development-induced displacement and resettlement processes: the *impoverishment risks and reconstruction* (IRR) model. This model is a conceptual and methodological tool which performs several essential functions in support of analytical and operational development work. The main functions for which the model can be employed are:

- a predictive function, to anticipate the main impoverishment risks involved in forced displacement and resettlement;
- a diagnostic function, to help assess in the field the content and the intensity of each major risk, in the context of a given project;
- a planning and problem resolution function, to guide the design of counter-risk measures and their incorporation in resettlement planning, for either preventing or mitigating risks;
- a research function, to serve as methodology in the scholarly analysis of resettlement impacts and to guide monitoring and evaluation studies on resettlement processes.

As a theoretical model, the IRR also makes the link between the conceptual apparatus used in the analysis of displacement processes, on the one hand, and the theory of poverty, impoverishment prevention and poverty reduction, on the other.

Knowledge has forewarning power. The research utility of the IRR model results from using knowledge about past processes, which is accumulated, 'packaged' and synthesized in the model. This research utility also comes from its ability to guide data collection in the field and to coherently aggregate disparate empirical findings along key variables. In the practice of planning or executing projects, the use of the IRR model can help prevent, or at least mitigate and gradually reverse, the impoverishment risks embedded in development projects that involve involuntary resettlement.

Theoretical modelling in resettlement research has been made possible by the vast body of empirical findings, generated by numerous researchers worldwide, about the adverse consequences of forced displacement. The accumulation of empirical data enables us to reveal basic regularities within a multitude of similar and comparable processes. In forced displacement, *the dominant regularity is the impoverishment of most resettlers*. This impoverishment is deconstructed and explained in the IRR model, which also outlines the key reconstruction strategies to counteract impoverishment.

The IRR model was formulated in the early 1990s (see Cernea 1990, 1991) and has been refined considerably since then (see Cernea and McDowell 2000). The model has been widely discussed in the development literature (e.g. Mathur and Marsden 1998; Mahapatra 1999) and has become the leading conceptual model in resettlement research.

Basic concepts

At the core of the IRR model are three basic concepts: *risk, impoverishment* and *reconstruction*. The related aspects of risks in development and risk-related social behaviour can be addressed with a set of more specific, focused risk concepts, such as risk exposure, risk aversion, risk prevention, risk taking, risk reduction, risk reversal and risk coping. The theoretical underpinnings of the IRR model are informed by sociology, economics, anthropology and ethics, and, more specifically, by concerns for equity, human rights and social justice in development, rather than by economic efficiency alone.

Resettlement needs and trends

Involuntary population displacement results from the imperative need to build modern industrial and transportation infrastructure, expand power generation and irrigation, implement urban renewal and enhance social services – schools, hospitals, water supply. Nonetheless, by its adverse effects, forced population displacement remains a social pathology of development, and first efforts must always be to avoid displacement wherever possible. Unfortunately, increases in population density, land scarcity and growing socio-economic needs maintain resettlement as a continuous companion of development. During the last two decades of the twentieth century, the magnitude of forced population displacements brought about by development projects was estimated at 10 million people annually, or some 200 million people over two decades. In the first decade of the twenty-first century, the amount of displacement caused by development is estimated at 15 million people annually. This clearly indicates the global dimension of this social pathology.

De-capitalization of resettlers

In developing countries (to which this article mainly refers), forced resettlement carries severe *risks of impoverishing the uprooted people*, many of whom were very poor even before displacement. Socio-anthropological research documents that resettlement operations tend to cause the de-capitalization and pauperization of vast numbers of resettlers. They lose capital in all its forms: natural capital, man-made physical capital, human capital and social capital. Eliminating or mitigating such impoverishment risks and improving resettlers' livelihoods is incumbent on governments, agencies and private-sector corporations responsible for projects that cause forced displacement.

Poverty reduction policies

If development's fundamental objective is to reduce poverty and promote growth, then development policies must attempt, among other goals, to minimize resettlement occurrences and (when resettlement is unavoidable) to carry out impoverishment-free relocation.

This chapter argues that efforts towards reducing *existing* poverty must go hand in hand with goals to *prevent the onset of new processes* of impoverishment. Development itself is not free from risks and adverse impacts. Such risks of potential impoverishment surface regularly in development projects that require involuntary resettlement, and sometimes in other projects as well. If project planning and execution fail to anticipate the potential risks, and to prevent them from becoming reality, severe problems in resettlement operations will inevitably occur. This is why the socio-economic and moral principles embedded in poverty reduction policies must be translated into targeted actions against adverse impacts and new impoverishment processes.

In practice, resettlement plans (RP) are mandatory in most internationally assisted projects. However, they are far less frequently mandated by governments of developing countries in projects financed from domestic sources alone. Therefore, the requirement for explicit, adequately financed and culturally sensitive RPs must be generalized in all countries.

Analytical and planning tools are often not sharp enough or sufficiently flexible to lead to differentiated and effective responses to risks. Improving the analytical methodology for regular risk assessment is therefore indispensable and should result in the formulation of *specific* risk management actions.

Usefulness of IRR in planning

Applying the IRR conceptual template to the circumstances of each development project has several advantages.

- It ensures, most importantly, that no major risk to resettlers is overlooked during the feasibility analysis of planned developments.
- It prompts planners to distinguish the different levels of *intensity* of each risk (high risks from low or moderate risks in a given project context), rather than treating all risks uniformly.
- It demands a *proactive risk-reversal* approach in project design, planning, financing and implementation.

The deconstruction of the impoverishment process into a template of eight basic risks facilitates the mobilization of proportionate resources for the highest risk or the risk affecting larger numbers of people, while allocating less to risks with lower incidence or intensity in a certain context. In practice, this differential approach may vastly increase equity by rationalizing resource allocation. *Early risk analysis* may also conclude that in certain projects, some of the IRR model's risks are not likely to occur; but it can also reveal some locally specific risks that are not part of the template but need to be addressed.

The major risks of impoverishment

The IRR model captures impoverishment not only in terms of income poverty, but also in terms of losing employment opportunities, shelter, health, nutrition, education or community power. The modelling of the main risks results from deconstructing the multifaceted displacement process into its essential and most general risks, each of which is presented briefly below. Further, we will point out how the IRR model is to be turned on its head to help derive counter-risk strategies and to measure projects against each of the eight basic risks.

1 *Landlessness*: Expropriation of land needed for the project's 'right of way' removes the main foundation on which many people build productive systems, commercial activities and livelihoods. Often land is lost for ever; sometimes it is partially replaced; and seldom is it fully replaced or fully compensated. This is the main form of de-capitalization and pauperization of the people who are displaced. Both natural and man-made capital are lost.

2 *Joblessness*: Loss of wage employment occurs in both rural and urban displacement. People losing jobs may be landless agricultural labourers, service workers or artisans. The unemployment or underemployment among resettlers may linger long after physical relocation. Creating new jobs is difficult and requires substantial investment, new creative approaches and greater reliance on sharing project benefits.

3 *Homelessness*: Loss of housing and shelter may be only temporary for many people, but for some it remains a chronic condition and is felt as a loss of identity and as cultural impoverishment. Loss of dwelling may have consequences on family cohesion and mutual help patterns if neighbouring households of the same kinship group are scattered. Group relocation of related people and neighbours is therefore preferable to dispersed relocation.

4 *Marginalization*: Marginalization occurs when relocated families lose economic power and slide down towards lesser socio-economic positions – middle-income farm households become small landholders; small shopkeepers and craftspeople lose business and fall below poverty thresholds. Economic marginalization is often accompanied by social and psychological marginalization, expressed in a drop in social status, and in resettlers' loss of confidence in themselves and in society.

5 *Increased morbidity and mortality*: The vulnerability of the poorest people to illness is increased by forced relocation, as it tends to be associated with increased stress, psychological trauma and the outbreak of parasitic and vector-born diseases. Serious decreases in health levels result from unsafe water supply and sewage systems, which cause the spread of epidemic infections, diarrhoea, dysentery, and so on, and may lead to higher mortality rates, particularly among children and the elderly.

6 *Food insecurity*: Forced uprooting diminishes self-sufficiency, dismantles local arrangements for food supply and thus increases the risk that people will fall into chronic food insecurity. This is defined as calorie-protein intake levels below the minimum necessary for normal growth and work.

7 *Loss of access to common property*: Poor farmers lose access to the common property assets belonging to communities that are relocated (e.g. loss of access to forests, water bodies, grazing lands). This type of income loss and livelihood deterioration is usually overlooked by planners and remains uncompensated.

8 *Social disarticulation*: The dismantling of community structures and social organization, the dispersal of informal and formal networks, local associations, and so on, is a massive loss of social capital. Such disarticulation undermines livelihoods in ways not recognized and not measured by planners, and results in disempowerment and further pauperization.

The risks discussed above affect non-uniformly various categories of people: rural and urban dwellers, tribal and non-tribal groups, children and the elderly, or, in river-based projects, upstream and downstream people. Research findings show that women suffer the impacts of displacement more severely than men. Host populations are also subjected to new risks, resulting from increased population densities and competition for resources.

How to reverse risks and reconstruct?

Before displacement actually begins, the social and economic risks of impoverishment are only impending risks. But if preventive counteractions are not initiated, these potential hazards convert into actual, dire impoverishment processes.

Robert K. Merton has shown insight in his observation that the prediction of an undesirable chain of events may become a 'self-destroying prophecy' if people respond adequately to the prediction (Merton 1979). It follows that a risk prediction model becomes most useful not when it is confirmed by adverse events, but rather when, as a result of its warnings being taken seriously and acted on, the risks are prevented from becoming reality, or are minimized. The prophecy destroys itself and the consequences announced by the model do not occur, or occur in a limited way.

The internal logic of the IRR model as a planning tool suggests that in order to defeat its impoverishment prediction it is necessary to attack the looming risks *early on* in the preparation of a development project. In the same way in which it deconstructs the process of displacement into eight major risks of impoverishment, the IRR model also deconstructs the process of resettlement and reconstruction into a set of definable *risk-reversal activities,* which can lead from:

1 landlessness to land-based resettlement;
2 joblessness to re-employment;
3 homelessness to house reconstruction;
4 marginalization to social inclusion;
5 increased morbidity to improved health care;
6 food insecurity to adequate nutrition;
7 loss of access to restoration of community assets and services;
8 social disarticulation to rebuilding networks and communities.

These strategic directions for reconstruction indicate that the IRR model is not just a predictor of inescapable pauperization: on the contrary, it maps the way to restoring and improving the livelihoods of the displaced. As in the case of other models, the components of the IRR model can be acted on and influenced through planning and resource allocation, in order to diminish the impact of one or several risks.

Risk reduction through policy measures

Development knowledge teaches us that measures to reduce risks can be taken at both the project level and the policy level. For instance, policies that keep the costs of energy too low tend to encourage over-consumption and tolerate waste, thus leading to the construction of more dams or thermal plants, with entailed displacements risks. This suggests that the risks of resettlement can also be diminished through better demand-management policies. Ultimately, the interlocked risks inherent in displacement can be controlled when governments adopt broad national policies for safety nets and risk reversals. Single means – for instance, cash compensation – are insufficient on their own to counterbalance all risks.

Maximum safeguarding is achieved when involuntary displacement is avoided altogether. This is the response to risks that should be considered first and foremost. Recognizing risks and their financial implications at the outset is often a powerful stimulus to search for an alternative that will eliminate the need for displacement or reduce the number of people affected. This is technically possible in some cases, for example, by changing the site of a dam, or by re-routing a highway around (rather than through) a village; many other technical options can be found through creative thinking.

Social research on resettlement has identified specific risk management strategies that can be employed against the common risks in resettlement, to prevent landlessness, joblessness, higher morbidity, and so on. In turn, social research on *voluntary* settlement schemes, and on patterns of self-management *after relocation,* has documented effective approaches (some replicable in involuntary resettlement) that can help those resettling in new lands to overcome the risks and difficulties of resettlement. (For empirical documentation on the impoverishment risks and impacts, as well as on results of risk reduction measures, please consult the 'Guide to further reading'.)

GUIDE TO FURTHER READING

Cernea, M.M. (ed.) (1999) *The Economics of Involuntary Resettlement. Questions and Challenges,* Washington, DC: World Bank. This book sharply criticizes economic methodologies used for the analysis and financial provision of resettlement operations, particularly the cost–benefit analysis. See particularly Chapter 1 (by Michael M. Cernea) and Chapter 6 (by Warren van Wicklin) about economic fallacies in resettlement analysis and sharing project benefits with displaced groups.

Cernea, M.M. (2007) 'Financing of development and benefit-sharing mechanisms in population resettlement', *Economic and Political Weekly*, 42(12): 1033–46 (available at http://www.epw.org.in).

Cernea, M.M. and McDowell, C. (eds) (2000) *Risks and Reconstruction. Experiences of Resettlers and Refugees*, Washington, DC: World Bank. The volume includes 18 chapters documenting experiences from all continents, with replicable approaches to risk prevention and risk management.

Mathur, H.M. (1998) 'The impoverishment risk model and its use as a planning tool', in H.M. Mathur and D. Marsden (eds) *Development Projects and Impoverishment Risks: Resettling Project Affected People in India*, Oxford and New Delhi: Oxford University Press.

REFERENCES

Cernea, M.M. (1990) *Poverty Risks from Population Displacement in Water Resources Development*, Cambridge, MA: Harvard University Press.

Cernea, M.M. (1991) 'Involuntary resettlement: Social research, policy and planning', in M.M. Cernea (ed.) *Putting People First. Sociological Variables in Development*, New York and London: Oxford University Press.

Cernea, M.M. and McDowell, C. (eds) (2000) *Risks and Reconstruction. Experiences of Resettlers and Refugees*, Washington, DC: World Bank.

Mahapatra, L.K. (1999) *Resettlement, Impoverishment and Reconstruction in India*, New Delhi: Vikas.

Mathur, H.M. and Marsden, D. (eds) (1998) *Development Projects and Impoverishment Risks: Resettling Project Affected People in India*, Oxford and New Delhi: Oxford University Press.

Merton, R.K. (1979) *The Sociology of Science: Theoretical and Empirical Investigations*, Chicago, IL: University of Chicago Press.

9.9 Ethnicity, identity and nationalism in developing countries

Katharine Adeney and Andrew Wyatt

Ethnicity and nationalism

Several violent conflicts in the 1990s, especially those in Rwanda and the Balkans, drew attention to the terms 'ethnicity' and 'nationalism'. Ethnic conflict is not new, but the revival of nationalist sentiment, the notion that the boundaries of 'the people' should coincide with the boundaries of the state, has been a common theme in contemporary conflicts. These conflicts also fuelled an interest in the nexus between security and development. However, in what follows we argue that the relationships between ethnicity, identity and nationalism have had important consequences for development over a longer time period. A historically informed perspective on these issues will create a better understanding of development.

'Ethnicity' is a contested term. Walker Connor (1994: 100) notes that the origins of the word refer to 'a group characterized by common descent'. He cautions against using the word as a synonym for minority, as majorities also possess an ethnicity. At its most basic, ethnicity refers to an identity that is shared among a group of people. This shared identity can be based on many markers, including language, religion, race and/or culture. Some scholars, including Connor, claim it is unhelpful to conflate different types of identity under the term 'ethnicity'. But it is unavoidable because a variety of markers can be used to create a perception of common descent. In any analysis of ethnic conflict, the type of ethnicity involved must be identified, as it may affect the scope, and the likelihood of resolution. Ethnicity is also contested according to whether it is other- or self-defined. An ethnic group may be defined by outsiders (other-defined) as a collectivity, even if the group itself does not possess a sense of self. But for ethnic conflict to take place, a group must possess a self-awareness of what differentiates 'us' from 'them'.

To note that ethnicity is related to common descent, or a perception of common descent, is not to argue that ethnic identities are immutable. These identities are subject to interpretation and change over time. Languages, cultures and religions are not static (Horowitz 1985). In addition, individuals possess multiple identities as well as political and social affiliations. This is important because identities are not only multiple, they are also situational (Manor 1996). The importance of one facet of an individual's identity is dependent on the context – often related to the perceived security, or otherwise, of that identity. These different identities interact, oppose and complement each other.

Nations may be ethnically defined, and Walker Connor's assertion that a nation is 'a self-differentiating ethnic group' (1994: 42) is a useful one because it implies a sense of self, defined against an 'other'. However, non-ethnic nations also exist. Civic nations define their members as those living within a territory (regardless of ethnic background). Citizenship rules help to define civic nations. So, being born in the territory of a state, as is the case in France, entitles you to become a member of a civic nation (Brubaker 1992: 18). Both ethnic and civic nations have a sense of a self, and an other, which often produces a political programme. This political orientation is captured in Ernest Gellner's famous definition of nationalism as 'a political principle which holds that the political and the national unit should be congruent' (1983: 1). Nationalism arose in the late eighteenth century, primarily as a result of the ideologies espoused by the French revolution – the people were sovereign, and *the* people became synonymous with *my* people. Though, of course, conflict between different communities had existed before this date and many European states had earlier attempted to create homogeneous populations along lines of religion and language. It is important to note that nationalist movements do not always seek independence; many are concerned with securing autonomy or greater rights within an existing state.

Three important processes during the colonial period shaped the politics of nationalism and ethnicity in the developing world. First, and very ironically, Western colonialists introduced many of the ideas that motivated nationalist campaigns to end colonial rule. This was very clear in the rhetoric used by the Indian National Congress to contest the legitimacy of British rule in India. Second, the drawing of political boundaries, on the basis of international power politics, often created very heterogeneous states. The boundaries of most states in sub-Saharan Africa were determined during the colonial period, and largely without regard to the ethnic composition of the territories in question (Handelman 2006: 80). Third, Western colonialism shaped the way that many identities in the developing world were presented and understood. Colonial administrators did not simply redefine identities. This would imply that colonial societies were a blank canvas on which existing identities and societies were not represented. Rather, colonialism might be said to the crucible in which identities were re-formed. Colonialism often divided groups against each other, especially when the opportunities provided by colonialism were taken up by one group more than another. Hindus in northern India, compared to Muslims, gained a disproportionate share of government education and employment, by virtue of their earlier embracing of the available opportunities. Also, colonialism often affected the internal labour market of colonized states – as seen by the introduction of Indian labourers to Malaysia and elsewhere. Finally, the 'simple' process of taking a census codified groups along lines that may not have been recognized by the population as a whole, and also made groups aware of the demographic composition of the state. If demography assumes political significance, for example if democratic elections are imminent, this awareness can cause conflict. This was seen strikingly in Sri Lanka, shortly after independence from Britain. The minority Tamil community suffered, as political leaders from the majority Sinhala community competed to represent themselves as guardians of a 'beleaguered' community (Horowitz 1985).

Nationalist movements

As noted above, nationalist movements in the developing world often took an anticolonial form. They highlighted the exploitative character of colonial rule and frequently celebrated the glories of their indigenous traditions. These traditions, often extensively re-narrated for political convenience, were used as the basis for 'imagined communities', united by a common culture (Anderson 1991: 6–7). These communities were 'imagined' because, while the population would never meet more than a fraction of its fellow nationals, images of their common features (standardized by modernity), such as language and history, brought the nation together. Nationalist movements in the developing world often faced difficulties in articulating a unified identity because of the diversity of the population living within the borders defined by the colonial powers. Nationalists agreed on demanding independence from the colonial powers and argued that self-determination was the only legitimate way to build a political community. Partha Chatterjee (1993) is critical of Anderson. He argues that too much attention is paid to the political activity of elite nationalists, whereas more creative forms of nationalism were expressed in cultural activity where the influence of Western ideas was much weaker. After independence, elite nationalists often emulated the material achievements of the West. They frequently ignored their own culture(s), especially dissenting and subaltern expressions of nationalism (Gandhi 1998: 120), as they sought to build a modern, and often centralized, state. Not all nationalist aspirations were achieved and some movements seeking independence for their unit, such as Aceh in Indonesia, were not recognized. Strong nationalist movements have frequently challenged the central state, as in the cases of Biafra in Nigeria, Katanga in the Congo and Kashmir in India. Only in rare cases, such as Bangladesh, Eritrea and East Timor, have these movements been successful.

Economic themes have been very prominent in the nationalist ideologies of developing countries. Anticolonial nationalists argued that colonial rule resulted in economic exploitation and poverty. The political elites of newly independent states were therefore obliged to redress this problem. The legitimacy of post-colonial states rested on the promotion of economic growth. Grand schemes of economic development, such as the Volta Dam in Ghana, were objects of national pride and demonstrated commitment to modernization (Wyatt 2005). Nationalist ideology often encouraged policies of import substitution that favoured national producers over foreign interlopers. In some cases, such as Taiwan and South Korea, nationalist development strategies resulted in rapid economic growth. In other cases, such as India, nationalist policies produced only modest growth, encouraging liberal critics to claim that vested interests were exploiting the nationalist label and gaining at the expense of the majority. Leftist critics, including many in the dependency school, were more circumspect (Hoogvelt 2001: 48). They were suspicious that nationalist policies favoured the dominant classes, but they also felt that a weak national bourgeoisie would continue a state of dependency on the former colonial powers. Nationalist ideology is out of favour with institutions of global governance, including the World Bank, the World Trade Organization and the International Monetary Fund, but most states continue to seek nationalist advantage, even when proclaiming their commitment to economic liberalism.

The relationship between identity and development

Early thinkers about development often distinguished between traditional, undeveloped societies and modern, usually Western, developed societies. They considered cultural norms and social identities to be determinants of development. Some social identities were held to be primitive and backward-looking, and so detrimental to development. Religious beliefs, based on superstition, were at odds with 'rational' science. Networks based around kinship or ethnicity were assumed to encourage nepotism and undercut the efficiency that would arise with a more merit-oriented society. It was hoped, and often assumed, that as economic growth occurred, some of these 'primordial' identities would give way to modern ways of self-identification, such as class or civic nationalism. National identities based around religious and ethnic affiliations were viewed with suspicion because they might encourage chauvinism towards other groups. Many of the leaders of the developing world also operated on these assumptions, including India's first prime minister, Jawaharlal Nehru (Adeney and Lall 2005). In practice, the distinction between tradition and modernity was overstated. 'Traditional' identities continued to adapt after the end of colonial rule. For example, caste in India remains a set of rules that determine marriage and social interaction, but it is also a badge of identity that is used in politics and the labour market (Gorringe 2005). The rise of mass politics and elections introduces identities into new arenas, as parties and governments seek to make connections with the 'people'. Economic growth and development has also led to adaptation. The spread of communication technology, such as film and television, helps create an awareness of a mass society and the location of social identities in those societies. Mass communication facilitates the development of an 'us' and a 'them', although (as noted above) individuals are usually members of multiple communities. Contrary to Karl Deutsch's assertion (1966), communication has not led to integration and the end of nationalism. Those working with a Marxist perspective on development are still keen to emphasize class identities and are wary of more 'cultural' identities. However, some policymakers are happy to shape development initiatives around cultural identities. The World Bank, under James Wolfensohn, was keen to explore the potential of faith-based groups as agents of development. There has been a long tradition of religious NGOs promoting social reform and development.

Social identities, ethnic and otherwise (including class), often form the basis of differential development. Nationalism, defined in an ethnic fashion, often excludes some communities within the state. Some development policies have been designed to create parity between communities. The New Economic Policy in Malaysia was designed to help 'ethnic' Malaysians catch up with the economically dominant Chinese. In Sri Lanka, policies were introduced to restore a 'balance' between the Sinhalese and Tamils. Such policies, even with the apparently laudable aim of promoting equality between communities that produce differential development for different groups, often lead to conflict, as has been the case in Sri Lanka. In some cases, development policies privileged one group over another, with little attempt at justification. Before 1971, East Pakistan experienced limited development, while West Pakistan moved ahead. The break-up of Pakistan and the creation of Bangladesh was driven by a nationalist movement with a strong economic dimension.

Nationalism and ethnicity have shaped development policies and opportunities. Nationalism has motivated exceptional levels of economic development in a few cases. Development policies have become intertwined with group aspirations. Conflicts between ethnic groups, as in the case of Rwanda or Sri Lanka, have limited the spread of human development. The political accommodation of identities has limited conflicts in other states. This needs to be understood as part of a broadly defined process of development. Identity remains an important variable which has affected development, and will continue to do so.

GUIDE TO FURTHER READING

Connor, W. (1994) *Ethnonationalism: The Quest for Understanding*, Princeton, NJ: Princeton University Press.

Handelman, H. (2006) *The Challenge of Third World Development*, Upper Saddle River, NJ: Prentice Hall.

Horowitz, D. (1985) *Ethnic Groups in Conflict*, Berkeley, CA: University of California Press.

REFERENCES

Adeney, K. and Lall, M. (2005) 'Institutional attempts to build a "national" identity in India: Internal and external dimensions', *India Review*, 4(3–4): 258–86.

Anderson, B. (1991) *Imagined Communities: Reflections on the Origin and Spread of Nationalism*, London: Verso.

Brubaker, R. (1992) *Citizenship and Nationhood in France and Germany*, Cambridge, MA, and London: Harvard University Press.

Chatterjee, P. (1993) *The Nation and its Fragments: Colonial and Postcolonial Histories*, Princeton, NJ: Princeton University Press.

Connor, W. (1994) *Ethnonationalism: The Quest for Understanding*, Princeton, NJ: Princeton University Press.

Deutsch, K. (1966) *Nationalism and Social Communication: An Inquiry into the Foundations of Nationality*, Cambridge, MA: MIT Press.

Gandhi, L. (1998) *Postcolonial Theory: A Critical Introduction*, Edinburgh: Edinburgh University Press.

Gellner, E. (1983) *Nations and Nationalism*, Oxford: Blackwell.

Gorringe, H. (2005) *Untouchable Citizens: Dalit Movements and Democratisation in Tamil Nadu*, New Delhi: Sage.

Handelman, H. (2006) *The Challenge of Third World Development*, Upper Saddle River, NJ: Prentice Hall.

Hoogvelt, A. (2001) *Globalization and the Postcolonial World: The New Political Economy of Development*, Basingstoke: Palgrave.

Horowitz, D. (1985) *Ethnic Groups in Conflict*, Berkeley, CA: University of California Press.

Manor, J. (1996) 'Ethnicity and politics in India', *International Affairs*, 72(1): 459–75.

Wyatt, A. (2005) '(Re)imagining India's (inter)national economy', *New Political Economy*, 10(2): 163–79.

9.10 Faith and development

Emma Tomalin

Introduction

Faith traditions continue to exert a strong influence on the lives of many people in developing countries. Religious beliefs can shape values about key development concerns, such as education and economics, and they frequently have an impact on styles of social and political organization. Moreover, many faith-based organizations are engaged in development-related activities, from service delivery to humanitarian aid and disaster relief. Nevertheless, in recent years, there has been a growing number of scholars and practitioners who have expressed concern at the failure of mainstream development theory and practice to consider the relationship between faith traditions and development (White and Tiongco 1997; Selinger 2004). A survey of three major development studies journals, between 1982 and 1998, revealed that religion and spirituality are 'conspicuously under-represented in development literature and in the policies and programmes of development organizations' (Ver Beek 2002: 68). There is, however, a burgeoning literature from 'within' religious traditions on development-related topics such as economics, sustainability and human rights. These themes have also been taken up within academic research outside the field of development: for instance, in religious studies, anthropology, sociology and economics (see the working papers of the Religion and Development Research Programme Consortium, available at http://www.rad.bham.ac.uk).

This short chapter will provide an overview of some of the main debates that have emerged around the topic of faith and development. What are the reasons for the marginalization in development studies of issues around religious faith? In what ways is religion relevant to the development project, and to what extent could considerations of faith and spirituality be 'mainstreamed' in development? By 'development' I mean primarily the agenda of the (predominantly) Western-driven development agencies and NGOs that have emerged since the 1950s (this does not deny that development has taken place in other settings, or that there are competing and critical visions). Although there have been shifts in understandings of development in the West during this period, none of the dominant conceptualizations has incorporated a consideration of the ways in which religious beliefs, practices and organizations relate to their agenda for change.

Understanding why faith traditions have been ignored

One reason why religion has not received attention within the development debate is due to the idea dominant in modernization theory that secularization (that is, the removal of the influence of religion from public or social life, and the separation of religion and the state) goes hand in hand with the transition to modernity and economic development. Thus, religion was expected to either disappear altogether or to become a purely private matter with a limited effect on public life. It was anticipated that people would give up their 'primitive superstitions' and 'backward religious world views' (particularly in their application to social matters) as their communities evolved into developed societies modelled on the West. However, this 'secularization thesis' has come under attack, since religion continues to play a significant role in public life in many developed as well as developing contexts.

Another reason for this apparent avoidance of religion concerns the difficulties that face secular development agencies (governmental and non-governmental) if they are seen to be supporting or opposing particular faith traditions. The politicization of religious affiliation is all too apparent (from the Muslim-Jewish conflict in Israel to the Hindu-Muslim tensions in India), and to enter into debates or alliances that can be construed as partisan could jeopardize development goals and exacerbate existing tensions. However, it is arguable whether this means that secular development agencies should never support the work of religious groups. Instead, common sense suggests the adoption of a careful and informed approach when building alliances with religious organizations. Nevertheless, inter-religious tensions can contribute to poor levels of development, by increasing economic and political instability and the marginalization of some religious groups. There is a need for development agencies to understand the controversial and complex links between religion, politics and social development, and their implications for policy.

A final reason for the uneasy relationship between development and faith is the fact that religious values may act against the interests of the development process (see the special edition of *World Development* 1980 in the 'Guide to further reading' at the end of this chapter). For instance, the rise of 'fundamentalist' or 'conservative' religious forms is often considered to have negative consequences for women's human rights. The Catholic Church's prohibition on condom use can increase women's chances of contracting HIV when their husbands have been unfaithful, or can lead to unwanted pregnancies, which in some Catholic contexts cannot legally be terminated. In some Muslim countries, Islamic law is interpreted to deny women any form of political participation, while in others women are virtually confined to the home due to religious attitudes towards maintaining their sexual modesty (Bayes and Tohidi 2001).

However, in such situations we often find the emergence of styles of 'religious feminism', which argue for reinterpretations of religious beliefs that are consistent with the 'core' values of the tradition as well as various types of feminist thinking. Such a strategy is attractive to women who wish to employ a religious narrative to guide their quest for empowerment, rather than relying on the secular rhetoric of mainstream (Western) feminist discourse. Thus, breaches of women's human rights in the name of religion suggest the need for a research agenda on religion and development that is concerned to understand the roots of such oppression and to identify ways of tackling it (see the special editions of *Gender and Development* 1999 and 2006 in the 'Guide to further reading').

The above discussion suggests a number of reasons why development has avoided consideration of religious issues. However, there is a growing number of scholars, both outside and within religious traditions, who are critical of this neglect and of the overtly secularist framework that guides the Western development project. Not only has religion continued to be important in people's lives and in the political economy of developing countries, but secular development agencies, such as the UK government's Department for International Development, also disburse funds to faith-based NGOs (such as the Catholic Agency for Overseas Development (CAFOD) and Islamic Relief). Nevertheless, there has been little research on the nature of the relationships between secular and faith-based organizations (FBOs), or on the contribution that religion makes to the lack of development and its role in the identification of possible solutions to this. In the next section I will discuss the synergies and tensions between faith and development: in what way does religion complement, oppose or offer viable alternatives to the development agenda?

Religion and the development project: Synergies and tensions

While the contemporary Western development agenda is secular in nature, Christian missionaries carried out most early development work. Manji and O'Coill (2002) argue that missionary organizations prefigured modern development NGOs. In Africa, for instance, Christian Aid emerged at the end of the colonial period from a network of such missionary bodies. Although the colonial governments were less concerned with the social welfare of their subjects than with extracting maximum profit from their empires, they nevertheless benefited from the services provided by missionary societies (who were also intent on evangelizing: for poor communities, the promise of development often went hand in hand with the abandonment or suppression of their own religio-cultural traditions). The provision of education and health care, for example, served to produce a pool of literate workers for administrative jobs and to help maintain a functional workforce. Scholars suggest that the social welfare provided by missionaries helped to maintain a satisfied population, thereby lessening the chance of civil unrest (Manji and O'Coill 2002).

While missionary organizations in many ways appended the aims of colonial rule, Christianity also challenged some of the racist values underpinning the colonial endeavour. The most important example is the antislavery movement, promoted by evangelical Anglican philanthropists, such as William Wilberforce, from the late eighteenth century. Calls to end slavery in the colonies represent the beginnings of a global humanitarianism, where, according to Howse, we find 'a new doctrine of responsibility towards the unprivileged, a doctrine which received its chief impulse from the Evangelical emphasis on the value of the human soul, and hence, of the individual' (1952: 7). Thus, although the contemporary development project is secular, its roots arguably rest in the morals and institutions established by Christian missionaries abroad, as well as the philanthropic movement within evangelical Christianity back home.

Today, despite efforts by post-independence states to assume responsibility for development work and service delivery, much development continues to be carried out by faith-based organizations of various types, as well as within religious communities (such as activities organized around churches, mosques or temples). While the work of the larger international FBOs, such as CAFOD, Christian Aid or Islamic Relief, is well known, there are numerous smaller groups and organizations working at the grass-roots level that are not documented or in receipt of international funds. There is some indication that the development establishment is beginning to take an interest in the links between religious organizations and poverty reduction. For example, in 1998 an organisation/network called the World Faiths Development Dialogue (WFDD) was set up by the president of the World Bank, James D. Wolfensohn, and Lord Carey, Archbishop of Canterbury, to encourage dialogue between religious traditions in the South and international development institutions. More recently, the UK government's Department for International Development (DFID) has produced booklets about world religions and poverty reduction, and its Commission for Africa report (2005: 120–1) highlights religion as an area for consideration. Many remain sceptical, however, about the motives of major donors who suddenly want to 'understand' religion. Some maintain that it is a knee-jerk reaction which aims to calm nerves after 11 September 2001, and there are concerns among faith groups that religion is being co-opted to serve a narrowly defined, economically driven development agenda.

Religion may also offer alternatives to the conventional development paradigm. It is not uncommon for religious groups to voice objections to the materialism inherent in Western development models, or to stress that spiritual development must not be precluded by economic considerations. Hence, the development alternatives produced by religious thinking may not always map the mainstream development agenda. Therefore, cooperation with religious organizations could be potentially threatening to the hegemony of Western development priorities and policies. Central to the issue of mainstreaming religion in international development is an assessment of the contradictions that arise between religious world views and the secular agenda of the development establishment. While in some cases such contradictions might reveal violations of human rights or the assertion of unjust power relations (e.g. with respect to the treatment of women), this is not always the case. For instance, there are significant differences between Islamic economics or Buddhist economics and the neoliberal model, yet advocates argue that they are viable alternatives (Zadek 1993; Vogel and Hayes 1998). Similarly, the Western secular model of human rights, adopted within rights-based approaches to development, can fail because it does not account for the impact of religion on the formation of social ethics. While religion can often act against the interests of human rights there is evidence to suggest that there are areas of overlap between secular understandings of human rights and religious values (Tomalin 2006).

Conclusion

One of the aims of development studies should be to produce systematic and reliable knowledge, and a better understanding of the social world, to aid the pursuit of development goals. It should not make judgements about the truth or desirability of particular religious values or beliefs, or urge a greater or lesser role for religion in achieving development objectives. However, the failure to consider the intersections between religion and development, and the ways in which religious organizations might be more fully engaged in the definition and achievement of development goals, is arguably detrimental to the development process.

GUIDE TO FURTHER READING

Development (2003) 46(4): at the core of this special edition on religion is the apparent paradox between the exclusion of religion in the development debate and its actual involvement in development on the ground.

Gender and Development (1999) 7(1) and *Gender and Development* (2006) 14(3): two special editions on religion, gender and development. The articles demonstrate that while religion can be an obstacle to women's development, it can also provide a basis for the pursuit of social, political and economic empowerment.

Journal of Religion in Africa (2002) 32(1): this special issue on religious non-governmental organizations comprises four articles that provide a discussion of the work, funding and ideological frameworks of Christian (Zimbabwe, Kenya) and Islamic (Senegal, Ghana) NGOs.

World Development (1980) 8(7/8): this volume is atypical in reflecting an 'early' interest in the relationship between religion and development. It has a number of articles that focus on religion as an obstacle to development, as well as several that aim to identify a more positive correlation.

USEFUL WEBSITES

World Faiths Development Dialogue: http://www.wfdd.org.uk – this website has information about the organization/network, as well as access to publications and reports.

Religions and Development: http://www.rad.bham.ac.uk – this website gives details of a Department for International Development-funded Research Programme Consortium on the topic of religions and development, based in the International Development Department at Birmingham University; it also provides access to a series of working papers.

Religion and Development Bibliography: http://environment.harvard.edu/religion/disciplines/economics/bibliography/noyce_index.html – this bibliography is divided into different headings, by both region and religion.

REFERENCES

Bayes, J.H. and Tohidi, J. (eds) (2001) *Globalization, Gender, and Religion: The Politics of Women's Rights in Catholic and Muslim Contexts*, New York and Hampshire: Palgrave.

Commission for Africa (2005) *Our Common Interest: Report of the Commission for Africa*, London: Penguin (available at http://www.commissionforafrica.org/english/report/introduction.html).

Howse, E.M. (1952) *Saints in Politics: The 'Clapham Sect' and the Growth of Freedom*, London: George Allen & Unwin Ltd.

Manji, F. and O'Coill, C. (2002) 'The missionary position: NGOs and development in Africa', *International Affairs*, 78(3): 567–83.

Selinger, L. (2004) 'The forgotten factor: The uneasy relationship between religion and development', *Social Compass*, 51(4): 523–43.

Tomalin, E. (2006) 'Religion and a rights-based approach to development', *Progress in Development Studies*, 6(2): 93–108.

Ver Beek, K.A. (2002) 'Spirituality: A development taboo', in T. Verhelst and W. Tyndale (eds) *Development and Culture*, Oxford: Oxfam, pp. 60–77.

Vogel, F.E. and Hayes, S.L. (1998) *Islamic Law and Finance: Religion, Risk, and Return*, The Hague: Kluwer Law International.

White, S. and Tiongco, R. (1997) *Doing Theology and Development: Meeting the Challenge of Poverty*, Edinburgh: St Andrew Press.

Zadek, S. (1993) 'The practice of Buddhist economics? Another view', *American Journal of Economics and Sociology*, 52(4): 433–45.

9.11 Global war on terror and the Global South

Klaus Dodds

The attacks of 11 September 2001 on the United States shocked Americans and the world community alike. On 7 October 2001, President George W. Bush declared that the United States would be engaged in a global war on terror (GWOT), which would seek not only to capture the mastermind behind this attack (the Saudi-born Osama bin Laden), but also to degrade those states and terror networks that provided the funding and planning support. With the support of the United Nations, the President sent US forces to Afghanistan in order to pursue the Taliban regime, which had hosted bin Laden after his exile from Sudan. After a short but intense conflict, the Americans and local allies, such as the Northern Alliance, routed the Taliban. Subsequently, a new government was elected and a slow process of reconstruction has been attempted, involving overseas agencies including the United Nations. Despite the apparent success of the military action, coalition partners of the United States, such as Britain and Canada, remain embroiled in a costly struggle with residual resistance groups, loyal either to the Taliban or to the Al-Qaeda network. Attempts to regulate the trade in opium have also failed because farmers have been unable to switch production to other forms of cash crops, not least because the profit margins attached to opium are far greater.

While the ongoing military campaign in Afghanistan remains controversial, the US-led assault in 2001 had the imprimatur of the United Nations. The same could not be said for the invasion of Iraq in March 2003. Frustrated by Saddam Hussein's continued defiance of United Nations weapons inspectors, the United States effectively bypassed the United Nations Security Council and decided to invade on the basis that the Iraqi regime represented a clear and present danger. It stood accused of supporting the Al-Qaeda network and stockpiling illegal supplies of weapons of mass destruction (WMD). With the support of a so-called 'coalition of the willing', the Americans and their allies overthrew the regime and captured Saddam Hussein, but failed to find any evidence of WMD. Four years on from the invasion (at the time of writing, 2007), it was increasingly clear that the Bush administration had been determined to pursue this regime regardless of any clear evidence of linkage to September 11th and/or WMD capacity. As a consequence, and in the face of continued high losses of civilian life in Iraq, through coalition bombing or suicide attacks by anti-American forces, the US occupation of Iraq had been accused of energizing still further radical Islamic militancy. This is a view that has been expressed by antiwar critics in North America and Europe, and within the Islamic community (umma) more generally.

The impact of 11 September 2001 has been keenly felt elsewhere in the Global South, although we have to be careful not to ascribe too much immediate significance to one particular event. For example, the fact that 15 of the 19 hijackers were Saudi passport holders could be used to focus attention on the relationship between Saudi Arabia and the United States, which stretches back at least to 1945 (Unger 2007). In effect, the United States promised to protect the Saudi Kingdom in return for generous access to the oilfields. In 1990–91, the US military was based in Saudi Arabia for the purpose of launching an assault on Saddam Hussein's forces stationed in Kuwait. While the Americans successfully removed the Iraqi invaders from Kuwait, Osama bin Laden, among others, was outraged at the presence of troops in the land of Mecca and Medina.

Earlier events in Afghanistan in the 1980s also contributed to the geopolitical milieu. In response to the Soviet invasion of Afghanistan in 1979, the USA and its allies, including Pakistan and Saudi Arabia, funded and trained resistance movements against Soviet troops. For the Reagan administration at the time, the logic of the cold war was overwhelming – the Soviets needed to be contained, and their enemy was potentially America's friend. In helping these anti-Soviet forces, the United States, perhaps unwittingly, was to help fund and arm a network of veterans, including bin Laden, who would come to resent the presence of America and regional governments such as Israel, Pakistan and Saudi Arabia. By the time of the Gulf War in 1991, bin Laden and his associates were already planning further assaults on America, in the Middle East and beyond. The World Trade Center was bombed in 1993; American embassies in Kenya and Tanzania were attacked in 1998; and the USS *Cole* was nearly sunk in Aden harbour in 2000.

GWOT and the reimagining of global political space

As part of his response to 9/11, President Bush declared in his 2002 State of the Union Address that the country was confronted by an axis of evil, composed of at least Iran, Iraq and North Korea. All three states stood accused of amassing WMD, abusing human rights and, in the case of Iraq, being connected to the perpetrators of the September 11th attacks. While Iraq was eventually to be targeted with direct military action in March 2003, the Islamic Republic of Iran is judged to be the greater threat, not least because it is seen as a regional sponsor of terror in Iraq, Lebanon and Syria. Given that the United States' principal ally in the Middle East is Israel, the identification of Iran as a member party of the 'axis of evil' is significant in reassuring a government that the United States is committed to rooting out terror, regardless of geographical location. Strikingly, Israel and others, such as Russia, have been supportive of the GWOT because it has helped to legitimate their own counterterror operations in the West Bank/Gaza and Chechnya respectively. At the time of writing (2006), it is still a matter of speculation whether the United States will carry out bombing raids designed to destroy Iran's suspected WMD capabilities, and/or encourage a regional ally, such as Israel, to implement a pre-emptive bombing mission. The possibility of a military invasion has also been discussed, and, as with Iraq, the fact that Iran is a major oil and natural gas exporter is a further complicating factor, as the United States is increasingly dependent on imported oil in order to service its energy needs. It is also eager to reduce its dependence on imported Saudi oil.

While some countries in the Global South have been branded as 'evil', others have been engaged by the United States with regard to the GWOT. In sub-Saharan Africa, for example, the Bush administration has supported the Pan-Sahel Initiative, which involves Chad, Mauritania, Mali and Niger, and is designed to enhance antiterror operations in the regions (Kraxberger 2005). Participants received military training and equipment so that these governments would be better able to prevent flows of people, weapons and finance from enabling terror groups from flourishing. In a striking reversal of previous disinterest in Africa – especially those states considered as 'failing' – the Bush administration is now interested in preventing the free movement of Islamic militants in Saharan Africa. In the Horn of Africa, US forces are now stationed in Djibouti, and the Pentagon is keen to establish further bases in central and West Africa, not least because interest is growing in the resource potential of states such as Angola and Guinea. Plane refuelling agreements have been signed with a host of African countries, including Kenya, Namibia and Zambia. In short, the political geographies of Africa are being changed by the GWOT. US funding for HIV/AIDS and development programmes, such as the Millennium Challenge Account, has also expanded in a further, albeit modest, attempt to improve relations with African countries.

In Asia, the USA has been engaged in two major policy initiatives: first, antiterror operations and, second, resource management. In South East Asia, America has been eager to improve relations with Indonesia (the most populous Muslim country in the world), following the Bali bombing of 2002 and the devastating tsunami in December 2004. US aid following the tsunami was considered critical, not only as a humanitarian gesture, but also as a mechanism for improving America's image in the Muslim world and the Global South more generally. This last point is of critical importance, as the invasion of Iraq, in combination with mounting evidence of US disregard for international law and conventions, has served to besmirch the reputation of the USA as a country characterized by liberty, freedom and human rights. Much to the disgust of Islamic militants, the USA also continues to work very closely with regional allies such as Pakistan in the GWOT. This has had severe implications for internal relations within Pakistan, and, in turn, has affected relations with neighbours such as Afghanistan and India.

The second dimension that has become more apparent in recent years has been resource competition between the USA and China in regions such as central Asia. Both countries are energy importers and their dependencies are increasing with regard to foreign sources. The Caspian Sea is often described as one of the most important and largely untapped resource areas in the world. Since the 1990s (in other words, prior to 11 September 2001), America increased its political and military presence in central Asia. The collapse of the Soviet Union in 1991 created an opportunity, which was seized by the Clinton administration. Both economic superpowers are investing in pipeline projects and resource extraction, and Russia is also a major interested party. Other regional powers, such as Iran, have negotiated energy deals with China, and this explains, in part, why China has been unwilling to support US plans for more coercive forms of diplomacy with regard to suspected WMD development.

The impact of the Global South, following the declaration of a US-led GWOT, has been substantial but uneven. While a few states have been labelled 'evil', others have received antiterror funding and other forms of support, and a small group have been invaded or threatened with possible invasion, as is the case with Iran. This is likely to continue as long as the Bush administration remains in office (until January 2009). The next US president will need to reconsider the human and material consequences of the GWOT and the corresponding implication for America's standing in the world. At present, it stands accused of being unilateral, pre-emptive and dismissive of international law and bodies such as the United Nations.

Conclusions

In September 2006, Hugo Chavez, the President of Venezuela, gave a speech to the United Nations General Assembly. He denounced President Bush as the 'devil', while holding a book by the veteran academic commentator, Noam Chomsky. While it is easy to mock such a performance, Chavez's speech, alongside his other pronouncements, such as an 'axis of good' involving Bolivia, Cuba and Venezuela, highlight how global political space is not only represented, but also contested. Although the USA remains the sole military superpower in the world, its impact on the Global South has been mixed. In the case of this political leader of oil-producing Venezuela, the GWOT is interpreted as part of a longer history of post-colonial experience, indelibly shaped by the hemispheric hegemonic power of the USA. For many countries in the Global South, acts of terror – whether state-sponsored or not – have been a feature of everyday life (one would only have to consult citizens living in Latin America, in places such as Buenos Aires, Lima and Montevideo). Likewise, it has been the fate of the Global South, almost since the Colombian encounter, to be unable to control flows of people, finance and even terror.

If we adopt a more generous historical and geographical framework, we would see that 11 September 2001 was truly shocking for the people of the United States because it happened *there*, and not somewhere else. For other people, living in other places, 'September 11th' is not without precedent – just ask the Chileans and the supporters of the late Salvador Allende.

GUIDE TO FURTHER READING

For general summaries of the war on terror and US relations with the Global South, especially the Middle East and south Asia:

Burke, J. (2004) *Al-Qaeda*, London: Penguin.

Clarke, R. (2004) *Against all Enemies*, New York: Free Press.

Unger, C. (2007) *House of Bush, House of Saud*, London: Gibson Books.

On resource competition:

Klare, M. (2001) *Resource Wars*, New York: Metropolitan.

Klare, M. (2004) *Blood and Oil*, New York: Metropolitan.

On Africa and the GWOT:

Kraxberger, B. (2005) 'The United States and Africa: Shifting geopolitics in an "age of terror" ', *Africa Today*, 52: 47–68.

On Iraq and the occupation:

Cockburn, P. (2006) *Occupation*, London: Verso.

Gregory, D. (2004) *The Colonial Present*, Oxford: Blackwell.

Packer, G. (2005) *The Assassins' Gate*, New York: Farrer, Straus and Giroux.

REFERENCES

Kraxberger, B. (2005) 'The United States and Africa: Shifting geopolitics in an "age of terror" ', *Africa Today*, 52: 47–68.

Unger, C. (2007) *House of Bush, House of Saud*, London: Gibson Books.

9.12 Corruption and development

Susan Rose-Ackerman

Economic development depends on good policies and effective institutions to carry out those policies. A country that tries to follow the prescriptions of macroeconomists will not succeed in promoting growth if its public and private institutions are very corrupt and dysfunctional. It is true that some countries are able to grow in spite of pervasive corruption, but extremely corrupt countries are not in that group, and even corrupt countries that manage to grow would do better with more effective institutions that need not be circumvented with bribes.

Tracking the connection between corruption and growth, however, is a difficult empirical exercise because the perpetrators of corrupt acts understandably wish to keep them secret. Nevertheless, a start has been made. Economists have generated a range of productive research, focusing mostly on bribery and illegal kickbacks.

Some of the first studies were contrarian. Economists saw bribes changing hands, and their first instinct was to applaud rather than condemn. In a bribe-maximizing system, government services go to the high bidders who value them most. Although other scholars quickly demonstrated that this perspective was radically oversimplified, the essential focus on bribes as prices and on the impact of corruption on resource allocation remains central to economic work. However, contemporary research demonstrates that corrupt payments do not usually further efficiency, and that illegal systems of bribe-prices undermine other public goals. From a policy point of view, economic research seeks both to isolate the economic effects of corruption and to suggest how legal and institutional reforms might improve the efficiency and fairness of government.

Conceptual underpinnings

Corruption occurs where private wealth and public power overlap. It represents the illicit use of willingness-to-pay as a decision-making criterion. Frequently, bribes induce officials to take actions that are against the interest of their principals, who may be bureaucratic superiors, politically appointed ministers, or multiple principals such as the general public. Pathologies in the agency/principal relation are at the heart of the corrupt transaction. Here, we differentiate between low-level opportunistic pay-offs, on the one hand, and systemic corruption, on the other, that implicates an entire bureaucratic hierarchy, electoral system or governmental structure, from top to bottom.

Low-level corruption occurs within a framework where basic laws and regulations are in place, and officials and private individuals seize on opportunities to benefit personally. There are several generic situations.

First, a public benefit may be scarce, and officials may have discretion to assign it to applicants. Then the qualified applicants with the highest willingness to pay and the fewest scruples will get the benefit in a corrupt system. This would seem to be the least problematic case. The pay-off is a transfer, and the benefits go to those who value them the most in dollar terms. The obvious policy response is to sell the benefit legally. For example, if a country has a limited supply of import licences to allocate, selling them to the highest bidders will usually be the efficient strategy.

Second, suppose that low-level officials are required to select only qualified applicants and that their exercise of discretion cannot be perfectly monitored. The overall supply may be scarce (for example, government-subsidized apartments), or open-ended (for example, driver's licences). In either case, the officials' discretion permits them to collect bribes from both the qualified and the unqualified. Incentives for pay-offs will also depend on the ability of superiors to monitor allocations, and on the options for the qualified – for example, can they approach another, potentially honest, official?

Third, the bureaucratic process itself may be a source of delay. Incentives for corruption arise as applicants try to get to the head of the queue. To further exploit their corrupt opportunities, officials may create or threaten to create more delay as a means of extracting bribes.

Some government programmes impose costs – for example, tax collection or the possibility of arrest by the police. Officials can then extract pay-offs in return for overlooking the illegal underpayment of taxes or for tolerating illegal activities. They can demand pay-offs in exchange for refraining from arresting people on trumped-up charges.

Low-level corruption can lead to the inefficient and unfair distribution of scarce benefits, undermine the purposes of public programmes, encourage officials to create red tape, increase the cost of doing business, and lower state legitimacy.

'Grand' corruption shares some features with low-level pay-offs, but it can be more deeply destructive of state functioning – bringing the state to the edge of outright failure and undermining the economy. Three varieties can be distinguished.

First, a branch of the public sector may be organized as a bribe-generating machine. For example, top police officials may organize large-scale corrupt systems in collaboration with organized crime groups. Tax collection agencies and regulatory inspectorates can also degenerate into corrupt systems managed by high-level officials.

Second, a nominal democracy may have a corrupt electoral system. Corruption can undermine limits on spending, get around limits on the types of spending permitted, and subvert controls on the sources of funds.

Third, governments regularly contract for major construction projects, allocate natural resource concessions, and privatize state-owned firms. High-level politicians can use their influence to collect kickbacks from private firms.

Much empirical work conflates these varieties of corruption into a single index number for each country. These indices capture the overall scale of the problem, but they are not much help in directing reform efforts to the most vulnerable sectors. Nevertheless, they do help to document the broad consequences and causes of corruption. Some of that work is summarized below, followed by suggested directions for reform.

Consequences of corruption

Modern empirical work began with the development of cross-country indices measuring the perception of corruption. The most widely used are compiled by Transparency International (http://www.transparency.org), an anticorruption non-governmental organization, and by the World Bank Institute (http://www.worldbank.org/wbi/governance). (See also the website of the U4 Anti-Corruption Resource Centre: http://www.u4.no/)

Richer countries and those with high growth rates, on average, have less reported corruption and better-functioning governments (Kaufmann 2003). However, it is unclear whether low levels of income and growth are a consequence or a cause of corruption. Most likely, the causal arrow runs both ways, creating vicious or virtuous spirals.

High levels of corruption are associated with lower levels of investment and growth, and corruption discourages both capital inflows and foreign direct investment. Thus, Wei (2000) finds that an increase in the corruption level from relatively clean Singapore to relatively corrupt Mexico is the equivalent of an increase in the tax rate of over 20 percentage points. Corruption lowers productivity, reduces the effectiveness of industrial policies, and encourages business to operate in the unofficial sector, in violation of tax and regulatory laws. According to Lambsdorff (2003b), if a country such as Tanzania could achieve the corruption score of the UK, its GDP would increase by more than 20 per cent, and net annual per-capita capital inflows would increase by 3 per cent of GDP. Highly corrupt countries tend to underinvest in human capital by spending less on education (Mauro 1997), to overinvest in public infrastructure relative to private investment (Tanzi and Davoodi 2002), and to have lower levels of environmental quality (Esty and Porter 2002). High levels of corruption can produce a more unequal distribution of income and can undermine programmes designed to help the poor. (The connection to income distribution may be complex; see Gupta, Davoodi and Alonso-Terme 2002.) For example, Olken (2006) shows how corruption and theft undermined a rice distribution programme in Indonesia.

Corrupt governments lack political legitimacy. Surveys carried out in four Latin American countries showed that those exposed to corruption had both lower levels of belief in the political system and lower interpersonal trust (Seligman 2002). Surveys in countries making a transition from socialism provide complementary findings (Fries, Lysenko and Polanec 2003).

In circumstances of low government legitimacy, citizens try to avoid paying taxes, and firms go underground to hide from the burden of bureaucracy. High levels of perceived corruption are associated with high levels of tax evasion and a lower obligation to pay taxes. As a consequence, corrupt governments tend to be smaller than more honest governments (Johnson et al. 2000).

Causes of corruption

Low levels of income and growth are both a cause and a consequence of corruption. Furthermore, trade openness and other measures of competitiveness appear to reduce corruption. Lambsdorff (2003a), for example, finds that weak law and order and insecure property rights encourage corruption, which, in turn, discourages foreign capital inflows.

Inequality has a negative effect on growth and that connection may be the result of its impact on corruption. An unequal system may be maintained by corrupt links between wealthy elites and the state (You and Khagram 2005).

Historical and social factors help explain cross-country differences. Acemoglu, Johnson and Robinson (2001) find that the type of colonial regime helps predict corruption levels after independence at the end of the twentieth century. La Porta et al. (1999) find that colonial heritage, legal traditions, religion and geographical factors are associated with corruption. These factors are not policy variables that present-day reformers can influence. The key issue, then, is whether they affect government quality directly, or whether they help determine intermediate institutions and attitudes that present-day policies can affect. If the latter, there may be alternative routes to the creation of institutions that facilitate economic growth and high income. Latitude and history need not be destiny.

Reform proposals

Much has been made of the importance of moral leadership from the top, but this is not sufficient. Too much moralizing risks degenerating into empty rhetoric – or worse, witch-hunts against political opponents. Policy must address the underlying conditions that create corrupt incentives, or it will have no long-lasting effects.

Some argue that the main cure for corruption is economic growth, and that economic growth is furthered by good policies, especially the promotion of education (Glaeser and Saks 2006). However, that claim reflects an overly simple view of the roots of economic growth and of corruption. Corruption is a symptom that state/society relations are dysfunctional. Pervasive corruption undermines the legitimacy of the state and leads to wasteful public policies. Good policies are unlikely to be chosen or to be carried effectively without honest institutions. The options for institutional reform fall into several broad categories: programme redesign, polices that increase transparency and accountability, and, in severe cases, constitutional change.

The first line of policy response is the redesign of programmes to limit the underlying incentives for pay-offs. This might mean eliminating highly corrupt programmes, but, of course, the state cannot abandon its responsibilities in many areas where corruption is pervasive. One response is to limit official discretion, for example, by streamlining and simplifying regulations, expanding the supply of benefits, making eligibility criteria clear, introducing legal payments for services, giving officials overlapping jurisdictions to give citizens choices, or redesigning systems to limit delays. Reformers should consider if clean-ups in one area will just shift corruption to another part of the government. Programmes may need to be comprehensive to have any impact. In addition, service delivery can be improved by civil service reforms that provide better salaries, improved monitoring, and the use of incentives.

The second collection of reform strategies focuses on the accountability and transparency of government actions. For example, a freedom-of-information law can give people access to government information, and many government decision-making processes should be open to public scrutiny and participation. Other options to improve accountability are the creation of independent oversight agencies and the use of external and internal benchmarks. Ongoing experiments with grass-roots democracy need more study to determine their impact and their transferability to other contexts (Rose-Ackerman 2004). Open government also depends on a vigorous and free media that can perform a watchdog function. International treaties, and organizations such as Transparency International, the World Bank and the United Nations, can help to create an environment in which multinationals limit their corrupt activities.

Third, some countries may need to consider more radical reforms in government structure. Democracy is valuable for many reasons, but, taken by itself, is hardly a cure for corruption. Some evidence suggests that presidential systems, especially those using proportional representation in the legislature, may be especially corrupt (Kuniková and Rose-Ackerman 2005). Furthermore, elections are not sufficient. The state must protect civil liberties and establish the rule of law. Rules must be clear and fair, and must be administered competently and fairly. This implies an honest, professional and independent judiciary, and police and prosecutors who have similar levels of integrity and competence.

We conclude with a word of caution. Clever, technical solutions, based on economic incentives, are not enough (Johnston 2005). If corruption is one of the pillars supporting a political system, it cannot be reduced substantially unless an alternative source of revenue replaces it. Powerful groups that lose one source of patronage will search for another vulnerable sector. Tough political and policy choices need to be faced squarely. It is little wonder that effective and long-lasting corruption control is a rare and precious achievement. But it is not beyond the power of determined and intelligent political reformers.

GUIDE TO FURTHER READING

Bardhan, P. (1997) 'Corruption and development: A review of issues', *Journal of Economic Literature*, 35: 1320–46.

Glaeser, E.L. and Goldin, C. (2006) *Corruption and Reform: Lessons from America's Economic History*, Chicago, IL: Chicago University Press for the National Bureau of Economic Research.

Rose-Ackerman, S. (1978) *Corruption: A Study in Political Economy*, New York: Academic Press.

Rose-Ackerman, S. (1999) *Corruption and Government: Causes, Consequences and Reform*, Cambridge: Cambridge University Press.

Rose-Ackerman, S. (ed.) (2006) *International Handbook on the Economics of Corruption*, Cheltenham: Edward Elgar.

Svensson, J. (2005) 'Eight questions about corruption', *Journal of Economic Perspectives*, 19(3): 19–42.

REFERENCES

Acemoglu, D., Johnson, S. and Robinson, J.A. (2001) 'The colonial origins of comparative development: An empirical investigation', *American Economic Review*, 91: 1369–401.

Esty, D. and Porter, M. (2002) 'National environmental performance measurements and determinants', in D. Esty and P.K. Cornelius (eds) *Environmental Performance Measurement: The Global Report 2001–2002*, New York: Oxford University Press.

Fries, S., Lysenko, T. and Polanec, S. (2003) *The 2002 Business Environment and Enterprise Performance Survey: Results from a Survey of 6,100 Firms*, London: European Bank for Reconstruction and Development (available at http://www.ebrd.com/pubs/econo/wp/0084.pdf).

Glaeser, E.L. and Saks, R. (2006) 'Corruption in America', *Journal of Public Economics*, 90(6–7): 1053–72.

Gupta, S., Davoodi, H.R. and Alonso-Terme, R. (2002) 'Does corruption affect income inequality?', *Economics of Governance*, 3: 23–45.

Johnson, S., Kaufmann, D., McMillan, J. and Woodruff, C. (2000) 'Why do firms hide? Bribes and unofficial activity after communism', *Journal of Public Economics*, 76: 495–520.

Johnston, M. (2005) *Syndromes of Corruption: Wealth, Power, and Democracy*, Cambridge: Cambridge University Press.

Kaufmann, D. (2003) *Rethinking Governance: Empirical Lessons Challenge Orthodoxy*, Discussion draft, Washington, DC: World Bank (available at http://www.worldbank.org/wbi/governance/pdf/rethink_gov_stanford.pdf).

Kunicová, J. and Rose-Ackerman, S. (2005) 'Electoral rules and constitutional structures as constraints on corruption', *British Journal of Political Science*, 35: 573–606.

Lambsdorff, J. Graf (2003a) 'How corruption affects persistent capital flows', *Economics of Governance*, 4, 229–43.

Lambsdorff, J. Graf (2003b) 'How corruption affects productivity', *Kyklos*, 56: 457–74.

La Porta, R., Lopez-de-Silanes, F., Shleifer, A. and Vishny, R. (1999) 'The quality of government', *Journal of Law, Economics, and Organization*, 15: 222–79.

Mauro, P. (1997) 'The effects of corruption on growth, investment, and government expenditure: A cross-country analysis', in K.A. Elliott (ed.), *Corruption and the Global Economy*, Washington, DC: Institute for International Economics.

Olken, B. (2006) 'Corruption and the costs of redistribution: Micro evidence from Indonesia', *Journal of Public Economics*, 90(4–5): 853–70.

Rose-Ackerman, S. (2004) 'Governance and corruption', in B. Lomborg (ed.) *Global Crises, Global Solutions*, Cambridge: Cambridge University Press, pp. 301–44.

Seligman, M. (2002) 'The impact of corruption on regime legitimacy: A comparative study of four Latin American countries', *Journal of Politics*, 64: 408–33.

Tanzi, V. and Davoodi, H. (2002) 'Corruption, growth, and public finance', in G.T. Abed and S. Gupta (eds) *Governance, Corruption and Economic Performance*, Washington, DC: IMF.

Wei, S.-J. (2000) 'How taxing is corruption on international investors?', *Review of Economics and Statistics*, 82: 1–11.

You, J.-S. and Khagram, S. (2005) 'A comparative study of inequality and corruption', *American Sociological Review*, 70: 136–57.

Governance and development

Editorial introduction

Development activity was for long virtually the monopoly of the state. However, the lack of alternatives did not mean the state was always a positive force for development. Moreover, in the late twentieth century, the state's claim to this monopoly weakened, while other agencies of development, such as the World Bank, the IMF and non-governmental organizations (NGOs), gained a higher profile. Development has to be seen in the economic context of global capitalism, but also in the political context. The most crucial relationship is between the state and the economy: states participate directly in processes of productive capital formation (establishing a set of economic policies favourable to capitalist accumulation), provide infrastructure and affect private-sector resource allocation through monetary and fiscal policies. The state provides an enabling environment/structure for development by other agencies. The state is the network of government, quasi-government and non-government institutions that coordinates, regulates and monitors economic and social activities. The role of non-state actors seems destined to grow as the power of the nation state declines and global economic activity intensifies.

Total official development assistance (ODA) allocated by all major donors is low and declining. Even though some ODA appears altruistic, much is manifestly deployed to promote the political and economic concerns of donors. Increased emphasis on aid conditionality underlines this, which has been controversial. Now not only the World Bank and the IMF but also many bilateral ODA programmes require recipients to adhere to certain policies. Aid is viewed as a means of promoting donors' perceptions of 'good governance' and 'sound' economic practices, leading many analysts and politicians to become very critical of aid. Research has indicated that economic growth has taken place post structural adjustment and reforms. Good governance is defined as sound management of a country's economic and social resources for development. What is 'sound' for the World Bank and others holding the view that 'democratization stimulates development' is a range of management techniques that are believed to work well within a standardized liberal democratic model. Critics contend that there are, and ought to be, different paths for development; they are not opposed to 'good governance' but urge that this is compatible with alternatives to liberal democracy in poor countries with different institutional contexts. Despite various campaigns led by various advocacy groups, such as Jubilee 2000 and Make Poverty History, urging for debt cancellations, progress on this front has been very slow. Since 1999 governments in the South are also required to develop pro-poor policies (poverty reduction strategies – PRSPs) by consulting local stakeholders, especially civil society and cultivating 'partnership'. The question remains if aid is effective in alleviating poverty and making a difference. What has become evident over the last few decades is that the two multilateral institutions and their sister agencies, the regional development banks, occupy a dominant position in the global political economy, with increasing involvement in the whole range of cross-cutting themes and politicised agendas, making their role very difficult.

Trade plays an important role in the promotion of economic development and the alleviation of poverty. With the changing structure of the world economy, 150 member countries have joined the World Trade Organization, especially as a result of the great dynamism of the new emerging economies of China, India, Japan, South Africa, Brazil and Mexico. There has also been an increase in South–South trade. The challenge is to contribute to the liberalization of trade for the particular interest of the developing countries, which has been slow and conflictual. This reflects the inherent complexities of the issues involved as the significant interests that are at stake for all countries involved in the process. This is very much reflected in issues related to intellectual property rights, and the protection of public health and access to medicine, agriculture, genetic resources, traditional knowledge and local farmers' rights in developing countries.

Throughout the 1990s the private sector's role in public service delivery has generated significant opposition and protest. It emphasizes the renewed interest of the markets in the development process, in the context of the state failure and a possible solution to respond to the vast needs of the low-income citizens of the developing countries. Search continues for combining the assumed efficiency of the private sector and the democratic accountability of the public bodies.

The purpose of giving ODA and its deployment is more open to scrutiny. One response has been increased funding for NGOs, generally thought more able to reach the local grass-roots level.

In the New Policy Agenda, combining market economics and liberal democratic politics, NGOs are simultaneously viewed as market-based actors and central components of civil society. NGOs fill gaps left by the privatization of state services as part of a structural adjustment or donor-promoted reform package. Governments need NGOs to help ensure their programmes are effective, well targeted, and socially responsible and well understood, hence the importance of the NGO–state relationship, which exists in diverse forms in different countries.

There are various types of NGO. At the international level we can differentiate between campaigning and charitable or service-providing NGOs. Both of these are generally based in the North. International campaigning NGOs are epitomized by Greenpeace. Such NGOs will address development policy issues from a distance. Northern-based, service-providing NGOs include Save the Children, Oxfam, Christian Aid, and so on. These generally have branches in the Southern countries in which they work. Often they will run their own projects, sometimes setting up their own partnerships with NGOs in the South, effectively bypassing those of the state. In other circumstances they will fund and monitor local service-providing NGOs or membership organizations. In recent years the NGO–donor relationship and its mutual trust have been tested mainly because of governments' reactions against terrorism, insecurity and instability. This has led to a shift in governments' attitudes towards non-governmental donors and civil society at large.

At the national level many NGOs are public-interest research or campaigning organizations. Some are Western-style human rights or conservationist NGOs. Usually relatively few, they often represent the concerns of particular groups. Other types of NGO are indigenous, national (and provincial) service-providing NGOs – mostly concerned with welfare and development. Many international NGOs have moved from directly running projects to working through partnerships with such NGOs. Lastly, there are membership organizations, often called 'grass-roots organizations', which exist to further their members' interests.

Recent findings have shown that NGOs are weak in contextual analysis of societies in which they work and that their approaches to monitoring and evaluation are rarely adequate. Further, certain key technical skills are frequently seen as lacking in their human resource base and many are more concerned with micro- than macro-context work. The practice of participation and innovation in project implementation can be poor too. Questions are asked about their accountability, legitimacy, performance and effectiveness. On the other hand, drawing on the new opportunities afforded by growth in their numbers and size and in the resources available to them, and facilitated by advances in communication technologies, NGOs want to scale up advocacy activities. NGOs have increasingly globalized, and are working through transnational networks, forging new enduring alliances and networks to maximize their impact, and engage in global policy processes. NGO campaigning (sometimes also through media) has led to NGOs being represented at important UN conferences and contact with the World Bank has grown rapidly over the 1990s, especially in the context of policy debates (e.g. environment, debt relief, gender, participation strategies and service delivery). NGOs are now also invited for formal consultations as part of civil society, on various sector policies and on the themes of the annual World Development Reports. NGOs have also been very critical of World Bank-financed infrastructural projects (e.g. involuntary resettlement, energy, forestry and dams) and have contributed to policy changes.

As economic inequalities have grown throughout the world, the political conditions required to overcome democratic deficits in decision making have become very crucial, especially in the context of discrimination on the grounds of race, colour, sex, language, religion, political or other opinions. Universal international human rights provide hope for many of the oppressed. It is also about generating accountability of states and security to citizens, and upholds national and international standards.

10.1 Foreign aid in a changing world

Peter Burnell

Official development assistance (ODA) is at the heart of foreign aid. The Development Assistance Committee (DAC) of the Organization for Economic Cooperation and Development (OECD) defines ODA as resources transferred on concessional terms, with the promotion of the economic development and welfare of the developing countries as the main objective. In addition, the early 1990s witnessed a growth in 'official aid' to 'Part II' countries, which shared ODA's essential features but was targeted on 12 'transition' countries in the former communist world, primarily Russia, and advanced developing countries like Israel. Concessionality ('softness') refers to grants or loans on especially favourable terms. Over time, grants have become the dominant mode of bilateral aid to the least developed countries, many of which have experienced difficulties in servicing their foreign debt, including loans formerly acquired on concessional terms.

Aid takes several forms, including transfers of finance, commodities and other goods, technical cooperation (around half of all bilateral aid) and debt relief. A conventional distinction is made between development aid and humanitarian or disaster relief aid. Military assistance, which was substantial, especially from the United States and Soviet Union during the cold war, is now relatively insignificant. Although the distinctions between different types of aid are theoretically coherent, in reality the boundaries sometimes break down: aid intended for one particular purpose may end up serving very different ends – the problem of 'fungibility'.

The big picture

In the 1960s the Development Assistance Committee (DAC) was established to improve and coordinate international aid efforts. Probably over 95 per cent of ODA now comes from DAC members, comprising 22 countries plus the European Commission, whose own contribution ranks around sixth after leading bilateral donors. In 2005, ODA to developing countries from DAC members increased to a record high of over US$100 billion, representing 0.33 per cent of these countries' gross national income (GNI), up from 0.26 per cent in 2004. Debt relief grants made a significant contribution to these figures, having grown by more than 400 per cent over one year. Debt forgiveness grants to Iraq and Nigeria alone accounted for US$14 billion and US$5 billion. Because these special cases are unlikely to be repeated, total ODA in the years ahead will be lower, but development aid still seems set to increase, so long as the promises made by donors are kept – something that some observers consider unlikely.

The United States, historically the top donor by volume, lost this position to Japan for much of the 1990s, but has since reclaimed the position, reconstruction aid to Iraq becoming a considerable component. ODA from EU countries provides more than half of all ODA. When measured against their gross national income, the country league tables for aid tell a very different story from the volumes (see Table 1). Approximately 30 per cent of ODA is managed by the multilateral donors, including the World Bank group's International Development Association, which makes interest-free loans to least developed countries. In addition, non-governmental agencies like Oxfam routinely provide sums totalling at least US$6 billion annually. This understates their role because official donors channel substantial additional amounts through them, especially for administering humanitarian aid.

Table 1 Net official development assistance, leading donors, 2005 (preliminary totals)

By volume			By percentage of GNI		
	Volume (US$ billion)	Percentage of GNI		Percentage of GNI	Volume (US$ billion)
United States	27.45	0.22	Norway	0.93	2.77
Japan	13.10	0.28	Sweden	0.92	3.28
United Kingdom	10.75	0.48	Luxembourg	0.87	0.26
France	10.05	0.47	Netherlands	0.82	5.13
Germany	9.91	0.35	Denmark	0.81	2.10

Source: Organization for Economic Cooperation and Development

The US Marshall Plan (1948–51) aid to economic reconstruction in Western Europe set a successful precedent of promoting development, which aid to other countries since has never really matched. But the pattern whereby US aid was strongly motivated by political reasons of national security and superpower rivalry has been an enduring feature. Other donors who became prominent later have also pursued multiple goals, although with individual characteristics. These range from economic objectives (Germany and Japan, for example), and a *mission civilisatrice* (France), to maintaining close historical relationships (around two-thirds of Britain's aid has traditionally gone to Commonwealth countries). The Netherlands, Canada and the Scandinavians are sometimes called 'like-minded' donors: they are presumed to share an attachment to goals of 'humane internationalism'. Before 1989, the USSR was a leading provider of technical and economic assistance, and military aid. For several years after the 1973–74 oil price rise, some oil-exporting countries (OPEC), chiefly Saudi Arabia and small Gulf states, were also important donors – Saudi Arabia being in the top five until the 1990s.

Among recipients, sub-Saharan Africa has steadily increased its share of all ODA, now approaching 40 per cent. Elsewhere, India and China are of greatly reduced importance. Bangladesh, Pakistan and Nicaragua continue to receive sizeable amounts. The most aid-dependent countries are not the major recipients (see Table 2). Smaller countries are treated more favourably, on a per-capita basis, and feature prominently among the most aid-dependent, especially emerging entities like Timor Leste and the Palestinian territories. A few former aid recipients have 'graduated' to donor status, most spectacularly Japan, and on a small scale Taiwan, South

Table 2 Net official development assistance, leading recipients, 2004

By volume			By percentage of GNI		
	Percentage of GNI 2003	Volume (US$ billion) 2004		Percentage of GNI 2003	Volume (US$ million) 2004
Iraq	N/A	4.65	Democratic Republic of Congo	98.61	1,815
Afghanistan	34.74	2.19	São Tomé and Principé	66.59	33
Vietnam	4.51	1.83	Guinea-Bissau	63.59	76
Ethiopia	23.54	1.82	Micronesia	47.26	86
Democratic Republic of Congo	98.61	1.81	Eritrea	42.38	260

Source: Organization for Economic Cooperation and Development

Korea and Turkey. China is expected to become increasingly important, not so much by total volume but in offering some developing countries an alternative source of support, which they can use to leverage greater independence from their traditional donors. The quid pro quos are economic benefits to China and diplomatic support against Taiwan.

Aid debates

In the early decades of development assistance, it was underpinned by an economic logic that stressed its contribution to filling two 'gaps' constraining development. Aid supplements savings and enhances investment, making possible an expansion of productive capacity. It furnishes foreign exchange for essential imports like machinery and, in many cases, fuel and food. Aid built large construction projects. Later, the remit was to lift the limits to the absorptive capacity for such capital inflows, for instance those deriving from technological backwardness.

By the 1970s heavy criticism was directed at most forms of aid, by dependency thinkers and others in the North and the South, many of whom viewed aid as an instrument of domination and exploitation. They doubted that it could be an effective means for reducing Third World poverty, and noted that it benefited privileged elites in the South as well as in donor countries. In the 1980s ODA was challenged by the rise of the neoliberal agenda in the West. Aid was now held to contribute to excessive government and to harm economic markets. Both groups of critics saw aid as part of the problem, not part of the solution to weak development. Neoliberals, especially, claim it can damage donor economies too, by distorting resource allocations. This applies particularly to tied aid, which, although much reduced, still persists in the form of the bulk of technical assistance.

The 1980s saw a dramatic expansion of conditionality-based lending linked to recommendations for economic policy and institutional reform. The advice embraces neoliberal tenets and embodies what became known as the 'Washington consensus' – structural adjustment loans (SALs) for structural adjustment programmes (SAPS) became a major feature. The 'conditionalities' incurred much resentment, not least because they appeared to be coercive and offensive to sovereignty. However, they are difficult to enforce. Their ineffectiveness (see Killick 1998) led to two new directions. First, the former belief that it is essential to get the economics right has now been supplemented by the notion that, to improve the chances of sound economic management and make development aid effective, the political environment must be addressed as well. 'Getting the politics right' gave aid a new role, introducing a second generation of conditionalities, focused on securing 'good governance' in particular.

The second new direction followed from Dollar and Burnside's influential World Bank report, *Assessing Aid: What Works, What Doesn't and Why* (Dollar and Burnside 1998), which recommended moving towards greater selectivity in aid allocation. That meant favouring countries who had already demonstrated a commitment to sound development policy and good governance, rather than using conditionality-based lending as an instrument to try to achieve those ends. Critics say this penalizes some societies which desperately need help. It offers no solution to their problems, which potentially could have damaging international repercussions. Critics also argue that, far from contradicting conditionality, selectivity simply replaces the *ex post* by an *ex ante* form of conditionality.

Moreover, a further additional generation of aid conditionality came into being in the second half of the 1990s, giving increased emphasis to pro-poor policies. And with the introduction of the poverty reduction strategy process after 1999, this was compounded with the new idea of process conditionality. Governments who are seeking concessionary funding from the Bretton Woods institutions, and debt relief in particular, are now required to internalize processes for embedding a pro-poor dimension into their development policy and budgetary arrangements, by consulting local stakeholders, specifically civil society. This is supposed to generate 'ownership', thereby countering many of the traditional failings of conditionality and development aid more generally.

Since the early 1990s, there has been an increasing amount of democracy assistance, perhaps reaching US$5 billion annually for democratic governance broadly defined, with the United States Agency for International Development, the European Union, the United Nations Development Programme and several government-funded but semi-autonomous democracy foundations being leading actors. Projects and programmes aimed at strengthening judicial autonomy, increasing legislative oversight, assisting with elections management, capacity-building in civil society and even promoting the development of viable political parties now form a notable sector in the aid industry. Like the other sectors, they engage a range of policymakers and practitioners in governmental and non-governmental organizations, independent think tanks and academic advisers. Carothers (1999) offers a classic overview. Both the actual contribution of democracy aid to democratization, and democratization's benefits to development and the performance of development aid specifically, are areas of considerable uncertainty. Although problematic, methodologies for evaluating the effectiveness of democracy assistance are now being pioneered by a few aid agencies. An example is Finkel et al.'s (2006) quantitative study of USAID democracy and governance assistance, which reached positive conclusions.

Recent trends

Since the 1950s, aid has undergone significant changes in respect of what we understand about it and our expectations. In the 1990s, some observers claimed that aid was in crisis. Its achievements were questioned by many shades of opinion. There seemed to be minimal support for aid in the USA, because its instrumental value for traditional foreign policy goals had obsolesced. A number of other donors manifested 'aid fatigue'. Aid in real terms and expressed as a percentage of donor wealth was declining, in contrast to increasing flows of private international finance. The corner was turned around the time of the UN-hosted conference on Financing for Development, staged in Monterrey in 2002. President Bush and the Europeans vied for the moral high ground, by announcing plans to increase their overseas aid substantially. But even before then, the events of 9/11 and subsequent reflections on the economic origins of international terrorism offered a new rationale for providing aid, and was beginning to drive thinking about aid's usefulness and influence its geopolitical allocation.

The post-cold war disorder has seen the emergence of more new kinds of security 'threats'. Substate violent conflict has the potential to cross borders. Issues like international migration, internationally organized crime, drug trafficking, global environmental threats and the challenge of mainstreaming gender all command attention. These have expanded aid's horizons significantly. Moreover, poverty is seen to be connected with all these issues, and aid agencies have rearticulated poverty reduction as their priority. The traditional language of giving has given way (at least in the rhetoric) to ideas of cultivating development 'partnership'. The emphasis now is supposed to be on achieving results, rather than 'moving the money', and the burden of responsibility rests with the recipients. Current thinking is that both the policy and the institutional environment, governance institutions especially, hold the key. It is expressed nowhere more vividly than in the Commission for Africa report, *Our Common Interest* (2005), launched just months before the G8 summit at Gleneagles, Scotland, which pledged to double aid by 2010, including an extra $25 billion for Africa and debt write-offs for 18 of the world's poorest countries. Nevertheless, that the leading aid organizations themselves, and the Bretton Woods institutions in particular, could do much more to institutionalize good governance in their own arrangements continues to be a live issue among their critics (see Woods 2006).

It remains to be seen whether development cooperation can deliver the wide-ranging mandate that it has acquired, even with increasing resources. An important lesson from the aid experience points to the magnitude of the problems it seeks to address – complex problems, requiring interdisciplinary approaches geared to 'holistic' solutions. 'Policy coherence', which means compatible policies in such matters as international trade, is also deemed to be crucial, as is more support for a wide range of global public goods. The moral is that we should moderate our expectations that aid by itself will make a difference.

GUIDE TO FURTHER READING

Browne, S. (2006) *Aid and Influence. Do Donors Help or Hinder?* London: Earthscan. A critical account of distorting influences behind aid-giving, together with practical recommendations, drawing on Browne's lengthy field experience and work for the United Nations.

Burnell, P. (1997) *Foreign Aid in a Changing World*, Buckingham and Philadelphia, PA: Open University Press. A widely available, accessible and broad-based account of the philosophy, politics and economics of foreign aid since 1945, although not abreast of recent issues.

Burnell, P. and Morrissey, O. (eds) (2004) *Foreign Aid in the New Global Economy*, Cheltenham: Edward Elgar. Thirty-two notable articles on aid published from the 1980s onwards, ranging from trade and fiscal linkages to environmental and gender perspectives, all framed by the editors' Introduction.

Easterly, W. (2006) *The White Man's Burden: Why the West's Efforts to Aid the Rest Have Done So Much Ill and So Little Good*, New York: Penguin. The book's subtitle needs no elaboration. Provocative.

Lancaster, C. (2007) *Foreign Aid. Diplomacy, Development, Domes*, The University of Chicago Press. Compares the domestic drivers of Germany and Denmark.

USEFUL WEBSITES

http://www.oecd.org/dac — site of the Development Cooperation Directorate (DAC) of the Organization for Economic Cooperation and Development (OECD), containing a wealth of regularly updated statistical information on aid flows and analytical reports.

http://www.worldbank.org — site of the World Bank, including the International Development Association.

http://www.dfid.gov.uk — site of the British government's aid agency, the Department for International Development.

http://www.usaid.gov — site of the United States Agency for International Development, containing, inter alia, the 2006 report, *Effects of US Foreign Assistance on Democracy Building: Results of a Cross-National Quantitative Study*, by S. Finkel, A. Pérez-Liñán and M. Seligson with D. Azpuru.

http://www.ned.org — site of the US's National Endowment for Democracy, a leading private non-profit provider of democracy assistance, funded by congressional grant.

REFERENCES

Carothers, T. (1999) *Aiding Democracy Abroad*, Washington, DC: Carnegie Endowment for International Peace.

Commission for Africa (2005) *Our Common Interest: An Argument*, London: Commission for Africa.

Dollar, D. and Burnside, C. (1998) *Assessing Aid: What Works, What Doesn't, and Why*, Washington, DC: World Bank.

Finkel, S., Pérez-Liñán, A. and Seligson, M. with Azpuru, D. (2006) *Effects of US Foreign Assistance on Democracy Building: Results of a Cross-National Quantitative Study*, Washington, DC: USAID.

Killick, T. with Gunatilaka, R. and Mar, A. (1998) *Aid and the Political Economy of Policy Change*, London and New York: Routledge.

Woods, N. (2006) *The Globalizers: The IMF, the World Bank and their Borrowers*, Ithaca, NY: Cornell University Press.

10.2 Third World debt

Stuart Corbridge

In 1982, Mexico defaulted on its external debt and the financial press announced the start of the 'debt crisis'. In the years that followed, enormous sums of money have been recycled from low- and middle-income countries to their creditors in the North. Campaigning groups have arisen (such as the Jubilee 2000 Coalition in the 1990s) which have called for a cancellation of the debts of the poorest countries. This demand has been made mainly on the ground that the original sums borrowed have been paid back many times over, because of the interest payments attached to the principal sum. It has also been made with regard to the damage that is being done to human development. According to a report prepared for Oxfam, in Africa as a whole in the mid-1990s, 'only one child in two [went] to school, [and] governments transfer[red] four times more to northern creditors in debt payments than they spen[t] on health and education' (UNDP 1999a: 14, citing Oxfam 1998).

How can this be? Why are the 'sins' of one generation visited on the next? And why and to what extent is this still happening today, after the long economic boom of the 1990s in the Organization for Economic Cooperation and Development (OECD), and following the 2005 G8 Summit at Gleneagles, Scotland, when the Make Poverty History coalition pushed key donors to cancel outstanding debt? We have to begin our analysis with geography, or with where the debt crisis is assumed to have broken out first. Although countries as diverse as Zaire and Poland had defaulted on their external debts in 1975 and 1981 respectively, it was not until the Mexican default of 1982, and the defaults which followed in Brazil and some other South American countries in 1983, that the international financial community began to speak of an 'international debt crisis'. The fact that they did so, of course – the fact that the front cover of *Time* in January 1983 featured the earth as a ticking debt bomb – was because large sums of money were owed by Latin American countries to a group of money-centre banks from the USA, Western Europe and Japan. It is estimated that nine leading US money-centre banks (a group including Citibank, Chase Manhattan, Chemical Bank and Bank of America) were owed US$48.6 billion in late 1984 by just five countries in Latin America (Mexico, Brazil, Venezuela, Argentina and Chile), a sum equivalent to 166.5 per cent of their shareholders' equity (after Kaletsky 1985). These and other commercial banks had made large profits by recycling petrodollars from the Organization of Petroleum Exporting Countries (OPEC) to countries which found it hard to pay for higher oil bills, or which needed funds to finance their programmes of industrial development.

Most of these loans were made for a period of five to seven years, were denominated in the US dollar, and were repayable at floating rates of interest. Real rates of interest were sometimes negative in the mid-1970s because of spiralling world inflation. This changed when the new Chairman of the Federal Reserve, Paul Volcker, began to tighten the US money supply in 1979. In just three years, the main index of the price of an international loan, the London Inter-Bank Offered Rate (LIBOR), climbed from an average of 9.2 per cent (in 1978) to 16.63 per cent (in 1981). As money became more expensive, the world economy was thrown into depression. Many countries in Latin America were unable to service their debts. Faced with a 'scissors' crisis of declining exports to the USA and Europe, and higher debt payments in a strengthening dollar, most of these countries sought to reschedule their debts (pay them back over a longer period, sometimes at higher rates of interest, and always for a fee) in the context of 'London Club' negotiations which brought debtors and creditors together with institutions like the World Bank and the International Monetary Fund (IMF). The Bretton Woods institutions typically used these meetings to persuade the defaulting country to 'put its house in order' by agreeing to a structural adjustment programme. A standard programme involved currency devaluation, tax and public spending cuts, and incentives to support export-led growth. As such, it embodied the view that the debt crisis of any given country was caused by domestic economic mismanagement rather than by an uncontrollable change in external economic circumstances.

The USA encouraged the World Bank and the IMF to deal with the crisis in Latin America in a more pragmatic manner than some on the right would have liked. Neoliberals have insisted that debt in itself is not a bad thing, nor is it in any way unnatural (Beenstock 1984). Just as young people take out mortgages in their twenties and thirties (to be repaid over 15, 25 or 30 years), so too should 'young' countries expect to take out loans from the older or richer countries which developed before them. But these loans have to be serviced. Just as a person in default on his or her mortgage must expect to lose that property to the mortgage company, so too should a country in default on its debt expect to be dealt with harshly. Failure to punish a defaulter would encourage what economists call 'moral hazard' – or the disposition to act badly again in the knowledge that one had got away with something the first time round. In addition, a policy aiming for a write-down of some or all of the debts of a country in default on its external loans would impose a hidden cost on those countries which did not default on their debts (South Korea was often mentioned in this context), or which were too poor to attract large bank loans in the first place (for example, India or Bangladesh). Debt write-downs in this light could be considered 'unfair' or even 'immoral' (Buiter and Srinivasan 1987).

The left has objected strenuously to these arguments. It has blamed US economic policy and an ideology of untamed 'developmentalism' for the plight in which many debtor countries have found themselves (George 1989). In making this critique it enjoyed the support of the (late) Latin American economist, Carlos Diaz-Alejandro. In a much-cited paper, Diaz-Alejandro argued that almost all Latin American countries were forced to default on their debts in the 1980s, notwithstanding the fact that they had run very different trading, monetary and fiscal policies. The default was prompted by the unilateral decision taken by the USA to raise interest rates. He further suggested that commercial banks had acted unhelpfully when they refused to make new loans to Latin America in 1982–83, and that while some economic reforms were required in some Latin American countries, 'nothing in the situation [before 1982] called for traumatic depressions' (Diaz-Alejandro 1984: 382).

In a curious way, this argument was echoed by some exporting groups in Florida, Texas and California, which put pressure on the administration in Washington to treat the crisis in Latin America as a trade crisis as well as a banking crisis. The USA was also keen to police the debt crisis in Latin America in such a way that the principle of repayment was consistently entrenched, but not so deeply that Latin countries would join together in a collective repudiation of their debts (as was proposed by Castro in Cuba and García in Peru). There is evidence to suggest that the USA pushed for Mexico to be dealt with more leniently than some other countries, in order to dissuade Mexico from siding with Brazil against the USA. In time, too, the USA took a lead in making debt management proposals that promised better times ahead for countries faced with 'a lost decade of development'. These proposals included the Baker Plan of 1985 (Adjustment with Growth) and the Brady initiative of 1989 (which promised financial support for those severely indebted middle-income countries (SIMICs) which agreed to avail themselves of debt write-downs in the secondary markets). In this manner, the USA demonstrated its willingness to temper a concern for moral hazard with a measure of realpolitik. The Bretton Woods institutions had to acknowledge these twin motives.

Positive net flows of money into Latin America in the 1990s encouraged the view that the banking crisis was over, and that sound economic management had laid the foundation for a group of 'emerging markets'. But if these claims were overstated, and ignored both the volatility of short-term money flows to Latin America (as witnessed by the Mexican peso crisis in 1994–95) and the continuing depredations suffered by the poor or those dependent on public spending, the spotlight did at last turn to the debt crises which were affecting some parts of Asia and large parts of Africa. And these crises, which had been going on for at least as long as the crisis in Latin America, were sometimes of a different hue to those in Brazil or Mexico, and arguably were more traumatic for their debt-encumbered populations.

In Latin America, just over half of the external debt outstanding in 1982 was owed to private creditors. In sub-Saharan Africa, in contrast, and in some poorer countries in Asia (including Pakistan and the Philippines), loans had been taken out mainly from official creditors like the World Bank or the European Union (or from sovereign nations), and their renegotiation was discussed in the Paris Club. In Africa, too, the total dollar value of the stock of loans outstanding as late as 2003 was often quite small when compared with the total external debt stock of Brazil or Mexico (both in excess of US$150 billion) or the USA (by far the largest debtor, but with no hint of a default): the total external debt of Mozambique stood at US$5 billion; Angola owed US$9.7 billion; Congo US$5.5 billion; and Kenya US$6.8 billion. But when these sums are compared to the gross national products (GNP) of these countries, we see that the crisis continues to be more severe in sub-Saharan Africa: whereas in Brazil and Mexico the ratio of external debt to GNP stood at less than 40 per cent in 2003, in Mozambique, Angola, Congo and Kenya, the average ratio was close to 200 per cent.

These figures, and the often crippling debt–export ratios under which some African countries labour, help to explain why it is that the debt crisis has become a crisis of development in parts of that continent. But if African countries owe so little to their creditors, why was this situation allowed to persist, and are there any signs of change? An answer to the first of these questions must begin, again, with geography and geopolitics. The USA policed the debt-cum-banking crisis in Latin America in order to maintain the integrity of the international financial system, while at the same time recognizing the political and economic importance of Latin America to the USA. Sadly, there are few signs that African countries can exert a similar pull on their creditors. Africa's debts might not count for much in the grand schemas of international money, but even in the midst of the so-called 'war on terror' there is little evidence to suggest that Africa 'itself' matters much today. Inaction, then, is a corollary of 'unimportance', and of the difficulties that African debtors have faced in organizing themselves as a collective presence akin to the Paris Club of official creditors. That said, it would be wrong to assume that Africa or even sub-Saharan Africa is a single entity. Not all countries in sub-Saharan Africa have high debt–GNP ratios (for example, Malawi, Chad and Burkina Faso have generally been under 50 per cent since the early 1990s), and some African countries have benefited belatedly and slowly, and after massive transfers of funds to richer countries, from the enhanced heavily indebted poor countries (HIPC) initiative that was announced at the 1999 G7 summit, and from the multilateral debt relief initiative (MDRI) that was created in 2006, following the Gleneagles agreement. Neither of these initiatives has come close to the outright debt cancellations demanded by Jubilee 2000 (now Jubilee Research) or the Make Poverty History coalition, but by 2006 more than 20 countries had qualified – reached their 'completion points' in terms of agreed policy changes – for irrevocable debt relief from participating creditors. There is progress, but it remains slow.

GUIDE TO FURTHER READING

Buiter, W. and Srinivasan, T. (1987) 'Rewarding the profligate and punishing the prudent and poor: Some recent proposals for debt relief', *World Development*, 15: 411–17. A provocative critique of liberal proposals for debt relief.

Corbridge, S. (1993) *Debt and Development*, Oxford: Blackwell. A guide to competing interpretations of the debt crisis.

Diaz-Alejandro, C. (1984) 'Latin American debt: I don't think we are in Kansas anymore', *Brookings Papers on Economic Activity*, 2: 335–89. Possibly the best single article on the crisis in Latin America.

Jubilee 2000 (1998) *Debt Education Package*, Washington, DC: Jubilee 2000. Up to date, and useful as an anti-dote to 'creditor' accounts of the debt crisis.

Woodward, D. (1992) *Debt, Adjustment and Poverty in Developing Countries*, 2 volumes, London: Pinter/Save the Children. Probably still the best book on the debt crisis. Can be updated by reference to various publications of the World Bank or the United Nations Development Programme (UNDP).

REFERENCES

Beenstock, M. (1984) *The World Economy in Transition*, second edition, London: George Allen and Unwin.

Buiter, W. and Srinivasan, T. (1987) 'Rewarding the profligate and punishing the prudent and poor: Some recent proposals for debt relief', *World Development*, 15: 411–17.

Commission for Africa (2005) *Our Common Interest*, London: Penguin.

Diaz-Alejandro, C. (1984) 'Latin American debt: I don't think we are in Kansas anymore', *Brookings Papers on Economic Activity*, 2: 335–89.

George, S. (1989) *A Fate Worse Than Debt*, Harmondsworth: Penguin.

Jochnick, C. and Preston, F. (eds) (2006) *Sovereign Debt at the Crossroads*, Oxford: Oxford University Press.

Kaletsky, A. (1985) *The Costs of Default*, New York: Twentieth Century Fund.

Oxfam (1998) *Making Debt Relief Work*, Washington, DC: Oxfam.

Sachs, J. (2002) 'Resolving the debt crisis of developing countries', *Brookings Papers on Economic Activity*, 1.

UNDP (1999a) *Debt and Sustainable Human Development*, Technical Advisory Paper No. 4, New York: United Nations Development Programme, Management Development and Governance Division.

UNDP (1999b) *Human Development Report, 1999*, Oxford: United Nations Development Programme and Oxford University Press.

10.3 Aid conditionality

Tony Killick

Meaning and significance

Much aid comes with requirements attached, specifying actions which recipient governments should undertake in return for the assistance. This practice of 'conditionality' has been particularly central to the operations of the International Monetary Fund (IMF), and conditional lending is also important for the work of the World Bank and other development agencies. Bilateral donors – mainly the governments of major industrial nations – also rely on conditionality, often by supporting the stipulations of the IMF and World Bank (the international finance institutions, or IFIs), but sometimes by laying down requirements of their own (e.g. to promote human rights, reduce corruption or protect the environment).

We are here concerned with *policy and institutional* conditionality. We differentiate this from the formal provisions – relating to the financial terms, and provisions for accounting and auditing – which are also written into aid agreements. We also differentiate it from non-controversial points of mutual agreement which the parties often put into agreements, and from the manifold other ways in which donors seek to influence the governments they aid. According to *The Oxford English Dictionary*, a condition is 'something demanded or required as a prerequisite to the granting or performance of something else; a stipulation'. Applying this to the present case: 'conditionality consists of actions, or promises of actions, made by recipient governments only at the insistence of aid providers; measures that would not otherwise be undertaken, or not within the time frame desired by the providers'.

The content of conditionality has evolved over time. In the 1980s and earlier, it was generally addressed to specific actions of policy reform: a devaluation, for example, or the privatization of a public enterprise. Later, more attention was paid to 'structural' matters relating to the general framework of policy (e.g. as it affected the regulation of private investment or the effectiveness of the central bank). Also, from the 1990s, increasing attention was paid to questions of 'governance', addressing more institutional issues, such as the enforcement of contracts, and the management and accountability of the public finances. So-called 'process conditionality' also began to emerge from the later 1990s, addressing *how* policies should be arrived at, most notably requiring that the poverty reduction strategies (PRSs), to which aid and debt relief were increasingly tied, should be founded on broad-based participation and consultation.

Being widely practised, conditionality is important for the way aid monies are spent, particularly the loans of the IFIs. Indeed, some writers have asserted that the comparative advantage of these institutions is that they are better able to enforce conditionality than private lenders (e.g. Hopkins et al. 1997).

Nature of the controversy

Conditionality has long been controversial. Some see it as an unacceptable interference with sovereignty, although, by and large, the principle has not been the centre of dispute. It is recognized that, in principle, conditionality can usefully act as a substitute for the collateral assets which private lenders would insist on. It can safeguard against the danger that aid will weaken a government's will to undertake policy reforms – the problem of moral hazard. Many see a link between domestic policies and the effectiveness of aid – although the evidence for this is contested – and assert that this gives donors a legitimate interest in the policies of recipient governments. Sometimes conditionality can be used as a resource by reformers within a government, and this may tip the political balance in their favour. Conditionality can induce greater consistency over time: governments with low credibility can use external conditionalities to lock in policies which otherwise may not command much confidence.

Essentially, these justifications all boil down to the claim that conditionality improves economic policies and institutions, promoting development and raising countries' creditworthiness. The corollary of this is that *the justification for conditionality stands or falls on its ability to induce change for the better*. The controversy is about whether the policy stipulations are well chosen and effective.

Evidence of effectiveness

The evidence indicates that the high-conditionality adjustment programmes of the IFIs achieve their objectives only to a very limited degree. Neither the IMF nor the World Bank has been able to show a systematic connection between their own programmes and improvements in economic policies. The revealed leverage of programmes over various policy instruments is quite weak. It appears that they can make a decisive difference to policy instruments (like the exchange rate) which can readily be monitored, are directly controlled by the government, involve a few individuals and agencies, and are not easy to organize against. But the results are more problematical when it comes to complex structural, distributional or institutional measures.

Worse still, IFI policies may impede economic reform. Recent cross-country research on the IMF, for example, has found that the influence of Fund programmes on reform is negative, tending to delay reforms (Dreher and Rupprecht forthcoming). This may happen through the moral hazard problem already mentioned. It may show up statistically because IFI assistance also goes to regimes resistant to reform. There is too much politics in the allocation processes to prevent this from happening. Poor programme implementation is another significant problem, manifested by programmes which break down or take far longer than originally planned. There is a lot of pretending that conditions have been met when the reality is otherwise.

This limited effectiveness of conditionality is regrettable because the evidence further shows that, when executed, the IFIs' approach to policy does improve economic performance. In the words of a 1995 World Bank report, 'generally adjustment lending has mostly promoted good policies, but got weak program results'. Research indicates that economic growth is improved when IFI-style adjustment policies are implemented and is significantly worse among the non-implementers (Noorbakhsh and Paloni 2001; World Bank 2004; Bedoya 2005).

But if the policies are broadly sound, why might implementation be so imperfect? In the general case, domestic politics appears stronger than financial pressures from donors. This seems also to extend to donor attempts to influence political reforms: in only 2 out of 29 cases examined by Crawford (1997) was donor pressure judged as significant in bringing about political change.

Explaining weak implementation

The *ownership* of policies is a key factor here. Government ownership is at its strongest when the political leadership, with broad support among agencies of state and civil society, itself decides that policy changes are needed, chooses what should be done and how quickly it should be executed. It is now widely accepted that domestic ownership of policy reforms is crucial for effective implementation and that donor pressures by themselves rarely produce reform. Change must have local champions; domestic leadership is essential.

Ownership is important because of disagreements between recipient governments and aid agencies, whose objectives and interests rarely coincide. The two parties are conditioned by different historical and institutional backgrounds; they are answerable to different constituencies; they each have their own internal political and managerial imperatives; it is recipients rather than donors who bear the costs of reforms, which makes them more cautious about the desirable extent of change; and nationalistic resentment of donor 'interference' undermines the legitimacy of externally promoted policy reforms.

Rewards, punishments and domestic politics

Interest conflicts could be overcome if incentives were in place that made it rewarding for recipients to comply with donor stipulations. This would require rewards for compliance *and the withholding of aid from non-compliers*. However, the evidence suggests that neither dimension of the incentive system is adequate. Programmes may be underfunded. Governments may have little incentive to accept unwanted policy stipulations because they can borrow elsewhere or because the domestic economy is strong enough without borrowing. There is also little evidence that, in practice, conditionality enhances the credibility of government policies, as suggested earlier. Reform programmes have proved too unreliable to have strong credibility effects.

Above all, governments often see that they have little to fear if they do not keep their side of the policy-for-money bargain. Killick (1998: Chapter 6) finds 'an overwhelming body of evidence' that non-implementation is rarely punished effectively and, therefore, that domestic politics override the requirements of conditionality. Other studies confirm this dominance of domestic influences (e.g. Ivanova et al. 2006). The appearance of punishment conveyed by programme cancellations (in the case of the IMF) or the withholding of payments (World Bank) is misleading because the costs to a government of waiting out a delay are generally not great and new credits can usually be negotiated. In fact, research has shown that delinquent governments are just as likely to be able to negotiate new credits as those who have complied with IFI conditions.

Delinquency goes unpunished for various reasons. There are often external pressures on donor agencies to continue aid. The institutional interests of the aid agency often push in the same direction. Except in extreme cases, it is difficult to act strongly against sovereign governments (who are themselves shareholders of the IFIs). There are fears that withdrawal of aid will have damaging human and macroeconomic effects. Staff promotion criteria and accounting systems create powerful pressures to keep on spending, even when governments break their promises.

The search for alternatives

The weight of evidence has increasingly persuaded its practitioners that conditionality is often unable to deliver what it is intended to achieve. Thus a senior World Bank official states: 'Conditionality as we know it does not work. If the policymakers are persuaded, conditionality is not needed, and if they are not persuaded, conditionality does not work...' (Chhibber, Peters and Yale 2006: xxiii). While the IMF has been more reticent, similar admissions have been made at senior levels. Partly in response to growing scepticism, both IFIs undertook reviews of their conditionality policies (van der Willigen 2005; World Bank 2005) and these led to the promulgation of new policy guidelines. Both sought to reduce their reliance on conditionality; 'streamlining' became the dominant theme. Some bilateral donors also moved away from the use of this instrument.

Both IFIs can show that the average number of conditions per new loan has gone down, as has the aggregation for the two institutions combined. There has also been some greater experimentation with more flexible forms. But there has been no renunciation of the principle of conditionality to strengthen policies and institutions, and both IFIs' streamlining efforts have been quite limited, leading the UK's Minister for International Development in September 2006 to threaten to withhold funds from the Bank because of its continuing overuse of conditionality.

An alternative model of aid relationships has emerged, which might be labelled 'selectivity plus partnership', but this too is problematic. This calls for the IFIs and other donors to concentrate their assistance on developing countries whose governments are regarded as pursuing broadly satisfactory policies, and whose goals largely coincide with those of the donors. Execution of this approach would screen out much of the money going to governments which are not serious about broad-based development and policy reform. And, because of the good level of prior agreement about goals and priorities, old-style conditionality could be replaced by the support of mutually agreed programmes of desired actions, meeting the criterion of ownership. In one version of this, conditionality is defined in terms of agreed outcomes, with governments left to choose the policies that would achieve the outcomes, known as 'results-based conditionality'.

The difficulties of this selectivity-plus-partnership model include:

- withholding aid from countries whose governments pursue perverse policies would penalize many people living in great poverty; conversely, countries with strong policies for need have less aid;
- government performance changes over time – the present is not necessarily a good predictor of the future;
- judging performance by results presumes that government policies exert a greater and more predictable degree of leverage over outcomes than is often the case;
- what constitutes 'good policies' is still being defined externally and this is difficult to reconcile with ownership;
- given the intrinsic imbalance in negotiating strength between rich donor agencies and poor recipient governments, the idea of an equal partnership is difficult to implement; 'mutually agreed' measures can often seem little different from old-style conditionality.

Conclusion

The present situation, therefore, is unsatisfactory. There is growing acceptance that conditionality is not a reliably effective instrument for the allocation of aid monies, but there is much institutional inertia and, in any case, the alternatives to conditionality also pose serious challenges. Considerable efforts are being made to improve the effectiveness of aid but the outcomes are as yet unclear. In the meantime, the governments of poor countries continue to be confronted by an array of demands from those who would provide them with support – demands they have become adept at avoiding.

GUIDE TO FURTHER READING

The best recent source is Koeberle et al. (2005), which contains a wide review of the subject, although largely from a World Bank perspective. Coverage of IMF-related issues is weaker, on which see van der Willigen et al. (2005). Influential earlier critiques are to be found in Killick (1998) (of which Killick (1997) provides a more summary statement) and Collier et al. (1997).

REFERENCES

Bedoya, H. (2005) 'Conditionality and country performance', in S. Koeberle, H. Bedoya, P. Silarszky and G. Verheyen (eds) *Conditionality Revisited: Concepts, Experiences and Lessons*, Washington, DC: World Bank.

Chhibber, A., Peters, R.K. and Yale, B.J. (eds) (2006) *Reform and Growth*, New Brunswick, NJ, and London: Transaction Publishers.

Collier, P., Guillaumont, P., Guillaumont, S. and Gunning, J.W. (1997) 'Redesigning conditionality', *World Development*, 25(9): 1399–1407.

Crawford, G. (1997) 'Foreign aid and political conditionality: Issues of effectiveness and consistency', *Democratization*, 4(3): 69–108.

Dreher, A. and Rupprecht, S.M. (forthcoming) 'IMF programs and reforms: Inhibition or encouragement?', *Economic Letters*.

Hopkins, R., Powell, A., Roy, A. and Gilbert, C.L. (1997) 'The World Bank and conditionality', *Journal of International Development*, 9(4): 507–16.

Ivanova A., Mayer, W., Mourmouras, A. and Anayiotos, G. (2006) 'What determines the implementation of IMF-supported programs?' in A. Mody and A. Rebucci (eds) *IMF-Supported Programs: Recent Staff Research*, Washington, DC: International Monetary Fund.

Killick, T. (1997) 'Principals, agents and the failings of conditionality', *Journal of International Development*, 9(4): 483–95.

Killick, T. with Gunatilaka, R. and Marr, A. (1998) *Aid and the Political Economy of Policy Change*, London: Routledge and Overseas Development Institute.

Koeberle, S., Bedoya, H., Silarszky, P. and Verheyen, G. (eds) (2005) *Conditionality Revisited: Concepts, Experiences and Lessons*, Washington, DC: World Bank.

Noorbakhsh, F. and Paloni, A. (2001) 'Structural adjustment and growth in sub-Saharan Africa: The importance of complying with conditionality', *Economic Development and Cultural Change*, 49(3): 479–501.

van der Willigen, T. et al. (2005) *Review of the 2002 Conditionality Guidelines*, Washington, DC: International Monetary Fund.

World Bank (1995) *Higher Impact Adjustment Lending*, Report of a Working Group to SPA Plenary, Washington, DC: World Bank.

World Bank (2004) *2003 Annual Review of Development Effectiveness*, Washington, DC: World Bank, Operations Evaluation Department.

World Bank (2005) *Review of World Bank Conditionality*, Washington, DC: World Bank.

10.4 The emergence of the governance agenda: Sovereignty, neoliberal bias and the politics of international development

Rob Jenkins

During the 1990s, governance emerged as a catch-all term in both the study and practice of development. It can be defined generically as the prevailing patterns by which public power is exercised in a given social context. Official and non-governmental development agencies have sought to operationalize the idea of *good* governance by restructuring state bureaucracies, reforming legal systems, supporting democratic decentralization and creating accountability-enhancing civil societies. The notion of good governance should, in principle, refer to any mode of public decision making that helps to advance human welfare, *however conceived*. But because of the heavy influence of aid donors, governance has come to be associated with institutions designed to support market-led development.

This built-in ambiguity finds its parallel in the imprecision of the cognate terms on which has been built the D&G (democracy and governance) sector, the term invented by the aid business for the set of programmatic initiatives funded by foreign assistance. Development consultants deployed to overhaul failing Third World states have seized on two suitably plastic ideas in particular: participation and accountability. Improving both, while not undermining managerial efficiency, has been the focus of intensive development intervention (Carothers 1999).

Classifying governance's many meanings

One of the most useful ways of classifying governance's many meanings is to begin with the rather fundamental division alluded to above: the difference between the concerns of theorists and practitioners. These are not, of course, air-tight categories: development agencies increasingly cultivate internal analytical capacities and contribute to governance debates; academic theorists engage more than ever in 'applied' advisory work on behalf of development agencies. Still, the distinction is valid. While academics can explore complicating factors that explain divergent patterns of governance, practitioners do not have this luxury: they cannot hope to replicate complex historical conditions.

As Hirst (2000) argues in his survey of governance, the study and practice of development is just one of several contexts in which the term has taken root. Hirst identifies five 'versions', corresponding to the fields of: (i) 'economic development'; (ii) international institutions and regimes; (iii) corporate governance; (iv) new public management; and (v) 'network governance', the increasingly popular deliberative forums found in (mainly) Western polities that address sets of related issues through a structured process of consultation and negotiation among relevant civil society and governmental actors.

It is worth noting that, among the five categories, the experience in the field of economic development has been uniquely all-encompassing. Debates on how understandings of governance can be applied to development problems by aid-recipient governments and external agencies have drawn promiscuously on ideas contained in each of the other four fields. International institutions, for instance, are expected to constrain the performance-inhibiting instincts of Southern (and Northern) governments by subjecting them to multilateral policy 'disciplines'. And since the birth of new public management in the late 1980s, its proselytizers have been exported to the South as fast as consultancy contracts could be written. Corporate governance reforms were a later addition in many places, but the demand for them rose as access to private capital led internationally inclined Southern firms to clothe themselves in organizational forms, and present their accounts in formats, that globally roaming investors would find familiar. The resistance to network governance by Southern bureaucracies, many of which still possess distinctly colonial characteristics, has not prevented a proliferation of consultative mechanisms and public–private management structures; indeed, these are a mainstay of the governance agenda.

Origins and the sovereignty context

The idea that governance was central to official development assistance received one of its earliest manifestations in a 1990 speech by British Foreign Secretary Douglas Hurd. Over the next two years, Hurd's statement was echoed by similar declarations from his counterparts in other rich countries. The shift towards governance thus coincided with the end of the cold war. This was in fact no coincidence, as the governance agenda represented – whatever the merits of its conception or execution – a further intrusion on the sovereignty of aid-recipient states. Today, externally funded 'national' anticorruption agencies probe the finances of key political elites in developing countries and are 'advised', often in fairly substantial detail, by foreign aid agencies and consultants. Even the courts that theoretically define the chief executive's authority are in many cases undergoing comprehensive organizational restructuring under the auspices of donor-funded governance programmes. These sorts of external intervention would have been unacceptable to Third World leaders during the cold war, when bipolarity placed more leverage in their hands by making it possible for the more capable among them to play off East against West.

In assessing the sovereignty implications of this level of external intervention, it is worth taking note of Hirst's observation that sovereignty consists of *both* states' ability to make decisions independently of external authorities *and* their capacity actually to govern – that is, to effect at least a respectable percentage of intended outcomes. This latter dimension of sovereignty had long been lacking in many countries that attained 'independence' in the great wave of decolonization from 1945 to 1975. This has been analysed by Robert H. Jackson (1991), whose work introduced a new term into the study of development: 'quasi-states'. The term quasi-states is now routinely associated with the lost independence of action implied by foreign economic intervention in the form of World Bank and International Monetary Fund (IMF) policy conditionalities. But this obscures a key aspect of its theoretical relevance, which is that the advent of strings-attached structural adjustment lending was merely the second half of a larger story of sovereignty lost.

The first half was the dismal failure of Third World states at translating priorities into policies and executing them effectively – that is, governing. Many states were not even fully in control of their territories, let alone able to regulate authoritatively, implying failure on an even less demanding definitional threshold for sovereignty. Thus, many Third World states had lost one dimension of sovereignty before the other was forfeited in exchange for continued access to international financing. The former helped to make possible the latter: the impositions of international financial institutions would have been more successfully resisted had developing countries possessed a more credible claim to having in practice exercised the governance aspect of sovereignty, defined in terms of minimal levels of societal penetration, not on the basis of how 'good' any such governance might have been.

When, from 1980, external agencies began using conditionality-based lending to pursue their policy agendas, they initially controlled only policymaking, not the structures through which policies were enacted and applied. Thus the shift towards governance in the 1990s – including 'political conditionality', the conditioning of aid on the existence of liberal constitutionalism and multi-party electoral contestation – must be understood as the culmination of a larger process through which sovereignty slipped from the grasp of Southern states. By pursuing a governance agenda throughout the 1990s, development agencies were able to substantially enhance their hold over the functioning of aid-recipient states.

Feasibility and necessity of governance interventions

While the end of the cold war made increased penetration of Southern states by development agencies more politically *feasible*, other trends seemed to make it *necessary*. Within multilateral organizations, one of the main justifications for conditioning aid on the reform of domestic agencies was that suboptimally designed institutions were ruining otherwise sound policy initiatives. This view served several useful purposes for the beleaguered aid agencies. It helped to ward off criticism of structural adjustment's marked failure to bring results in most places it was tried: 'it wasn't the policies, but the governance framework' became part of the revised 'Washington Consensus'. At the same time, by speaking in terms of correcting perverse organizational incentives, unblocking institutional bottlenecks, diversifying civil society, reorienting the citizen–state interface and other such 'technical' solutions, external agencies were able to disavow any interference in the 'domestic politics' of the states in which they operated. While the World Bank's Articles of Agreement prohibit such intrusive practices, they *do* permit the organization to address 'managerial' issues, to the extent that they are relevant to the effective discharge of the Bank's responsibilities as a creditor agency (World Bank 1994). This, in effect, meant that the more technical-sounding the interventions, the more publicly justifiable they would be. Gradually, this gave way to less carefully camouflaged forms of intervention. A watershed of sorts was passed in 1997, when the World Bank, IMF, United Nations Development Programme (UNDP) and other traditionally non-interfering institutions placed the issue of corruption firmly on their agendas, and even cut off aid to Kenya for a time, partly on grounds of the government's failure to tackle corruption.

The idea that fundamental governance reform was necessary found its way into academic writings on development around the same time that agencies took up the idea. These studies were based largely on detailed empirical investigations, rather than on abstract model-building. Atul Kohli's (1990) dissection of India's crisis of (un)governability was followed by a raft of popular articles, such as Robert D. Kaplan's 'The coming anarchy', which analysed the collapse of so-called 'failed' states in large parts of sub-Saharan Africa (Kaplan 1994).

In short, several trends combined to facilitate the emergence of a composite notion known as governance: geostrategic realignments, bureaucratic convenience, the legacy of previous policy failures. It would be wrong, however, to ignore the contribution of important ideological transformations. The vastly increased emphasis on market-based solutions naturally had its influence on the full range of ideas about governance. This 'neo-liberal bias' has undermined many otherwise useful insights about the nature of institutions in structuring dissent and, under some circumstances, promoting accountability (Kaufman, Kraay and Zoida-Lobaton 1999). Attempts to use foreign aid to build the sort of civil society that would check the power of government, without capturing it, were all but destined to fail. They did so spectacularly at times, such as when a non-governmental organization (NGO) leader, funded by American 'democracy assistance' programmes, seized power in a coup in Burundi in 1996 (Jenkins 2001).

Governance in practice: The fear of success

Indeed, the manner in which governance objectives were pursued points to a larger pattern in the linkage between theory and practice. This is what might be called a fear of success. By seeking to recreate a badly flawed vision of how 'functional' civil societies in the West actually operate – or, even worse, operated at an earlier stage in their developmental trajectories – both social theorists and development practitioners have betrayed an instinctive reluctance to face up to civil society's inherently precarious condition and sometimes ugly character, or to let democracy do its unpredictable work (Gellner 1994). Private associations which aid agencies, for one reason or another, found distasteful were excluded from their civil society 'strategic frameworks', and denied funding, just as civil society groups that upset the predictions of academic theorists were banished from their carefully constructed models. Usually, the problem concerned their contribution to undesired ends.

The same is true for other aspects of democratic governance in which both development theorists and practitioners have been involved – for instance, elections, where outcomes can be injurious to democracy's long-term health and yet still be democratic. In such instances, the international community has demonstrated a palpable fear of democracy – or at least a strong desire to retain control over what should, by definition, be a local process of conferring legitimacy. The incumbent government of Algeria was permitted by otherwise governance-conscious donor governments, and large sections of the associated development intelligentsia, to simply ignore the results of the 1992 elections, because the group widely believed to have won, an avowedly Islamist party, did not conform to the recipe for good government promoted by theorists and advanced by agency staff.

The institutional arena in which development policy is least elaborated is international and transnational governance. The fear of democracy partly explains this as well. Genuine governance reforms that would reduce the North–South disparities that characterize, for instance, *participation* within international organizations (to say nothing of the *accountability* deficit within even rule-based institutions of global governance such as the World Trade Organization) would represent a substantial challenge to the very governments that control development agencies. Even technical assistance to encourage poorer countries (and poorer groups within them) to participate more wholeheartedly in these organizations is heavily slanted away from programmes that might assist them in negotiating for such things as enhanced terms of trade, new rules for enforcing international agreements, and compensation for global environmental protection measures.

The extreme versatility of the idea of governance will ensure its survival for the foreseeable future. But it will continue to be shaped by political constraints, including the interests of powerful actors, the changing nature of sovereignty, and the performance of development agencies and Southern states.

GUIDE TO FURTHER READING AND REFERENCES

The following text references provide the basis for further reading.

Carothers, T. (1999) *Aiding Democracy Abroad: The Learning Curve*, Washington, DC: Carnegie Endowment for International Peace.

Gellner, E. (1994) *Conditions of Liberty: Civil Society and its Rivals*, London: Hamish Hamilton.

Hirst, P. (2000) 'Democracy and governance', in J. Pierre (ed.) *Debating Governance*, Oxford: Oxford University Press.

Jackson, R.H. (1991) *Quasi-States: Sovereignty, International Relations and the Third World*, Cambridge: Cambridge University Press.

Jenkins, R. (1999) *Democratic Politics and Economic Reform in India*, Cambridge: Cambridge University Press.

Jenkins, R. (2001) 'Mistaking governance for politics: Foreign aid, democracy and the construction of civil society', in S. Kaviraj and S. Khilnani (eds) *Civil Society: Histories and Possibilities*, Cambridge: Cambridge University Press.

Kaplan, R.D. (1994) 'The coming anarchy', *Atlantic Monthly*, February.

Kaufman, D., Kraay, A. and Zoida-Lobaton, P. (1999) 'Governance matters', World Bank Policy Research Working Paper 2196, Washington, DC: World Bank.

Kohli, A. (1990) *Democracy and Discontent: India's Growing Crisis of Governability*, Cambridge: Cambridge University Press.

World Bank (1994) *Governance: The World Bank's Experience*, Washington, DC: World Bank.

10.5 Strengthening civil society in developing countries

Alison Van Rooy

(This chapter draws substantively on Van Rooy 1998.)

Why bother about civil society?

The answer is that talk about civil society is shaping the very way in which we 'do' international relations today. That conversation pulls together global ideas, values, institutions and dollars in a vibrant, and sometimes violent, fashion. In many ways, civil society is the Rome of today's internationalism; wherever we begin, we will arrive at this debate sooner or later.

Certainly, writing about the role of civil society has grown in volume and depth since the mid-1980s. From this sphere are to come agents of change to cure a range of social and economic ills left by failures in government or the marketplace: autocracy, poverty, oppression, social malaise. Cornucopian expectations for social change have been heaped on this idea and for some Northern donors, in particular, the 'discovery' of civil society has promised a solution to the enduring problems of development and democracy. Many have devoted official development assistance dollars to a range of civil society projects throughout the world, and the number and variety of those projects increase daily.

Yet serious questions remain about the whole enterprise. What are people talking about when they use the term 'civil society'? What are the issues and implications, both for good and ill, of this growing debate in the international aid business? This chapter poses, and begins to answer, some of these vexing questions.

What does 'civil society' mean?

What do we mean, *precisely*, when we use the term 'civil society'? The term has a long history in political philosophy, and its definition has altered with Roman, Lockean, Hegelian, Marxist and Gramscian interpretations, long before it was resurrected in the 1990s. Out of that long debate, what messages have we brought forward today? I think there are at least six different elements, and at least as many dangers in turning them into policy directions.

Civil society as values and norms

For some, the 'civil' in civil society is the operative word: the term describes the kind of well-behaved society that we want to live in, the goal for our political and social efforts. This ideal society is trustful, tolerant, cooperative – ambitions held to be universal and to be universally good.

Note the 1990s conversation about 'social capital', for instance, invigorated by Robert Putnam's *Making Democracy Work* (1993) and 'Bowling alone' (1993, 1995). Building on the work of others, Putnam illustrated – in Italy and the United States – that communities held together by overlapping memberships in neighbourhood associations were more prosperous, healthy and livable. The bonds of trust and reciprocity created in these neighbourhood civil society organizations (CSOs) are called social capital.

Faced with such a normative and ideologically laden concept, the policymaker's first task may be simply to recognize the ethical motors that shape the civil society (and social capital) debates.

Civil society as a collective noun

While the normative note is always present, civil society is most commonly defined as a collective noun: synonymous with the voluntary sector (or the third sector), and with advocacy groups, non-governmental organizations (NGOs), social movement agents, human rights organizations and other actors explicitly involved in change work. The definition most often excludes those groups belonging to the marketplace and the state, and further specifies that civil society organizations do not include those groups interested in acquiring political power, hence the usual exclusion of political parties.

The response from the academic community has been to start counting: just how many CSOs are there? The prominent and important work of Salamon (2004), for example, shows variations in the shape and structure of the sector, and historical and cultural patterns.

From a policy perspective, however, there are difficulties with the empirical focus alone. One problem is that the term is equated, in practice at least, with particular sectors or kinds of organization (those that we like), even if the definition is meant to encompass a larger population. In development circles, civil society is further reduced to 'NGO'. If we are trying to understand processes of social change, we must go beyond exercises in cataloguing.

Civil society as a space for action

Civil society has also been used to describe the sphere or arena in which civil organizations prosper (or wilt). The United Nations Development Programme's (UNDP) definition is typical: 'UNDP takes a broad view of CSOs, of which non-governmental organizations (NGOs) are an important part. In this perspective, civil society constitutes a third sector, existing alongside and interacting with the State and profit-seeking firms' (UNDP 2002: 1).

Throughout the policy literature, we see circles (like the ones shown in the figure) used to describe civil society, drawn with clear boundaries around the state, the market and a 'residual' category of non-state, non-market actors. One problem is that the circles are frequently drawn in even, egalitarian sizes. The intent is schematic, but the effect is to depict a vision of balance and segregation which may not exist in reality. Another problem is that this description divides the world by organizational type, hiding other aspects of an organization's role or function in society. Even if one allows overlapping identities (unions, for example, as part-market, part-civil society), the effect is nonetheless of sorting by organizational identity rather than by purpose, goal, vision, method, function or other more interesting distinctions.

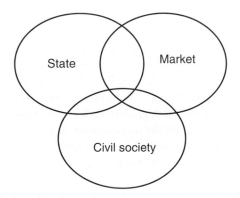

Modelling civil society

Civil society as a historical moment

Others describe civil society as a historical moment, either a real or idealized description of society that exists when a set of prerequisites was in place. Adam Seligman's (1992) prerequisites were the primacy of the individual, rights-bearing and autonomous, and a shared public space in which agreed rules and norms are sustained. Blaney and Pasha, searching for civil society in India and Africa, similarly argue for 'the stabilization of a system of rights, constituting human beings as individuals, both as citizens in relation to the state and as legal persons in the economy and the sphere of free association' (1993: 4). They suggest that this mix of prerequisites cannot simply be assumed to exist in other countries.

The interesting thing about a historical view of civil society is that it raises questions about how civil society emerges and why it might disappear. The goal for policymakers has subsequently been a quest for the foundations, the prerequisites of civil society. Can one create a system of rights? What about a culture of association? Obviously, the potential for intervention on such an enormous field becomes small – or, at best, very long term.

Civil society as anti-hegemony

One of the most radical optics on the debate argues that civil society is not conducive to modern liberalism (in politics or economics), but is instead its antithesis.

First, many CSOs are disengaged from formal political processes and work partly underground, outside conventional institutions of civil society and the state, or are mobilized in opposition to prevailing cultural norms. In positing alternate visions of society (about gender and power, sexual identity, anticonsumerism, antiglobalization or anti-Westernism), movements may never join in formal political action. If one defines civil society primarily in terms of its relationship with the state, one may well miss this aspect of civil organizing.

For policymakers trying to work in other cultures, or in subcultures within their own, the implication is that their intervention may be utterly unwanted – a symptom of the perceived cultural and economic dominance of 'hegemonic' institutions.

Civil society as an antidote to the state

The sixth overlapping optic describes civil society by its activities in opposition to a centralized or autocratic state. Promoting civil society has come to mean limiting the state.

Part of the reason is a loss of faith in both the abstraction and the physical manifestation of the state. Jessica Mathews, then with the Council of Foreign Relations, suggested that 'The end of the Cold War has brought no mere adjustment among states but a novel redistribution of power among states, markets, and civil society', such that today, 'NGOs are able to push around even the largest governments' (1997: 50, 52). For Mathews, not only *should* states wield less power, they actually *are* less powerful in the face of the civil society onslaught. Today, a raft of backlash responses have appeared to counter that perceived upsurge: asking whether CSOs are 'merchants of morality', 'too big for their boots', or even a good thing for global development (Bond 2000; Bob 2002; Florini 2004).

Another concern focuses on the implications for sovereignty in a *globalizing* civil society. Lipschultz (1992) argues that we are seeing an increase in international activism *because* of a leaking away of sovereignty. Environmental degradation, the universalization of human rights (and the notion that foreign actors can act on the transgression of rights in other countries), civil wars, drug trafficking and other transborder activities are no longer seen to belong to the governments that govern the territory in which they take place.

The legitimacy of the state itself thus becomes less certain. In the world of international activism, there is a growing notion that true democracy may involve the circumvention of some governments altogether. That position presents a very serious challenge to policymakers.

Strengthening civil society in developing countries?

The debates and rebuttals presented here do not mean, however, that there is no role for the international community in supporting CSOs and a broader civil society in the South. I think that there is a role, but one that must be taken with more self-criticism and public debate. Working with CSOs, after all, is both practically and politically complex. One set of guidelines, therefore, first asks donors to interrogate, and to seek help in interrogating, their own goals.

Interrogate goals

Because the debate on civil society is normatively convoluted, it is important that all players are aware of their own motivations. What is the aid agency doing? Why? Who wants the donor to be there? It is important that the philosophical underpinnings of programmes are described and understood; only then can they be debated.

Get the lay of the land

It is also important that one's own philosophies of change bear some relevance to the countries in which one works. Donors need to develop knowledge of the dynamics of power among CSOs, the market and the state. For example, what level of political and financial support or resistance is put up by home governments, international agencies and powerful domestic players?

Getting the big picture also implies an examination of the other forces that are working on civil society. Socially and culturally, one needs to learn about the informal or unregistered organizations of civil society – clan associations, extended family networks, church affiliations – which nonetheless carry tremendous weight in social change. One also needs to offer at least a passing consideration of international factors of debt; economic liberalization, protectionism and globalization; trans-border flow of ideas, people and illicit and legal goods; and environmental problems.

Make political assessments

If anything, the debate on civil society has shown that political motivations for aid have come out from under the table. Can donor politics be justified in the context of local agendas? Whose agendas are those? What impact might intervention make on shaping political outcomes? Civil society organizations at the heart of much donor attention are often political (if not partisan) bodies at the centre of real conflicts, real debates. The question is not whether politics can be avoided, but whether one's particular choice of political stance and partnerships can be justified, and to whom.

Plan strategically

Given these considerations, donor planning should consider at least three facets: the organizations themselves, their relationships and the environments in which they work. A metaphor of civil society as a building of bricks, mortar and site is used to make the distinctions clearer.

Bricks
The bricks, the constituent parts of the building, are organized groups. They may be morally good, bad or neutral in function. Donor programmes could be designed to help the activities and influence of particular bricks in the civil society edifice.

Mortar
Relationships are the mortar that holds the building together. One needs to ask how organizations are related: are they disparate and atomized, or tightly woven into coalitions? What groups exist in

opposition to or in support of their work? Programmes to increase the strength of that mortar might fund umbrella organizations, meetings, training centres and networking travel.

Building site
This building is not drawn from thin air; there are preconditions or enabling environments necessary for its existence. The metaphorical equivalents might be the building site and its zoning laws, union rules and bank practices. In political terms, these include a system of rights, a culture of association, legal protection, the role of the state and market, and the availability of financing, among other factors – some of which an outside donor agency might affect.

Moving forward

What, then, are we to make of all this? Is there any point in development practitioners, North or South, getting on board the 'strengthening civil society' bandwagon?

This chapter suggests that the idea of civil society has become omnipresent in donor language today, in large part because it rings many political, economic and social bells. The ideas packed into the two familiar words are rich, contradictory and in danger of being all things to all people. At the same time, both the ideas embedded in 'civil society' and the manifestation of CSOs themselves hold out tremendous inspiration for change. Indeed, in treading very carefully in the world of real politics, the task for a new generation of development activists, North and South, is not to throw the baby out with the bath water.

GUIDE TO FURTHER READING AND REFERENCES

Theoretical history

Chandhoke, N. (1995) *State and Civil Society: Explorations in Political Theory*, New Delhi, Thousand Oaks, CA, and London: Sage Publications.
Cohen, J.L. and Arato, A. (1992) *Civil Society and Political Theory*, Cambridge, MA, and London: MIT Press.
Hall, J.A. (ed.) (1995) *Civil Society: Theory, History, Comparison*, Cambridge and Cambridge, MA: Polity Press.
Seligman, A.B. (1992) 'Trust and the meaning of civil society', *International Journal of Politics, Culture and Society*, 6(1): 5–21.

Critiques

Blaney, D.L. and Pasha, M.K. (1993) 'Civil society and democracy in the Third World: Ambiguities and historical possibilities', *Studies in Comparative International Development*, 28(1): 3–24.
Bob, C. (2002) 'Merchants of morality', *Foreign Policy*, 129 (March/April): 36–45.
Bond, M. (2000) 'The backlash against NGOs', *Prospect Magazine*, April.
Florini, A. (2004) 'Is global civil society a good thing?', *New Perspectives Quarterly*, Spring: 4.
Harbeson, J.W., Rothchild, D. and Chazan, N. (eds) (1994) *Civil Society and the State in Africa*, London and Boulder, CO: Lynne Reinner.

Trends and issues

Lipschultz, R.D. (1992) 'Reconstructing world politics: The emergence of global civil society', *Millennium*, 21(3): 389–420.
Mathews, J.T. (1997) 'Power shift', *Foreign Affairs*, January/February.
Salamon, L.M., Wojciech Sokolowski, S. and associates (2004) *Global Civil Society: Dimensions of the Nonprofit Sector*, Volume 2, Bloomfield, CT: Kumarian Press.

Civil society and donors

Carothers, T. (1999) *Aiding Democracy Abroad: The Learning Curve*, Washington, DC: Carnegie Endowment for International Peace.

Van Rooy, A. (ed.) (1998) *Civil Society and the Aid Industry: The Politics and Promise*, London and Ottawa: Earthscan and the North–South Institute.

Other references

Putnam, R.D. (1995) 'Bowling alone: America's declining social capital', *Journal of Democracy*, 6(1): 65–78 (expanded in Putnam, R.D. (2000) *Bowling Alone: The Collapse and Revival of American Community*, New York: Simon and Schuster).

Putnam, R.D. with Leonardi, R. and Nanetti, R.Y. (1993) *Making Democracy Work: Civic Traditions in Modern Italy*, Princeton, NJ: Princeton University Press.

UNDP (2002) *UNDP and Civil Society Organizations: A Policy Note on Engagement*, New York: United Nations Development Programme.

10.6 The role of non-governmental organizations (NGOs)

Vandana Desai

The growth of the NGO sector

The term NGO is applied to many kinds of organization, ranging from large Northern-based charities, such as Oxfam, to local self-help organizations in the South, with an aim to improve the quality of life of disadvantaged people. They are mainly private initiatives, involved in development issues on a non-profit basis. The term 'NGO' is understood to refer to those autonomous, non-membership, relatively permanent or institutionalized (but not always voluntary) intermediary organizations, staffed by professionals or the educated elite, which work with grass-roots organizations in a supportive capacity. Grass-roots organizations (GROs), on the other hand, are issue-based, often ephemeral, membership organizations; they may coalesce around particular goals and interests, and dissipate once their immediate concerns have been addressed. Non-governmental organizations (NGOs) have become an important and vocal platform for the involvement of civil society in public affairs.

NGO partnerships

Since the 1950s, NGOs have come to play an increasingly important part in the formulation and implementation of development policy, becoming key actors in the political economy of development. There has been increased collaboration with both governments and aid agencies, based on a growing belief over the period that the promotion of NGOs could offer an alternative model of development and play a key role in processes of democratization (see Mercer 2002). NGOs were seen as more administratively flexible, closer to the poor, innovative in problem solving and more cost-effective than corresponding state partners. Donor pressure towards structural reform and privatization underlies the increased interest in NGOs as 'service deliverers' – part of a wider and explicit objective to facilitate productive NGO–state partnerships. There is a realization among donor countries that aid is becoming ever more complex, with new instruments and players, and increasing criticism of its effectiveness. Private financial flows increased rapidly in the wake of increased liberalization of trade. The increase in private capital flows was unprecedented in the 1990s, driven by market reforms, the rise in global trade, lowering investment barriers in developing countries, and the fall in communications and transport costs.

The expansion in partnership between Northern and Southern NGOs originated in changing attitudes in the North in the 1960s and 1970s. A view took hold that merely transferring resources in the form of tools or funds was not an adequate response to poverty when that was rooted in structural problems. Indeed such transfers could just preserve the situation by creating financial dependency. The establishment of research departments and policy units in Northern NGOs marked this change in approach and contributed to its sustainment (Ebrahim 2006). The humanitarian function of NGOs evolved to embrace poverty reduction, environmental sustainability, gender equality and democracy.

Northern NGOs repond to emergencies, short-term relief and long-term rehabilitation, such as victims of war and of natural or man-made disasters. They raise money in the North, from the general public, the private sector and governments, to pay for their work and to share as much as possible with their Southern counterparts, to help in building the capacity of Southern NGOs and to educate their own constituencies in the North about the underlying causes of poverty, as well as drawing people into active lobbying and campaigning for change.

Southern NGOs have the basic responsibility among NGOs for leading the development process in developing countries and the expertise to do so. Relationships between Northern and Southern NGOs must be based on an equal partnership incorporating transparency, mutual accountability and risk sharing. An important accountability problem concerns the unequal relationship between donors, Northern NGOs (see Bebbington 2005) and Southern NGOs (see below)

Roles of NGOs

NGOs are popular because they demonstrate unique characteristics and capabilities – they are perceived to be flexible, open to innovation and able to access the poor through work at the grassroots level.

NGOs play two main roles, either service delivery or policy advocacy. As service delivery agents, NGOs provide welfare, technical, legal and financial services to the poor, or work with community organizations in basic service and infrastructure provision. This is frequently a matter of filling the gaps left by the partial service delivery of governments withdrawing from involvement in provision. In the past, governments of developing countries were seen as spearheading the development process. However, such paternalism reached its limits when it became clear that government did not have the financial resources to pay for the essential services of the poor and lacked the organizational expertise to be effective. In such an environment, the important role for NGOs since the mid-1980s has been in mitigating the adverse costs of structural adjustment and promoting donor reform packages in offering insurance against a political backlash against harsh adjustment regimes. Such a role raises important questions. Patterns of service delivery through the voluntary sector may lack compatibility and coordination. In so far as such efforts rely on government funding, their ultimate durability may also be queried. At a deeper level, there are worries about the long-term impact of NGO service provision on the sustainability of national health and education systems (rather than programmes) and access to quality services for all.

Networking and building movements

The other frequent role for NGOs is policy advocacy, seeking social change by influencing attitudes, policy and practice, seeking to reform state services on the basis of NGO experiences and to lobby directly for the policy changes. This is involvement in participatory, public-interest politics, and NGOs engaging in such activity realize the increasing importance of information (which they gather through their own experience of working at the grass-roots) as they begin to utilize the power of ideas and information to promote positive change in the wider structures of government and the official aid community. These NGOs often play a catalytic or seeding role – demonstrating the efficacy of a new idea, publicizing it, perhaps persuading those with access to greater power and budgets to take notice, and then encouraging the widespread adoption of the idea by others.

Neither of these roles needs exclude the other. Some NGOs naturally progress from filling a gap in service delivery to recognizing the need to look to the wider context in which the need arises, finding themselves drawn, possibly through involvement in NGO networks (Bebbington 2003), into national or global policy advocacy (Keck and Sikkink 1998).

NGOs work with grass-roots organizations/community organizations which often comprise poor and marginalized groups. In this respect they both widen (in social and geographical terms) and deepen (in terms of personal and organizational capacity) the possibilities for citizen participation. NGOs have been important in mobilizing large numbers of people against either entrenched elites or state interests, campaigning on their behalf and seeking to influence public policy (e.g. the cancellation of debt of heavily indebted nations, placing it on the agenda of the G8 summit at Gleneagles in July 2005). This type of bottom-up democracy has been successful in many instances where it might eventually lead to top-down political change. NGOs have become key actors in a process of transformatory development. They can affect norm changes that lead to regime change or the restructuring of world politics. They do this (especially Northern NGOs) through the communicative power of information, lobbying, research, campaigning or media work, acting on the basis of their moral authority (e.g. in the areas of human rights, free trade, debt relief and child labour).

NGOs create alliances and networks to place pressure on the state (DeMars 2005). NGOs have been drawn into networks of growing complexity. Many Northern NGOs, such as Christian Aid, have moved away from the direct implementation of projects to a 'partnership approach' with Southern NGOs, but the precise nature and terms of such partnerships often remain unclear (Lewis 1998).

The role of NGOs in strengthening civil society and democratic development

The point that NGOs' contribution to development might be more important for political rather than economic reasons was first made in the late 1980s by Michael Bratton (1989), and there is increasing interest in the role of NGOs in promoting democratic development. The perspective of 'security policy' democracy poses the threat of opening a Pandora's box of ethnicity, conflict and instability.

Their role is emphasized in this context by virtue of their existence as autonomous actors; NGOs are said to pluralize and therefore to strengthen and expand the institutional arena, bringing more democratic actors into the political sphere. More civic actors mean more opportunities for a wider range of interest groups to have a 'voice', more autonomous organizations to act in a 'watchdog' role vis-à-vis the state, and more opportunities for networking and creating alliances of civic actors to place pressure on the state (e.g. Jubilee 2000 debt initiative). NGOs enhance democracy by expanding the number and range of voices addressing government. NGOs have a key role to play during and after democratic transitions. For example, in Chile, NGOs played a vital role in opposing the Pinochet regime throughout the late 1970s and 1980s, and their role has undergone some degree of change since the early 1990s (Lambrou 1997).

NGOs have become inextricably implicated in civil society, democracy, good governance and social capital. Clarke (1998a), in one of the few studies which examines the role of NGOs in the politics (see Devine 2006) of development across the developing world, opines that the failure to theorize the political impact of NGOs has led to an overly 'inadequate, explicitly normative inter-pretation of NGO ideology' (1998a: 40). This failure has encouraged a tendency to take NGOs' positive political role as natural or self-evident.

NGOs and the state

NGOs provide expertise in 'development software' (participatory approaches, community organ-izing, public-private partnerships, stakeholder ownership strategies); they are more innovative, adaptable, cost-effective and aware of the local situation; and their grass-roots representation brings legitimacy and community mobilization to programmes and projects. NGOs strengthen the state through their participation in improving the efficiency of government services, acting as strategic partners for reform-oriented ministries, filling the gaps in service provision, and helping the government to forge ties with the grass roots.

The impact of states on NGOs is absolutely central in defining the role that NGOs can play in national development, for it is governments which give NGOs the space and the autonomy to organize, network and campaign (Clarke 1998a, b). Of course, it is difficult to generalize about state–NGO relations, as local political networks are always diverse.

NGOs and accountability

NGOs are increasingly being funded by states and official aid agencies, and questioning what impact this trend has on NGO accountability. Concerns are raised by many regarding the internal and external accountability of NGOs. NGOs have downward accountability to members and upward accountability to donors/governments (patrons). NGOs are internally accountable to ben-eficiaries, donors, boards of directors, trustees and advisory committees. They are externally accountable to organizations and actors with which they affiliate, international government organ-izations, states and people throughout the world. Accountability is crucial for NGOs as they have only their reputation for credibility on which to base their actions. Accountability in NGOs needs to be appropriate for their work, for the needs of the beneficiaries (clients) and for the values of the organization itself. There is *functional accountability* in relation to accounting for resources and their impacts, and *strategic accountability*, which relates to the wider implications of an NGO's work (especially in the context of impacts on other organizations or the wider environment in which NGOs operate) (see Edwards and Hulme 1995). These are basically mechanisms for assess-ing effectiveness, and for the monitoring and evaluation of NGOs in relation to their effectiveness. Accountability in NGOs is quite complex.

Conclusion

The key issue for the future is whether and how NGOs will adapt to the global changes which are currently under way. NGOs are constantly having to link both local and global agendas if they are to be effective, and they will increasingly be forced to learn from and adapt to changing demands and opportunities.

The increased availability of large-scale funding has been one of the primary factors driving NGO growth in the 1980s, encouraging the proliferation of social welfare organizations which often had little or no political agenda. The 'inherent' advantages of the NGOs themselves are grad-ually worn away by increased funding, professionalization, bureaucracy and the shifting of objec-tives away from 'social mobilization' (which might be less attractive to donors) towards service delivery. This process may lead to a widening rift between well-resourced service providers and poorly funded social mobilization organizations. This highlights the fact that NGOs exhibit potentially illuminating contrasts in emphasis and packaging of activities, in client groups and organizational style. Considerable diversity exists in relation to how autonomous NGOs are from the influence of funding agencies or donors. Increasingly, questions have been asked. Can NGOs deliver all that is expected of them? Is the glowing image realistic? How effective are NGOs? There seems to be more concentration on success stories such as the Grameen Bank and Seva, and a gap appears to be emerging between rhetoric and practice, which raises issues of objective monitoring and evaluation of NGOs' projects, effectiveness, legitimacy, performance and accountability. Despite growing interest in evaluation, there is still a lack of reliable evidence on the impact of NGO development projects and programmes. If NGOs want to continue to sustain their claim to moral authority, they need to maintain attributes such as impartiality and independence, veracity and reliability, representiveness, accountability and transparency.

GUIDE TO FURTHER READING AND REFERENCES

Bebbington, A. (2003) 'Global networks and local developments: Agendas for development geography', *Tijdschrift voor Economische en Sociale Geografie*, 94(3): 297–309.

Bebbington, A. (2005) 'Donor–NGO relations and representations of livelihood in nongovernmental aid chains', *World Development*, 33(6): 937–50.

Bratton, M. (1989) 'The politics of government–NGO relations in Africa', *World Development*, 17: 69–87.

Clarke, G. (1998a) *The Politics of NGOs in South-East Asia: Participation and Protest in the Philippines*, London: Routledge.

Clarke, G. (1998b) 'Non-governmental organisations (NGOs) and politics in the developing world', *Political Studies*, XLVI: 36–52.

DeMars, E.D. (2005) *NGOs and Transnational Networks: Wild Cards in World Politics*, London: Pluto Press.

Devine, J. (2006) 'NGOs, politics and grassroots mobilisation: Evidence from Bangladesh', *Journal of South Asian Development*, 1(1): 77–99.

Ebrahim, A. (2006) *NGOs and Organizational Change: Discourse, Resources and Learning*, Cambridge: Cambridge University Press.

Edwards, M. (2000) *NGO Rights and Responsibilities: A New Deal for Global Governance*, Cambridge: Cambridge University Press.

Edwards, M. and Hulme, D. (eds) (1995) *Beyond the Magic Bullet: NGO Performance and Accountability in the Post-Cold War World*, London: Macmillan.

Hulme, D. and Edwards, M. (1997) (eds) *Too Close for Comfort? NGOs, States and Donors*, London: Macmillan.

Keck, M.E. and Sikkink, K. (1998) *Activists Beyond Borders: Advocacy Networks in International Politics*, Ithaca, NY, and London: Cornell University Press.

Lambrou, Y. (1997) 'The changing role of NGOs in rural Chile after democracy', *Bulletin of Latin American Research*, 16: 107–16.

Lewis, D. (1998) 'Development NGOs and the challenge of partnership: Changing relations between North and South', *Social Policy and Administration*, 32(5): 501–12.

Mari, F. (2004) *NGOs at the Table: Strategies for Influencing Policy in Areas of Conflict*, Rowman & Littlefield Publishers.

Mendelson, S.E. and Glenn, J.K. (eds) (2002) *The Power and Limits of NGOs*, New York: Columbia University Press.

Mercer, C. (2002) 'NGOs, civil society and democratization in the developing world: A critical review of the literature', *Progress in Development Studies*, 2(1): 5–22

Sheth, D.L. (2004) 'Globalisation and new politics of micro-movements', *Economic and Political Weekly*, 39(1), 3 January: 45–58.

Welch, C.E. Jr (ed.) (2001) *NGOs and Human Rights: Promise and Performance*, Philadelphia, PA: University of Pennsylvania Press.

10.7 NGOs and the state

John D. Clark

This chapter reflects the author's views and not necessarily those of the World Bank or affiliated organizations.

What do NGOs offer?

When I raised money for Oxfam at school I first heard the proverb: 'Give a man a fish and you feed him for a day; teach a man to fish and you feed him for a lifetime'; it seemed a profound statement on the need for development and self-reliance, not handouts. But I have come to see it as an eloquent parody of all that is wrong with so much that passes for 'development'. It begs important questions and is based on dubious assumptions.

Do the experts teach *everyone* to fish, or just the poor? Without targeting, there may be little left for the most deserving. If you teach the poor to fish, do they have the nets and boats they need; will they be able to buy or rent them? Do they have access to the fishing grounds, or are these monopolized by the local elite? If they catch fish, are they able to market them and get a fair price – or are they exploited by middlemen? Are they equipped to withstand the risks of fishing in dangerous waters? Are the waters polluted, either killing the fish or rendering them inedible? How environmentally sustainable is the trade? If you teach only the *man* to fish, will the benefits be shared within his family? These questions are unanswered. And, by the way, has anyone bothered to ask the poor whether they *like* fish? Is it a culturally appropriate skill to teach them?

The proverb's assumptions insult the intelligence of the poor. It paints a picture of ignorant, hungry people sitting idly beside well-stocked waters, just waiting for the expert to arrive from outside and show them how it is done. Anyone who has come close to poor people knows how hardworking and resourceful they generally are. But the greatest false assumption is that the problem of hunger is reduced to a technical issue of production, when in reality it is largely a political issue of distribution and inclusion.

Keeping with the metaphor, there may be a compelling case for helping people catch fish, but unless the approach taken is founded on realistic assumptions and addresses the above questions, the programme will at best be irrelevant and could well be harmful. It is for these reasons that NGOs and other civil society actors have vital roles to play in development; hence governments and development agencies such as the World Bank are increasingly working with NGOs and promoting the growth of the sector. For this reason, too, in 2003 the Secretary General of the United Nations established a high-level panel to advise on strengthening UN relations with civil society. He recognized that, while the UN is primarily a forum for the world's governments, to remain fully relevant it also has to engage more fully with NGOs and other civil society actors.

NGOs can offer essential 'local knowledge' about local conditions and the poor. They can deliver services to vulnerable and difficult-to-reach population groups. Their parallel activities may make the programme much better for the poor (by providing credit for nets and boats, for example, or by setting up a refrigeration plant so the catch can be frozen and sent to market, so ending the stranglehold of the one local merchant). Through social assessments and participatory research, NGOs can point out how the programme can better serve different communities, and be tailored differently for different ethnic groups. By sensitizing authorities about the ideas and preferences of the poor, they can help attune the project to their real needs. Through gender training and mobilizing the women, they can ensure equity within the family. And through social mobilization they can help the poor to organize themselves, either to form cooperatives, to demand changes or to ensure the accountability and probity of the programme's officers (Clark 1995).

These are vitally important roles, best served by NGOs, community-based organizations and others in civil society who are close to the poor and enjoy their trust. Some argue that NGOs are *better* at development than government or official donors. This is a sterile line of argument. There are many things that NGOs will never be able to do, and they cannot acquire the scale of government programmes. Their value is that they do *different* things.

Generalizations are dangerous. Not all NGOs are effective; some talk a fine patter but do little for the vulnerable. In some countries, NGOs congregate close to big cities and do not reach into the poverty belts. There are important questions of accountability and legitimacy, for example, regarding their claim to 'speak for the poor' (Edwards and Hulme 1995). But the sector as a whole plays important and increasingly powerful roles. This may include challenging the decisions of individual states, but in ways which shift governments to better serve their responsibilities vis-à-vis their populations, and therefore enhance their legitimacy. Legitimate governments, therefore, have no need to fear a well-functioning and responsible NGO sector.

Why states need NGOs

Governments, therefore, need NGOs to help ensure that their programmes are effective, well targeted, socially responsible and well understood. The media likewise need NGOs because they trust the local knowledge and alternative perspectives they offer. The public needs them because of their services and their mobilizing capacity – helping citizens to express their voice or challenge authority. Parliamentarians need them for policy guidance, for feedback on what people want, and as watchdogs in monitoring public programmes and enhancing the accountability of officials.

The legitimacy of individual NGOs rests not necessarily in their mass membership or their budget, but in their *usefulness* to these constituencies. The NGO sector, therefore, is symbiotic with a well-functioning, democratic state, not parasitic or undermining.

Since the earliest days of tribal government, the keenest goal of leaders has been to hold on to the reins. This is achieved through wielding power over competitors (especially through military might), and cultivating popularity by allowing important population groups to do what they want as long as it does not undermine the leadership, and by making plausible promises of rewards to come (in this, and subsequent lives).

Cultivating popularity needs channels for eliciting what would be popular, for providing people with what they need, and for enabling people to do the things they want. Over the centuries, civil society has evolved to provide these channels. Some states muzzle or do not permit free civil society; these risk being isolated from their populations. At times, civil society pressure might be antisocial or reinforce appalling regimes. The vibrant citizens' organizations in Weimar Germany in the 1920s and 1930s, for example, demanded more and more from a weak government and, some argue, precipitated a shift towards the populist government form of the Nazi Party (Berman 1997). But in general, civil society helps attune governments to their populations and strengthens mechanisms of democracy and accountability. This is more so where states have coherent and transparent mechanisms for policymaking. For example, vigorous environmental campaigning in the USA drove the creation and expansion of government environmental agencies, laws and enforcement mechanisms (Carothers 1999/2000).

Electoral democracy is valuable for assessing the main concerns of the majority. But everyone is a minority in one respect or another – due to our age, religion, location, ethnic group, physical attributes, employment status, sexual orientation, hobbies, convictions or passions. And we tend to see ourselves as defined more by these factors than our nationality, but national democratic processes are often blind to them. For thousands of years, throughout the world, therefore, civil society has emerged in varying degrees to represent these interests. Some causes may be detested by others (such as those promoted by the National Rifle Association in the USA, and racist groups), but citizens' advocacy, in general, reinforces democracy and strengthens state capacity. By aligning ourselves with civil society organizations of our choice we extend our democratic reach; *representative* democracy (in which we select our delegates for decision-making forums through elections) is supplemented by *participatory* or *deliberative* democracy (in which we engage more directly in the debates that particularly interest us, through civil society channels) (Clark 2003).

In summary, NGOs are important to states in that (according to Clark 1991) they can

- encourage governments to adopt innovations from the voluntary sector;
- educate and sensitize the public about their rights and opportunities;
- collaborate in making government programmes more effective;
- attune programmes to public needs;
- strengthen local institutions and make them more accountable;
- act as conduits for citizen consultation and advocacy.

How states shape civil society

Though civil society has become important in virtually every country, its magnitude, scope and influence – hence its contribution to society and to development – varies enormously. A number of factors account for this – including the tradition for philanthropy, exposure to Western ideas and education, national religions, and so on – but one factor is of paramount importance: the NGO–state relationship. NGOs sometimes prefer to keep their distance from government, or side with the opposition. Sometimes governments resent and mistrust NGOs. Tandon (1991) describes a typology of state–NGO relations, according to whether the regime is autocratic, weak and unpredictable, or a mature democracy.

The key determinant of this relationship is often the framework of laws and regulations governing the formation and operation of NGOs. Ideally this framework is fully enabling while encouraging some discipline. Laws which hamper the formation of independent NGOs, which deny citizens rights to join or support NGOs, or which subject NGO operations to strict government control and unpredictable intervention, fetter the NGO sector. Not only are citizens thereby denied the positive contributions NGOs offer, but they are denied the 'rights of association' guaranteed by most states (including, in theory, China) who have signed the UN International Covenants on Civil and Political Rights. Conversely, where laws are so lax that it is trivially easy to register an NGO for tax and fund-raising advantages, and where there are no requirements for transparency and accountability, the public is unprotected from unscrupulous NGO operators. NGOs have therefore been major conduits for corrupt leaders to siphon funds out of developing countries into their personal bank accounts (e.g. in Indonesia in the late 1990s), and the Organization for Economic Cooperation and Development's (OECD) Financial Action Task Force (FATF) suggests that NGOs can be conduits for money laundering and the financing of terrorism (FATF 2004).

Getting the balance right is not easy, and will depend on the legal tradition and other aspects of the country in question (Irish, Kushen and Simon 2004). Governments should not seek to manage NGOs – this would undermine NGOs and inappropriately stretch government capacity. Instead they should create conditions that encourage effective self-regulation of the sector. NGOs that seek benefits from the state or the public should be expected to be transparent and accountable, proportionate to the scale of these benefits. Unfortunately, in recent years, many governments (particularly in the former Societ Union) have developed laws that restrict NGO freedoms, especially in the case of advocacy and human rights groups. Some advance concerns regarding terrorism or national security to justify their repressive legislation (National Endowment for Democracy 2006).

How states can work well with NGOs

Governments' stance towards NGOs can be either non-interventionist, encouraging, offering partnership, seeking co-option or controlling (Brown 1990). In addition to promoting a healthy policy environment, there are at least five ways in which governments can ensure a positive NGO relationship (Clark 1995).

First, governments can provide NGOs with information about state programmes and policies for dissemination to their constituencies and gathering feedback. NGOs can help governments strengthen citizen consultation and public awareness of rights and opportunities. While in 1990 only 13 countries had access to information laws, by 2006, 65 countries had such laws and 30 more were developing them (Rodrigues 2006).

Second, governments can offer opportunities for operational collaboration, commissioning NGO activities that complement their programmes and strengthening the NGOs. This partnership approach is strongly encouraged by the World Bank and other donors. Even where governments are suspicious or hostile towards NGOs it may be that some line ministries are disposed towards partnership.

Third, governments can involve NGOs in policy debate and public consultations on new policies or major government projects. For example, NGOs can help orchestrate effective public hearings about infrastructure projects. The World Bank now *requires* public hearings, including civil society, for all projects it funds that may have a significant environmental impact.

Fourth, governments can coordinate – or encourage coordination – between the various agencies (non-governmental, governmental, donors and private sector) who work in a common field. This was strongly promoted by a former president of the World Bank (Wolfensohn 1999).

Finally, governments can help finance NGOs, through grant funding, loans, contracts and opportunities to be conduits for government resources provided to communities. The World Bank, for example, supports 'Social Funds' in many countries in which funds are often provided through NGOs to poor communities for village infrastructure, community investments or micro-credit.

Conclusion

In all these areas there is potential for conflict and difficulties. NGOs may be at odds with governments; collaboration by some may appear to undermine advocacy efforts of others. Government agencies may seek to co-opt (and possibly corrupt) the NGOs they work with, or NGOs may find that their own agendas get lost.

There are many reasons to promote close state–NGO relations. NGOs may be cost-effective, work in remote areas or be innovative. But their most important potential is for engaging citizens, particularly the poor, in shaping the decisions that affect them and in allocating associated resources. Popular participation is the main argument for improving state–NGO relations and fostering an enabling environment for NGOs, because ultimately 'development' is what is done *by* people, not *to* people.

GUIDE TO FURTHER READING

Chambers, R. (1983) *Rural Development: Putting the Last First*, Harlow: Longman.

Clark, J. (1991) *Democratizing Development: The Role of Voluntary Organizations*, London and West Hartford, CT: Earthscan and Kumarian Press.

Edwards, M. (1999) *Future Positive: International Cooperation in the 21st Century*, London: Earthscan.

Fowler, A. (1997) *Striking a Balance: A Guide to Enhancing the Effectiveness of NGOs in International Development*, London: Earthscan.

Salamon, L. and Anheier, H. (1998) *The Emerging Sector Revisited*, Baltimore, MD: Johns Hopkins University, Institute of Policy Studies.

REFERENCES

Berman, S. (1997) 'Civil society and the collapse of the Weimar Republic', *World Politics*, 49: 401–29.

Brown, L.D. (1990) *Policy Impacts on the NGO Sector*, Washington, DC: World Bank.

Carothers, T. (1999/2000) 'Civil society: Think again', *Foreign Policy*, Winter 1999–2000.

Clark, J. (1995) 'The state, popular participation and the voluntary sector', *World Development*, 23(4): 593–601.

Clark, J. (2003) *Worlds Apart: Civil Society and the Battle for Ethical Globalization*, London and West Hartford, CT: Earthscan and Kumarian Press.

Edwards, M. and Hulme, D. (eds) (1995) *NGO Performance and Accountability: Beyond the Magic Bullet*, London and West Hartford, CT: Earthscan and Kumarian Press.

Financial Action Task Force (FATF) (2004) *Report on Money Laundering Typologies 2003–4*, Paris: Financial Action Task Force.

Irish, L., Kushen, R. and Simon, K. (2004) *Guidelines for Laws Affecting Civic Organizations*, New York: Open Society Institute.

National Endowment for Democracy (2006) *The Backlash Against Democracy Assistance*, Washington, DC: National Endowment for Democracy.

Rodrigues, C. (2006) *Promoting Public Accountability in Overseas Development Assistance: Harnessing the Right to Information*, New Delhi: Commonwealth Human Rights Initiative.

Tandon, R. (1991) *NGO Government Relations: A Source of Life or a Kiss of Death*, New Delhi: Society for Participatory Research in Asia.

Wolfensohn, J. (1999) *A Proposal for a Comprehensive Development Framework*, Washington, DC: World Bank.

10.8 NGDO–donor relationships: partnership in an era of disrupted continuity

Alan Fowler

The story updated

This chapter in the previous edition of the compendium focused on the concept and practice of partnership between non-governmental development organizations (NGDOs) and agencies responsible for allocating official development assistance (ODA). It did so from a perspective of convergence in their language, priorities and ideas about how development works and in the taxation-based resources they rely on. It was argued that this process was accompanied by intensifying interaction that seldom reflected the quality of relationship that partnership implied (Fowler 2002). There was a use and abuse of the partnering label that obscured the asymmetries involved: in power, in access to information, in establishing and playing by the rules of the game and in a fair sharing of risks and responsibilities (Groves and Hinton 2004). These relational features have changed little and, as described later, in some respects are regressing. However, they are now located in a significantly different geopolitical context.

Whether or not the partnership label is justified, continuity remains in donor recognition of NGDOs as part and parcel of the development landscape. While firm, aggregate amounts are impossible to calculate, the volume of official aid dedicated to NGDOs continues to grow directly within the overall budgets of many donors. Official aid is also financing NGDOs indirectly from other allocations, often through decentralized donor decision making and from loans made by development banks. (See OECD/DAC statistical tables). For example, it is estimated that half of the US$1.1 billion allocated to World Bank Multi-Country Aid Programmes is disbursed through civil society organizations (CSOs) (Reynolds Mandell 2006).) Some aid agencies are refining their NGDO funding methods, which, on a limited scale, is opening up interesting relational modalities (Adams, Pratt and Warren 2006). Be that as it may, the tendency towards competitive approaches to the allocation of aid to NGDOs continues unabated. Moreover, the sometimes uneasy, mutually necessary symbiosis between donors and NGDOs described by Tej Tvedt (1998, 2006) is now located within an accelerated process of aid rationalization. In the name of efficiency and effectiveness, the framing and technocracy of the aid system is altering in ways that are pulling NGDO–donor relations along in their wake.

Simultaneously, a discontinuity has emerged in how states view NGDOs. The benign acceptance of their merits is giving way to critical scrutiny. One reason for this shift is that NGDO–donor relations are now caught up in government reactions against terrorism, insecurity and instability. Aid is becoming part and parcel of a comprehensive security strategy for a donor's own country (Beall, Goodfellow and Putzel 2006). Significant growth in amounts committed at the G8 summit in Gleneagles in 2005 is premised on ODA acting as a preventive investment in and beyond failed or fragile developing states. The full impact of this shift on NGDO relations with donors remains to be seen. But given concerns about CSOs as channels for terrorist financing, the mutual trust required for authentic partnership is less forthcoming.

Paradoxically, at a time when relations with governments are coming under strain, commitments to significantly boost aid volumes will challenge governmental 'absorptive capacity', so increasing opportunities for NGDOs to help with disbursement. (For example, at the G8 conference at Gleneagles, the EU pledged to increase aid to an average of 0.5 per cent of GDP of member states; on absorption, see *IDS Policy Briefing*, Issue 25, Institute of Development Studies, September 2005.) With these contrary drivers, the complicated relational development foreseen in the previous edition of this volume is playing itself out, but in many ways that were not anticipated.

An updated story of NGDO–donor relationships in an era of continuity and disruption can be told through lenses of rationalization and securitization. Because of its overarching nature and features described in other chapters in this volume, we start with a brief and narrow look at securitization (Duffield 2002).

Securitization

For donor countries, securitization involves a strategy with three interlocking components. One is a cluster of traditional instruments of foreign relations: diplomacy, trade, military force and (humanitarian) post-conflict reconstruction. Second are counterterrorism measures. Third, ODA is directed at reducing inequality and poverty while increasing the policy capability, institutional efficacy and democratic robustness of statehood (Fowler forthcoming). NGDO–donor relations are being strongly conditioned by the technical and coordination demands of the third component, but also by a significant shift in governments' attitude towards NGDOs and civil society more broadly.

> A number of governments and political actors seem to regard the third sector as a source of insecurity, not as a civil society but as encouraging uncivil society, not as strengthening peace and human security but as willing conduit for, or an ineffective, porous and ambivalent barrier against insecurity in its most prominent modern forms, terrorism and violence (Sidel 2006: 201).

In the North and the South, there is more government circumspection about NGDOs. Caution is arising in terms of NGDOs and political issues, as well as doubts about their operating at the cutting edge of development practice and hence their greater effectiveness. One consequence is a growing demand for NGDO accountability (Bendell 2006; Jordan and Van Tuijl 2006), which adds weight to the performance-driven rationalization of ODA, which is a critical factor impacting on donor–NGDO relations and the prospect of attaining authentic partnership.

Rationalization

Since 2000, the aid system has evolved into a more complex architecture of policies, priorities, instruments and channels (Fowler 2003; Burrell and Maxwell 2006). Overarching features of aid impacting on donor–NGDO relations are:

*   policy frameworks set at the Monterrey conference on aid financing; the still to be completed development round of the World Trade Organization initiated in Doha; and the Johannesburg conference on sustainable development;
*   the UN Global Compact with business in support of international development;
*   the Millennium Development Goals and Millennium Project 2005–2015.

Significant operational elements are:

*   good governance initiatives;
*   poverty reduction strategies;
*   general budget support;
*   sector-wide approaches to allocating aid;
*   results-based management;
*   rights-based approaches.

With these goals, policy frameworks and methods in place, to improve effectiveness by reducing transaction costs, a donor meeting in Paris in 2005 agreed to actively harmonize and align their efforts (OECD/DAC 2005). The extent to which the effects of better collaboration between donors will be achieved is very much open to question. Be that as it may, exclusion of civil society in these deliberations, and virtual neglect of this actor in the final document, are indicative of sidelining within the thinking and preoccupations of the prevailing aid system.

The landscape for NGDO–donor relationships is pretty much unilaterally set. The comprehensiveness of the architecture and the coercive strength of funding appear to leave little NGDO room for negotiation about fundamentals. NGDO–donor partnership around jointly conceived agendas is less probable. Moreover, trust and mutuality is giving way to apprehension of being openly critical or too 'alternative' (Wallace, Bornstein and Chapman 2006: 129). Minor innovations aside, the 'partnership' issue for NGDOs is if and how (far) to comply with what donors require. (For example, the Swedish and Norwegian development agencies are exploring new, core financing arrangements with a limited number of Southern and Northern NGDOs.)

Rationalization using the generally centralizing, prescriptive implements shown above is accompanied by a security-related impetus to 'bring the state back in' as the primary agent of development. Government in the South has to be in the driving seat of and responsible for change. Supposedly, participatory planning and monitoring processes will generate the desired wider citizen ownership and acceptance of state-initiated development. The Paris agreement includes a preference for providing general budget support, rather than funding discrete public service programmes. A relational implication is to reorient service-oriented NGDOs away from direct relationships with foreign donors towards recipient governments. The consequences for reduced NGDO autonomy and potential for co-optation loom even larger than before (ActionAid/Care 2006).

Conversely, the good governance agenda requires civil society to have a sufficiently independent position with respect to the state. To attain this condition, donors will need to channel finance outside of government structures. Contending forces will shape how this process plays out in different contexts of relations between states and civil society, and to whose benefit. Southern NGDOs are pressuring to be 'empowered', by taking Northern NGDOs out of aid flows and implementation. But delegated decision making means that ODA is increasingly negotiated and committed by donor agencies within recipient countries. In response to localization of funding, some Northern NGDOs are strategically (re-)registering themselves as 'local' entities. This may involve membership building of an international federation, with advantages in terms, for example, of accessing information and expertise. A potential consequence already being seen is the 'squeezing out' of more truly local civil society actors.

With what rationale and how carefully and insightfully donors act in this situation will be a significant factor shaping NGDO–donor relations in the years to come. Donor complicity in displacement of southern NGDOs is one scenario. Giving preference to Southern NGDO-led civic evolution and strengthening, perhaps with Northern NGDOs as junior parties, is another option. The general point is that NGDO–donor relations are becoming more of a trilateral interplay, increasingly located in the South, both lessening and complicating the chainlike binary, linear sequence from North to South.

An additional aspect shaping relations is that funders will supposedly forego their 'own' projects on the ground. Consequently, they will be looking to NGDOs for intelligence about the lived reality of the poor and information about government performance in meeting agreed development targets. This suggests a relational evolution around potentially more risky roles for NGDOs in 'reporting' on their government to 'foreign masters'. To counter this possibility, countries such as India and Russia are increasing or taking initiatives to tighten regulations that restrict, control and monitor foreign finance to NGDOs. A general expectation, therefore, is that donor–NGDO relations will be interpreted through a more overtly political lens than has previously been the case.

Prospects

With the state being reinstated as development actor *primus inter pares*, a case can be made for a general decrease in donor regard for NGDOs as significant or vitally 'alternative' development agents. A similar argument has been voiced in a reappraisal of the developmental importance of civil society more widely (Edwards 2005). This does not imply that NGDOs will no longer feature in the donor funding repertoire. Rather, their leverage on the relational conditions they face or can negotiate is unlikely to increase. In fact, the opposite seems more probable.

GUIDE TO FURTHER READING

Adams, J., Pratt, B. and Warren, H. (2006) *Official Agency Funding of NGOs: Mechanisms, Trends and Implications*, Occasional Paper Series No. 46, Oxford: International NGO Training and Research Centre. A comprehensive review of the mechanics of NGDO financing arrangements across a range of donors. It serves as a useful guide to variations around common relational problems as well as elaboration on the contending ideas that guide donor behaviour.

Fowler, A. (2005) *Aid Architecture: Reflections on NGO Futures and the Emergence of Counter Terrorism*, Occasional Paper Series No. 45, Oxford: International NGO Training and Research Centre. This paper was written at a time when a fuller picture of reforms in the aid architecture, counterterrorism and the securitization of aid were starting to emerge and intertwine. It contains ideas for the sort of strategic responses that NGDOs could contemplate.

Tvedt, T. (1998) *Angels of Mercy or Development Diplomats? NGOs and Foreign Aid*, London: James Currey. A critically insightful analysis of the donor–state–NGO relational triangle and how it serves mutually institutional interests rather than the oppositional premise more usually portrayed.

Wallace, T., Bornstein, L. and Chapman, J. (2006) *The Aid Chain: Coercion and Commitment in Development NGOs*, Rugby: Intermediate Technology Development Group. Tracing the way that aid conditions and donor behaviours are transmitted by and impact on NGDOs is no easy task. This multi-country study shows the ways in which the discourse and technologies of ODA do just that.

REFERENCES

ActionAid/Care (2006) *Where To Now? Implications of Changing Relations Between DFID, Recipient Governments and NGOs in Malawi, Tanzania and Uganda: Implications of Direct Budget Support for Civil Society Funding and Policy Space*, London: ActionAid/Care UK.

Beall, J., Goodfellow, T. and Putzel, J. (2006) 'Introductory article: On the discourse of terrorism, security and development', *Journal of International Development*, 18: 51–67.

Bendell, G. (2006) *Debating NGO Accountability*, Geneva: NGLS Development Dossier, UN-Non-Governmental Liaison Service.

Burrell, S. and Maxwell, S. (2006) *Reforming the International Aid Architecture: Options and Ways Forward*, Working Paper 278, London: Overseas Development Institute.

DFID (2006) *Civil Society and Development: How DFID Works with Civil Society to Deliver the Millennium Development Goals*, London: Department for International Development.

Duffield, M. (2002) *Global Governance and the New Wars: The Merging of Development and Security*, New York: Zed Press.

Edwards, M. (2005) *Have NGOs Made a Difference? From Manchester to Birmingham with an Elephant in the Room*, Working Paper Series 028, Manchester: Global Poverty Research Group, Manchester University.

Fowler, A. (2002) 'NGDO–donor relationships: The use and abuse of partnership', in V. Desai and R. Potter (eds) *The Companion to Development Studies*, London: Hodder Arnold, pp. 508–14.

Fowler, A. (2003) *International Development Frameworks, Policies, Priorities and Implications: A Basic Guide for NGOs*, Toronto: Oxfam.

Fowler, A. (forthcoming) 'Development and the new security agenda: W(h)ither(ing) NGO alternatives?', in A. Bebbington, S. Hickey and D. Mitlin (eds) *Can NGOs Make a Difference? The Challenge of Development Alternatives*, London: Zed Books.

Groves, L. and Hinton, R (eds) (2004) *Inclusive Aid: Changing Power and Relationships in International Development*, London: Earthscan.

Jordan, L. and van Tuijl, P. (eds) (2006) *NGO Accountability: Politics, Principals and Innovations*, London: Earthscan.

OECD/DAC (2005) *Paris Declaration on Aid Effectiveness*, Paris: Organization for Economic Cooperation and Development.

Reynolds Mandell, C. (2006) 'Willing to learn', *Alliance*, 11(4): 29–30.

Sidel, M. (2006) 'The third sector, human security, and anti-terrorism: The United States and beyond', *Voluntas*, 17(3): 199–210.

Tvedt, T. (1998) *Angels of Mercy or Development Diplomats? NGOs and Foreign Aid*, London: James Currey.

Tvedt, T. (2006) 'The international aid system and non-governmental organisations: A new research agenda', *Journal of International Development*, 18: 677–90.

Wallace, T., Bornstein, L. and Chapman, J. (2006) *The Aid Chain: Coercion and Commitment in Development NGOs*, Rugby: Intermediate Technology Development Group.

10.9 Non-government public action networks and global policy processes

Barbara Rugendyke

Historically, non-government development assistance organizations (NGOs) based in Northern donor nations delivered assistance, primarily at the local scale, to disadvantaged communities in Southern nations. Their primary mandate was to contribute to improved quality of life for people in those communities. However, rather than continuing to concentrate on the 'development project', in order to provide services like water supplies and sanitation systems, or to encourage income-generation activities and alternative livelihood strategies, increasingly NGOs have devoted their energies to advocacy campaigns. In doing so, drawing on new opportunities afforded by growth in their numbers and size and in the resources available to them, and facilitated by advances in communications technologies, NGOs have increasingly globalized, working through transnational networks to maximize their impact on global policy processes.

This trend is epitomized in the ongoing Global Call to Action Against Poverty (GCAP) campaign, a global coalition of national antipoverty campaigns. At the launch of the affiliated Make Poverty History campaign in London in 2005, Nelson Mandela called for a 'public movement' to eliminate poverty, likening this to international solidarity movements to abolish slavery and apartheid, and urging that 'poverty is man-made and it can be overcome and eradicated by the actions of human beings' (in Bedell 2005: 10). With over 540 organizations in the United Kingdom alone committed to it, within six months of its launch, 87 per cent of the UK's population was aware of the campaign and 8 million people wore a white wristband signifying their support. Organizations from over 100 countries joined GCAP, which aims to tackle global poverty by lobbying for further cancellation of the debt of heavily indebted nations, trade justice and increased quantity and quality of aid. A concerted lobbying campaign in the UK culminated in an estimated 250,000 people marching through Edinburgh on 6 July 2005 to demand that world leaders act in the interests of poverty reduction. The fact that debt relief was so firmly on the agenda at the Gleneagles G8 meeting that month is widely attributed to the campaign.

Its precursor, the Jubilee 2000 Campaign, was the first global campaign through which development NGOs united over a single issue – debt relief for the world's most heavily indebted nations. Jubilee 2000 mobilized more than 24 million people from over 60 nations to sign a petition (Mayo 2005: 174), drawing supporters from faith-based and secular organizations, trades unions and businesses, of all ages and occupations. With 110 member organizations, within four

Debt protest: campaigners in Prague, during the World Bank/IMF Annual Meeting in 2000, call for G7 members to deliver their promise to drop the debt of 25 developing nations
Source: Photo by James Hawkins/Oxfam

years of its launch in 1997, 'Jubilee 2000's campaign for the remission of unpayable Third World debt made a remarkable impact, raising the issue's profile internationally as well as locally' (Mayo 2005: 172). After a concerted lobbying campaign, in 1999, at the Cologne G8 Summit, world leaders agreed to cancel US$100 billion of debts owed by the poorest nations (Bedell 2005: 19). The campaign is credited with having contributed to poverty alleviation, enabling diversion of resources from debt repayment to increased spending on health care, housing provision and education.

NGOs' attempts to mobilize the public into widespread social movements are clearly having an impact and seem to be realizing the calls of commentators to 'scale up' advocacy activity (Edwards and Hulme 2000). What has led to this growing focus by NGOs on working in global alliances to advocate for changed policies?

Among NGOs, development practitioners and development theorists, debate about the most appropriate forms of development intervention has not subsided. NGOs have grappled with the uncertainties of development practice, struggling to find the best ways to improve quality of life for those suffering the ravages of poverty and disadvantage. Decades of local-level development efforts led to the realization that project work in communities is insufficient to bring about broader changes to address the ongoing causes of poverty. Indeed, one common criticism of NGOs was that, in focusing on development and empowerment at the local level, they had failed to consider the wider structural factors which perpetuated poverty (Edwards and Hulme 1992). These factors were the focus of theorizing about development in the 1980s. The radical development theories which predominated at the time contributed to new understandings that 'underdevelopment' was a condition maintained by inequitable global structures, such as entrenched unfair terms of trade, poor commodity prices, oppressive debt obligations and inequitable distribution of resources between different social groups and nations. In seeking to tackle these causal factors, in the following decades NGOs increased their commitment to advocacy, believing that this would maximize the impacts and cost-effectiveness of their work.

NGOs also responded to calls from their southern partners to increase their engagement in advocacy. In the early 1980s, when questioned about how best to help the poor in Tanzania, Julius Nyerere's response was: 'change public opinion in your own country' (Burnell 1991: 240). Southern NGOs have consistently called for Northern NGOs to express concern about the global crises of poverty and environmental destruction through lobbying and campaigning, for Northern NGOs are more likely to have the power and resources to engage with global institutions and to impact on their policies. In addition, evolving development practice increasingly emphasized the importance of empowering local communities and of their participation in all stages of the development process. This resulted in recognition that growing numbers of Southern NGOs were best placed to initiate and manage development work in local communities. Northern NGOs responded by looking for new ways to contribute to poverty alleviation.

Thus, since the 1990s, NGOs have increasingly prioritized advocacy as a poverty alleviation strategy. Broadly, advocacy includes campaigning (aiming to change public opinion) and lobbying (attempting to change policy). The objectives of both forms of advocacy are to influence policy formation, particularly of policies which could lead to positive change in people's lives. Harnessing public support, the NGOs believe, gives them the potential to impact on the policies of the global and national institutions which determine access to resources and power. The revolution in communications technology which enabled increased sharing of information, and access to and contact with the public, has facilitated this, rapidly expanding the spheres of influence of activist organizations.

Many Northern NGOs have increased the proportion of their budget and staff time allocated to advocacy, establishing departments dedicated to research and lobbying. While expenditures on advocacy by international NGOs increased between 1984 and 1996, in 1996 just 4.1 per cent of their total expenditure was on advocacy (Anderson 2007a). Total staff resources committed to the NGOs' advocacy also increased over the 12 years; however, the small percentage of total expenditure devoted to advocacy did not reflect confidence in it as the strategy most likely to contribute to poverty alleviation. By 2005, though, the financial commitment of 14 of the same NGOs to policy research, lobbying and public campaigning had, in general, increased dramatically. Only three had increased their resource allocation to advocacy by less than 100 per cent. More than half increased the financial and human resources allocated to advocacy by three or six times between 1996 and 2005 (Anderson 2007a). Thus, in the last decade, NGOs have given greater priority to advocacy, prompted by the success of earlier campaigns.

In seeking to optimize the reach of their advocacy, and reflecting broader processes of economic globalization, NGOs forged new alliances and increased their engagement in global networks. In one sense, NGO operations have always been 'global', with Northern donors traditionally operating through expatriates in Southern nations and, later, through 'southern partners'. Thus, NGOs have long worked through networks 'through which people, ideas and resources circulate and in which material interventions in particular locations are conceptualised and executed' (Bebbington 2003: 300). However, in attempting to increase their influence in national and global affairs, NGOs have formed national and international networks. For example, by 2003, 90 per cent of Australian NGOs had participated in campaigns with other Australian NGOs, and 44 per cent had joined campaigns coordinated by the Australian Council for International Development (ACFID), a national council of Australian NGOs. Seventy-five per cent of Australian NGOs had either participated in global alliances or cooperated with international NGOs in advocacy, and 37 per cent had joined international advocacy networks, such as Jubilee 2000. Themes of advocacy campaigns conducted within alliances tended to be broad, most commonly debt (38 per cent), aid (27 per cent) and a range of others, including banning landmines, the environment and the extension of education (Rugendyke and Ollif 2007).

NGOs have also globalized their activities through formalizing and strengthening existing alliances. For example, influenced by the globalization of economic and political systems, and to facilitate global coordination and expansion of previously independent Oxfam affiliates, nine previously independent national Oxfam affiliates merged to form Oxfam International (Stichting Oxfam International – OI) in January 1996 (Anderson 2007a). Thirteen affiliates now belong to Oxfam International. Oxfam International also established its Washington Advocacy Office (WAO) in 1995 to coordinate the development of joint policy and strategies for the Oxfams. The advocacy office is located in Washington, DC, to facilitate direct access to the Washington-based multilateral agencies (MLAs), the World Bank, the International Monetary Fund (IMF) and the United Nations (UN), headquartered in New York.

In working together to broaden their impact, NGOs have been drawn into networks of growing complexity. The primary impetus for this has been growing awareness of the power of public action through experience of its successes. Although it has been argued that NGOs have made 'little progress at the level of ideology and global systems' (Nyamagasira 2002: 8), through uniting in alliances, NGOs have 'materially contributed to policy changes by Northern and Southern governments' (Anderson 2002: 84). These have included the success of campaigns relating to baby milk marketing codes, drafting an international essential drugs lists, trade liberalization relating to clothing manufacture in Southern nations, action against global warming and rainforest destruction, debt relief to African nations, and the imposition of sanctions to combat apartheid (Anderson 2002).

Responding to the growing influence of NGOs, in 1997 the United Nations Security Council held its first meeting with NGOs. In 1968, 377 NGOs had consultative status with the UN, but by 2001 this had expanded to include over 1550 organizations (Opuku-Mensah 2001). NGO campaigning has included representation at important UN conferences, including the 1992 Earth Summit, and NGOs have now 'become *incorporated* into the UN system' (Martens 2006: 692). Thus, NGOs have become increasingly integrated into global decision-making processes.

There is growing evidence that NGOs have influenced policy formation within the World Bank and other multilateral organizations and development banks, including shaping World Bank policies related to poverty alleviation, participation and gender issues. NGO lobbying has led to cancellation or modification of major projects, including dam construction and related resettlement schemes (Anderson 2002). In relation to debt relief for heavily indebted poor countries (HIPCs), a significant shift in World Bank policies towards proposals made by Oxfam International and other NGOs has been traced (Anderson 2007b).

Development NGOs continue to contribute directly to material changes at the local level. However, through their advocacy they now also provide for their constituencies 'a conduit for voluntary participation in global issues outside the formal political realm of the states' (Taylor 2004: 273). Simultaneously, NGOs' participation in global advocacy alliances provides 'a legitimizing platform for dissident and diverse voices from regions where economic and political power is lacking' (ibid.).

GUIDE TO FURTHER READING

Mayo, M. (2005) *Global Citizens: Social Movements and the Challenge of Globalization*, London and New York: Zed Books. This accessible volume discusses the development of campaigning alliances by NGOs, community-based organizations and labour movements, presents case studies of social mobilization and speculates about the challenges facing future attempts to transform global society.

Smith, J. and Johnston, H. (eds) (2003) *Globalization and Resistance: Transnational Dimensions of Social Movements*, Oxford: Rowman & Littlefield Publishers. The relationships between globalization processes and social movements are explored through case studies of activism focused on local and global issues.

Rugendyke, B. (ed.) (2007) *NGOs as Advocates for Development in a Globalising World*, Abingdon and New York: Routledge. Devoting increasing resources to advocacy campaigns directed at global actors, NGOs have globalized to maximize their impact. Reasons for these changes, and the strengths, limitations and impacts of NGO advocacy at a range of scales, are discussed.

Yanacopulos, H. (2002) 'Think local, act global: Transnational networks and development', in J. Robinson (ed.) *Development and Displacement*, Oxford: Oxford University Press, pp. 205–244. This introductory chapter explores relationships between networks of NGOs, social movement organizations, international financial institutions and state actors, both within and across nations.

USEFUL WEBSITES

Global Call to Action Against Poverty Poverty Online: http://www.whiteband.org/
Jubilee Debt Campaign: http://www.jubileedebtcampaign.org.uk/
Make Poverty History: http://www.makepovertyhistory.org/

REFERENCES

Anderson, I. (2002) 'Northern NGO advocacy: Perceptions, reality, and the challenge', in D. Eade (ed.) *Development and Advocacy*, Oxford: Oxfam Great Britain, pp. 84–94.

Anderson, I. (2007a) 'Global actions: International NGOs and advocacy' in B. Rugendyke (ed.) *NGOs as Advocates for Development in a Globalising World*, Abingdon and New York: Routledge, pp. 71–95.

Anderson, I. (2007b) 'Oxfam, the World Bank and heavily indebted poor countries', in B. Rugendyke (ed.) *NGOs as Advocates for Development in a Globalising World*, Abingdon and New York: Routledge, pp. 96–124.

Bebbington, A. (2003) 'Global networks and local developments: Agendas for development geography', *Tijdschrift voor economische en sociale geografie*, 94 (3): 297–309.

Bedell, G. (2005) *Makepovertyhistory: How You Can Help Defeat World Poverty in Seven Easy Steps*, London: Penguin Books.

Burnell, P. (1991) *Charity, Politics and the Third World*, London: Harvester Wheatsheaf.

Edwards, M. and Hulme, D. (eds) (1992) *Making a Difference: NGOs and Development in a Changing World*, London: Earthscan.

Edwards, M. and Hulme, D. (2000) 'Scaling up NGO impact on development: Learning from experience', in D. Eade (ed.) *Development, NGOs and Civil Society*, Oxford: Oxfam Great Britain, pp. 44–63.

Martens, D. (2006) 'NGOs in the United Nations system: Evaluating theoretical approaches', *Journal of International Development*, 18: 691–700.

Mayo, M. (2005) 'Learning from Jubilee 2000: Mobilizing for debt relief', in *Global Citizens: Social Movements and the Challenge of Globalization*, London and New York: Zed Books, pp. 172–92.

Nyamugasira, W. (2002) 'NGOs and advocacy: How well are the poor represented?', in D. Eade (ed.) *Development and Advocacy*, Oxford: Oxfam Great Britain, pp. 7–22.

Opoku-Mensah, P. (2001) 'The rise and rise of NGOs: Implications for research', *Tidsskrift ved Institutt vor sosiologi og statsvitenskap*, 1: 1–3.

Rugendyke, B. and Ollif, C. (2007) 'Charity to advocacy: Changing agendas of Australian NGOs', in *NGOs as Advocates for Development in a Globalising World*, Abingdon and New York: Routledge, pp. 17–43.

Taylor, P. (2004) 'NGOs in the world city network', *Globalizations*, 1: 265–77.

10.10 Public–private partnerships

Alex Loftus

Introduction

From the 1980s onwards, public–private partnerships (PPPs) have increased in number and scope around the world. The defining feature of these, developing a partnership between government and one or more private company, is clearly not a recent innovation. However, since the mid-1980s, the dramatic increase in such partnerships, their expansion to services normally considered to be protected from market forces and their active promotion as development strategies in the Global South have been remarkable. From the provision of basic services such as electricity, health, education and water, to the development of vast urban spectacles, the boom in public–private partnerships emphasizes the renewed primacy of the market in the development process. In what follows, I consider some of the arguments for and against public–private partnerships. Then, in concluding that the evidence for their benefits is often lacking, I consider the reasons for their continued prevalence and promotion.

Variations in partnering arrangements

Local and national states have, of course, always worked with the private sector. Historically and geographically, these partnerships have varied. In the case of public services, partnering arrangements can range from one- or two-year service contracts with the private sector, to outright divestiture. With the former, the state would retain overall ownership and management of the service and the private sector's role would be limited to one aspect of service provision, such as billing or infrastructural works. With the latter, the state's role is reduced to a simple regulatory one. This is more often considered a form of outright privatization. Somewhere between these two extremes, there is a variety of other arrangements. Management contracts generally last for between five and ten years and permit the private sector to take over the management of a service, while both risk and ownership remain with the state. Concession contracts have a longer duration, often for between 25 and 30 years. Overall responsibility for the provision of a service is transferred to the private sector for this period, following a competitive tendering process. Build, operate, train and transfer (BOTT) contracts rely on the private sector to construct new infrastructural works, before an eventual transfer of responsibility to the state. This final category has similarities with the UK government's Private Finance Initiative, in which new infrastructural projects are undertaken and financed by the private sector before being leased to and eventually handed over to the public sector. The exact division of risks and responsibilities varies within each of these contractual agreements (see Bakker 2003).

Arguments for public–private partnerships

Perhaps the central argument for the development of PPPs in the Global South lies in the real or perceived inadequacies of the state sector. States, it is sometimes argued, are under-resourced, bureaucratic, inefficient and simply unable to deliver the services expected of them. In contrast, partnerships will bring together the finance, efficiencies and dynamism of the private sector with the (assumed) accountability of government agencies. In a context of state failure, it is argued that utilizing the private sector is the only possible response to the vast needs of low-income citizens. In addition, the speed with which the private sector can be mobilized to construct infrastructural works is often seen to be advantageous. In the case of South Africa, for example, the ambitious targets set by the post-apartheid government for connection of rural households to an improved water supply would, it was argued, necessarily have to take place through a PPP arrangement. In this instance, the assets were transferred to the state once operational. Crucially, this made the involvement of the private sector much less of a sensitive issue.

Aside from the argument that the state cannot cope with the scale of the demands being placed upon it, the private sector is said to bring benefits through: competitive tendering of contracts; the use of a more flexible workforce; and being more demand-led and thus more responsive to signals within the market. These benefits, it is hoped, can be shared with the public sector, although for much of the time the state's role is reduced to that of a regulatory entity.

Arguments against public–private partnerships

Many, perhaps the majority, of the arguments in favour of public–private partnerships have proven chimerical. Depending on one's perspective, the failures of PPPs can be put down to state interference, market failure or the profit motive itself. New infrastructural works commissioned under public–private partnerships have encountered several problems. First, in sectors that have been failing, new investments represent a high risk. It is very difficult to encourage the private sector to invest in new long-term projects when profits might be low and risks might be high. In the Global South, examples range from failed water contracts (in Buenos Aires or Jakarta) to problems in ensuring investment in costly energy infrastructure. Within complex infrastructural projects, often involving many different public and private actors, it becomes difficult to design an incentive structure that might encourage investments in those areas that really need them. For many, this is a concern at the heart of efforts to rectify market failures. However, for others, the central problem lies in the fact that the private sector's predominant concern must be the ability to ensure profitable returns on its investments. Extending infrastructural projects to low-income populations is unlikely to be the most pressing concern here. In the case of water provision, under the concession contract signed in Buenos Aires in 1993, the result of this was an extension of the water network to higher-income residents and a failure to keep up with extensions to the (less profitable) sewerage network (Loftus and McDonald 2001).

In many cases, service delivery through existing infrastructure has also been negatively affected by the expansion of PPPs. One of the central battlegrounds here has been the fact that costs are often passed directly on to consumers in the form of higher user charges. The development of PPPs has gone hand in hand with an emphasis being placed on what is termed full cost recovery. Operation and maintenance costs (and often new investments in expanding service provision) are passed directly on to consumers. Cross-subsidization between sectors and between high- and low-income groups is explicitly discouraged. The aim in promoting this is to ensure that a service operates on a sound financial footing. However, questions around cost recovery raise important debates about the role of subsidies, who benefits from these (often this is the private sector), as well as issues around the new social inequalities emerging under PPPs. Within South Africa, struggles over cost recovery (within corporatized service delivery) have brought this to vivid light. The scale of the problem faced by citizen-consumers is emphasized by an extensive survey conducted in 2001, suggesting that 10 million people had been affected by water disconnections in the post-apartheid period (McDonald and Pape 2003). Relying on subtle alliances of public and private, the South African example emphasizes that such criticisms should not turn a blind eye to the failings of the state sector: it would be very wrong to idealize public service provision in the Global South. However, a rush to involve the private sector through PPPs, more often than not, compounds such problems.

If the picture for the consumer is often mixed, it is almost wholly negative for labour. While PPPs have often been regarded as a necessary corrective to a bloated state sector, this has frequently been at the cost of secure, good-quality jobs. Case studies of waste workers show the health and safety implications of these changing working conditions for municipal employees (see http://www.queensu.ca/msp).

Clearly, some of these failings could be blamed on inadequate regulation, weak contractual obligations and poor enforcement of labour laws. In this regard, much greater stress has been placed on the importance of regulatory bodies. In several situations, tighter regulation has, perhaps inevitably, curtailed short-term profits and sparked protests from the private sector. Welsh Water's transformation into a 'mutual' firm in 2001 (a not-for-profit partnership) has been linked to an ongoing process of re-regulation, with the state redefining environmental and cost targets (Bakker 2003). With a hope that the private sector might look to a longer-term accrual of profits, some attention has focused on the growth in pension fund investment in public–private partnerships.

Shifting the public–private boundary

Often overlooked in simple cost–benefit analyses of the advantages and disadvantages of PPPs are the more qualitative changes effected. Though less tangible, these may be of greater long-term significance. In particular, as more and more aspects of social reproduction are served by entities whose main motivation is the accrual of profit, our daily lives have become inextricably interwoven with a capitalist system of accumulation. Political life has also witnessed a transformation through the increasing prominence of PPPs. The result is that the main locus of decision making has shifted from the state to a broader range of public and private actors. This is often captured through reference to the shift from government to governance. While the rise of new forms of governance is often welcomed, frequently this overlooks the ways in which profit motives, rather than democratic accountability, become central to the provision and upkeep of a service. In Stiglitz's (2002) words, privatization has often served as willing handmaiden to 'briberization'.

For Harvey (2005), public–private partnerships epitomize some of the changes in governance that have accompanied the ascendancy of the neoliberal state. Owing to the neoliberal suspicion of democracy, an attempt has been made to integrate state decision making into the dynamics of capital accumulation and networks of class power. Capital thereby acquires a much stronger role in writing legislation, determining public policies and setting regulatory frameworks (ibid.: 76–8). While there is an air of conspiracy theory about some of this, Harvey's earlier writings (Harvey 1989) show how a context of inter-urban competition (highlighted in the rise of urban entrepreneurialism) serves as the hidden hand that disciplines local and national governments into PPPs. Competition compels PPPs, rather than an elite cabal hijacking the state for its own purposes. At the same time, attention has turned to what some term ongoing primitive accumulation (de

Angelis 2001) or accumulation by dispossession (Harvey 2003), through the colonization of every-day life by the profit motive. Accumulation by dispossession captures the process through which capital seeks to prise open communal resources as a source of profitable investment. During periods of crisis, brought about through the over-accumulation of capital and an apparent dearth of outlets for capital investment, the opening up of resources through a variety of public–private partnerships permits profits to be made in new areas. New PPPs in such areas as the provision of water represent the cutting edge of accumulation by dispossession.

Future prospects

Throughout the 1990s, the private sector's role in public service delivery has generated significant opposition and protest. Bechtel's contract with the departmental government of Cochabamba in Bolivia ignited one of the largest and most iconic protests of the new millennium, with many thousands of protestors marching in the streets of the city and galvanizing international support. Similar new social movements have developed around public service delivery elsewhere, initiating important scalar strategies for challenging the social relations of contemporary capitalist society. Because of this, and also in response to falling profit rates, the wave of PPPs in the water sector developed in the 1980s and 1990s seems to have slowed. However, PPPs have also transformed. Tri-sector partnerships have subsequently emerged. These new partnerships seek to bring civil society groups into public–private arrangements – whether through NGOs or grass-roots organizations. The UK's main international development agency, the DFID, responded enthusiastically to such initiatives, arguing that they achieved a win-win-win situation for countries in the Global South (DFID 2002). Research on one such partnership in Durban's water sector, however, would suggest that most of the winnings are likely to go, once again, to the private sector (Lumsden and Loftus 2003). The DFID's enthusiasm appears at best naive, and at worst somewhat cynical. Elsewhere in South Africa, attempts to develop PPPs through union groups and to share experiences have produced some mixed but also some hopeful findings.

Overall, public–private partnerships tell us much about the changing fortunes of global capitalism. Evidence for their purported benefits is often highly dubious. Arguments that private investment in infrastructure will lessen the burden on the public purse are based on a short-term view of public spending and an initial accounting fallacy. The efficiency gains and environmental benefits that the private sector is said to bring are often not based on solid evidence either. Experiments in developing new forms of public partnering offer interesting antidotes to the dogmatic insistence on the priority of the private sector. Struggles against public–private partnerships have been at the forefront of the battle to confront the inequalities of global capitalism in hopeful ways.

GUIDE TO FURTHER READING

Budds, J. and McGranahan, G. (2003) 'Are the debates on water privatization missing the point?', *Environment and Urbanization*, 15(2): 87–114.
McDonald, D.A. and Ruiters, G. (2004) *The Age of Commodity: Water Privatization in Southern Africa*, London: Earthscan.

USEFUL WEBSITES

Some of the most extensive and well-researched resources are available as open-source documents through the Public Services International Research Unit at the University of Greenwich, see http://www.psiru.org
Other useful research reports on PPPs in sub-Saharan Africa are available through the Municipal Services Project, based at Queens University in Canada, see http://www.queensu.ca/msp

REFERENCES

Bakker, K.J. (2003) 'From public to private to…mutual? Restructuring water supply governance in England and Wales', *Geoforum*, 34: 359–76.

de Angelis, M. (2001) 'Marx and primitive accumulation: The continuous character of capital's "enclosures"', *The Commoner*, 2, September (available at http://www.commoner.org.uk).

DFID (2002) 'Tri-sector partnerships: how do they work?', *Developments*, 18, July, London: Department for International Development.

Harvey, D. (1989) 'From managerialism to entrepreneurialism: The transformation of urban governance in late capitalism', *Geografiska Annaler, Series B: Human Geography*, 71B(1): 3–17.

Harvey, D. (2003) *The New Imperialism*, Oxford: Oxford University Press.

Harvey, D. (2005) *A Brief History of Neoliberalism*, Oxford: Oxford University Press.

Loftus, A.J. and McDonald, D.A. (2001) 'Of liquid dreams: A political ecology of water privatization in Buenos Aires', *Environment and Urbanization*, 13(2): 179–99.

Lumsden, F. and Loftus, A. (2003) 'Inanda's struggle for water through pipes and tunnels: Exploring state–civil society relations in a post-apartheid informal settlement',

McDonald, D.A. and Pape, J. (2002) *Cost Recovery and the Crisis of Service Delivery in South Africa*, Pretoria: HSRC.

Stiglitz, J.E. (2002) *Globalization and its Discontents*, London: Penguin.

10.11 Multilateral institutions and the developing world – Changes and challenges

Morten Bøås

Multilateral institutions occupy a dominant role in the developing world as they provide both much-needed loans and technical assistance. Much has been written about them, and there is no shortage of technical information concerning their financing, lending and impact, but what is often lacking is a concise introduction, focusing on key aspects of these institutions that are important for understanding both the politics of their functioning and the changes and challenges that affect them. Multilateral institutions as a term is used to describe many different global institutions; however, in this chapter it includes the major multilateral development banks (MDBs) – the World Bank, the three largest regional development banks, the African Development Bank (AfDB), the Asian Development Bank (ADB) and the Inter-American Development Bank (IDB), and the International Monetary Fund (IMF). As these institutions are not only complex, but also perform a wide range of different tasks, they cannot be approached as unitary actors. What is needed is an approach that highlights its internal processes and politics. The first part of this chapter looks at power and organization in such institutions, while the second part addresses the changes and challenges they have encountered.

In 1944, a conference was convened in Bretton Woods in the USA by the emerging victorious countries in the Second World War. It was here that the World Bank and the IMF were born – in the hope that they would provide the foundations for a peaceful and prosperous future for the world. In the first decade of the twenty-first century, these two multilateral institutions, and their sister agencies the regional development banks, occupy a dominant position in the global political economy, but not only are they the target of powerful attack – both in the streets and in the media – they also have to face up to the fact that the world is changing rapidly (Bøås and McNeill 2003).

The 50-year anniversary of the World Bank and the IMF was met with the 'Fifty years is enough' campaign, which subsequently developed into a loosely knit confederation of non-governmental organizations (NGOs) which has continued to demonstrate against 'globalization' in general, and its institutional manifestations – the World Bank, the IMF and the regional development banks – in particular (see Brown and Fox 2001). While some people see these institutions, and the multi-lateralism they promote, as playing an important role in the elimination of world poverty, others see them not as the solution, but as part of the problem.

Power and organization

The multilateral institutions represent a form of international cooperation the world had not experienced prior to 1945, an evolution from the League of Nations and United Nations models, in which all member countries formally have an equal voice and vote. Their structure is inspired by the joint-stock model of private capitalist corporations, in which member countries are shareholders whose voting powers vary with their relative economic importance. In other words, each member country's share of the votes is weighted in accordance with the combined amount of capital it has paid in and is guaranteeing. All member countries are organized in a country constituency, headed by an Executive Director who controls the combined votes of his or her constituency, and who sits on the institution's Board of Directors. The size and composition of the country constituencies vary across the universe of multilateral institutions, but the principle of organization is similar.

The capital construction of all multilateral institutions was established with the formation of the World Bank. It was established as an institution, which was to be owned, and whose capital would be provided, by government, not by private sources. Its initial authorized capitalization of US$10 billion consisted of 20 per cent in the form of paid-in capital and 80 per cent in the form of guaranteed capital. This distinction is crucial for our understanding of these institutions. Each country subscription is divided into two parts. The larger one is the so-called *guaranteed capital*. This amount is not actually paid by the member countries to the multilateral institution, but each member guarantees for a certain sum of money. The credit rating of the World Bank and the other multilateral institutions is based on the amount guaranteed by rich industrialized member countries. This gives these institutions the best possible international credit rating (e.g. triple A) and makes it possible for them to lend money on international capital markets and re-lend it to poorer countries with a lower credit rating. This would not be possible without rich member countries, and therefore it constitutes the backbone of their power. The institutions could not function without them, and this knowledge, which is shared by all the actors involved, also implies that votes rarely are used. They are simply not needed very often as the power relations on the Board of Directors are so transparent, and the consequences of constantly working against them so obvious to everybody concerned.

Multilateral institutions therefore reflect the power relations prevailing at their point of origin, and tend, at least initially, to facilitate world views and beliefs (for instance in the merits of neoliberal economics) in accordance with these power relations (c.f. Cox 1992; Wade 2002). Outcomes, however, are determined not simply by the distribution of power among the members that constitute the institution in question, but also by the multilateral institution itself, which can affect how choices are framed and outcomes reached. All multilateral institutions should therefore be approached, first and foremost, as social constructions (see Kratochwil and Ruggie 1986). Those involved are political, economic and social actors, operating not just through the state's foreign policy apparatus, but also transnationally.

Changes and challenges

All multilateral institutions are originally established in order to solve problems. After the completion of the reconstruction of Europe, the 'problem' was development (or the lack of it). President

Truman's inaugural speech on 20 January 1949 is commonly held to mark the beginning of the modern development practice (Nustad 2004). In this speech, the transfer and transfusion of scientific and expert knowledge was presented as the solution to poverty and misery. This was the means, and the objective – increased prosperity and closer resemblance to Western societies – was the original goal of multilateral institutions; despite all the new policies and approaches that have emerged this has remained at the heart of their activities.

What have changed are the means, not the ends. And the changes that have taken place have been incremental – most often without any attempt to place new objectives in a logical, prioritized order. The process of change that has taken place in multilateral institutions thus resembles what Ernst Haas has called 'change by adaptation' (see Haas 1990).

In comparison to other social units, multilateral institutions confront rather special challenges when faced with demands to incorporate new issue areas. Their mission is never simple and straightforward because both member states and other actors in their external environment may disagree on the interpretation of the mission (the ends), as well as on the tasks (the means) that need to be carried out if the mission is to be completed. In social units that function under such circumstances, organizational routines and standard operating procedures will be preferred to substantive change. Multilateral institutions will therefore favour one particular way of arranging and routinizing their activities. Since they have to satisfy different constituencies (that is, borrowing countries, donor countries and, increasingly, NGOs and civil society), multilateral institutions will try to avoid articulating competing views. Consensus therefore becomes an objective in itself, but the kind of consensus established in multilateral institutions is constructed on the power relationships prevailing in the institution in question. This means that consensus in multilateral institutions is usually artificial.

This way of reasoning also helps us to understand why the favoured approach of multilateral institutions in promoting development was that of the 'engineer'. Development (or the lack of it) was seen as a technical issue, and not as a political question. If the challenges of development, and the new ideas supposed to resolve them, could be defined in technical terms, this increased the possibility of getting a proposal for action approved by staff and borrowing-country governments. Over time, a limited re-examination of the means utilized to reach their ends was made possible when new issue areas were presented to the multilateral institutions in the same language as the old and familiar knowledge. By applying such a strategy of depoliticization, new and potentially challenging discussions were kept within the framework of already existing standard operating procedures. It was therefore possible to treat potentially highly political issues, such as governance, as technical issues, and thereby the underlying political conflicts could be controlled, at least in part. For example, it was the ability to define governance in strictly economic and technical terms that facilitated this issue area's incorporation into multilateral institutions.

Projects have been modified by the inclusion of new social and environmental components and regulatory safeguards in order to ensure that environmental and social damage is avoided as much as possible. The approach of multilateral institutions, however, is still of an engineering problem-solving type, with policies and project papers written in the technical language that staff, management and the boards of multilateral institutions are used to.

In the 1950s and 1960s, this strategy worked remarkably well. But in the 1970s and 1980s, it was gradually called into question, and by the mid-1990s it was fully apparent that new development challenges could no longer be tackled by narrow technical approaches, and multilateral institutions started to experience more severe difficulties. The issue was no longer simply a matter of finding the right technical solution to a functional problem. Today, the challenge is to construct some sort of consensus around an increasingly politicized agenda, constituted around a whole range of new cross-cutting themes, such as governance, involuntary resettlement and indigenous people. The technocratic consensus has reached its limits. It is no longer possible, in any credible way, to define development solely in a technical and functional manner. As a consequence, the internal artificial consensus is disappearing, not only between donor and borrowing member countries of multilateral institutions, but also internally in these institutions. An increasingly political agenda will make the process of political manoeuvring between donor and recipient countries and other stakeholders (civil societies and the private sectors) increasingly difficult for multilateral institutions.

Concluding remarks

The questions concerning the future of multilateral institutions and how they respond to changes and new challenges are many, and the answers too few. However, what is more important than finding answers is to ask the right questions, and they can be coined only if we grasp the realities of these institutions. They do reflect the power relations prevailing when they were established, but they have also been subjected to change, and the new issue areas that they have had to tackle has challenged the old technocratic mode of these institutions. They have also been forced to deal with criticism from a wide range of civil society actors. However, these changes apart, they still operate in a way that gives power to rich member countries, and this is not likely to change, as the entire modus operandi of multilateral institutions is based on their ability to secure loans from international capital markets on the basis of the credit rating they achieve from the guaranteed capital of the rich member countries.

USEFUL WEBSITES

Bank Information Centre: http://www.bicusa.org
Bretton Woods Project: http://www.brettonwoodsproject.org
World Bank: http://www.worldbank.org
Structural Adjustment Participatory Review International Network: http://www.saprin.org

REFERENCES

Brown, L.D. and Fox, J. (2001) 'Transnational civil society coalitions and the World Bank: Lessons from project and policy influence campaigns', in M. Edwards and J. Gaventa (eds) *Global Citizen Action*, London: Earthscan, pp. 43–58.
Bøås, M. and McNeill, D. (2003) *Multilateral Institutions: A Critical Introduction*, London: Pluto Press.
Cox, R. (1992) 'Multilateralism and world order', *Review of International Studies*, 18(2): 161–80.
Haas, E. (1990) *When Knowledge is Power – Three Models of Change in International Organizations*, Berkeley, CA: University of California Press.
Kratochwil, F. and Ruggie, J.G. (1986) 'International organization: A state of the art or an art of the state', *International Organization*, 40(3): 753–75.
Nustad, K. (2004) 'The development discourse in the multilateral system', in M. Bøås and D. McNeill (eds) *Global Institutions and Development: Framing the World?* London: Routledge, pp. 13–23.
Wade, R. (2002) 'US hegemony and the World Bank: The fight over people and ideas', *Review of International Political Economy*, 9(2): 201–29.

10.12 The World Bank and NGOs

Paul J. Nelson

Although the world's largest lender for development is owned and governed by its 185 member governments, its contact with non-governmental organizations (NGOs) grew rapidly in the 1980s and 1990s, both in policy debates and in service delivery. A wide variety of NGOs, based in the industrial countries and in the World Bank's borrowing countries, were drawn into lending and policy processes that were long almost exclusively the province of national governments. By 2007, as the resignation of Paul Wolfowitz from the Bank's Presidency sparked broad debates about the institution, many of the issues – debt relief, corruption, environmental impact and the constant broadening of the Bank's agenda – were issues in which NGOs had been critically involved.

Three clear types of contact have emerged: NGO collaboration in World Bank-financed projects; invited consultation in policy discussions; and confrontations over projects or controversial policies. Both project collaboration and more confrontational critiques have helped to make way for changes in the World Bank policy, forced a more open information disclosure policy, and, in a few cases, influenced its lending practice. The World Bank now refers to its engagement with 'civil society' or with 'civil society organizations', including not only NGOs, but also religious leaders, trades unions, manufacturers' associations and other organized groups. The term NGO is retained in this chapter, but the organizations discussed often include social movements and other forms of association.

Three forms of interaction

NGO involvement in World Bank-financed projects

The World Bank makes loans to governments to finance development projects, and encourages policy changes through non-project 'development policy loans'. NGO involvement in implementing World Bank-financed projects grew rapidly during the 1980s and 1990s, as many governments' service delivery capacities were shrinking. Fewer than 10 per cent of projects between 1973 and 1988 were reported to involve an NGO, but the World Bank (2007a) reports that half of projects approved in 1990 and 70 per cent of those approved in 2006 involved an NGO in some role.

These roles are variable, and NGO involvement does not necessarily signal a change in the character of the project or in decision making about the project. Many projects in the early 1990s, for example, involved NGOs in a single project 'component', or as recipients of small grants through special social service funds known as emergency social funds (ESF) or social investment funds (SIF), and many in the 2000s involve 'one-off consultations' in the early stages of the project (World Bank 2007a: 25).

'Consultation' in policy formation

'Consultation' is a buzzword at the World Bank. In addition to project-level talks with NGOs or community organizations, the World Bank regularly sponsors dialogues or formal consultations (face-to-face or virtual) to elicit NGO input on sector policies (forestry, energy, extractive industries, social policy, etc.), and on the themes of the annual *World Development Report*. The Bank has co-sponsored conferences and consultations on social policy issues such as hunger alleviation, gender, participation, globalization and micro-enterprise lending, and circulates a guide for governments on consulting with civil society (World Bank 2007b). These consultations are frequent, relatively public and do not usually create binding commitments for the World Bank, nor have immediate implications for any particular loan or member state.

The Bank's promotion of participatory processes in development also leans heavily on the practice of 'consultation' between borrowing governments and civil society groups. The Bank promotes the use of public budget oversight methodologies in many countries, and insists on at least nominal talks between governments and civil society stakeholders in certain policy areas. The Poverty Reduction Strategy Papers (PRSPs), for example, which every low-income borrowing country must complete as a condition of low-interest lending, are to be developed through a process of consultation with civil society organizations. Forty-nine countries had approved PRSPs as of 2007; the Bank reports that 88 per cent of recent national processes involved 'consultations with civil society', but that the 'scope and intensity' of that consultation varied greatly (2007a: 16).

Confrontation: The NGO critique

The World Bank has also become a lightning rod for policy advocacy and for criticism of the international economic system and of development aid. NGOs have pressed the Bank to become more generous, egalitarian and responsive to gender and minority concerns; more transparent and open to effective civil society participation; and more sensitive to natural resource use and human rights standards.

Resistance to World Bank-financed infrastructure projects has been the most visible form of NGO criticism, and has forced the Bank to give attention to environmental and social issues involved in major dam and energy projects. NGO critics have blocked at least one project, provoked amendments to others, and helped to motivate the creation of an independent inspection panel to which affected communities can appeal (Clark, Fox and Treakle 2003). They also motivated the Bank to carry out a thorough and self-critical review of its role in involuntary resettlement of communities for major infrastructure projects (Fox and Brown 1998).

One blocked project – a proposed loan for a major dam on Nepal's Arun river – was proposed for World Bank funding in 1994, and vigorously opposed by some of the indigenous residents of the remote river valley, whose objections had little influence with the Nepalese government. NGOs lobbied the Bank directly, pressured member governments' representatives on the Bank's Board, and finally filed a claim with the new Independent Inspection Panel. The claim, submitted by anonymous residents of the river valley and a national NGO, the Arun Concerned Group, was investigated by the Panel, which found that the Bank had violated its own policies in preparing the project. Then-President James Wolfensohn ended World Bank involvement in the project in June 1995.

These strategies – working in coalitions to gain influence on the Board of Executive Directors, and lobbying the World Bank directly and through the media – have sometimes worked effectively. But even when targeting specific projects, NGOs often find that their influence is limited. The Chad–Cameroon pipeline, financed in part by two branches of the World Bank, was perhaps the most systematically monitored project in history, with human rights, development and environmental NGOs from Europe, North America and Chad and Cameroon pressing for unprecedented safeguards in an effort to minimize environmental damage and ensure that oil revenues were invested in development, rather than funnelled into civil war and personal gain. A complex system of trust funds, national and international oversight bodies, and reporting requirements, however, failed to prevent the feared outcome: in July 2006, the World Bank cut off lending to Chad in response to the government's refusal to hold to an agreement to devote fixed percentages of oil revenues to development objectives, but lending was restarted in January 2007 after new negotiations (Horta, Nguiffo and Djiraibe 2007).

Effects on policy and practice

The World Bank's activities are of interest to a wide range of actors in the international political economy. Organization for Economic Cooperation and Development (OECD) governments, international organizations and borrowing country governments have strong interests in virtually all decisions at the World Bank. Within each government there may be distinct views among the Central Bank, Treasury, Development Ministry or Agency, or export agency. Other organizations in the UN system sometimes take an interest in World Bank policies that affect their mandates, and see the Bank as an important potential source of co-financing for projects. As the World Bank recreates itself as the centre of a web of 'partnerships', NGOs are not alone in trying to win influence.

Effects at the World Bank

What effects has all this attention had on the World Bank? The complex political environment makes it difficult to sort out causes of policy change, but NGOs have arguably had important roles in four trends at the World Bank, both intended and unintended. They have helped to make greater space for innovators on staff, greater openness to external scrutiny and extensive changes in formal policy, and they have helped to expand the World Bank's influence over many borrowing governments.

Space and support for internal innovators
Staff who want to use participatory methods, or innovate in other ways, have benefited from external pressure on the Bank (Miller-Adams 1999). Internal advocates for more participatory project design and implementation brought NGO advocates into the internal 'participation learning group' that documented participatory strategies, made policy recommendations and led to the creation of a widely distributed *Participation Sourcebook*. Internal working groups on micro-enterprise lending and gender issues also relate closely to interested NGOs.

Greater openness
NGO pressure also contributed directly to adoption of a new, more liberal information policy in 1993, under which the public can gain access to at least summaries of most project-related documents. The information disclosure policy's implementation, however, has been uneven, especially when corporate interests are involved directly (Nelson 2003).

Formal policy changes
In a handful of environmental and social policy areas it is clear that NGOs have contributed to policy changes. Confrontational strategies have led to new environmental and rights policies in fields such as energy, forestry and involuntary resettlement related to major infrastructure projects (Fox and Brown 1998). Involuntary resettlement, perhaps the area of most intense NGO advocacy, is also the area where internal and independent reviewers have found the clearest evidence of changes in practice.

NGO pressure has had other, unintended effects as well. The Bank is an increasingly agile institution, capable of policy change and of taking on new issues to satisfy important stakeholders. Its anticorruption programmes, its somewhat heterodox position in the debate over the Asian financial crisis, support for debt relief initiatives in the late 1990s and its interest in corporate governance are all pertinent examples.

Expanding influence over borrowers
In expanding its policy domain and the safeguards it applies to lending, the World Bank has also expanded its authority over its borrowers. Among the requirements it demands of its borrowers, new since 1980, are environmental impact assessments, national environmental action plans, disclosure of certain documents, poverty assessments, and a variety of safeguards and reports regarding 'good governance' (Goldman 2005), all of which create new, externally mandated duties for governments.

Effects on the NGOs

The World Bank, too, has an agenda in working with NGOs. Like most development aid agencies, it treats NGOs as an important constituency in securing political support. The World Bank's economic policy framework of liberalization, privatization, export promotion and reshaping the welfare state also depends on NGOs to manage social programmes and emergency social funds. But the Bank's continued encouragement of private-sector provision of key services, including water and sanitation, has sparked a new round of opposition from NGOs, consumer organizations and labour unions, often organized around claims to the human right to water (Conca 2005).

Network links built among the World Bank's NGO critics help to shape the structure, orientation and capacity of civil society organizations. Sustained NGO campaigns to influence World Bank projects and policy in involuntary resettlement and energy policy have built enduring networks. These links between civil society organizations in the Global North and South can help to build capacity for self-representation, an important addition to other service delivery-related capacity-building programmes among NGOs, which often focus on capacities for service delivery.

But NGO networks themselves will likely be asked to meet a standard of democracy and accountability, if they are to be considered legitimate political actors. International NGOs, particularly environmental advocates, have figured prominently in advocacy networks and coalitions, and the World Bank's borrowing governments and Southern NGOs themselves are increasingly demanding greater clarity about who represents whom, and on what agendas, in advocacy towards international organizations such as the World Bank (Jordan and van Tuijl 2006).

Prospects

NGOs have won a seat at many World Bank policy discussions, and the Bank has established mechanisms to tap the service-delivery capacity and knowledge of NGOs, including those in its borrowing countries. Both parties face challenges in building on these arrangements. The World Bank will need to devise ways to bring NGOs and its borrowing governments into more consistent, effective contact, if it is to continue to benefit from NGOs' cooperation without further undercutting the role of borrowing governments.

NGOs will need to build the local capacity to monitor and force implementation of the policy commitments won at Bank headquarters, and devise ways to give increasing voice and control to NGOs based in the borrowing countries. In the process, they may find ways to make the World Bank a source of leverage for humane and accountable solutions to a new round of international finance and development issues.

GUIDE TO FURTHER READING

Fox, J. and Brown, L.D. (eds) (1998) *The Struggle for Accountability: The World Bank, NGOs and Grassroots Movements*, Cambridge, MA: MIT Press. A detailed account of the interactions between international NGOs, grass-roots movements and the World Bank in shaping controversial projects and policies.

Goldman, M. (2005) *Imperial Nature: The World Bank and Struggles for Social Justice in the Age of Globalization*, New Haven, CT: Yale University Press. A highly critical study of the World Bank's environmental and social policies, focusing on the Bank's relations to community and social movement activists.

World Bank (2007a) *World Bank–Civil Society Engagement: Review of Fiscal Years 2005 and 2006*. Washington, DC: World Bank. The Bank's report on recent interactions with civil society, including 'operational collaboration', global and national consultations, and policy debates. Positive and thorough.

USEFUL WEBSITES

http://www.worldbank.org – the World Bank maintains one of the most informative and best documented websites of any international organization, including a major section on civil society.

http://www.bicusa.org – the Bank Information Center, a Washington, DC-based NGO that monitors World Bank projects and policies, especially (but not only) those with environmental impacts.

http://www.brettonwoodsproject.org – the independent, London-based NGO Bretton Woods Project is critical of the Bank and carries coverage of a wide range of issues of interest to NGOs.

REFERENCES

Clark, D., Fox, J. and Treakle, K. (eds) (2003) *Demanding Accountability: Civil Society Claims and the World Bank Inspection Panel*, Oxford: Rowman & Littlefield.

Conca, K. (2005) *Governing Water: Contentious Transnational Politics and Global Institution Building*, Cambridge, MA: MIT Press.

Fox, J. and Brown, L.D. (eds) (1998) *The Struggle for Accountability: The World Bank, NGOs and Grassroots Movements*, Cambridge, MA: MIT Press.

Goldman, M. (2005) *Imperial Nature: The World Bank and Struggles for Social Justice in the Age of Globalization*, New Haven, CT: Yale University Press.

Horta, K., Nguiffo, S. and Djiraibe, D. (2007) *The Chad–Cameroon Oil Pipeline Project: A Project Non-Completion Report*, Washington, DC: Environmental Defense (http://www.environmentaldefense.org/documents/6282_ChadCameroon-Non-Completion.pdf).

Hulme, D. and Edwards, M. (eds) (1997) *NGOs, States and Donors: Too Close for Comfort?* New York: St Martin's Press in association with Save the Children.

Jordan, L. and van Tuijl, P. (2006) *NGO Accountability: Politics, Principles and Innovations*, London: Earthscan.

Miller-Adams, M. (1999) *The World Bank: New Agendas in a Changing World*, London: Routledge.

Nelson, P.J. (2003) 'Multilateral development banks, transparency and corporate clients: "Public–private partnerships" and public access to information', *Public Administration and Development*, 249–57.

World Bank (2007a) *World Bank–Civil Society Engagement: Review of Fiscal Years 2005 and 2006*, Washington, DC: World Bank.

World Bank (2007b) *Consultations with Civil Society: A Sourcebook*, Washington, DC: World Bank.

10.13 The role of the United Nations in developing countries

Jim Whitman

The United Nations as a development actor

Three factors inform and constrain the role of the United Nations in developing countries. The first is that the United Nations is a political organization, not a developmental one. Development is an intensely political and often highly contested matter and, unlike dedicated development organizations or individual nation-states, the UN, its organs, agencies, funds and programmes have very little room for independent initiative. The UN's developmental roles are shaped directly and indirectly by the priorities of its more powerful member states.

The second factor is that, beyond general statements about human betterment in the UN Charter and elsewhere, the ends and means of development have been subject to very considerable change since the founding of the UN – again, much of it politically determined. Decolonization more than tripled the number of UN member states and brought nearly all of humanity within its remit. As much of the 'underdeveloped' world became the 'Third World' of cold war competition, development was subject to strategic considerations. More recently, globalization has begun to alter the perceptions and expectations of governments and peoples, rich and poor alike. In addition, development thinking on every scale is subject to economic trends and prevailing ideologies; the perceived needs of the poor; and factors once peripheral which take on considerable significance – human rights, gender, environment. The United Nations does not stand above or outside any of these currents.

Third, in development matters as in most other fields, the UN is not a single actor. In operational terms, there is a good case to be made for specialization in health (World Health Organization), food (World Food Programme), agriculture (Food and Agriculture Organization), education and culture (UNESCO) and the like, but there are more fundamental divisions at work. The Bretton Woods institutions (the World Bank and the International Monetary Fund) are part of the UN 'family' but not part of the UN 'system' – essentially, they have functional independence (see ul Haq 1995). In practice, this means that the developing country initiatives of a number of UN agencies, even including the World Bank, can run counter to the structural adjustment programmes of the IMF. The debt burden of many developing countries has been exacerbated by structural adjustment programmes, while many of the UN's agencies work to mitigate the consequences. A more disturbing dysfunction has been visible in Iraq for more than a decade. While the UN acts under its Charter remit to maintain international peace and security through its sanctions regime against Iraq, UN development agencies struggle to deal with the resultant human suffering, including a dreadful surge in child malnutrition.

However, the role of the United Nations in developing countries is not merely a lowest common denominator of its more powerful member states – sometimes expressed as the notion that the UN is no more than the sum of its parts. The eradication of smallpox in the 1970s, led by the WHO, is a case in point, as is the achievement of access to clean water for tens of millions of people. Food dependency has been eliminated from many regions and the UN also provides the technical expertise and administrative oversight for an impressive range of international regulation and global monitoring, from telecommunications to disease surveillance. Nor is the UN confined to operational matters. Development has no clear boundaries and since many of the most fundamental human needs also find expression in human rights laws and norms – clearly embodied in the UN Charter and the Universal Declaration of Human Rights, as well as in extensive international law – the UN embodies powerful and near-universal ideals. The United Nations Development Programme's annual *Human Development Report* is as important in normative terms as its rankings are in political terms. The eventual inclusion of 'human liberty' as a crucial indicator beside life expectancy, income and education is important in ensuring that measures of development are not confined to technical matters and aggregate statistics such as Gross Domestic Product. The United Nations also provides a focal point for new thinking, 'bottom-up' agenda-setting and the articulation and dissemination of norms. UN summits have been central to the inclusion of human rights, the claims of indigenous peoples, the needs of children, gender issues, population control and environmental considerations as part of development. Through a combination of norm-setting, data-gathering and monitoring, the UN and its various agencies have been instrumental in such substantial if undramatic advances as improvements in agriculture, literacy and infant mortality rates in many parts of the world.

Current trends

Yet as the gap between rich and poor continues to widen and as a spiral of poverty, environmental degradation and violent conflict become all but a way of life in some regions (Suliman 1999), the difference between what the UN enshrines and what it is able to accomplish threatens its legitimacy. When the cold war ended, much hope was invested in UN peacekeeping, occasionally to the detriment of development, as considerable resources were devoted to the demands of emergency humanitarianism. Even when peacekeeping or peace enforcement are relatively successful, the demands of post-conflict reconstruction and development are typically complex, politically volatile and indifferently funded. The operational budgets of those UN agencies most closely involved – UNDP, WFP, the UN Refugee Agency (UNHCR) – are donor-driven, which means that their ability to move from relief to development is conditioned not only by the immediate political interests of states, but also by the general trend in decreasing overseas aid budgets.

The decline in assistance to developing countries, in combination with unmet but growing emergency needs, are mutually reinforcing. Between 1996 and 1997, world aid declined from US$55.4 billion to US$47.6 billion; and aid to the poorest countries is at its lowest level for a decade (Randal, German and Ewing 1998: 4). Stretched UN capacity cannot address even the worst need; and capacity-short operational failures are not uncommon. While more populations sink from 'underdeveloped' to 'conflict-ridden', matters not commonly regarded as development issues, such as the global refugee crisis or the proliferation of landmines, impact on UN development initiatives and it becomes ever more difficult to address local manifestations of international iniquities and inequities in isolation. This trend is furthered by a variety of globalizing forces – most notably the harmonization of international trade being ushered in by the World Trade Organization; and also trans-boundary issues as diverse as the HIV/AIDS pandemic, regional water scarcity, resource depletion and the arms trade.

These trends make UN development initiatives all the more important, since the alleviation of human suffering, the empowerment of the dispossessed and the extension of universal norms to marginalized populations is what gives development its moral force. They are also a large part of what gives the UN its standing and legitimacy, which it will need to preserve and strengthen in order to address threats to human welfare, particularly in poorer states. The difficulty facing the UN and its operational agencies is how to deal with immediate and burgeoning need, while planning for a very different development future. In fact, the role of the UN in developing countries is becoming ever more difficult to separate from the role of the UN in framing an equitable and humane international order. In a rapidly globalizing world (Thomas and Wilkin), the interests of powerful states are no less subject to change than poorer ones, and reconsidered calculations of costs and benefits make plain the advantages of peace and stability over containment; the worth of vaccination and literacy programmes; the social and economic conditions that make and sustain export markets; and the importance of balancing trade and environment. It is plain that if the role of the United Nations in developing countries is to remain programmatic rather than events-driven, and if it is to sustain an inclusive and long-term approach to the welfare of humanity, then 'high-level' deliberations and country-level operations must come to be expressions of a single ethos. In other words, we must come to see the development of impoverished nations and peoples as the development of global society; and our own welfare as closely bound up with the welfare of humanity.

The prospect

At present, state-based fears about empowering the UN are coupled with fierce criticism of its operational deficiencies, while debate about UN reform is sidetracked into matters of bureaucratic streamlining. This pernicious cycle can be broken only by recognizing the worth of the UN's inclusiveness and standing, and its very considerable expertise, both strategically and operationally. The UN's role in developing countries properly begins with ensuring that the elimination of poverty is an inescapable requisite of international agreements that include or affect poor states, much as the UN has been instrumental in ensuring the same for human rights and for the environment. Macroeconomic strategy, currency stabilization, food production, trade regimes, employment and other large-scale considerations are not the backdrop against which 'development' can commence; if the former are not human-centred, culturally attuned and equitable, then UN agency involvement will be largely curative and, often, merely palliative.

There is no shortage of modernizing (as opposed to merely 'reform') proposals to ensure that the UN's existing organs and agencies further a 'culture of development', from a re-orientation of the Bretton Woods institutions, to the establishment of an Economic Security Council. Better coordinated programmes between various UN agencies and between the UN and various government and non-government bodies are also necessary. Concerted initiatives that capture the public imagination and garner official support – the anti-landmines campaign, or the progress made towards eliminating polio, for example – more easily dissolve barriers and open the door on political possibility than declarations. And, at every level, the legacy of development as large-scale intervention must be replaced by the goal of human emancipation, which means forging working partnerships with those whom we would assist.

Conflicting interests, unrecognized difficulties and all manner of obstacles and dilemmas are the stuff of development work, but these will only become more entrenched when the aspirations of the United Nations Charter do not find expression in practical programmes. Article 55 of the Charter states that the United Nations 'shall promote solutions to international economic, social, health, and related problems'. Vision and commitment will be required to summon the necessary political engagement at a time when the restoration of war-torn societies, the majority of which are in the developing world, absorb so much political capital, often with disappointing results. A more strategic, regional approach to resolving impacted conflict holds open possibilities for combining relief with longer-term and more broadly conceived development, since so many violent conflicts range across borders. The role of the UN in these instances should extend well beyond familiar technical matters, into the restoration of justice systems, building or restoring civil administration, income generation and ensuring that the delicate fabric of social welfare provision is not left to the mercies of market forces. The sum of UN initiatives should nurture war-torn societies back into the community of states, not propel them as full players on to the 'level playing field' of the world political economy.

A more integrated, less sectoral approach to underdevelopment will be essential for development planners facing problems which are global in character as well as extent. HIV/AIDS, for example, now affects 24 million people in sub-Sarahan Africa (UNAIDS figures), driving a downward spiral of disease, impoverishment and social splintering. Development initiatives as conceived in previous decades cannot be undertaken in such circumstances, nor in places where violence has become entrenched or social stability and coherence has been under siege for a generation or more. Perhaps the biggest obstacle in the way of creative thinking and concerted political initiative would be an alarmist or defensive reaction on the part of governments in the developed world, which would further erode United Nations capacity.

Conclusion

In a world full of 'lessons' from recent events, one widely shared perception about the Gulf War should give us pause: it is that when the cause is sufficiently important, we – the international community – can move swiftly; can find in the United Nations the legal and political means to address a gross injustice; and can marshal the diplomatic, financial and logistical means few would have thought possible beforehand. A true culture of development can not grow out of charitable impulses, narrow self-interest or emergency provision. Nor, more importantly, is the way of life enjoyed by the developed world sustainable in a world of 800 million malnourished human beings. The role of the United Nations in developing countries is ultimately the work of uniting all nations in equality; facilitating this work will be the principal characteristic of enlightened self-interest in the twenty-first century.

GUIDE TO FURTHER READING AND REFERENCES

Klingebiel, S. (1999) *Effectiveness and Reform of the United Nations Development Programme*, London: Frank Cass.

Norgaard, R. (1994) *Development Betrayed: The End of Progress and a Coevolutionary Revisioning of the Future*, London: Routledge.

Randel, J., German, T. and Ewing, D. (eds) (1998) *The Reality of Aid, 1998/1999*, London: Earthscan.

Suliman, M. (ed.) (1999) *Ecology, Politics and Violent Conflict*, London: Zed Books.

Thomas, C. and Wilkin, P. (eds) (1997) *Globalization and the South*, Basingstoke: Macmillan.

ul Haq, M. (ed.) (1995a) *The UN and the Bretton Woods Institutions: New Challenges for the Twenty-First Century*, Basingstoke: Macmillan.

ul Haq, M. (1995b) *Reflections on Human Development*, Oxford: Oxford University Press.

United Nations Development Programme (2000) *Human Development Report, 2000*, Oxford: Oxford University Press.

10.14 Challenges to the World Trade Organization

Pitou van Dijck and Gerrit Faber

The authors would like to thank Marinella Wallis at CEDLA for her contributions.

From GATT to WTO

Since 1 January 1995, the World Trade Organization (WTO) has provided the all-embracing framework for the conduct of its members in a broad range of trade-related policy areas. The WTO replaced the General Agreement on Tariffs and Trade (GATT), established in 1947, and aims at the realization of similar objectives, operates on the basis of the same principles and encompasses all the results achieved in the GATT rounds of multilateral trade negotiations. As laid down in the Marrakesh Agreement Establishing the World Trade Organization, which resulted from the Uruguay Round of the GATT, the main objective of the WTO is to contribute to the welfare of its members, and particularly of developing countries, by improving the functioning of the multilateral trade system. This objective is meant to be realized through the liberalization of world trade and the creation of a transparent, reliable and fair rules-based system for trade relations. Among its most essential principles are 'general most-favoured-nation treatment' and 'national treatment on internal taxation and regulation', as laid down in Article I and Article III of the GATT respectively. Article I refers to non-discrimination between imports from different member countries in the trade regime of a member country, while Article III refers to non-discrimination between domestic supply and imports from member countries after customs clearance. Many GATT-WTO articles deal with circumstances and conditions allowing countries to intervene in trade flows by levying import tariffs and using subsidies to protect or support domestic producers and consumers for reasons related to unfairness of competition, safety and health, and emergency conditions. More specifically, a substantial number of articles stipulate exceptions made for developing countries, and particularly for least-developed countries in order to support their development process.

GATT was probably the most successful contractual arrangement among countries after the Second World War. In successive rounds of negotiations, tariff barriers to international trade in manufactured products were cut substantially, particularly in developed countries, and many non-tariff barriers to trade, like regulations and standards, were taken up for harmonization. Finally, a large number of trade disputes among contracting parties of the GATT were settled.

The GATT agenda had expanded continuously. The Tokyo Round (1973–79) included codes on standards, subsidies, government procurement, and the agreements on harmonization of regulations regarding Technical Barriers to Trade and on the Application of Sanitary and Phytosanitary Standards. Agreements on services, investment, intellectual property rights, subsidies and agriculture expanded the agenda further during the Uruguay Round of the GATT (1986–94).

Notwithstanding these significant achievements, which contributed greatly to the liberalization of world trade and global welfare, GATT did not make much progress in liberalizing international trade in agricultural products and services, or in some labour-intensive manufactured products of particular interest to developing countries. International trade in textiles and clothing was largely regulated outside the GATT, in a series of successive Multi-Fibre Arrangements, aiming at curtailing and regulating the expansion of exports of such products by developing countries to the markets of developed countries.

The role of developing countries in the long series of successive GATT rounds preceding the Uruguay Round was rather limited, and the agenda was used to reflect issues of particular importance to developed countries. Non-reciprocity, preferential treatment for their exports and more space for their trade policies were the major elements of the 'special and differential treatment' offered to developing countries. The role of developing countries became somewhat more prominent during the Uruguay Round, in which the issue of market access for export products from developing countries was addressed – most notably agricultural products, clothing and textiles – as well as the issue of service exports by developed countries to the markets of developing countries. However, the 'dirty tariffication' of agricultural trade barriers, and the back-loading of the abolition of quantitative import restrictions on developing countries' exports of clothing and textiles, as arranged in previous Multi-Fibre Arrangements, constituted a dilution of the benefits of the Uruguay Round for developing countries.

Interestingly, a group of Latin American and east Asian developing countries and some developed countries, which all had a stake in the liberalization of international trade in temperate zone agricultural products, cooperated in the so-called Cairns Group, and managed to have a significant impact on the negotiations by making agriculture a key issue in this last of the GATT rounds. This form of cooperation among countries with more or less similar interests was to become one of the characteristics of subsequent negotiations in the first WTO round.

Challenges to the WTO

The challenges the WTO has faced from its inception are daunting for several reasons. First, the agenda has broadened substantially and includes many issues that were not dealt with before at the multilateral level, or were postponed deliberately by the key role players because of their political sensitivity. This had been the case with agriculture, which had been kept off the agenda of the GATT until the Uruguay Round came up with a first Agreement on Agriculture, which was, to a large extent, a framework agreement for future negotiations. The broad agenda of the WTO includes not only measures to liberalize and discipline trade in manufactures, agricultural products and services, but also regulations pertaining to a broad range of issues, such as intellectual property rights, trade-related investment measures and standards. Moreover, it contains a new mechanism to settle disputes among its members that improved discipline substantially, particularly with regard to the major and most powerful member countries. This mixed bag, with many types of new issues differing substantially by nature from the topics that used to dominate the agenda in the past, has complicated the quantification and valuation of concessions made in different areas.

Next, membership has increased, and with it the number of countries participating in the negotiations. At the time of the first GATT round in 1947, the number of so-called contracting parties which participated in the negotiations was only 23; this rose to 124 at the Uruguay Round that finalized the GATT in 1994. During the 1980s particularly, a large number of developing countries joined the GATT and committed themselves to the multilateral system by binding their most-favoured nation import tariff rates, applicable to all countries in the GATT, by reducing their applied tariff rates and by abandoning their non-tariff barriers. In the meantime, the number of members of the WTO has increased to 150 countries (as at January 2007), while still more countries are negotiating accession.

Moreover, the structure of negotiations changed with the changing structure of the world economy. In earlier times, the world economy used to be strongly dominated by two economic superpowers, the USA and the EU, which used to play a key role in agenda setting and the overall negotiation process. It is true that the USA and the EU are still by far the two largest economic powers in the world economy, as measured by their gross national product at purchasing power parity (GNP-PPP), and that the trade flow between them is the largest inter-regional trade flow in the world economy. As shown in the figure, a multipolar world economy is emerging, as reflected

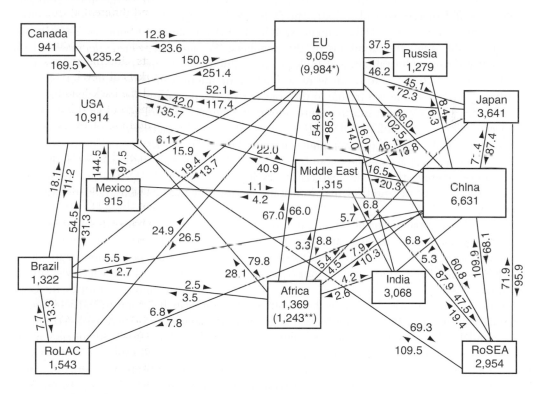

Main countries and regions according to GNP-PPP, and main trade flows in billions of US dollars, 2003

Source: Dijck and Faber 2006; data on GNP-PPP taken from World Bank 2004; export data (DOTS) taken from IMF 2004.

Notes: RoLAC = Rest of Latin America and the Caribbean (western hemisphere less Brazil and Mexico); RoSEA = Rest of South East Asia (Cambodia, Indonesia, Korea, Lao PDR, Malaysia, Philippines, Singapore, Thailand and Vietnam).

(a) = including the new members since 1 May 2004
(b) = sub-Saharan Africa

It should be noted that measuring GNPs at PPP yields results that may differ strongly from the results of more traditional valuations using annual averages of exchange rates, and tends to increase the size of developing economies as compared to the EU and the USA. Moreover, statistical deficiencies and biases may affect the presentation, as depicted in the figure, particularly in the case of China.

by the size of the economies of China, Japan and India, and to a lesser degree Russia, Brazil and Mexico. The emergence of these economies has a significant impact on the direction of trade flows and has resulted in great dynamism in the world trade system, as reflected by the increasing role of South–South trade, and particularly of east Asia in world trade. These changes are reflected also in the interests and the say of countries, and consequently the agenda of the negotiations.

Finally, by adhering to the principle of a 'single undertaking', all countries are required to accept the complete negotiating result as a whole. This, of course, does not imply that all rules and concessions apply in the same way to all member countries.

The Doha Development Agenda

The ultimate decision-making body in the WTO is the Ministerial Conference, composed of representatives of all member countries. This Conference meets at least once every two years. The European Union was among the initiators of the first, ambitious, WTO round. After a failed start at the third Ministerial Conference of Seattle, the new round started at the next Ministerial Conference of Doha in November 2001. The Doha Declarations, which lay down the principles and objectives of the Doha Development Agenda (DDA) for the new 'round' of negotiations, leave no doubt about the ambitions of the members: 'We are determined…to maintain the process of reform and liberalization of trade policies…and pledge to reject the use of protectionism.' In Doha, much time and words were devoted to the interests of developing countries, and the title of the new round is a tribute to the objective of creating a multilateral trading order in which 'trade can play a major role in the promotion of economic development and the alleviation of poverty'. To be successful, the DDA has to contribute to the liberalization of trade in product groups of particular interest to developing countries. This holds for developing countries' export interest in the markets of developed countries as well as for their trade potentials in South–South trade. Hence, liberalization of the markets of developing countries themselves, and particularly the large middle-income countries, may contribute significantly to gains from trade in developing countries.

Since Doha, negotiations on liberalization of the world trading system have met much resistance and progressed at a slow pace. The fifth Ministerial Conference at Cancun in September 2003 was characterized by controversies and conflict over the centrepiece of the negotiations: agricultural reform. A bone of contention was the joint EU-US paper on agricultural reform, which was considered unacceptable and triggered the creation of a diverse group of developing countries, the G-20, with Brazil as their acting leader. Among the countries participating in this group are India, Indonesia, Nigeria, Pakistan, South Africa, China, Mexico, Argentina and many other South American countries. The EU and the USA initially expected this coalition to be short-lived, but this was not the case, at least up to the time of writing (2006). On the contrary, at the sixth Ministerial Conference in Hong Kong the G-20 played a crucial role, and even managed to issue a common declaration on agriculture with the G-90, which is all the more remarkable as the latter coalition of predominantly very poor and least-developed countries in many respects have interests contrary to those of the G-20.

Centrepiece of the negotiations on the Doha Development Agenda are concessions by developed countries regarding access to their markets of agricultural products and domestic support for their agricultural producers, and by developing countries – particularly large middle-income countries – regarding market access for non-agricultural products, and to a lesser extent services. These critical issues are strongly interrelated, as the level of ambition in market access for agriculture and manufactures should be 'comparably high'. Moreover, the level of ambition achieved regarding these three critical issues would serve as the benchmark for all the rest of the Doha Agenda. A breakthrough in what is referred to as the 'triangle of make-or-break issues' is key to the success of this first WTO round, and requires initiatives by the main players in the WTO negotiations, and indeed in the world trade system itself, most notably the EU, USA, Japan, China, India and Brazil.

The conflictive nature of the negotiations and the length of time involved to come to multilateral trade agreements reflect as much the inherent complexities of the issues involved as the significant interests that are at stake for all countries involved in the process. At the same time, the way negotiations are organized and decisions are made contributes to the complexity. The requirement of transparency, which is essential for a democratic validation, does not fit naturally with strategic operations in negotiations, and full participation of an increasing membership concerning an expanding agenda does not facilitate rapid decision making either, particularly not in the context of a single undertaking, implying that nothing is decided until everything is decided. All this indicates that there are good reasons indeed to assess critically the way the WTO has been operating since 1995, and to improve the organization's capability to deal with its formidable task in the years to come.

GUIDE TO FURTHER READING AND REFERENCES

Dijck, P. and Faber, G. (eds) (1996) *Challenges to the New World Trade Organization*, The Hague, London and Boston, MA: Kluwer Law International.

Dijck, P. and Faber, G. (eds) (2006) *Developing Countries and the Doha Development Agenda*, London and New York: Routledge.

GATT (1994) *The Results of the Uruguay Round of Multilateral Trade Negotiations, The Legal Texts*, Geneva: GATT Secretariat.

Hoekman, B., Mattoo, A. and English, P. (eds) (2002) *Development, Trade, and the WTO*, Washington, DC: World Bank.

IMF (2004) *Direction of Trade Statistics Yearbook*, Washington, DC: International Monetary Fund.

Ingco, M. and Nash, J. (eds) (2004) *Agriculture and the WTO, Creating a Trading System for Development*, Washington, DC: World Bank and Oxford University Press.

World Bank (2004) *World Development Report 2005: A Better Investment Climate for Everyone*, Washington, DC: World Bank.

USEFUL WEBSITES

http://worldbank.org
http://unctad.org
http://WTO.org

10.15 Intellectual property rights and multilateral institutions

Duncan Matthews and Viviana Munoz Tellez

Introduction

Since the mid-1980s, there has been an unprecedented increase in the substantive and territorial scope of intellectual property rights, which has had profound implications for developing countries. This chapter explains why intellectual property rights are an important topic for development studies and outlines the response of multilateral institutions to the issues involved.

What are intellectual property rights?

Intellectual property rights are granted to individuals or organizations in order to give protection over inventions, literary or artistic works, symbols, names, images and designs, and allow the inventor or creator the right to prevent others from making authorized use of their property for a limited period. The main categories of intellectual property rights are: patents, trademarks, geographical indications, copyright, design rights and plant breeders' rights (for a detailed explanation of the different categories of intellectual property rights and the justifications for granting these rights, see Bently and Sherman 2004).

Key events in the history of international intellectual property rights

The history of international intellectual property rights is marked by a number of key events, as follows.

- 1883: The principle of non-discrimination in the granting of intellectual property rights is established by the Paris Convention on the Protection of Industrial Property Rights so that foreigners are treated in the same way as national citizens for the purposes of domestic patent, industrial design and trademark laws.
- 1886: Berne Convention on the Protection of Literary and Artistic Works is signed to provide similar provisions for copyright works.
- 1893: Responsibility for administering the Paris and Berne Conventions is handed over to the United International Bureaux for the Protection of Intellectual Property (known by its French acronym, BIPRI).
- 1974: World Intellectual Property Organization (WIPO), a specialized agency of the United Nations, takes over administration of the Paris and Berne Conventions from the BIPRI.
- 1984: Multilateral negotiations to revise the Paris Convention and introduce effective enforcement mechanisms capable of combating international piracy and counterfeiting of intellectual property end in failure. Attention switches to linking intellectual property enforcement to the General Agreement on Tariffs and Trade (GATT).
- 1986: Ministerial Declaration, launching the Uruguay Round of GATT, includes the mandate to negotiate on trade-related aspects of intellectual property rights.
- 1994: GATT ministers conclude the Uruguay Round by signing a Final Act, establishing the World Trade Organization (WTO), and the Agreement on Trade-Related Aspects of Intellectual Property Rights (TRIPS). The Paris and Berne Conventions remain in force, but now coexist with the more far-reaching intellectual property standards and stricter enforcement provisions of TRIPS.

The impact of intellectual property rights on developing countries and the response of multilateral institutions

In terms of the impact of intellectual property rights on developing countries, two sets of issues have been particularly contentious: (i) public health and access to medicines; and (ii) agriculture, genetic resources and traditional knowledge.

Public health and access to medicines

TRIPS requires that WTO members grant patents for pharmaceutical products. This has raised concerns about the protection of public health and access to medicines because patented medicines cost much more than the equivalent, unpatented, 'generic' versions. As well as requiring patent protection to be available for pharmaceutical products, TRIPS also limits the extent to which WTO members can produce, import and export cheaper, 'generic' copies of the patented medicines. With rising prices for patented pharmaceutical products, the concern is that the problem of access to medicines in developing countries will become more acute.

The cost and availability of antiretroviral (ARV) drugs for people living with HIV is a particular concern, and has led non-governmental organizations (NGOs) and developing country governments to challenge the intellectual property rights of multinational drug companies. In South Africa, for instance, concerns about the high cost and availability of ARVs led the South African courts to declare, in 2003, that multinational drug companies GlaxoSmithKline and Boehringer Ingelheim had abused their patents and had kept the price of ARV drugs unnecessarily high. Similarly, in Brazil (2006) and Thailand (2007), controversy has surrounded the high price of the ARVs such as Kaletra, for which multinational drug company Abbott holds the patent.

At the level of multilateral institutions, WTO members acknowledged concerns about the problems that intellectual property rights can create for access to medicines in developing countries by adopting a Declaration on TRIPS and Public Health (the Doha Declaration) at the Fourth Ministerial Conference in Doha on 14 November 2001. In response to the Doha Declaration, on 30 August 2003, WTO members agreed to a temporary solution that would make it easier for developing countries to import generic medicines to meet public health needs (Matthews 2004). On 6 December 2005, WTO members agreed to an amendment of TRIPS to make this temporary solution permanent (Matthews 2006), but concerns remain about the high price and the availability of medicines in developing countries.

These concerns about the link between intellectual property rights and access to medicines are being discussed at the World Health Organization (WHO). In May 2006, following the publication of a report by the WHO Commission on Intellectual Property Rights, Innovation and Public Health (CIPIH), the World Health Assembly adopted a Resolution on Public Health, Innovation and Essential Health Research and Intellectual Property, and established an Intergovernmental Working Group (IGWG). The IGWG has a mandate to investigate further the risks associated with high prices of patented pharmaceutical products and to propose solutions to the paradox that the patent system does not encourage pharmaceutical companies to invest in research into so-called 'neglected diseases'. The 'neglected diseases' problem occurs because, if diseases are common in developing countries but are not a particular public health problem in the developed world, there is unlikely to be a profitable market for new drugs, even if pharmaceutical companies invest heavily in expensive research and development to bring new products to the market.

Agriculture, genetic resources and traditional knowledge

The relationship between agriculture, genetic resources, traditional knowledge and intellectual property rights is also contentious. Of particular concern is the trend, since 2001, to extend intellectual property rights (specifically patents and plant breeders' rights) to plant genetic resources. The commercial possibilities of plant genetic resources could potentially benefit the national economies of many countries rich in biodiversity, most of which are developing countries. Potentially, traditional communities could also reap gains from the exploitation of genetic resources. However, if access is not managed appropriately at the international level, it may also result in the misappropriation of biological and genetic resources and traditional knowledge (known as biopiracy).

A well-known example of alleged biopiracy is the case of the San tribes of the Kalahari. The San, one of the oldest communities in southern Africa, are the holders of traditional knowledge on the use of *Hoodia gordonii*, a plant they have historically consumed to stave off hunger on their long journeys. The San were initially unaware that a patent had been granted on an appetite suppressant derived from an extract of the plant, but, following the intervention of NGOs, such as the South African San Institute and Biowatch, an agreement was signed in 2003 so that the San people will benefit financially from commercialization of the patented product (Wynberg 2004).

Farmers in developing countries are also increasingly concerned about the granting of intellectual property rights on plants, particularly patents on plant genes and the granting of plant breeders' rights. The concern is not only that the cost of seeds will increase due to the plant breeders' monopoly, but also that access to agricultural resources will be inhibited by the use of these intellectual property rights. Traditionally, farmers could freely replant, exchange and sell seeds. However, patents and plant breeders' rights typically impose restrictions on farmers' ability to sell (or sometimes even reuse) seeds from plants that they have grown. In India, NGOs such as Navdanya and the Gene Campaign have been campaigning to highlight the role of farmers in the conservation of plant genetic resources, and India has now introduced legislation to protect farmers' rights in India alongside the rights of plant breeders (Sahai 2002).

In intellectual property negotiations taking place in multilateral institutions, developing countries have been proposing measures to ensure that the appropriate mechanisms are in place to deal with concerns about agriculture, genetic resources and traditional knowledge. Their proposals include:

- balancing the rights of breeders with the rights of local farmers in developing countries to save, share, sell and replant seed;
- equitable sharing of benefits between plant breeders and farmers to take account of the latter's contribution to innovations in plant breeding and plant patenting;
- the protection of genetic resources through measures which prevent the grant of patents over genetic resources;
- the protection of the innovations of indigenous and other traditional communities, and the recognition of their traditional knowledge.

Several multilateral institutions deal with the above-mentioned issues and the treatment of agriculture, genetic resources and traditional knowledge cuts across a number of forums. These include: the WTO; the WIPO; the Convention on Biological Diversity Conference of the Parties (CBD-COP); the International Union for the Protection of New Plant Varieties (UPOV); and the United Nations Food and Agriculture Organization (FAO). These multilateral institutions administer a number of interrelated international agreements that include: the Convention on Biological Diversity (CBD); the TRIPS Agreement; the International Convention for the Protection of New Varieties of Plants, administered by UPOV; and the FAO International Undertaking on the Utilization of Plant Genetic Resources for Food and Agriculture, and the subsequent FAO International Treaty on Plant Genetic Resources for Food and Agriculture. The fact that several instruments touch on issues related to genetic resources and traditional knowledge ultimately complicates their implementation and allows for different interpretations of the obligations.

Developing countries, supported by NGOs, have highlighted the need for coherence between the various international agreements. However, the negotiations continue, with few concrete outcomes as regards introducing measures that developing countries could use in order to prevent the misappropriation of genetic resources and traditional knowledge (as at the time of writing, 2006).

The problem caused by the interrelationship between different international agreements is itself being addressed in several multilateral institutions, most notably the WTO TRIPS Council and the WIPO Intergovernmental Committee on Intellectual Property and Genetic Resources, Traditional Knowledge and Folklore (IGC). Generally, developing countries and NGOs consider that the FAO International Undertaking on the Utilization of Plant Genetic Resources for Food and Agriculture is in harmony with the CBD. The former covers the specific needs of agriculture, and is considered to hold the middle ground between the CBD (which focuses on the protection of biodiversity) and TRIPS (which extends intellectual property rights over intangible assets, including plant genetic resources).

The relationship between TRIPS and the CBD is one of the most contentious. While TRIPS is seen by many developing countries and NGOs to be in tension with the CBD, many developed countries maintain that no conflict exists between the two instruments. NGOs emphasize the importance of implementing the CBD and creating coherence between the various international agreements that deal with genetic resources and traditional knowledge. They point, in particular, to the importance for developing countries of harmonizing TRIPS with the CBD in order to ensure the sustainable use of biodiversity and prevent misappropriation, and for the protection of traditional knowledge.

Both TRIPS and the CBD touch on issues concerning genetic resources and intellectual property. On the one hand, the CBD deals with access to genetic resources and creates an obligation for the fair and equitable sharing of benefits arising out of the utilization of genetic resources on mutually agreed terms and informed consent. On the other hand, TRIPS allows intellectual property rights to be extended to genetic resources. The agreement obliges WTO members to protect plant varieties, through a patent or through a *sui generis* (own kind) regime, or through a combination of both. It does not, however, mention benefit sharing or informed consent.

In order to create coherence with the CBD, on 1 June 2006 a group of six developing countries, led by India, submitted a proposal to the WTO TRIPS Council for an amendment to TRIPS, to introduce specific requirements in patent applications for disclosure, indicating where biological material has been obtained from.

Conclusion

Given the potential impact of intellectual property rights on developing countries, the complexity of the issues and the plethora of multilateral institutions involved, there is no doubt this will remain a controversial topic for development studies and will be the subject of intense debate for many years to come.

GUIDE TO FURTHER READING AND REFERENCES

Bently, L. and Sherman, B. (2004) *Intellectual Property Law*, Oxford: Oxford University Press.

Matthews, D. (2002) *Globalising Intellectual Property Rights: The TRIPS Agreement*, London: Routledge.

Matthews, D. (2004) 'The WTO decision on implementation of Paragraph 6 of the Doha Declaration on the TRIPS Agreement and public health: A solution to the access to essential medicines problem?', *Journal of International Economic Law*, 7(1): 73–107.

Matthews, D. (2006) 'From the August 30, 2003 WTO decision to the December 6, 2005 agreement on an amendment to TRIPS: Improving access to medicines in developing countries?', *Intellectual Property Quarterly*, 2: 91–130.

Sahai, S. (2002) 'India's plant variety protection and farmers' rights legislation', in P. Drahos and R. Mayne (eds) *Global Intellectual Property Rights: Knowledge, Access and Development*, Basingstoke: Palgrave.

Wynberg, R. (2004) 'Rhetoric, realism and benefit-sharing: The use of traditional knowledge of the hoodia species in the development of an appetite suppressant', *Journal of World Intellectual Property*, 4(4): 851–76.

USEFUL WEBSITES

NGOs, intellectual property rights and multilateral institutions: http://www.ipngos.org/

TRIPS material on the World Trade Organization website: http://www.wto.org/english/tratop_e/trips_e/trips_e.htm

World Intellectual Property Organization – IP for Development: http://www.wipo.int/ip-development/en/

10.16 Universal rights

Peris Jones

Introduction

Re-emerging into the daylight, rubbing tired eyes, exhausted-looking delegates exit a smoke-filled meeting room at the United Nations. It is 1948. At stake, no less than two and a half years into negotiations, was the final round of amendments – 168 in all – with delegates working every day for more than two months in order to finalize the Universal Declaration of Human Rights (UDHR). How dated and naive this invocation of a common humanity and universal values associated with human rights must appear to critics of 'grand narrative' ideas and proponents of post-modernism and post-development. And the contemporary era, characterized as it is by 'regime change' in Iraq and elsewhere, underscores the tendency more generally of Western interventions to 'generate seemingly timeless and spaceless versions of sovereignty, rights, the law, and the nation abstracted not only from violence and force, but also from any questioning of geo-political interventions in less developed societies' (Slater 1997: 64).

While particularly significant for debates on 'development', arguably such critiques also contributed to creating an overly myopic inward gaze, in which our collective eye has been taken off the political ball at a time when economic inequality worsens across and within the Global 'North' and 'South'. Put simply, the problem does not lay in imagining the universalism of 'rights' per se, but rather the political conditions required to overcome democratic deficits in decision making at global and national levels.

But such critiques are nevertheless sobering when attempting to read the blueprint for humanity proposed along the lines of Article Two of the UDHR (see 'Useful websites' at the end of this chapter). This declares freedom from discrimination on the grounds of 'race, colour, sex, language, religion, political or other opinion, national or social origin, property, birth or other status', in which we face being swept away on a wave of romantic platitudes somewhat reminiscent of the famous John Lennon song 'Imagine'. However, the UDHR, and more particularly the substantial international human rights edifice carved out of the post-war era, are much more nuanced than the most obvious criticisms allow.

International human rights are imbued with a spirit of providing a focus to and authoritative language for the 'hopes of the oppressed' and 'replacing efficacy of force by the force of ethics' (Alves 2000: 478). These lofty ideals inevitably find resonance with the universalistic drive and impulse of the project of 'Development' itself (and hence also encounter the considerable body of critique made of 'development'). At the outset of the chapter, however, human rights are regarded as a mechanism for generating accountability of states and scrutiny to both its citizens and agreed-upon national and international standards. Inevitably, it must be conceded that one should accept the parameters of the creation of the UDHR: a product of its specific time (post-Second World War) and particular place (state representatives at the United Nations), meaning that the 'universalism' of the UDHR, and more recent subsequent human rights agreements, can and must inevitably be qualified. But acknowledging this context, and contemporary geopolitical constraints, does nothing to diminish the relevance of human rights. On the contrary, as more critical accounts suggest, the challenge is to reconstruct them through acknowledging that a politics of rights is key to their implementation (Jones and Stokke 2005). This involves seeking ways to create a democratic politics of rights wherein the relationship between citizen and state is fundamentally altered through ensuring national and locally driven accountability. This democratizing impulse to reconnect citizens to state obligations (and protection from private actors) would also serve to re-equip international human rights for the considerable challenges of development in the twenty-first century.

But let us return to the specific context of time and place of the UDHR – our bleary-eyed UN delegates – and one of the most common allegations directed against human rights: the alleged incompatibility of universal rights and cultural relativism.

The West as champion of human rights?

The most common complaint raised against the UDHR is that it is a Western-created document, derived from Western cultural, philosophical and political values. Human rights, for example, are premised upon principles such as political pluralism and non-discrimination, particularly the rights of women and children, and individual claims rather than collective responsibilities. Furthermore, as a product of that era, the 1948 UDHR process clearly omitted the representation of vast swathes of Africa, Asia and elsewhere, still under the yoke of colonial rule. But the delegates emerging from the meeting hall included those from India, China, Lebanon, Cuba and other Latin American countries, among others, reflecting different cultural traditions and regional influences on the drafting process. Indeed, the complaint of cultural bias in human rights has prompted revisionist approaches, since the mid-1990s, as to the context and process leading to the creation of the UDHR.

According to Waltz (2002), while it is relatively straightforward to locate Western philosophical writings in support of human rights, they should not be *equated* with them. Furthermore, not all Western thinkers or states historically welcomed or supported human rights. In terms of geopolitics, Waltz shows that some of the most influential Western powers were themselves sceptical about human rights. In particular, the colonial powers resisted the idea of universal rights, the USA resisted reference to discriminatory practices and, significantly, socio-economic rights, and the USSR 'adamantly' opposed the idea of inherent rights that might be beyond the control of the state. It is therefore important to separate the geopolitical ambitions and interests of the great powers then, as now, from the *intent* of universal norms and standards of international human rights. The revisionism refocuses the key role played by many smaller (non-Western) states in defining and pushing the UDHR, over and above the role usually ascribed to Western powers. (On 10 December 1948, the UDHR was adopted by 46 votes to zero, with eight abstentions, including apartheid South Africa, Saudi Arabia and a socialist bloc of East European countries.)

Inclusion of socio-economic rights, such as housing, health and social security, among others, interestingly, were vehemently opposed by the USA, deemed too radical. But due to the insistence of some non-Western countries, such as Syria, they were finally included (Waltz 2002). Other key human rights documents include the International Covenant on Civil and Political Rights (ICCPR) and the International Covenant on Economic, Social and Cultural Rights (ICESCR; see 'Useful websites' at the end of this chapter). (In fact, the USA ratified the ICCPR only in 1992, and despite signing the ICESCR in 1977, it has still not ratified the Covenant.) These central pillars of human rights were negotiated and finally agreed on in the 1960s, when most countries had gained independence from colonial rule, and therefore reflected broad state participation and negotiation. Kabasakal Arat (2006: 423) therefore contends that the current international human rights regime is an 'amalgamation or an unspecific, yet complex, theoretical heritage, if any', reflecting 'an improvised and negotiated design'. These are important counterpoints to outright dismissal of the International Bill of Human Rights (as human rights covenants and conventions and the UDHR are collectively termed) as an overly Western project. Indeed, these international standards have been used to hold both governments and private actors accountable in both the North and South. The ICESCR, for example, and, more specifically, the right to health, has been pivotal to global civil society struggles waged against governments and pharmaceutical companies in order to create universal access to AIDS medication. As such, these and other universal human rights standards can be co-opted for the ends of social justice and, in the process, can also serve to break out of the spatial straitjacket imposed by the topography of development.

Cultural politics/political cultures and rights

But with these observations made, cultural, religious and national differences continue to be invoked in criticism of human rights. Sometimes these can be revealed as cynical use of culture to deflect political criticism of a regime's human rights abuses: President Robert Mugabe of Zimbabwe (in)famously condemns any outside criticism of his human rights record as nothing more than attempts at (Western) 'regime change'; the United States currently invokes its 'war against terror' as justification for suspending civil and political rights, most notably in Guantánamo Bay. For many years, though, some South East Asian countries claimed that their so-called 'Asian values', such as communitarian welfare and social order, were contradicted by human rights standards – individual freedoms – and, especially, that rights are considered a brake on economic transformation. However, many of these claims have been refuted, with positive (albeit often insufficient) links identified between economic development and level of respect for civil and political rights by a regime. Many Asian leaders and scholars dissent from the rather polarized view of 'Asian' values versus the 'West'. Instead, many regard these categories as compatible and reflecting internal heterogeneity in either case.

In 1993, an important milestone in reconciling cultural relativism with human rights was reached at the World Conference on Human Rights in Vienna. Representatives from 170 countries adopted by consensus Article 1 that: 'The universal nature of these rights and freedoms is beyond question.' Generally speaking, today, cultural relativism is noticeably less likely to be used by states as an argument to oppose human rights. Instead, it is much more commonplace for states to nominally demonstrate commitment to international human rights and to 'buy in' to accepting their cultural legitimacy at that level. That said, of course, it is quite another matter for states to domesticate and implement these standards within their countries.

Certainly, it would appear sensible to recognize the need for the cultural norms, symbols and traditions of non-Western societies to enter into international human rights discourse, lest these continue to be seen in the 'Third World' as 'invasive of sovereignty, a result of imbalances of power and ethnocentric' (Penna and Campbell 1998: 7). And to some extent this is already being done, for example, through regional documents such as the African Commission on Human and *Peoples'* Rights (emphasis added; see 'Useful websites' at the end of this chapter). But a more pressing issue is unavoidable: how should states accommodate and reconcile cultural differences with domestication of human rights standards? One might suggest that progressive development discourse has tended to avoid the difficulties associated with dialogue and action surrounding oppressive cultural practices. Indeed, proponents of cultural relativism should be met with challenges as to what kind of 'culture' is being talked about, who defines the content and what types of coercive practices serve to place constraints on equal enjoyment of that culture and rights. Because it is usual that the gatekeepers to particular cultures have most to lose by reconciling practices with human rights standards, we must consider the power relations before uncritically accepting 'culture' at face value. A fundamental issue for reflection, therefore, should be whether members of particular cultural (ethnic, national, minority, religious) groups have the choice and possibility to opt out of certain cultural practices. In other words, whereas a one-size-fits-all critique is often levelled against human rights, we might also level this accusation against proponents of cultural relativism.

In South Africa, for example, like many parts of sub-Saharan Africa, there is a range of cultural practices contributing to subordination of women, wherein 'culture' is invoked to justify particular behaviour. Take customary law of succession, which demands that when a woman in a customary marriage dies, her husband carries on controlling the family property. However, if the husband dies before the wife, the heir, the eldest male, takes over the control of the family property and becomes the head of the family. This system discriminates against women and girls, who are not allowed to inherit the property. Why should this be an acceptable cultural practice? Why not seek to ensure, as the South African Constitution does, that cultural practices and customary laws are not in conflict with the principle of and legislative clause for equality and non-discrimination? A case challenging unfair discrimination against women and girls came before the South African Constitutional Court in 2004, in which it was decided that the customary law of succession did discriminate against women and girls. This is particularly significant because it recognizes that while people have a right to their culture, this should not mean that women or others should be placed in an unequal or vulnerable position in society (see 'Guide to further reading' at the end of this chapter for attempts to reconcile culture and rights through alternative female circumcision rites).

Conclusion

It should be clear by now that the UDHR and subsequent human rights instruments should not be read narrowly as a clash of cultures or philosophies, nor dismissed merely as an expression of geopolitical domination of Western powers and donor-driven agendas in development. It is about far more than this. Its impact has been to open up decision making nationally and internationally, in order to scrutinize the quality of governance within a state, to hold it and other actors accountable. But what appears critical is to hold participatory public debate and to inform on ways to accommodate cultural differences and to justify when cultural – and, we can add, 'developmental', practices – are *not* deemed legitimate. The same is also true when discussing different sets of human rights, for example, socio-economic rights, wherein the state may have certain positive duties regarding improving access to health, housing, and so on. Human rights have been critical to framing national and global movements' struggles to contest certain democratic deficits, as mentioned, for example, in advocating for *universal* access to antiretroviral AIDS medication.

For both sets of rights, court cases can sometimes be effective vehicles to air these differences, depending on the quality of the legal debate, whether access to justice is possible for marginalized groups, as well as the authority of the judgements given. But whether discussing cultural differences or socio-economic inequality, the fundamental point is that citizens require both legal and non-legal means and political opportunities to actually acquire and transform rights (Jones and Stokke 2005). An important starting point is to strengthen a democratic politics of rights, capable of linking across different terrains from the global to national decision-making processes, and, especially, locally driven meanings of human rights. The challenge, no less, is to democratize the human rights 'project' itself.

GUIDE TO FURTHER READING

For ways of reconciling culture and rights to do with female genital circumcision and the creation of 'alternative circumcision rites', see Ibhawoh, B. (2000) 'Between culture and constitution: Evaluating the cultural legitimacy of human rights in the African state', *Human Rights Quarterly*, 22: 838–60.

For an interesting empirical examination of state behaviour in reporting to specific human rights committees, and obstacles to deeper implementation, see Harris-Short, S. (2003) 'International human rights law: Imperialist, inept and ineffective? Cultural relativism and the UN Convention on the Rights of the Child', *Human Rights Quarterly*, 25: 130–82.

For more on the politics of rights, and specifically socio-economic rights, and their potential and pitfalls in development, see Jones, P.S. and Stokke, K. (2005) *Democratising Development: The Politics of Socio-Economic Rights in South Africa*, Leiden: Martinus Nijhoff/Brill.

USEFUL WEBSITES

For key human rights documents and information, such as the Universal Declaration of Human Rights, and workings of UN human rights bodies, see http://www.un.org/rights/

For African-related instruments, see the African Commission on Human and Peoples' Rights, at http://www.achpr.org

REFERENCES

Alves, J.A.L. (2000) 'The declaration of human rights in postmodernity', *Human Rights Quarterly*, 22: 478–99.

Jones, P.S. and Stokke, K. (eds) (2005) *Democratising Development: The Politics of Socio-Economic Rights in South Africa*, Leiden: Martinus Nijhoff/Brill.

Kabasakal Arat, Z.F. (2006) 'Forging a global culture of human rights: Origins and prospects of the International Bill of Rights', *Human Rights Quarterly*, 28: 416–37.

Penna, D.R. and Campbell, P.J. (1998) 'Human rights and culture: Beyond universality and relativism', *Third World Quarterly*, 19(1): 7–27.

Slater, D. (1997) 'Spatialities of power and postmodern ethics: Rethinking geo-political encounters', *Environment and Planning D: Society and Space*, 15: 55–72.

Waltz, S. (2002) 'Reclaiming and rebuilding the history of the Universal Declaration of Human Rights', *Third World Quarterly*, 23(3): 437–48.

Index